Shari'ah
The Islamic Law

'Abdur Raḥmān I. Doi

Ta Ha Publishers
London. United Kingdom

Reprint 1997

Published by:
TaHa Publishers Ltd.
1, Wynne Road
London SW9 OBB
website:http://www.taha.co.uk/
email: sales@taha.co.uk

British Library Cataloguing in Publication Data
Doi, A Rahman I.
Shariah the Islamic Law
1.Islamic Law
I. Title
340.5'9

ISBN 0 907461 38 7 (Paperback)

Printed and Bound by- De-Luxe Printers,
London NW10 7NR.
website: http://www.de-luxe.com
email: naresh@aapi.co.uk

بسم الله الرحمن الرحيم
نحمده ونصلي على رسوله الكريم، وآله وأصحابه أجمعين

PREFACE

Islam is a religion and a way of life based on the commandments of Allah contained in the Holy Qur'ān and the Sunnah of the Prophet of Islam, Muhammad (Ṣallallāho 'Alaihi Wasallam). Every Muslim is under an obligation to fashion his entire life in accordance with the dictates of Qur'ān and Sunnah. So he has to observe at every step the distinction between what is right *(Ḥalāl)* and what is wrong *(Ḥarām)*. This highlights the need and importance of his acquaintance with the corpus juris of Islam (Sharī'ah). I, therefore, developed a keen interest in the study of the Holy Qur'ān during my student days.

But as is so common these days, the strong wind of "progressive" and "modern" ideas also took me off my feet particularly when listening as a student to the persuasive discourses of learned teacher Professor M. J. Sethna on "synthetic criminology". I started doubting the wisdom of *Ḥadd* punishments and this trend seeped into other areas of the Shari'ah. Fortunately, my exposure to fashionable influences ended too soon when I proceeded to Cambridge (England) to work as a research scholar in the areas of *Fiqh* and *Uṣūl al-Fiqh*. As I grappled on my own with the new problems concerning the Sharī'ah, it soon began to dawn upon me that this legal system based on divine guidance has immense potentialities to check the evils which beset the world today.

I carried this idea with me when I received a chance to work as a student at the Inns of Court at Middle Temple in London, an opportunity to attend the short courses in International Law at the Hague Academy of International Law, the Hague (Netherlands) and an occasion to pursue a course in Comparative Law at the Universite Internationale Sciences Droit Comparee, Luxembourg. In all these places, I continued to check and recheck my conclusions with other western scholars and I was confirmed in my belief that no legal system deriving its sustenance only from human intelligence can cure our society of the evils of criminality and exploitation. Seeing the high rate of crimes in the Western World, I was completely disenchanted with the high-sounding theories of synthetic criminology and this conditioned my thinking on other aspects of man-made legal systems.

I, therefore, began thinking that in order to save others from falling into the same error I owed a duty that I must not only acquaint them with the injunctions scattered throughout the Holy Qur'ān and the Sunnah which form the basis of Shari'ah but also enlighten them about the rational and comparative importance of such injunctions. The present book is in fulfilment of this desire.

This book developed out of my lectures delivered to my students of the Centre of Islamic Legal Studies and Faculty of Law, Ahmadu Bello University, Zaria, Nigeria. This book, I strongly feel, is different from other books currently available in English on 'Islamic Law' or to be correct, Anglo-Muhammadan Law. Unlike those books, this work takes as its starting point the Qur'ān and the Sunnah rather than the decisions of the courts.

I must, however, admit here that the interpretation of the Divine Message is not an easy task. I seek Allah's guidance and pray for His forgiveness for my shortcomings in undertaking it. But I am doing so in the hope that the book may stimulate further thought and research in this fascinating area and be of use to those interested in the subject.

I take this opportunity to thank my students, friends and other scholars whose comments and suggestions have helped me in the preparation of this book. I owe a special debt of gratitude to Shaikh Mannā' Al-Qaṭṭān, Director of *Al-Ma'had al-'Āli lil Qaḍā* of Riyadh for providing me with valuable original source books on the subject during my visit to Imam Muḥammad bin Sa'ūd University and to many of my colleagues who have given their valuable contribution in the preparation of this book.

Wa mā taufīqi illā billāh:

Rabī' al-Awwal, 1404 A.H.

Abdur Rahman I. Doi
Centre of Islamic Legal Studies
Ahmadu Bello University
Zaria, Nigeria

CONTENTS

PART I
The Fountain Head of Shari'ah

Chapter 1

Chapter 2

Chapter 3

Chapter 4

The Secondary Source of Shari'ah

Chapter 5

The Four Schools of Fiqh and Their Leaders

PART II

Family Relations

Chapter 8

Chapter 9

Chapter 10

Chapter 11

Chapter 12

PART III

Crime and Punishment

Chapter 16

PART IV

Inheritance and Disposal of Property

Chapter 17

Chapter 18

Chapter 19

PART V

The Economic System

Chapter 20

***Tijarah:* Trade and Commerce**

Chapter 21

Chapter 22

PART VI

External and Other Relations

Chapter 23

Chapter 24

Chapter 25

Chapter 26

PART I

THE FOUNTAIN HEAD OF SHARĪ'AH

Chapter 1

What is Sharī'ah

Allah is the Law Giver

Shari'ah is an Arabic word meaning the Path to be followed. Literally it means 'the way to a watering place.' It is the path not only leading to Allah, the Most High, but the path believed by all Muslims to be the path shown by Allah, the Creator Himself through His Messenger, Prophet Muḥammad (P.B.U.H.). In Islam, Allah alone is the sovereign and it is He who has the right to ordain a path for the guidance of mankind.[1] Thus it is only Sharī'ah that liberates man from servitude to other than Allah. This is the only reason why Muslims are obliged to strive for the implementation of that path, and that of no other path.

«ثُمَّ جَعَلْنَاكَ عَلَىٰ شَرِيعَةٍ مِنْ الأَمْرِ فَاتَّبِعْهَا وَلَا تَتَّبِعْ أَهْوَاءَ الَّذِينَ لَا يَعْلَمُونَ».

"We made for you a law, so follow it, and not the fancies of those who have no knowledge."[2]

The absolute knowledge which is required to lay down a path for human life is not possessed by any group of people. In the words of Sayyid Quṭb, "They are equipped with nothing but fancies and ignorance when they undertake the task which is no concern of theirs and does not properly belong to them. Their claim to one of the properties of divinity is a great sin, and a great evil.[3]

The Injunctions on Justice in the Divine Revelations

There are a number of Qur'ānic injunctions commanding Muslims to do justice. Right from the beginning, Allah sent with His Apostles three gifts which aim at rendering justice and guiding the entire human society to the path of peace. In *Sūrah al-Ḥadīd,* the Qur'ān says:

«لَقَدْ اَرْسَلْنَا رُسُلَنَا بِالبَيِّنَاتِ وَانْزَلْنَا مَعَهُمُ الكِتَابَ وَالميزَانَ لِيَقُومَ النَاسُ بِالْقِسطِ».

"We sent aforetime our Apostles with Clear Signs and sent down with them The Book and the Balance (of Right and Wrong), that men May stand forth in Justice."[4]

Three things are mentioned as gifts of Allah. They are the Book, the Balance, and Iron, which stand as emblems of three things which hold society together, *viz* – Revelation, which commands Good and forbids Evil; Justice, which gives to each person his due; and the strong arm of the Law, which maintains sanctions for evil-doers.

Justice is a command of Allah, and whosoever violates it faces grievous punishment:

«انَّ اللّٰهَ يَأْمُـرُ بِالْعَـدْلِ وَالأحسَـانِ وَايتَـاىءِ ذي الْقُرْبى وَينْهٰى عَنِ الفَحْشَاءِ وَالمُنْكَرِ وَالبَغيِ ، يَعِظُكُمْ لَعَلَّكُم تَذَكَرُونَ».

"Allah command justice, the doing of good, and charity to Kith and Kin, and He forbids all shameful deeds, and injustice and rebellion: He instructs you, that ye may receive admonition."[5]

Justice is a comprehensive term, and may include all the virtues of good behaviour. But the religion of Islam asks for something warmer and more human, the doing of good deeds even where perhaps they are not strictly demanded by justice, such as returning good for ill, or obliging those who in worldly language "have no claim" on you; and of course the fulfilling of the claims of those whose claims are recognised in social life. Similarly the opposites are to be avoided: everything that is recognised as shameful, and everything that is really unjust, and any inward rebellion against Allah's Law or our own conscience in its most sensitive form.

The Prophet of Allah is asked to tell to people to do justice as the Creator, the Nourisher and the Cherisher of all has commanded it:

«قُلْ اَمَرَ رَبّي بِالقِسْـطِ».

"Say: My Lord has commanded justice."[6]

The command is repeated in *Sūrah al-Nisā:*

«اَنَّ اللّٰهَ يَأْمُـرُكُمْ اَنْ تُؤَدّوُا الاَمَـانَـاتِ اِلٰى اَهْلِهَـا وَاِذَا حَكَمْتُم بَيْنَ النَّـاسِ اَنْ تَحْكُمُوا بِالْعَدْلِ».

> "Allah commanded you to render back your trusts to those to whom they are due. And when you judge between man and man, that you judge with justice."[7]

The Prophet is asked to administer justice according to the *Kitāb-Allāh* (Book of Allah):

«إنَّا أنْزَلْنَا اَلَيْكَ الكِتَابَ بِالحَقِّ لِتَحْكُم بَيْنَ النَّاسِ بِمَا أرَاكَ اللّٰهُ - وَلاَ تَكُنْ لِلْخَائِنِينَ خَصِيماً».

> "We have sent down to thee the Book in truth, That you might judge between men, as guided By Allah: so be not (used) as an advocate by those who betray their trust."[8]

The Commentators explain this passage with reference to the case of Ta'imah ibn Ubairaq, who was nominally a Muslim, but in reality was a hypocrite, and given to all sorts of wicked deeds. He was suspected of having stolen a set of armour, and when the trail was hot, he planted the stolen property into the house of a Jew, where it was found. The Jew denied the charge and accused Ta'imah, but the sympathies of the Muslim community were with Ta'imah on account of his nominal profession of Islam. The case was brought to the Apostle, who acquitted the Jew according to the strict principle of justice, as "guided by Allah". Attempts were made to prejudice him and deceive him into using his authority to favour Ta'imah.

The general lesson is that the righteous man is faced with all sorts of subtle wiles: the wicked will try to appeal to his highest sympathies any most honourable motives to deceive him and use him as an instrument for defeating justice. He should be careful and cautious, and seek the help of Allah for protection against deception and for firmness in dealing the strictest justice without fear or favour. To do otherwise is to betray a sacred trust: the trustee must defeat all attempts made to mislead him.

Justice must be done equally to all and sundry, even if it is to be done against one's self, or one's parent or relatives. There must be no difference between rich and poor. All are servants of Allah, and must be judged according to the Book of Allah:

«يَا أَيُّهَا الَّذِينَ آمَنُوا كُونُوا قَوَّامِينَ بِالْقِسْطِ شُهَدَاءَ لِلّٰهِ وَلَوْ عَلَى أنْفُسِكُمْ اَوِ الْوَالِدَيْنِ وَالاَقْرَبِينَ - اِنْ يَكُنْ غَنِيًّا اَوْ فَقِيراً فَاللّٰهُ اَوْلَى بِهِمَا فَلاَ تَتَّبِعُوا الْهَوَى اَنْ تَعْدِلُوا - وَاِنْ تَلوُا اَوْ تُعْرِضُوا فَاِنَّ اللّٰهَ كَانَ بِمَا تَعْمَلُونَ خَبِيراً».

"O ye who believe: Stand out firmly for justice, as witnesses to *GOD*, even as against Yourselves, or your parents, or your Kin, and whether it be (against) rich or poor. For *God* can best protect both. Follow not the lusts (Of your hearts), lest ye swerve, and if you distort (justice) or decline to do justice, Verily Allah is well-acquainted with all that you do."[9]

Justice is Allah's attribute, and to stand firm for justice is to be a witness to Allah, even it it is detrimental to our own interests, as we conceive them, or the interests of those who are near and dear to us. According to the Latin saying, "Let justice be done though heaven should fall".

But Islamic justice is something higher than the formal justice of Roman Law or any other human Law. It is even more penetrative that the subtler justice in the speculations of the Greek philosophers. It searches out the innermost motives, because we are to act as in the presence of Allah, to whom all things, acts, and motives are known.

Some people may be inclined to favour the rich, because they expect something from them. Some people may be inclined to favour the poor because they are generally helpless. Partiality in either case is wrong. We are asked to be just, without fear or favour. Both the rich and the poor are under Allah's protection as far as their legitimate interests are concerned, but they cannot expect to be favoured at the expense of others. Allah can protect their interests of all, far better than any man.

In the Sharī'ah, therefore, there is an explicit emphasis on the fact that Allah is the Lawgiver and the whole *Ummah*, the nation of Islam, is merely His trustee. It is because of this principle that the Ummah enjoys a derivative rule-making power and not an absolute law-creating prerogative. The Islamic State, like the whole of what one might call Islamic political psychology, views the Dār al-Islam (Abode of Islam) as one vast homogeneous commonwealth of people who have a common goal and a common destiny and who are guided by a common ideology in all matters both spiritual and temporal. The entire Muslim Ummah lives under the Sharī'ah to which every member has to submit, with sovereignty belong to Allah alone.[10]

Every Muslim who is capable and qualified to give a sound opinion on matters of Sharī'ah, is entitled to interpret the law of Allah when such interpretation becomes necessary. In this sense Islamic policy is a democracy. But where an explicit command of Allah or his Prophet already exists, no Muslim leader or legislature, or any religious scholar can form an independent judgement; not even all the Muslims of the world put together have any right to make the least alteration in it.[11]

The executive function, therefore, under the Sharī'ah vest solely in the just ruler or a group of such people who appoints his delegates and is responsible only to the Sharī'ah as represented by the Council of Jurists

('Ulamā and Fuqahā') in whom the legislative function of deriving laws from the Book of Allah and the Sunnah is vested. New laws according to the needs of the time and circumstances are only made by these men learned in the guiding principles of law, men chosen by the popular assembly from among the multitudes of those learned in the Shari'ah on account of their enlightenment and understanding of the need of the people.[12]

But the fundamental principles on which rests the Islamic legal system is that the laws of Islam are not passed in a heated assembly by men who ardently desire the legislation in their interest, against men who ardently oppose it in their interest. The laws of Islam are firmly based upon the Sharī'ah and are, therefore, in the interest of the people as a whole. They are not the work of warring politicians, but of sober jurists.[13]

This is the reason why there is a greater degree of stability in the Shari'ah mainly due to its Divine Origin as compared to any other man-made secular legislation in the world.

The difference between other legal systems and the Sharī'ah is that under the Sharī'ah its fountainhead is the Qur'ān and Sunnah, the Waḥy al-Jalī (the revelation *per se*) and the Waḥy al-Khafī (the hidden revelation). The Qur'ān and the Sunnah are the gifts given to entire Ummah. Therefore the Ummah as a whole is collectively responsible for the administration of Justice. This is the reason why any legislative or consultative assembly in any Muslim land has no power of encroachment on any legal right of the members of the Ummah and those who live with them in peaceful co-existence.

The other important point in this regard is that in Sharī'ah, Justice is administered in the name of Allah, one of Whose attributes is Al-'Ādil (the Just and the Giver of Justice). Any injustice or any tribal or racial consideration is nothing but a grave sin and disobedience to Allah. "To judge justly" is, therefore, a religious duty and a devotional act. Neither a king, nor a caliph or a sultan can ever claim his words are laws as was done by tyrant rulers from Pharroh to Louis XIV. They are not the fountainhead of justice even though some wrong-headed Muslim rulers might have posed as if they possessed such authority. With this in mind, we shall proceed to examine briefly the sources and the aims of Sharī'ah.

The Aims of Shari'ah

The Sharī'ah, originated from the direct commandment of Allah; but there is the provision or power given to man in order to interpret and expand Divine commandment, by means of analogical deductions and through other processes.[14] Unlike the Roman law which developed from the actionorEnglish Common Law which developed from the writs[15] the very first source of Sharī'ah is the Holy Qur'ān. The second source is the Sunnah or the Practice of Prophet Muḥammad (S.A.W.) who has rightly explained:

> "I leave two things for you. You will never go stray while holding them firmly. The Book of Allah and the Sunnah of His Prophet".

The third source which may be classified as both "Ijmā'" consensus of opinion of 'Ulamā', and 'Qiyās' analogical deductions provide detailed understanding derived from the Qur'ān and Sunnah, covering the myriads of problems that arise in the course of man's life.[16] As a matter of fact, the ideal code of conduct or a pure way of life which is the Sharī'ah, has much wider scope and purpose than an ordinary legal system in the western sense of the term.[17] The Sharī'ah through this process aims at regulating the relationship of man with Allah and man with man. This the reason why the Sharī'ah law cannot be separated from Islamic ethics. The process of revelation of various injunctions (Aḥkām) of the Qur'ān shows that the revelation came down when some social, moral or religious necessity arose, or when some Companions consulted the Prophet concering some significant problems which had wide repercussions on the lives of Muslims.

The Qur'ān, therefore, is the best commentary (*Tafsīr*) of the Qur'ān and the main sources of the Sharī'ah.

The scholars of the Qur'ān have enumerated varying number of verses of legal injunctions, but the number is approximately considered to be 500.[18] They deal with marriage, polygamy, dower, maintenance, rights and obligations of the spouses, divorce and various modes of dissolution of marriage, the period of retreat after divorce ('Iddah), fosterage, contracts, loans, deposits, weights and measures, removal of injury, oaths and vows, punishments for crime, wills, inheritance, equity, fraternity, liberty, justice to all, principles of an ideal, state, fundamental human rights, laws of war and peace, judicial administration etc.[19]

The Qur'ānic injunctions, from which is derived the Sharī'ah, are further explained and translated into practice by the Sunnah of the Prophet. Sunnah literally means a way, practice, rule of life; and refers to the exemplary conduct or the model behaviour of the Prophet in what he said, did or approved. Thus it became a very important source of the Sharī'ah only second in authority after the Holy Qur'ān.

Besides the Qur'ān and the Sunnah, the consensus of the opinion of the learned men and jurists, known in the Shari'ah terminology as the Ijma, plays an important role in Islamic law since it provides a broad vehicle of progress and reconstruction. Qiyās or analogical deduction is also recognised as the source of Islamic legal system since it gives an instrument to cope with the growing needs and requirements of society. But such analogical deduction is based on very strict, logical and systematic principles and is not to be misconstrued as mere fancies and imaginations of men. Alongside these four sources, the Shari'ah takes into consideration Istihsan or juristic preference or equity of a jurist as against Qiyās which helps in providing elasticity and adaptability to the entire Islamic legal system. The concept of al-Masalih al Mursalah (the matters which are in public interest and which are not specifically defined in the Sharī'ah) was enunciated by Imām Mālik bin Anas (d. 795 A.D.) and has also become a part of the Sharī'ah system.

Justice as Respect to People

The central notion of Justice in the Sharī'ah is based on mutual respect of one human being by another. The just Society in Islam means the society that secures and maintains respect for persons through various social arrangements that are in the common interests of all members. A man as Khalifat-Allāh (vice-regent of Allah) on earth must be treated as an end in himself and never merely as a means since he is the cream of Creation and hence the central theme of the Qur'ān. What is required is the equal integrity of each person in the society and his loyalty to the country concerned which in turn will make it the duty of the society to provide equally for each person's pursuit of happiness. This is the reason why things unlawful (Ḥarām) for Muslims but lawful for non-Muslims will not be made forbidden for them in the Muslim country.

Politically, respect for persons was the motivating thought behind the Kalimah al-Shahādah, the creed of confession of Islam, which neglected any other diety other than Allah who created all human beings as equal irrespective of their tribes or clans. It was this teaching which made the Quraishites, Prophet Muḥammad's tribesmen, angry when he helped to liberate the slaves and destitutes like Bilāl, Zaid and many others in the early days of Islam. It is a fact of history that all of Khadījah's wealth was spent after freeing the slaves; and before her death she, along with the Prophet, could hardly get a square meal a day. It was the same principle which guided the first city state of Medina as shown in its charter which guaranteed individual rights irrespective of religious beliefs of the communities living in Medina.

Respect for persons in the Shari'ah is rooted in the Divine injunctions of the Qur'ān and the precepts of the Prophet. The Bill of Rights, Suffrage, Civil Rights and the slogans for political equality as we know today are of a very recent origin and seem to be mere reflections of what the Sharī'ah taught 1400 years ago from now. The treatment accorded by the Sharī'ah made the aristocracies of birth, race, wealth, language, the features which vary from person to person, all suspect as disrespectful of persons. The criterion of respect was only the Taqwah, the fear of Allah.

«ان أكرمكم عند الله أتقاكـــم»

"The best among you in the eyes of Allah are those who are stronger in Taqwah (fear of Allah)"

The Sharī'ah, it should be noted, gives priority to human welfare over human liberty. Muslims as well as non-Muslims living in a Muslim state are duty bound not to exploit common resources to their own advantage, destroy good producing land, and ruin the potential harvest or encroach upon a neighbour's land. Since a man in Islam is not merely an economic animal, each person's equal right to life, and to a decent level of living, has priority over the so called economic liberty.

Behind every legal, social or political institutions of Islam, there is a divine sanction which every believer is expected to reverence no matter where he lives. He cannot change his own whims into laws. There are the limits of Allah (Ḥudūd-Allāh) which are imposed in order to curtail man's ambitions and devices. Ḥalāl (lawful) and Ḥarām) unalwful) are clearly mentioned and these are the boundaries which every Muslim as well as non-Muslim living with them must respect. If he transgresses any of these limits, he is doing wrong or committing a crime. Even between these two boundaries of 'lawful' and 'unlawful', there exists the things which are doubtful (Mushttabiḥāt), which must be refrained from in order to avoid excesses. The ḥadīth of the Prophet says:

«ان الحلال بين، وإن الحرام بين، وبينهما أمور مشتبهات لا يعلمهن كثير من الناس - فمن إتقى الشبهات فقد أستبرأ لدينه وعرضه - ومن وقع في الشبهات وقع في الحرام - كالراعي يرعى حول الحمى يوشك أن يرتع فيه. الا وأن لكل ملك حمى، الا وأن حمى الله محارمه. الا وأن في الجسد مضغة، إذا صلحت صلح الجسد كله، وإذا فسدت فسد الجسد كله، الا وهي القلب».

"That which is lawful is plain and that which is unlawful is plain and between the two of them are doubtful matters about which not many people know. Thus he avoids doubtful matters clears himself in regard to his religion and his honour, but he who falls into doubtful matters fall into that which is unlawful, like the shepherd who pastures around a sanctuary, all but grazing therein. Truly every kind has a sanctuary, and truly Allah's sanctuary is His prohibitions. Truly, in the body there is a morsel of flesh which, if it be whole, all the body is whole and which, if it be diseased, all of it is diseased. Truly, it is the heart."[20]

In reality, these limits provide safeguards of the rights of men and nations and give men sense of responsibility to Allah and hence to the entire mankind. These limits stop him from being inhuman, and make him respect the blood and property of another man, and give equality of treatment to all individuals, male and female before law. In commercial dealings, these limits provide for respect for contractual dealings and pledged words and the prohibition of usury and gambling. In the case of individual conduct, these limits provide for the prohibition of intoxicants and not to do injustice to servants and give charity to poor relations and provide for the strict law governing inheritance. In the dealings with nations, these limits provide for respect for treaties, and give strict code of conduct for one's dealings with the fellowmen by not destroying even the enemies means of sustenance, and show mercy to the surrendered enemy and show respect for non-combatants. In short, in every action of a man's dealings with fellow men there are limits (Ḥudūd) imposed by Allah which are nothings but the sanctions of the Divine Shari'ah.

Judicial power, according to Sharī'ah, must always operate in conformity with equity, even to the benefit of an enemy and to the detriment of a relative. Shari'ah does not allow the slightest modification in the rule of perfect justice, or any form of arbitrary procedure to replace it. It firmly establishes the rule of law, eliminating all differences between the high and the low.

Qur'ān asserts that all mankind, born of the same father and mothers, forms one single family, that the God of men is Unique, that the Creator has ordered men according to nations and tribes so that they may know, and assist one another, for the good of all.

In the administration of justice, therefore, a Judge must be upright, sober, calm and cool. Nothing should ruffle his mind from the path of rectitude. If he does wrong, he is not only responsible to the people but also to God. The noble Prophet (S.A.W.) advised: "No judge shall pass a judgement between two men while he is angry."[21] He must not feel kindness in executing the ordained sentences for the prescribed crimes. The Qur'ān says: "Let not pity detain you in the matter of obedience to Allah if you believe in Allah and the Last Day and let a party of believers witness their sentences."[22] He must decide disputes with as much speed and promptness as possible, for delayed justice produces no appreciable good. He must not accept any present or bribery from the parties concerned. He must exert hard to arrive at a just conclusion. The Prophet said: "Verily Allah is with a judge so long as he is not unjust. When he is (willingly) unjust, he goes off him and the devil keeps attached to him."[23] To a judge, all are equal in the eye of the law. As *God* dispenses justice among His subjects, so a judge should judge without any distinction whatsoever. The Prophet said: "The previous nations were destroyed, because they let off persons of high rank and punished the poor and the helpless". In the Sharī'ah, a judge is a judge for every matter – civil, criminal and military. There is no separate Judiciary for separate civil, criminal and military departments.

The basic principles of Sharī'ah, therefore, can be summed up as follows:

(a) The larger interest of society takes precedence over the interest of the individual.
(b) Although 'relieving hardship' and 'promoting benefit' are both among the prime objectives of the Sharī'ah the former takes precedence over the latter.
(c) A bigger loss cannot be inflicted to relieve a smaller loss or a bigger benefit cannot be sacrificed for a smaller one. Conversely, a smaller harm can be inflicted to avoid a bigger harm or a smaller benefit can be sacrified for a larger benefit.

Al-Qāḍi (The Judge) and His Responsibilities Under Sharī'ah

Qualification of a Qāḍi:

As we have seen, Islam has given a great importance to Justice which must be done at all cost. Those who perform the function of the *Qāḍis* (judges) or *Qāḍī al-Quḍāt* (Chief Justice) must be not only men of deep insight, profound knowledge of the Shari'ah, but they must also be Allah-fearing, forth right, honest, sincere men of integrity. The Holy Prophet (S.A.W.) has said:

> The Messenger of Allah said: "The *Qāḍis* are of three types. One type will go to paradise and the remaining two will end up in the fire of hell. The person who will got to paradise is one who understood the truth and judged accordingly. One who judged unjustly after understanding the truth, they will go to hell. Likewise, Qāḍi who judged in ignorance also will go to the hell."[24]

The above Ḥadīth shows how delicate and responsible job of Qāḍī is in Islam. His knowledge of Qur'ān and Sharī'ah must be very deep and that he judges justly. Otherwise, it can really ruin a man's spiritual future in the next world. The life in this world is only for a limited period while the life in the next world is for ever. Then why should one really undertake to be a judge when he does not have the required qualifications and character to be a judge? In another Hadith, one who is given this responsibility to be a Qāḍī as if he is slaughtered without a knife.

عن أبي هريرة قال قال رسول الله صلى الله عليه وسلم: «من جعل قاضيا بين الناس فقد ذبحُ بغير سكـــين».

It is reported by Abū Hurairah that the Messenger of Allah said: "One who is made a Qāḍi to administer justice among people as if he is slaughtered without a knife".

Naturally, a man who is appointed as a Qāḍi or a judge does not have an easy job to perform. If he becomes slightly irresponsible and unjust, he will be caught on the Day of Judgement. On the other hand, when he is just and administers justice according to the Book of Allah and the Sunnah of the Prophet (S.A.W.), he is taken as an enemy of highly influential people in the society. The responsibility of a Qāḍī is like a double-edged sword, and one has to be extraordinarily careful in fulfilling it. The following is the guidance from the Sunnah of the Prophet which every judge must follow in their task of administering justice:

(1) *Equality of All Litigants:* A Muslim judge must treat all his litigants equal whether he is a king or his page, a master or his servant, a rich man or a poor man, a relative or a stranger and a friend or a foe:

عن عبادة بن الصامت قال قال رسول الله صلى الله عليه وسلم: «أقيموا حدود الشرع في القريب والبعيد ولا تأخذكم في الله لومة لائم».

It is reported by Ubādah bin al-Ṣāmit that the Messenger of Allah (S.A.W.) said: "Let the *ḥudūd* of Allah be applied equally on your relatives and the total strangers. You should not care a bit for the reproachment of any critic whatsoever."[25]

The Prophet (S.A.W.) has also said:

عن عائشـــة رضي الله عنهـا أن النبي صلى الله عليـه وسلم قال: «أقيلوا ذوى الهيآت عثراتهم الا الحدود».

It is reported by 'Āishah that the Messenger of Allah said: "Forgive the shortcomings of highly respected people but certainly do not forgive them in awarding the *ḥadd* punishment to them."[26]

(2) *The Defendant and Appeallant must appear before the Qāḍī:* Even though one is a highly placed person or a king or an emperor or an administrator of a country, he must not be exempted from appearing before the judge to answer the charges levelled against him:

It is reported by 'Abdullah bin Zubair that the Messenger of Allah said: "Both the parties in a dispute must be brought before the judge."[27]

(3) *The Defendant should be given right to take an oath:* Human being, being what he is, will keep on grumbling and blaming others for his own faults or in order to hide his faults and escape punishments. If every

one's claim is taken seriously, there would appear so many claimants of people's life and property. The remedy is suggested by the Holy Prophet as follows:

عن ابن عباس عن النبي صلى الله عليه وسلم قال: «لو يعطى الناس بدعواهم لا دعى ناس دماء رجال وأموالهم ولكن اليمين على المدعى عليه».

> It is reported by 'Abdallah bin 'Abbas that the Messenger of Allah (S.A.W.) said: "If people were to be judged merely on account of their claims, there would appear claimants of the life and property of everyone (so that there would remain none whose life and property can remain safe.) So, the defendant must be given right to take an oath (concerning the charge levelled against him)."[28]

The above guidance of the Prophet will provide the defendants with an opportuntiy to get acquitted of the calumny put against them.

(4) *The judge must be careful in awarding Ḥadd punishment:* Ḥadd punishment is meant to be a deterrent so that people may not become complacent and commit crimes simply because they find punishment to be just nominal. But while awarding *Ḥadd* punishment, the Judge must make sure that the crime is definitely committed. If there is a slight doubt in establishing the crime, he should refrain from awarding *ḥadd* punishment. The Prophet has said:

> It is reported by Aishah that the Messenger of Allah (S.A.W.) said: "As far as possible, refrain from awarding *Ḥadd* punishment to a Muslim. If there is found slight excuse (or doubt), leave him alone because it is better for the judge to err in acquitting the accused rather than erring in awarding him punishment."[29]

From the above *Ḥadīth*, it is also clear that in order to find out the crime committed by the accused, the judge must endeavour to the best of his ability. To keep an accused in unlawful custody without due process of Law is also against the spirit of Justice.

Should We Shun Our Responsibility In Accepting the Position of a Judge?

Although the responsibility of a *Qāḍī* or a Judge are very great, it is essential that the learned jurists must accept the position of a Judge in order to administer justice and save humanity from chaos, anarchy and law of the jungle. The Messenger of Allah said to Amr bin al-'Ās:

> "If the Judges exercise *Ijtihād*, and arrives at the correct decision he is doubly rewarded, and if he arrives at a wrong decision, he is still rewarded singly provided he exercised *Ijtihād*."[30]

The best instrument in the hands of a Qāḍi are the *Book of Allah*, the *Sunnah of the Prophet*, the *decisions of the Ṣaḥābah, Tābi'in* and *Tābi' Tābi'īn* and above all *Taqwah* (fear of Allah). With these, if he adminsiters justice and makes a mistake, Allah will forgive him and reward him. Some people erroneously put forward the case of Imam Abū Ḥanīfah who refused to accept the position of a Judge on account of his personal piety. But they forget that although Imām Abū Ḥanīfah himself refused to be a judge, he did not stop his companion and disciple Abū Yūsuf to render the same services to the *Ummah*. The Prophet once said:

> "I am but a human, and I give judgement according to what I hear (from the parties), but should I decide in favour of a party because that party is better in tendering their own case, when in fact the other party to the dispute is the one in the right then the party in whose favour judgement was erroneously rendered has reserved for himself a place in hell".

When this could happen to the rightly guided Messenger of Allah, what about any ordinary member of his Ummah?

Caliph ʿUmar's Guidance for Judges

The Judges were appointed for the administration of justice by the Prophet (S.A.W.) himself. He sent Mua'dh bin Jabal to Yemen as Judge. Likewise, he had entrusted Judicial task to ʿAlī bin Abū Ṭālib and Ibn Yasār. The *Rāshidūn* Caliphs continued with the same practice and sent judges to different parts of the Muslim world. Sayyidnā ʿUmar appointed Abul Dardā to help him as a *Qāḍi* in Medina. Shurayḥ was appointed as a judge in Basrah, and Abū Mūsa al-Ashʿari in Kūfah in Iraq.

The memorable letter of Sayyidnā ʿUmar written to Abū Mūsā al-As'harī on the eve of his appointment as the *Qāḍī* outlines the functions and responsibilities of a Muslim Judge and is equally relevant even today. Among other things he said in the letter:

> "Try to understand the depositions that are made before you because it will be useless to consider a plea that is not valid. Consider all equal before you in the court and (consider them equal) in giving your attention to them so that the highly placed people may not expect you to be partial and the humble may not despair of justice from you. The claimant must produce evidence. An oath must be taken from the defendant. It is permissible to have compromise among Muslims but not an agreement through which *Ḥarām* (unlawful) would be turned to *Ḥalāl* (lawful) and vice versa.
>
> If you have given a judgement yesterday and today you may arrive to a correct opinion upon re-thinking, you must not feel prevented from retracting from your first judgement, because justice is primeval, and it is better to retract than to continue in error. Use your own individual judgement about matters that perplex and about which neither an answer is found in the Qur'ān and the Sunnah. Know the similitude and weigh the issues accordingly (here Abū Mūsā is asked to use individual judgement and arrive to a logical conclusion through the use of *Qiyās* and *Ijtihād*).[31] If one brings a claim, which he may or may not be able to prove,

decide a time-limit for him. If he produces evidence within the time-limit set (by you), you should allow his claim, otherwise you are at liberty to give judgement against him. This is the best way to forestall or clear any possible doubt. All Muslims are acceptable as witnesses against each other, except those who have received a punishment (earlier) provided by the *Sharī'ah*, and those who are proved to have given false witness, and those who are suspected partially on the ground of client status or relationship because Allah praised be His name, forgives one because of taking oaths and postpones punishment in the face of the evidence. Avoid weariness, fatigue and annoyance at the litigants. Allah will grant you a great reward and give good reputation for establishing justice in the courts of justice. Good bye."

Shūrā: The Mutual Consultation in Sharī'ah

Since the Ummah has the first allegiance to be paid to Allah, all the affairs of Muslims should be guided by the Divine Book (*Kitāb-Allāh*). Human inspiration, intellect and judgement to run their affairs should be based on the authority of power and Wisdom of Allah. Unlike human power, this power is good and merciful. Unlike human wisdom, this wisdom is necessarily complete and indisputable.

Whatever Allah has given us is merely for the convenience of this life, but we should always be mindful of the fact that whatever is with Allah is better and more lasting.[32] Therefore our efforts should be directed to make not only this life better but the life hereafter secure. Those who are believers should put their trust in God while executing all their affairs, should avoid greater crimes and shameful deeds and should forgive even they are angry.[33] After making us aware of our responsibility, verses 42 of *Sūrah al-Shūrā* says:

«وَالَّذِينَ اسْتَجَابُوا لِرَبِّهِمْ وَأَقَامُوا الصَّلَوٰةَ وَأَمْرُهُمْ شُورَىٰ بَيْنَهُمْ وَمِمَّا رَزَقْنَٰهُمْ يُنْفِقُونَ».

"Those who answered the call of their Lord, and establish regular prayer, and whose affairs are a matter of counsel (i.e. they are conducted by mutual consultation), and who spend out of what we bestow on them for sustenance".[34]

The Muslim Jurists have said that when mutual consultation was made necessary for the Prophet himself to follow, it really becomes incumbent upon his followers to resort to *Shūrā* in all our activities whether individual, social or politicial matters. The Messenger of Allah used to receive revelation from Allah, hence, seemingly he was not in need of mutual consultation but still he was asked to do so through divine commandment. It is on this basis that Ibn Taimiyyah has said that "The leader has no other option but to resort to *Shūrā* since Allah had commanded his Prophet to do so. All others, therefore, have a special need for mutual consultation."[35] The Prophet has said in a

Ḥadīth: "If I were to make any one a caliph without consultation, I would have named Abdallah bin Mas'ūd.[36] Likewise, Caliph 'Umar has also said that caliphate can never function without mutual consultation.[37]

عن عمر بن الخطاب قال: «لا خلافة الا عن شــــوري».

In the Battle of Uḥud, the companions of the Prophet had recommended that it is better that they defend against the enemies coming from Mecca while keeping themselves in Medina. But Hamza, the uncle of the Prophet and other young men were of the opinion that they should bravely go out of Medina and fight the incoming enemies. After viewing their opinions the Prophet resolved (*Azm*) to go out of Medina and fight. Later the elderly companions persuaded the young men to withdraw their suggestion. The young men went to the Prophet and with repentance withdrew their opinion but the Prophet said that now after weighing the view points in the consultation he had already resolved and it would be against the prophetic mission to go back on the final resolution.[38]

The other fine example to show how the righteous caliphs depended on the mutual consultations of the public is that of caliph 'Umar who was of the opinion that after the conquest of Iraq and Syria the land should not be divided among the warriors as booty but should be made the property of the state so that through its produce and income the essential works of public welfare can be carried out. But some companions opposed the view of the caliph. When they could not find any solution through mutual consultation, the caliph called a public meeting in the prophetic mosque for general consultation and addressed the public in the following words: "I have not just gathered you here and given you the trouble for nothing. The reason for inviting you is that you should also participate in the trust of the caliphate which has been trust upon me by you. Undoubtedly, I am an ordinary human being like you. I want that those who have opposed my point of view and those who have favoured it should declare it openly. I do not wish that you should follow my point of view because you all possess the Book of Allah (from which you may derive guidance to resolve the issue).

Mutual consultation is, therefore, one of the great qualities that the Faithful (*Mu'min*) has to cultivate in himself. It is ordained by Allah in Ayah 159 of *Sūrah āl-Imrān:*

«فَبِمَا رَحْمَةٍ مِنَ اللّٰهِ لِنْتَ لَهُمْ وَلَوْ كُنْتَ فَظّاً غَلِيظَ الْقَلْبِ لَا نْفَضُّوا مِنْ حَوْلِكَ فَاعْفُ عَنْهُمْ وَاسْتَغْفِرْ لَهُمْ وَشَاوِرْهُمْ فِي الاَمْرِ فَاذِاَ عَزَمْتَ فَتَوَكَّلْ عَلَى اللّٰهِ، اَنَّ اللّٰهَ يُحِبُّ الْمُتَوَكِّلِينَ».

> "It is part of the Mercy of Allah that you do deal gently with them, were you severe or harsh hearted, they would have broken away from about you: So pass over their faults and ask for Allah's forgiveness for them, and consult them in affairs. Then when you have taken a decision, put your trust in Allah."[39]

On this basis, consultation among Muslims is an important pillar of the beautiful and elaborate building of the Islamic way of life. To do any collective work without prior mutual consultation is not only a way of the ignorant but is also a clear defiance of the regulation laid down by Allah. The great importance give to the whole process of consultation is based upon three reasons:

Firstly, it is very unfair to decide alone a matter concerning two or more people. In collective matters nobody has a right to do according to one's sweet will. All the people concerned with the matter should be consulted, and if it is concerned with a very large number of persons then their representatives should be sounded for their considered opinion.

Secondly, if a man tries to act autocratically or arbitrarily, either he wants to usurp the right of others or he considers himself superior to others whom he holds in contempt. From moral point of view both these attitudes and bad and reprehensible. However, even a trace of these wrong attitudes cannot be found in the Faithful (*Mu'min*), who is neither selfish so as to take unfair advantage of others, nor is proud and self-conceited so as to believe himself a paragon of intelligence and knowledge.

Thirdly, it is a concern of great responsibility to take decisions on matter relating to the rights and interests of others. Anyone, who is conscious of Allah and His inevitable judgement, cannot dare to bear the burden of such responsibility all alone. Such reckless acts are done by only those people who are devoid of fear of Allah and are without care of the hereafter. Allah-fearing person with conscious awareness of the Day of Judgement will necessarily try to consult all the people or their trusted representatives concered with a collective matter in coming to a decision and line of action so that a just and impartial decision is made and if ever a mistake is made the burden of responsibility does not fall on one person alone.

These are the three reasons about which if one ponders, one can well understand why mutual consultation is a necessary requirement of the type or morality taught by Islam to man, and why violation of it is such an immoral and unethical act that Islam can never allow it. Islamic way of life requires that the principle of consultation should be applicable to every small or big collective affair. In the affairs of the household husband and wife should consult each other before doing anything, and then the children attain the age of puberty their opinion should also be taken into account. If the affairs of the whole family are being dealt with, then counsel should be taken with every sane adult member of the family.

If the affairs are of relatives, a clan, a tribe, a whole village, or an entire town or city and it is not possible to take counsel with everybody, then the decisions should be taken by an assembly of trusted representatives of the people, who are selected or elected according to an agreed method and set procedure. If the affairs belong to a whole nation then the national head should be appointed after knowing the opinion of all. The head in turn should run the affairs of the country with the help of such counsellors who command the confidence of the nation. Such a leader should remain at the help of the affairs of the nation until the time set by the nation and no longer. No honest person can ever desire to try to become the head of a nation or to continue to be the head by coercion or forceful means, nor can he use deceitful ways and means in order to appoint himself as the principal authority of the nation by using force and then demanding approval from the people by means of a coerced obedience, nor can he use crafty tactics, so that the people instead of choosing, of their own free will, persons of their liking should select those who would vote and wait for him and support his wrong policies. Such desires and actions are only present in a person whose intentions are bad and corrupt.

To present a false appearance of "and whose affairs are a matter of counsel", and to make its basic requirements practically ineffective can only be the motives of a person who is unscrupulous enough to try to deceive Allah and the general public despite the fact that neither Allah can be misled nor the public can be so blind that a person openly commits an act of daylight banditry and he continues to believe sincerely that he is not committing robbery with violence but is serving the public. The rule of "and whose affairs are a matter of counsel" by its very nature demands five things for its fulfilment.

First, those people, whose rights and interests are involved, should have full freedom of expression and should be kept informed about how their affairs are being run. They should have also the full right to protest if they see any deficiency, negligence or error in the proper discharge of the duties of leadership pertaining to their affairs. Still if they find no improvement in the performance of such duties they should be able to change their leaders appropriately. To order the collective affairs of the people after stifling their voice, fettering their hands and feet and keeping them in the dark is a clear-cut dishonesty and nobody can agreed that it is an implementation of "and whose affairs are a matter of counsel".

Secondly, the person for shouldering the responsibility of managing the collective affairs should be appointed with the express approval of the people. This approval should be freely given without let or hindrance. It should not be obtained with coercion, intimidation, bribery, temptation, intrigue, deceit or trickery. The real and rightful leader of a nation is not the one who imposes himself upon it by every possible artifice, but who is chosen by the people of their free will.

Thirdly, the advisers of the head of the nation should also have full confidence of the people and should prove worthy of it. It is very obvious that the people cannot trust men who gain representative places through pressure, monetary temptation, falsehood and skill in trickery.

Fourthly, the people who give their counsel or considered opinion should do so according to their knowledge and consicence in full freedom. If it is not so and the counsellors give their opinion under duress of their knowledge and conscientious beliefs, then this is manifest dishonesty and treachery and not any compliance with "and whose affairs are a matter of counsel".

Fifthly, the collective advice or decision arrived at by the principle of unanimity or majority should be accepted without reservation, because if one clique is free to follow its whims in spite of listening to the consultative assembly then the process of consultation becomes meaningless and null and void. Allah ordains that their affairs are run by mutual consultation, but does not say that they are consulted in their affairs. Thus this commandment is not to put into practice by merely consulting one another but it is very essential that the actual affairs be conducted according to the decisions reached unanimously or by the majority at the end of the process of consultation.

With the above explanation of the Islamic principle of consultation (shūra) this basic fact should also be kept in full view that 'shūra' is not the last word, nor the absolute authority in running the affairs of Muslims, but it is definitely limited within the confines of "Al-Dīn" of Islam, the code of life of Islam which has been decreed and codified by Allah himself. It is dependent upon the fundamental principle that in whatever matter there is difference of opinion between the Muslims they should refer to His Book, the Holy Qur'ān, and the Sunnah of the Holy Prophet. According to this basic principle Muslims can consult each other about matters in the Sharī'ah regarding the correct meaning of a particular clause and correct observance of it in order to fulfil its purposes; but they cannot confer together with the purpose of replacing or altering in any manner the ruling or decision of Allah and His Prophet by their own conclusions.

This is a vast topic, but albeit, the outlines have been sketched.

Notes

1. Sayyid Qutb, *Hadha al-Din* (This Religion of Islam), U.S.A., I.I.F. S.O. Publication, undated, p. 19.
2. Qur'an, ch. 65:18
3. Sayyid Qutb, *op. cit.* p. 22.
4. Qur'ān, ch. 57:25.
5. Qur'ān, ch. 16:90.
6. Qur'ān, ch. 7:29.
7. Qur'ān, ch. 4:58.
8. Qur'ān, ch. 4:105.
9. Qur'ān, ch. 4:135.
10. Kumo Sulaiman, *The Rule of Law and Independence of Judiciary under the Shari'ah*, C.I.L.S. Publication, Zaria.
11. Maududi, A.A., *Political Theory of Islam*, a chapter in *Islam - Its Meaning and Message*, edited by Khurshid Ahmad, London, 1976. p. 161.
12. Cf. Pickthal, Marmaduke Muhammad, *Cultural Sides of Islam*, Lahore, 1976, p. 181.
13. *Ibid*, p. 181.
14. Hamidullah, Muhammad, *Muslim Conduct of State*, op. cit., p. 6.
15. Coulson, N.J., *A History of Islamic Law*, Edinburgh, p. 8.
16. Maudūdi, *Toward Understanding Islam*, I.I.F. Publication, 1970, p. 143.
17. Coulson, N.J., *A History of Islamic Law*, op. cit., p. 83.
18. Suyuti, Jalal al-Din, *Al-Itqan fi ulum al-Qur'an.*.
19. Abdal-Wahhab Ibn Khallaf has tried to classify these verses in following order: 70 verses on family law, 70 verses on civil law, 30 verses on penal law, 13 verses on jurisdiction and procedures, 10 verses on constitutional law, 25 verses on international law, 20 verses on economic and financial order and 50 verses on sources of law in general. C.f. Usul al-Fiqh, Cairo, 1956, pp. 34-35.
20. Related by Al-Bukhari and Muslim.
21. Mishkat al-Masabih, 26:55.
22. Qur'ān, ch. 24:2.
23. *Mishkat al-Masabih*, 26:61.
24. Abū Daud and Ibn Mājah.
25. Ibn Mājah and Mishkāt – *Kitāb al Hudūd.*
26. Abū Daud. See *Mishkāt, Bāb al-Hudūd.*
27. Ahmad and Abū Daud. Also see *Mishkat, Bāb al-Aqdiyah.*
28. Muslim. Also see *Mishkat, Bab al-Aqidiyah.*
29. Tirmizi, also see *Miskhat*, Kitab al-Hudud.
30. Muslim, Bukhāri, Abu Daud and Tirmidhi.
31. The words in brackets are mine.
32. Surah al-Shura (ch. 42:36).
33. *Ibid*, ch. 42:38
34. *Ibid*, ch. 42:38
35. Al-Siyāsah al-Shariyyah, page 75.
36. Mustadrak of Al-Hakim.
37. Kanz al-'Ummal.
38. Fath al-Bāri Vol. 7. See the page of Battle of Uhud.
39. Qur'an, ch. 3:159.

Chapter 2

Holy Qur'ān: The First Primary Source of Sharī'ah

The Book of Allah:

The Holy Qur'ān is the Book of Allah (Kitāb Allāh)[1] sent through the last of the Prophets, Muhammad. It contains the knowledge (*al-'Ilm*)[2] imparted by Allah and the guidance (*Al-Hudā*) for men who are righteous for all time to come. It is a declaration (*Bayān*)[3] of the truth and light (*Nūr*)[4] to show the right path. It is the wise (*al-Ḥakīm*)[5] the complete exhortation (*maw'uẓat*)[6] and the clear message (*al-Balagh*).[7] It is a rope of Allah (*Ḥubl-Allāh*)[8] by holding which individuals and nations can achieve salvation. It is the remedy (*al-Shifā'*)[9] for all the spiritual ailments of men. It is a constant reminder (*al-Dhikr*)[10] for all of us that Prophets will not come any more for our guidance. It acts as the criterion (*al-Furqān*)[11] to choose between the truth and the falsehood.

As the final revelation (*Tanzīl*)[12] from Allah, it is the embodiment of the fairest statements (*ahsan al-Ḥadīth*)[13] and Divine words of wisdom (*Ḥikmah*).[14]

The Qur'ān provides a code of conduct for every believer and is the commandment (*Amr*)[15] and a warrant (*Tadhkirah*)[16] for him. Its injunctions are manifest (*Mubīn*)[17], sublime (*'Ālī*)[18] and blessed (*Mubārak*)[19].

Early religious books were either very short (e.g., the Budddhist books) or very long (e.g., the Bible). But the Qur'ān falls in between them and is of medium size.

Its composition in the desert of Arabia, was a remarkable feat considering the fact that very little writing had taken place before the revelation of the Qur'ān.[20]

The Qur'ān is divided into 114 chapters and contains 86430 words and 3,23,760 Letters of the Alphabet. The total number of verses are 6666. In order to facilitate its reading the Qur'ān is divided into 30 convenient sections and 540 *Ruku'* and 7 *manāzil.* There are fourteen (according to some fifteen) places in the Holy Qur'ān where the words used are so commanding that the reciter feels liking bowing down in awe to glorify Allah; at these places the reader is required to prostrate.

The Qur'ān was revealed piecemeal within a period of 22 years, 2 months and 22 days according to the needs of time and to provide solutions to the problems which came before the Prophet (S.A.W.).

The first revelation of the Qur'ān began on the 15th night of the month of Ramadān in the 41st year of the Prophet's life. Its first *Surah* was revealed in the Cave of Hira when the verse, *"Recite in the name of thy Lord and Cherished who created man our of a (mere) clot of congealed blood. Proclaim and thy Lord is Most Bountiful"*[21] was revealed.

The last verse of the Qur'ān, "This day we have perfected for you Your religion and I have completed My bounties and I am pleased with the Religion of Peace (Islam),"[22] was revealed on the 9th Dhul Ḥajjah in the 10th Year of Hijra when the Prophet was running in the 63rd year of his life.

Tafsīr of the Holy Qur'ān (Exegesis):

The *Ṣaḥāba* or the companions of the Prophet saw the Qur'ān as a rich mine of Divine wisdom and spent their lives in the search of the treasures lying buried in that mine. Their labour brought out those pearls of wisdom which illuminate our thought pattern even today.

The first output of the intellectual activity of the *Ummah*, therefore, was the *Tafsīr* or the Exegesis of the Qur'ān which, in a way, helped in explaining the norms of Sharī'ah contained in the Qur'ān.

The word *Tafsīr* is derived from the Arabic word *'Fasara'* which means 'to make clear', 'to show the objective', or 'to life the curtain'. *Tafsir,* therefore, would mean the science through which the Book of Allah can be understood. According to 'Allāmmah Shāh 'Abdul 'Azīz Dehlavi, an exegesis-writer should keep in mind the following three conditions when he seeks to interpret the Qur'ān:

1. Every word should be explained with its real meaning so that it shows the reality of its objective. In order to achieve this, the scholar has to employ linguistic knowledge and grammar.
2. Everything should be explained with reference to the context of the main theme of the revelation.
3. The interpretation should not be contrary to the writings of the *Ṣahāba,* who witnessed the coming of the revelations to the Messenger of Allah.

Tafsīr, therefore, means the science with the help of which the meaning of the Qur'ānic injunctions and the causes of their revelation can be understood.

Qur'ān is the Best Tafsīr of the Qur'ān

The first and the foremost *Tafsīr* or Commentary of the Qur'ān is the Qur'ān itself,[23] one part of which helps to elucidate the other part. This can be seen throughout the Qur'ān. As for example, when we pray in *Sūrah al.Fātihah: "Guide us unto the Sirāt al-Mustaqīm (the straight path)"*[24] We like to know what is that straight path? The entire Qur'an is full of examples to show us that path, as if the Holy Qur'ān is the answer to that prayer and yearning of the believers. Likewise, in the same *Sūrah*, we read: *"The path of those on whom you have showered your bounties,"*[25] we like to know, who are these blessed and fortunate people? The Holy Qur'ān gives us the categories of these truthful, pious, martyrs through the examples of His Prophets and Messengers as well as other true believers. When various *(mujmal)* Qur'ānic statement is elucidated in the light of the specific *(mubayyan)* one. To take a concrete example, Allah Says "Permitted to you is the beast of the flocks, except that which is now recited to you."[26] The purpose of this statement becomes comprehensible in the light of another verse of the same chapter: "Forbidden to you are carrion, **blood, and the flesh of swine** . . . "[27] Similarly, explaining the absolute *(mutlaq)* by the restricted *(muqayyad)* and the general *('āmm)* by the particular *(Khass)* is a part of the method of explaining parts of the Qur'ān in the light of other related parts of the Qur'an.[28] By applying this method Muslim scholars also try to oviate the problems posed by the verses which seem to be mutually contradictory. The work of Muqatil b. Sulayman (d. 150/767), *Mutashābih fī al-Qur'an*[29] is a good example of a relatively early grappling with this problem. The clarification of the meaning of the Qur'ānic verses was one of the main functions of the prophetic office. Ibn Khaldun said: "The Prophet (peace be upon him) used to clarify the *mujmal* and to distinguish between the abrogating verses and the abrogated ones, and to make this clear to his Companions."[30] We learn from Ahadith that the Prophet (peace be upon him) at times used to explain some verses. For example, he explained that the words: *"Those with whom Thou art wrathful"* (occuring in *Surah al-Fatihah*) allude to the Jews. Again, he explained *"nor of those who are astray"* (in the same chapter) as alluding to the Christians.[31] There are several other instances of the same nature in Hadith works which illustrate this point.

When the Messenger of Allah (peace by upon him) was asked about some verses, the answers he gave became authoritative explanations of those verses. For instance when the verse 6:82 was revealed, people found it difficult to comprehend its import, and hence asked the Prophet (peace be upon him) as to who of them did not commit wrong against himself. The Prophet (peace be upon him) made it clear that here is meant *"Shirk associating others with Allah"* which has been characterised elsewhere in the Qur'an (31:13) as a "mighty wrong".[32] There were occasions when the Companions consulted the Prophet (peace be upon him) and his silence, or corrections were themselves considered a kind of commentary. When the verse 2:187 was revealed *("And eat and drink, until the white thread shows clearly to you from the black thread")*, 'Ābid b. Ḥātim took two robes, one white and the other balck, and looked at them, but failed to distinguish one from the other. Then he went to the Prophet in the morning and told him about what had happened. The Prophet explained that was meant by it was day and night.[33] This Prophetic Commentary (*al-Tafsīr al-Nabawī*) is to be found in the collections of traditions made by al-Bukhari, Muslim, Tirmidhi, and others.[34]

The Birth of the Science of Tafsīr

The Holy Qur'ān has given rise to so voluminous a literature in languages in the last century. And the activity in this blessed field goes Urdu, Swahili, Hausa – that a single man cannot even peruse the whole of it in his lifetime. Apart from these languages, a lot of Qur'ānic literature has come into existence in many European, African and Asian languages spoken in the Muslim world alone – Arabic, Persian, Turkish, in our present time. It has been rightly remarked: "... there is no book in whose service so much talent, so much labour, so much time and money have been expended as has been the case with the Qur'an."[35] If one looks at *Al-Itqan fi 'Ulūm al-Qur'an* by Imam Jalal al-Din Suyuti (d. 911 A.H.) one can realise the encyclopaedic volume of the Qur'ānic sciences. During the life-time of the Prophet (S.A.W.), the *Ṣaḥāba* used to ask him questions relating to the interpretation of the Holy Qur'an and the different aspects of the injunctions *(Aḥkām)* contained in it. The Prophet (S.A.W.) used to explain to them matters concerning all the Qur'ānic verses.

The result of these exercises was that the *Ṣaḥāba* came to know all about the Causes of Revelation *(Asbāb al-Nuzūl)*, of different verses. They were also able to distinguish between the *Nāsikh* (abrogated) and *Mansūkh* (Non Abrogated) from amongst the verses.

The Prophet (S.A.W.) stood to explain and interpret the verses of the Holy Qur'ān to the *Ṣaḥāba* as was directed by Allah. This fact is evident in the Qur'ānic verse which reads:

«وأنزلنا اليك الذكر لتبين للناس ما أنزل اليهم ولعلهم يتفكرون».

"And we have sent down unto thee (also) the Message, that thou mayest explain clearly to men what is sent for them, and that they may give thought."[36]

All things he had said in explanation or to which he had given silent approval were committed to memory by the *Sahabah*. Those who embraced Islam or were born after the death of the Prophet used to inquire from the *Sahābah* about the Prophet's explanations to the various verses of the Holy Qur'ān. The *Sahābah* on their own part used to tell their followers – (*Tābiūn*) not only the Prophet's explanations of the various verses, but also of other interpretations to which the Prophet had given his silent approval.

Most of these *Ṣahābah* were men of great learning. A majority of them had committed the whole of the Qur'ān to their memories. Almost all of them had emerged as great Qur'ān reciters right from the time of the Prophet.

In fact, it will be fair to say that the *Ṣaḥāba* were tutored by the Prophet himself and they knew the Qur'an better than all great scholars of our time. The *Ṣaḥāba*, as has been noted above, transmitted the Sunna of the Prophet to the followers (Tābi'ūn) and the followers in their turn transmitted it to their own followers *(Tab'Tābi'ūn).*

Abū Abd al-Rahmān al-Sulamī al-Tābi'ī (d. 82 A.H.) has said: "Those who recited Qur'ān to us like Uthman bin Affan and Abdallah bin Masud and others that when they learnt ten verses from the Prophet, they did not go beyond that unless they thoroughly understood them and put them into practice."[37] Thus the Ṣāḥabah used to spend years in learning the *Sūrahs* of the Qur'ān. Imām Mālik says in his *Muwaṭṭa* that Abdallah bin Umar spent eight years in memorizing the *Sūrah al-Baqarah.*[38]

The four Rāshidūn or Rightly Guided Caliphs were undoubtedly the early Tafsīr scholars (commentators) of the Qur'ān since they witnessed the coming of the revelations *(Waḥy)* and learnt directly from the Prophet their inner meanings. Other recognized scholars of the Qur'ān in the time of the Prophet, who may aptly be described as scholars of *Tafsīr* were:

1. 'Abdallāh bin 'Abbās (d. 68 A.H./687 A.D.)
2. 'Abdallāh bin Mas'ūd (d. 32 A.H./653 A.D.)
3. Ubayy bin Ka'b (d. 20 A.H./040 A.D.)
4. Zayd bin Thābit (d. 45 A.H./665 A.D.)

5. Abū Mūsa al-Ash'ari (d. 44 A.H./664 A.D.) and
6. 'Abdallāh bin al-Zubayr (d. 73 A.H./692 A.D.)[39]

The leaders of *riwāyāt* in *Tafsīr*, taken in order of the amount they related, were: Ibn 'Abbās, Ibn Mas'ūd, 'Ali, and Ubayy bin Ka'b. Ibn 'Abbās was called the rabbi of the community *(ḥibr al-ummah)*, the interpreter of the Qur'ān *(tarjumān al-Qur'ān)*, and the Sea *(al-Baḥr)*. It was related that Gabriel told the Prophet (S.A.W.) that Ibn 'Abbās was the best *(khayr)* of the community.[40] Ibn 'Abbās, as some scholars observe, was the father of *Tafsīr*. His wide knowledge in many fields assisted him in this arduous task. His knowledge of the Arabic language and literature too was very extensive, which is illustrated by the following incident. Nāfi'bin al-Azraq once asked a large number of questions relating to the Qur'ān, asking him to provide corroborative evidence from Arabic poetry. Ibn Abbās gave the meanings of two hundred words and a verse of pre-Islamic poetry for each in proof of his contentions.[41]

Many Companions of the Prophet were proud of Ibn 'Abbās and praised him. Among them was 'Alī bin Abī Tālib who said of his *Tafsīr*. "It is as if he were looking at the unseen through a thin veil." There was also Ibn 'Umar who said: "Ibn 'Abbās is the most knowledgeable person of the community of Muhammad about what was revealed to him (S.A.W.)."[42]His being the forefather of the 'Abbāsids no doubt played some part in the attribution of a large number of traditions to him.

The other great scholar of the Qur'ān in the early days was 'Abdallah bin Mas'ūd. He spent his time in understanding the deeper meaning of the Qur'ān. The recognition of his depth of knowledge is given even by Sayyidna 'Ali, the fourth Caliph of Islam. Once he was asked about 'Abdallah bin Mas'ud and his scholarship, he replied as follows: "He knows the Qur'ān and the *Sunnah*, and his knowledge is the best.[43] His *qirā'ah* (method of recitation) is well known, and his opinions relating to *Tafsīr* in the books of Hadith and *Tafsir* are considered highly authentic. After Ibn Mas'ūd comes 'Alī followed by Ubayy b. Ka'b, Ubayy is a great authority in Qur'anic Commentary. Hajji Khalifa states: "There is a big copy which Abu Ja'far al-Rāzī related from al-Rābi'bin Anas from Abū al-'Āliyah from Ubayy bin Ka'b."[44] Nothing is known of what happened to this copy but his explanatory opinions are found in the books of *Tafsīr* and Ḥadīth. Those four Companions were the greatest Companions in the field of *Tafsīr* and much more is related from them to others. There are some Companions who related traditions relevant to questions of *Tafsīr* such as A'ishah (d. 58/675), Abū Hurayrah (d. 57/677), 'Abdallāh bin Amr bin al-'Aṣ (d. 63/683), 'Abdallah bin 'Umar bin al-Khaṭṭāb (d. 73/692) Jābir bin ʻAbdallāh al-Anṣāri (d. 74/693), and Anas bin Mālik (d. 91/709).[45]

The great Companions of the Prophet (Ṣaḥābah) who had learnt the Qur'ān and its living *Tafsīr* from the Prophet himself passed away one by one. The task of developing the science of *Tafsīr*, therefore, rested on the *Tābi'ūn* (the successors of the *Ṣaḥābah*) who were tutored by the noble companions of the Prophet.

There were three main schools of Qur'ānic Commentary which had developed by the end of the first half of the first century. The first was that of Makka whose master was ʻAbdallāh Ibn 'Abbās and whose students were Sa'id bin Jubayr (d. 94/712 or 95/713), Mujāhid bin Jabr al-Makkī (d. 104/722), 'Ikrima, the *mawlā* of Ibn 'Abbās (d. 105/723), Tāwūs bin Kaysān al-Yamānī (d. 106/724) and 'Aṭā' bin Abī Rabāh (d. 114/732).[46] The second school was that of Iraq which recognised Ibn Mas'ūd as its master (and also some other Companions, but the school accepted him to be its main authority). Its students were 'Alqama bin Qays (d. 102/720), al-Aswad bin Yazīd (d. 75/694), Masrūq bin Al-Ajda' (d. 63/682), Mara al-Hamadāni (d. 76/695), 'Amir al-Sha'bi (d. 105/723), al-Ḥassan al-Baṣrī (d. 121/738), Qatāda al-Sadusī (d. 117/735), and Inbrāhīm al-Nakha'ī (d. 195/713).[47] Finally, there was the school of Madina which, as the first capital of the Islamic Caliphate, was full of Companions and Muslim scholars, the most famous being Ubayy bin Ka'b. His students were Abū al-'Āliyah (d. 90/708), Muḥammad bin Ka'b al-Qarzī (d. 117/735), and Zayd bin Aslam (d. 130/747), under who his son 'Abd al-Raḥmān bin Zayd and Mal ik bin Anas studied.[48]

The works of *Tafsīr* at this stage included comments on more verses than before, and the successors *(Tābi'ūn)* began to compose their Commentaries as well. Although some of them transmitted the opinion of Companions outside their school, most of their material was attributed to the founder of their own school. In the immediate period following, we find the following prominent scholars in the field of *Tafsir*: Isamī'il al-Suddī (d. 128/745), al-Daḥḥāk bin Muzāhim (d. 105/723), al-Kalbī (d. 146/763), Muqatil bin Ḥayyān (d. before 150/767) and Muqātil bin Sulaymān (d. 150/767).

Since the Tafsīr-writing began in the life time of the Prophet Muḥammad (S.A.W.), it is not possible to pin-point and say that such and such Tafsīr is the oldest extant. It is likely that there were many works of *Tafsir*, but some of them have not survived till the present time. It is, however, generally believed that the oldest extant work on *Tafsīr* is that of Al-Tabari who died in 310 A.H./922 A.D. as believed by classical scholars like Muḥammad Al-Dhahabī[49] in his famous work *Al-Tafsīr wal Mufassirūn* and modern scholars like Aḥmad Amīn.[50] This is really not true since the *Tafsīr* of Mujāhid bin Jabr al-Makkī (d. 104 A.H./722 A.D). Zaid bin 'Alī (d. 122 A.H./740 A.D.), 'Ata al-Khurāsānī (d. 133/755 A.D.), Muḥammad bin al-Saib al-Kalbī (d. 146 A.H./763 A.D.) and Muqātil bin Sulaimān al-Khurāsāni (d. 150 A.H./767 A.D.) are still extant and available.[51] The process of *Tafsir*-writing has continued right to our day and would go on for ever.

After these famous people came the four Great Imams, (Imam Mālik, Imām Abū Ḥanīfā, Imām Shafie, Imām Aḥmad bin Ḥanbal) who established the principles of the science of Islamic Jurisprudence. Due to the efforts a scientific form of study, collection and compilation of the Sunna (Ḥadīth) evolved. Rules were established by different scholars for the determination of the authenticity of any Hadith ascribed to the Prophet and for the detection of weakness in it either on the ground of doubt in the character of one of the narrators or on the ground of the unsoundness of the language.

One of those who so formulated these rules was Muhammad al-Ṭabarī who was a contemporary of al-Bukhārī, the great collector of *Aḥādīth*. He was the first man to write on the Qur'ānic exegesis explaining it side-by-side with the Sunnah. He was, indeed, the first scholar to make the study of the exegesis a distinct discipline. In his 30-volume book[52] he gave a *Tafsir* of the Qur'an on the basis of what had been explained by the *Ṣaḥāba*.

In later years, commentators and Qur'ānic scientists formulated various rules of interpretation, which enabled both the Arab as well as the non-Arab Muslim scholars to write the works of *Tafsīr* in Arabic and other languages.

Some of these rules related to *I'rāb* and *Balāghah*. They were collected in the form of books. The most famous of such books is Al-Zamakhashari's *Al-Kashshaf*[53] which literally means "the book that explains". Al-Zamakhsharī was an eminent Mu'tazilite, a rationalist and a philosopher. Therefore, many scholars of the Qur'anic exegeis have criticized his work as consisting of most of the Mu'tazilite thoughts. But despite this criticism, this book remains as one of the most authoritative works on the subject.

The period of the 'Abbāsid Caliphate was the period of intellectual renaissance *(Al-Naḥḍa Islāmiyya)* in which the Muslim world was exposed to different foreign ideas. The knowledge gained in this manner was weaved into the fabric of Islamic thought and culture. Consequently, there emerged the *scholastic* theology *('Ilm al-Kalām)* wherein the articles of Islamic faith and the Attributes of Allah were discussed to establish the unity *(Tawhīd)* of Allah. The most celebrated work on the subject of *'Ilm al-Kalām* is Sayyed Sharif Jurjani's *Sharḥ al-*

Mawāqif. *'Ilm al-Kalām* was also used in the development of the Ṣūfī intellectual movement. Imām Fakhr al-Dīn al-Rāzī, author of a voluminous *Tafsīr* and *Mafātīḥ al-Ghayb,* was the most outstanding product of this movement.

Al-Isrā'iliyyāt in Tafsīr

In the late centuries, Muslims used to seek information from the Jews newly converted to Islam, about the stories of the ancient civilizations mentioned in the Holy Qur'ān. The narration and explanations of old events by these *Ahl al-Kitāb* (People of the Book) used to be taken as authentic and final by the Arabs for they did not know anything about them. One such narrator was Ka'ab al-Aḥbār, a learned Jew who was converted to Islam. But the Arabs later discovered their mistakes as most of these explanations and narrations were proved to be flase. These false explanations and narrations are called Al Isra'illiyat.[54] and some of them can still be found in the words of *Tafsir*.[55] The reason for the acceptance of the explanations and narrations of these stories from the newly converted Jews was the following Traditions:

> "Preach from me even if it is one single verse and narrate from the Israelites and there is no harm. Whosoever attributes a lie on me intentionally, he prepared his residence from the fire of Hell."[56]

There is a limit in what one can accept from the People of the Book. Some commentators have differed in giving the names of *Ashab al-Khaf*[57] (People of the Cave), the colour of their dog and their actual number. Allah says: "Say, my Lord knows their number best, it is but few that know their case. Enter not therefore in controversies concerning them except in the matter that is clear."[58] There is also a difference about the name of a boy killed by Aliser the names of the birds enlivened for Ibrahim by Allah, and the type of wood of the staff of Musa, etc.[59]

Some scholars held the opinion that wherever the texts of the Qur'ān and the Ḥadīth are silent on a particular story, the direction contained in the aforesaid Ḥadīth would suffice, and a Muslim allowed to accept the explanations or narrations given by the People of the Book. They further expiated on their stand and said that such explanations and narration should be classified into the following categories:

1. Those which our texts approve; we must accept all of them.
2. Those which our texts reject; we must reject all of them.
3. Those about which our texts are silent; we have the freedom to explore.

Kinds of Tafsīr:

There are two kinds of *Tafsīr:*

1. *Al-Tafsīr Bil Ma'thūr*
The first books of this class of Tafsīr are:
(1) Tafsīr attributed to Ibn ʿAbbās
(2) Tafsīr Ibnʿ Utaibah
(3) Tafsīr Ibn Abi Khātim
(4) Tafsīr Abi al-Shaikh Ibn Habbān
(5) Tafsīr Ibn 'Atiyyaḥ
(6) *Al-Durr Al-Manthūr Fi al-Tafsīr Bil Ma'thūr* by Imām al-Suyūṭī
(7) Tafsīr Abil Layth al-Samarqandī called *Baḥr al-ʿUlūm*
(8) Tafsīr Abi Ishaq called *Al-Kashf wal Bayān an Tafsīr al-Qur'ān*
(9) *Jāmiʿ Al-Bayān Tafsīr Al-Qur'ān* by Jarīr al-Ṭabarī.
(10) Tafsīr Ibn Abī Shaybah
(11) Tafsir al-Baghawī called *Ma'ālim al-Tanzīl*
(12) Tafsir by Ibn Kathir called *Tafsir al-Qur'an al-' Azim*
(13) Tafsīr al-Shaukānī called *Fath al-Qādir.*

2. *Al-Tafsīr Bil Ma'qūl Wa Bil Darāyah:*
In this kind of Tafsir, the commentator relies much on his own intellectual reasoning and initiative to interpret the verses of the Holy Qur'ān. It subsequently led to the development of exegesis writing in the light of linguistic and mystical interpretations of the Qur'ān and took the following forms:

(A) *Al-Tafsīr al-Lughvī (The Linguistic Tafsīr):*
This is the linguistic interpretation of the Holy Qur'ān. The notable works in this class are:
(i) *Tafsīr al-Kashshāf* by Mahmūd Binʿ Umar al-Zamakhsharī, the Muʿtazilite scholar. Al-Zamakhsharī has described the beauty of language and style of the Holy Qur'an, and shown that the Holy Book is a great miracle *(Muʿjizah).*
(ii) *Tafsīr al-Baḥr al-Muḥīṭ* by Abī Hayyān al-Andalūsi.

(B) *Al-Ta'wīl, Falsafa wal Taṣawwuf (The Sūfī or Philosphical Interpretations):*
This is purely philosophical and mystical exposition of the Holy Qur'ān. The most famous works of this kind are:
(i) *Mafāthīḥ al-Ghayb by Imām Fakhr al-Dīn al-Rāzi.*
(ii) *Al-Lubāb fi Ma'ānī al-Tanzīl* by al-Khāzin.

(C) *Al-Isrāīliyyāt:*
These works are based on the explanations and narrations received from the Jews newly converted to Islam regarding the stories mentioned in the Holy Qur'ān. The works in this category are:
(i) *Tafsīr Ibn Hayyān* by Ibn Ḥayyān.

(ii) *Tafsīr al-Qurṭabī* by al-Qurṭabī. It sorts out the authentic ones from among the various explanations.

(D) *Tafsir Āyāt al-Ahkam (Commentary on the Verses of Injunctions:*

These works contain explanations of the verses of injunctions *(Āyāt al-Aḫkām)* in the Holy Qur'ān. The outstanding works in this class are:

(i) *Ahkām al-Qur'ān* by Ibn al-'Arabī al-Māliki.
(ii) *Tafsīr al-Qurtabi* by al-Qurṭabī.
(iii) *Tafsīr al-Jaṣṣāṣ* by al-Jassas al-Ḫanafi.

(E) *Tafsīr al-Riwāyah wal Darāyah (Commentary through Narration and Proof);*

These works have taken into consideration both the narration *(al-riwāyah)* and the Proofs *(al-darāyah)* of the verses of the Holy Qur'ān. The outstanding works in this category are:

(i) *Tafsīr al-Kathīr* by Ibn Kathīr.
(ii) *Fatḥ al-Qadīr* by al-Shawkānī.

The other works of Tafsīr that can be listed in the category of *Tafsir bil Ra'y* are the following:

1. Tafsīr 'Abd al-Raḥmān bin Kaysān al-Asamm.
2. Tafsīr Abi al-Jabai
3. Tafsir 'Abd al-Jabbār
4. Tafsīr al-Nasafi called *Madārik alTanzīl wa Haqāiq al-Ta'wīl*
5. Tafsīr al-Baidāwi called *Anwār al-Tanzīl wa Asrār al-Ta'wīl*
6. Tafsīr al-Jalālayn by Jal āl-Din al-Maḥalli and Jalal al-Dīn al-Suyuti.

Risk of Imaginary Tafsīr:

It is very risky to undertake the interpretation of the Holy Qur'ān on the basis of a personal opinion without reference to the authorities stated above. The Prophet (S.A.W.) has warned:

«من قال في القرآن برأيه أو بما لا يعلم فليتبوأ مقعده من النار».

"Whosoever said anything in the matter of the Qur'ān according to his own thoughts or anything about which he did not know, he is making his residence in the fire of hell."[60]

Some *Ṣahābah* were very careful and remained silent in commenting on the Qur'ān. It is narrated from Sa'īd bin al-Musayyib:

انه كان إذا سئل عن تفسير آية من القرآن قال: انا لا أقول في: «القرآن شيئا».

"When ever he was asked about the Tafsir of any verse from the Qur'ān, he said: We do not say anything in the matter of Qur'an."[61]

The risk involved in embarking on personal interpretation of the Holy Qur'ān can be best understood by considering the example of the explanation of the following verse of the Holy Qur'ān.

«وَالّـلاتي يَأْتِـينَ ٱلْفَـاحِشَـةَ مِنْ نِسَـائِكُمْ فَاسْتَشْهِـدوُا عَلَيهِنّ اَرْبَعَةً مِنْكُمْ فَانْ شَهِدُوا فَاَمْسِكُوهُنَّ فِي الْبُيُوتِ حَتّىَ يَتَوَفّهُنَّ ٱلْمَوْتُ اَوْ يَجْعَلَ اللّٰهُ لَهُنَّ سَبيلاً».

"If any of your women are guilty of lewdness, take the evidence of four (reliable) witnesses amongst you against them; and if they testify, confine them until death do claim them, or Allah ordain for them some (other) way." 62

Some of the Commentators maintain that this verse relates to women committing fornication among themselves. But other Commentators argue that it applies to those women who commit adultery with men or women. So far so good. But a major difference among the Commentators has arisen on the question whether this particular verse has been abrogated by another verse on the same subject,[63] or whether it has been given a permanent place in the Holy Qur'ān.

«اَلـزّانِيَـةُ وَالـزّاَني فَاجْلِدُوا كُلَّ وَاحِدٍ مِنْهُمَا مِائَة جَلْدَةٍ وَلاَ تَاْخُذْكُمْ بِهِمَا رَاْفَةٌ فِي دِينِ اللّهِ اِنْ كُنْتُمْ تُؤْمِنُونَ بِاْللّهِ وَاْليَوْمِ ٱلاخِرِ وَلْيَشْهَدْ عَذابَهُمَا طَائِفَةٌ مِنَ ٱلْمُؤْمِنِينَ».

"The woman and the man guilty of adultery or fornication, flog each of them with a hundred stripes: let not compassion move you in their case, in a matter prescribed by Allah, if you believe in Allah and the Last Day: and let a party of believers witness their punishment."

A majority of the Commentators agree that this verse has been abrogated by the other verse. But there are other Commentators who say that it has not been abrogated. They include Ibn al-'Arabī. He has advanced the argument that this is a verse setting a limit for its own operation and application, namely that women should be kept in the house until death has overtaken them or until Allah in His mercy has revealed a new verse. According to him if the latter situation takes place, the first part of the injunction will still have applied. The other verse does not abrogate it since it does not contradict the first part of the injunction from Allah, namely, taking the evidence of four reliable witnesses. But commenting on the controversial verse and the other verse.[64]

Ibn 'Abbās says:

كانت المرأة إذا زنت حبست في البيت حتى تموت والرجل أوذي بالتعزيب والضرب بالنعال: فنزلت: «اَلـزَّانِيَـةُ وَٱلـزَّانِي فَاجْلِدُوا كُلَّ وَاحِدٍ مِنْهُمَا مِائَةَ جَلْدَةٍ». وان كانوا محصنين رجما بسنة رسول الله صلى الله عليه وسلم فهو سبيلهما.

> "When a woman committed adultery, she should be confined in the house until she dies and a man should be punished through Ta'zir and beating with shoes."

Then was revealed the following verse:

> "The woman and the man guilty of adultery or fornication, flog each of them with hundred stripes" (Qur'ān, 24:2) if they both were married, they should be stoned to death according to the *Sunnah* of the Prophet since that was their path."[65]

The Established and Allegorical Meanings of the Qur'ān

According to the Qur'ān; there are two systems of meanings; the fundamental *(muḥkam)* and the derivative *(mutashābih)*.[66]

«هُوَ ٱلَّذِي اَنْزَلَ عَلَيْكَ ٱلْكِتَابَ مِنْهُ آيَاتٌ مُحْكَمَاتٌ هُنَّ أُمُّ ٱلْكِتَابِ وَأُخَرُ مُتَشَابِهَاتٌ فَأَمَّـا ٱلَّـذِينَ فِي قُلُوبِهِمْ زَيْـغٌ فَيَتَّبِعُـونَ مَا تَشَـابَـهَ مِنْهُ ابْتِغَاءَ ٱلْفِتْنَةِ وَٱبْتِغَاءَ تَأْوِيلِهِ وَمَـا يَعْلَمُ تَأْوِيلَهُ اِلَّا ٱللّٰهُ وَٱلـرَّاسِخُونَ فِي ٱلْعِلْمِ يَقُولُونَ آمَنَّا بِهِ كُلٌّ مِنْ عِنْدِ رَبِّنَا وَمَا يَذَّكَّرُ اِلَّا أُولُوا ٱلْاَلْبَابِ».

> "He it is who has sent down to thee the Book: In it are verses Basic and Fundamental (of established meaning); They are the foundations of the Book; others are Allegorical. But those in whose hearts is pervesity follow the part thereof that is allegorical, seeking discord, and searching for its hidden meanings. But no one knows its hidden meanings except Allah. And those who are firmly grounded in knowledge say: 'We believe in the Book; the whole of it is from our Lord:' and none will grasp the Message except men of understanding".

This verse gives us an important clue to the interpretation of the Holy Qur'ān.

Broadly speaking the Qur'ān may be divided into two portions, not given separately but intermingled, *viz:*

1. The portion which is the nucleus or foundation of the Book; literally "the mother of the Book", and
2. The portion which is figurative, metaphorical, or allegorical.

It is fascinating for people to take up the later portion and exercise their ingenuity about its inner meaning; but it refers to such profound spiritual matters that human language is inadequate to deal with them and no human being can be sure about their meanings which are known to Allah alone. On the other hand, the verses of "established meaning" *(muḥkam)* refer to the categorical orders of the *Sharī'ah* (or the Law), which are plain to human understanding. In other words, the verses which are "The mother of the Book" include those which form the very foundations on which rests the essence of Allah's Message, and in this respect they are distinguishable from the various illustrative parables and allegories contained in the other type of verses.

It is also worth noting that in a sense the whole of the Qur'ān has both *"established meaning"* and *"allegorical meaning"* [67] In this sense the division between *Muḥkam* and *Mutashābih* would not be between the verses but between the meanings to be attached to them. Each verse is but a sign or symbol. What it represents is something which is immediately applicable, and something which is eternal and independent of time and space. The wise man will understand that every verse possesses an "essence" and as well, carries an illustrative clothing given to that essence. So he would try to understand the essence as best he can, but not waste his energy or time in logic-chopping and hair-spliting about the illustrative clothing.

The Prophet (S.A.W.) has, on his own part, transmitted every word and letter of the Holy Qur'ān to humanity and explained all of them with clear details to preclude every possibility of confusion or change in their form, content and meaning. He did it with such vigour and assuidity that even Allah had to say:

«فَلَعَلَّكَ بَاخِعٌ نَفْسَكَ عَلَى آثَارِهِمْ إِنْ لَمْ يُؤْمِنُوا بِهٰذَا الْحَدِيثِ أَسَفًا»

"Then may be thou wilt kill thyself with grief, sorrowing after them if they believed not in this Message".[68]

The Requisities for Tafsir Writing

Tafsir-Writing is a very serious matter because it is so intimately concerned with the faith *(Imān)* of every Muslim. Explaining the Qur'ān on the basis of its translations or on the basis of one's own personal opinions and reasoning cannot be regarded as Tafsir-Writing. Those who indulge in interpreting the Qur'ān with the help of their fertile brains and unbridled whims would do well to remember the following warning of the Prophet (S.A.W.): "Whosoever speaks about the Qur'ān without knowledge should prepare his seat in the Hell-Fire."

Before a person should take up Tafsīr-Writing he should:

(i) possess a sound and thorough knowledge of the Arabic language because, as Mujahid has said: "Tafsīr is not permissible for one who is not an Ālim (Scholar) in the Arabic Language;"[69]

(ii) be well-grounded in ʿIlm-al-Maʿānī *(Knowledge of Rhetoric);*

(iii) have a sound and thorough knowledge of the Hadith literature and the science of Ḥadīth.

(iv) should have an ability through the knowledge of the Ḥadiths, to recognize that which is *Mubham* (ambiguous) and to elaborate on that which is *Mujmal* (brief or abridged).

(v) have a sound knowledge of *Asbab al-Nuzul* (Reasons for Revelation) of the different verses from Ḥadīth.

(vi) have a thorough knowledge of *Nāsikh* and *Mansūkh* (abrogation of one verse by another);

(vii) possess good knowledge of Uṣūl al-Fiqh (Principles of Islamic Jurisprudence);

(viii) possess knowledge of ʿIlm al-Tajwīd (the science of recitation of the Qur'ān); and

(ix) be a man of *taqwah* (piety).

Besides the above requirements there are others as well which a person should possess before he can be qualified as a *Mufassir.*

When a man whose Islamic knowledge is inadequate and superficial resorts to "Interpreting" the *Āyāt* of the Qur'ān he seeks refuge in the figments of his own imagination in order to conceal his ignorance of the subject and in this process makes the Holy Qur'ān a victim of his logic and reason. It was for this reason that Caliph ʿUmar branded such 'Commentators' of the Qur'ān as *"Aʿdā al-Sunnah"* or "Enemies of the Sunnah", he says:

> "There will be people who will dispute with you by producing the Qur'ān as their proof. You should apprehend them with al-Ḥadīth because the Companions of the Sunnah have the best knowledge of the Book of Allah."

In the light of the above discussion, the following emerge as the qualities of a Mufassir:

(i) He should never entertain any doubts as to the principles and injunctions contained in the verses of the Qur'ān for Allah says:

«ذٰلِكَ الكِتَابُ لَا رَيْبَ فِيـــهِ».

"Undoubtedly there is not doubt in it". [70]

(ii) He must be a righteous man *'Muttaqī'* as Qur'ān gives guidance to those who are God fearing.[71]

«هُدًى لِلْمُتَّقِيــــنَ».

"In it is guidance sure to those who fear Allah".

(iii) He must also believe in Allah and the Unseen and should not be an atheist.[72]

«ٱلَّذِينَ يُؤْمِنُونَ بِالغَيْــــبِ».

"(In it is guidance) for those who believe in the unseen".

(iv) He must be regular in his five daily prayers for Qur'ān says:

«وَيُقِيمُــونَ الصَّلاةَ».

"(In it is guidance) for those who are steadfast in prayers"

«ان الصلاة تنهى عن الفحشاء والمنكر».

"Without doubt, the prayer restrains you from shameful and unjust deeds."[73]

(v) He must be charitable.[74]

«وَمِمَّا رَزَقْنَاهُم يُنْفِقُــونَ».

"(In it is guidance) for those who spend out of what we have provided for them".

The Legal Injunctions of the Qur'ān (Āyāt al-Ahkām)

The Importance of Āyāt al-Aḥkām:

The *Aḥkām* (Injunctions) of the Qur'ān are of primary importance in the life of Muslims. They form the sources of the Sharī'ah. They are contained in *Āyāt al-Aḥkām.* According to *Imam* Al-Suyūṭī[75] there are five hundred verses with legal connotation in the Qur'ān. But some other scholars feel that the number of verses of Ahkam is more than this number and yet other consider their number to be less than five hundred. Whatever may be the case, these *āyat al-Aḥkām* form the code of conduct for every Muslim from birth to death. They provide the touchstone to distinguish true from false, good from bad and *Ḥālāl* (lawful) and *Ḥarām* (unlawful) in every sphere of life. This is the reason why the Holy Qur'ān is also called *al-Furqān*, the criteria. The Qur'ān unlike the other man-made laws, is not amendable. Therefore, the Qur'ānic *Aḥkām* have remained the same for the last 1400 years. With these preliminary remarks, we may proceed to some some of these *Āyāt al-Aḥkām*.

General Classification of the Verses of the Qur'ān:

The verses of the Holy Qur'ān can be classified into four categories as follows:

(i) *those which teach mankind through the remembrance of the gifts of Allah: (ʿIlm al-Tadhkīr bi ala al-Allah)*

There are numerous gifts of Allah like water, air, sun, moon, day, night, heavens, earth, children, vegetation, animals, etc. which point out the existence of Allah, the Divine Lordship of Allah, Oneness of Allah, etc.

«انَّ فِي ذٰلِكَ لَآيَاتٍ لِقَوْمٍ يَتَفَكَّــرُونَ».

"In these things there are signs for those who consider".[76]

«فَبِأَىِّ الاٰءِ رَبِّكُمَا تُكَذِّبَـــانِ».

"Which bounties of Allah will you reject".[77]

(ii) *those which teach mankind through the remembrance of various happenings, incidents, etc. (ʿIlm al-Tadhkīr bi Ayyām Allāh)*

«علــم التذكير بأيــام الله».

A number of events show how Allah had helped His Prophets and other pious people, and how He had punished the wrongdoers. The examples of Allah's help to Prophets Ibrāhim, Ismāil, Mūsa, Hārūn, Isa and Muhammad can be seen throughout the pages of the Holy Qur'an.

Also the examples of Allah's punishment on the wrong-doers can be observed in the Holy Qur'ān in the cases of Firaun (Pharaoh), Nimrud, Qārūn, Abu Lahab and the communities of Ad and Thamud.

(iii) *those which teach mankind through the remembrance of death and Eschatology; (ʿIlm Al-Tadhkīr bil Maut wa Mābaʿd Al-Maut)*

«علم التذكير بالموت وما بعد الموت».

Death and all the events which follow death are mentioned in the Holy Qur'ān. These events are as follows:

a) Question in the grave by Munkar and Nakir,
b) Barzakh, the intermediate state after the death till the day of resurrection,
c) Resurrection,
d) The Day of Judgement,
e) Rewards and Punishments,
f) Heaven and Hell, and
g) The Beautific vision (seeing Almighty Allah face to face).

(iv) *those which teach mankind the injunctions of the Qur'ān: ('Ilm Al-Tadhkīr bi Āyāt Al-Aḥkām)*

«علم التذكير بآيات الاحكــام».

Many verses contain the commandments or injunctions of Allah for governing the conduct of every Muslim from birth to death; their observance will bring him his eternal happiness. These verses are called *Āyāt al-Aḥkām.* They may be grouped into four categories:

أحكــام المجمــل:

(i) *The Consise Injunctions:*
These are the precise commandments contained in the Holy Qur'ān. But the Holy Qur'ān does not give the detailed rules regarding these commandments. For example, the injunctions concerning purification *(Taharah),* prayers *(Ṣalāt),* fasting *(Ṣaum),* poor rate *(Zakāt),* and pilgrimage *(Ḥajj),* etc., are all mentioned in the Qur'ān, but the detailed rules about these are to be found in the traditions of the Prophet (Ṣ.A.W.).

أحكــام المجمل والمفصل:

(ii) *The Concise-cum-Detailed Injunctions:*
The concise-cum-detailed injuctions are those which are contained in verses some of which mentioned the commandments in brief but others mention them in detail and further leave them to the Ḥadīth and Sunnah. As for example injunctions on War, Peace, Jihād, Prisoners of War, Booty and Relations with non-Muslims. These details are not merely left to the Hadith and the Sunnah alone but *Ijtihād* can also be a method to find suitable solution to the problems.

(iii) *The Detailed Injunctions:* أحكـام المفصـل

These injunctions are contained in the verses of the Qur'ān which give complete details of the commandments. Therefore, there is no room for *Ijtihād,* e.g., all the Hadd Punishments Qisās, Equitable Relations, Unintentional Homicide, Murder, Thēft *Sariqah),* Robbery *(Hirābah),* Zinā *(Fornication),* and Qadhaf *(Defamation).*

(iv) *Fundamental Principles of Guidance Derived from Injunctions:*

The Holy Qur'ān also mentioned certain fundamental principles for the guidance of Muslims in acting according to other injunctions. But these principles have no clear-cut definitions either in the Qur'ān or the Sunnah except basic norms. They are to be provided through the due process of Ijtihād. These principles are:

a) principles of freedom,
b) principle of justice,
c) principle of consultation,
d) principle of public interest,
e) principle of equality.

It is the consensus opinion among the interpreters of Qur'ān and Muslim jurists that any Muslim who legislatively innovates, or enacts laws inconsistent with what *God* has revealed, enforcing his own laws while renouncing the revealed ones - unless he believes that his innovated or self-imposed laws are a correct interpretation of Allah's revelation - would be *classified* under one of the categories of either *Fāsidūn, Fāsiqūn, Ẓālimūn* and finally *Kāfirūn.* For example, if a ruler does not apply the Islamic penalty for theft or slander or adultery, preferring the judgements of man-made law, such a ruler would be considered definitely an unbeliever. If a ruler fails to apply *Islamic jurisprudence* for reasons other than disbelief, he is considered a wrongdoer, and if, as a result of neglecting *Islamic jurisprudence,* he violates a human right or overlooks a principle justice and equality, he is considered a rebel.78.

List of Some of the Legal Injunctions of the Holy Qur'ān

The Sources of Sharī'ah:
Qur'ān and the Suunah are the Primary Sources of the Islamic Legal System

Ijmā' (Concensus of Juristic Opinion):	Al-Nisā ch. 4 v 59, 115
Qiyās (Analogy)	Al-Baqara ch. 2 v. 227
	Al-Ḥashr ch. 59 v. 2
Ijtihād:	Al-'Ankabūt ch. 29 v. 69
Istihsān (Juristic Reference):	Al-Baqara ch. 2 v. 185
	Al-Ḥajj ch. 22 v. 78
Marriage:	Al-Baqara ch. 2 v. 222, 235
	Al-Nisā ch. 4 v. 4, 19, 21, 23, 24, 25,
	Al-Māida ch. 5 v. 5, 7.
	Al-A'rāf ch. 7 v. 189.
	Al-Nūr ch. 24 v. 3, 22, 26, 32, 33.
	Al-Aḥzāb ch. 33 v. 37
	Al-Rūm ch. 30 v. 21
	Al-Mumtahina ch. 60 v. 10, 11, 12.
Purpose of Marriage:	Al-Rūm ch. 30 v. 21
	Al-Nisā ch. 4 v. 1.
	Al-Naḥl ch. 16 v. 72.
Choice of Partners:	Al-Nūr ch. 24 v. 31
	Al-Nisā ch. 4 v. 3
Polygamy:	Al-Nisā ch. 4 v. 3, 129
Mahr (Dower):	Al-Nisā ch. 4 v. 4, 20, 21, 24, 25
	Al-Māida ch. 5 v. 6.
	Al-Baqara ch. 2 v. 236
Nafaqa (Maintenance):	Al-Baqara ch. 2 v. 233, 241.
	Al-Nisā ch. 4 v. 34.
	Al-Ṭalāq ch. 65 v. 6, 7.
	Al-Aḥzāb ch. 33 v. 50
Good Behaviour Between Spouses:	Al-Nisā ch. 4 v. 19, 129, 130
Code of Conduct for Believing Women:	Al-Nūr ch. 24 v. 30, 31.
Responsibilities of Man:	Al-Nisā ch. 4 v. 34, 35, 128
Marriage with Unbelievers:	Al-Baqara ch. 2, v. 221

Marriage with Ahl Al-Kitāb (People of the Book):	Al-Mā'ida ch. 5 v. 6
Prohibited Degree of Relationship:	Al-Nisā ch. 4 v. 22, 23, 24.
Ẓihār (Injurious Assimilation):	Al-Aḥzāb ch. 33 v. 4
	Al-Mujādila ch. 58 v. 2, 3, 4.
Ilā (Vow of Desertion):	Al-Baqara ch. 2 v. 226
Li'ān (Mutual Cursing):	Al-Nūr ch. 24 v. 4, 5, 6, 7, 8, 9, 10, 12.
Ṭalāq (Divorce):	Al-Baqara ch. 2 v. 227-232, 236-237, 241, 242
	Al-Nisā ch. 4 v. 20, 21, 35, 128, 130
	Al-Aḥzāb ch. 33 v. 49
	Al-Ṭalāq ch. 65 v. 1, 2, 6, 7.
Khul'a (Redemption):	Al-Baqara ch. 2, v. 229
	Al-Nisā ch. 4 v. 128.
'Idda (Retreat):	Al-Baqara ch. 2 v. 228, 234, 235.
	Al-Ṭalāq ch. 65 v. 1, 2, 3, 4.
Raja'a (Revocation of Divorce):	Al-Baqara ch. 2 v. 228.
	Al-Aḥzāb ch. 33 v. 49.
Suckling (Raḍā):	Al-Baqara ch. 2 v. 233
Orphan and Guardianship:	Al-Nisā ch. 4 v. 2, 3, 5, 6, 8, 10, 127
	Al-Baqara ch. 2 v. 220.
Succession or Inheritance:	Al-Baqara ch. 2 v. 180, 181.
	Al-Nisā ch. 4 v. 7, 9, 11, 12.
Waṣiyya (Wills):	Al-Nisā ch. 4 v. 7, 8, 11, 12, 33, 176.
Legal Transactions	
Trade and Business (Sale):	Al-Baqara ch. 2 v. 188, 275
Writing and Deeds of Sale:	Al-Baqara ch. 2 v. 282
Ribā (Usury):	Al-Baqara ch. 2 v. 275, 276, 278, 279, 280, 281.
	Āl-Imrān ch. 3 v. 130
Debt:	Al-Baqara ch. 2 v. 245, 280.
	Al-Muzzamil ch. 73 v. 20
	Al-Taghābun ch. 64 v. 17
Mortgage:	Al-Baqara ch. 2 v. 283

Trust (Amāna):	Al-Nisā ch. 4 v. 35 Al-Anfāl ch. 8 v. 27
Measurement:	Banī Isrā'īl ch. 17 v. 35 Al-Shūrā ch. 42, 181, 182. Hūd ch. 11 v. 85
Food and Drinks:	Al-Baqara ch. 2 v. 168, 172.
Justice:	Al-Nisā'ch. 4 v. 58, 135. Al-Māida ch. 5 v. 9, 45, 47 Al-A'rāf ch. 7 v. 29 Al-Nahl ch. 16 v. 90
Crimes:	
Theft (Sariqa):	Al-Baqara ch. 2 v. 286. Al-Māida ch. 5 v. 41, 42.
Zinā (Fornication):	Banī Isrā'il ch. 17 v. 32 Nūr ch. 24 v. 2, 3, 4, 5, 6, 7, 8, 9.
Wine (or any Intoxicant):	Al-Baqara ch. 2 v. 219 Al-Māida ch. 5 v. 93
Highway Robbery (Hirāba):	Al-Māida ch. 5 v. 36, 37.
Killing (Oath):	Al-Baqara ch. 2 v. 178, 179. Al-Māida ch. 5 v. 35
Defamation (Qazf):	Al-Nūr ch. 24 v. 4, 5, 11, 20, 23, 24
Witnesses:	Al-Baqara ch. 2 v. 140, 282, 283 Al-Nisā ch. 4 v. 15, 135. Al-Māida ch. 5 v. 9, 109, 110, 111. Al-Nūr ch. 24 v. 13 Al-Furqān ch. 25 v. 72.
Oaths (Al-Yamīn):	Al-Baqara ch. 2 v. 224, 227. Al-Māida ch. 5 v. 92 Al-Naḥlch ch. 16 v. 94 Al-Nūr'ch. 24, v. 22, 53.
Punishments:	Al-Baqara ch. 2 v. 178, 179. Al-Nisā ch. 4 v. 15, 16, 92, 93. Al-Māida ch. 5 v. 36, 37, 41, 42, 48 Al-Nūr ch. 24 v. 2, 3, 4, 5.
Repentance (Tauba):	Al-Tauba ch. 9 the whole chapter *especially* v. 29 which deals with legal injunctions.
Lawful Relation (Qaṣāṣ):	Al-Baqara ch. 2 v. 178 Al-Māida ch. 5 v. 35, 48.
Consultation (Shūrā):	Āl-'Imrān ch. 3 v. 158

	Al-Shūra ch. 42 v. 38
Law of War and Peace:	Al-Baqara ch. 2 v. 217.
	Al-Nisā ch. 4 v. 71, 100
	Al-Anfāl ch. 8 v. 41, 61.

---

1. Qur'ān, 2:1-2.
2. Qur'ān, 2:145.
3. Qur'ān, 3:138.
4. Qur'ān, 4:4.
5. Qur'ān, 10:1.
6. Qur'ān, 10:57.
7. Qur'ān, 14:52.
8. Qur'ān, 3:103.
9. Qur'ān, 17:82.
10. Qur'ān, 21:50.
11. Qur'ān, 25:1.
12. Qur'ān, 39:23.
13. Qur'ān, 54:5.
14. Qur'ān, 65:6.
15. Qur'ān, 69:48.
16. Qur'ān, 43:1-2.
17. Qur'ān, 43:4.
18. Qur'ān, 85:21.
19. Qur'ān, 21:50. For detailed discussion on the subject, see Al-Qaṭṭān, Mannā', *Mabāhith fī Ulūm al-Qur'ān,* Riyadh, 1976, pp. 21-23.
20. For details of the contents of the Qur'an, See Doi, A. Raḥman I., *Introduction to the Qur'ān,* 34-37 (Lagos, 1972).
21. Qur'ān, 96:1-3.
22. Qur'ān,
23. See for details on this subject, Al-Zarakhshī, Badr al-Dīn, *Al-Burhān fī Ulūm al-Qur'ān*, edited by M. Ibrahim, 2 volumes, Cairo 1957-58.
24. Qur'ān, ch. 1:6
25. Qur'ān, ch. 1:7.
26. Qur'ān, ch. 5:1.
27. Qur'ān, ch. 2:173.
28. For details see Al-Dhahbī, Muḥammad, *Al-Tafsīr wal Mufassirūn*, Cairo 1961, Vol. 1, pp. 38-39.
29. See Al-Malāti, 'Abul Husain Muḥammad bin Aḥmad, *Al-Tanbīh wal Radd,* Istanbul 1936, pp. 44-63.
30. Ibn Khaldūn, *Al-Muqaddimah*, Cairo (undated), p. 382.
31. Tirmidhī, Muḥammad bin 'Isā, *Al-Ṣaḥiḥ*, Bulaq 1875, p. 48.
32. Al-Dahahabi, op. cit., vol. 1, p. 46.
33. Al-Jaṣṣaṣ, Aḥmad bin 'Alī al-Razi, *Ahkam al-Qur'ān*, Istanbul 1916, vol. 1, p. 288.
34. Al-Bukhārī, *Al-Ṣaḥīḥ*, op. cit., vol. 3, pp. 60-137; also see Al-Tirmidhī, *Al Ṣaḥīḥ*, op. cit., vol. 2, pp. 156-242.
35. Yūsuf 'Ali, *The Holy Qur'ān* . . .
36. Qur'ān, ch. 16:44

37. Al-Qaṭṭān, Mannā' *Mabāḥith fī 'Ulūm al-Qur'ān*, Riyadh, 1976 p. 347.
38. *ibid.*
39. Al-Suyūṭi, *Al-Itqān*, op. cit., p. 968.
40. Ibid, p. 909.
41. Al-Suyūṭī, *Al-Itqān*, op. cit. pp. 282-309.
42. Al-Dhahabi, Al-Tafsir wal Mufarsirūn, op. cit., vol. 1, p. 69.
43. Al-Dhahabī, op. cit., vol. 1, p. 86.
44. Haji Khalīfah, *Kashf al-Ẓunūn*, Istanbul 1941, vol. 1, p. 429.
45. Ibid, vol. 1 430.
46. Al-Dhahabī, op. cit., vol. 1, p. 101.
47. Ibid, vol. 1, p. 118.
48. Ibid, vol. 1, p. 114.
49. Al-Dhahabī, *Al-Tafsīr Wal Mufassirūn*, op. cit., Vol. 1, p. 209.
50. Ahmad Amin, *Fajr al.Islām*, Cairo 1928, p. 274.
51. See Al-Sawwāf, Mujāhid Muḥammad, Early *Tafsīr – A Survey of Qur'ānic Commentary up to 150 A.H.*, an article in *Islamic Perspective* ed. Khurshid Aḥmad and Z. Anṣāri, Leicester 1979, pp. 135-145.
52. Al-Tabari, Ibn Jarīr.
53. A. Al-Zamakhshari.
54. For details of *Isra'iliat*, cf. Abū Shahbā, Muhammad, *Al-Isrā'iliāt wal Mauduaī Fil Kutub al-Tafsīr.*
55. As example may be cited; the stories of Adam and Eve, Hārut and Mārut, Prophet Yūsuf, the building of the Ka'bah, the killing of Jālut by Prophet Dāud, the Ark of Noah, the corruption of the Israelites, of the Companions of the Cave *(Aṣḥāb al-Kahf)* Dhul Qarnain, the Gog and Magog, the Queen of Sheba Bilqis, etc.
56. Al-Bukhārī.
57. See Qur'ān, ch. 18 *(Sūrah al-Khaf)*.
58. Qur'ān, ch. 18:22.
59. For further details on *al-Isrāiliyyāt*, see Mannā al-Qattān, *Mabāhith fī 'Ulūm al-Qur'ān*, op. cit., p. 349.359.
60. Al-Tirmidhi, Al-Nasai and Abu Daud.
61. Narrated by Imam Malik in Muwattā. Also cf. Mannā 'al-Qaṭṭān, *Mabāḥith*, op. cit., p. 352.
62. Qur'ān, ch. 4:15.
63. Qur'ān, ch. 24:2.
64. Qur'ān, ch. 4:16 "If two men are guilty among you of adultery punish them both. If they repent and amend, leave them alone for Allah of Oft-returning, Most Merciful".
65. Ibn 'Abbās.
66. Qur'ān, 3:7.
67. Qur'ān, 11:1; 39.23.
68. Qur'ān, 18:6.
69. Mujāhid.
70. Qur'ān, 2:2.
71. Qur'ān, 2:3.
72. Qur'ān, 2:4.
73. Qur'ān, 29:45.
74. Qur'ān, 2:5.
75. Al-Suyūṭī, *Itqān fī 'Ulūm al-Qur'ān.*
76. Qur'ān, ch. 13:3. Also cf. 16:11; 16:69; 30:21; 39:42; 45:13.
77. Qur'ān, ch. 55:13. In Sūrah *Raḥmān*, this verse is repeated 31 times.
78. 'Audah, 'Abdul Qādir, *Islam Between Ignorant Followers and Incapable Scholars*, I.I.F.S.O., Kuwait 1971, p. 48.

Chapter 3

The Sunnah: Second Primary Source of Sharī'ah

The Ḥadith Literature as the Exegesis of the Qur'ān

The Holy Qur'ān was revealed to Prophet Muhammad (S.A.W.) who never spoke from his own imagination but told only what Allah had revealed unto him. The Holy Qur'ān bears witness to this fact:

«وَمَا يَنْطِقُ عَنِ ٱلْهَوى اِنْ هو اِلاّ وَحْيٌ يُوحَي».

"Nor does he say (ought) of his own desire. It is no less than inspiration sent down to him."[1]

This verse was revealed to counter the three wrong charges levelled by the Qurashites of Makka against the Prophet to the following effect:

(i) that he was going astray either through the defect of intelligence or through carelessness.
(ii) that he was being misled or deceived by evil spirits (jin) and was a *Majnūn* (one possessed by a jin); and
(iii) that he was speaking out of his whim or impulse, or from a selfish desire to impress his own personality. It confirmed that the Prophet (S.A.W.) received direct inspiration from Allah which guided all his thoughts and actions. The real import of the above verse is that it shows the importance of the Hadith and the Sunnah in the interpretation of the entire message of the Qur'ān and in the formation of the Islamic system.

It is for this reason that after Qur'ān, which is *God's* word and the first source of Islamic Sharī'ah, Ḥadīth stands second as the 'hidden revelation' *(waḥy khafī)*. The Qur'ānic verse lends support to this fact when it says:

«وَاَنْزَلْنَا اِلَيْكَ الذِّكْرَ لِتُبَيِّنَ لِلنَّاسِ ما نُزِّلَ اِلَيْهِم وَلَعَلَّهُمْ يَتَفَكَّـرُوْن».

"And we have sent down unto You also the Message; that You may explain clearly to men what is sent for them, and that they may give thought."[2]

In addition to the above Qur'ānic authority there is an authority available in the Ḥadith confirming that Sunnah no less important in interpreting the Qur'ān:

«الا وأني قد اوتيت القرآن ومثله معـــه».

"Undoubtedly, I am given the Qur'ān and the like of it (i.e. Sunnah) with it."[3]

This is permitted by the Holy Qur'ān itself.[4] There is also an authority in the Sunnah to the same effect:

«الا واني قد أوتيت القرآن ومثله معـــه».

"Beware, I am given the Qur'ān and something like it along with it."[5]

But in cases where the Sunnah is also silent as to the interpretation of Qur'ānic verses, recourse may be had to the way the Companions of the Prophet (Sahāba) had interpreted them. This is underscored by a saying of Ibn Mas'ūd:

«كان الرجل منا إذا تعلم عشر آيات لم يجاوزهن حتى يعرف معانيهن والعمل بهن فتعلمنا القرآن والعمل جميعا».

'These were people among us when they learnt ten verses, they would not go further unless they knew their meanings properly and acted upon them. Thus we learnt the Qur'ān and based all our actions on it."[6]

This statement shows that the Ṣaḥāba were well versed in the interpretation of the Holy Qur'ān and that in the absence of any guidance from the Holy Qur'ān and the Sunnah of the Prophet (S.A.W.) the interpretation of the verses of the Holy Qur'ān by the Sāhāba will be binding on the future generations.

The following example shows how the Sahaba used to interpret the verses of the Holy Qur'ān.

A lady came to 'Abdullāh Ibn Mas'ūd and said:

"I have learnt that you preach certain things, and you say that those who tattoo and have themselves tatooed have been cursed by Allah Ta'ālā, whereas I have read the Qur'ān from cover to cover and did not find therein what you are saying."

Ibn Masū'd said:

"Go and read the Qur'ān again."

After carrying out the order of Ibn Mas'ūd she presented herself again and said:

"Even now I have not yet discovered in the Qur'ān what you say."

Ibn Mas'ūd replied:

أما قرأت «وَمَا اتَاكُمُ الرَّسُولُ فَخَذُوهُ وَمَا نَهَاكُمْ عَنْهُ فَانْتَهُوا».

"What, have you not recited, 'Whatever the Messenger brought to you take hold of it, and whatever he forbids you of, abstain from it."[7]

When the Lady replied in the affirmative, Abdullah Ibn Mas'ud said:

«فهـــو ناك».

"That is it. i.e. What I have said."

In other words, whatever is in the Ahādith is covered by the Ayah of the Qur'ān mentioned by Ibn Mas'ūd.

In reality, the entire life of the Holy Prophet (S.A.W.), whatever he did or said, was according to the teachings of the Qur'ān and hence, if all the events of his life and teachings are taken together with all the authentic *Aḥādīth*, we get a complete *Tafsir* of the Qur'ān put into practice by the Messenger of Allah himself, the bearer of the Divine Revelations.

The causes of revelations (*asbab al-Nuzul*) and other explanations of the verses of the Qur'ān that we find in the collections of Aḥādīth of Imām al Bukhārī, Imām Muslim and Imām Tirmidhī, which form the Tafsir *al-Nabawī*, is not complete, although they have been arranged according to the chapters of the Qur'ān by these great scholars of Hādith." There might be traditions from the Prophet (S.A.W.) relevant to three of four verses of a chapter while there might be nothing relating to its remaining verses. There are scholars, however, who believe that the Prophet commented on the whole Qur'ān, and one of these is the famous scholar Ibn Taimiya.[8] What seems more plausible is the statement of 'Ā'isha: The Prophet (peace be upon him) commented only on some verses of the Book of Allah (and his commentary consisted of) what Gabriel had taught him.[9]

'Abdāllah Ibn 'Abbās used to comment on the Qur'ān even in the presence of the Companions. 'Umar b. al-Khaṭṭāb used to give priority to Ibn 'Abbās, over the Companions, so they complained to him about this. 'Umar called Ibn 'Abbas and asked the Companions about the explanation of chapter 110: "When comes the help of Allah and victory." The Companions remained silent. Ibn 'Abbās said that it referred to the time of the death of the Messenger of *Allah*. 'Umar endorsed that opinion and thereby justified his preference for the young Ibn 'Abbās.[10]

It is significant that there is no explicit mention in the chapter of the time of death of the Prophet. What the statement of Ibn 'Abbas implies is that when victory comes everything is completed, meaning that the Prophet (S.A.W.) had completed his task. Hence, nothing lay in store for him except to return to the mercy of Allah.

The Prime Sources of the religion of Islam are the Qur'ān and the Hadith. The Qur'ān is the word of Allah to all Muslims. The Prophet did not have anything to do with its words; it was revealed to him as it is now read. Whilst the Qur'ān gives the Muslims a primary rule of life, there are many matters where guidance for practical living is necessary but about which the Qur'ān says nothing. In such cases the obvious thing was to follow the custom or usage of the Prophet (i.e. Sunnah). There were ancient customs which could be accepted in some matters, but on matters peculiar to the religion of Islam there was the custom of the earliest believers who had been the contemporaries and companions of the Prophet and who presumably would act in matters of religion according to the custom of the Prophet himself. Eventually there came into existence traditionals which gave formal statement to what the Sunnah of the earliest Muslims was on a variety of matters. Literally, Sunnah means a way or rule or manner of acting or mode of life. In consequence of this, there arose in Islam a class of students who made it their business to investigate and hand down the minutest details concerning the life of the Prophet.

Before long attention came to be concentrated on the Prophet and his manner of life became in their eyes the ideal Muslim to be imitated by his followers. In other words the Sunnah of the Prophet became a standard of living which every Muslim should aspire to reach. Certainly, who else could be a better guide for Muslims that the Prophet himself. His words and deeds, therefore, became a source of inspiration for all Muslim in all time to come.

After his death, reports of the Prophet's wonderful sayings and doings began to circulate. These sayings continued to increase from time to time as they were collected from the *Ṣaḥāba*, the Companions of the Prophet and became subject to standardization and selection.

This represented the word of the Prophet as supplemented to the word of Allah. The Ḥadīth, in other words, is the second pillar after the Qur'ān upon which every Muslim rests the fabric of his faith and life. The body of traditions circulated orally for some time, as indicated by the word *'Ḥadīth'*, commonly used for tradition and which literally means a saying conveyed to man either through hearing or through witnessing an event. It is also used to denote "conversation" i.e. the telling of something new. The records of the sayings, therefore, were called *Ḥadīth*; the rest, as a whole, was called *Sunnah* (custom or usage). For its details the plural *Sunan* meaning customs was used.

The Ḥadīth, in short, is the storerooms of the Sunnah of the Prophet,[11] serving an essential need of the Muslims, be they individuals or communities. It was for this reason that they were taught by the Prophet in the following manner :

1. Verbal Teaching was done by the Prophet himself respecting important things three times.[12] Then he used to listen to the Companions to make sure that they had learnt them correctly.[13] Even when delegations arrived in Medina, the Prophet had charged the Medinites not only to accomodate them but to teach them the message of Islam and its practices through the Qur'ān and the Sunnah. The Prophet used to ask them questions to find out as to how much they had learnt.[14]
2. Teaching through writing was done by the Prophet through various letters that he wrote to kings, rulers, chieftains and Muslim governors. These letters contain instructions concerning zakat, taxes, forms of worship, etc. etc.[15]
3. Teaching done by the Prophet through practical demonstration like the way how to perform ablution, how to say prayers (Ṣalāt), performing *Hajj* and observe fasts. His instruction in respect of the Salat was:

«صلوا كما رأيتموني أصلـــــي».

"Pray as you see me offering prayers."[16]

Importance of Hadīth for both Religious and Legal Purposes in Islam

As we have seen earlier, the Ḥadīth has come to supplement the Qur'ān as a source of the Islamic religious law. Muslims can always turn to both sources for answers to all problems. Be they legal or religious. The importance of the Ḥadīth in this regard can be realized when one considers the zeal and enthusiasm with which every group of Muslims, every party, every movement supplied itself with a selection of Traditions which would give Prophetic authority for its particular point of view.

After the death of the Prophet, every case that came up for decision had to be referred either to the Holy Qur'ān or to some judgement or saying of the Holy Prophet, which judgements or sayings therefore, obtained a wide reputation. There are a number of numerous cases on record in which a right was claimed on the basis of a judgement or saying of the Holy Prophet, and evidence was demanded to the authenticity of that saying.

For instance, Fāṭimah, the Prophet's daughter claimed that she was entitled to an inheritence from the Holy Prophet. But according the Bukhārī, chapter 85, traditions 2, the Holy Prophet said: "We prophets do not inherit nor leave an estate for an inheritence: Whatever we leave is a charity". This saying was cited by Abū Bakr as against the claim of Fāṭimah. The truth of this Hadīth was not questioned by anyone and Fāṭimah's claim was rejected. Incidents of this type occurred daily and became the occasion of establishing the truth of many sayings of the Holy Prophet.

Not only was the truthworthness of the particular Hadīth established all doubt, but the Ḥadīth also obtained a wide circulation, and from being the knowledge of one man only, passed to that of many. The Ḥadīth Literature, as we now have it, provides us with apostolic precept and example covering the whole duty of man; it is the basis of that developed system of law, theology and custom which is Islam. Muslim law is so very comprehensive that all the minute acts of a Muslim are guarded by it. A Muslim, in reality is told by his code not only what is required under penalty, but also what is either recommended or disliked after giving illustrations of the Prophet and his nearest companions. This is done without involving any reward or penalty since a pious believer is interested to know the praiseworthiness or 'blameworthiness' and thus reform his action to please Allah and His Prophet.

In Sharī'ah (Islamic Theology), therefore, actions are divided into five classes, as follows:

1. *Farḍ* or *Wājib:* a compulsory duty the omission of which is punished.
2. *Mandūb* or *Mustaḥab:* An action is rewarded, but the omission is not punished.
3. *Jāiz* or *Mubāḥ:* An action which is permitted but is legally indifferent.

4. *Makrūh:* An action which is disliked and disapproved by the Shari'ah but it is not under any penalty.
5. *Ḥarām:* An action which is forbidden. It is punishable by law.

After understanding the above framework of Muslim law, it is understandable that it was essential to receive guidance from the life history of the Prophet. For this reason, all the records of the manners and customs of the Prophet, of the little details of his life and conversation were collected.

Thus traditions of the Prophet were important in the development of Islamic Legal System and Jurisprudence. The Muwatta of Imam Malik bin Anas (d. 179 A.H.) shows, for example, how the law can be drawn from these usages and Traditions of the Prophet. This book, the first of its kind, helped to build up a system of law based partly on Traditions. It was followed by the Musnad of Imām Aḥmad bin Ḥanbal (d. 241 A.H.).

In short, after the Holy Qur'ān the Hadith is the primary source of Muslim law.

The Growth and the Development of the Science of Ḥadīth

Islam spread throughout the world with miraculous speed. Within a century, the names of Allah and His Prophet, Muhammad, (S.A.W.) were loudly cried out in the words of Mu'addhin from the minarettes of the mosque buildings throughout the *whole* world. It is very interesting to note that Islam was preached by Prophet Muhammad both as a religion and as a way of life. Therefore, the Holy Qur'ān contains the revelations from Allah pertaining to all aspects of human beings both in the mundane existence and the existence hereafter. It contains a number of laws, as for example, rules in regard to marriage, inheritences and the law or a book the care of orphans, etc. etc. But the Qur'ān is not meant to be a book of law or a book of history or sociology. It is, as a matter of fact, a book of guidance where Allah speaks to his creatures to lead a decent and refined life. The Qur'ān does not settle the question arising from diverse categories, as systematic and moral theology, ritual civil and military law.

The Holy Qur'ān with its wealth of detail is still insufficient by itself without the assistance of Fatāwā (a religious decision) and Tradition, and the Hadīth arose to supply this need. As far as the other eastern religions are concerned, their followers built gorgeous temples for their deities but the Muslims on the contrary, wrote systematic science like Asma al-Rijal the science to verify the narrators of the Traditions of Muhammad as to who reported and from who and what was the character of the reporter both in public and his private life. This was a tremendous task but the early Muslim devoted their life-time to this study of the science of theology, the commentaries of the Qur'ān, the Ḥadīth and the like.

Bukhārī, a notable traditionist, whose compilation of the Ḥadīth is known among the Muslims as the most correct one, recalls a Ḥadīth from Muhammad as reported by 'Abdallah bin Mas'ūd that the best Ḥadīth is the book of God' (Bāb Ītiṣām, ed Krehl, iv. p. 240). Hadith is a noun derived from the word Hadatha which means in a broad sense, a tale or verbal communication of any kind. The Holy Qur'ān is, as it was revealed to the Prophet Muḥammad and as it was heard from the tongue of the Prophet Muḥammad since he led his life according the teachings of the Qur'ānic and his whole life was inspired by Allah himself.

The Ḥadīth of the Prophet enshrines the Sunnah or the "Way of life" the custom and practice of the early Muslim Community. The Ḥadīth of the Prophet invoked to prove that certain acts were performed by the Prophet and therefore they were to be imitated by all faithful Muslims. It is from this point of view that Ḥadīth and Sunnah are sometimes names of the same things.

During the life-time of the Prophet, the Muslims did not need any other guide in the matters of both spiritual and secular nature. After his death, the early pious Muslims imitated him and strictly followed his examples. Therefore, they always referred to the words and deeds of Muhammad. Their work of collections of the traditions was a separate thing from the study of law although it was eventually connected with it. They began to compile everything that he had said and done; what he had refrained from doing; what he had given quasiapproval to by silence. Above all, a record was being gathered of all the cases he had judged and of his decisions; of all the answers which he gave to formal questions on the religious life and faith.

At first a particular companion of the Prophet had his own collection in memory or in writing. Then these collections were passed on to others. This is how the chain ran on and in time a Tradition evolved which consisted formally of two essential parts – the text (math) so handed on, and the chain of transmitters (Isnad) over whose lips it had passed. As for example, X said, "therefore narrated Z 'saying . . . So far it is the Isnad until it came to the last link and then followed the math, "The Messenger of Allah may benediction and salutations of Allah be on him, said "Acquisition of knowledge is compulsory for Muslim men and women." Thus the writing down of the Traditions aided the memory to hold that which was already learned.

Asma Al-Rijal

In order to know the life and the career as well as the character of the various persons who constituted the various links in the chains of the different Isnads, there developed the science of Asmā al-Rijāl which literally means the names of the men. In fact, it is the biography and criticism of the narators of the Hadith or any such aspect of their life as may be helpful in determining their identity, veracity and reliability.

The earliest formal collections of traditions were generally in the form known as Musnad. In these, each Hadith or statement which gave the saying or described the action of the Prophet was preceded by Isnad, or chain of transmitters. This took it back to the companion intimate of the Prophet who had himself heard the statement or witnessed the event given in the matan or text of the Hadith, as authority for the Sunnah of the Prophet. These were then listed under the name of the final link in the Isnad, as we have mentioned before.

The following example will show how clearly this was done.

According to Bukhārī (chapter 30, Tradition 26) "Abdan related to us (saying) Yazid B Zurai informed us saying: Hisham related to us saying: Ibn Sirin related to us from Abu Huraria from the Prophet may benediction and salutation be upon him – that he said 'If anyone forgets and eats and drinks, let him complete his fast, for it was Allah who caused him thus to eat or drink." Similarly one finds a chain or narrations in the recorded Traditions.

From these examples it will be observed that the narrations are generally done in direct speech thus A told me, saying that B said C had informed him saying I mentioned that he hear relate "I heard F ask the Apostle of God so and so.

A more practical arrangement, however was by subject-matter since at an early period the working jurists needed collections of Traditions which they might use in rendering decisions or practical cases. There grew up the practice of arranging collections under the rubrics suggested by the need of the Jurists in the matter of inheritance, debts, ritual practices etc. Thus Al-Bukhārī groups together a number of Aḥādīth concerning "fasting". Some of these include Ahadith "on the necessity of the Fast of Ramaḍān." On the fast who eats and drinks from forgetfulness, etc.

The latter development in the method of arranging collections took place about the middle of the third century when Ḥadīth had attained such importance as a means of determining the practice and beliefs of the Community. The primary aim of the reporters was to establish unerring authority for laws and custom; thus though the collectors (or reporters) devoted scrupulous attention to the isnad; so far as the arrangement of Traditions was concerned the isnad was subordinate to the musnad (i.e.) the subject-matter of the tradition). Traditions were recorded according to their subject and the subject matter was arranged under the headings of law books. Such collections were "*Musnannafat.*"

Gradually six of such collections which were made in the latter part of the third century of Islam succeeded in gaining such general approval that later generations, tacitly accepted them as the six Cononical Collection (Sahah Sittah). They are:

1. The Ṣaḥīḥ of al-Bukhārī (d. 256 A.H = 870 A.D.)
2. The Ṣaḥīḥ of Muslim (d. 261 A.H. = 875 A.D.)
3. The Sunan of Ibn Majah (d. 273 A.H. = 887 A.D.)
4. The Sunan of Abu Da'ud (d. 275 A.H.) = 888 A.D.)
5. The Jāmiʿ of al-Tirmidhī (d. 279 A.H. = 892 A.D.)
6. The Sunan of al-Nasā'ī (d. 303 A.H. = 915 A.D.)

In preparing their collections, these Traditions obviously used a critical technique of selection to decide what they would include and what they would reject. Bukhārī, for example, examined 600,000 traditions of which he accepted only 7,397. Their purpose was to assemble a body of traditions which would serve as a rule of life for practising Muslims, so their primary interest was in selecting such Traditions as would give clear guidance concerning what Muslims belief and practice should be, what things were permissible and approved, and what were not permissible and disapproved.

In their attempt to set up tests of authenticity which would exclude unauthentic material, these Traditionists picked on the *isnad* as the testing point and worked out an elaborate system for testing the trustworthiness of these "chains" and of the individuals who formed the links therein, so that an isnad could be labelled "excellent", "good", "fair", "weak", etc., and the Tradition itself rated accordingly.

To a Muslim therefore, the *isnād* is quite as important an element in a Ḥadīth as the *matn* itself. Since the Hadith consists of two parts – the *isnad* and the Matn as we have already seen there grew up the principles of the criticism of the Hadith as the Traditionists began to write their commentaries of the Ḥadith literature in general.

Thus, there came into existence the criticisms of the Hadith relating to the Isnad and those relating to the Matn. The following is a summary of the principles of criticisms of the Isnad:

1. All the Traditions must be traced back to its original reporter

through a chain of transmitters. These transmitters must be of excellent character, truthful and must have a good retentive memory and high qualities of head and heart.
2. Every Tradition which reported an event or happening that occurred frequently in the presence of a large number of people, must have been originally reported by several narrators.

On the basis of these strict principles, many Traditions narrated by a single companion (Ṣaḥābī) of the Prophet were rejected. As for example, a Ḥadīth is said to have been reported by Sayyidnā Abū Bakr alone in which he says that at the time of the call for prayers (Adhān), the Muslims kissed their thumbs when the Holy Prophet's name was recited. Since this event took place in the presence of a large number of Muslims, five times a day without fail, it should have been reported by a number of narrators. Since it is reported by only one companion, the Ḥadīth is rejected.

As far as the Matn is concerned, the following principles of criticism of the Hadīth are laid down:

1. The Ḥadīth should not be contrary to the text or the teachings of the Qur'ān or the accepted basic principles of Islam.
2. The Ḥadīth should not be against the dictates or reasons or laws of nature and common experience.
3. The Hadith should not be contrary to the Traditions which have already been accepted by the authorities as reliable and authentic by applying all the principles.
4. The Ḥadīth which sings the praises and excellence of any tribe, place or persons should be generally rejected.
5. The Ḥadīth that contains the dates and minute details of the future events should be rejected.
6. The Hadith that contains some remarks of the Prophet which are not in keeping with the Islamic belief of the Prophethood and the position of the Holy Prophet or such expression as may not be suitable to him, should also be rejected.

Such strict principles of the criticism of the Ḥadīth are extremely necessary since the Traditions of the Prophet are of great importance, second only to the Qur'ān. This is the reason why all the important Muslim jurists belonging to the first three generations of the Muslims era preferred the Traditions to the Qiyās (analogical deductions). In some cases, some of them refused to express their individual opinion on legal matters in cases in which the Hadith was known to them. The jurists like Imām Mālik also accepted the practice of the Companion of the Prophet as an important legal authority since the practices followed by the companion were based on the practices of the Prophet. The Companion of the Prophet followed the footsteps of their master scrupulously.

The Holy Qur'ān advocates the acceptance of Ḥadīth as a source of Islamic legal system. It says "Whatever the Messenger givesyou, take it, and whatever he forbids you, abstain it."[17]

Qualification of a Transmitter of the Hadīth

It is agreed by all the scholars of Hadith as well as the jurists of Islam that a transmitter of the Hadith should possess certain qualifications to be acceptable. He must be of firm faith, truthful, matured in age and a person of great integrity. He must also be conversant with the names, careers and characters of the earlier reporters of the Traditions. In short, Imām al-Shāfi'ī has summed up the qualifications of a transmitter in the following words in his Risālah. "He must be of firm faith, well-known for his truthfulness in whatever he reported. He should understand its contents and should know well how the change in expression affects the ideas expressed therein. He should report verbatim what he learnt from his teacher, and not narrate in his own words the sense of what he had learnt. He must possess a retentive memory and if he has reported from a book, he should remember his book well. He should refrain from making a report on the authority of those whom he met but from whom he did not learn anything. His report must be in agreement with what has been reported by those who are recognised to have good memory, if they also have transmitted these reports.

Classification of the Ḥadīth:

The scholar of the Ḥadīth literature have divided the Traditions into three categories according to the degree of their reliability. This classification was based on:

1. The perfection or imperfection of the chain of their transmitters
2. The freedom of the texts from any concealed defects
3. Acceptance or rejection of any Ḥadīth by the Companions (Aṣḥāb)

Their followers (Tabi'um) and their successors (Tab': Tābi'ūn) *Aḥādīth* can be classified as *Mutawātir* (of consecutive testimony) *Mashur* (famous). *Ahadi* or *Khabar al-Wahid* (one man's narrative) or *Mursal* (incomplete in Isnād). The three categories of the Hadīth according to their quality are:

1. The *Sahīḥ:* These are the genuine Traditions so declared after applying all tests.

2. The *Ḥasan:* These are the fair Traditions although inferior in the matter of authenticity to the *Ṣaḥih.*
3. The *Ḍa'īf:* These are the weak Traditions which are not so very reliable.

The *Ḍa'īf* or weak Traditions are divided further as follows, taking into consideration the degree of their defects in their reporters *(ruwwāt)* or in the text *(Matn)* of the reports:

a. The *Mu'allaq* Traditions: These are those Traditions in which one or two transmitters are omitted in the beginning of the *Isnad.*
b. The *Maqtū'* Traditions: These are those Traditions which are reported by a *Tabi'i*, a man of second category after the Prophet.
c. The *Munqaṭi'* Traditions: These are the broken Traditions.
d. The *Mursal* Traditions: These are the incomplete Traditions in the *Isnad* of which a companion *(Ṣaḥābī)* is omitted, e.g. A *Tābi'ī* says, the Prophet said . . . . . .
e. The *Muṣaḥḥaf* Traditions: These are the Traditions which have a mistake in the words or letters of the *Isnād* or the *Matn* e.g. Ḥasan is written as Hashan.
f. The *Shādh* Traditions: These are the Traditions with a reliable chain of reporters but their meanings are contrary to other similarly attested Traditions narrated by the majority of the contemporary transmitters.
g. The *Mauḍū'* Traditions: These are the fabricated and untrue Traditions.

Al-Ḥadīth al-Qudsī

Al-ḥadīth al-Qudusī is a special type of *hadīth* where, although worded, according to the majority of jurists, by the Prophet (S.A.W.) unlike the Qur'ān, the meaning or content is inspired by Allah. The normal type of *ḥadīth*, on the other hand consists of the statements of the Prophet (S.A.W.) himself on his own initiative and it augments the *waḥy*. An example of *al-ḥadīth al-qudusī* related in the *Ṣaḥiḥ* of Muslim is: "Worshippers, I have prohibited myself from being unjust and ordained that injustice is *ḥarām* amongst you, so do not be unjust to each other". The *Qudsī* Ḥadīth begins in a slightly different manner as follows:

«قال رسول الله صلى الله عليه وسلم فيما يرويه عن ربه عز وجل ......».

"Said the Messenger of Allah (S.A.W.) in what is narrated by his Lord, the Almighty and Glorified ......

or it reads as:

«قال رسول الله صلى الله عليه وسلم: قال الله تعالى ....».

"Said the Messenger of Allah (S.A.W.) that Almighty Allah said .... "

In the *Ḥadīth al-Qudsī*, the wording is that of the Messenger of Allah while its meaning and contents are from Allah. It is *Wahy* in meaning without words *(Wahy bil ma'nī bidun al lafz)*[18] prayers (ṣalāt)[19] and its recitation is a devotion (ʿibādah) because the Hadīth says that one who recites – a word from the Book of Allah does a good deed and will be reward ten times."[20]

But the Ḥadith al Qudsī is not to be recited in prayers nor has it this kind of reward.

Ahadi: One Man Narrative

The Aḥādī, or one man narrative is also called *Khabar al-Wahid.* The bulk of traditions fall into this category. Jurists differ on what conditions qualify an *aḥādī* tradition for acceptance. Mālik insisted that it should not contravene the practice of the people of Medina; al-Shafi'i demanded authenticity, the chain of narration to be continuous and the narrator to be renowned for his honesty and ability to comprehend and quote accurately. Aḥmad bin Ḥanbal agreed with al-Shāfi'ī on the importance of continuity in the chain of transmission and the Hanafis acepted the *aḥādī* traditions provided the narrator was trustworthy and the narration made good sense. An example of an *aḥādī* is "No bequest in favour of an heir."

The Four Period of Ḥadīth Scholars

The following is a list of great scholars of Ḥadīth who have contributed a great deal to the science of Ḥadīth right from the time of the Prophet (S.A.W.) to the end of the first century of Hijrah. This can be considered as the first period of Ḥadīth Scholars.

First Period

The Companions of the Prophet

Those who have narrated more than 1000 Aḥādīth

	Name	*Year of death*	*Age at death*	*Number of Narrations of Ḥadīth*	*Number of pupils*
1.	*Abū Hurairah 'Abdur Rahmān*	*59 A.H.*	*78 yrs*	*5374*	*800*
2.	*'Abdallāh bin 'Abbās*	*68 A.H.*	*71 yrs*	*2660*	
3.	*Ummal-Muminīn*	*58 A.H.*	*67 yrs*	*2210*	
4.	*'Abdallah bin 'Umar*	*78 A.H.*	*94 yrs*	*1560*	
6.	*Anas bin Mālik*	*93 A.H.*	*103 yrs*	*1286*	
7.	*Abū Sa'id Khudrī*	*74 A.H.*	*84 yrs*	*1170*	
Those who narrated between 500 and 1000 Aḥādīth					
8.	'Abdallāh bin 'Umru bin al-'Āṣ	63 A.H.			
9.	Sayyidinā 'Umar	23 A.H.			
10.	Sayyidinā 'Alī	40 A.H.			
Those who have narrated more than 100 and less than 500 Aḥādīth					
11.	Sayyidinā Abū Bakr	13 A.H.			
12.	Sayyidinā Uthman	36 A.H.			
13.	Umm Salmah	59 A.H.			
14.	Abū Mūsā Ash'arī	52 A.H.			
15.	Abū Dhar Ghaffārī	32 A.H.			
16.	Abū Ayyūb Anṣārī	51 A.H.			
17.	Ubayy bin Ka'ab	19 A.H.			
18.	Mu'ādh bin Jabal	18 A.H.			

Famous Tābi'in (Successors of the Ṣaḥābah)

The following are the famous *Tābi'in* who have rendered a great service to the science of Ḥadīth.

1. Saʿīd bin Musayyib: Born in the second year of Sayyidnā ʿUmar's Caliphate and died in 105 A.H.
2. Urwah bin Zubair: Died in 94 A.H.
3. Salim bin ʿAbdallah bin ʿUmar: Died in 106 A.H.
4. Nafi Maula ʿAbdallah bin ʿUmar: Died in 117 A.H.

The Great Ḥadīth Scholars of the Second Period

The second period of the development of Science of Ḥadīth ends roughly at the middle of the second century of the Hijra Calendar. A group of *Tābi'in* rendered a great service to this cause, they are as follows:

1. Muḥammad bin Shitāb Zuhrī: Died in 124 A.H. in Mecca.
2. ʿAbdal-Mālik bin Jarīḥ: Died in 150 A.H. in Mecca.
3. Imam Auzai in Syria: Died in 157 A.H..
4. Ma'mar bin Rashīd in Yemen: Died in 153 A.H.
5. Sufyān al-Thawrī in Kūfah: Died in 161 A.H.
6. Ḥammād bin Salmah in Basrah: Died in 167 A.H.
7. Abdallah bin Mubarak in Khurasan: Died in 181 A.H.
8. Imām Mālik bin Anas in Medina: Died in 179 A.H.

The Great Scholars of Ḥadīth of the Third Period

In the third priod of Ḥadīth studies, scholars tried to separate the Aḥādith of the Prophet from the words and deeds of the *Saḥābah* (Athār al-Ṣaḥābah) and the statements of the *Tābi'in* (Aqwāl al-Tābi'in). This was the period of valuable research which yielded the following Hadith sciences for the protection of the Ḥadīth Literature:

1. The Science of *Asmā'al Rijāl:*

It was through this science that the study of the life history of 500,000 narrators has been done as preserved for posterity. In no other religion has so much pain been taken for such detailed studies, and this is the reason why the lives of their religious personalities are shrouded in mystery. The famous works like *Tahdhīb al-Kamāl* by Imām Yūsuf Mazī (d. 742 A.H.) *Tahdhīb al-Tahdhīb* by Ḥāfiẓ Ibn Ḥajar and *Tadhkirah al Ḥuffāẓ* by Al-Dhahabī (d. 748 A.H.) are the treasures in this field of studies.

2. The science of *Mustaliḥ al-Ḥadīth:*

It was through this science that the classification of Hadīth as authentic or weak and their criteria are studied. In this field the famous work of Abū 'Umaru'Uthman bin Ṣalāḥ, (d. 577 A.H.) named *'Ulūm al-Ḥadīth* well known as *Muqaddimah Ibn al-Ṣāliḥ* is well known.

3. The Science of *Gharīb al Ḥadīth:*
It was through this science that the difficult words of *Ahadith* were studied and research were made on their linguistic origins. The famous work of Al-Zamakhshari (d. 538 A.H.). In this field is *Al-Fā'iq* and that of Ibn Athīr (d. 606 A.H.) is his Nihāyah.

4. The Science of *Fiqh al-Ḥadīth:*
It was through this science that the research was carried out in the Ahadith which is concerned with the legal injunction of the Qur'an. The books like *I'lām al-Muwaqqi'īn* of Ḥafiz Ibn Qiyum(d. 751 A.H.) and *Ḥujjaj – Allāh al-Balighah* of that *Walī Allāh al-Dihlavī* are well known in this field.

5. The Science of *Aḥādīth al-Mauḍū'ah:*
It was through this science that the authentic Ḥadīth were separated from the fabricated narrations. *Al-Fawāid al-Majmū'ah* of Imām Shaukānī (d. 1255 A.H.) and *Al-Liali al-Masmau'ah* of Jalāl al-Dīn al-Suyūṭī (d. 911 A.H.) are the famous works on this subject.

6. The Science of *Aṭrāf al-Ḥadīth:*
It was through this science that one can know which narration will be found where and who is actually its narrator. Even if one knows a small portion of a Hadith and wishes to know it all, and its chain of narrations, it will be known through this science. The famous works like *Tuhfat al-Ashraf* of Ḥafiz Mazī (d. 742 A.H.) gives full index of the *Ṣaḥaḥ sittah* (the six authentic collections of Aḥādīth). The great scholar of Ḥadīth took 26 years to complete this book. The orientalist has used such works and with a little addition, here and there have written their 'voluminous' works of Aḥādīth which are considered to be 'original' works even by Muslims all over the world simply because the knowledge of religious science has declined a great deal after the Muslim land fell in the hands of the imperialists. The Western scholars as well as the Muslim scholars who have studied in the West mostly refer to the second hand works of the orientalists rather than the original works of muslims servants, and thus criticise unduly the Hadith literature like their masters.

This list can be very lengthy since there are about one hundred such sciences on which Ḥadīth scholars have worked. These sciences helped tremendously in the growth and development of Islamic jurisprudence and they become the very basis of Sharī'ah.

The scholars of Ḥadīth of the third period and their works are as follows:

Name	Work
1. Imām Aḥmad bin Ḥanbal (d. 241 A.H.)	*Musnad Aḥmad*
2. Imām Muslim bin Ḥajjāj al Qushayrī (d. 261 A.H.)	*Ṣaḥīḥ Muslim*
Imām Muḥammad bin Ismāīl al-Bukhārī	*Sahih al-Bukhārī*
Imām Abū Dāūd Ash'ath al Sijistani (d. 275 A.H.)	*Sunan Abū Dāūd*
5. Imām Abū Ismāil-Tirmidhi (d. 279 A.H.)	*Jami al-Tirmidhī*
6. Imām Aḥmad bin Shu'aib al-Nisai (d. 303 A.H.)	*Al-Sunnan al-Mujtaba*
7. Imām Muḥammad bin Yazīd Ibn Majah al-Qazwini (d. 273 A.H.)	*Sunan Ibn Mājah*

The Fourth Period of Ḥadīth Scholars

The fourth period begins from 5th Century of Hijrah Eve and continues until today. In this period, mostly works of commentaries (Sharḥ) on the earlier works have been written, and some scholars are busy explaining points arising out of these works even today. The famous works of early writers of the fourth period are as follows:

1. *Mishkāt al-Maṣābih* by Wali al-Din al-Khatib
2. *Riyāḍ al-Ṣāliḥīn* by Abū Zakariyā Yahyā bin Sharf al Nawawi (d. 676 A.H.)
3. *Muntaqi al-Akhbār* by Abul Barakāt Abdus Salām Ibn al Taimiyyah (d. 652 A.H.). This was the grandfather of Shaikh Taqī al-Din Ahmad Ibn Taimiyyah (d. 728 A.H.) Imām al-Sahukanī wrote *Nail al Autār* in 8 volumes is the commentators of this work.
4. *Bulūgh al-Marām* by Ḥāfiz Ibn Ḥajar (d. 752 A.H.)
5. *Subul al-Salām* by Muḥammad bin Ismā'īl (d. 1182 A.H.) This book is the commentary of Bulūgh al-Marām of Hafiz Ibn Ḥajar.

There are many other commentaries written in many languages of Muslims all over the world. The work still continues.

Notes

1. Qur'ān, 53: 3-4.
2. Qur'ān, ch. 16:44.
3. Al-Bukhāri
4. Qur'an, ch. 59:7
5.
6.
7. Qur'ān, ch. 59:7.
8. Al-Suyūti, Jalāl *al-Dīn, Al Itqan fi-'Ulūm al Qur'ān, Calcutta.* 1856, p. 822; see also Al-Dhahabi, Al-Tafsir-Wal Mufassirun op. cit. vol. 1. p. 499.
9. Al-*Mabani, Muqaddimatān*, p. 182; *Al-Muqaddamah, p. 263.*
10. Al-Sayis, Muḥammad Ali, Tafsīr Āyāt al-Qur'āni Cairo, 1953, vol. 4, p. 128.
11. For further details see M. M. 'Azamī, Studies in Ḥadīth Methodology and Literature, Indianapolis, 1977. pp. 9-31.
12. Ṣaḥīh al-Bukhārī, Chapter on Islam, 30.
13. Ibid, chapter on Wudu, 75.
14. Aḥmad bin Ḥanbal, Musnad, Cairo, 1313, vol. 4. p. 206.
15. Ḥamidullah, Al-Wathāiq al-Siyāssiyah, Beirut 1968.
16. Ṣaḥiḥ al-Bukhārī, chapter on Adhān, 18.
17. Qur'ān, ch. 59:7.
18. Al Qaṭṭān, Mannā', Mabāḥith 'Ulūm al Qur'ān, Riyadh, 1976 p. 26
19. Qur'ān, Al-Muzammil: 20.
20. Narrated by Tirmidhi from Ibn Masud.

Chapter 4

The Secondary Sources of Sharī'ah

The primary sources of the *Sharī'ah*, Islamic Legal system, are the *Qur'ān* and the *Sunnah*. The Secondary sources are *al-Ijmā', al-Qiyās* and *āl-Ijtihād* – which are derived fromt he legal injunctions of the Holy Qur'ān and the Sunnah of the Prophet. Hence, the final sanction for all intellectual activities in respect of the development of Shari'ah comes from no where else but the Qur'ān. Even any Hadith which goes contrary to the Qur'ān is not to be considered as authentic. We shall examine in detail the secondary sources of the Shari'ah and their Qur'ānic sanctions.

Al-Ijmā': The Consensus of Opinions

Apart from the Qur'ān and the Sunnah, the two primary sources of the Sharī'ah, there are two secondary sources. One of them is *al-Ijmā'*, the consensus of Juristic opinions of the learned *'Ulama* of the *Ummah* after the death of the Messenger of Allah.

Ijma can be defined as the consensus of opinion of the companions of the Prophet *(Ṣaḥābah)* and the agreement reached on the decisions taken by the learned *"Muftis"* or the Jurists on various Islamic matters.

Almighty Allah himself encourages seeking the opinions of others on religious matters as is said in the Holy Qur'ān:

«فَبِمَا رَحْمَةٍ مِنَ اللّٰهِ لِنْتَ لَهُمْ وَلَوْ كُنْتَ فَظّاً غَلِيظَ الْقَلْبِ لَا نْفَضّوا مِنْ حَوْلِكَ فَاعْفُ عَنْهُمْ وَاسْتَغْفِرْ لَهُمْ وَشَاوِرْهُمْ فِي الاَمْرِ فاذا عَزَمْتَ فَتَوَكَّلْ عَلَى اللّٰهِ، اَنّ اللّٰه يُحِبُّ الْمُتَوَكّلِينَ».

> "It is through the mercy of Allah that you are lenient with them; if you were to be hard-hearted; they would have deserted you; pardon them and seek for the forgiveness for them and seek their opinion in the matters; whenever you decide upon something, have belief in Allah surely Allah loves those that rely on Him."[1]

Almighty Allah has also said:

«اَلذَّينَ اُسْتَجَابُوا لِرَبِّهِمْ وَاَقَامُوا الصَّلَاةَ وَاَمْرُهُمْ شُورٰى بَيْنَهُمْ وَمِمَّا رَزَقْنَاهُمْ يُنْفِقُونَ».

> "Those who answered the call of their Lord, and establish regular prayer *(Salāt)* and whose affairs are a matter of counsel and spend out of what we bestow on them for sustenance."[2]

Prophet Muḥammad (S.A.W.) also supported the process of *Ijmāʿ* when he says in a Ḥadīth:

«لا تجتمع أمتي على ضلالـــــة».

> "My people would never agree on whoever leads them astray".

The practice of *Ijmāʿ* can be traced back to the days of the companions of the Prophet as can be seen from the following example. Almighty Allah does not state the type of punishment that should be applied to one who drinks alcohol. But the agreement was reached by the consensus of opinions of the *Ṣaḥābah* when Sayyidnā ʿAlī bin Abū Ṭālib said: "He who drinks, gets drunk; he who gets drunk, raves; he who raves, accuses people falsley; and he who accuses people falsley should be given eighty strokes of cane according to the injunction of the Holy Qur'ān. Almighty Allah has said:

«الـذين يرمـون المحصنت منكم ولم يأتـوا بأربعـة شهداء فأجلدوهم ثمانين جلدة ولا تأخذوا لهم شهادة ابدا».

> "Those that accuse the innocent women falsley, and they do not bring forth four witnesses, flog them eighty strokes of cane and do not accept their witnesses, they are the wrong-doers."[3]

Ijma owes its origins to the following Qur'ānic verses in *Surah al-Nisa:*

«وَمَنْ يُشَاقِقِ اُلـرَّسُـولَ مِنْ بَعْـدِ مَا تَبَيَّنَ لَهُ اُلْهُدٰى وَيَتَّبِعْ غَيْرَسَبيلِ اُلْمُؤْمِنينَ نُوَلِّهِ مَا تَوَلّٰى وَنُصْلِه جَهَنَّمَ وَسَاءتْ مَصيراً».

"But whoso make a breach with the Messenger after the guidance has become clear to him, and follows a way other than that becoming to men of faith, We shall leave him over to what he has chosen and We shall land him in the fire of hell – an evil refuge."[4]

«يَـا أَيُّهَـا ٱلَّـذِينَ آمَنُـوا أَطِيعُـوا ٱللَّهَ وَأَطِيعُـوا ٱلرَّسُولَ وَأُولِي ٱلأَمْرِ مِنْكُمْ فَإِنْ تَنَازَعْتُمْ فِي شَيْءٍ فَرُدُّوهُ إِلَى ٱللَّهِ وَٱلرَّسُولِ».

"O believers, obey Allah and obey the Messenger and those in authority among you. If you should quarrel on anything, refer it to Allah and the Messenger."[5]

The healthy consultation *(Shūrā)* and the use of Juristic reason *(Ijtihād)* are normal preliminaries for arriving at a binding *Ijmāʿ.* The Rāshidūn Caliphs always consulted the *ṣaḥābah* whenever a novel issue arose. The Caliphate of Abubakr was based and run on the process of *Ijmā'* of the *ṣaḥābah*.

The following few examples are based on such process of *Ijmāʿ:* The validity of a contract for the purchase of goods *yet to be manufactured (aqd al-Istisnā')* is based on an *Ijmāʿ.*

The normal rule is that a sale of non-existent goods is not valid because of uncertainty. The Jurisitc consensus was aiming at providing a practical solution. In the field of inheritance, for an example, it was agreed that if a person is predeceased by his father, then the grandfather participates in the inheritance of the estate with the son taking the share of the father.

It was also agreed that a grandmother is entitled to a sixth of the estate of the propositus. This *Ijmāʿ*, on this issue, is based on a decision attributed by al-Mughīrah ibn Shuʿbah (d. 50 A.H.) to the Prophet (S.A.W.).

In the field of family law it was agreed that since the Qur'ān prescribed marriage with mothers and daughters then grandmothers and granddaughters (however removed) by the same token fall within the prohibited degrees.

The minimum period of gestation is six months according to all *Fiqh* schools, but an example of lack of *Ijmāʿ* is in fact the disagreement over the maximum period of gestation.

The consensus of the *ʿUlama* must be based on the Book of Allah, the instructions of the Prophet *(Qaul al-Rasūl),* the actions and demonstrations of the Prophet *(Fiʿl al-Rasūl).* But some actions of the Prophet can be of a very special nature which cannot be applicable to an ordinary man. Lastly, the consensus should be based on preachings and speeches of the prophet *(Taqrīrāt al-Rasul).*

The *Ijmaʿ* could be divided into three broad categories: *Ijmaʿ al-Qawl* (the verbal consensus of opinion), *Ijma' al-Fi'l* (the consensus of opinion on an action) and *Ijma' al-Sukut* the silent consensus).

The *Ijma'* could also be sub-divided into two broad categories: *Ijmā' al-'Azīmah* (the regular consensus of opinion) and *Ijma' al-Rukhṣah* (the irregular consensus of opinion).

As regards the verbal consensus of opinion, if an issue is raised and all the Jurists assent to it by voicing out their approval, the consensus of opinion is regular. But if it is raised but none of them says anything, the consensus of opinion is irregular. Nonethless both of them are valid in Islamic Law system.

As regards the practical *Ijmā'*, if a Jurist does something and none of the other Jurists challenges him, the *Ijma'* is regular; but if a Jurist does something, and one or more Jurist question him, the *Ijmā' al-Fi'l* is irregular. Nonetheless, both of them are valid as far as Islamic Law is concerned. During the time of the Imāms Mālik and Abū Ḥanīfah, the eligibility of Jurists who could sanction the *Ijmā'* became a matter of controversy. According to some Jurists, it is only the Companions of the Prophet who were in a position to sanction the *Ijmā'*. According to the Shi'ites, however, the *Ijma'* can only be sanctioned by *Ahl-al-Bayt* (the people of the House of the Prophet), that is the descendants of 'Alī and Fatimah, the daughter of the Prophet.

According to Imām Mālik, the *Ijmā'* can only be sanctioned by the Jurists of Madīnah. But as far as the Ḥanīfah school of thought is concerned, the *Ijmā'* can be sanctioned by any qualified Jurists irrespective of his geographical place of abode or the religious sect that he belongs to. The Jurists also disagreed amongst themselves as to the number of the Jurists who can ratify the *Ijmā'*. According to Imāms Mālik and Abū Ḥanīfa, the number must not necessarily be very great. Some Jurists put the number to three Jurists while some others say that two will suffice the purpose. The Jurists also say that any *Ijmā'* sanctioned by the companions of the Prophet could only be rep ealed by no one else but by the Jurists who lived during their period. But any *Ijmā'* sanctioned by the Jurists who are not the companions of the Prophet can be repealed by the Jurists of their generation as well as the Jurists of the generation after them are empowered to do so, because people consider their opinion as of the same weight in the Islamic legal system.

The Jurists say that any *Ijmā'* that has to do with some marginal issue on *'Ibādāt* (religious worship), must be ratified by every member of the community that is concerned. If a layman says that he does not agree to a matter raised, it must be accepted as invalid. But, on the other hand, if the *Ijmā'* has anything to do with *Mu'āmalāt* which need thorough reasoning, the layman's point of view must not be considered.

The Māliki school considers that the established practice of the people of Medina *('amal ahl al-Medina)* provided valid *Ijmā'*. But other schools disagreed on this point. Some Ḥanbalis (as well as some other Jurists) accept only the agreement of the four Rāshidūn Caliphs as the only binding *Ijmā'*.

Similarly other Jurists consider the *Fatwas* (Juridical opinions and decisions) of the *Ṣaḥābah* as binding *Ijmā'* for the *Ummah*. To the Shi'ites, however, the binding *Ijma'* is that of the *ahl-al-Bayt*, as well have seen before. Some Ḥanbalī scholars are of the view that *Ijma'* is not binding if reached more than one generation after the Prophet's death, because it is nearly impossible to obtain the express agreement of every single qualified jurist after that stage of the spread of Islam.

Most Jurists have agreed that only an express *Ijmā'* is binding. But the Hanafi Jurists consider the silence of the Jurists with regard to the vocal expression of a particular opinion as an effective implied agreement provided that *(a)* there is an evidence that the silent Jurists were really well acquainted with the issue and *(b)* a reasonable period of time passed after the view was expressed to enable other Jurists to devote sufficient time for research and analysis. If both conditions are met, say the Hanafi Jurists, silence of Jurists amounts to an approval.

No matter the rank of the pious *'Ulamā* and their thorough deliberations, no amount of *Ijma'* can abrogate a text *(nass)* i.e., a provision laid down in the Qur'ān or the Sunnah of the Prophet. It should also be remembered that no *Ijma'* was reached or could have been reached except after the Prophet's death, that is after all the texts were revealed or stated, for *Ijmā'* is based always on the interpretations of the Qur'ān and the Sunnah.

If any *Ijmā'* is soundly founded on the texts of the Qur'ān and the Sunnah it cannot be repealed by any subsequent consensus; but if the *Ijmā'* is merely based on public interest *(Maṣāliḥ al-Murslah)*, it may be repealed if the public welfare so requires.

In the fourth century of Hijrah era that is the tenth century A.D., some Muslim Jurists took a passive attitude and said that the *Ijtihād* and *Tafsīr* had been exhaustively accomplished by the early scholars of peerless ability.

Later, in the seventh century of Hijrah era (the middle of the 13th century A.D.), a great catastrophe struck the Muslim world and the Tartars, headed by Halaku Khan the grandson of Chengis Khan, captured Baghdad and killed the 'Abbasid Caliph al-Musta'si on 1258 A.D. The Mamluks who overthrew the Ayyūbids in Egypt in 1205 A.D. fought the central Asian invaders and defeated the Mongols on more than one occasion, starting their campaigns as early as 1260 A.D. But it was only in 1302 A.D. under al-Sulṭān al-Nāṣir, a former army commander under the Ayyubids, that the Tartars were finally defeated. During the period when Baghdad was under the mercy of the nomadic warriors of Central Asia, the Jurists in 'Iraq reached a wrong consensus to close the door of *Ijtihād* which they had not practised much anyway since the tenth century A.D. No one, in fact, had the right to put a stop to the process of *Ijtihād*.

In short, *Ijmā'* is *Ḥujjah* for all the four-schools of Islamic Jurisprudence.

Imām al-Shāfi'ī has fully discussed *Ijma'* as one of the sources of Sharī'ah in his famous *Risālah*.[6]

The following discourse of al-Shafi'i throws enough light on *Ijma'*. Imām Shāfi'ī says:

> Some one asked me: "Do you assert, with others, that the consensus of the 'Ulama should always be based on an established Sunnah even if it were related (on the authority of the Prophet)?"
>
> He replied: "That on which the 'Ulama are agreed and which, as they assert, was related from the Messenger of Allah, that is so. As to that which the 'Ulama do not relate (from the Prophet), which they may or may not relate as a tradition from the Prophet, we cannot consider it as related on the authority of the Prophet because one may relate only what he has heard, for no one is permitted to relate (on the authority of the Prophet) information which may or may not be true. So we accept the decision of the 'Ulama because we have to obey their authority, and we know that wherever there are Sunnahs of the Prophets, the 'Ulama cannot be ignorant of them, although it is possible that some of them are, and we know that Ulama can neither agree on anything contrary to the Sunnah of the Prophet nor on an error."
>
> Someone may ask: Is there any evidence in support of what you hold?
>
> Imām Shāfi'i replied: "Sufyān (b. 'Uyayna) told us from 'Abd al-Mālik b. 'Umayr from 'Abd al-Raḥmān b. 'Abd-Allah b. Mas'ud from his father, who said: The Messenger of Allah said: "Allah will grant prosperity to His servant who hears my words, remembers them, guards them, and hands them on. Many a transmitter of Law is no Lawyer himself, and many may transmit law to others who are more versed in the Law than they, etc.

Sufyan (also) told us from 'Abd-Allah b. 'Alī Sulaymān b. Yasār from his father, who said: 'Umar b. al-Khaṭṭāb made a speech at al-Jabiya in which he said: The Messenger of Allah stood among us by an order from Allah, as I am now standing among you, and said:

> "Believe my Companions, then those who succeed them (The Successors), and after that those who succeed the Successors; but after them unfaithfulness will prevail when people will swear (in support of their saying) without having been asked to swear, and will testify without having been asked to testify. Only those who seek the pleasure of paradise will follow the Ummah, for the devil can pursue one person, but stands far away from two. Let no man be alone with a woman, for the devil will be the third among them. He who is happy with his right (behaviour), or unhappy with his wrong behaviour, is a (true) believer."[7]

He asked: What is the meaning of the Prophet's order to follow the Ummah?

Imām Shāfi'ī replied: There is but one meaning for it.

He asked: How is it impossible that there is only one meaning?

Imam Shāfi'ī replied: When the Ummah spread in the lands, (of Islam), nobody was able to follow its members, who had been dispersed and mixed with other believers and unbelievers, pious and impious. So it was meaningless to follow the community (as a whole), becuase it was impossible (to do so), except for what the (entire) Ummah regarded as lawful or unlawful (orders) and (the duty) to obey these (orders).

He who holds what the Muslim Ummah holds shall be regarded as following the Ummah, and he who holds differently shall be regarded as opposing the community he was ordered to follow. So the error comes from separation: but in the Ummah as a whole there is no error concerning the meaning of the Qur'ān, the Sunnah, and Analogy.

Al-Qiyās: Analogical Deduction

Al-Qiyās could be defined, in Islamic theological parlance, as analogy, or analogical deduction. In other words, *al-Qiyās* is the legal principle introduced in order to derive at a logical conclusion of a certain law on a certain issue that has to do with the welfare of the Muslims. In exercising this, however, it must be based on Qur'ān, Sunnah and *Ijmā'*.

This legal principle was introduced by Imam Abu Hanifah, the founder of the Ḥanafī school, in Iraq. The reason why he introduced it was not unconnected with the intention of curbing the excessive thinking and disgression of the people from the Islamic legal point.

During the period of the 'Abbāsids, people engaged themselves in reading various text books on logic philosophy, etymology, linguistics, literatures of various places, foreign text books, which to some extent tended to corrupt their minds and lead them astray. They wanted to apply what they had studied in these foreign text books to Islamic Jurisprudence. Many new Muslims in far away lands had brought with them their philosophical outlook, their culture and even some religious and legal notions in the fold of Islam. Abū Ḥanīfah introduced *Qiyas* as a measure to curb their excessive thinking and to keep them on check.

However, there are some people who go against this legal principle. In this regard, there are scholars and Jurists who may be termed as *anti-Qiyās* and *Pro-Qiyās*. Each and every one of them brought forth evidence to support his stand.

Those who are against *Qiyās* have said that Almighty Allah revealed the Holy Qur'ān to us for our guidance, no more, no less. A Muslim must look for the solution of his problems in the Qur'ān. Almighty Allah has said:

«ما فرطنا في الكتاب من شىء ثم إلى ربكم تحشرون».

"We do not omit anything in the Holy Qur'ān; surely, to your Lord shall you return."[8]

They also supported their argument with the tradition of the Prophet. Above all, they doubted the proper functionality of *Qiyās* in Islamic Legal point of view. The *Pro-Qiyās* also supported their stand with the Qur'ānic verse, the traditions of Prophet Muhammad and the statements of his companions. Almighty Allah has said:

«فأعتبروا يا أولى الأبصار».

"Think deeply, O ye who are understanding."[9]

The *Pro-Qiyās* say that the people of understanding referred to in this verse must use their common sense to deduce Islamic Law. They supported their argument by quoting the Ḥadīth of the Prophet which says:

> "The Prophet sent Mu'ādh bin Jabal to Yemen as their Judge and governor. Before Mu'ādh left the Prophet, he asked the latter on what basis would he judge if he was confronted with a problem. Mu'adh said that he would judge on the basis of the contents of the Qur'ān. The Prophet asked him: "assuming that you do not find it in the Qur'ān, on what basis would you judge", Mu'ādh said he would judge on the basis of the Sunnah of the Prophet. The Prophet also asked him: "assuming you do not find it in both the Qur'ān and the Sunnah of the Prophets, on what basis would you judge", Mu'ādh bin Jabal replied that he would use his own individual judgement. And the Prophet Muḥammad was very happy to hear this statement".

Ḥadīth also has it that the Prophet sent Abū Mūsā al Ash'arī to Yemen during his life-time, and he told him to judge on the basis of the Qur'ān, and that if he did not find solution in the Qur'ān, he should make use of the traditions of the Prophet, and that if he did not find the solution in the tradition of the Prophet, he should use his own judgement.

During the life-time of the companions of the Prophet the companions arrived at various decisions on analogical deductions. As for example on the punishment that should be given to a drunkard, Sayyidnā ʿAlī concluded by saying: "He who drinks, get drunk; he who gets drunk, raves; he who raves, accuses people falsley and he who accuses people falsely should be given eighty strokes of cane. Therefore, he who drinks should be given eighty stroke of cane". From all that has been said so far, we can deduce that there is nothing wrong in using *al-Qiyās* in deriving at a logical conclusion in Islamic Law in as much as that conclusion does not go against the injunctions of the Holy Qur'ān or the Sunnah of the Prophet.

Similarly, there arose a problem about the appointment of a Caliph after the death of the Prophet. Before reaching an *Ijmāʿ* on Abūbakr's Caliphate, the Prophet's choice of Abūbakr as spiritual leader to act as an *Imām* in congregational prayers was the comparative basis for the selection of Abubakr as temporal Leader.

Another interesting example of analogical deduction is that of the Qiyās and Ijtihād by Sayyidnā Umar, the second Caliph. He asked the Prophet whether a kiss during the fast vitiates the fast even though no orgasm is reached. The Prophet posed a question: "Does rinsing one's mouth vitiate the fast?" ʿUmar replied: "No, it was all right to do so." So the Prophet indicated that the fast is similarly not vitiated by a kiss if it is not accompanied by an orgasm.

Similarly, when a Muslim breaks his fast during the month of Ramaḍān intentionally, he is obliged to expiate (Kaffārah) for it in the following manner:

a) Manumitting a slave;
b) Or he ought to fast for two months consecutively in lieu of manumission;
c) If his health will not stand 2 months' fasting, then he must feed 60 paupers.

Another example of *Qiyās* is provided in the case of beduin who had a sexual intercourse with his wife during the period of fasting. He went to the Prophet and confessed of his sin. The Prophet told him that he should give a *Kaffārah* (expiation). The *'illah* (effecting cause for extending a rule by analogy) was deliberate breaking of the fast, and therefore since the sexual intercourse vitiates the fast, *Kaffārah* (expiation) becomes incumbent upon the defaulter.

Imām Mālik has also given a verdict issued on *Qiyās* by a remarriage of the wife of a missing person after the court has issued a decree deeming him dead, although he subsequently appears, with the re-marriage of a divorced wife who has been recalled by her husband into the matrimonial bond but who has remarried because the recall was not communicated to her. In both cases the wives observe a waiting period (The *'Iddah* of death in the first case, and the *'Iddah* of Talaq in the second case); in both cases the women enter into the second marriage in good faith. Sayyidnā 'Umar had given a *fatwah* that in the case of the woman who was not made aware of the recall becomes the lawful wife of the new husband, Imām Mālik said the same applies in the case of the former wife of the missing person as she becomes the legal wife of the new husband.

The Prophet was asked by a woman whether she could perform the *Ḥajj* on *behalf* of her *aged* father. The Prophet replied in affirmative just as she may discharge on his behalf a pecuniary debt.

Imam al-Shafi'i was asked a question about Qiyas or analogical deductions as one of the sources of Shari'ah, and the Imam has given reply to this question in his *Risālah*:[10]

On what ground do you hold that on matters concerning which no text is to be found in the Book of Allah, nor a Sunnah or consensus, recourse should be had to Qiyās? Is there any binding text for the use of Qiyās, analogical deduction?

Imām Shāfi'i replied: If Qiyas were stat ed in the text of the Book or the Sunnah, such a text should be called either Allah's command or the Messenger of Allah's order rather than Qiyās.

He was asked about Qiyās and whether it is *Ijtihād*, or they are the two different things?

According to Imam Shafi'i, they are the two terms with the same meaning. When he was asked about their common basis, he replied: "On all matters touching the life of a Muslim there is either decision or an indication as to the right answer. If there is a decision, it should be followed: If there is no indication as to the right answer, it should be sought by *Ijtihād*, and *Ijtihād* is *Qiyās* (analogy).

He was asked that if the scholars apply *Qiyās* correctly, will they arrive at the right answer in the eyes of Allah and will it be permissible for them to disagree in their answer through Qiyās? Have they been ordered to seek one or different *Qiyās?* Have they been ordered to seek one or different answers for each questions? What was the proof for the position that they should apply Qiyās on the basis of the literal rather than the implicit meaning of a precedent, and that it is permissible for them to disagree in their answers? Should (Qiyās) in matters concerning the scholars themselves be applied differently from the way it is applied in matters concerning others? Who is the person qualified to exercise *Ijtihād* through Qiyās in matters concerning himself, not others, and who is the person who can apply it in matters concerning himself as well as others?

Imam Shafi'i replied: If Qiyās were stated in the text of the Book or The first consisted of the right decisions in the literal and implied senses; the other, of the right answer in the literal sense only. The right decisions (in the literal and implied senses) are those based (either) on Allah's command or on a Sunnah of the Messenger of Allah related by the Ijma from an (earlier) Ijmā'.

These commands of Allah and the Sunnah are the two sources by virtue of which the lawful is to be established as lawful and the unlawful as unlawful. This is (the kind of knowledge) of which nobody is allowed to be ignorant or doubtful (as to its certainty).

Secondly, (Legal) knowledge of the specialists type consists of traditions related by a few and known only to scholars, but others are under no obligation to be familiar with it. Such knowledge may either be found among all or a few of the scholars, related to a reliable transmitter from the Prophet. This is the (kind of) knowledge which is binding on scholars to accept and it consistutes the right decision in the literal sense such as we accept the validity of the testimony of two witnesses. This is right (only) in the literal sense, because it is possible that evidence of the two witnesses might be false.

Thirdly there is legal knowledge derived from *'Ijmā'* (consensus).

Finally, there is legal knowledge derived from *Ijtihād* (personal reasoning) through *Qiyās*, by virtue of which right decisions are sought. Such decisions are right in the literal sense to the person who applies analogy; not to the majority of scholars, for nobody knows what is hidden except Allah.

He asked: if (legal) knowledge is derived through *Qiyās* provided it is rightly applied – should (the scholars) who apply analogy agree on most (of the decisions), although we may find them disagreeing on some?

Imām Shāfi'ī replied that *Qiyās was of two kinds: the first, if the case in question was similar to the original meaning of the precedent, no disagreement of this kind is permitted.* The second, if the case in question is similar to several precedents, Qiyās must be applied to the precedent nearest in resemblance and most appropriate. But those who apply *Qiyās* are likely to disagree in their answers.

When he asked to give examples explaining that legal knowledge is of two kinds, the one consisting of the right decisions in the literal and implicit senses, and the other of the right decisions in the literal, not the implicit, sense?

Imām Shāfi'ī replied: if we were in the Sacred Mosque and the Ka'ba is in sight, do you not agree that we should face it (in prayer) with certainty?

He said: That is right.

Imām Shāfi'ī asked: (since) the duties of prayer, the payment of Zakāt, performance of pilgrimage, and the like have been compulsory on us, are we not under obligation to perform them in the right ways?

He replied: That is right.

Imām Shāfi'ī asked: since the duty imposed on us to punish the fornicator with a hundred stripes, to scourge him who casts an imputation (of adultery) with eight, to put to death him who apostatizes, and to cut off (the hand of) him who steals, are we not under obligation to do so (only) to him whose offence is established with certainty on (the basis of) his admission?

He replied: That is right.

Imām Shāfi'ī asked: Should not (the decisions) be the same whether we were obligated to take them against ourselves or others although we realize that we know about ourselves what others do not know, and we do not know about others but outward observation what we know about ourselves inwardly?

He replied: That is right.

Imām Shāfi'ī then asked: Are we not under obligation to face Sacred House (in prayer) where we may be?

He replied: That is right.

Imam Shāfi'ī asked: Do you hold that we (could always) face the Sacred House correctly?

He replied: No, not always as correctly as when you were able to see (the Sacred House); However, the duty imposed on you was fulfilled.

Imām Shāfi'ī asked: Are we not obligated to accept the Just Character of a man on the basis of his outward behaviour, and establish marital and inheritance relationship with him on (the basis of) his outward acceptance of Islam?

He replied: That is right.

Imām Shāfi'ī said: Yet he may not be just in character inwardly.

He replied: That is quite possible; but you are under no obligation to accept save what is explicit.

Imām Ṣhāfi'ī asked: So it is not lawful for us to establish marital and inheritance relationship with him, and to accept his testimony, and is it unlawful for us to kill him on the basis of (our) explicit (knowledge) of him? But if others should discover him to be an unbeliever, would it not be lawful for them to kill him and to repudiate marital and inheritance relationship or whatever else he had been permitted to do?

He replied: That is right.

Imām Shāfi'ī then asked: Thus the obligation imposed on us toward the same person differs in accordance with the degree of our understanding of it and other's understanding of it.

He replied: Yes, for each one fulfils his obligation on the basis of his own understanding.

Imām Shāfi'ī said: Thus we hold concerning matters on which there is no binding explicit text that these should be sought by *Ijtihād* – through *Qiyās* because we are under obligation to arrive at the right answers according to us.

He asked: Are you not seeking the answer to one question through different means?

Imām Shāfi'ī replied: Yes, whenever the grounds are different.

He asked: Give me an example.

Imām Shāfi'ī replied: If a man admits an obligation on his part to Allah or to another person, I should take a decision against him on the strength of his admission; if he does not admit, I should take the decision on the evidence established against him; if no evidence can be established against him, I should take the decision on the basis of an oath taken by him which might acquit him; if he refuses (to take the oath), I should ask the other party to take an oath and I should make the decision against him on the basis of the oath of the other party. it is understood that (one's own) admission against himself-owing to (one's natural) covertousness and greed is more certain than the evidence of others, since they might make a mistake or tell a lie against another. The evidence of witnesses of just character against a person should be regarded as nearer the truth) than (the accused) refusal to take an oath, or (nearer to the truth) than the oath taken by the other party (against him), since the latter might not be just in character. Thus the decision is taken on several grounds, some of them stronger than others.

He said: That is all right, but if he refuses to take an oath, we (the Ḥanafī school) will take the decision (against him) on the ground of his refusal.

Imām Shāfi'ī said: But you will have taken a decision on an evidence weaker than ours.

He said: Yes, however, I disagreed with you on the source of evidence (on the strength of which you have taken the decision).

Imām Shāfi'ī said: The strongest evidence for your decision was his admission, although one is liable to make an unfounded or erroneos admission (on the strength of which) a decision might be taken against a person.

He said: That is correct; for you are under no other obligation than that.

Imām Shāfi'ī asked: Do you not agree that we are under an obligation to take the right decision by one of two means; either by certainty based on literal, not implicit meanings?

He replied: Yes, but is there any explicit text in the Book or the Sunnah in support (of your opinion)?

Imām Shāfi'ī said: Yes, in such examples as I have (already) discussed concerning the determination of the *Qiblah* for myself and others. (For Allah said:

> "And they comprehend not anything of His knowledge save what He wileth."[11]

Having considered the pros and cons of the Qiyās, Imām Shāfi'ī, who had at the intitial stage antagonised it, agreed that *Qiyās* also can be accepted as one of the principles of Islamic Law provided it is strict Qiyās. What he means by strict *Qiyās* is that it must be based on the Qur'ān, the Sunnah and the *'Ijmā'* (the consensus of opinion of the companions or the Jurists).

The Jurists have laid down the conditions which *al-Qiyas* can be accepted: among them are:

a) that the Qiyās must be applied only when there is no solution to the matter in the Qur'ān or in the Hadith.
b) that *al-Qiyās* must not go against the principles of Islam.
c) that *al-Qiyās* must not go against the contents of the Qur'ān neither must it be in conflict with the traditions of the Prophet.
d) that it must be a strict *Qiyās* based on either the Qur'ān, the Hadith or the *Ijmā'*.

There are two types of *al-Qiyās*: *(a) Qiyās al-Jalīyy* (the translucent or transparent *Qiyās*, and *(b) Qiyās al-Khafīyy* (the hidden *Qiyās*).

With regard to *Qiyās al-Jalīyy*, alcohol is forbidden on the grounds of its being intoxicant can also be equally forbidden in Islam.

As regards the *Qiyās al-Khafīyy*, Almighty Allah asks us to give out Zakāt. It was the Prophet Muhammad who explained how it should be given out. He said among other things, that one goat must be given out as Zakāt on every forty goats. Giving a poor man a goat would do him little or no use. Therefore, we are allowed to sell that goat and give him the money. He would appreciate perhaps the money more than he would appreciate the goat.

There are some Jurists who oppose the use of *Qiyās.* The Mu'tazilites like Ibrāhīm bin Sayyār, and the Scholars of Ẓāhirī school including Ibn Ḥazm of Andalusia, also opposed the use of *Qiyās.*

The Shī'ites sects like the Ithnā 'Ashariyyah (the twelves), the Uṣūlis and the'Ibādites (a Khārajite sect) employ the terms *'aql* and *ra'y* for the same concept of Qiyās.

Al-Ijtihād:

The Arabic word for *Ijtihād* literally means an effort or an exercise to arrive at one's own judgement.

In its widest sense, it means the use of human reason in the elaboration and explanation of the Shari'ah Law. It covers a variety of mental processes, ranging from the interpretation of texts of the Qur'ān and the assessment of the authenticity of Ahadith. *Qiyās* or analogical reasoning, then, is a particular form of *Ijtihād*, the method by which the principles established by the Qur'ān, Sunnah, and *Ijma'* are to be extended and applied to the solution of new problems not expressly regulated before.

Al-Ijtihād, therefore, is an exercise of one's reasoning to arrive at a logical conclusion on a legal issue done by the Jurists to deduce a conclusion as to the effectiveness of a legal precept in Islam. Imām Muḥammad Idrīs al-Shāfi'ī has supported the idea of *Ijtihād* by quoting a verse of the Qur'ān to substantiate his conviction over the issue. Almighty Allah has said:

وَمَنْ حيث خرجت فولّ وجهك شطر المسجد الحرام وحيث ماكنتم فولوا وجوهكم شطره.

"Wherever you go, face the Mosque of Haram, and wherever you are, turn your face towards it".

Imām Shāfi'ī maintains that if one does not exercise his intellect, he would not be able to know where Masjidal-Ḥaram is. Therefore, Allah himself indirectly encourages us to exercise our faculty of reasoning, a great gift to mankind, to derive a logical conclusion on certain matters.

The Jurists have laid down certain conditions under which *al-Ijtihād* must *not* be exercised:

a) *Ijtihād* must not be exercised as to the existence of Allah. It is certain that Allah does exist and any attempt to think in His existence or not would lead to disbelief.

b) *Ijtihād* must not be exercised as to the truism of the Prophets of Allah who were sent by Allah Himself and any attempt to ponder over the idea of their Prophethood is tantamount to disbelief.

c) *Ijtihād* must not be exercised on the authenticity of the Holy Qur'ān.

Before one can be *al-Mujtahid,* one has to be knowledgeable about the religion of Islam, the Sunnah, *Fiqh* and *Uṣūl-al-Fiqh.* He should possess the following qualities:

a) He must be so very well versed in the study of Qur'ān. That he must know the reason why the verses and chapters of the Qur'ān were revealed and when each one of them was revealed *(Asbāb al-Nuzūl).*
b) He must be well versed in the study of the traditions of the Prophet *Muḥammad.* That is, he must know the distinction authentic between Hadith from the surious Hadith; he must know *Ḥadīth* and *Ḥasan* (good Ḥadīth)*Ḥadith alDa'if* (weak Ḥadīth) and so on.
c) He must know the principles of *Ijmā'* very well.
d) He must know the injunctions of Qiyās and the conditions that surround it.

The *Mujtahid* in other words must possess good character apart from academic excellence. Among the moral qualities he must possess are:

a) He must be a good Muslim. That is he must not be a nominal Muslim; rather, he must be a practicing one.
b) He must be very pious and law-abiding to all the injunctions of the Holy Qur'ān.
c) He must not be influenced by an heretical influences.
d) He must be just, reliable, trustworthy and pure from iniquitous practices.

The Mujtahid's can be classified into three broad categories:

a) *Al-Mujtahid fil Sharī'ah:* These they were those who did *Ijtihād* in the matter of Shari'ah. There were the companions of the Prophet till the third century of Islam.
b) *Al-Mujtahid fil-Madhhab:* These were those who did *Ijtihād* and later founded schools of jurisprudence.

These are the Mujtahids that followed them:

c) *Al-Mujtahid fil-Masā'il:* These are the Present day Mujtahids who give *Fatawa* or Juristic opinions on religious matters.

Any form of *Ijtihād* must have its starting point in a principle of the Qur'ān, Sunnah, or *Ijmā'* and cannot be used to achieve a result which contradicts a rule established by any of these three fundamental sources; whenever a new case of issue presents itself, reasoning by *Qiyās* with an original case covered by the Qur'ān the Sunnah or *Ijmā'* is possible provided the effective cause *('illah)* is common to both cases.

As for example, wine is prohibited by the the texts, and the *'illah* for this prohibition is an intoxication. Therefore, other intoxicants like spirits, and drugs like hemp and marijuana are prohibited by *Qiyās* becuase they also lead to drunkeness and loss of senses. In this way the prohibition is extended by analogical deduction. The majority of Muslims, including the four major Sunni schools, accept *Qiyās* and *Ijtihād* to determine Juristic basis for reasoning on an issue:

a) There should be an original subject *(aṣl)*;
b) There should be an object of the analogy, being a new subject *(far')*;
c) There should exist effective cause common to both subjects *('illah)*;
d) There should also be a rule arrive at by *Qiyās (ḥukm)*.

In the case of the prohibition of an intoxicant like gin, the following four cardinal points must exist:

(i) Wine (ii) Gin (iii) intoxication (iv) prohibition

The following are some other examples of arriving at an *Ijtihād* through the use of analogical deductions:

1. In Sūrah al-Jum'ah the Qur'ān prohibits sale transactions after the last call to Jumah prayer. The rule is extended by *Qiyās* to other kinds of transactions and engagements which distract Muslims from attending the Jum'ah prayer.
2. In the Sunnah of the Prophet a killer is deprived from sharing in the inheritance of his victim. This rule is extended to the law of *Waṣiyyah* (bequests) as well.

The Shī'ites believe that *Ijtihād* is only the prerogative of their *Imāms* who are presumed to be infallible. In the modern times, Muslim scholars like Jamāl al-Dīn al-Afghānī and his disciple Shaikh Muḥammad Abduh have written about the "re-opening of the door of *Ijtihād*". Al-Afghānī tried to justify in the presence of a group of Muslim scholars in Cairo that the importance of reopening the door of *Ijtihād* was an Islamic response to imperialism prevalent in the Muslim world at that time. Muḥammad 'Abduh, Afghānī's disciple gave fresh interpretation of the principles embodied in the divine revelation as a basis for legal reform. Although engendered violent controversy, the supporters of the fresh *Ijtihād* argued that the doctrine of "the closure of the door of *Ijtihād* had not been established by an infallible *Ijmā'* as alleged by the opponents of *Ijtihād*.

It was argued that any *Ijmā'* of the 'Ulamā in the period intellectual stagnation and under fear as well as during any foreign domination like that of the Mongols in Baghdad around 1258 A.D. and afterwards could lead to harmful consequences. Therefore fresh *Ijtihad* was launched in the 19th Century in the public interest and thus it was believed that the door of *Ijtihād* was re-opened and the *Ijmā'* reached in Baghdad in the 13th Century was repealed. But the question is: was the door of *Ijtihad* ever closed. To my mind, perhaps Shaikh Afghānī and 'Abduh, however great scholars they were over-played their role.

Istiḥsān or Istiṣlāḥ or Maṣāliḥ Al-Mursalah: Public Interest

Istiḥsān or *Maṣāliḥ al-Mursalah* has been mentioned indirectly in the Holy Qur'ān in the following verse:

«ٱلَّذِينَ يَسْتَمِعُونَ ٱلْقَوْلَ فَيَتَّبِعُونَ أَحْسَنَهُ أُولَٰئِكَ الَّذِينَ هَدَاهُمُ اللَّهُ وَأُولَٰئِكَ هُمْ أُولُوا ٱلْأَلْبَابِ».

> "Those who listen to the word, and follow the best meaning in it: Those are the ones Whom Allah has guided, and those are the ones endued with understanding."[12]

The Mufarsirūn (commentators) have interpreted this verse in two ways. If "word" in this verse is taken as any word, the clause would mean that good and pious men should listen to all that is said and choosen the best of it for general good – as long as that word is according to the spirit of the Divine Message. But if "word" is taken here to mean the Word of Allah, it would mean that they should listen reverently to it, and where permissive and alternative courses are allowed for those who are not strong enough to follow the higher course, those "endued with understanding" should prefer to attempt the higher course of conduct. For example, it is permitted within limits to punish those who wrong us, but the nobler course is to repel evil with good.[13] We should try to follow the nobler course.

Public interest is also regarded in Shari'ah as a basis of law. The jurists of different schools have used different Arabic terms to describe it. The Hanafis call it *istihsan* meaning equitable preference to find a just solution. Imam Malik calls it *Al-Masalih al-Mursalah that is the public* benefit or public welfare. The Arabic word mursal literally means to set loose from the texts and *masalih* means welfare. Imām Aḥmad bin Ḥanbal calls it *istislah* seeking the best solution for the general interest. The Ḥanbalī scholar Ibn Qudāmah as well as the Māliki jurist Ibn Rushd have occasionally used the term *istiḥsān.* The only school which does not recognise *Istihsān* as a source is the Shāfi'ī school. According to Imām Shāfi'ī, if it is allowed, it can open the door to the unrestricted use of fallible human opinions since the public interest, will vary from place to place and time to time.

It should be noted that the concept of public welfare and general interest can really be very helpful particularly in cases which are not regulated by any authority of the Book of Allah, the Sunnah or *ijmā'*. In that case, equitable considerations may override the results of strict Qiyās taking into consideration the public interest. Shāfi'ī jurists have employed *Istidlāl* to achieve similar results by avoiding merely the application of strict *Qiyas. Istidlāl* is the process of seeking guidance, basis and proof from the sources although its dictionary meaning is merely an argumentation. With this brief introduction, we shall examine some examples of *istihsan.*

1. The *Bay' bi al-Wafā* or the sale subject to any future redemption which can be construed as a kind of mortgage was allowed because of the practical need for such transactions in the interest of public welfare.
2. Islam attaches a great importance to the proper dress of a woman *(satral-'Aurah).* No man except her husband can see certain parts of her body. But, on account of necessity, a physician may be allowed to medically examine and diagnose a woman in the interest of saving her life.
3. *Divorce* given in death, sickness *(marḍ al-maut),* even though effected as irrevocable *talaq*, it will not deprive the divorced wife from her share in the inheritance. The husband in reality was trying to deprive her of her rights and he wanted to shun his obligations. It was merely the divorce for an escape *(ṭalāq al-far).* Some Shāfi'ī and Ẓāharī jurists disagree with the majority of *'Ulamā* on this issue. The Ḥanafī jurists maintain that the entitlement of the divorced wife lasts during her *'iddah* period while the Hanbalis take the view that she will be entitled to participate as long as she has not remarried again. The Mālikis however, accord her the right to participate in the inheritance even if she has remarried provided the deceased did not recover in between the death illness and his ultimate death.
4. The *ḥadd* punishment of amputation of hands in case of a theft will not be applied even if all the evidences proved that it was really committed during the period of a famine when no food was available and one was forced to steal. Imam Shāfi'ī says that he will apply this rule simply because Sayyidnā 'Umar decided a case in this way. He does not think that it was done on the principle of *Istiḥsān.*
5. The eating of meat which has not been slaughtered according to

the Islamic ritual *(Dhabīḥah)* permissible where no other lawful food is available.

6. Destruction of lawful food-stuff is not allowed without any special reason. Byt Sayyidnā 'Umar ordered the spilling of milk mixed with water as a punishment that would prevent deceit of dishonest persons engaged in the sale of adulterated milk.

7. The second call of the *adhan* for Jumah prayer was not a practice in the time of the Prophet and the two Rāshidūn Caliphs. Sayyidnā '*Uthman bin 'Affan,* the third Caliph, started it as a reminder for the public benefit. Imām Mālik bin Anas gave several juristic decisions *(fatwas)* based on *maṣāliḥ al-Mursalah* (public-interest). Some of them are listed as follows:

a) The Muslim ruler may exact additional taxes from the wealthy citizens in the period of emergency.

b) A Caliph or a ruler does not have to be the most meritorious claimant, otherwise strife will be inevitable.

c) Imam Malik as well as Imam Ahmad bin Hanbal prohibited the sale of grapes, which is otherwise legal, to a wine merchant as he will use them to ferment wine which is unlawful.

d) The sale of arms during a civil disturbance is prohibited as it may intensify the struggle.

Most of these rules could fit into Ḥanafī *Istiḥsān* or Shāfi'ī *Qiyās.*

Istishab: Legal Presumption

Istishab means a rule of *evidence* or a legal *presumptin* of continuance (*istishab*) of conditions (*al-hal*). In other words, it is the presumption in the laws of evidence that a state of affair known to exist in the past continues to exist until the contrary is proved. *Istisḥāb* is accepted by all schools of Islamic Jurisprudence as a subsidiary source of the Sharī'ah. There is a presumption of innocence until the guilt is established. This presumption, is based on *istisḥāb.* There will be a similar presumption of *ḥalāl* things in the absence of its specific prohibition. A debt is presumed to subsist until its discharge is evidenced. Likewise a marriage is presumed to continue until its dissolution (Ṭalāq) becomes known. In the case of *Ibadat,* mere doubt does not vitiate the validity of rituals. Supposing a man after ablution entertains a mere doubt as to whether he is still has his ablution to perform the prayers, then there is a presumption of purity *(ṭuhr)* and, similarly, if he thinks genuinely that he has performed the correct number of prostrations (*Sajadah*) then a mere doubt will not affect his genuine belief. In the case of an ownership title, a judge will presume ownership from valid title deeds until the contrary is proved. If a person is missing *(Mafqūd),* his wife remains his legal wife until the court, after due enquiries issues a decree presuming the contrary, namely death.

Sadd al-Dharā'i (Blocking the ways)

Sadd al-Dharai really means blocking the ways even if the method involved is otherwise legal. In fact, this source of Shari'ah is not much different from the *Maṣāliḥ al-Mursala,* but it is used by Maliki jurists and some Ḥanbalis under this name. Most of the rules categorised under Sadd al-Dharāi can conveniently fit into the various subsidiary sources related to public interest or public welfare.

'Urf and 'ādāt (Custom)

'Urf, the known practices and *'Ādāt* or Customs are recognised as a subsidiary source by all schools of Jurisprudence. The Māliki school attaches more importance to custom than other schools. But customary rules are valid as long as there is no provision on the matter in the Qur'ān and the Sunnah. If any of the customs contradict any other rule of Sharī'ah, they will be considered outside the pale of Islamic Law.

Notes

1. Qur'ān, ch.
2. Qur'ān, ch. 42:38.
3. Qur'ān, ch.
4. Qur'ān, ch. 4:115
5. Qur'ān, ch. 4:59.
6. Al-Shāfi'ī *Risālah* translated by Majīd Khadduri, Baltimore 1961 pp. 285-287.
7. In the year 638 the Caliph 'Umar went to al-Jābiya, a village on the outskirts of Damascus, where he met several leading Companions. For the text of the tradition, see Shāfi'ī, *Musnad,* vol. II, p. 187; and Ibn Ḥanbal, vol. I, pp. 112-12, 176-81.
8. Qur'an ch.
9. Qur'an ch.
10. Al-Shafi'i, *Risalah* translated by Majid Khadduri, Baltimore 1961, pp.288-293.
11. Qur'ān, ch. 2:256.
12. Qur'ān, ch. 39:18.
13. See Qur'ān, ch. 33:96, see Yusuf Ali, *The Holy Qur'ān* p. 1241.

Chapter 5

The Four Schools of Fiqh and their Leaders

The Sharī'ah as we have seen before is derived from a high divine source, embodying the Creator's *(khāliq)* will and Justice. The main task of the Prophet was to correctly interpret the Divine Will and spread justice *('Adl)*, and to establish peace between man and man, and man and his Creator. The Qur'ān and the Sunnah were put into practice by the Prophet and his companions, who in turn studied the life-giving principles contained in the Book of Allah and the Sunnah of the Prophet. This is the reason why Imām al-Shāfi'ī has ranked the study of Sharī'ah which is based on these sources as higher than supererogatory prayers *(Nawāfil)*. The famous Muslim thinker and the poet of the East Dr. Muḥammad Iqbal, after producing voluminous books of poetry on mainly Islamic themes wished in the last years of his life that it would have been better if he has spent all his energy in the service of *Fiqh al-Islām*. It is to fulfil the unfulfilled desire of his life that he contacted, the late Maulānā Maudoodi and other *'Ulamā* to join hands with him to work on *Fiqh*. His famous book, the *Reconstruction of Islamic Thought*[1] was the beginning of the shaping of his future deliberations. Sharī'ah undoubtedly is the backbone of the religion of Islam. The 'Ulamā took to this study right from the time of the *Ṣaḥābah*.

The Difference of Opinions (Ikhtilaf) is Mercy (Raḥmah):

Imāms, Abū Ḥanīfah, Mālik, Shāfi'i and Aḥmad bin Ḥanbal, the leaders of four Sunni schools of law, have rendered a great service to the cause of Islamic Jurisprudence. Neither did they want to alter the spirit of the Qur'ān, nor the *Sunnah* of the Prophet as is harped by some non-Muslims as well as brain-washed scholars of Islam. If one closely examines the *fiqh* of the four schools, one will never come across any difference of opinions as far as the basic principles of Islam are concerned. The differences mainly centre around the *furūāt* (tiny branches) of theology rather than the *Uṣūl* (the fundamental principles) of belief. It is about such differences that the Messenger of Allah has said: "Difference of opinion (*Ikhtilaf*) in my *Ummah* is (a form of) blessing." It is through this blessing, that Muslims of today have inherited such comprehensive *corpus juris* which provides guidance in every walk of life. Imām Abū Ḥanīfah (80-150 A.H.) and Imām Mālik Ibn Anas (93-179 A.H.) were the jurists who really speaking, inherited the legacy of the special 'knowledge' of the *Tābiin* with all its 'bearings' – agreements and controversies. They adopted the similar attitudes of their predecessors in relying on the Qur'ān, the Sunnah and the opinions of the companions especially the cause of *Ijmāʿ* as the main source of Islamic Law, followed by their *Ijtihād* although Imam Malik placed more reliance on the opinions of teachers than Abu Hanifah. But in cases where there was an irreconcilable conflict of or difference of opinion among the Ṣaḥabah, the Iraqi Jurists and Hijazi Jurists followed what was narrated, opined or practised by their predecessors.

The two leaders as well as their disciples came closer after the travels made by Imām Abū Ḥanīfah and his illustrious companions Imām Abū Yūsuf and Imām Muḥammad bin al-Ḥasan al-Shaibānī to Makka and Medina where Imām Abū Ḥanīfah met Imām Mālik and the companions of ʿAbdallāh bin ʿAbbās. Abu Yusuf and Muḥammad Ibn al-Ḥasan also studied the *Muwaṭṭā'* of Imām Mālik with the author himself.

The famous Jurist and scholar of Egypt, Laith bin Saʿd (d. 175), and many other scholars elsewhere were engaged in jurisprudential discussions and because of the good of the *Ummah* at heart, he sent a brotherly message to Imām Mālik objecting with strong arguments to the insistence of Imām Mālik on the ʿ*Amal Ahl-al-Madina* or the practice of the people of Medina as the main criteria to be followed. Muḥammad bin al-Ḥasan al-Shaibānī, the disciple of Imām abū Ḥanīfah, wrote a book on jurisprudence dealing with these matters. Imam Shafi'i (150-204 A.H.) bridged the gap by visiting Iraq and acquainting himself with the difference between the Ḥijāzis and Iraqis wrote 'al Risālah' pointing out the defect and the weaknesses in the legal thinking of his contemporary jurists and emphasising the importance of adhering to the Qur'ān, the Sunnah, the conclusive *Ijmāʿ* of the Muslim jurists, and the appropriate Qiyas — as the main sources of Law — excluding arbitrary judgements (i.e. Istiḥsān), local and partial agreements, unauthentic narration and unfounded practices (e.g. Practice of the people of Medina). The Risālah of Shāfiʿī (by taking the jurists from the area of details *(Furūʿāt)* to the area of fundamentals gave a timely birth to the science of '*uṣūl al Fiqh*' – jurisprudence upon which the Sharīʿah safely and systematically developed. Thus it was the joint efforts of the three Imams which brought about a healthy development.

The effort made by Shāfi'ī for systematic jurisprudence was paralleled by another type of specialised research namely, the collection of all the traditions from their different provinces, shifting them out, the acceptable narrations from the unacceptable ones. Imām Aḥmad bin Ḥanbal, the fourth leader and jurist (164-241) wrote the Musnad, the most comprehensive book on Sunnah, through his special research and relied mostly on the Qur'ān, the Sunnah, whatever be the number of the narrators, the opinions of the companions and the successors – irrespective of their home towns, and the process of Ijtihad.

The love and respect of these jurists was so great to each other that they visited and sat in the study-circles of each other. They disagreed on certain matters but remained brothers and friends. Imām Abū Ḥanīfah, thirteen years older than Imām Mālik sat in the lessons of Imām Mālik who respectfully welcomed him and made himself next to him.

Imām Muḥammad bin al-Ḥasan, the famous disciple of Imām Abū Ḥanīfah, went to Medina and learnt *al-Muwaṭṭā* from Imām Mālik for three years after the death of his teacher, Abū Ḥanīfah. Imām Mālik and Imām Abū Ḥanīfah, both learnt Ḥadīth from Imām Muḥammad bin Shihāb al-Ẓuhrī, and Ẓuhrī, the teacher did not feel it was below his dignity to learn from Imām Mālik, his pupil. Imām Ja'far al-Ṣādiq (d. 198 A.H.) was the teacher of both Imām Abū Ḥanīfah as well as Imām Mālik.[1] Likewise, both the Imāms also learnt from a famous *Tābi'ī* scholar Muḥammad bin al-Munkadir al-Madanī (d. 131 A.H.). The great Imāms, had such love and respect towards each other that even Imām Abū Ḥanīfah, a senior contemporary of Imām Mālik, would attend the lectures of Imam Malik, particularly when he was dictating *Aḥādīth*.[2] Imām Shāfi'ī also became a student of Ḥadīth under the guidance of Imām Mālik. When some one asked Imām Shāfi'ī about Imām Mālik, he said, "If Imām Mālik and Sufyān bin 'Uyaynah were not there, there would not have existed the science of Ḥadīth in Ḥijāz". About *al-Muwaṭṭā* of Imām Mālik, Imām Shāfi'ī says: "There has never appeared on earth a book that is closest to the Qur'ān than the Book of Mālik".

Imām Shāfi'ī says about a Ḥanafī Imām that when Imām Muḥammad bin al-Ḥasan, the disciple of Abū Ḥanīfah, used to discuss any juristic point, it seemed as if a revelation was descending. He used to write down his lectures.[3] Imām Muḥammad also paid a great respect to Imām al-Shāfi'ī. Once he was going to the court of Hārūn al-Rashīd and met Imām al-Shāfi'ī on the way. Imām Muḥammad got down from his horse and asked his servant to go and inform the caliph that he would not be in a position to remain present at the court that day. Imām Shāfi'ī insisted that he should go to the court and that he would see him another day to which Imām Muḥammad replied that it was not essential for him to go to the Caliph's court.[4] Imām Shāfi'ī and Imam Muḥammad used to have debates *(Manāẓirāt),* and used to agree and disagree on many points, a sign of healthy academic discussion, which was a common practice in those days.

Likewise, Imām Aḥmad bin Ḥanbal learnt *Aḥādīth* from Yaḥyā bin Sa'īd al-Qaṭṭān, the famous disciple of Imām Abū Ḥanīfah. It is said that while asking questions, Imām Aḥmad would stand up out of respect for the teacher from the time of *'Aṣr* prayer to the *Maghrib* (sunset) prayer.[5] Imām Aḥmad used to say about his teacher that he had not seen one like him.[6] Imām Aḥmad bin Ḥanbal also used to say about 'Abdallāh bin al-Mubārak, another pupil of Imām Abū Ḥanīfah, that during the period of this scholar, nobody has ever tried to exert so much efforts in acquiring the knowledge of Ḥadīth as 'Abdallāh bin al-Mubārak. Khaṭīb al-Baghdādī, the famous historian, narrates the statement of Imām Aḥmad bin Ḥanbal who said that when he first wanted to learn the science Ḥadīth, I first went to Imām Abū Yūsuf, another disciple of Imām Abū Hanifah. He has narrated many *Aḥādīth* from Abū Yūsuf.[7]

The above examples show that all the Imāms were teachers and pupils of each other, all working for a common goal that is to serve the posterity in enhancing their knowledge about the Sharī'ah. The treasures of knowledge that they have left behind guides the *Ummah* even today and *in all time* to come. We shall now see the life and works of the four leaders of Islamic Jurisprudence.

The Founders of the School of Fiqh

1. *Imām Abū Ḥanīfah*

The Ḥanīfah school of *Fiqh* was the first to be founded by Nu'mān bin Thābit bin Zūta bin Māh, an 'Ajami or a non-Arab scholar who is well known by his *Kunyah* Imām Abū Ḥanīfah (d. 150 A.H.) in Kūfah in Iraq. Kūfa during this period had become well known as a seat of learning. The legacy of 'Abdallāh bin Mas'ūd (d. 32 A.H.), the *Ṣaḥābī* and a great scholar of the Qur'ān and the Sunnah had flourished in Kūfa as it was there that he taught from the time that he was sent by caliph 'Umar as a *Qāḍī* and a scholar-teacher.

His Early Life:

Imām Nu'mān bin Thābit Abū Ḥanīfah belonged to that pious period of the *Tābi'īn,* the successors of the *Ṣaḥābah* (the companions of the Prophet). The famous historian *Khaṭīb* of Baghdad says that Abū Ḥanīfah was born in the year 80 A.H. His father Thābit called upon Caliph 'Alī to pray for him and his family. Khaṭīb says: "I believe that his prayer bore fruit."[8] Abu Hanifah was a *Tābi'ī,* since he had the good fortune of witnessing the period in which some *Ṣaḥābah* still lived till his early youth. The notable names of Anas bin Mālik (d. 93 A.H.) the personal attendant of the Holy Prophet, and Sahl bin Sa'd (d. 91 A.H.) while Abul Ṭu'fail 'Āmir bin Wāthilah (d. 100 A.H.) when Abu Ḥanīfah was twenty years old. 'Aini, the commentator of *Hidāyah* says that Abū Ḥanīfah even heard *Ḥadīth* from the *Ṣaḥābah.*

Abū Ḥanīfah was first brought up as a trader like his ancestors; but he soon started taking deep interest in education. During this period Islamic learning was being spread by great Tābi'ī scholars and Imāms like Auza'i in Syria, Ḥammād al-Baṣrah, Sufyān al-Thaurī in Kūfah, Mālik bin Anas in Medina, and Laith in Egypt.[9]

His Education:

One day, when Abū Ḥanīfah was passing by the house of Imām Sha'bī, a learned scholar of Kūfah, Sha'bī mistook him as a student, and asked: "Where are you going, Youngman?" Abū Ḥanīfah named a merchant whom he was going to see. "I meant to ask", said Sha'bī, "whose classes you attend", "Nobody's Sir". Sha'bī said: "I see signs of intelligence in you. You ought to sit in the company of learned men". As if it sparked a new light in Abū Ḥanīfah's heart, he embarked on studies, and became a great Imām in the field of *Fiqh* and Ḥadīth.

He attended lectures of Ḥammād in Fiqh and then began his study of Ḥadīth. Abul Maḥsin al-Shāfi'ī gives a list of Hadith teachers of Abū Ḥanīfah, ninety-three of whom belonged to Kūfah who were *Tābi'īn.*[10]

The Scholars from whom he learnt in Kūfah were Sha'bi, Salamah bin Kuhail, Manarib bin Dithār, Abū Isḥāq Sabi, 'Aun bin 'Abdallāh, Amr bin Murrah, A'mash, Adīb bin Thābit al-Anṣārī, Samak bin Ḥarb and many others. In Baṣrah, he learnt from Qatādah and Shu'bah, famous *Tābi'ī* scholars who had studied *Ḥadīth* under *Ṣaḥābah* of the Prophet. Sufyān al-Thaurī calls Shu'bah "*Amīr al-Mu'minīn fil Ḥadīth*", the leader of the believers in Ḥadīth. Shu'bah was so much impressed by and attached to Abū Ḥanīfah that once he said of him: "just as I know that the sun is bright, I know for certain that learning and Abū Ḥanīfah are doubles of each other."[11] Shu'bah had permitted Imām Abū Ḥanīfah to teach Ḥadīth and narration. Someone asked Yaḥyā bin Mu'īn, one of the teachers of Imām al-Bukhārī about Abū Ḥanīfah. He replied: "It is enough for me to know that Shu'bah had permitted him to teach Ḥadīth and narration. Shu'bah after all was Shu'bah."[12]

After completing his education in Kūfah and Baṣrah, Imām Abū Ḥanīfah went to Makka and Medina, the fountain heads of religious learning, and enrolled as a student of the famous scholar 'Aṭā bin Abī Rabāḥ. 'Abdallāh bin 'Umar, the son of Caliph 'Umar, recognising merits of 'Aṭā bin Abī Rabāḥ, "why do people come to me when 'Aṭā bin Abī

Rabāḥ is there for them to go to?"[13] During the Ḥajj period, there used to be a government proclamation prohibiting anybody but 'Aṭā bin Abī Rabāḥ from giving *Fatāwa* (Juristic decision).[14] The great scholars like 'Auzāi, Zuhrī and 'Umar bin Dīnār were alumni of his school.[15] 'Aṭā bin Rabāḥ interviewed him about his beliefs while enrolling him in his class. Abū Ḥanīfah replied: "Sir, I do not speak ill of the *Aslāf* (people of earlier generations), do not call sinner *Kāfirs* and believe in *Qaḍā* and *Qadar* (Predestination and Freewill)". 'Aṭā was pleased on hearing this and permitted him to be his student.[16] Until 'Aṭā's death in 115 A.H. Abū Ḥanīfah always visited him when-ever he visited Makka and respectfully sat in his study circles. While in Makka, he also attended the classes of Ikramah, a disciple of the famous scholar 'Abdallah bin 'Abbās. He had the good fortune of learning Ḥadīth and points of Fiqh from Sayyidnā 'Alī, Abū Hurairah, 'Abdallah bin 'Umar, 'Aqabah bin 'Umar, Ṣafwān, Jābir and Abū Qatādah apart from his master 'Abdallāh bin 'Abbās. It is said of Ikramah that he taught at least seventy *Tābiīn.* Saʻīd bin Zubair was once asked: Did he know of someone more learned than him among his contemporaries? He replied that it was Ikramah. Ikramah taught Imām Abū Ḥanīfah with great care and personal attention, making him so very proficient that he gave Abū Ḥanīfah to exercise personal judgement and rulings in his life-time.[17]

His Encounter with Imām Bāqir

Imām Abū Ḥanīfah's fame as a great scholar and his intellectual gifts and originality had spread far and wide. But along with his fame also increased the adverse remarks of some superficial observers of his being a *Qayyās*, one who made analogical deductions. On his second visit to Medina, he met Imām Bāqir, when he was introduced to Imam Baqir, the latter addressed him in these words:

> "So it is you who contradicts the traditions of my grandfather on the basis of *Qiyās*. Abū Ḥanīfah said: "May Allah forbid. Who dare contradict the Ḥadīth? After you sit down, Sir, I shall explain my position". The following conversation that took place between the two great men, explains how much attached Imām Abū Ḥanīfah was to the fundamental principles of Islam:
> **Abū Ḥanīfah:** "Who is the weaker, man or woman?"
> **Imām Bāqir:** "Woman"
> **Abū Ḥanīfah:** "Which of them is entitled to the larger share in the inheritance?"
> **Imām Bāqir:** "The man"
> **Abū Ḥanīfah:** "Now, if I had been making more deductions through analogy, I should have said that the woman should get the larger

share, because on the face of it, the weaker one is entitled to more consideration. But I have not said so".

"To take up another subject, which do you think is the higher duty, prayer *(Ṣalāt)* or fasting *(Ṣaum)*?"

Imam Baqir: "Prayer *(Ṣalāt)*".

Abu Hanifah: "That being the case, it should be permissible for a woman during the period of her *Ḥayḍ* (menstruation) to postpone her prayers and not her fasts (which is lower than prayers). But the ruling I give is that she must postpone her fasting and not her prayers (following the foot steps of the Messenger of Allah)".

Imām Bāqir was so much impressed by this dialogue and the firmness of Imām Abū Ḥanīfah's faith and his love for the Prophet that immediately got up and kissed Imām Abū Hanīfah's forehead."[18]

His Humility:

Imām Abū Ḥanīfah later learnt for some time from Imam Baqir and Imām Ja'far al-Ṣādiq. Imām Abū Ḥanīfah as a keen scholar never felt below his dignity to learn from anyone. Imām Mālik was thirteen years his junior, but he often attended his lectures and learned *Aḥādīth* from him. Imām Mālik used to receive him with a great respect and used to make him sit beside him. Imām Abū Ḥanīfah is particularly famous for having had innumerable teachers. Abū Ḥafṣ says that Abū Ḥanīfah learnt *Aḥādīth* from at least four thousand scholars. One main reason why Imām Ḥanīfah attached himself to so many teachers and attended so many schools was that he wanted to acquaint himself with the different principles and methods in vogue so that by a comparative study of them he could arrive at some system of his own.[19] Although his merit was recognised by his teacher Ḥammād, and had become a real *Mujtahid*, due to his sincere regard he refrained from establishing a school of his own even though he was forty years of age. As long as Ḥammād lived, he never stretched his feet towards his house out of respect for his teacher. When Ḥammād died in 120 A.H., he was offered his chair though reluctantly. He saw a dream at this juncture in which he saw a dream that he was digging up the Prophet's grave. He was very much frightened and wanted to give up the chair. Ibn Sīrīn comforted him and interpreted the dream as an indication that he was the dead branches of learning in Islam. It was then that Abū Ḥanīfah settled down to teach. He became so very famous that everywhere he travelled, people gathered round him for interviews, discussions and debates with him. His students came from all over the Muslim World. He was visited by a large number of people to listen to his religious discourses so much that he began to be suspected of complicity in every upheaval that took place in that country.

Imām Abū Ḥanīfah's Rejection of Qāḍis Post:

In 132 A.H. Umayyads dynasty was overthrown by the ʿAbbāsids. The first ʿAbbāsid Caliph died only after his rule for four years, and was succeeded by his brother Manṣūr. Apart from the extermination of Umayyads, Manṣūr starting pouring out his hatred against the *Ahl al-Bait.* In 145 A.H. the followers of Muḥammad Nafs Zakiyyah took up arms against Manṣūr. The latter died fighting against Mansur's forces, and his brother Ibrāhīm continued the fight after him. Imam Abu Ḥanīfah had supported Ibrahim because of his just cause. Later when Ibrahim was overpowered in 146 A.H. by the Caliph, he began to arrest the supporters of Ibrāhīm, one of whom was Imām Abū Ḥanīfah. But when he was brought to the court, his courtiers recognised and respectfully presented him to the Caliph, saying: "This man is the greatest living ʿĀlim (learned man)". When Manṣūr listened to the Imam and realised how learned he was, he offered him the post of *Qāḍī* (Judge). Imām Abū Ḥanīfah declined the offer, saying: "He was not fit for the post". Manṣūr became angry and shouted: "You are a liar." He immediately retorted: "If I am a liar, then my statement that I am not fit for the post of a Qāḍī is true since a liar cannot be appointed as a Judge."

Manṣūr, in anger, took a vow that he would make Abū Ḥanīfah accept the post, but the Imām too, boldly vowed not to accept it. The Caliph ordered that he should be imprisoned. But his reputation as a scholar and teacher made the Caliph to allow him to teach even in the prison. Imām Muḥammad bin al-Ḥasan, the famous disciple of Imām Abū Ḥanīfah was tutored while in prison. When more and more people visited the prison to listen to the Imām, Manṣūr saw another danger to his authority, and decided to poison the Imām.

His Death:

In the month of Rajab 150 A.H., the great Imam died due to the effect of poison while he was saying his prayers. The *Janāzah* prayer was performed six times, and each time fifty thousand people took part in the prayers. Even after his burial, people kept on coming from different places saying funeral prayers for about twenty days.

In 459 A.H., a mausoleum was built on his tomb the Seljuqī ruler Alp Arsalān, and he also built a large *Madrasah* nearby.

Disciples of Imām Abū Ḥanīfah:

Imām Abū Ḥanīfah left a large number of disciples behind him. Abul Maḥāsin Shāfiʿī has listed the names of nine hundred and eighteen disciples. But the most well known of them are the following:

1. Qāḍī Abū Yūsuf: He was born 113 A.H. and was a son of a poor

labourer. Imām Abū Ḥanīfah helped financially to relieve his problems. After Imām Abū Ḥanīfah's death, he was appointed *Qāḍī* in the year 166 A.H. Caliph Mahdi. Harun al-Rashid appointed him *Qāḍī al-Quḍāt,* the Grand Qāḍi or Chief Justice. As a versatile scholar: Apart from his masters over *Fiqh*, he was very well versed in Ḥadith. He has written many books which are quoted by Ibn al-Nadīm in his famous work *Kitāb al-Fihrist*,[20] but the most well known is his *Kitāb al-Kharāj* which is a collection of Justice views on *Kharāj* (tribute), *Jizyah* Tax, classification of lands according to its productivity, etc. etc. He has also fearlessly admonished the Caliph in this book. He died in 182 A.H.

2. *Muḥammad bin al-Ḥasan al-Shaibānī:*

Imām Muḥammad was born in 135 A.H. near Damascus. He came to Kūfah for his studies. He learnt from Imām Abū Ḥanīfah while he was in prison, and after his death, he completed his education under Imām Abū Yūsuf and went to Medina, where he learnt Ḥadīth from Imām Mālik. Imām Shāfi'ī is one of his eminent pupils. Imām Shāfi'ī has said: "Whenever Imām Muḥammad expounds a point of law, it seemed as if the revealing angel had descended upon him. According to al-Nawawī, the famous *Muḥaddith,* Imām Shāfi'ī once said: "I learnt a camel load of learning from Imām Muḥammad". Imām Aḥmad bin Ḥanbal was once asked as to where from he had learnt all the subtle points of law, he replied: "From the books of Muḥammad bin al-Ḥasan". His famous works are the *Mabsut*, originally written by Abū Yūsuf but revised and edited by him. The other works are *Jāmi' al-Saghir, Jāmi' al-Kabīr, Ziyādāt, Kitāb al-Ḥujaj* and *Siyar Saghīr wa Kabīr.* He died in 189 A.H.

3. *Imām Zufar:*

He was born in 110 A.H., and was a great scholar of Ḥadīth and very well versed in *Qiyās.* Imām Abū Ḥanīfah used to call him the greatest of his companions in the field of analogical deductions. He died in 158 A.H.

The followers of the Ḥanafī school have spread throughout the world particularly in Asia and Middle East.

2. *Imām Mālik Bin Anas*

The period of the *ṣaḥābah* (companions of the Prophet) had just come to an end when Imām Mālik bin Anas was born. Medina, the city of the Prophet *(Madīnah al-Rasūl)* and the city *par-excellence,* was the centre of Islamic learning during that period since the disciples or pupils of the *ṣaḥābah* (companions of the Prophet), known as the *Tabiun*,were the recognised masters of Islamic learning who attracted scholars from different parts of the Muslim world to Medina.

His Early Life:

Imām Mālik was born in the year 93 A.H. as mentioned by Saʿmānī in his famous work on genealogy *Kitāb al-Ansāb* and Dhahabī in his *Tadhkirkah al-Huffaz*[22]

There is little difference of opinion about this date as some scholars like Ibn Khallikān have recorded that the Imām was born in 95 A.H. and Yāfi'ī has said that he was born in 94 A.H.[23]

The Imām belonged to a royal Arab family of Ḥumair from Yemen which had settled in Medina after the advent of Islam. Just as the family of Imām Mālik was famous for their hospitality and other qualities before Islam, they became equally well known after they had accepted Islam but in a different way altogether. Their services to the cause of Islam will be remembered in Islamic history for all time to come. The genealogy of the Imām runs as Mālik, the son of Anas, the son of Abū Āmir, the son of ʿUmar, the son of Hārith, the son of Ghiman, the son of Habthil, the son of ʿUmrū, the son of Ḥārith who was also well known as *Dhil-Ṣubḥ.* It was Abū ʿĀmir who accepted Islam in the family. Imām Mālik's nickname (Kuniyyah) was ʿAbdallah but when he became very famous as a great scholar in Medina, people referred to him as *Imam Dar al-Hijrah,* 'the Leader of the House of Migration' meaning the leader of thought in Medina.

The period of Imām Mālik's birth was the period of rule of the Umayyad Caliphate and the reign of Caliph Walid bin ʿAbd al-Malik, the third ruler of Umayyad dynasty, whose territories had expanded up to Spain in Europe, the Maghrib in Africa and India in Asia. Although the Umayyads had shifted their capital from Medina to Damascus in Syria, the importance of the city of the Prophet had continued as every Muslim worth his name would take pride in visiting the Holy City even if he had to travel a long distance to fulfil his life-long desire. Since Medina was no longer the political capital of Islam, it continued its spiritual and educational role as was the case in the life time of the Prophet. But Islam had spread far and wide, and enthusiastic Muslim scholars, Arabs and non-Arabs alike, came and lived in Medina to sit at the feet of the famous scholars like Imām Mālik bin Anas.

His Education:

The family of Imām Mālik, during his early childhood, had already become well known as scholars and teachers in Islamic learning. Imam's grandfather, who also bore the same name as the Imām, was a famous scholar of Ḥadīth and is considered to be one of the authentic narrators of Ahadith was alive until Imām Mālik reached the age of ten years. By that time Imām Mālik had started his schooling, although as a child he could not directly benefit from his deep learning except the everlasting impressions and the encouraging words of counsel and love played an important role in building the character and zeal for learning for the Imām. Imām's uncle Abū Suhail Nāfi' was a recognised scholar of Ḥadīth and has the fame of being the teacher of Imām Ẓuhrī, a very famous contemporary of Imam Malik. Imam Malik learnt *Aḥādīth* from his uncle. Imām's father Anas and his uncle Rābi'were also scholars of Ḥadīth as they have narrated *aḥādīth* from their father Mālik (Imām Mālik's grandfather). Imām Mālik was such a keen scholar right from the childhood that once his teacher was lecturing to his students and a snake fell into his lap from the ceilings. All his students ran away while he kept sitting undisturbed as if nothing had happened at all. He was so much engrossed in his studies, that even a snake did not move him.

Imām's Teachers:

1. *Abū Radīm Nāfi' bin 'Abd al-Raḥmān:*

In the field of Qur'ānic studies, Imam learnt how to read and recite the Holy Qur'ān according to the established principle, of *Tajwid* from the very famous scholar Abū Radīm Nāfi' bin 'Abd a Raḥmān who is well known in this field throughout the Muslim world even today. Abu Radim died in the year 169 A.H.

2. *Nāfi:'*

Nāfi'was a great scholar of Ḥadīth during the early years of Imām Mālik's life. He learnt this science from his famous master 'Abdallāh bin 'Umar since Nāfi'was his freed slave who served him for 30 years of his life. Those who knew the place of 'Abdallah bin' Umar in Ḥadīth literature would realise what a great opportunity it was for Nāfi'to learn from such a great scholar who was always surrounded by pupils. 'Abdallah bin 'Umar as the son of 'Umar bin al-Khaṭṭāb, the second caliph of Islam, and one of the closest companions of the Prophet (S.A.W.)

Apart from learning Aḥādīth from 'Abdallah bin 'Umar, Nāfi' had also the good fortune of serving the other companions and servants in the field of Ḥadīth 'Āishah, Umm-Salmah, Abū Hurairah, the famous narrator of Aḥādīth, and Abū Sa'īd al-Khudrī and many others. His pupils include not only Imām Mālik but other luminaries of that period whose names are famous in Islamic learning like Ibn-Jārij, Imām Ẓuhrī, Imām Auzā'ī and Ayyūb Sakhtiyānī. Imām Mālik was in a habit of asking juristic opinions of his great teacher adding: What did Ibn'Umar say about these issues:?" who could be a greater authority ont he juristic decisions and opinions of ʻAbdallah bin ʻUmar than his closest man like Nāfiʻ. The Imam also loved his teacher for his devotion, integrity and honesty that he often used to say that once he heard an opinion on Ḥadīth narrated by Ibn Umar from his teacher Nāfiʻ, he does not need any further proof on the issue.

This is the reason why *Muwaṭṭā* is full of various *Aḥādīth* which are narrated by Imām Mālik on the authority of Nāfiʻ who heard them from ʻAbdallah Ibn ʻUmar.

The pious caliph ʻUmar bin ʻAbdul ʻAzīz, who himself was a great scholar, chose Nāfiʻ as a teacher of Egyptians and sent him there. It is only in Islam that a slave, through his piety, devotion and scholarship, could be raised to such a high authority that *Aḥādīth* narrated by him were considered to be authentic and he was respected as a great scholar by the ruling caliphs. He died in 117 A.H.

3. *Ja'far al-Ṣādiq:*

Imām Ja'far al-Ṣādiq was also one of the teachers of Imām Mālik. Apart from being a great scholar, he belonged to the family of the Prophet. He was a great grand son of Imām Ḥussain, the grand son of the Prophet. His father, Imām Bāqar, was also a great scholar. The chain of his narration of Ahadith goes back to his father Imām Muḥammad Bāqar, ʻUrwah bin Zubair, Muḥammad bin Munkadir and 'Aṭā.[23] Apart from Imām Mālik, his pupils included Sufyān al-Thawrī, Ṣhʻabah, Abū ʻĀṣim Yaḥyā Anṣārī, Imām Abū Ḥanīfah and Sufyān bin ʻAiyiyyah. Imām Jaʻfar al-Ṣādiq died in 198 A.H.

4. *Muḥammad bin Yaḥyā al-Anṣārī:*

Muḥammad bin Yaḥyā was another teacher of Imām Mālik. He was also a *Tābi'ī*. He used to teach in *Masjid al-Nabawī*, the Prophetic Mosque in Medina. Muḥammad bin Yahya died in 121 A.H. at the age of 74 years.

5. *Abū Ḥāzim Salmah bin Dīnār:*

Abū Ḥāzim was another *Tābi'ī* scholar and a teacher of Imām Mālik. He also used to teach in the Prophetic Mosque, and died in 140 A.H.

6. *Yaḥyā bin Saʻīd:*

Yaḥyā bin Saʻīd was also a *Tābi'ī* scholar and pupil of Imām ʻAlī bin Zain al-ʻĀbidīn bin Ḥusain and ʻAdi bin Thābit and Anas bin Mālik. Apart from Imām Mālik, Ḥammād, Shaʻabah, Sufyān al-Thaurī were his illustrious pupils. He died in 143 A.H.

7. *Hishām bin ʻU'rwah:*

Hishām bin ʻU'rwah a venerable and well known *Tābi'ī*, was also a teacher of Imām Mālik. He had heard traditions from many companions and was the teacher of several other great scholars of Ḥadīth, like Sufyān al-Thawrī and Sufyān bin ʿAyniyyah. Later, he went to Kūfah in the period of Khalīfah Abū Ja'afar Manṣūr, the ʿAbbāsid, and people flocked round him to listen to his lessons on Tafsīr and Ḥadīth. Caliph Manṣūr greatly respected him and led the funeral prayers when Hishām died. According to Ibn Sa'd, he was reliable in the science of Ḥadīth and knew large number of *Aḥādīth.* Abū Ḥātim was described him as the *Imām* in the science of Ḥadīth.

The Famous Pupils of Imām Mālik and the Authentic Copyist of The Muwaṭṭā:

Imām Mālik's fame spread far and wide and the contemporary scholars from different parts of the Muslim world of that period considered it to be a great privilege to sit in the circle of the great Imām and listen to his lessons on Ḥadīth and exhortations on various juristic and legal issues. Many of them took down full notes and copied the text of the *Muwaṭṭā,* the famous collection of Ḥadīth by their teacher. This activity helped a great deal since these scholars returned to their respective countries with an authentic copy of the *Muwaṭṭā* on which they based their teachings of Aḥādīth and jurisprudence of Imām Mālik. Their number reaches to about 1300 scholars who came to learn from him. We shall give a brief biographical sketch of the most prominent of these scholars which would also help us to see why their copies of the *Muwaṭṭā* have remained the most authentic so far.

1. *Yaḥyā bin Yaḥya al-Masmūdī (d. 234 A.H.)* belonged to the Berber tribe of Spain. He travelled twice to see Imām Mālik to learn from him and then returned to his country to teach the science of Ḥadīth and Jurisprudence. The Emir of Cordova asked him to accept an appointment as the *Qāḍī* of Cordova, but he declined. He was a very pious man of his time. Yaḥyā went to Medina in the last year of Imām Mālik's life and learnt from him the famous *Muwaṭṭā* except three chapters from the Book of I'tikāf since Imām Mālik died later in the year in 149 A.H. Yaḥyā was present in his funeral prayers and burial. Yaḥyā also came closer to other pupils of Imām Mālik like ʿAbdullāh bin Wahāb, Laith bin Sa'd al-Maṣrī, Sufyān bin ʿAiyinah and Ibn al-Qāsim, the author of *Al-Mudawwahah.*

   It is through his narrations that *al-Muwaṭṭā* became well known in the Maghrib. He died in 234 A.H.

2. The other famous pupil of Imām Mālik was Ibn Wahb Abū Muḥammad ʿAbdallah bin Salmah al-Fahrī al Maṣrī. His famous works include *al-Jāmiʿal-Ḥadīth, Kitāb al-Manāsik, Kitāb al-Maghāzī*

and *Kitab Tafsir al-Muwatta*. He died in 199 A.H.

3. Abī ʿAbdallāh ʿAbd al-Raḥmān ʿAbd al-Raḥmān bin al-Qāsim bin Khālid al-Thasrī was another illustrious pupil of Imām Mālik. He died in Egypt in 191 A.H.

The other pupils were:
Abū ʿAbd al-Raḥmān ʿAbdallah bin Muslimah al-Ḥārith. (d. 221 A.H.)
ʿAbdallāh bin Yūsuf al-Damishqī
Abū Yaḥyā Ma'ān bin ʿĪsā bin Dīnār al-Madanī (d. 198 A.H.)
Saʿīd bin Kathīr bin Afīr bin Muslim al-Anṣārī (d. 226 A.H.)
Yaḥyā bin Yaḥyā bin Bikir al-Maṣrī (d. 231 A.H.)
Abī Maʿsab al-Zuhrī, Qāḍī of Medina (d. 242 A.H.)
Maʿsab al-Zubairī
Muḥammad bin al-Mubārak
Muḥammad bin al-Ḥasan al-Shaibānī.

All the above scholars have left the most authentic copies of *al-Muwaṭṭā* which they learnt from Imam Malik.

Those who benefited from the study circle of Imām Mālik included the ʿAbbāsid Caliphs like Abū Ja'far Manṣūr, Mahdī, Hārūn al-Rashīd and his sons Amīn and Maʾmūn al-Rashīd, and the learned Jurists like Abū Ḥanīfah, Imām Shāfi'i, Imām Muḥammad bin al-Ḥasan al-Shaybānī, Qaḍī Abū Yūsuf and Imām Ibn Qāsim al-Mālikī.

Imām Mālik as a Teacher

According to Dhahabī in his famous work *Tadhkirah al-Ḥuffāẓ*, even Imām Abū Ḥanīfah used to sit in the presence of Imām Mālik with such respect as one sits in the presence of one's teacher. Although it reflects great humility on the part of the older scholar Abū Ḥanīfah, it never the less shows the great respect with which Imam Abu Hanifah held Imam Mālik bin Anas.

Imam Malik's method of teaching his pupils was also unique in his time, and it is the same system which is followed in our traditional Qur'ānic schools and in the mosque-teachings and preachings in West Africa till today. Imām Mālik liked his pupils to read aloud while he himself listened.[24] Some people objected to this system. Yaḥyā bin Salām did not like this method and left his school simply on this ground.

Imām Mālik, the teacher would sit on a high seat with the book of Allah and his collection of Ḥadīth by his side and the students will sit around the teacher, and they would jot down notes of the lectures of the Imām. If the number of pupils grow very large, one of the most bright pupils with strong memory would stand up and repeat the teacher's words without altering the theme and substance of the master's words. The person chosen by Imām Mālik to do this job was Ibn Ulliyyah and Imām's contemporary scholar, Ibn Shu'ba, had chosen Ādam bin Abi Ayas for the same function.

Imām Mālik's contemporaries were luminaries in the field of Islamic scholarship and particularly Islamic jurisprudence. The scholars who were alive at that time were Imām Auzāi in Syria, Ḥammād at Baṣrah, Imām Abū Ḥanīfah and Sufyān al-Thawrī at Kūfah, Laith in Egypt.

Imām Mālik as a Muḥaddith and a Jurist

As a great *Muḥaddith* that is a scholar and authority on the science of *Ḥadīth*, he scrutinized all kinds of narrations, sermons of the Prophet, expatiation on Qur'ānic and other stories, sayings about excellences and the biographical narrations by the *Ṣaḥāba* of the Prophet, the explanations of Qur'ān and Hadith by the *Ṣaḥāba* and their way of life. He then compiled about a thousand *aḥādīth* after careful consideration in his famous *Muwaṭṭā*.

All his legal theories and its codification is based on the *Ḥadīth* and *Sunnah* of the Prophet. Weakness in quoting the traditions and giving a legal judgement based on them would always create problems for the later generation. This is the reason why Auzāi, a recognised *Mujtahid* and a great scholar and contemporary of Imām Mālik in Syria, could not influence people to accept him as a master and founder of a school of jurisprudence as is acclaimed Imām Mālik. This is further confirmed whem someone asked Imam Aḥmad bin Ḥanbal his opinion of Auzāi. He replied: "He is weak in Ḥadīth and weak in judgement."

Although Imām Mālik is a famous *Muḥaddith* (Traditionist) his legal theories and decisions required the use of *Ijtihād*. Ibn Qutaibah (d. 276 A.H.) the famous traditionist, therefore has enumerated him as one of the *Ahl al-Ray* in a chapter of the same name in his *Kitāb al-Ma'ārif.*

During the period of Imām Mālik, the famous scholars of Ḥadīth were of two categories although both of them were engaged in rendering their best servies to the science of Ḥadīth with utmost respect to the Prophet and his companions. One group concerned themselves with collecting *Aḥādīth* and *Riwāyāt* (narrations). The collection of Ḥadīth was also a marathon task, and it required travelling from place to place even to record one Ḥadīth and establish the chain of its narrators. The other group of pious scholars collected and examined the Aḥādīth with a view to deducing from them commandments and juristic decisions.

Imām Mālik was so very careful in selecting the Ḥadīth while compiling his famous word *Al-Muwaṭṭā* that he even did not include the narrations made by his father Anas and his uncle Rabī on the authority of his grandfather.

As a jurist he fearlessly gave his *fatāwa* (juristic decisions) even if the ruling Caliphs disliked it. Once he was asked to give *fatwah* about a divorce given under durress. Other Imams said that it will be considered as a divorce even if given forcibly, but Imām Mālik said that there would be no divorce. Ja'far bin Sulaimān, the governor of Medina and a cousin brother of Caliph Manṣūr ordered Imām Mālik not to give such *Fatwah,* but the Imām publicly gave his opinion and was flogged because of this.

Imām Mālik used to refrain from giving *Fatwah* if they were asked from distant places. Once a man came after travelling for about six months and sought Imām's legal opinion, the Imām replied: "Please tell your people that Imām Mālik has said that he cannot give answer to that question." Ibn Abi ʻUways has said that once Imām Mālik told him that sometimes such questions are posed to him that out of anxiety he cannot eat or drink. If someone corrected him in any juristic opinion, the Imām used to accept it immediately.[25]

Imām Mālik has not narrated any Ḥadīth or opinion from the great scholars of Iraq. Shu'aib bin Harab once asked Imām Mālik: "Why have you not narrated anything from the people of Iraq? Imām replied: "Our elders *(aslāf)* have not narrated anything from them, hence our youngers have also not narrated anything from their youngers." In reality, he had nothing against the *ʻUlamā* of Baṣrah, Baghdad and Kūfah. One of his Shuyūkh (teachers) was Ayyūb Sakhtiyānī, a well known *Tābiʻī* who came from Baṣrah, and he respected his contemporary scholars from Iraq whenever they visited him and sat in his lessons. Many of his renowned pupils also came from Iraq.

The Medinan Fiqh:

The greatest contribution that Imām Mālik made was the codification of the Medinan *Fiqh*. Medina was the centre where all branches of Islamic learning were taught by great scholars and dedicated persons who had learnt the science of the Qur'ān, the Hadith and the principles of jurisprudence from the Prophet and his companions. The companions having all departed one after another, the famous *Tābiʻīn* scholars were still living in Medina in the time of Imām Mālik. There were seven outstanding *Tābiʻīn* who have become central figures in *Fiqh* and *Ḥadīth,* and all questions of law were generally referred to them. Two such names are Sulaimān and Salīm bin ʻAbdullāh. Sulaimān was a slave of Maimūnah, the mother of Muslims and wife of the Prophet and Salim was the grandson of ʻUmar and was taught by his father ʻAbdullāh bin ʿUmar. These *Tābiʿīn* constituted a consultative body to which all *Sharīʿah* questions were referred.[26] The Medinan Fiqh that Imam Mālik codified was the outcome of the exercise of these pious *Tābiʿīn* based on the authority of the opinions of the *sahabah* and the Prophet.

Imām Mālik died on 11th *Rabīʿal-Awwal,* in the year of 179 A.H. at the age of 86 years, and was buried in *Jannat al-Baqīʿ* in Medina.

The Muwaṭṭā of Imām Mālik: As Assessment

Professor N. J. Coulson, in his book *"A History of Islamic Law"* has said that "In the jurisprudence of the years 770-800 the reasoning of individual scholars, local consensus and the reported precedents (Sunnah) of Muḥammad (S.A.W.) lay in uneasy juxtaposition. This stage of legal development is mirrored in the first written compending law produced in Islam – the *Muwaṭṭā* of the Medinan scholar Mālik bin Anas (d. 796)".[27] Those who are well versed in *Fiqh* and *Uṣūl al-Fiqh* as well as the science of Ḥadīth will be able to realise that this is far from truth. The *Muwaṭṭā* of Imām Mālik does not 'mirror' in any sense the *uneasy juxtaposition* of the reasoning of individual scholars, local consensus and the reported precedents of the Prophet, but it is the most authentic compilation of *Aḥādīth* and some of their interpretations by the *sahabah* and the Tabi'un on all important aspects of a Muslim's way of life. Hence, the *Muwaṭṭā* begins with the *ṣalāt* (Five Daily Prayers) and then goes on the *Ahadith* dealing with other pillars of Islam, and then comes to various legal aspects as taught through the precepts of the Prophet and understood and practised by the *sahabah* and the *Tābiʿūn.*

The style of *Muwaṭṭā* followed by Imām Mālik is such that it helps a reader to understand, first of all, what the Holy Prophet (S.A.W.) has to say on the subject. Since, the final authority in Sharīʿah is to be derived from the Qur'ān and the Sunnah, any Ḥadīth conflicting with the teachings and the spirit of the Qur'ān is not to be regarded as a Ḥadīth but a mere fabrication. The invariable practice of Mālik to begin his discussion of legal topic by quoting relevant *Aḥādīth* or a precedent of the *ṣaḥābah* based on these authorities, makes the *Muwaṭṭā* most authentic. Imām Muḥammad bin Idris al Shāfiʿī has rightly said, therefore, that "there is no book that has come up on the surface of the earth, after the book of Allah, more authentic than the Book of Mālik.

There has never appeared a book after the Book of Allah more authentic than the book of Mālik (i.e. *Muwaṭṭā*)." In another narration, Imām Shāfiʿī is reported to have said:

«ما وضع على الأرض كتاب هو أقرب إلى القرآن من كتاب مالك».

"There has never appeared on earth a Book that is closest to the Qur'ān than the Book of Mālik".

In yet another narration, Imām Shāfi'ī has narrated that *Muwaṭṭā* is most useful book after the Qur'ān.[28]

Imām Shāfi'ī authenticity is unquestionable, as he is also the Imām of a school of Islamic theology and jurisprudence. Imām Aḥmad bin Ḥanbal has said about Imām Shāfi'ī's mastery over *Muwaṭṭā* in the following words:

«كنت سمعت طوطاء من بضعة عشر رجلا من حفاظ أصحاب مالك فأعدته على الشافعي لاني وجدته أقومهم».

I studied *al-Muwaṭṭā* under ten of Mālik's students who used to memorize it. Finally I checked my memorization by reading it to al-Shāfi'ī's because he was the most perfect among them."[29]

Now whose opinion are we going to consider more reliable? The Western scholars or Imam al-Shāfii's? Naturally, every Muslim the world over, will accept the judgement of the latter. The Western scholars view about the *Muwaṭṭā* is merely as follows:

"Mālik's chosen method of composing his treaties *(Muwaṭṭā)* was first to report such precedents as were known, and then to consider them, interpret them, and accept them or otherwise in the light of his own reasoning and the legal tradition of Medina. His supreme criterion was the local consensus of opinion, and *there was nothing so sacrosanct about Traditions (Aḥādīth)* from the Prophet or other precedents that enabled them to override his authority in cases of conflict. The *Muwaṭṭā* is essentially a manual of the doctrine currently endorsed by the establishment in Medina.[30]

One wonders whether it is true that Imām Mālik ever wanted to report the precedents which were known in Medina circles and then consider, interpret and accept or reject them according to his mere reasoning and whether his supreme creation was really to obtain the local consensus of opinion as mentioned by the Western scholars and that in reality he did not hold anything sacrosanct about *Aḥādīth* from the Prophet or other precedents from the *ṣaḥāba* and *Tābi'ūn* Imām Mālik's intention as can be understood from the following incident narrated by Al-Ṭabarī, was to render the guidance of the authentic *Aḥādīth* and the exact practice of the time – of the *ṣaḥāba* and the *Tābi'ūn* in the heartland of Islam and in the city of the Prophet, city par excellence. This was the reason why he actually collected ten thousand chapters which he calls book (Kitāb).[31] It is narrated by Muḥammad bin 'Umar who said that he heard from Imām Mālik bin Anas the following:

"When the ʿAbbāsid Caliph Abū Ja'far al-Manṣūr performed his pilgrimage (and came to Medina), he called me. When I met him, I narrated Aḥādīth. He asked me some questions and I replied. Then he said 'I desire that I may make copies of your book *Muwaṭṭā* and then send them to all the Muslim countries and order people to act upon them, and do not cross the limits'. He (Imām Mālik) replied: 'O Amīr al-Mu'minīn, do not do so".[32]

Imām Mālik was a great Imām who wished to revive the practice of the Sunnah of the Prophet and he spent his life in collecting the *Aḥadith* and chose the most authentic ones to be included in his *Muwatta*. To say that there was nothing sacrosanct about the *Aḥādīth* of the Prophet, is to put a very grave charge against the pious life of Imām Mālik and amounts to the Imām's lack of respect and love for the Prophet. The *Muwaṭṭā* is not merely a manual of doctrines but is in the foremost a manual of Hadīth and the authentic guide on the Sharī'ah of Islam.

The same Western Scholar, while discussing the genesis of Sharī'ah law, further confuses the prevailing situation in Imām Mālik's time. He says: "It should finally be stressed that there was no suggestion, at this stage, that the Prophet was other than a human interpreter of the Divine Revelation, his authority lay in the fact that he was closest, in time and spirit, to the Qur'ān and as such was the ultimate starting-point of the Islamic sunnah."[33] This is a widespread misunderstanding among the non-Muslim scholars of Islam who write their books on Islam without any respect to the *Īmān* (belief) of all Muslims. In the time of Imām Mālik, before this period and in subsequent stages, that every Muslim, through his commitment to the *shahādah*, believes that Prophet Muḥammad is *not* merely "a human interpreter of the Divine revelation", but he was the Messenger of Allah (Rasūl Allāh). His authority did *not* lie merely "in the fact that he was closest, in time and spirit, to the Qur'ān", and as such was the ultimate starting-point of the Islamic Sunnah, but he was the person on whom the Holy Qur'ān was revealed for the guidance of mankind, and, hence, he was the best interpreter of the Qur'ān.

3. *Imām Muḥammad Idrīs al-Shāfi'ī*

Abū Muḥammad ʿAbdal Raḥmān bin Abī Ḥātim al-Rāzī[34] who died in 327 AH/938 AD is the earliest and most accurate biographer of Imām Al-Shafi'i who says that Muḥammad Idris Al-Shāfi'ī was born at Gaza, a small town on the Meditterean Sea. Some other biographers say that he was born in Asqalān (Askelon) which is not far from Gaza in the year 150 AH/767 AD. He belonged to the tribe of Quraish, and thus was a descendant of Prophet Muhammad. After his father's death, his mother took him to Palestine and lived with a Yamenic tribe to which her ancestors belonged. Later she travelled to Mecca with Al-Shāfi'ī when he was ten years old.[35] From his early childhood he displayed a sharp intelligence and was excellent in memorizing things. He was eloquent in speech and was very good in poetry and Arabic language apart from his legal studies.

His Early Life

As a child Shāfi'i was a very intelligent and a bright boy, always very keen to learn the traditional Islamic sciences. Like every Muslim child in those days, he began his studies with the learning of the Qur'ān and memorized it at the early age of seven years. During that time Imam Mālik's famous work *Al-Muwaṭṭā* was a very well known book on *Ḥadīth* and *Fiqh* in Ḥijāz and other parts of the Muslim world. We are told that Al-Shafi'i memorized complete *Al-Muwaṭṭā* at the age of fifteen.[36] He studied Islamic jurisprudence under the well known scholar Muslim bin Khālid al-Zanjī, the *Muftī* of Mecca (died in 180 AH/796 AD) and Sufyān bin'Uyayana (died 198 AH/813 AD).[37]

He left Mecca for Medina to study at the feet of Imām bin Anas, a well known scholar and jurist in Medina during that time. Imām Al-Shāfi'ī was then twenty years of age, and continued his study with Imām Mālik until the latter's death in the year 179 AH/796 AD. By the time of Imām Mālik's death, Al-Shāfi'ī had already gained reputation as a famous jurist in Ḥijāz and other places.[38]

Al-Shāfi'ī in Iraq

When the governor of Yemen visited Medina, he was so much impressed by the great learning of Al-Shāfi'ī that he persuaded him to take up a government position as an administrator which al-Shafi'i accepted for a short while. We were told that Al-Shāfi'ī's frankness brought him in conflict with the government officials and was deported to Iraq in heavy chains in 187 AH/803 AD. Various unfounded allegations including that of conspiracy were levelled against him. This happened during the Caliphate of Hārūn al-Rashīd of the 'Abbāsid dynasty.

Al-Shāfi'ī was presented to the Caliph along with other conspirators but he was pardoned by the Caliph when the eloquent Al-Shāfi'i successfully defended himself. In the court of Hārūn al-Rashīd, it is said, he discussed with the Caliph every conceivable branch of knowledge including Greek medicine and philosophies in their original languages. Fortunately for him Imām Muḥammad bin Al-Ḥasan al-Shaybānī (died 189 AH/805 AD) the famous Ḥanafī jurist, was present in the court of Hārūn. He helped him by saying that Al-Shāfi'ī was a famous scholar of

Fiqh and his life must be spared. Al-Shāfi'ī's discussion with Hārūn so much delighted the Caliph that he became his patron.[39] Al-Shāfi'ī found peace of mind and heart in Baghdad and devoted his time to serious studies with Imām Al-Shaybānī.

With his bitter experience of the past government service, he vowed not to take up any government job again, although he was patronised by the Caliph.

Al-Shāfi'ī who had so far studied in depth under Imām Mālik had made him an expert on the Mālikī school of thought, but now, in Baghdad, he had a new opportunity to go deep into the Ḥanafī school of Islamic jurisprudence. He lived with the Ḥanafī jurists and discussed with them on various legal issued defending the position of his master Imām Mālik,[40] and became reputed as an upholder of *Aḥādīth*. Thus, Al-Shāfi'ī had the privilege of studying in depth of both the Mālikī and Ḥanafī systems.

His Study of Ḥanafī and Mālikī Schools

Al-Shāfi'ī then moved to Egypt in the year 188 AH/804 AD via Ḥarīrān, Syria and Mecca. Because of his earlier stay in Mecca, as well as his growing fame as an eminent jurist, he was well received in Mecca where he delivered lectures in *Ḥaram al-Sharīf.* During the course of his lectures, Al-Shāfi'ī who was an expert on both Mālikī and Ḥanafī schools of thought, expressed various differences of opinions with and departures from the legal position of Imām Abu Ḥanīfah and Imām Mālik. Many of his supporters, who followed the Mālikī system, were disappointed on listening to his discourses, but he still made impact on some scholars, one of whom was Imām Aḥmad bin Ḥanbal, who was then studying in Mecca. In spite of his difference of opinion with Imām Mālik, Imām Al-Shāfi'ī respected the *Muwaṭṭā* of Imām Mālik so much so that he says: "there has never appeared on earth a book that is closer to the Qur'ān than the book of Mālik. In yet anothr narration he has said that *Muwaṭṭā* is the most useful book after the Qur'ān.[41]

Later he returned to Baghdad to spend a short period of three or four years in 194 AH/810 AD. While he was in Baghdad, Caliph Mamun Al-Rashīd (died 218 AH/833 AD) invited him to occupy the position of *Al-Qāḍī* (judge), but Al-Shāfi'ī refused to accept the position.[42] In the meantime, he was invited to come to Egypt by 'Abdallāh bin Mūsā. He left Baghdad finally in the year 198 AH/814 AD at the age of 50 years. Some of his biographers say that since Al-Shāfi'ī vehemently opposed the *Mu'tazilite* doctrine, which the ruling Caliph also supported, he decided to leave Baghdad as quickly as possible.[43]

Al-Shāfi'ī in Egypt

Al-Shāfi'ī found himself in a peaceful and congenial atmosphere in Egypt. It was here that most of his mature works were written. He was always surrounded by large numbers of scholars from different parts of the world who came to learn *Fiqh* and *Uṣūl al-Fiqh* from him. His leading disciples like Rabī' bin Sulaimān al-Marali (died 270 AH/880 AD) Abū Yakub al-Ruwayti (died 231 AH/845 AD) and Abu Ibrahim bin Yahya al-Muzanī (died 274 AH/877 AD) and many others keenly heard his discourses and every word that the great master uttered was recorded by them. It was the practice of Imām al-Shāfi'ī that whatever was written down by his disciples was read aloud to him and he would go on correcting the text.[45] This is the reason why the most accurate discourse of Imām al-Shāfi'ī has come down to us. The famous works of Al-Shāfi'ī like *Kitāb al-Umm* and *Risālah* are the most famous contributions in the field of Islamic legal system.

Imām Shāfi'ī was a man of impressive personality and was well-known for his straight forwardness and *taqwah* (piety). He lived his life with meagre resources. Still he was very generous to the poor and the needy. His biographer Al-Rāzī says that he was in a habit of giving away to the poor everything that he could lay his hands on.

His Death

It is a pity that at times the difference of opinion of *'Ulamā* are not tolerated by some shallow minded followers of certain savants as can be seen in the case of Al-Shāfi'ī's differences of opinion from his master Imām Mālik. It is said that a man called Fityān, a follower of Imām Mālik in Egypt was defeated in arguments by Al-Shāfi'ī during his learned lectures and discourses, as a result Fityan's followers attacked Al-Shāfi'ī after one of his lectures, and badly injured him. A few days later Al-Shafi'i died.[46] There is another view as well that Imām Al-Shāfi'ī suffered from a serious intestinal illness which made him very weak during the last years of his life, and he died as a result of the natural illness on the last day of Rajab in the year 204 AH/20th January 820 AD in the old Cairo, in Egypt. He was buried near Mount al-Muqattam. About four centuries after his death a big domed Mausoleum was built at his grave by the Ayyūbid Sulṭān, Mālik al-Kāmil in the year 608 AH/1212 AD.

Al-Shāfi'īs Famous Works

Out of the two great works of Imām Al-Shāfi'ī, *Kitāb al-Risālah Fī-Uṣūl al-Fiqh,* commonly known as *al-Risālah,* the most famous book of Islamic Jurisprudence. Imam al-Shafi'i himself refers to *al-Risālah* very often as *"our book"* or *"my book",* showing the importance he himself attached to *al-Risālah.*

Perhaps there were two books of the same name. The old *risālah* and the new *Risālah*. In the old *Risālah*, Shāfi'ī set forth the system of the Qur'ān including those general and particular rules, abrogating and abrogated communications and the *Sunnah* as the authoritative source of the Shari'ah. It also included discourse on *Ijma* and *Qiyas*. Unfortunately, this text of old *Risālah* has not reached us except a few passages which are reproduced by some other scholars in their books.

The new *Risālah* which has come down to us has made a great impact on the Islamic Jurisprudence in general. It gained him a title of the father of Islamic Jurisprudence. *Risālah* was composed in Egypt after Al-Shāfi'ī had settled there. Therefore, it reflects the mature legal opinions of Imam Al-Shafi'i while he was at the Zenith of his career as a learned man in the field of Jurisprudence. In the *Risālah* Imām Shāfi'ī has not only emphasized the *Sunnah* as the source of Shari'ah but also draws heavily on *Sunnah* in formulating the rules of law. In reality, the *Risālah* was written mainly to defend the view points of traditionalists concerning the over-riding authority of the *Sunnah*. His greatest authority on *Sunnah* was Imam Malik and Sufyan bin Uyayna, whom he quotes time and time again.

On the other hand, his main experience was derived from intense debates that he had written with the Hanafi jurists during his stay in Baghdad. His discussions with the Hanafi jursits had made a great influence in his legal thoughts particularly during his stay with Imām Muḥammad al-Shaibānī. In his other famous book, *Kitāb al-Umm* Imam Al-Shafi'i has devoted the whole section of the book to his discussion with eminent jurists of his time like Imam Malik, Imam Auzāī, Imām Abū-Ḥanīfah, Imām Abū-Yūsuf and Imām Muḥammad Al-Shaibānī. This book shows how great a scholar Imām Shāfi'ī was that he had studied the works of these eminent jurists with great care and profoundity.

Imām Al-Shāfi'ī was undoubtedly a great jurist and an eminent scholar of Ḥadīth who will always be remembered by people for all time to come. So much impact has been made by Al-Shāfi'i in the field of Islamic jurisprudence that the Shāfi'ī school is named after him, and millions of followers today are proud to follow his footsteps in various juristic opinions that he has left behind for their guidance. His followers are mainly found in Yemen, Egypt, Syria, in countries of south East Asia like Malaysia, Indonesia, East Africa and to some extent scattered in all parts of the Muslim World.

4. *Imām Aḥmad bin Muḥammad bin Ḥanbal*

Imām Abū 'Abdallāh Aḥmad bin Muḥammad bin Ḥanbal was born in Marw on 20th of Rabī' al-Awwal in the year 164 AH. His father, Muḥammad was reputed as a warrior *(Mujāhid)* who lived in Baṣrah in Iraq. It is said that when his father went to Marw as a *ghāzī* Imām Aḥmad was born during his sojourn in Marw. While still an infant he was brought to Baghdad where his father died at a very early age of thirty. The entire responsibility of bringing him up was thus thrown on his mother Ṣafiyah bint Maimūnah bint Malik Al-Shaibānī.

His Early Life

Imām Aḥmad was a very inquisitive and intelligent child, keenly interested in furthering his education. He began his early study of Ḥadīth literature in the year 179 AH; when he was only sixteen years old. It is said that he became such a great scholar of Ḥadīth that he remembered almost a million *Aḥādīth*. He based, therefore, his juristic opinions solely on *aḥādīth* and became an eminent jurist in his time as well as all the time to come.

Imām Aḥmad's Teachers

The following scholars were the teachers of Imām Aḥmad bin Ḥanbal. Imām Muḥammad al-Shāfi'ī, Bishr bin al-Mufaḍḍal, Ismā'īl bin Ulayyah, Jarīr bin 'Abdul Ḥamīd, Yaḥyā bin Sa'īd bin al-Qaṭṭān Abū Dā'ūd. 'Abdallāh bin Namīr, Waki bin al-Jarrāḥ, some of his teachers have narrated *Aḥādīth* from this illustrious pupil. They are Abū Dā'ūd, Aswal bin Āmir, Imām al-Shāfi'ī, Yaḥyā bin Ādam; Imām Bukhārī, Imām Muslim and Yazīd bin Hārūn.[47]

His illustrious pupils include Abū Bakr al-Alhram, Ḥanbal bin Isḥāq, Abul Qāsim al-Baghwī and many others.

Relationship Between Imam Ahmad and Imam Shafi'ī

The famous scholar Abu-Bakr al-Baihaqi has mentioned Shafi'i as the most important teacher of Imām Aḥmad. It is true that Imām Aḥmad had special attachment with Imām Shāfi'ī as seen through most of his narrations in his famous book *Musnad Aḥmad* which are derived from Imām Shāfi'ī. Imām Shāfi'ī also had a great respect for Imām Aḥmad because of his sincerity of purpose and outstanding scholarship. Once, when Imām Shāfi'ī met Imām Aḥmad in Baghdad in 199 AH, the former asked Imām Aḥmad to acquaint him with any *aḥādīth* that he had traced as correct either from Ḥijāz, Syria or Iraq which he would like to put into practice. He further added that he was not like the theologians of Ḥijāz who would not like to accept their *ḥadīth* which has spread in other parts of Muslim world branding as untrue or about which the Ḥijāz

'Ulamā say, "We do not consider them true nor untrue", but as far as I am concerned I act on the true *ḥadīth* no matter from where I find it. Imam Shafi'i, in spite of his being the most learned in his time, used to refer to Imam Ahmad whenever he had any difficulty about *aḥādīth.*[47] Imām Shāfi'ī has described Imām Aḥmad as the "Most learned in the affairs of *aḥādīth.*"

Imām Aḥmad's Taqwah

Imām Aḥmad was a very pious scholar who devoted all his life in the service of *aḥādīth* and *Fiqh.* Once, when 'Abbasid Caliph Hārūn al-Rashīd told Imām Shāfi'ī that he needed a *Qāḍī* to be sent to Yemen, Imām Shāfi'ī spoke to Imām Aḥmad bin Ḥanbal who was then thirty years of age and a student in the study circle of Imām Shāfi'ī. Imām Aḥmad refused blunty saying, "I came to your place in search of knowledge and not that you thrust upon me a delicate position of a *Qāḍī.*" Imām Shāfi'ī then kept quiet. Imām Aḥmad was so very pious that even he did not like to pray behind his son or his uncle nor he went to their houses to eat because both of them had accepted government positions under the Caliph. It is said that once he was very hungry for three days, and he did not have anything in the house. His wife borrowed a little flour from a neighbour and wanted to make bread as quickly as possible. She rushed to her son's house to bake the bread. Imām Aḥmad did not like it and from that day onwards asked that the door leading to his son's house be closed. He did so because his son was an employee of the Caliph.

Once Caliph Ma'mūnal-Rashīd distributed some gold as *Ṣadaqah* among the scholars of *Aḥādīth.* While all the traditionists accepted it, Imām Aḥmad refused to accept. When Imām Aḥmad was in Yemen, his financial condition was very weak. His teacher, Shaikh Abdur Razaq the famous *Muhaddith* and author of *Muṣannaf* came to know about it, and took a handful of *dīnār* and presented it to Imām Aḥmad. Imām Aḥmad replied, "I do not need them" His condition at that time was such that his clothes had almost worn out, and he had no other dress to put on. He tried to hide himself in his house and closed the doors. People came in search of him and came to know the reason for his hide out. They tried to offer a little money but Imam only accepted one *dīnār* out of it on a condition that he would repay by rendering some service by writing or copying a book.

The famous *Muḥaddith* Abū Dā'ūd says about Imām Aḥmad that to sit in his company was a matter of gaining great reward in the next world *(al-Ākhirah).* He never quarrelled with any one in all his life. The scholar Baihaqī has reported from Imām Aḥmad that when someone asked him a definition of a *Mutawakkil* (one who relies on Allah), Imām Aḥmad that one who does not pin any hope on any one but Allah.

His Inquisition

Imām Aḥmad bin Ḥanbal in the later years of his life challenged even the Caliph and his religious authority. As a result, he was imprisoned for a long time and was treated very harshly by the rulers. But as a man of conscience, he never surrendered to the wrong-headed views of the authorities. There exists a lot of material on his inquisition. The suffering of Imām Ahmad really started when he came into conflict with the mutazilites and their philosophical ideologies. The muʿtazilites were the free thinkers and were patronized unfortunately by Caliph Maʾmūn al-Rashīd, Mūtaṣim Billāh and Al-Wāthiq who had accepted the Mutazilite view-point and made it an official creed and had imposed it as a duty on all Muslims to follow it. Imam Ahmad and other traditionists flatly refused muʿtazilites doctrines and condemned the mischief of the creation of the Qur'ān which was supported by the ruling ʿAbbāsid Caliphs. It was for this reason that he was brought before the inquisition from Baghdad to Tarsus in very heavy chains. Particularly, it was during the reign of Caliph Muʿtaṣim Billāh, that he patiently suffered corporal punishment and secluded imprisonment.

The Caliph recognising the learning and piety of Imām Aḥmad went to him from time to time to request him to accept the creed of the Muʿtazilites in which case the Caliph himself would free him from all the chains and would become his follower and he would become the most favourite courtier. But Imām Aḥmad refused to surrender to the confused Muʿtazilite ideology. In anger, Caliph Muʿtaṣim ordered his servants to trample him under their feet and many of his joints were dislocated as a result of this cruelty.

The Imām was kept in heavy chains. He was thrown in a prison in Baghdad where he spent nearly thirty months. There was no light in the cell, and he was not given a lamp at night. When the Imām insisted on his traditional belief and did not agreed with the muʿtazilite doctrines put forward by ʿAbdal-Raḥmān al-Muʿtazilī and Isḥāq bin Ibrahim al Muʿtazilī, a large group of executioners were brought, his hands were tied and he was whipped until unconscious. But in spite of all the atrocities, and blood flowing due to flogging, Imām Aḥmad kept on saying that Qur'ān is uncreated, it is the knowledge of Allah *(ʿIlm Allāh)* and one who said that the knowledge of Allah is created has committed the sin of disbelief *(Kufr)*. Mutasim, the Caliph was scared of his future in this world and the next world, and ordered the punishment to be stopped and chains to be removed on 25th Ramaḍān in the year 221 A.H.[21] The wounds began to heal and Mutasim made sure that his deputies came and enquired of the health of the Imām. He repented for his actions. Imām Aḥmad forgave all except those who had committed a great sin against the Book of Allah. Imām Bukhārī says that when news of Imam's suffering reached Baṣrah, Abul Walīd Tiyalsī said: "If Imām Aḥmad had been born among the Israelites, perhaps he would have been a Prophet of Allah."

<u>*His Works*</u>

Imam Ahmad has written many books, but the most important of them are *Kitāb al-ʿAmal, Kitāb al Tafsīr, Kitāb al Nāsikh wal Mansūkh, Kitāb al-Zāhid, Kitāb al Masāʾil, Kitāb al-Faḍāʾil, Kitāb al-Mansik* and *Kitāb al-Iman* . The most well known work of Imām Aḥmad is his *Al-Musnad* in which the Imām has narrated more than fifty thousand and seven hundred thousand *aḥādīth* that he had collected. Imām Aḥmad died in 241 AH. The people of Baghdad turned for his funeral prayers.

By the end of the ninth century AD, the four major Sunnī schools had come to subscribe to a common theory, namely that the primary sources of Islamic law are:

1. The Qur'ān
2. The Sunnah
3. The *Ijmāʿ* (juristic consensus of opinion) and
4. Qiyās (reasoning by analogy).

Notes

1. **Iqbal, Muhammed (Dr.),** *The Reconstruction of Islamic thought* Lahore 1951.
2. See Ibn Khallikan on Ja'far al-Sadiq.
3. See *Taz'in al-Malik*, reported from Abu Nu'aim, pp. 13-16.
4. Ibn Hajar, *Tawali al-Ta'sis*, Cairo, p. 69.
5. Ibid.
6. *Fath al-Mughith.*
7. Al-Dhahabi, *Mizan al-I'tidal,* See Introduction.
8. Khatib, *Tarikh Baghdad.*
9. *Ibn Jazlah, Mukhtasar Ta'rikh Khatib Baghdadi,* see notes on Imam Abu Hanifah.
10. Abdul Qasim bin Kas, *Manaqib al-Nu'man,* quoted very often in al-Damishqi's Uqud al-Juman fil Manaqib al-Nu'man.
11. See Afandi, Muhammad Kamil (Qadi of Baghdad), *Manaqib al-Imam al-A'zam, 1136 A.H. (in Turkish).*
12. *Al-Damishqi, Muhammad bin Yusuf bin Ali, Uqud al-Juman fi Manaqib al-Numan*, op. cit., chapter 10.
13. Ibid.
14. Shi-bli Nu'mani, *Sirat al-Nu'man* (Urdu) translated into English by Hadi Husain, Lahore 1977 p. 25.

15. Ibid.
16. Ibid.
17. Cf. Ibn Jazalah, Mukhtasar Ta'rikh Khatib Baghdadi, op. cit.
18. Shibli Nu'mani, *Sirat al-Nu'man*, op. cit., pp. 25-6.
19. Al-Damishqi, *'Uqud al-Juman*, op. cit., see chapter 16.
20. Shibli Nu'man, *Sirat al-Numan*, op. cit., pp. 31-2.
21. Ibn al-Nadim, *Kitab al-Fihrist.*
22. Dhahabi, *Tadhkjrah al-Huffaz* vol. 1 p. 175-190 also cf. Samani, *Kitab al-Ansab.*
23. cf. Yafii, *Tabaqāt al-Fugaha*
24. Ibn Khallikan, Abul Abbas Shams al-Din, *Wafayat al-Ayan*, ed. Muhammad Muhyi al-Din, Cairo 1948. See notes of Imam Malik.
25. Fath al-Mugith, p. 238-239.
26. Al-Zawadi, *Manaqib Malik*, p. 131.
27. Fath al-Mugith.
28. Coulson, N.J. A History of Islamic Law. Edinburgh 1964, p. 43.
29. Cf. Abd al-Baqi, Muhammad Fuad, (edited by), *Al-Muwatta.* Kitab al-Sha'b, Cairo (undated), p. 1.
30. Ibid.
31. Coulson, N.J., A History of Islamic Law, op. cit., p. 46-47.
32. Al-Tabari, *Dhail al-Mudhail*, p. 107.
33. Al-Dibaj, p. 25.
34. Al-Dibaj, p. 43.
35. Al-Razi, Ibn Abi Hatim, *Kitab Adab al-Shafi'wa Manaqibuh*, ed. Muhammad Zahid al-Kathari, Cairo 1953.
36. Al-Baghdadi, Khatib, *Tarikh Baghdad*, Cairo 1931, vol. 2, p. 59.
37. Ibn 'Abdal-Barr, *Al-Intiqa*, Cairo 1932, p. 71.
38. Ibn Hajar, *Tawali al-Tasibi ma'ali Ibn Idris*, Cairo 1301 AH, pp. 79—82.
39. Abu Maimal-Isfahani, *Kitab Hilyat al-Auliya*, Cairo 1938, vol 9, p. 29.
40. Ibn Abdal-Barr, op. cit., pp. 94-98.
41. Al-Baghdadi, Khatib, op. cit., vol. 2, p. 68.
42. C.F. Abdul Baqi, Muhammad Fuad, (edited by) *Al-Muwatta*, Cairo (undated) p. 1.
43. Ibn Hajr, *Tawali al-Tasis*, op. cit., p. 84.
44. Abu Zahra, *Al-Shafi'i*, Cairo, 1948, p. 28.
45. Ibn Abī Ḥatim, op. cit., p. 71.
46. Ya'qūt, *Mujamal al Udabā*, ed. Margolioth, London, 1931, vol. 4 pp. 394-395.
47. Al-Dhahabī; *Tadkhirah-Ḥuffāẓ* See also Ibn Abī Yala; *Ṭabaqāt.*
48. Shāh Wali-Allāh Dihlawī, Ḥujjat-Allāh *al-Bāligah,* Vol. 12, p. 148.
29 *Subkī, Ṭabaqāt al-Shāfi'iyyah al-Kubrā,* p. 250.

PART II
Family Relations

Chapter 6

Al-Zawāj: Marriage

The Purpose of Marriage:

Allah created men and women so that they can provide company to one another, love one another, procreate children and live in peace and tranquility to the commandments of Allah and the directions of His Messenger. The Qur'ān says:

«وَمِنْ اياته انْ خَلَقَ لَكُمْ مِنْ انْفُسِكُمْ ازْوَاجاً لِتَسْكُنُوا الَيْهَا وَجَعَلَ بَيْنَكُمْ مَوَدَّةً ورَحْمَةً إِنَّ فِي ذَلِكَ لآياتٍ لِقَوْمٍ يَتَفَكَّرُون».

"And among His signs is this, that He created for you mates from among yourselves, that you may dwell (live) in tranquility with them, and He has put love and mercy between your hearts. Undoubtedly in there are signs for those who reflect."[1]

The Qur'ān further says:

«وَاللّهُ جَعَلَ لَكُمْ مِنْ أَنْفُسِكُمْ ازْواجاً وَجَعَلَ لَكُمْ مِنْ ازْواجِكُمْ بَنِينَ وَحَفَدَةً وَرَزَقَكُمْ مِنَ الطَّيِّبَاتِ..»

"And Allah has made for you your mates of your own nature and made for you, out of them sons and daughters, and grandchildren, and provide for you sustenance of the best."[2]

Apart from the Book of Allah, there are many traditions of the Holy Prophet Muhammad (S.A.W.) which further explain the Islamic institution of marriage. The Prophet (S.A.W.) has said:

"There is no mockery in Islam".

«لا رهبانية في الاسلام».

Celibacy is not considered a virtue in Islam or taken as a means of getting closer to Allah as is done by other religions like Christianity, Budhdhism and Jainism, etc. . . .

The Prophet (S.A.W.) has advised:

«يـامعشـر الشبـاب من استطـاع منكم البـاءة فليتـزوج فإنـه اغض للبصر واحصن للفرج».

"O you youngmen, whoever is able to marry, should marry, for that will help him to lower his gaze and guard his modesty."[3]

And the Prophet (Ṣ.A.W.) has referred to modesty as a "part of Īmān".

«الحياء من الايمان»

"Modesty is part of the faith."[4]

In order to achieve modesty and complete one's Iman, marriage is prescribed by the Prophet (Ṣ.A.W.):

«النكاح من سنتي فمن رغب عن سنتي فليس مني».

"The marriage is my tradition whosoever keeps away therefrom, is not from amongst me".

With these Qur'ānic injunctions and the guidance from the Prophet in mind, we shall examine the institution of marriage in Shari'ah.

The word *zawj* is used in the Qur'ān as a pair or a mate; in usage it connotes marriage. "Do they not look at the earth, how pairs of noble things we have produced therein."[5] Even in Paradise, the Qur'ān informs us that we shall have mates.[6] Allah created humans from one soul, from it He created the male and female. The story of creating Eve (the first female) from a rib of Ādam (the first male) is not mentioned in the Qur'ān.

"And among His signs is this, that He created for you mates from among yourselves that you may dwell in (peace) with them."[7]

"O mankind, heed (in reverence) your Lord who created you from single soul and from it created its mate and from them twain both spread multitude of men and women."[8]

The Prophet orders Muslims to get married as soon as they can. The family is the nucleus of the Islamic society, and marriage is the only way to bring about such an institution. Extra-marital relations are categorically condemned and prohibited.

"Do not come nearer to adultery (or fornication) for it is a shameful deed and an evil, opening the road to other evils."[9]

It is only logical that Islam sets up the rules to regulate the functioning of the family whereby both spouses can find peace, love, security, and relatedness. The elements are necessary for accomplishing the greatest purpose of marriage: the worship of Allah (al-ʿIbādah). By worship it is not only meant the performance of rituals merely having sex with your wife, but it essentially implies righteousness in all transactional behaviour. The concept of *ʿIbādah* is very wide. Every good deed, every service to humanity, every usual productive effort, and even every good word is a part of a true Muslim's worship of his creator. If both husband and wife observe this main purpose, this cardinal purpose of their union, they would easily learn how to help each other achieve this goal – a goal greater than themselves. They would learn how to tolerate each other, how to love Allah in themselves and in other beings, and how to overcome their difficulties and their shortcomings.

The second purpose of marriage is to respond to the basic biological instinct of procreation. Children are the realization of motherhood and fatherhood. Islam is particular in providing the most possible wholesome atmosphere for bringing up the offspring. To give birth to children and neglect them is a crime toward society, towards the children, and even towards the parents themselves. The child who is deprived of the ample love of his or her parents, and if such a child is not properly tutored in Islamic way of life at an early age, and who is left to babysitters and nurseries will develop many anti-social behavioural patterns and may end up with crime, perversion and corruption. Such a child may never find his or identity as he or she could have felt it in a systematic manner during his or her childhood. Without a family life, governed by Islamic order and discipline, how can we expect a child to have the Muslim conscience and the Islamic value of righteousness?

Islam prescribes clear rights and obligations on parents and their descendants: Parents are legally responsible for the education and maintenance of their children. These by turn, are legally responsible for accommodating and maintaining their parents, if they so require, in their old age. Both parents and children inherit from each other according to a prescribed and accurate law of *Mīrāth* (inheritance) specified in the Qur'ān. Neither of them can deprive the other of their respective shares in the legacy.

This is only one part of the long family code in Islam. What is of importance here is the husband-wife relationship – their sex roles with the context of Islamic comprehension:

> "and among His Signs is this, that He created for you mates from among yourselves, that you may dwell in peace with them. And He has put love and mercy between your hearts; Undoubtedly, in this are signs for those who reflect."[10]

Despite the importance of these moral values: rest, peace, love, and mercy, Islam did not stop there. It bolstered its original concept of the family by defining the roles of man and woman in such a manner that each should act in accordance with his or her biological merits. The man, with his aggression, is charged with what is called the "instrumental" functions: maintenance, protection, dealings with the outworldly matters and leadership within the family. The woman is entrusted with caring for and rearing the children, organising the home, and creating the loving atmosphere inside her matrimonial home. In an Islamic society the wife is not expected to be pushed to work to gain money. Even the unmarried woman, the divorced woman and the widow are guaranteed, by law, an income that helps them lead a reasonably comfortable life. Work or trade are not prohibited to woman in Sharī'ah provided they do it within the framework of modesty and with the permission of the husband, they are not recommended to undertake such activities unless there is a justification for them to go to work and should be without prejudice to their husband's rights. Once the woman gets married, she accepts the Islamic ruling on the functioning of the family. Her role becomes mainly to achieve the welfare of her household and to look after the internal family affairs. If she has her own property or fortune, and if she opts to run or invest such wealth she is entitled to do so without her husband's permission, provided this does not infringe upon her marital obligations, and responsibilities to her children.

Therefore, marriage in Islam, broadly speaking, is:

- a means of emotional and sexual gratification,
- a mechanism of tension reduction,
- a means of legitimate procreation,
- Social placement,
- an approach to inter-family alliance and group solidarity,
- an act of piety *(Taqwah)*[11]
- It is a form of *Ibadah*, i.e. worship of Allah and obedience of His Messenger.

Both above definitions and purposes are quite elaborate and comprise many views about functions of the family. Nevertheless, there is an intricate cause and effect relationship between the family and society.

Islam is integral, and Muslims are supposed to adopt it in its entirety.

> "Believe ye in part of the Scripture and disbelieve ye in part thereof? And what is the reward of those who do so save ignominy in the life of this world, and the Day of Resurrection they will be consigned to the most grevious doom . . ."[12]

From the foregoing discussion it becomes clear that Islam does not approve of celibacy and enjoins upon Muslims to get married. The purpose of marriage in Islam, as we have seen, is not mere carnal pleasure but the establishment of an institution whereby men and women may guard against lewdness and indecency, procreate children for preserving the human race and satisfying normal sexual urge for securing comfort and happiness.

Is Marriage Obligatory?

According to Imāms Abū Ḥanīfah, Aḥmad bin Ḥanbal and Mālik bin Anas, although marriage in its origin may be deemed to be recommendatory, in cases of certain individuals, it becomes obligatory *(Wājib)*[13]

However, Imām Shāfi'ī[14] considers marriage to be superogetory *(Mubāḥ).*

What emerges from a careful consideration of the Qur'ānic injunctions and the traditions of the Prophet (S.A.W.) is that marriage is compulsory *(Wājib)* for a man who has the means to easily pay *(Mahr*, (Dower), and maintain a wife and children and who is healthy and fears that if he does not marry he may commit fornication *(zinā)*. It is also compulsory for a woman who has no other means of maintaining herself and fears that her sexual urge may push her into fornication. But it is recommendatory *(Mandūb)* for a person who has a strong will to control his sexual urge and not to fall prey to the evil temptations of shaitan but whose only aim is to have children. However, marriage is superogatory *(Mubāḥ* or *Nafl)* for a person who can control his sexual desire; who has no wish to have children and who feels that marriage will not keep him away from his devotion to Allah.[15]

However, according to the Mālikī school, it is obligatory *(Farḍ)* for a Muslim to marry even though he may not be in a position to earn his living on the following three conditions:[16]

1. If he fears that by not marrying he will commit fornication *(al-Zinā)*
2. If he is unable to fast to control his passion or that he can fast but his fasting does not help him to refrain from adultery.
3. He cannot even find a slave girl or an utterly poor girl to marry.

Some Jurists disagree on this point, and suggest that if he cannot procure lawful livelihood, he must not marry. If at all he married without any hope of getting lawful bread, he will commit theft. Thus, in order to avoid one evil, he will be a victim of another evil.[17]

The Ḥanafī school considers marriage obligatory on the following four conditions:

1. If a man is sure that he will commit *Zinā* if he did not marry.
2. If he cannot fast, or even if he can fast, it does not help him to control his passion. If fasts help him, he must fast rather than marry.
3. If he cannot get a slave-girl to marry.
4. If he is able to pay dower *(Mahr)* and is capable to earn lawful livelihood. If he is not capable to earn his livelihood lawfully, it is not obligatory for him to marry.[18]

Marriage if forbidden *(ḥarām)* to a man if he does not possess the means to maintain his wife and children or if he suffers from an illness serious enough to affect his wife and his progeny.

It is not desirable *(Makrūh)* for a man who possesses no sexual desire at all or who has no love for children, or who is sure to be slackened in his religious obligations as a result of marriage.[19]

The Prophet (Ṣ.A.W.) enjoined upon his followers to contract marriage because he had a definite object in view for them. There is a Ḥadīth which says:

عن أنس: قال رسـول الله صلى الله عليـه وسلم: «إذا تزوج العبـد فقـد استكمل نصف الدين فليتق الله في النصف الباقي».

"It is narrated by Anas (may Allah be pleased with him) that the Messenger of Allah (Ṣ.A.W.) said: "When a man marries, he has fulfilled half of his religion, so let him fear Allah regarding the remaining half".

The Prophet (Ṣ.A.W.) considered marriage for a Muslim as "Half of his Religion" because it may shield him from promiscuity, adultery, fornication, homosexuality, and the life which ultimately lead to many other crimes including slander, quarrel, homicide, loss of property and finally the disintegration of the ideal family system on which so much stress has been placed by the Holy Prophet (Ṣ.A.W.).

According to the Prophet (Ṣ.A.W.) the remaining half of the faith which is complimentary to the first half, can be saved by *Taqwah* (i.e. fear of Allah and righteousness).

In yet another Ḥadīth, the Holy Prophet (Ṣ.A.W.) has mentioned the best thing that a Muslim can aspire to have after *Taqwah*, is a good pious and obedient wife.

عن أبي أمـامة عن النبي صلى الله عليـه وسلم أنه قال: «ما استفاد المؤمن بعـد تقـوى الله خيراً له من زوجـة صالحة، إن أمرها أطاعته، وإن نظر اليها سرته، وإن أقسم عليها أبرته، وإن غاب عنها حفظته في نفسها وماله».

Abu Imanah said, the Prophet (S.A.W.) used to say:

> "After fear of Allah and righteousness, a believer gets nothing for himself than a pious wife who obeys him if he gives her a command, pleases him if he looks at her, she is true to him if he commands her to do something (of course not *Haram*), and is sincere to him regarding her person and his property whenever he is absent from her".

The Holy Prophet (S.A.W.) laid great stress on righteousness, piety and faithfulness as the main criteria in the choice of life partners. "Whoever marries a woman", said the Prophet (S.A.W.) "solely for her power and position, Allah but increases his humiliation, whoever marries a woman solely for her wealth, Allah but increases his poverty.

But whoever marries a woman in order that he may restrain his eyes, observe cautiousness and treats his relations kindly, Allah puts a blessed ness in her for him and in him for her". Thus, piety and righteousness shall be uppermost in the motives of marriage. The Prophet (S.A.W.) has also said: "There are three persons whom the Almighty Himself has undertaken to help: first, he who seeks to buy his freedom (i.e. discards the concept of slavery); second, he who marries with a view to secure his chastity; and the third, he who fights in the cause of Allah' *(Jihād)*"

Celibacy: An Un-Islamic Practice

Islam is the only religion that does not subscribe to the view that the exercise of the natural instinct of sex is not compatible with the highest degree of dignity or with the cultivation of the highest values. Such a view is contrary to the whole concept of moral and spiritual values inculcated by Islam. Natural instincts, even as mental faculties and physical prowess, are a gift of Allah. Their nature is not evil: If they are properly used, they become good; if improperly used, they become evil. Sexual excesses impede intellectual activity. In order to reach full intellectual power, the presence of well-developed sexual glands and effective control of the sexual appetite are both necessary. If this capacity is neglected it becomes an evil.

Therefore celibacy in reality is a violition of human nature. This is the reason why Islam does not permit celibacy or monasticism as a way of life. The Holy Qur'ān says: "And, (as for) monkery, they innovated it – We did not prescribe it to them – only to seek Allah's pleasure, but they did not observe it with its due observance."[20] In the Qur'ānic verse 37:20, we are first told that we should not run after the gaieties of the world and make the amassing of wealth the pursuit of our life; but in this verse we are reminded that we should not go to the other extreme and give up worldly pursuits and adopt such practices as monkery. Celibacy is expressly forbidden in Islam.[21] We are thus required to keep the balance between the material and moral sides of life. It was carnal-minded men who invented the doctrine of original sin. "Behold", says the Psalmist, "I was shapened in iniquity, and in sin did my mother conceive me."[22] This is entirely against Islam in which the office of father and mother is held in the highest veneration. Every child of pure love is born pure. Celibacy is not necessary a virtue, and may be a vice.[23]

This attitude of Islam towards marriage contrasts with the teaching of Christianity which is, that virginity is best but that for those who find this impossible, marriage is permissible. "It is better to marry than to burn," St. Paul brutally puts it.[24] "To the unmarried and the widows I say it is well for them to remain single as I do". St. Paul further explains: "I want you to be free from anxieties. The unmarried man is anxious about the affairs of the Lord, how to please the Lord; but the married man is anxious about worldly affairs, how to please his wife; and his interests are divided. And the unmarried woman or girl is anxious about the affairs of the Lord, how to be holy in body and spirit; but the married woman is anxious about worldly affairs, how to please her husband. I say this for your own good, not to lay any restraint upon you, but to promote good order and to secure your undivided devotion to the Lord."[25]

The Holy Prophet said, "The marriage is our Sunnah. He who deliberately turns against our way is not of us." Islam considers parenthood to be the duty of every human being. In the civilised world of today most persons refuse to take over the responsibility of parenthood, offering as an excuse the insufficiency of their means to support a family. The Holy Qur'ān disposes of this flimsy excuse in these simple words, "If they are needy, Allah will make them free from want out of His Grace."[26] Celibacy is thus unnatural and un-Islamic.

Selection of a Bride

The Prophet (S.A.W.) recommended that in the selection of a bride, a man shall see before betrothal the intended bride lest a blunder in choice or an error in judgement should defect the very purpose of marriage. However, a man should not throw a passionate gaze at the would be bride but only have a critical look at her face and hands to gain sufficient idea about her personality and beauty.[27]

If a man so desires he may appoint a woman to go, see, and interview the would-be bride, so that she could fully describe the type of woman she is.[28]

Since believing men and women are referred in the Holy Qur'ān a woman also has the right to look at her would-be husband.[29]

The special permission to have a glance at the would-be wife does not contravene the following code of conduct for believing men and women: given in the Holy Qur'ān:

«قُلْ لِلْمؤمِنِينَ يَغُضّوا مِنْ أبْصَارِهِمْ وَيَحْفَظُوا فُرُوجَهُمْ ذلِكَ ازْكى لَهُمْ إنَّ اللّهَ خَبيرٌ بِمَا يَصْنَعُون».

"tell the believing men to, lower their gaze and be modest. That is proper for them. Lo! Allah is aware of what they do."[30]

«وَقُلْ لِلْمُؤ مِنَاتِ يَغْضُضْنَ مِنْ أَبْصَارِهِنَّ وَيَحْفَظْنَ فُرُوجَهُنَّ وَلَا يبْدِينَ زِينَتَهُنَّ إلّا مَا ظَهَرَ مِنْهَا وَلْيَضْرِبْنَ بِخُمُرِهِنَّ عَلىٰ جُيُوبِهِنَّ وَلَا يُبْدِينَ زِينَتَهُنَّ إلَّا لِبُعُولَتِهِنَّ أوْءابَآئِهِنَّ أوْ آبَآءِ بُعُولَتِهِنَّ أوْ أبْنَآئِهِنَّ أوْ أَبْنَآءِ بُعُولَتِهِنَّ أوْ إِخْوَانِهِنَّ أوْ بَنِي إِخْوَانِهِنَّ أوْ بَنِي اخَوَاتِهِنَّ أوْ نِسَآئِهِنَّ أوْ مَا مَلَكَتْ ايْمَانُهُنَّ أوِ التَّابِعِينَ غَيْرِ أُولِي الأَرْبَةِ مِنَ الرِجَالِ أوِ الطِفْلِ الَّذِينَ لَمْ يَظْهَرُوا عَلىٰ عَوْرَاتِ النِّسَآءِ وَلَا يَضْرِبْنَ بِأرْجُلِهِنَّ لِيُعْلَمَ مَا يُخْفِينَ مِنْ زِينَتِهِنَّ وَتُوبُوآ إلَى اللّهِ جَمِيعاً أيُّهَ المُؤ مِنُونَ لَعَلَّكُمْ تُفْلِحُون».

"And tell the believing women to lower their gaze and be modest, and to display of their adornment only that which is apparent, and to draw their veils over their bosom, and not to reveal their adornment save to their own husbands or fathers or husband's father, or their sons or sister's sons or their women or their slaves or male attendants who lack vigour or children who know naught of woman's nakedness. And let them not stamp their feet so as to reveal what they hide of adornment. And turn unto Allah together O believers, in order that ye may succeed."[31]

The Choice of Partner and the Power of Ijbār

A. In no circumstances would the suitor and the would-be bride be allowed to remain alone in a room, because the Holy Prophet (S.A.W.) says that whenever you leave a man and a woman alone there is always a third person present and that is the shaitan. There is no notion of *courtship* in Islam as it is the practice in the West where a man willing to marry a girl dates with her for six months and sometimes a year or two on the pretext that they would known their common interests better. But is is a sad commentary on the Western world that in spite of all this intimacy, courting couples grossly fail to understand each other and end into a broken romance; if by any chance they get into marriage they usually find that the elongated period of courtship has not helped to yield any better understanding between them. The present alarming rate of divorce in the West proves this point.

It is reported that when Mughīra ibn Shu'bah made a proposal of marriage to a woman the Holy Prophet asked him if he had seen her and on his replying in the negative, he enjoined him to see her, because "it was likely to bring about greater love and concord between them" The jurists are almost all agreed upon the *istiḥbāb* (approval) of looking at the woman whom one intends to marry. And since the contract is effected by the consent of two parties, the man and the woman, and one of them is expressly told to satisfy himself about the other by looking at her, it would seem that the woman has the same right to satisfy herself before giving her assent. The consent of both the man and the woman is an essential of marriage, and the Holy Qur'ān lays down expressly that the two must agree:

> "Do not prevent them from marrying their husbands when they agree among themselves in a lawful manner."[32]

B. The choice of partner by a Muslim girl is subject to the overriding power of *Ijbār* granted to her father or guardian under Mālikī School. This is a safety measure in the interest of the girl herself. If the father or the guardian of the girl finds that in her immaturity or overzealousness the girl is going to marry a man possessing a bad character or lacking proper means of livelihood, he may restrain her from marrying that man and can find a suitable person to be her husband and may give her marriage to him. Generally speaking, such marriages arranged by fathers and guardians work better than the marriage brought about through courtship.

Free Consent of the Parties

Marriage in reality is a *Mīthāq*[33] meaning a solemn covenant or agreement between the husband and wife – which must be reduced to writing.[34] They should agree in a lawful manner.[35] As there can be no agreement, unless both parties give their consent to it, marriage in Islam can only be contracted with the free consent of the two parties. The Holy Prophet said: "The widow and the divorced woman shall not be married until her order or ordained, and the virgin shall not be married until her consent is obtained.[36] And Bukhārī's next chapter is entitled thus: "When a man gives his daughter in marriage and she dislikes it, the marriage shall be repudiated";[37] and a hadith is quoted showing that the Holy Prophet repudiated such a marriage. A virgin girl came to the Holy Prophet and said that her father had her married against her wishes, and the Holy Prophet gave her the right to repudiate the marriage.[38] With regard to divorced women, the Holy Qur'ān says, "And when you divorce women, and they have come to the end of their waiting period, hinder them not from marrying other men if they have agreed with each other in a fair manner."[39] With regard to widows the Holy Qur'ān says: "And if any of you die and leave wives behind they bequeath thereby to their widows (the right to) one year's maintenance without their being obliged to leave (the dead husband's home), but if they leave (the resident) of their own accord there is no blame on you for whatever they do with themselves in a lawful manner";[40] for instance, by remarrying, in which case they forego their claim to additional maintenance during the remainder of the year. The Maliki School, however, gives power of Ijbar to the guardian.

Prohibited Degrees of Marriage

The laws of marriage have been so framed by the Sharī'ah that they may help to establish an ideal *Ummah*. To this end the Qur'ān and the Sunnah, have prescribed the prohibited degrees in marriage which can be divided into two categories:

1. The permanently prohibited degrees and
2. The temporarily prohibited degrees.

The Permanent Prohibitions

The permanently prohibited degrees are contained in Sūrah al-Nisā':

«وَلَا تَنْكِحُوا مَا نَكَحَ ابَآؤكُم مِنَ النسَآءِ إلّا مَا قَدْ سَلَفَ انّهُ كَانَ فَاحِشَةً وَمَقْتاً
وَسَآءِ سَبِيلا . حُرِّمَتْ عَلَيْكُمْ أُمهّاتُكُمْ وَبَنَاتُكُمْ وَاخَوَاتُكُمْ وَعَمَّاتُكُمْ وَخَالَاتُكُمْ
وَبَنَاتُ الْاخِ وَبنَاتُ الاُخْتِ وَأُمَّهَاتُكُمُ الّتي ارْضَعْنَكُمْ وَاخَوَاتُكُمْ مِنَ الرَّضَاعَةِ
وَامَّهَاتُ نِسَآئِكُمْ وَرَبَائِبُكُمُ الَّتي فى حُجُورِكُمْ مّنْ نِّسَائِكُمُ التي دَخَلْتُمْ بِهنَّ فَإنْ لَمْ
تَكُونُوا دَخَلْتُمْ بِهنَّ فَلا جُنَاحَ عَلَيْكُمْ وَحَلَآئِلُ ابْنَائِكُمُ الّذينَ مِنْ اصْلَابِكُمْ وَانْ
تَجْمَعُواْ بَيْنَ الأُخْتَيْنِ إلّا مَا قَدْ سَلَفَ إِنَّ اللّهَ كَانَ غَفُوراً رّحيماً».

"And marry not those women whom your fathers married, except what hath already happened (of that nature) in the past. Lo! it was even lewdness and abomination; and an evil way. Forbidden unto you are your mothers, and your daughters, and your sisters and your father's sisters, and your mother's sisters and your brother's daughters and sister's daughters, and your foster-mothers, and your foster-sisters, and your mothers-in-law and your step-daughters who are under your protection (born) of your women unto whom you have gone in – but if ye have not gone into them, then it is no sin for you (to marry their daughters).

And the wives of your sons who (spring) from your own loins. And (it is forbidden unto you) that ye should have two sisters together, except what hath already happened (of that nature) in the past. Lo! Allah is ever Forgiving, Merciful."[41]

From the above verses, it is clear that a Muslim must not marry the following:

1. His mother
2. His step mother(s): In the Jahiliyyah period a step son or brother inherited his father's widow(s). Similar practice continued in Yorubaland of Nigeria, where, in some cases, the oldest son inherits the youngest wife of his father;
3. His grand mother(s) (Grand mothers include father's and mother's mothers howsoever high);
4. His daughter(s): (Daughters include the grand daughters i.e. sons or daughters howsoever low);
5. His sister(s); (including Full, or consaguine and uterine, sisters);
6. His father's sister(s): (including the grand father's sister(s));
7. His mother's sister(s): (including the grand mother's sister(s));
8. His brother's daughters;
9. His foster mother;
10. His foster mother's sister(s);
11. His sister's daughter(s);
12. His foster sister;
13. His wife's mother;
14. His step daughter: (such a daughter should have been born to his wife with whom he has consumated his relationship. If the marriage was not consumated there is no prohibition);
15. His son's wife: (this will not include wives of persons whom one treats as one's adopted.

Temporary Prohibitions

Temporary prohibitions are those which can be removed by a change of circumstances. They are as follows:

1. A man must not marry two sisters in marriage at one and the same time. The temporary prohibition here gets removed as soon as, his wife dies and he takes her sister in marriage. This provision also applies to a man's aunt as well as niece;
2. A man must not marry a married woman. But the impediment is removed immediately on the dissolution of her marriage either by death of her husband or divorce followed by completion of the period of *ʿiddah* (retreat);
3. A man must not have more than four wives at a time. But the impediment is removed as soon as one of the wives dies or is divorced;
4. A man must not marry a woman during her *ʿiddah*. But the impediment is removed as soon as the period of *ʿiddah* expires.

The Qur'ān says:

«... ولا تُواعِـدُوهُنَّ سِراً الّا انْ تَقُـولُـوا قَوْلاً مَعْـرُوفا وَلا تَـعْزِمُوا عُقْدَةَ النِّكَاحِ حَتى يَبْلُغَ الكِتَابُ اَجَلَهُ....»

". . . But do not make a secret contract with them except in terms honourable, nor rescue on the tie of marriage till the term prescribed is fulfilled."[42]

This means that a man shall not make a specific proposal to a woman in *'Iddah*. However, one can send implied words like the following to a woman whose husband dies or who has been irrevocably divorced:

"I wish to find a woman of good character."

But even here if a woman is having the *iddah* of *ṭalāq* where *raj'ah* is still possible, a man should not send her even implied words for she is still considered as a legal wife of the ex-husband. By doing so, one is becoming instrumental in breaking up a family where there are still chances of reconciliation.

The Case of Two Suiters after a Girl:

The Prophet (S.A.W.) disapproved two suitors vying with one another for marriage with one girl. This is so because such a situation is likely to create enmity between two Muslim brothers. The Prophet (Ṣ.A.W.) said:

«المؤمن أخ المؤمن فلا يحل له أن يبيع على بيع أخيه أو يخطب على خطبة أخيه حتى يترك».

"A believer is a brother of a believer, hence it is not lawful for him to bargain upon the bargain of a brother; nor propose (the hand of a girl) on the marriage proposal of his brother, until the latter (voluntarily) withdraws the proposal"!

But the guardians' right of *Ijbār* stands at a different level. If he finds that the girl under his guardianship is going to marry a man who is of bad character or a man who is not in a position to take a family he may restrain the girl from going ahead with the proposal.[43]

Some people regard this as only a moral obligation where as others view it as a moral as well as legal obligation. But to reduce the efficacy of the above tradition to the level where the proposer second in time would not be compelled to opt out of his proposal will be tantamount to paying less attention to the Qur'ānic injunctions;

"Whatever the Prophet has brought to you, accept it, and deny yourselves that which he withholds from you."[44]

The only person given the power to make proposals upon the proposal of a suitor is the guardian; who has been vested with the power of *Ijbār* where he forsees some detrimental effects resulting from the marriage.

Imam Abu Hanifah, Imam Shafi'i and Imam Malik hold the view that it is a sin to put a proposal on the proposal of a brother, and if marriage is contracted it will suffice if the second suitor who was successful seeks the forgiveness of the first suitor and of Allah.[45] But the Ẓāhirīs consider such a marriage as void. It is submitted that the former view appears more rational and sound in comparison to the latter view for it may create more problems than it seeks to solve.

1. Qur'ān, 30:21.
2. Qur'ān, 16:72.
3. Saḥīḥ al-Bukhārī.
4. Ibid.
5. Qur'ān, ch. 31:10; Sūrah 50:7; Sūrah 26:7.
6. Qur'ān, ch. 2:25; Sūrah 4:57.
7. Qur'ān, ch. 4:1.
8. Qur'ān, ch. 4:1.
9. Qur'ān, ch. 17:22.
10. Qur'ān, ch. 30:21.
11. cf. ʿAbd al-ʿAṭī, Ḥammudah, *The Family Structure in Islam*, Indianapolis 1957, p. 54-55
12. Qur'ān, ch. 2:85.
13. *Ḥāshiyah al-Dasūqī* on the *Sharḥ al-kabīr*, vol. II, p. 9:215, *Qawwānīn al-Aḥkām al-Sharī'ah* by ibn-Juzay p. 9:217.
14. See Abū Zahra, *Aḥwāl Shaksiyyah* p. 9. 24.
15. *Mawāhib al-Jalīl*, vol. II, p. 403-404.
16. Al-Jazīrī, ʿAbdur Rahamān, *Kitāb al-Fiqh alal Madhāhib al-Arabʿah,* vol. IV, pp. 4, Cairo 1970.
17. Ibid, p. 5.
18. Ibid, p. 6.
19. Ibid.
20. Qur'ān, ch. 57:27.
21. Bukhārī, 67:8.
22. Psalmist 51:5.
23. Yusuf Ali, *The Holy Qur'ān*, Note No. 249.
24. Corinthians 7:9.
25. Ibid 7:8.
26. Qur'ān, ch. 24:32.
27. cf, *Ḥāshiyah al-Dasūqī*, vol. 2, p. 215.
28. *Muwāhib al-Jalīl* vol. III, p. 405.
29. *Ḥāshiyah al-Dasūqī*, vol. II, p. 215.
30. Qur'ān, 24:30.
31. Qur'ān, 24:31.
32. Qur'ān, ch. 2:232.
33. Qur'ān, ch. 4:21.
34. Qur'ān, ch. 2:282.
35. Qur'ān, ch. 2:232.
36. Bukhārī, 67:42.
37. Bukhārī, 67:43.
38. Abū Dāʾūd, 12:25.
39. Qur'ān ch. 2:232.
40. Qur'ān, ch. 2:240.
41. Qur'ān, 4:22-24.
42. Qur'ān, 2:235.
43. *Muwāhib al-Jalīl* vol. III. The case of Abū Juham bin Ḥuzaifah and Muʿāwiyyah ibn abu Sufyān is relevant here. They proposed marriage to, Fāṭimah bint Ghaith. The Prophet (Ṣ.A.W.) advised Fāṭimah not to marry any of them on the ground that Muʿāyyiah was then a pauper and Abū Juham was cruel and harsh so she married Usāmah.
44. Qur'ān, ch. 59:7.
45. cf. Ibn ʿAsākir in his book *Kitāb Ashal-al-Madazik* vol, II, p. 68.

Chapter 7

Marriage Relationship in Islam

Islam wants to build a model society. This is why it gives maximum attention to the family affairs of the believers. If the foundation of the family is strong, the foundation of the nation will be strong. Therefore, Islam does not leave the roles of individual members of the family to mere human speculation. Islam has put every member in his rightful place and charged him to carry out his responsibilities with *Taqwah* (fear of Allah). The Holy Qur'ān says:

«الرِّجَالُ قَوَّامُونَ عَلَى النِّسَاءِ بِمَا فَضَّلَ اللّهُ بَعْضَهُمْ عَلَى بَعْضٍ وَبِمَآ انْفَقُوا مِنْ
اَمْوَالِهِمْ فَالصَّالِحَاتُ قَانِتَاتٌ حَافِظَاتٌ لِلْغَيْبِ بِمَا حَفِظَ اللّهُ وَالَّتِي تَخَافُونَ
نُشُوزَهُنَّ فَعِظُوهُنَّ وَاهْجُرُوهُنَّ فِي الْمَضَاجِعِ وَاضْرِبُوهُنَّ فَاِنْ اَطَعْنَكُمْ فَلَا تَبْغُوا
عَلَيْهِنَّ سَبِيلًا....»

> "Men are the protectors and maintainers of women, because Allah has given the one more (strength) than the other, and because they support them from their means. Therefore the righteous women are devoutly obedient, and guard in (the husband's) absence what Allah would have them guard. As to those women on whose part fear disloyalty and ill conduct, admonish them (first), (next) refuse to share their beds, and (last) beat them (lightly); but if they return to obedience, seek not against them means of annoyance."[1]

In order to keep peace and order in the family life of Muslims, Allah has declared in this verse that men are *Qawwāmūn* i.e., protectors and maintainers of women. The word *Qawwāmūn* signifies a person who takes the responsibility of safe-guarding the interest of another person.

This position comes to men as opposed to women not only because, generally speaking, they have more physical strength and greater capacity for hard work, but also because it is extremely important that in every family, there should be a head who may give orders to and settle things among the members of the family. It is for this reason that the rest of the family – especially the wife – is asked to obey the husband. This is why Allah has described the obedient wife, as the most righteous.

However, it should be born in mind that the wife should not obey the husband if what he asks her to do is against Allah's injunctions, because obedience is first to Allah. The woman should observe chastity and guard her and her husband's honour, whenever the husband is away from home.

It is human nature that some squabbles and misunderstanding may arise in the family. Therefore, each member of the family has been asked to have fear of Allah, to be patient and to exercise self-restraint. The foregoing verse prescribes certain measures which should be taken in settling disputes among the couples. They are as follows:

1. *Admonition*

   Before taking any other measure which may be to the detriment of the couple, the wife should be admonished in a polite manner. And if this proves effective, there is no need to resort to a harsher measure.
2. *Severing of conjugal relations*

   If admonition by the husband fails to correct the wife, the husband may refuse to share his bed with his wife. But this must be confined to a reasonable period of time and should not be continued indefinitely.
3. *Light Beating*

   Wife-beating is generally discouraged by Muslim Jurists. However, if the wife's behaviour is against the injunction of Allah and the Sunnah of the Prophet, beating her in a light manner may become necessary. But the Prophet (S.A.W.) has enjoined that she must not be beaten on the face or in such a way as may leave some mark on her body.

Arbitration

Islam discourages, as much as possible, taking of family disputes to the courts of Law. This is why the preceding verse says that if there is a dispute between the wife and the husband arbiters, one from each side, should be appointed to resolve it.

Finally, the Qur'ān gives warning to the men that if the women obey and correct their ways, they should not be nagged or and the men should not find faults in them in order to annoy them.

The relationship between husband and wife in the Qur'ān is described thus: "They are as a garment to you, and you are as a garment to them."[2] Husband and wife are for mutual support, mutual comfort, and mutual protection, fitting into each as a garment fits the body. A garment also is both for show and concealment. The question of sex is always delicate to handle. Here we are told that, even in such matters, a clear, open and honest course is better than fraud or self-deception. A husband and wife who are bound together by love and tenderness "that God has put between them are indeed garments for each other." The Holy Qur'ān says, "the best garment is the garment of God-consciousness"[3] so that a husband and wife should be such a garment for each other.

"But in accordance with justice, the wives' rights (with regard to their husband) are equal to the (husband) rights with regard to them, although men are a degree above them. And Allah is Almighty Wise".[4] The statement that men are a degree above them simply shows that superior authority to run the house must be given to either the husband or the wife, and it is here given to the husband, as it is the duty of the man to maintain the woman. "Men shall take full care of women, because God has given the one more strength than the other, and because they support them from their means".[5]

Subject to this, the sexes are on terms of equality in law and, in certain matters, the weaker sex is entitled to special protection. Men are exhorted to consort with their wives in kindness and are told, "If you dislike them it may will be that you dislike something which God might yet make a source of abundant good".[6]

The last sermon of the Holy Prophet at Arafat has put this relationship in memorable words: "O ye people! You have some rights over your wives as they have over you. Your rights in them are that they have chaste life, and do not admit into their homes anybody whom you dislike, and they do not fall into manifest evil. If they do, Allah permits you to keep them away from your beds in order that they may improve and mend their ways. You may even resort to such light chastisement as may not produce any harmful effect on their body. But, in case they do no such thing you are duty-bound to arrange suitably for their food and clothing according to your means. Well, remember! your treatment of your wives should be righteous and kind, for they are in your custody and cannot safeguard their rights. The day you married them you considered them as a trust of Allah, and you brought them home according to His injunctions".

The Holy Prophet said, "The best among you is he who treats the members of his family best." He was himself always most careful and considerate in respect of all that concerned women. On one occasion he was on a journey when women were also in the party. At a certain stage in the journey, the camel drivers fearing that they were late began to drive the camel fast. The Holy Prophet told them, "mind the crystal", meaning that they should pay due regard to the comfort of the women.

The use of the term 'crystal' with respect to women implies that they are delicate and sensitive and are easily hurt. On another occasion he explained that a woman by her nature is like a rib, "You can straighten it out with persistent gentleness, but if you try to straighten it suddenly you are likely to break it".

In short, it is the right of the husband over his wife to obey him willingly in everything which is not forbidden, she does not have to obey if the husband asks her to do which is against the command of Allah and guidance given by His Messenger. She must try to keep herself as pleasant as possible to her husband and must not show her anger to him. It is reported by Ḥākim from 'Āishah:

سألت رسـول الله صلى الله عليـه وسلم: أي النـاس أعظم حقاً على المرأة؟ قال: «زوجها». قالت: فأي الناس أعظم حقاً على الرجل؟ قال: «أمه».

> She asked the Messenger of Allah: "Who has greater right over a woman?" He (the Prophet) replied: "Her husband". She asked: "Then who has a greater right over a man?" He replied: "His mother".

The Prophet has further said:

«لو أمرت أحد أن يسجد لأحد، لأمرت المرأة أن تسجد لزوجها من عظم حقه عليها».

> "If I had ordered anyone to prosterate before someone, I would have ordered a woman to prosterate before her husband, taking into consideration the great right he has over her."[7]

But religion of Islam teaches uncompromising montheism, and no one must prosterate before anyone except one's Creator, Allah. The above Hadith of the Prophet shows the right of a husband over his wife. If one compares the chaos in the modern world, one realises that women have been given so called 'freedom', 'liberty' or 'independence', but in reality she suffers a lot as she has lost her proper place and function in the society..

The Holy Qur'ān lays the greatest possible stress on kindly and good treatment towards the wife. The Holy Qur'ān asks men to "treat them kindly".[8] Kindness is even recommended in the case when a man dislikes his wife, for "it may be that you dislike a thing while Allah has placed abundant good in it".[9] The Holy Prophet laid great stress upon good treatment of a wife. He said: "The most excellent of you is he who is best in his treatment of his wife".[10] He also said: "Accept my advice in the matter of doing good to women".[11] In his famous address at the Farewell pilgrimage, he again laid particular stress on the good treatment of women: "O my people! You have certain rights over your wives and so have your wives over you . . . They are the trust of Allah in your hands. So, you must treat them with kindness".[12]

The woman's special function is to bring up the children. She has been created in such a way that the quality of love preponderates in her, and she is devoid of the sternness of man; she is therefore, inclined to one side sooner than the man, and on account of this quality, she is compared to the rib, in a Hadith of the Prophet.[13]

Her being bent like the rib is adduced as an argument for being kind to her and for leaving her in that state.

Marriage with Polytheists (al-Mushrikah)

While the marriage with the 'people of the Book' is permitted in Islam, it is completely forbidden to marry a polytheist in any form, whether she happens to be an idol-worshipper or one who has given up Islam *(al-Murtaḏah)* or a worshipper of a cow, or other animals, trees, or stones. The Holy Qur'ān commands in the following words:

«وَلاَ تَنْكِحُوا الْمُشْرِكَاتِ حَتّىٰ يُؤْمِنَّ وَلَأَمَةٌ مُؤْمِنَةٌ خَيْرٌ مِنْ مُشْرِكَةٍ وَلَوْ اعْجَبَتْكُمْ وَلاَ تُنْكِحُوا الْمُشْرِكِينَ حَتّىٰ يُؤْمِنُوا وَلَعَبْدٌ مُؤْمِنٌ خَيْرٌ مِنْ مُشْرِكٍ وَلَوْ اعْجَبَكُمْ أُولَئِكَ يَدْعُونَ الَى النَّارِ وَاللّٰهُ يَدْعُوآ الَى الْجَنَّةِ وَالْمَغْفِرَةِ بِإِذْنِهِ وَيُبَيِّنُ آيَاتِهِ لِلنَّاسِ لَعَلَّهُمْ يَتَذَكَّرُونَ».

> "Do not marry unbelieving women idolators until they believe: a slave woman who believes is better than an unbelieving woman, even though she allures you. Unbelievers do but beckon you to the Fire. But Allah beckons by His Grace to the Garden of bliss and forgiveness, and makes His signs clear to mankind that they may celebrate His praise."[14]

The causes of revelation of this verse was in respect of Kannāz Ibn Ḥaṣīn al-Ghanāwī whom the Messenger of Allah has sent to Mecca on a mission. He knew a woman called 'Anaq in Mecca with whom he was greatly in love from the days of *Jahiliyyah.* He came to her and told her that Islam has forbidden whatever used to happen in the Jahiliyyah period. She replied: "In that case marry me". Kannāz replied that he would ask for the Prophet's permission in the matter. When he sought Prophet's advice, he said that Kannāz should not marry her since he was a Muslim while she was a polytheist.[15]

There is yet another cause of revelation mentioned by ʿAbdallāh bin ʿAbbās in respect of ʿAbdallāh bin Rawāḥah, a companion of the Prophet who had a black slave girl. He once became angry with her. When the Prophet came to know about it, he asked 'Abdallāh bin Rawāḥah in the following words:

The Prophet: what is the matter, O'Abdallāh?
'Abdallāh replied: 'O Messenger of Allah, she (slave girl) fasts, offers her prayers and makes ablution properly and believes in Allah that there is no god but Allah and that you are the Messenger of Allah.
The Prophet: O 'Abdallah, she is then a believer.
'Abdallāh: Then, by Allah who has sent you with the truth, I will declare her a free woman and marry her.

When 'Abdallāh married her, many Muslims taunted him that he married a slave girl since they liked to marry polytheists simply because of their high lineage. It was on this occasion that the above verse was revealed.

If a Muslim woman subsequently renounced Islam, she does not remain any more a legally married wife. Her marriage with a Muslim husband becomes null and void automatically.

The reason given in the verse 2:221 as to why the believers have been prohibited from marrying *mushrik* spouses is that, 'they invite you to the Fire'.[16]

This means that such a marriage might mislead the Muslim spouses to the ways of *shirk*, for the relations between the husband and the wife are not merely sexual but spiritual and cultural as well. It is possible that the Muslim spouse may influence the *mushrik* spouse and his and her family and their offspring in favour of the Islamic way of life. But it is equally possible that the *mushrik* spouse may imbue the Muslim spouse, his (and her) family or their offspring, with the spirit and ways of *shirk*. Most probably as a result of such a marriage, a mixture of Islam and un-Islam will be bred in such a family. A non-Muslim might approve of this, but a Muslim cannot afford to do so as a monotheist. One who sincerely believes in Islam can never take such a risk merely for the sake of the gratification of his lust. He would rather suppress his passions than do anything that might mislead him to disbelief, blasphemy and *shirk* or, at least mislead his progeny.[17]

Marriage with the "People of the Book" (Ahl al-Kitāb)

In Islam, 'people of the Book' are the Jews and the Christians, those who believe in the Books of Allah like *Torait* and *Injīl* revealed to Prophets Mūsā and Isa respectively. Marriage with women of the people of the Book if permitted in Islam according to the following injunction in the Qur'ān:

«اليومَ أُحِلَّ لَكُمُ الطَّيِّبَاتُ وَطَعَامُ الذَّينَ أُتُوا الكِتَابَ حِلٌ لَكُمْ وَطَعَامُكُمْ حِلٌ لَهُمْ وَالمُحْصَنَاتُ مِنَ المُؤمِنَاتِ وَالمُحْصَنَاتُ مِنَ الَّذِينَ أُتُوا الكِتَابَ مِنْ قَبْلِكُمْ اذَا اتَيْتُمُوهُنَّ اجُورَهُنَّ مُحْصِنِينَ غَيْرَ مُسَافِحِينَ وَلاَ مُتَّخِذِي اخْدَانٍ.....».

> This day are all things good and pure made lawful to you. The food of the people of the Book is lawful unto you and yours is lawful unto them. Lawful unto you in marriage are not only chaste women who are believers, but chaste women among the people of the Book revealed before your time, when you give them their due dowers, and desire chastity and not lewdness nor secret intrigues."[18]

There is a consensus of opinion of the *ʿUlamā* of the *Ah l al-Sunnah Wal-Jama'ah* that marriage with Jews and Christian women is permitted as was the practice of the companions of the Prophet *(Ṣaḥābah)* like ʿUthmān, Ṭalḥā, Ibn ʿAbbās, Hudhaifah and their followers *(Tābiʿūn)* like Said bin al-Musayyib, Sāʿīd bin Jubair, Al-Ḥasan, Mujāhid, Tawus, Akramah and others.

In spite of the practice of the *Ṣaḥābah*, and the *Tābiʿūn*, ʿAbdallāh bin ʿUmar was of the opinion that one should not marry a Jewish or a Christian woman. He used to say: "Allah has forbidden to marry polytheists, and I do not understand anything other than greater polytheism when a woman says that her Lord is Isa who is a servant from the servants of Allah".[19]

Although, there are examples of the pious *Ṣaḥābah* and their followers *(Tābiʿūn)* who married the *Kitābiyyah*, one has to take enough caution before contracting such marriages. The *Ṣaḥābah* had exemplary characters and their lives were full of righteousness and piety *(Taqwah)*. After marrying such women who followed different religions and celebrated different festivals, they knew how to keep them under proper control so that their children were not influenced by their mothers. There is not a single example of the *Ṣaḥābah* or the *Tābiʿūn* whose children ever transgressed from the limits of Allah or changed over to their mother's religion. Therefore, marriage with such ladies is permitted but is generally discouraged as *Makrūh.*

I have seen in many such marriages the food problem, when mother even at times brings forbidden food and children partake of it. Likewise, she would sip wine as part of her religious ritual, and the habit slowly finds its way into the house. In some houses, I have even seen Christmas and Muslim festivals celebrated simultaneously. In extreme cases, boys of such marriage bear Muslim names, while girls bear the names common among the Christians and Jews.

If there are a good number of Muslim women to get married with, in any given country, it will be considered unlawful, according to the

Ijtihād of certain 'Ulamā,[20] to marry the *Kitābiyyah* women. Since Muslim women cannot marry the *Kitābī* men, who will marry them in those circumstances? It is better then that Muslim men marry Muslim women.

The jurists of the four schools of Islamic jurisprudence have discussed the marriage with the *Kitābiyyah* women and given their juristic views. According to the Hanafī school it is unlawful to marry a *Kitābiyyah* woman if she is in the country which happens to be an "abode of war *(Dār al-Ḥarb)*" because that can open up a door to mischief. In such conditions the children by that marriage will be more inclined towards the religion of their mother.[21] The Māliki school on the other hand, has two opinions. The first is that the marriage with a *Kitābiyyah* is completely disapproved *(Makrūh)* whether she is a *Dhimmī* or one belonging to the abode of war. The dislike for a woman of the latter category is greater. The second opinion is that there is no complete disapproval in marrying a *Kitābiyyah* because the Qur'ānic words has given a tacit approval. They show disapproval of such a marriage in the abode of Islam because it is not forbidden for a *Kitābiyyah* woman to drink wine or eat the flesh of a pig or going to the church and this affects the religious belief and behaviour of her children. It is not essential for a *Kitābiyyah* that both of her parents are ahl-al-kitāb. Her marriage will be valid even if her father is a kitābī and her mother is an idol worshipper. The Shāfi'ī and Ḥanbalī schools believe that both her parents must be ahl al-kitāb in order to have a valid marriage. If her father is a kitābī and her mother is an idol worshipper the marriage is unlawful even though she has reached the age of puberty and has accepted the religion of her father.[22]

Marriage with Ṣābiūn and Majūs

According to the jurists, the Ṣābiūns are the communities whose beliefs fall in between the belief of the Zoroastrians, Jews and the Christians. In other words, they do not have any particular religion. Mujāhid, an eminent theologian considers them as a sect of the *Ahl al-Kitāb* who read Zabūr, while Ḥasan, another theologian says that they worship angels. In the opinion of 'Abdur Raḥmān bin Zaid, they lived in the Island of Mosul and used to say *Lāilāha ill Allāh* (There is no deity worthy of worship but Allah), but do not practise it, and have no book or prophet. This is the reason why the polytheists of Mecca used to say to the companions of the Prophet as follows:

«هؤلاء الصابئون، يشبهونهم بهم في قول لا اله إلا الله».

"These Ṣābiūn resemble them (companions) in saying *Lāilāha illa Allāh*"

The Holy Qur'ān mentions the Jews, the Ṣābiūns, the Christians in the following words:

«انَّ الّـذينَ آمَنُـوا وَالَّذينَ هَادُوا وَالصَّابؤِنَ والنَّصَارٰى مَنْ آمَنَ بِاللّهِ واليَوْمِ الآخِرِ وَعَمَلَ صَالِحاً فَلا خَوْفٌ عَلَيْهِمْ وَلاَ هُمْ يَحْزَنُونَ».

"Those believe (in the Qur'ān), those who follow the Jewish (Scriptures), and the Sabiuns and the Christians, and who believe in Allah and the Last Day, and work righteousness, on them shall be no fear, nor shall they grieve."[23]

The same theme is repeated in Sūrah al-Baqarah, verse 62. According to Ibn Kathīr, the famous commentator of the Qur'ān, the Sabians used to pray in the direction other than the Qiblah, they used to read Zabur and worshipped angels. They knew Allah and had their own *Shari'ah* and lived in the vicinity of Iraq. It is also said that they believed in some Prophets, and fasted for 30 days in a year and even prayed five times a day.[24]

'Allāma Yūsuf 'Alī, quoting *Encyclopaedia Britannica* considers them as people who played an important part in the history of Arabia whose inscriptions were like those of Phoenicians and Babylonians, and had a flourishing Kudom in Yemen tract in South Arabia about 800 - 700 B.C. They worshipped the planets and he further conjectures that the Queen of Sheba of Bible and Bilqīs of the Qur'ān is connected with them.[25] In the period of Caliph Ma'mūm al-Rashīd in 830 A.D. a group of people in Harran in Syria claimed the privileges as the people of the Book. They wore a peculiar dress and had long hair, worshipped stars with Hellenic tendencies like the Jews contemporary with Jesus.[26]

It is on this ground that a Muslim is permitted to marry a Sabian lady. But I do not agree with 'Allāmah Yūsuf 'Alī, the celebrated commentator of the Qur'ān, when he extends the term *Ṣābiūn* to cover the followers of Budhdha, a confucius or Vedas, and marriage Hindus, Buddhists and the followers of confucius or Shinto will definitely come under the category of the marriage with polytheists.

Ibn al-Nadhir says concerning the Majus or Zoroastrians who worship the fire that marriage is not forbidden with Zoroastrian ladies or eat meat of animals slaughtered by them. They are not *Ahl-al-Kitāb* as they have no book, nor do they believe in Prophethood and worship fire. Imam al-Shafi'i narrates that Sayyidnā 'Umar once mentioned the Majus and said: "I do not know how do I treat the Majūs?". 'Abdur Raḥmān bin 'Awf, a famous companion of the Prophet replied to him:

سمعت رسول الله صلى الله عليه وسلم يقول: «سنّوا بهم سنة أهل الكتاب».

"I heard the Messenger,of Allah saying that treat them in the same way as *Ahl-al-Kitab*".

After understanding whom a Muslim is allowed to marry, it is important to note that, in no circumstances, is a Muslim lady permitted to marry a non-Muslim, whether he happens to be *Ahl-al-Kitāb* or otherwise.

The injunction is contained in the Holy Qur'ān in the following verse:

«يَـآءيُهَـا الَّـذينَ آمَنُـوآ اذا جَآءكُمُ المُـؤْمِنَاتُ مُهَاجِرَاتٍ فَامْتَحِنُوهُنَّ اللّهُ اعْلَمُ بايمَـانِهِنَّ فَانْ عَلِمْتُمُـوهُنَّ مُؤْمِنَـاتٍ فَلَا تَرْجِعُوهُنَّ الىَ الكُفَّارِ لَا هُنَّ حِلٌ لَهُمْ وَلَا هُمْ يَحِلّونَ لَهُنَّ....».

"O you who believe! when they come to you believing women refuges, examine and test them: Allah knows best as to their faith: If you are certain that they are believers, for the unbelievers, nor are the unbelievers lawful husbands for them."[27]

In this verse Allah has ordered the believers that when immigrant women come to them and once they realise that they are believers, they must, in no circumstances, be sent back to the disbelievers. Once they have left their original places due to their belief in Islam and love for Allah and his Prophet, they must not be allowed to suffer in the hands of disbelievers.

The disbelievers cannot treat the believing women in their marriage according to the principles of *Amr bil Ma'rūf* and vice versa, as is declared in the Qur'ān:

«ولن يجعل الله للكافرين على المؤمنين سبيلا».

"And never will Allah grant to the Unbelievers a way to triumph over the Believers".

Solemnizing of Marriage According to the Sunnah

There are two special rites of the Muslim marriage. They are: *Ijab* and *Qubūl* or a proposal and acceptance.

According to the Maliki School, there are five requirements of a marriage. The foremost is the guardian without whom there is no legal marriage. The second is dower. The third is the bridegroom. The fourth is the bride who is neither in Iddah nor in the state of *Ihram* and the fifth condition is the Sighah which means *Ijab* and *Qubūl*, i.e. the proposal and the acceptance.

The Shāfi'ites have enumerated the following five conditions: Husband, Wife, Guardian, Two Witnesses and the *Ṣighah* (*Ijab* and *Qubūl*).

The Ḥanafī school lays emphasis on the *Ṣīghah*. The definite and clear words must be uttered in the *Ijāb* and Qūbūl, and the acceptance must be made in the gathering where Ījāb is uttered *(Fī Majlis al-Ījab)*.

It is *Mustaḥab* or a commendable act to give a sermon *(Khutbah)* before the marriage rites are performed. This may provide a forum for informing and advising the bride and bridegroom of their marriage responsibilities in Islam.

It may belong as occasion demands, but the shortest recommended form is just to say:

«الحمد لله والصلاة والسلام على رسول الله»

"Praise be to Allah and benedictions and salutations be on the Messenger of Allah." of Islam."

After the above words of praise for Allah and the salutations and benedictions on the Messenger of Allah, it is the *Sunnah* of the Prophet (S.A.W.) to recite the following three verses of the Qur'an appropriate on this occasion:

«يَآءيُهَا الَذينَ آمنُوا اتَّقُوا اللّهَ حَقَّ تُقَاتِهِ وَلاَ تَمُوتُنَ إلاَّ وَانْتُمْ مُسْلِمُونَ»

"O you who believe! fear Allah as He should be feared, and die not except in a state of Islam".[28]

Fear of Allah or *Taqwah* mentioned in this verse gives a reasonable man to avoid harm to himself or to people whom he wishes to protect live his wife and children and other people in his family and friend circle. The verse also mentioned the life to be lived according to the principles laid down by Islam. It should not be merely an outward show that one lives as a Muslim but the whole being should be permeated with Islam.

«يَـآءيُهَـا النَّـاسُ اتَّقُـوا رَبَّكُمُ الذَّي خَلَقَكُمْ مِنْ نَفْسٍ وَاحِدَةٍ وَخَلَقَ مِنْهَا زَوْجَهَا وَبَثَّ مِنْهُمَا رِجَالاً كَثيراً وَنِسَآءَ، وَاتَّقُوا اللّهَ الذّي تَسَاءلُونَ بِهِ وَالأرْحَامَ اِنَّ اللّهَ كَانَ عَلَيْكُمْ رَقيباً».

"O mankind reverence your Guardian, Lord, who created from a single person, created, of like nature, his mate, and from them twain scattered like seeds countless men and women; reverence Allah, through whom you demand your mutual rights, and reverence the wombs (that bore you): for Allah ever watches over you."[29]

«يَـآءيُهَـا الذّينَ أمَنُوا اتَّقُوا اللّهَ وَقُولُوا قَوْلاً سَديداً يُصْلِحْ لَكُمْ اعْمَالَكُمْ وَيَغْفِرْ لَكُمْ ذُنُوبَكُمْ وَمَنْ يُطِعِ اللّهَ وَرَسُولَهُ فَقَدْ فَازَ فَوْزاً عَظيماً».

"O you who believe, fear Allah and always say a word directed to the Right: that He may make your conduct whole and sound and forgive you your sins: he that obeys Allah and His Messenger has already attained the highest achievement."[30]

In every *Khuṭbah,* whether for marriage, *Jum'ah* prayer or Id prayers or occasional sermons, if they do not contain *Tash-ahhud*, it is incomplete, as the following Ḥadīth suggests:

عن ابي هريرة أن النبي صلى الله عليه وسلم قال: «كل خطبة ليس فيها تَشَهُّدْ فهي كاليد الجذماء».

"It is reported by Abū Hurairah that the Prophet said: "Every Sermon that does not have *Tashahhud* in it, is like a hand of a leper."

It is also *mustahab* that a short prayer *(al-Duʿā),* should be said. The shortest prayer as a Sunnah of the Prophet is as follows:

«بارك الله لك وبارك عليك وجمع بينكما في خير»

"May Allah bless you, and may blessing be upon you and may your coming together be auspicious".

There is no harm in saying long prayers after this.

Likewise, *Walīma* (Marriage feast) to all the *ʿUlamā* of all the schools of law is *Sunnah al-Mu'akkadah.* There should be no extravagance or show business in the feast. It may be bread and meat or just a small goat slaughtered and feasted upon. This was a condition laid by the Prophet while giving *Fāṭimah* in marriage with ʿAlī:

قال رسول الله صلى الله وسلم: «انه لابد للعرس من وليمة».

The Messenger of Allah said: "The bridegroom will have to give *Walimah.*"

The Role of Guardians in Valid Muslim Marriage

The jurists of the Shāfi'ī and the Mālikī schools have considered the approval of the guardian to marry a certain person by his ward as one of the essential ingredients of valid Muslim marriage, but the Ḥanafi and the Hanbali schools consider the consent of the guardian merely as a condition. The later two schools put greater emphasis on the proposal and acceptance. All the four schools have derived their views from the Ḥadiths of the Prophet. The Shāfiʿī and Mālikī schools have based their view on the following Ḥadith:

ان النبي صلى الله عليه وسلم قال: «ايما امرأة نكحت بغير إذن وليها فنكاحها باطل».

"The Prophet (S.A.W.) said: Any woman who got married without the permission of her guardian, her marriage would be considered null and void." The Hadiths of the Prophet further clarifies as to who can play the role of guardian:

«لا تزوج المرأة المرأة، ولا تنكح المرأة نفسها».

"A woman cannot be married by a woman and a woman cannot be married by herself".

In the absence of father or a near relative, the king or Amīr or a ruler can be a guardian.[34] There is a case of a woman who came to the Holy Prophet and offered herself for marriage, and she was then and there married to a person who could not even settle any dowry due to his poverty. There was no natural guardian (father or other near relative) present at that time. Perhaps the Prophet played the role of the guardian or that she was matured enough to understand the pros and cons of her action.

In certain verses of the Qur'ān there is no mention at all of a guardian in express words. As for example, "And when you divorce women and they end their term of ʿIddah, do not prevent them from marrying their husbands when they agree among themselves in a lawful manner."[35] But there is another verse which speaks of the need of a guardian and his careful decision. As for example, in the case of a *thayyibah* (a woman who has seen a husband), the Qur'ān says: "And do not give believing women in marriage to idolators until they believe."[36] This verse is undoubtedly addressed to the guardians, who have therefore no right to give consent in such cases.

As we have seen before, a divorced woman is not to be prevented from marrying in a lawful manner."[37] In the case of a widow, the Qur'ān says: "But if they themselves go away, there is no blame on you for what they do of lawful deeds by themselves."[38] This verse recognises the widow's right to marry herself. These two verses clearly recognise the right of the *thayyiba* (the divorced woman or the widow) to give herself in marriage, and prohibit the guardian from interference wẖen the woman herself is satisifed. This is quite in accordance with a Ḥadīth quoted by Abū Dāʾūd that the widow and the divorced woman has greater right to dispose of herself (in marriage) than her guardian."[39] Although Imām Abū Ḥanifah gives freedom to the virgin who has reached the age of puberty to marry according to her choice, the consent of the guardian is still one of the conditions of marriage. He argues that a woman who has attained the age of majority can dispose of her property without reference to a guardian, so she is also entitled to dispose of her person. But at the same time it cannot be denied that there is a natural bashfulness about the virgin, and, moreover, she has not the same experience of men and affairs as has a widow or a divorced woman, and it is therefore in the fitness or things that her choice of a husband should be subject to the approval of a father or other guardian, who would also settle the terms, and guard her against being misled by unscrupulous people. But as the contract, after all, depends on her consent and not on the consent of the guardian, which in fact is only needed to protect her, her will must ultimately prevail according to the Ḥanafī school.

The Holy Prophet has said: "The widow and the divorced woman shall not be married until her order is obtained, and the virgin shall not be married until her permission is obtained."[40] Besides, "When a man gives his daughter in marriage and she dislikes it, the marriage shall be repudiated",[41] there is already a case in which the Holy Prophet once repudiated such a marriage.

Guardianship and Marriage of a Minor:

According to Ḥanafī School, the marriage of a minor boy or girl is lawful, whether the minor girl is a virgin or a *thayyibah*, provided the guardian is one of the *'aṣāba* (relations on the father's side). Imām Mālik also recognises such marriage only when the guardian is a father. Imām Shāfi'i recognises such marriage only when the guardian is a father or a grandfather. The Hanafi view is that if the minor has been given in marriage by a guardian who is not the father or the grandfather, the minor has the option on attaining majority of repudiating the marriage. But, as a hadith already quoted shows, even if the father gives away his daughter in marriage against her wishes, and she is of age, the marriage can be repudiated if the girl strongly desires. A minor girl too if on coming of age she finds the match unsuitable, marriage can be repudiated.[42]

1. Qur'ān, 4:34.
2. Qur'ān, ch. 2:187.
3. Qur'ān, ch. 7:26.
4. Qur'ān, ch. 2:228.
5. Qur'ān ch. 4:34.
6. Qur'ān, ch. 4:19.
7. Abū Daūd, Tirmidhī and Ibn Ḥabbān.
8. cf. Qur'ān, ch. 2:229; ch. 2:231, and ch. 4:19.
9. Qur'ān, ch. 4:19.
10. Muslim, 13:11.
11. Bukhâri, 67:19.
12. Muslim, 15:19.
13. Bukhāri, 67:80.
14. Qur'ān, ch. 2:221.
15. Al-Jāmi'li-ahkam al-Qur'ān, vol. 3, p. 67; also cf. Sayyid Sābiq, Fiqh al-Sunnah, vol. 6, Kuwait 1968, p. 206.
16. Qur'ān, ch. 2:221.
17. Maudūdī Abul A'lā, *Tafhim al-Qur'ān (The meaning of the Qur'ān)* vol. 1, Lahore 1971, p. 154-155.
18. Qur'ān 5:5
19. cf. Sayyid Sābiq. Fiqh al-Sunnah. op. cit. 6, pp. 208-209.
20. cf. Al-Qarḍāwī, Yūsuf, *Al-Ḥalāl wal Ḥarām fil Islām*, 1977 p. 245.
21. *Kitāb al-Fiqh 'alal Madhābib al-Arbi'ah* op. cit., vol. 4, p. 76.
22. Ibid p. 77.
23. Qur'ān, ch. 5:69.
24. Ibn Kathīr, *Tafsīr Ibn Kathīr* – see the commentary of the above quoted verse.
25. Yūsuf 'Ali, *The Holy Qur'ān* – see note 76.
26. Ibid.
27. Qur'ân, ch. 60:10.
28. Qur'ān, ch. 3:102.
29. Qur'ān, ch. 4:1.
30. Qur'ān, ch. 33:70-71.
31. Fatāwā 'Alamgīrī, vol. 2, p. 1.
32. Bukhāri, 67:37.
33. Bukhāri, 67:42.
34. Bukhāri, 67:41.
35. Qur'ân, ch. 2:232.
36. Qur'ân, ch. 2:221.
37. Qur'ān, ch. 2:232.
38. Qur'ân, ch. 2:240.
39. Abū Dāud, 12:25.
40. Bukhāri, 67:42.
41. Bukhāri, 67:43.
42. Abū Dāud, 12:25.

Chapter 8

Ta'addud Al-Zawjat: Polygamy

Polygamy or marrying more than one wife is not a new phenomenon. It has always been with mankind from time immemorial among different peoples in various parts of the world. The Arabians were polygamous even before the advent of Islam and so were other people on most parts of the world during that time. When one goes through the Jewish and Christian religious scriptures, one finds that polygamy was an accepted way of life. All the Prophets mentioned in the Talmud, the old Testament and the Qur'ān were polygamous with the exception of Prophet Jesus who if he had lived longer on this earth would have, perhaps, accepted the same system as his forefathers. In the Pre-Islamic Arabia there was the practice of limitless polygamy.

The Institution of polygamy was recognised among Medes, Babylonians, Abbysinians and Persians. Moses allowed polygamy among his people since it was practised by the Greeks among whom a wife was not only transferrable but also marketable already prevalent among them. It was customary among the tribes of Africa, Australia and the Mormons of America. Even the Hindu law of India does not restrict polygamy.[1] The laws of Manū have laid down specific conditions for celebrating subsequent marriages, it says: "A barren wife may be superseded in the eighth year; she whose children (all) die, in the tenth, she who bears only daughters, in the eleventh; but she who is quarrelsome, without delay.[2]

The Jāhiliyyah Arabs used to marry a large number of women and considered them as a chattel. In most cases even there was nothing like marriage as women could be bought and sold at will.

The Qur'ānic verses and Aḥādith on Polygamy

With the advent of Islam, the limitless polygamy was restricted to four wives at one time under special circumstances and that too with a number of rules attached to it which we will study here. The only Qur'ānic verse that refers to polygamy is as follows:

«وَإِنْ خِفْتُمْ الّا تُقْسِطوا فِي اليَتَامىٰ فَانْكِحُوا مَا طَابَ لَكُمْ مِنَ النِّسَآءِ مَثْنٰى وَثُلاثَ وَرُبَاعَ، فَإِنْ خِفْتُمْ الّا تَعْدِلُوا فَوَاحِدَةً....».

"If you fear that you shall not be able to deal justly with the orphans, marry the women of your choice, two, or three or four. But if you fear that you shall not be able to deal justly with them, then only one"[3]

The above rule on polygamy has been introduced conditionally. This verse more especially refers to justice to be done to the orphans. It was revealed immediately after the Battle of Uhud when the Muslim communities were left with many orphans and widows and some captives of wars. The treatment was to be governed by principles of greatest humanity and equality. As Yusuf Ali says, the occasion is past but the principles remain. Marry the orphans if you are quite sure that it is in that way you will protect their interest and their property with perfect justice to them and to your own dependants if you have any. The verse not merely limited to the orphans but it has a general application about the marriage laws in Islam. The Muslim jurists, therefore, have laid down the following conditions if at all someone wants to take more than one wife. (1) He should have enough financial capacity to look after the needs of the additional wives that he has undertaken. (2) He must do equal justice to them all. Each wife should be treated equally in fulfilling their conjugal and other rights.

If a man feels that he will not be able to treat them with equality and justice or he does not have the means to support them he should restrict himself to marrying only one wife. Imām Mālik says in the *Muwaṭṭā* that Ghaylān bin Salamah accepted Islam and he had ten wives. The Messenger of Allah said:

«امسك منهنّ اربعا وفارق سائرهن»

"Keep four out of them and make the others free."

Similarly Abū Dā'ūd mentions from Ḥārith bin Qays:

قال: اسلمت وعندي ثماني نسوة فذكرت ذلك للنبي صلى الله عليه وسلم، فقال: «أختر منهن اربعاً».

"I accepted Islam and I had eight wives. I mentioned it to the Prophet. He advised: 'Select four out of them." '

Taking more than one wife makes it absolutely essential for one to do as much justice as humanly possible to each of them. The very object of marriage in Islam is to have a healthy family where man and his wife or wives and children live in peace, love and harmony as is required in the injunctions of the Qur'ān.[4]

Among His Signs is this that He (Allah) created for you mates from among yourselves that you may dwell in tranquility with them, and he has put love and mercy between your hearts. Thus the man as the father and the woman as the mother of the children dwell together and bring up a family unity. Different people have different temperaments but if kindness, love, tenderness, tranquility can be maintained such a family unit is successful. If this is not possible then one must limit oneself with what one can easily manage, that is one wife.

The following situations will allow polygamy as the best solution:

1. When the wife is suffering from a serious disease like paralysis, epilepsy or a contagious disease. In this circumstance it will be better if there is another wife to look after the needs of the husband and children. Her presence will also help the sickly wife.
2. When the wife is proved barren and after the medical examination the experts have given their opinion that she is not capable of bearing a child. The husband then should marry a second wife so that he may have children since a child is a joy of life.
3. When she is of unsound mind. In that case the husband and the children will suffer a great deal.
4. When the woman has reached the old age and has become weak and infirm and cannot look after the house and the property of the husband.
2. When the husband finds out that she has a bad character and she cannot be reformed. He should then have another wife.
6. When she has moved away from the husbands' house and has become disobedient and the husband finds it difficult to reform her. He should then take another wife.
7. During the period of war when men are killed and women are left behind a very large number, polygamy can provide the best solution.
8. Apart from the above circumstances, if the man feels that he cannot do without a second wife in order to satisfy his natural desire which is very strong and when he has enough means to support her, he should take another wife. There are certain areas in the world where people are physically very virile and cannot be satisfied with one wife. In such cases polygamy can provide an answer.

Only limited Polygamy allowed:

Islam limited the limitless polygamy practised in the *Jāhiliyyah* society of Arabs and non-Arabs. It was a fashion with chiefs and of tribe rulers to keep big harems. Even some Muslim rulers had become victims of passion and practised limitless polygamy in the later periods of Islamic history. Whatever their practice, such polygamy has no place in Islam. If necessary a Muslim can marry up to four wives and not more at a given time. According to Imam al-Shafi'i, it is not lawful for anyone other than the Prophet to marry more than four wives at a given time.[5]

Some of the Ẓāhirites maintain that the Qur'ānic words *Mathnā* means "two, two"; *Thulāth* "three, three"; and *Rubā* "four, four", and thus the number permitted swells to eighteen in number. There are some who think erroneously that *"Mathnā wa thulātha wa Rubā"* put together comes to nine and thus up to nine wives are allowed in Islam. This is, in reality, a wrong interpretation of the Qur'ānic injunction. The P̱rophetic interpretation of this verse is contained in the following Ḥadīth of the Prophet:

أن النبي صلى الله عليه وسلم قال لغيلان بن اسية الثقفي وقد اسلم وتحته عشر نسوة: «أختر منهنّ اربعاً وفارق سائرهن».

The Prophet said to Ghilān bin Umayyah al-Thaqafī who had just accepted Islam and had ten wives: "Choose four out of them and give up all others."[6]

Once a Muslim marries more than one wife, it is essential for him to treat them equally in the matter of food, residence, clothing and even in sexual relationship as far as is possible. If one is a little doubtful in showing equal treatment in fulfilling thier rights, he must not take more wives. If he feels able to fulfil his responsibilities to only one, he should not marry two. Secondly; if he can do justice to two, he should not marry three. The final limit is that of four wives, if one feels necessary to do so.

«فَإِنْ خِفْتُمْ الاّ تَعْدِلوا فَوَاحِــدَة»

"If you fear that you will not be able to do justice, then marry only one."[7]

The justice referred to in this verse only relates to the humanly possible equitable treatment. In the matter of love, even if one really wants to do equal justice with sincerity of purpose, he will not be able to do so knowing human beings what they are.

The Qur'ān refers to this human weakness in the following words:

«وَلَنْ تَسْتَطِيعُوا أَنْ تَعْدِلُوا بَيْنَ النِسَاءِ وَلَوْ حَرَصْتُمْ، فَلا تَمِيلوا كُلَّ المَيْلِ فَتَذَرُوهَا كَالمُعَلَّقَةِ....».

> "You are never able to be fair and just as between women, if ever it is your ardent desire: but turn not away from a woman altogether so as to leave her as it were hanging in the air."[8]

Shaikh Muḥammad bin Sīrīn while explaining this verse said that this inability referred to in the Holy Qur'ān is in respect of love and sexual intercourse. Shaikh Abūbakr bin al-'Arabī says "No one can control one's heart since it is entirely in the hands of Allah". The same is the case of cohabitation when one may satisfay one wife better as compared to the other. Since this was not the intention of the man, it is not his fault and hence he will not be held responsible. The mother of the faithful, 'Ā'ishah, reported the Prophet saying:

كان رسـول الله صلى الله عليـه وسلم يقسم ويعـدل ويقـول: «اللهم هذا قسمي فيما املك فلا تلمني فيما تملك ولا املك».

> "The Messenger of Allah used to distribute things and do justice to all, and used to say: 'My Allah, this is my distribution which is in my control, but do not hold me responsible for what is in your control and I have no control over it'."*

Here the reference is to the heart and matters connected with the heart when the Ḥadīth speaks of "the thing under Allah's control."[10] After understanding the aspect of equal justice to one's wives, the following Hadith of the Prophet must be kept in mind to avoid excesses.

The Holy Prophet said, "A man who marries more women than one and then does not deal justly with them, will be resurrected with half his faculties paralysed." Preservation of the higher values and promotion of righteousness must be the constant objectives. Permission to marry more than one woman at a time is necessary emergency provision for the preservation of high social values and for safeguarding society against promiscuity. At this state it becomes relevant to quote Billy Graham on polygamy. "Christianity cannot do so, it is to its detriment. Islam has permitted polygamy as a solution to social ills and has allowed a certain degree of latitude to human nature, but only strictly within the framework of the law. Christian countries make a great show of monogamy, but actually they practise polygamy. No one is unaware of the part mistresses play in society. In this respect, Islam is a fundamentally honest religion and permits a Muslim to marry a second wife if he MUST, but strictly forbids all clandestine amatory associations in order to safeguard the moral probity of the community."

Modernist Approach to Polygamy

There is a growing tendency to consider some Islamic institutions to be out-modes when they do not conform to the western pattern of life. This is particularly true in the case of polygamy which some scholars have vehemently opposed. They have even tried to misinterpret certain verses of the Qur'ān saying that polygamy is not allowed in Islam. The two verses of the Qur'ān which they have referred to in strengthening their argument are verses 3 and 129 of *Sūrah al-Nisā'* (Chapter 4 of the Qur'ān). Verse 3 reads: "If you fear that you shall not be able to deal justly with the orphans, marry women of your choice, two or three or four; but if you fear that you shall not be able to deal justly with them, then only one." Verse 129 reads: "You will never be able to be fair and just as between women, even if it is your ardent desire."

The argument usually tendered in respect of the above two verses is that Islam has allowed marrying more than one wife on the condition that the man cannot be perfectly fair and just to all the wives. But this condition is almost impossible to fulfil as it is mentioned in verse 129 quoted above, hence they argue that polygamy is not allowed in Islam because a man who marries more than one wife puts himself in an impossible position. When they fear injustice, they must not marry more than one wife.

The modernists consider verse 129 as a clause and a legal condition attached to polygamous unions. Since impartial treatment cannot be possible, one must restrict oneself to monogamy. What they overlook in the fact that "impartial treatments" in the matter of residence, food and clothing is a relative term which will differ from person to person and country to country according to the economic standard of the society. What one would need to provide in a European country in terms of food, clothing and residence would not apply in certain countries in Asia and Africa where the standard and the cost of living are much lower. Hence, it is a matter of the conscience for the individual husband to provide his wives equal treatment according to his situation. Even in one given society the standard would differ – a business man will provide to his wives according to his standard; while a labourer, whose income is low, may provide according to his own standard of income. The women that the labourer would marry would be used to a lower standard as compared to a business man. Besides, the wives may voluntarily accept a lower standard and may live peacefully as it happens in many polygamous homes in Africa.

The impact of the colonial era on the Muslim countries was so great that they changed their law of personal Status and imposed restrictions on the husband marrying more than one wife. The first attempt of this kind was made by Syria in 1953. Syrian Law on Personal Status (Decree No. 59) of 1953 provides: " . . . The Judge is empowered to refuse permission to a married man to marry another woman if it is established that he is not in a position to support two wives . . . " (Art. 17). Here it was stipulated not to take an additional wife unless they were capable of supporting them.[11] In this case the Syrian jurists, trained in the western countries, maintained that the Qur'ānic provision in verse three of *Sūrah al-Nisā* should be regarded as a positive legal condition precedent to the exercise of polygamy and enforced as such by the courts on the principles that those that lead to abuses must be closed.

They made it essential for an intending husband to seek permission of the court to marry. It was required by Article 17 of the law that the *Qāḍī* may with-hold permission to a man who is already married to marry a second wife, where it is established that he is not in a position to support both. The defaulters, are considered to be liable to penalties and the court would not recognise the marriage, although in spite of the clause of penalty they did not go as far as declaring the marriage *invalid.*

In Tunisia, polygamy was prohibited outright by the law of Personal Status in 1957. The Tunisian Code of Personal Status, 1957 says: "Polygamy is forbidden. Any person who, having entered into a bond of marriage, contracts another marriage before the dissolution of the preceding one, is liable to one years' imprisonment and to a fine . . . " (Art. 18). Here too, the modern jurists, influenced by Western pattern of life, declared that the Qur'ānic verse 3 of *Sūrah al-Nisā* would not be construed strictly as a moral exhortation but as a legal condition precedent to polygamy, and therefore, no second marriage should be permissible unless and until adequate evidence was forthcoming that the wives would be treated impartially. Since they thought that in the modern social and economic condition such impartial treatment was practically an impossibility, they maintained that the essential conditions of polygamy was impossible of fulfilment. In other words, the Tunisian jurists even went a step further and completely prohibited polygamy against explicit Qur'ānic provision.

The Moroccan Code of 1958 took a middle course and prohibited polygamy conditionally when there was any apprehension of unequal treatment. The Moroccan Code of Personal Status, 1958 says: "Polygamy is prohibited where it is likely to involve injustice towards the wives . . . " (Art. 30). The marriage contract concerning the second wife shall not be drawn up until the latter has been informed that her prospective spouse is already married. The courts were only allowed to intervene by granting divorce on the grounds of unequal treatment which is not that much a departure from the Mālikī school of

Jurisprudence which is practised in Morocco and which allowed a co-wife to claim divorce if she was not given proper maintenance.

Similarly in Iraq, the law of personal status of 1959 did not declare polygamy as prohibited but imposed restrictions on the institution. The Iraqi Code on Personal Status, 1959 reads: " . . . It is not permissible to marry more than one woman without authorisation from the judge. The grant of permission is regulated by the conditions that the husband's financial status permits it for supporting the wives and it is for a genuine benefit" (Art. 3). One could not marry a second wife without the permission of the *Qādī* who will not grant permission unless he is satisfied that the husband is financially capable of supporting an additional wife and that some lawful benefit for the husband was found in such marriage. The *Qādī* will not give permission unless he was satisfied that there was no fear of any unequal treatment of the wives.

In Pakistan, the restriction was placed on polygamous marriage by the Muslim Family Law Ordinance of 1961 which required that a written permission of the Arbitration Council was required before one could marry a second wife. Pakistan's Family Law Ordinance, provides: "No man, during the subsistence of an existing marriage, shall, except with the previous permission in writing of the Arbitration Council, contract another marriage . . . " (Sec. 6). The permission would only be granted if the Arbitration Council was satisfied that the proposed marriage was necessary and just. In this case the consent of the existing wife was required except in the cases of insanity, physical infirmity or sterility. But in any case the council's permssion was essential to be obtained before contracting a second marriage. The defaulter was liable to be imprisoned for up to one year or had to pay a fine up to Rs.5000 or both. If the *Mahr* was deferred, he was required to pay it forthwith and the existing wife had the right to get a divorce. In spite of all these restrictions, if a second marriage was contracted without the council's permission it would not be considered legally invalid.

The above examples lead us naturally to a consideration of the conflict between the Qur'ānic Injunctions and the so-called reforms in respect of polygamy in some Muslim countries. There are countries where the Shari'ah Law of polygamy has not been tampered with by the modernist forces like Saudi Arabia, most countries in East and West Africa, and in Asia. Then there are countries like Syria and Tunisia where polygamy, obviously allowed in the Qur'ān and the Sunnah, has been made prohibited by law. There are some other countries where serious restrictions have been imposed by law in contracting a second marriage, but the marriage, if it takes place, is not rendered invalid. It is interesting to note that these law reforms in Muslim countries are of recent origin, since it was first introduced in Syria in 1953 and later, some other Muslim countries followed suit. It is my candid view that the countries which have just prohibited polygamy by law have gone against the injunction of the Qur'ān and the Sunnah of the Prophet and the practice of the *Tābi'ūn* and the *Tab' Tābi'ūn*.

It should be borne in mind that the role of the Prophet did not end with one announcement of the *Sunnah* or the way of life to the world at large. He had to guide the people who followed him, explaining to them the implications of all the approved actions, moral code, the divine injunctions and the form of law that sustained the whole system. If polygamy were not allowed, he should have stopped people from practising it in his life-time. There are a number of *Aḥādīth* of the Prophet in which cases from polygamous homes were brought to him. The solutions were found and justice was done, and in some cases marriages were dissolved, if they had become unworkable. But, there is not a single *Ḥadīth* that suggests that the polygamy was forbidden by the Prophet or the Rāshidūn Caliphs or Muslim rulers of the Umayyad and the 'Abbāsid dynasties.

There is the important question of the role of the *'Ulamā* and *Fuqahā* of Islam, the great learned men and jurists, who have tried to guide the *'Ummah* after the death of the Prophet. The great *Imāms* and the founders and leaders of the four schools of Islamic jurisprudence and their disciples have left behind volumes of their works. They too have tried to find a solution to the problems arising out of polygamous unions, but have never outright prohibited polygamy. Why did the great *'Ulamā* have to wait 1400 years to pronounce polygamy prohibited in 1953?

By declaring prohibition, the so-called modernist reformers have refused to accept the Qur'ānic injunction or have indirectly rejected the Sunnah of the Prophet declaring it unworkable and have also disregarded the opinions of the pious 'Ulamā.

More than twenty-seven years have passed since polygamy was banned in some Muslim countries. Much has been written to appreciate these reformers by European scholars. The existence of such reforms are cited as a factor which makes people more cautious in contracting a second marriage, or else moves them to be more reckless in marrying more wives. If one takes statistics of polygamous marriages before and after the prohibition in Syria and Tunisia, one would find few cases where people have refrained from contracting a second marriage. But at the same time it has heightened tensions in the minds of those who were capable, both economically and physically to marry and satisfy more wives. A few have married contrary to the law and undergone penalties, but many have taken a short cut of entering into extra-marital relations secretly following the style of life in the Western world in order to cling to monogamy.

There is a dearth of empirical evidence which might enable us to answer the crucial question: "Has the prohibition of polygamy served as a deterrent?" "Has the Muslim Society become more prosperous because of this prohibition?" Quite naturally, the empirical evidence in this field will remain as scare as possible.

It is common place to say that the imaginary fear of misuse of polygamy is widespread and abiding in the minds of the Western trained Muslim elites. The question is whether such fear, even if justified to some extent knowing the unpredictable human nature, will remain effacious when we think of the alternative of importing the moral vices of the Western culture. Knowing human beings how they are, even the provisions of marriage, divorce, trade and commerce and all other aspects of law stand to be misused.

Those Muslim countries which have imposed heavy fines and imprisonment (or both) for one who does not first obtain permission of the Arbitration Council, as in Pakistan, or an authorisation from the Judge, as in Morocco, here too is an obvious violation of the Shari'ah provision on polygamy. The permission will only be granted if the existing wife gives her consent except in the cases of insanity, physical infirmity or sterility. Thus obliging the man to justify his intention by giving convincing reasons would give the Arbitration Council or Courts far more power of restraining even necessary polygamy. Some women tend to be very jealous by nature, and in spite of the fact that husband needs a second wife on conditional grounds, she will not understand her husband, nor would the court understand the man's needs easily since "one would have great difficulty in explaining, biologically, such a sudden change of heart."[12] If his legitimate biological desires are supressed against his will, it would give rise to adultery, concubinage and prostitution. The best course open for Muslims, therefore is to strive to the Qur'ānic advice.

«وما اتاكم الرسول فخذوه وما نهاكم عنه فانتهوا»

"So take what the Apostle assigns to you, and deny Yourself that which he witholds from you."[13]

The *Ummah* has lived successfully for fourteen hundred years without these reforms, and it can *Inshā'Allāh* survive the future.[14]

Polygamy: A Sociological Issue in Africa

The main purpose of marriage in the mind of an African man is the production of children who are his glory. If children do not come, or not come fast enough, as the result of a marriage, the man increases the number of wives although he does not divorce his barren wife.[15] In the traditional African society, the number of man's wives and children was the measure of his success in life and the children were considered their fathers' chief assurance of protection and support in his old age. The possession of many wives and children was regarded as a sign of wealth and nobility. It was not unknown for a man to have as many as 200 children.[16]

Polygamy is an old established custom and, to the African, it appears not only a reasonable but almost an essential institution.[17] In Iboland of Nigeria in West Africa, it is traditionally obligatory on a father to marry the first wife for his sons.

The sons in turn are expected to marry additional one or two or three wives for themselves. Otherwise, they will be regarded as weaklings among their age grades and in the community. Even their wives do not object to the addition of other women in the life of their husbands; they believe that extra hands would lighten the work in the house and on the farm.

---

1. cf. Rashīd, Khālid, *Muslim Law*, Lucknow 1979, p. 73.
2. Manū, 9:81.
3. Qur'ān, ch. 4:3.
4. Qur'ān, ch. 30:20.
5. Cf. Sayyid Sābiq, *Fiqh al-Sunnah*, po. cit., vol. 6, p. 223.
6. Imām Mālik, *Al-Muwaṭṭā*, ed. Muḥammad Fuād 'Abd al-Bāqī-Kitāb al Sha'b, Cairo (undated).
7. Qur'ān, ch. 4:3.
8. Qur'ān, ch. 4:129.
9. Abū Dāūd, Tirmidhī and Nisāī.
10. cf. Abu Daud.
11. Cf. Coulson, *A History of Islamic Law*, Edinburgh, 1971, p. 208.
12. Ingells, N. W., *Biology of Sex*, quoted by Khalid Rashid op. cit. p. 72.
13. Qur'ān, ch. 59:7.
14. The author only argues objectively although he has only one wife.
15. Chief I. O. Delano, A Short Biography of Oba Akinyele, an unpublished manuscript in the Institute of African Studies, University of Ife, p. 11.
16. G. A. Olawoyin, *The System of Customary Marriage Among the Ifes*, a paper read at a Seminar of the Institute of African Studies, University of Ife, 1967/68/7 p. 2.
17. Sir Alan Burns, *History of Nigeria*, George Allen and Unwin, 1958, p. 252.

Chapter 9

The Unlawful Forms of Marriage

Mut'ah: The Temporary Marriage

This is a forbidden form of marriage which is contracted for a short period for a fixed remuneration. It was allowed in the early formative period of Islam before the *Shari'ah* of Islam reached its completion. It was allowed in the early days while one went on a journey or when people went in battles against enemies. The reason why it was allowed was that new Muslims were passing through a transitionary period from the Jāhilliyyah to Islam. In the Jāhilliyyah period adultery was so common that it was not considered a sin. Just as Islamic injunctions of usury *(al-ribā)* and wine-drinking *(al-Khamr)* came only gradually, since people were so much used to them, *Mutah* was only allowed in the early days for people going on *Jihād* or Ghazwat. Those whose faith was still weak prove to commit adultery while away on *Jihād.* Those who had strong *Īmān* expressed the desire to get castrated in order to curb their passion. 'Abdullāh bin Mas'ūd has said:

> "We used to go on Ghazawāt with the Messenger of Allah, and we did not take our women with us. We asked (the Prophet) if we could get ourselves castrated. The Messenger of Allah refused us to do so and allowed us to marry women by giving her clothes for a certain period."

It is also narrated by Sayyidnā 'Alī: I said to Ibn 'Abbās during the Battle of Khaibar:

أن رسول الله صلى الله عليه وسلم نهى عن المتعة وعن لحوم الحمر الألية زمن خيبر.

"The Prophet (S.A.W.) forbade the temporary marriage and the eating of the flesh of donkey."[1]

After the *Sharī'ah* of Islam reached its completion, it was made unlawful *(Ḥarām)*. Temporary permission due to force of circumstances that the Prophet had given was made *harām* immediately after the conquest of Makkah as narrated by 'Ali. 'Alī says:

أنه غزا مع النبي صلى الله عليه وسلم في فتح مكة فأذن لهم في متعة النساء فقال: فلم يخرج حتى حرمها رسول الله صلى الله عليه وسلم.

"He was with the Prophet on the occasion of the battle for the conquest of Mecca. The Prophet had permitted *Mut'ah* marriage for the Sahabah. He says that the Prophet declared it unlawful even before leaving that place."

According to yet another narration, the Prophet declared:

«وأن الله حرم ذلك الى يوم القيامة»

"Undoubtedly Allah made it unlawful until the day of Judgement."

Islam wants to build a healthy society in which *Mut'ah* marriage, if allowed, can create many problems than it can solve. If unchecked, it can give rise to prostitution. There is a consensus of *'Ulamā* that it is unlawful. The only opinion of Abdullah bin Abbas was contrary to this view, but soon he saw the gravity of the situation and misuse people made to this form of marriage which was only allowed in extreme circumstances of warfare, did no longer consider it lawful.[2]

Some Shi'ite school of law considers it lawful even today, although it is seldom practiced.

Al-Shigār

Al-Shighar is an Arabic term which means lifting of a dog while it is passing excreater. This is the reason why the same word has been applied to this undesirable form of marriage since there is a resemblance of picking up a woman without paying any dowry at the time of her marriage. *Mahr* is the right of a woman and is a means of her security and not merely a bride price to be enjoyed by her parents or to get undue advantage by giving one's daughter or sister in marriage as an exchange for taking in marriage the other man's daughter or sister or award without paying any dowry.

In pre-Islamic Arabia, *Shighār* was a recognised form of marriage which was forbidden by Prophet Muḥammad after the advent of Islam because this form of marriage deprives the woman of her right.[3]

Marriage with Foster Relations: The Curse of Modern Milk Bank

As it is conveyed in the verse 23 of sūrah *al-Nisā*, marriage is prohibited between a person having a foster relationship corresponding to a blood relationship. It renders a marriage unlawful in Islam. It is unfortunate that in modern times, there are increasing efforts to establish milk banks not only in Europe and America but even in some Muslim countries where all newly born babies are fed with human milk which according to the above verse brings them to the category of foster brothers and sisters. Once these children grow up, they marry each other which in actual fact means a foster brother marrying a foster sister without knowing such relationship. Such marriages are unlawful not only in Islam but even in other religions. The Prophet (S.A.W.) has said:

«نعم، الرضاعة تحرم ما تحرم الولادة»

"Yes, the foster relations make all those things unlawful which are unlawful through corresponding birth (blood) relations."[4]

Marriage of a Woman with a Man Who Marries Her Paternal or Maternal Aunt

It is narrated by Jābir that the Messenger of Allah (S.A.W.) forbade that a woman should be married to a man who has married her paternal or maternal aunt.[5]

سمع جابر رضي الله عنه قال: نهى رسول الله صلى الله عليه وسلم أن تُنكح المرأة على عمتها أو خالتها».

1. Al-Bukhārī, vol. VII, 50.
2. Al-Bukhārī; also cf. Zad al Ma'ad vol. 4.4, p.7.
3. Al-Bukhārī, ch. 67:29.
4. Al-Bukhārī vol. VII, Hadith 36.
5. Al-Bukhārī vol. III, Hadith 44.

Chapter 10

Mahr (Dower)

No Marriage without Mahr

Mahr (dower) has been mentioned in the Holy Qur'ān[1] as an essential part of a Muslim marriage. It is given by the bridegroom to his bride in accorance with their mutual agreement. It may be of any value from a quarter of a *Dinār* to a thousand *Dinār* or more.[2] *Mahr* is not like the African custom of giving a bride-price since marriage in Islam is not sale of a girl to a husband. It also differs from the old European system of dowry in which the father used to give his daughter a heavy dowry at the time of her marriage which became the property of the husband, as if it was an inducement to him to marry the girl. The same is the practice among the Christians and Hindus in Kerala and other parts of India. The fathers are required to pay very heavy dowries to find suitable husbands for their daughters. In the Jāhiliyyah society of the Arabs, *Mahr* was considered as the property of the guardian of a girl. The amount of dowry varies according to the educational qualifications, professional standing, wealth and social status of the boy.

In Islam, on the other hand, *Mahr* is a marriage gift from the bridgroom to his bride and becomes her exclusive property. Islam has elevated the status of women as *Mahr* is given as a mark of respect for her.[3] Even if marriage ends in divorce *(al-Ṭalāq),* the dowry remains the wife's property and the husband has no right to take it back, except in the case of *Khul'* where the divorce takes place at the request of the wife in consideration of the return of the whole or part of the *Mahr* paid to her.

In other words, *Mahr* is a sum of money or other property promised by the husband to be paid or delivered to the wife in consideration of the marriage.

The other word generally used for *Mahr* in the Holy Qur'ān is *ajr* meaning reward, and a gift that is given to the bride. In fact, *ajr* is that in which there is gain but no loss. The word *ṣadaqa* is also used in the Holy Qur'ān to signify the nuptial gift. Another word used in the Holy Qur'ān to indicate the nuptial gift is *fariḍah*,[4] literally what has been made obligatory or an appointed portion. The word *mahr* is also used in Ḥadith to signify dowry, or the nuptial gift. According to the Holy Qur'ān, the *mahr* is given as a free gift by the husband to the wife, at the time of contracting the marriage: "And give women their dowries as a free gift."[5] The payment of the *mahr* on the part of the husband is an admission of the independence of the wife, for she becomes the owner of property immediately on her marriage, though before it she may not have owned anything. The settling of a dowry on the woman at the marriage is obligatory: "And lawful for you are all women besides these, provided that you seek them with your property, taking them in marriage not committing fornication. Then as to those whom you profit by (by marriage) give them their dowries as appointed."[6] In the case of a Muslim marrying a Christian or a Jewish woman: the Qur'ānic injunction is: "And the chaste from among the believing women and the chaste from among those who have given the Book before you, when you have given them their dowries, taking them in marriage."[7]

It would appear from this that the Holy Qur'ān renders the payment of *Mahr* necessary for a valid marriage. The Hadith of the Prophet also leads to the same conclusion.

Sayyidnā 'Umar the second Caliph, and Qāḍī Shuraiḥ have decreed that if a wife remits the whole of her *mahr* or a part of it but later on demands it, the husband shall be compelled to pay it because the very fact that she demands it is a clear proof that she did not remit it of her own free will.

When is Mahr to be paid?

The payment of *Mahr* is necessary even though it might be a very small sum.[8] In exceptional cases, marriage is legal though the amount of *mahr* has not been specified, but it is obligatory and must be paid afterwards. Thus the Holy Qur'ān says, speaking of divorce: "There is no blame on you if you divorce women when you have not touched them, or appointed for them a dowry."[9] This shows that marriage is not valid without specifying a dowry. Ḥadith also speaks of the validity of a marriage, even though dowry has not been named.[10] But the dowry must be paid, either at the time of the consummation of marriage or afterwards. The amount of dowry in this case would depend upon the circumstances of the husband and the position of the wife. The Holy Qur'ān makes this clear by requiring the provision for wife to depend upon the circumstances of the husband, "the wealthy according to his means and the straightened in circumstances according to his means."[11] In a hadith it is related that the case of a woman, whose husband died before fixing a dowry and consummating marriage, was referred to 'Abd-Allah Ibn Mas'ud, who decided that she should be paid a dowry according to the dowry of the women of like status with herself *(Kasadaqi nisaihā*), and this decision was afterwards found to be in accordance with the decsion of the Holy Prophet in a similar case.[12] In Fiqh, it is called *mahr mithl* (lit., the *mahr* of those like her, or her equals) or customary dower. It is determined by the *mahr* of her sisters and paternal aunts and uncles' daughters that is to say, with reference to the social position of her fathers' family. Therefore even if the dowry has not been specified at the marriage, it is to be determined and paid afterwards, and if it remains unpaid in the husband's lifetime, it is a charge, on his property after his death. The words of the Holy Qur'ān require its payment at marriage, barring exceptional cases when it may be determined or paid afterwards. The Māliki school follows this rule and renders payment necessary at marriage, while the Hanafi school treats it more or less as a debt.

Let us now examine the injunctions in the Holy Qur'ān about dower:

وَاتُوا النِّسَآء صَدُقَاتِهِنَّ نِحَلَةً فَإِنْ طِبْنَ لَكُمْ عَنْ شَىْءٍ مِنْهُ نَفْساً فَكُلُوهُ هَنِيئاً مَرِيْئاً».

"And give the women (on marriage) their dower as a free gift but if they, of their own good pleasure, remit any part of it to you, take it and enjoy it with right good cheer."[13]

These words make it obligatory upon a Muslim to give dower to the woman whom he takes as a wife. It also exhorts Muslims to marry women with the permission of their (women's) guardians and payment of their dowers:

«فَانْكِحُوهُنَّ بِإِذْنِ اهْلِهِنَّ وَاتُوهُنَّ اجُورَهُنَّ بِالمَعْرُوفِ...»

"Wed them with the leave of their owners, and give them their dowers, according to what is reasonable."[14]

From the foregoing it is clear that *mahr* can be either specified or unspecified. The specified *mahr* is the amount settled by the parties at the time of marriage or after the marriage is solemnized. In the case of a bridegroom who is a minor, his father would settle the amount of *mahr*. The specified *mahr* can be either prompt *(mu'ajjal)* or deferred *(muwajjal)*. When the mahr is *mu'ajjal* it is payable on demand. If it is the deferred *mahr* it is payable only at the dissolution of marriage either by death of the husband or when the wife is divorced. The unspecififed *mahr* is the *mahr* which is not settled at the time of marriage or immediately after the marriage and is fixed according to the social position of the wife's family *(mahr -mithl)*.

What is a reasonable amount of dower will depend on the relative position in life and social status of parties to marriage and differ from place to place, period to period and country to country. The Prophet (S.A.W.) has also said:

«ولا نكاح إلّا بولي وصداق وشاهدين عدل».

"And there is no marriage except with the permission of guardian and payment of dower and two reliable witnesses."

Thus it is clear that dower is an essential ingredient in Islamic marriage without which the contract is not complete. This Āyah refers to dower as *ṣadaqah*. It has its own significance. Since the word *ṣadaqah* also means charity, it is implied that dower is to be given as a free gift which becomes the property of the wife. Therefore she has full authority to give any portion of her dower to her husband or guardian.

Another verse in the Holy Qur'ān declared:

«وَإِنْ أَرَدْتُمُ اسْتِبْدَالَ زَوْجٍ مَكَانَ زَوْجٍ وَآتَيْتُمْ إِحْدَاهُنَّ قِنْطَاراً فَلَا تَأْخُذُوا مِنْهُ شَيْئاً أَتَأْخُذُونَهُ بُهْتَاناً وَإِثْماً مُبِيناً».

"But if ye decide to take a wife in place of another, even if ye had given the latter a whole treasure for a dower, take not the least bit of it back. Would ye take it by slander and a manifest wrong?"[15]

This verse makes it clear that dower belongs to the divorced woman, whatever its value. The husband is not entitled to take it by force or duress or through slander. Every husband should fear Allah and have *Taqwah* (piety) and refrain from usurping the rights of his former wife. The Qur'ān further emphasises:

«وَكَيْفَ تَأْخُذُونَهُ وَقَدْ أَفْضَى بَعْضُكُمْ إِلَى بَعْضٍ وَأَخَذْنَ مِنْكُمْ مِيثَاقاً غَلِيظاً».

"And how could ye take it when ye have gone in unto each other, and they have taken from you a solemn covenent?"[16]

It shows that the dower belongs to the woman and not her former husband. So if he tries to get it back through foul means of putting a calumny against her and slandering her, he earns the disapproval of the Holy Qur'ān. In another verse, the Holy Qur'ān declared:

«وَالْمُحْصَنَاتُ مِنَ النِّسَآءِ إِلاَّ مَا مَلَكَتْ ايْمَانُكُمْ كِتَابَ اللّهِ عَلَيْكُمْ وَأُحِلَّ لَكُمْ مَا وَرَآءَ ذٰلِكُمْ اَنْ تَبْتَغُوا بِأَمْوَالِكُمْ مُحْصِنِينَ غَيْرَ مُسَافِحِينَ فَمَا اسْتَمْتَعْتُمْ بِهِ مِنْهُنَّ فَآتُوهُنَّ اجُورَهُنَّ فَرِيضَةً وَلا جُنَاحَ عَلَيْكُمْ.....».

"Also (prohibited are) women already married, except those whom your right hands possess (i.e. captives in a *Jihād*). Thus hath Allah ordained (prohibitions) against you; except for those all others are lawful, provided ye seek (them in marriage) with gifts from your property, desiring chastity, not lust. Seeing that ye derive benefit from them, give them their dowries (at least as prescribed), but if, after a dower is prescribed, ye agree mutually (to vary it), there is no blame on you."[17]

It means that dower is obligatory and without it no Muslim marriage can take place. It further shows that dower is a means of reward or remuneration. When a man takes a woman in marriage, she surrenders her person to him. So a man should also surrender some of his property to her. Of course, the woman has a right to release her husband from dower or to change its amount after mutual understanding with him.

The Qur'ān makes payment of dower obligatory not only in marriage between Muslims but also in marriage of a Muslim to a woman who is *Kitābiyah* (belonging to the people of the Book, i.e., Jews or Christians.)

«والمحصنات من المؤمنات والمحصنات من الذين اوتوا الكتاب من قبلكم اذا اتيتموهن اجورهن محصنين غير مسفحين ولا متخذي اخدان».

"(Lawful unto you in marriage) are (not only) chaste women who are believers, but chaste women among the people of the Book, revealed before your time, when you give them their due dowers and desire chastity, not lewdness, nor secret intrigues."[18]

The Holy Qur'ān also says:

«لا جُنَاحَ عَلَيْكُمْ إِنْ طَلَّقْتُمُ النِّسَاءَ مَا لَمْ تَمَسُّوهُنَّ اوْ تَفْرِضُوا لَهُنَّ فَرِيضَةً وَمَتِّعُوهُنَّ عَلَى المُوسِعِ قَدَرُهُ وَعَلَى المُقْتِرِ قَدَرُهُ مَتَاعاً بِالمَعْرُوفِ حَقّاً عَلَى المُحْسِنِينَ».

"There is no blame on you if ye divorce women before consummation or the fixation of their dower. But bestow on them (a suitable gift). The wealthy man according to his means, and the poor according to his means. A gift of a reasonable amount is due from those who wish to do the right thing."[19]

It shows that if a Muslim divorces his wife before the marriage is consummated or before dower is fixed he is required to give a suitable amount to the divorced woman according to his own capacity. But if *ṣadāq* is fixed before marriage and divorce is given before the consummation of marriage, he shall have to pay one half of the fixed *ṣadāq* to her.[20]

No Fixed Amount for Mahr

Looking at the Sharīʻah of Islam governing rules about *Mahr*, no definite amount or a thing of a definite value is fixed as *Mahr*. The injunctions of the Qur'ān are silent on this issue. It is narrated by Amir bin Rabiah that a woman belonging to Banu Fazarah was married on a pair of shoes as her *Mahr*.

The Messenger of Allah asked her:

«أَرَضِيتِ عَنْ نَفْسِكِ وَمَالِكِ بِنَعْلَيْنِ؟ فقالتْ: نَعَمْ، فأَجَازَه»

"Are you happy with yourself with a pair of shoes? She said 'Yes'. The Prophet (S.A.W.) then permitted her to marry."[21]

Likewise, a woman came to the Prophet (S.A.W.) and said: "O Messenger of Allah, I wish to give myself to you". Then she stood for a long time waiting for an answer. Then a man stood up and said: "O Messenger of Allah, if you do not need her, get her married to me". The Prophet (S.A.W.) then asked him:

«هَلْ عِنْدَكَ مِنْ شَيْءٍ تُصَدِّقُهَا إِيَّاهُ»

"Do you possess something that you can give as sadaq?" He replied that he had only a pair of trousers, which if given to her, he will be without one. He was asked to give even if he had an iron ring. Since he had none, the Prophet asked:

«هل معك من القرآن شيء»؟

"Do you have anything from the Holy Qur'ān?" He said: 'Yes', and enumerated the *Surahs* that he remembered. The Prophet then said:

«زوجتك بما معك من القرآن»؟

"I declare you two married with what you possess from the Qur'ān."[22]

In this case, the chapters or portions of the Qur'ān that the man remembered were considered as his *Mahr*. But Ḥadīth must be properly understood. It does not negate the minimum *Mahr* fixed by Imām Abū

Ḥanīfah or Imām Mālik. Ibn al-Qyim has explained this Ḥadīth that the *Mahr* is the right of a woman, and the pious lady mentioned in the above Ḥadīth was satisfied with the man who was at least knowledgeable in the Qur'ān.

«وهذا احب اليها من المال الذي يبذله الزوج فان الصداق شرع في الأصل حقاً للمرأة تنتفع به، فاذا رضيت بالعلم والدين، واسلام الزوج، وقراءته القرآن كان هذا من افضل المهور وانفعها».

"And this was dearer to her than proper ty given by her husband, because *Ṣadāq* in reality is meant for a woman to benefit her. If she became happy with knowledge and religion and Islam of her husband his recitation of the Qur'ān, this was the best *Mahr* and most beneficial to her."[23]

As for giving a large *Mahr*, there is absolutely no harm. Once Caliph 'Umar delcared that no one should increase *Mahr* more than 400 dirhams. When he descended, a Quriashite lady asked him: "Have you not heard Allah's injunctions?"

'Umar went back to the pulpit and declared: «واتيتم احداهن قنطارا»

«إني كنت قد نهيتكم أن تزيدوا في صدقاتهن على أربعمائة درهم، فمن شاء أن يعطي من ماله ما أحب».

"I was asking you not to give more than 400 dirhams as *Mahr*. Whosoever wishes may give as much property as one wishes to give."[24]

The husband however, has no right to demand back anything of the dowry given to the wife in consideration for the marriage or ornaments, clothes, etc., given to her as gifts. It is utterly against the moral principles of Islam to ask for the return of anything given to another as a present or gift.[25] The Holy Prophet likens this disgraceful behaviour to the licking up of his own vomit by the dog. It is indeed shameful on the part of a husband to keep back or demand, after the divorce, what he himself gave to his wife. As a matter of fact Islam exhorts the husband to give her something at her departure.[26]

Other Conditions in Respect of Mahr

The payment of Mahr should be in the form of something that has a value even though it may be small or very valuable. According to the Ḥanafī school the smallest amount of *mahr* is 10 dirhams but according to Mālikī schools the least *mahr* is equivalent to 3 dirhams. However, there is no fixed minimum in the Shāfi'ī and Ḥanbalī schools as well as among the Shi'ites. If one gets married on the dower in terms of a quantity of wine or pigs or anything that is unlawful in Islam which cannot be owned or bought or sold by a Muslim, the marriage is null and void. All the Jurists of the four schools agree upon this view. The Māliki school insists that half of the *mahr* should be given on the spot for the consummation of a valid marriage. *Mahr* can be given promptly on marriage or can be postponed until after the marriage. The Hanafi's point of view is that the payment of dower can be delayed, either part of it is delayed or the whole of it, but it must not be forgotten completely or the proposal for giving the *mahr* should not be made in an ambiguous way, saying: I marry you for £100 to be paid when the clouds come, or when the sky falls rain, or a traveller arrives etc. The Mālikīs say that the *mahr* may be a definite thing like a known animal, by looking at it or by describing it like this horse or a particular kind of horse like the Arabia horse, or it may be a definite amount of money as mentioned earlier. Even if the dower is not prompt it should not be delayed through a flimsy promise like "to be postponed until death or until our separation." According to the Shāfi'ī and Ḥanbalī school it is lawful if the entire *mahr* is paid later as long as it is not forgotten completely. Once the amount of *mahr* is fixed and it is ready in hand, the payment should not be delayed. According to the Mālikīs it may be given to the wife on the day of marriage except when the woman herself wants to take it later. The *mahr* should not be postponed simply because of the sickness of the wife. The Maliki school views that if it is fixed that half of the dower be paid promptly and half later on with the specific words that "I marry you on £50 to be paid promptly and the remaining £50 later on." It is necessary in this condition to pay her the amount before consummation. According to the Shāfi'ī school the wife can refuse consummation by the husband if the *mahr*, once agreed to be paid completely, is not paid. If the husband did not pay the *mahr* or maintenance to the wife, the wife can take action to annul the marriage. The Shāfi'ī jurists say that if the husband is unable to pay the *mahr*, as agreed, then it is up to the wife either to be patient or she may take the matter to the Qāḍī to annul the marriage.

No limits have been placed on the amount of *mahr*. The words used in the Holy Qur'ān show that any amount of dowry may be settled on the wife:

"-and you have given one of them a heap of gold."[27] Thus no maximum or minimum amount has been laid down. The Holy Prophet paid varying amounts to his wives; in one case when the Negus paid the amount to Umm Ḥabība (Abū Sufyān's daughter), who was by then in Abbyssinia, where the marriage took place, it being four thousand dirhams, while in the case of the other wives it was generally five hundred dirhams.[28] The *mahr* of his daughter Fatimah was four hundred dirhams. The lowest amount mentioned in Hadith is a ring of iron,[29] and a man who could not procure even that, was told to teach the Holy Qur'ān to his wife.[30] In some Hadith two handfuls of meal or dates are also mentioned.[31] The amount of dowry may however be increased or decreased by the mutual consent of the husband and wife, at any time after marriage; and this is plainly laid down in the Holy Qur'ān: "Then as to those whom you profit by (by marrying), give them their dowries as appointed; and there is no blame on you about what you mutually agreed after what is appointed of dowry."[32] The wife is the owner of *Mahr* and hence she may remit the dower wholly or partially. The remission of the *Mahr* in the terminology of *Fiqh* is called *Hibat al-Mah r*.

In the Ḥanafī school, however, if the dower has been specified *(al-Mahr al-Musammā)* then the question arises whether it is to be given promptly *(Mu'ajjal)* or is it to be deferred or delayed *(Mu'ajjal)*. *Mu'ajjal* or prompt *Mahr* is to be paid immediately after marriage if demanded by the wife. If it is agreed that it is *Mua'jjal* or delayed or deferred, it becomes payable on the dissolution of marriage or when some ugly event takes place rocking the happy family ties. When *Mahr* is fixed *Musammā)*, it may be split into two equal parts and it may be stipulated that one part shall be paid immediately on demand from the wife and the other part will be paid on the death of the husband or divorce or the happning of some special event.

---

1. Qur'ān, 4:4.
2. In Nigeria, the Jama'at Naṣril Islām has recently agreed upon the minimum amount of *Mahr* to be not less than five Naira since the cost of living has gone high and the purchasing power of five Naira today is not more than ¼ Dinar in the Prophet's time.
3. Sayyid Sābiq, *Fiqh al-Sunnah*, op. cit. vol. 7, p. 58.
4. Qur'ān, ch. 4:4
5. Ibid.
6. Qur'ān, ch. 2:24.
7. Qur'ān, ch. 5:5.
8. Bukhārī, ch. 678 Ḥadīth 51 and 52.
9. Qur'ān, ch. 2:236.
10. Abū Dāūd, ch. 12 Ḥadīth 31.
11. Qur'ān, ch. 2:236.
12. See Abū Dāūd, ch. 12, Ḥadīth 31.
13. Qur'ān, 4:4.
14. Qur'ān, 4:20.
15. Qur'ān, 4:20.
16. Qur'ān, 4:21.
17. Qur'ān, 4:24.

18. Qur'ān, 5:6.
19. Qur'ān, 2:236.
20. Qur'ān, 2:237.
21. Narrated by Ahmad, Ibn Mājah and Thirmidhī.
22. Bukhari and Muslim.
23. Quoted by Sayyid Sābiq, *Fiqh al-Sunnah*, op. cit., vol. 7 p. 63.
24. Narrated by Said bin Manṣūr and Abū Ya'lā.
25. Cf. Qur'ān, ch. 2:229.
26. Cf. Qur'ān, ch. 2:241.
27. Qur'ān, ch. 4:20.
28. Abū Dāūd, ch. 12, Ḥadīth 28.
29. Bukhārī, ch. 67, Ḥadīth 52.
30. Ibid, ch. 67, Ḥadīth 51.
31. Cf. Abū Dāūd, ch. 12, Ḥadīth 29.
32. Qur'ān, ch. 4:24.

Chapter 11

Ṭalāq: Divorce in Sharī'ah

There are times in a man's life when it becomes impossible to continue with cordial relationship with his wife and vice versa. It is a part of human nature that in spite of all his achievements and scientific progress his human frailties become apparent.

Satan, being an open enemy of man, comes to play his role at the height of glory of human civilisation. At times good preaching and wise counsel also do not work. It is in such times when marriage becomes impossible to work, it is better to separate amicably rather than drag on indefinitely, making the family-home a hell. In such circumstances the immediate victims are the children of such a family unit. In Islam marriage is a contract and the contract should be made to work but not when it becomes humanly impossible. It is only in such unavoidable circumstances that divorce is permitted in Sharī'ah. When such circumstances arise, one must still keep in mind that through marriage, she has taken from him a solemn covenant *(mīthāq)*:

«واخذن منكم ميثاقاً غليظاً».

"And they have taken from you a solemn covenant".[1]

Ṭalāq literally means to set an animal free. It is used in the Sharī'ah to denote the legal method whereby a marriage is brought to an end. Although Islam allows divorce if there are sufficient grounds for it yet the right is to be exercised only under exceptional circumstances. The Prophet (S.A.W.) has said:

«ابغض الحلال عند الله عزوجل الطلاق»

"Of all things which have been permitted, divorce is the most hated by Allah".[2] These words will always act as a strong check on the hasty recourse to and wanton absue of the permissibility of divorce. In yet another Hadith, the Prophet has said: "Marry and do not divorce; undoubtedly the throne of the Beneficient Lord shakes due to divorce."[3]

The aim of the Sharī'ah is to establish a healthy family unit through marriage, but if for some reasons this purpose fails, there is no need to linger on under false hopes as is the practice among the adherents of some other religions where divorce is not permitted. Islam encourages reconciliation between spouses rather than severance of their relations. But where good relations between spouses become distinctly impossible, Islam does not keep them tied in a loathsome chain to a painful and agonising position. It then permits divorce. This is made clear by the Holy Qur'ān. As soon as differences between spouses take a serious turn to endanger their contract, it ordains that arbiters be appointed to sort out these differences and bring about reconciliation between them, it says:

«وَإِنْ خِفْتُمْ شِقَاقَ بَيْنِهِمَا فَابْعَثُوا حَكَماً مِنْ اهْلِهِ وَحَكَماً مِنْ اهْلِهَا إِنْ يُرِيدَآ اصْلَاحاً يُوَفِقِ اللّهُ بَيْنَهُمَا انَّ اللّهَ كَانَ عَلِيماً خَبِيراً».

"If you fear a break between them two, appoint, (TWO) arbiters, one from his family, and the other from hers; if they wish for peace, Allah will cause them reconciliation: for Allah has full knowledge and is acquainted with all things."[4]

In case the arbitrators[5] fail to effect a repproachment between the spouses, the Qur'ān permits such spouses to part company.
It says:

«وَإِنْ يَتَفَرَّقَا يُغْنِ اللّهُ كُلاًّ مِنْ سَعَتِهِ وَكَانَ اللّهُ وَاسِعاً حَكِيماً».

"But if they disagree and must part, Allah will provide abundance for all from His all-reaching bounty: For Allah is he who cares for all and is wise."[6]

If the stage of parting has been reached, the Qur'ān enjoins upon husbands not to misuse or abuse their power position and leave the wife hanging but rather to dispose of the matter one way or the other.

«وَلَنْ تَسْتَطِيعُوآ انْ تَعْدِلُوا بَيْنَ النِّسَآءِ وَلَوْ حَرَصْتُمْ فَلا تَمِيلُوا كُلَّ المَيْلِ فَتَذَرُوهَا كَالمُعَلَّقَةِ وَإِنْ تُصْلِحُوا وَتَتَّقُوا فَإِنَّ اللّهَ كَانَ غَفُوراً رَحِيماً».

"You are never able to be fair and just between women, even if it is your ardent desire: but turn not away (from your wife) altogether, so as to leave hr (as it were) hanging (in the air). If you come to a friendly understanding, and practice self-restraint, Allah is oft-forgiving, Most Merciful."[7]

In order to put an end to all uncertainties the Qur'ān has laid down:

«لِلَّذِينَ يُؤْلُونَ مِنْ نِسَآئِهِمْ تَرَبُّصُ أَرْبَعَةِ أَشْهُرٍ ـ فَإِنْ فَآؤُا فَإِنَّ اللّهَ غَفُورٌ رَحِيمٌ. وَإِنْ عَزَمُوا الطَّلَاقَ فَإِنَّ اللّهَ سَمِيعٌ عَلِيمٌ».

"For those who take oath for abstention from their wives, a waiting for four months is ordained; if they return then, Allah is oft-forgiving, Most Merciful. But if their intention is firm for divorce, Allah hears and knows all."[8]

On the basis of these Qur'ānic injunctions and the guidance from the Sunnah of the Prophet, the jurists of the four schools of Islamic Jurisprudence have given clarifications on divorce. *Sharḥ al-Kabīr*[9] has given the following five categories of divorce:

1. Divorce becomes Wājib (most essential) in the case of *Ṭalāq al-Hukmain* in *Shiqāq*.
2. Divorce is *makrūh* (disapproved) when it is not essential. If there is no harm anticipated either to one's self or one's wife, and there is still some hope of reconciliation, which based on the Hadith: "Most hated among things permitted by Allah is divorce".
3. It is *Mubāḥ* when there is a need for it, particularly when wife's character is bad *(sū'khulq al-mar'ah)* and thus some harm is expected through the continued marriage.
4. It is *Mandūb* when the wife is not fulfilling the essential rights of Allah imposed on her, or if she happens to be unchaste.
5. It is *Mahzūr* when it is given during the days of her monthly periods.

In *Mughnī al-Muhtāj*,[10] all the first four categories of divorce are mentioned, but the fifth category is *Ḥarām* (unlawful), and it is the divorce of innovation *(Ṭalāq al-Bidī)* Imām al-Nawawī has mentioned only four kinds of divorce. They are *Haram, Makrūh, Wājib* and *Mandūb* as mentioned in his *Sharḥ* on *Ṣaḥiḥ al-Muslim.*[11] According to him, there is no divorce which can be called *Mubah.*

The Mālikī Jurist al-Dardīr also agrees with the above view in his famous commentary of *Al-Mukhataṣar* of Khalīl.[12]

Faskh: Annulment or Abrogation of Marriage

Like divorce, *Faskh* also brings an end to marriage. It literally means 'to annul a deed' or rescind a bargain? It is decreed by the *Qāḍī* after the careful consideration of an application made to him by the wife. The *Qāḍī* if satisfied that the woman is prejudiced by a marriage, he will annul the marriage. The conditions governing *Ṭalāq* (divorce) and *Faskh* are given details by jurists of the four schools of Islamic Law.

It is *Ṭalāq* in the following cases according to the Ḥanafi School:[13]

a) Pronouncements of divorce by husband
b) Ilā'
c) Khul'
d) Li'ān: Mutual Impercation
e) Separation because of sexual defect *('aib Jinsī)* in the husband
f) Separation due to denial *(Ibā)* by the husband of Islam.

It will be *Faskh* in the following cases according to the Ḥanafī Schools:

a) Separation due to apostacy of the spouses
b) Separation to spoiling *(fasād)* of marriage
c) Separation due to lack of equality of status *(kafā')* or lack of compatability of the husband.

It will be *Ṭalāq* according to the Shafi'i and the Hanbali Schools:[14]

a) Pronouncement of *Ṭalāq* by the husband
b) *Khul'*
c) Declaration of *ṭalāq* by the Qāḍī of the husband's refusal to give divorce because of *Ilā'*.

It will be *Faskh* according to the Shāfi'ī and Ḥanbalī Schools:

a) Separation due to defect in one of the spouses
b) Separation due to difficulties *(isar)* of the husband
c) Separation due to *Li'ān*
d) Separation due to apostacy of one of the spouses
e) Separation due to spoiling of marriage
f) Separation due to lack of equality of status *(kafā')* of the husband

It will be *Ṭalāq* according to the Mālikī School[15] in the following cases:

a) Pronouncement of *Ṭalāq* by the husband
b) *Kuhl'*
c) Separation due to defect in one of the spouses
d) Separation due to difficulties *(Isār)* of the husband from providing maintenance to his wife
e) Separation due to ḥarm *(ḍarar)*
f) Separation due to *Ilā'*

g) Separation due to lack of compatability or equality of status *(kafā)*'

It will be *Faskh* in the following cases:

a) Separation due to the process of *Li'ān*
b) Separation due to spoiling of marriage *(Fasād)*
c) Separation due to the denial of Islam by one of the spouses

Shiqaq: Breach of Marriage Agreement

Thus the *shiqaq* or breach of marriage agreement may arise from the conduct of either party as we have already enumerated. If either of the married partners misconducts himself or herself, or either of them is consistently cruel to the other, or, as may sometimes happen, they cannot live together in marital agreement. The *shiqāq* in these cases is more express, but still will depend upon the parties whether they can pull on or not. Divorce must always follow when one of the parties finds it impossible to continue the marriage agreement and is compelled to break it off.

There may also arise cases in which the husband is imprisoned for life, or for a long period, or if he is absent and no news can be heard of him, or he is maimed for life and is unable to provide maintenance for his wife, it will be a case of *shiqaq* if the wife wants a divorce, but if she does not, the marriage will remain. In case the husband is aggrieved in a similar manner, he has the option of taking another wife.

If either of the couple, apostalized, the marriage shall be judicially dissolved by a divorce. But according to the view of other jurists, such a marriage is to be dissolved without a divorce. If a non-Muslim couple embraced Islam, their marriage shall continue to subsist. But if only one of them accepted Islam such a marriage is to be dissolved without a divorce. If it is the wife who embraced Islam, and the marriage is subsequently so dissolved, and she started to observe the idda; now, if the husband followed suit during the idda, then the husband will have first claim to her. If the husband accepts Islam, while the woman is either a Jew or a Christian, he has the permission to retain her. But if, the husband accepts Islam while the woman was a Magian and she, also immediately accepts Islam after him; they can then continue as husband and wife; but if she did not accept Islam, immediately, then they are separated.[16]

Procedure of Divorce

There is a laid down procedure of divorce in Shari'ah such as to encourage reconciliation wherever possible. But if all the efforts to reconcile and establish good relationship between the two life partners fails, and the husband and wife consider it impossible to live together any longer, there is no loathsome chain to keep them together by force. They may separate in peace and each of them may seek fulfillment with somebody else with a new marriage relationship. Marriage is thus to be understood as a mere contract in Islam and should be made to work as long as love and respect for each other lasts. The aim of the Sharī'ah is to establish a healthy family unit through marriage, but if this purpose fails, there is no need to linger on under pretence as is the practice among the adherents of some other religions where divorce is not permitted and a vow is taken at the marriage ceremony that they will not break the marriage promise "until death do us part".

It is un-Islamic and unethical to leave one's life hanging in the air. The Qur'ān says:

«وَلنْ تَسْتَطِيعُـوآ انْ تَعْـدِلـوا بَيْنَ النِسَـآءِ وَلـوْ حَرَصْتُمْ فَلا تَمِيلوا كُلَّ المَيْـلِ فَتَذَرُوهَا كَالمُعَلَّقَةِ وَإِنْ تُصْلِحُوا وَتَتَّقُوا فَإِنَّ اللّهَ كَانَ غَفُوراً رَحِيماً».

"You are never able to be fair and just between women, even if it is your ardent desire: but not away (from your wife) altogether, so as to leave her (as it were) hanging (in the air). If you come to a friendly understanding, and practice self-restraint, Allah is oft-forgiving, Most Merciful."[17]

If there remains no chance for any compromise then divorce is only the last resort.

«وَإِنْ يَتَفَرَّقَا يُغْنِ اللَّهُ كُلّاً مِنْ سَعَتِهِ وَكَانَ اللّهُ وَاسِعاً حَكِيماً».

"But if they disagree and must part, Allah will provide abundance for all from his all-reaching bounty: for Allah is He who cares for all and is wise."[18]

In other words, the *Sharī'ah* only permits to divorce one's wife or wives under definite conditions. Muslims can only divorce their wives in three distinct and separate periods within which they might endeavour to become reconciled; but should all attempts at reconciliation prove unsuccessful, then in the third period the final separation becomes effective.[19]

Divorce may be given orally, or in writing, but it must take place in the presence of witnesses as we are told in the Qur'ān that when they have reached their prescribed time, then either retain them with kindness or separate them with kindness, and call to witness two men of justice from among you, and give upright testimony for Allah.[20] Whatever the actual words used for divorce, they must expressly convey the *intention* that the marriage tie is being dissolved. As to whether a divorce would be effective under certain circumstances, there are differences among the jurists or different schools. Evidently intention is as necessary a factor in the dissolution of marriage as in the marriage itself, but wh ile some recognise that divorce is ineffective if given under compulsion or influence, or in a state of intoxication, or in anger or jest, or by mistake or inadvertance, others hold it to be ineffective in some of these case and effective in others. The Ḥanafi school views that the divorce becomes effective whether the words be uttered in sport or jest or in a state of drunkeness and whether a person utters them willingly or under compulsion, but Imam Shafi'i says that divorce in such circumstances does not become effective.

When is the Ṭalāq Valid?

If one, due to extreme circumstances, has to pronounce divorce, the following conditions must be satisfied for a divorce to be valid:

1. He should be sane *('Āqil)*
2. He should not be a minor *(Bāliqh)*
3. He should have his own discretion *(Mukhtār)*

If a divorce is given by an insane person or a child, it will not be considered a valid *ṭalāq*. Abū Hurairah has narrated the following Hadith from the Prophet:

«كل طلاق جائز إلّا طلاق المغلوب على عقلـه».

"All divorce is lawful except the divorce given by a person whose intellect is overpowered."

If a divorce is given without an intention or choice, that is through duress, it will not be valid according to Imām Mālik, Imām Shāfi'ī, Imām Aḥmad bin Hanbal, 'Abdallah bin 'Abbās and others, but Imām Abū Ḥanīfah considers it to be valid.

If divorce is given by an intoxicated prson, it will not be valid according to all the schools of Islamic Law. If the *ṭalāq* is given in anger, it will be considered unintentional and therefore not valid as narrated in a Ḥadith, Imam Aḥmad, Abū Dā'ūd, Ibn Mājah and al-Ḥākim. Similarly, divorce given through mistake will not be binding according to all the jurists. There will be no divorce before marriage. The triple divorce pronounced at one and the same time, or when a wife is menstruating or in *afās* after child-birth, is a divorce of innovation and is *ḥarām* (unlawful) according to all the jurists.[21] This is the view of Abdallāh bin 'Umar, Sa'īd bin al-Musayyib and Ṭā'ūs.[22] The divorce given to a pregnant woman will be binding according to all jurists except the Ḥanafis.[23]

'Aḥsan' Form of Ṭalāq: A Check on Separation

Of the several forms of divorce recognised in Sharī'ah the one that bears the impress of the Holy Prophet's sanction and approval is the *'Aḥsan'* type of *'Ṭalāq'*.[24] This form of repudiation involves the following conditions, each of which is really intended to prevent a permanent breach:

a) The husband, in the first place, must pronounce only one *Ṭalāq* (repudiation), the object of this limitation is that he may subsequently, when better sense prevails, revoke the repudiation – if he has pronounced *Ṭalāq* from caprice or in a moment of excitement within the period of the wife's Iddah which begins after the pronouncement of divorce.

b) The *Ṭalāq* if necessary, is to be pronounced when the wife is in a state of purity *(Ṭuhur)* and there is no bar to sexual intercourse. It is declared unlawful to pronounce repudiation when she is in menses.

c) The husband mut abstain from intercourse with his wife after pronouncing *Ṭalāq* for the period of three months, the period of her'iddah.[25]

There is a tradition of accepted authenticity that throws considerable light on the wisdom of underlying the last two restrictions.'Abdullāh bin 'Umar divorced his wife while she was in her menses; and the matter was reported to the Prophet who, much exasperated at the levity of his conduct, said: "Let him take her back and retain her till she becomes pure and again have her courses and again gets pure. Then, if he thinks it prudent, let him divorce her, but he should do so when she is clean and has not been approached; and this is the period of *'Iddah* which Allah has ordered for divorce."

Some learned commentators observe in connection with this tradition that the purpose of this condition is, to avoid rash and hasty procedure on the part of the husband, through aversion arising from the wife's impurity, and, by fixing a long period of abstinence to give him opportunities to reconsider his decision about the divorce, so that perhaps he may repent, and exercise the right of return before the expiry of the period of *'iddah.*

During this period of retreat, the marriage subsists between the parties, and the husband retains his marital authority over his wife. He may, therefore, have access to the wife even without her permission, and can treat her as his wife, but this would actually amount to his exercising the right of *Rajāh* (return). During the *'iddah*, the husband is under an obligation to lodge the wife in his house in a separate apartment, and maintain her. The injunctions of the Qur'ān are quite clear on this point. "O Prophet, when ye divorce women, divorce them at their appointed time, and compute the term exactly, and fear Allah your Lord. Oblige them not to go out of their apartment nor allow them to depart, unless they be guilty of manifest lewdness."[26]

"House the divorced, as you house yourselves, according to your means, and distress them not, by reducing them to straits. And if they are pregnant, then bear charges for them, till they are delivered of their burden; and they suckle your children, then pay them their remuneration; consult among yourselves, and act generously."[27]

If, the husband has pronounced one, or even two *Ṭalāq*, and if within the prescribed period, he abstains from intercourse with his wife, and does not exercise the right of *Rajāh* (return) on the divorced wife, he loses the power of recantation at the expiration of the term, and complete cessation of the marital rights and duties takes place. A fresh marriage will be necessary for the parties to re-unite.[28]

Jurists however, differ in the interpretation of the above quoted verses of *Rajāh*. The Ḥanafī jurists are of the opinion that the husband retains the right of renunion up to the time of the purification of the wife by a bath after the third monthly course. The same is the opinion of Sayyidna Abū Bakar, Sayyidnā, 'Ali, 'Abdallāh bin Abbās, Abu Mūsā al-Ash'ari, 'Abdallāh bin Mas'ūd and some other *Ṣaḥabah*. The jurists of Māliki and Shāfi'i schools, however, are of the opinion that the husband forfeits the right of reunion as soon as the wife has a discharge of the third monthly course. This opinion is based on our Lady 'Aishah, 'Abdallāh bin 'Umar and the companion Zaid bin Thābit. It is a unanimous view of all jurists based on the Qur'ān that the husband retains the right of *Rajah* or reunion only when he has pronounced one divorce or two divorces, but he forfeits the right of reunion when he pronounced three divorces.

Furthermore, if the husband has divorced his wife three times, it will not be lawful for him to have relations with the wife unless she marries another husband and this second marriage is consummated and then she is divorced again. A triple divorce (i.e. three divorces at one and the same time) is regarded as an undesirable innovation *(Bidāh)*. If pronounced, however, it shall remain binding upon the husband. The lawful divorce decreed by the Sharī'ah is for the husband to divorce his wife when she is free from menstruation, and without having any relation with her after her previous menstruation; and the pronouncement shall be once only. Having done that, the husband must desist from pronouncing another divorce until the period of her retirement '*iddah*' expires.[29]

A husband has the right to take back his wife, who still menstruates, as long as she has not yet entered her third menstruation in the course of the '*iddah* retirement; – third in the case of a free woman, and second menstruation in the case of a slave woman.[30]

Divorce is of two types: *Ṭalāq al-Rajʿī* and *Ṭalāq al-Bā'in*. The first two pronouncements of divorce followed by the periods of retreat from the wife with whom marriage is consumated are called *Ṭalāq al-Rajʿī* in which return to the conjugal relationship is still possible. When the third divorce is pronounced it becomes *Ṭalāq al-Bā'in*.

Ṭalāq al-Rajʿī is based on the following Qur'ānic injunctions:

«الطَّلاقُ مَرَّتَانِ فَإمْسَاكٌ بِمَعْرُوفٍ اوْ تَسْرِيحٌ بِإحْسَانٍ....».

"A divorce is only permissible twice: After that the party should either hold together on equitable terms or separate with kindness."

This is a safety measure provided in the matrimonial relationship. Where divorce for mutual incompatability is allowed there always remains a danger that the parties might act hastily then repent and reconcile and then again wish to separate. To prevent a repetition of such capricious actions, this limit is prescribed by the Holy Qur'ān. Divorce with the possiblity of reconciliation is allowed only for two occasions. After that the parties must definitely make up their minds either to dissolve their marriage permanently or to live honourably together in mutual love and forebearance; neither party worrying the other nor grudging nor evading duties and responsibilities of marriage.[31]

In the *Ṭalāq al-Rajʿī* the spouses can still enjoy the usual benefit from each other since the marital relationship has not disappeared. If one of them dies, the other will inherit from him or her; as the case may be. Maintenance will still remain available to the wife and children. The *Rajah* or the return is the right of the husband. The Qur'ān says:

«وَبُعُولَتُهُنَّ احَقُّ بِرَدِّهِنَّ فِي ذلِكَ إنْ ارَادُوآ اصْلاحـاً».

"And the husband has the better right to take them back in that period if they wish for reconciliation."[32]

It will suffice just to utter the words like "I take you back" or the return can be effected through action like resuming sexual relation, or kissing each other. According to Imām Shāfiʿī the return cannot be possible except by uttering a specific word. According to Imām Mālik it is not permissible to be in privacy with the divorced wife or to have sexual relationship with her without her permission; but there is no harm in eating with her.

Ṭalāq al-Bā'in is divorced with three pronouncements or divorce before the consumation of marriage. There is no possibility of return to the conjugal relationship when the three divorces are completed. There are two kinds of *Ṭalāq al-Bā'in: Baynūnah Ṣughrā* and *Baynūnah Kubrā*. The *Baynūnah Ṣughrā* decreases the conjugal rights of the husband. In the event of the death of one of the parties, the other will not inherit from him or her as the case may be. While in *Baynūnah Kubra* all the conjugal rights cease. The former husband cannot even re-marry the former wife unless she marries another man and he voluntarily divorces her without any intention of *Taḥlīl.*

A Severe Restriction on Frequency of Ṭalāq

One can understand that the very spirit of the prescribed form of *Ṭalāq* is geared towards a revocation *(Rajah)* of the divorce and a reconciliation between the parties concerned. If, however, the parties fail to take advantage of the prescribed interim measures, and are determined to break from each other, the husband may pronounce the *Ṭalāq* for the third time and thus dissolve the marriage definitely. The divorced wife is forthwith rendered unlawful to him, and he cannot re-marry her, unless the wife marries first another person by a valid and binding contract, is divorced by this person, after a bona fide consummation of marriage, and completes the period of *'iddah* consequent upon such repudiation.[33]

This severe condition, has been the subject of much comment particularly by non-Muslim critics who forget that the very existence of such a condition demonstrates most strongly that the principles of Islam are entirely opposed to the alleged facility or ease in giving divorce. The object of laying down such a strict rule, was to prevent a definite dissolution of marriage, by appealing to the sense of honour of the people.

This rule restrains the frequency of divorce among Muslims. The condition is a very wise one, as it renders separation more rare, by imposing a check on its frequent practice among the Hebrews and the Heathen Arabs in the Jāhiliyyah Society. The check was intended to control a jealous, sensitive, but half cultured race, (the Jāhiliyyah Arabs) by appealing to their sense of honour.

Ṭalāq Ḥasan:

In this form, *ṭalāq* is pronounced as follows:

a) Three successive pronouncements of divorce are made.

b) They are made during three consecutive periods of *Ṭuhur* (purity).
c) There is no intercourse during any of the three periods of purity.
d) It remains revocable until the third, final pronouncement of divorce is made. On pronouncement of the final formula the divorce becomes irrevocable.

Ṭalāq al-Bid'ah: Innovated Divorce

Many years after the death of the Prophet (S.A.W.) a new form of divorce made its appearance as an innovation *(Bid'ah)*. In this form, *ṭalāq* becomes irrevocable as soon as it is pronounced. It happens this way: the husband utters the formula "I divorce you. I divorce you; I divorce you!!" in one sitting or conveys it to the wife in writing. This form of divorce leaves no room for reconsideration and no chance for repentance. This is usually done by ignorant Muslims to satisfy their selfish motives. When these ignorant people pronounce divorce thrice at one and the same sitting, they commit a henious sin against the precepts of the Sharī'ah. The Holy Prophet has very severely denounced this practice and Sayyidnā 'Umar used to whip the husband who pronounced divorce thrice at one and the same sitting.

In the event of a final divorce, the Sharī'ah laws are very particular in providing for the protection of the wife's property against the avarice of the husband. If the divorce is due to a cause imputable to the husband, he has to make over to her all property, and pay off the *Mahr* that has been settled upon her. If, however, the divorce has been resorted to at the instance of the wife, without any justifiable cause, she has simply to abandon her claim to the dower. "The wife thus occupies", observes Syed Ameer 'Alī, "a decidedly more advantageous position than the husband" in the Shari'ah.

At this juncture, it will be appropriate to look at the method of divorce that existed before the advent of Islam in order to understand the extent of reforms introduced by Kitāb-Allāh and the Sunnah of the Prophet.

The Method of Divorce Before the Advent of Islam

Divorce was practised in the pre-Islamic world, but the form and the method of divorce were inhuman. Whenever a man became angry, whether on account of valid reasons or just to show his dislike and hatred to the woman, she had no recourse to any legal procedure nor could she get any alimony or maintenance or any other kind of right from him.

Even when the Greeks were at the height of their glory of civilisation, their form of divorce was not guided by any rules and regulations or conditions and restrictions. Divorce had become a part of their matrimonial life, and even if the two parties vowed to a condition at the time of marriage not to separate from each other, the Judge will still grant them divorce if the matter was taken to the Court. The Romans on the other hand, looked upon divorce as an impossibility after a religious wedding rites were performed but the husband was given limitless rights over the wife up to the extent that in some cases after quarrelling with each other the husband used to murder his wife in order to get rid of her as there was no recourse to any legal action to separate according to their religious law. Later on, divorce was introduced among the Romans.

The Jewish religion improved upon the existing horrible conditions and legalised divorce but still men had immense powers to divorce his wife. He could easily get rid of his wife by levelling a flimsy charge of irreligiousity on her. Even if the husband intended to compromise, still he was bound by the religious code to divorce underground. Besides, according to their law if a woman had not given birth to a child after ten years of marriage, it was essential for the husband to divorce her.

According to the ancient Hebraic Law, a husband could divorce his wife for any cause which made her disagreeable to him and there were few or no checks to the arbitrary and capricious use of his power.

Women, however, were not allowed to demand divorce from their husbands for any reason whatsoever under that law.

Among the Athenians, the husband's right to repudiate his wife was as unlimited as among the ancient Israelites.

Among the Romans, divorce was recognised from the earliest times. The Laws of the Twelve Tables admitted divorce. In addition, a Roman had the power of summarily putting his wife to death for acts like drinking, poisoning and a substitution of a spurious child, but the wife had no right to sue for a divorce and, if she solicited separation, her temerity made her liable to punishment. In the later Republic, the facility and frequency of divorce could not contribute to happiness and virtue; and in fact, it tended to destroy all mutual confidence and to exaggerate every trifling dispute. Gibbon says: "In three centuries of prosperity and corruption, this principle of free divorce was enlarged to frequent practice and pernicious abuse. Passion, interest, or caprice suggested daily motives for dissolution of marriage; a word, a sign, a message, a letter, the mandate of a freedom, declared the separation; the most tender of human connections was degraded to a transient society of profit or pleasure".

Christianity has a unique system of divorce. It opposed the Jewish religion and declared divorce as unlawful, mainly attributed to the teachings of Jesus Christ. It went so far as declaring unalwful the second marriage by the person who divorced his wife as well as the woman who was divorced by him earlier.

It was said also in Matthew 5:31, 32: "It hath been said, whosoever shall put away his wife, let him give her a writing of divorcement: But I say unto you, that whosoever shall put away his wife, saving for the cause of fornication, causeth her to commit adultery: and whosoever shall marry her that is divorced committeth adultery".

Likewise it is reported in Mark 10:11, 12 as follows: "And he saith unto them whosoever shall put away his wife, and marry another committeth adultery against her. And if a woman shall put away her husband, and be married to another, she committeth adultery".

The whole subject of making divorce an impossibility is based on the following teachings of the Bible: "Whatsoever God has put together, let no man put assunder".[34] When one thinks on the Christian position of divorce, it is surprising it is allowed in a case of adultery of both parties – when God made them together who is then separating them. Likewise when there are pressing circumstances where the two life partners cannot live together under one roof and finally get separated it is also done by God Himself since He is the creator of the two partners. The Roman Catholics even interpret Matthew 5:31, 32 as not a ground for divorce at all. They say that there is no divorce in Christianity. Adultery automatically nullifies marriage. So in such cases it is not merely lawful but essential for the man to desert. The Protestants have allowed divorce on the grounds of adultery only, but if divorce is granted on any other grounds, including cruelty, highmindedness and prolonged quarrels, it has been declared unlawful for the two parties. The Orthodox Coptic Church of Egypt has made many amendments in the bibilical provision for divorce. They include the barrenness of the wife for three years, contagious disease and prolonged quarrels, where there is no hope for settlement. But these amendments are sociality and man-made rather than based on the commandments of the Bible.

Ancient Hindu Doctrine considered marriage as an indissoluble tie, enduring even after the death of either of the parties to it. This was the reason why a wife had to burn alive along with the dead body of the husband in the event of his death.

Among the Arabs also, the power of divorce possessed by the husband was unlimited. They recognised no rule of humanity or justice in the treatment of their wives.

In the Jāhiliyyah period before Islam, the Arabs used to divorce their wives at any time, for any reason, or without absolutely any reason whatsoever. They were also in the habit of revoking the divorce, and divorce again as many times as they liked. They could, if they were so inclined, swear by one of their idols that they would have no intercourse with their wives, though still living with them. They could arbitrarily accuse their wives of adultery, dismiss them and leave them with such notoriety as would deter other suitors, while they themselves would go exempt from any formal responsibility of maintenance or legal punishment.[35]

Imām Mālik, in his *Muwaṭṭā* has given the following two situations prevalent in the early days of Islam coming down from the Jāhiliyyah period:

> "A man divorced his wife, took her back, when the period of retirement was coming to an end, again divorced her, saying — By Allah, I will neither accept thee, nor allow thee freedom to marry another. So Allah revealed the verse: "You may divorce your wives etc."

Again:

> "Men used to divorce their wives, and take them back, not because they intended to retain them but because they wanted to tease their wives by putting off the divorce indefinitely; So Allah revealed the verse: "Retain them not by constraint etc."

'Āishah has reported that a man used to divorce his wife at will and took her back at will even though she was in *'iddah*,[36] even at times divorced her a hundred times or more. It is on such an occasion that the revelation came:

«الطَّلاقُ مَرَّتَانِ فَإِمْسَاكٌ بِمَعْرُوفٍ اوْ تَسْرِيحٌ بِإِحْسَانٍ...».

> "A divorce is only permissible twice: after that the parties should either hold together on equitable terms or separate with kindness."[37]

Tahlil or Halalah

Taḥlīl or *ḥalālah* which means legalising or making a thing lawful, was also a pre-Islamic practice. When the wife was divorced irrevocably, after thrice pronouncing the divorce formula, and the husband wanted to take her back, she had first to marry a third person on condition that he would divorce her after having sexual connection with her. This was called *ḥalālah*. It is a mistake to confound the *ḥalālah* with the marriage, since *ḥalālah* is a kind of punishment for the woman who had to undergo the disgrace of sexual connection with someone else while the marriage is a perpetual marital tie, and the divorce in that case may not follow at all; in fact the normal course of things it would not follow at all. It is for this reason that the Holy Prophet cursed those who resorted to this practice. He said: "The curse of Allah be on the man who commits *halālah* and the man for whom the *ḥalalāh* is committed.[38] Sayyidnā 'Umar is reported to have said that if there were brought to him two men who took part in the practice of *ḥalālah*, he would treat them as adulterous people. The three divorces, as allowed in the Holy Qur'ān, of which the third is irrevocable, were of very rare occurance, as such divorced naturally occurred at long intervals. The case of Rukana is mentioned in the reports; he first divorced his wife in the time of the Holy Prophet, then re-married her and divorced her a second time in the reign of 'Umar, and finally in the caliphate of 'Uthmān.

The Qur'ānic verse specifies as follows:

«فَإِنْ طَلَّقَهَا فَلَا تَحِلُّ لَهُ مِنْ بَعْدُ حَتَّىٰ تَنْكِحَ زَوْجاً غَيْرَهُ ـ فَإِنْ طَلَّقَهَا فَلَا جُنَاحَ عَلَيْهِمَا أَنْ يَتَرَاجَعَا إِنْ ظَنَّا أَنْ يُقِيمَا حُدُودَ اللّٰهِ وَتِلْكَ حُدُودُ اللّٰهِ يُبَيِّنُهَا لِقَومٍ يَعْلَمُونَ».

> "So, if a husband divorces his wife (irrevocably), he cannot, after that, remarry her until after she has married another husband and he has divorced her. In that case, there is no blame on either of them if they re-unite, provided they feel that they can keep the limits ordained by Allah. Such are the limits ordained by Allah, which he makes plain to those who understand."[39]

The custody of children will be the responsibility of the mother after divorce. This condition shall remain in force until a boy becomes sexually mature; and until a girl is married away and the marriage is consummated. And, if the mother dies or marries another husband, the right of custody shall pass into the hands of the grandmother; after her comes the maternal aunt. But if there is none of the mother's maternal relations the right shall pass into the hands of sisters and paternal aunts. And, if there are none of these, the right passes into the hands of agnates.[40]

In other words Qur'ān and Sunnah of the Prophet warn against any pre-arranged scheme that a certain man should marry a certain divorced woman with the understanding that he would divorce her again to enable the former husband to re-marry his divorced wife. This shall be an unlawful act and such a marriage shall be no marriage at all but adultery and the woman shall not become the lawful wife of the first husband by such a pre-arranged scheme. Sayyidnā 'Alī, 'Abdāllah bin Mas'ūd, 'Abū Hurairah and 'Uqbah bin 'Amir, all relate the Ḥadīth to the effect that the Holy Prophet cursed all the persons who indulge in such devices.

Differences of opinions of the four schools of Islamic Jurisprudence in the matter of Divorce are listed below:

The Ḥanafi school is of the view that it is unlawful *(ḥarām)* to divorce one's wife as long as there is stability in the relations of the two life partners. Imām Shāfi'i however, does not consider it unlawful. Imām Abu Ḥanifah considers the pronouncement of tripe divorce as *ḥarām*, and one who gives it is a sinner, Imām Aḥmad bin Ḥanbal and Imām Shafi'i do not reckon the act as *ḥarām*.

The sickness like lukoderma (Barṣ) cannot be a ground for divorce according to Imām Abū Hanifah, but Imām Shafi'i and Imām Malik say that this can be grounds for divorce. If a man gives a divorce in the death sickness *(marḍ al-Maut)*, and he dies while she is still in *'iddah*, the wife will still be entitled to her share of inheritance from the estate of the deceased according to the Ḥanafi school, but according to Imām Shāfi'i she will not be entitled to inheritance. Imām Shāfi'i considers sexual intercourse with a woman who has been given a divorce of *rajah* as *ḥarām* (unlawful), but Imām Abū Ḥanifah says that in such a case, the husband can have intercourse with her and it will amount to *raj'ah*. It is not necessary to mention in specific words that he intends her to return *(raj'ah)* back to normal family life, the mere act will suffice the purpose. But Imām Shafi'i insists on declaration of the intention that he wants her to return back *(rajah)*. Imām Shāfi'i even emphasises on the witnesses for *rajah*, but Imām Abu Ḥanifah says that if witnesses are not easily available, there is no need for them.

Evil Treatment Through Pagan Practices

Ẓihār: Injurious Comparison

The word *Ẓihār* is derived from *Ẓahr* meaning 'back'. An Arab, in the days of ignorance, would say to his wife, *anti 'alayya; Ka-ẓahri Ummī*, i.e. "You are to me as the back of my mother". This was called *Zihar*. No sooner were these words pronounced, than the relation between husband and wife would come to an end in the case of a divorce, but the woman was not at liberty to leave the husband's house and to drag on as a deserted wife. The Sharī'ah prohibits this ugly practice of the Jāhilliyyah society. One of the Muslims, Aus Ibn Samit treated his wife Khaulah in a similar manner. Khaulah came to the Holy Prophet and complained of her husband's ill-treatment. The Holy Prophet told her that he was unable to interfere. She went back disappointed and it was then that the Prophet received the revelation contained in verse 1-2 in Sūrah al-Mujādilah that Allāh indeed knows the plea of her, who pleads with thee about her husband and complains to Allah, and Allah knows the contentions of both of you, surely Allah is Hearing and Seeing.

As for those of you who put away their wives by likening them to the backs of their mothers, they are not their mothers; their mothers are no others than those who gave them birth; and most surely they utter a hateful word and falsehood. The man who resorted to this practice was ordered to free a slave; or if he could not find one, then to fast for two successive months, and if unable to do that, to feed sixty poor people.[41]

The following injunction of the Qur'ān condemns the evil practice of *Ẓihār*:

«مَـا جَعَـلَ اللّهُ لِرَجُـلٍ مِنْ قَلْبِيْنِ فِي جَوْفِهِ وَمَا جَعَلَ أَزْوَاجَكُم اللاَئي تُظَاهِرُونَ مِنْهُنَّ أُمَّهَـاتِكُمْ وَمَـا جَعَـلَ ادْعِيَائَكُمْ ابْنَاءكُم ذَلِكُمْ قَوْلُكُمْ بِأفْوَاهِكُمْ وَاللّهُ يَقُولُ الحَقَّ وَهُوَ يَهْدِي السَّبيل».

"Allah has not made any man two hearts in his own body: nor has He made your wives whom you divorce by *Ẓihār* your mothers: nor Has He made you adopted sons your sons. Such is only your manner of speech by your mouths. But Allah tells you the truth, and He shows the Right Way."[42]

This was in fact an evil custom, through which the husband selfishly deprived his wife of her conjugal rights and yet kept her tied to himself as a slave without her being free to remarry. Through this practice one pronounced words implying that she was like his mother, she could not demand conjugal rights but was not yet free from his control and could not contract another marriage. The Shari'ah condemned *Ẓihār* in the strongest terms and punishment is provided for it, as we have seen before. A man sometimes says such words in a fit of anger; they did not affect him as such, but they degrade the position of a woman.

Similarly, the Qur'ān further clarifies on the practice of *Ẓihār* in the following verses of Sūrah *Al-Mujāddidah:*

«الَّذينَ يُظاهِرُونَ مِنْكُمْ مِنْ نِسَآئِهِمْ مَا هُنَّ أُمَّهَاتِهِمْ اِنْ أُمَّهَاتُهُمْ الاَّ الائى وَلَدْنَهُمْ وَانَّهُمْ لَيَقُولُونَ مُنْكَراً مِنَ القَوْلِ وَزُوراً وَأن اللّهَ لَعَفُوٌّ غَفُورٌ».

If any men among you divorce their wives by *Zihar* (calling them mothers), they cannot be their mothers. None can be their mothers except those who gave them birth. And in fact they use words (both) iniquitous and false: but truly God is One that blots out (sins, and forgives [again and again].[43]

The immediate occasion as we have noted before was what happened to Khaulah bint Tha'labah wife of 'Aus, son of Ṣāmit. Though in Islam, he divorced her by an old Pagan custom. Such a custom was in any case degrading to a woman. It was particularly hard on *Khaula*, for she loved her husband and pleased that she had little children whom she had no resources herself to support and whom under *Ẓihār* her husband was not bound to support. She urged her plea to the Prophet and in prayer to Allah. Her just plea was accepted, and this iniquitous, based on false words, was abolished. Anyone was found guilty of this practice had a heavy penalty to pay as mentioned in the following *āyah*:

«وَالَّـذِينَ يُظَـاهِـرُونَ مِنْ نِسَآئِهِمْ ثُمَّ يَعُودُونَ لِمَا قَالُوا فَتَحْرِيْرُ رَقَبَةٍ مِنْ قَبْلِ اَنْ يَتَمَآسَّا ذٰلِكُمْ تُوعَظُونَ بِهِ وَاللّٰهُ بِمَا تَعْمَلُونَ خَبِيرٌ».

But who divorce their wives by *Ẓihār* then wish to go back the words they uttered, (it is ordained that such a one) should free a slave before they touch each other, thus are ye admonished to perform and God is well-acquainted with (all) that ye do."[44]

If one does not find means to free a slave as a *Kaffārah*, then he should add the following:

«فَمَنْ لَمْ يَجِـدْ فَصِيَـامُ شَهْـرَيْنِ مُتَتَـابِعَـيْنِ مِنْ قَبْلِ اَنْ يَتَمَاسَّا فَمَنْ لَمْ يَسْتَطِعْ فَاِطْعَامُ سِتِّينَ مِسْكِيناً ذَلِكَ لِتُؤْمِنُوا بِاللهِ....».

"And if any has not (the wherewithall) he should fast for two months consecutively before they touch each other. But if any is unable to do so, he should feed sixty indigent ones. This, that ye may show yourfaith in God."[45] *(Sūrah LVIII, 4).*

Apart from *Kaffārah* (expiation), she can sue for maintenance for herself and her children, but her husband could not claim his conjugal rights. If it was a hasty act and he repented of it, he could not claim his conjugal rights until after the performance of his penalty as mentioned above. If she loved him, as in Khaulah's case, she could also herself sue for conjugal rights in the legal sense of the term and compel her husband to perform the penalty and resume marital relations.

Ilā' like *Ẓihār* was also an evil practice of the pre-Islamic days by which the wife was kept in a state of suspense, sometimes for the whole of her life. *Ila',* which means literally swearing, signifies technically the taking of an oath that one shall not have sexual relations with one's wife. In the pre-Islamic days the Arabs used to take such oaths frequently, and as the period of suspension was not limited, the wife had sometimes to pass her whole life in bondage, having neither the position of a wife, nor that of a divorced woman free to marry elsewhere.

After the advent of Islam, the situation was corrected through the divine revelation commanding that if the husband did not re-assert conjugal relations within the period of four months, the wife should be divorced:

«لِلَّذِينَ يُؤْلُونَ مِنْ نِسَآئِهِمْ تَرَبُّصُ أَرْبَعَةِ اشْهُرٍ فَإِنْ فَاؤُا فَإِنَّ اللّهَ غَفُورٌ رَحِيمٌ، وَإِنْ عَزَمُوا الطَّلاقَ فَإِنَّ اللّهَ سَمِيعٌ عَلِيمٌ».

"In the case of those who swear that they will not go into their wives, the waiting period is four months; then if they go back, Allah is surely forgiving, Merciful. And if they resolve on a divorce, then Allah is surely Hearing, Knowing."[46]

Ilā', in reality, was meant to trouble a woman by keeping her hanging in the air.[47]

Although it is true that relations between husband and wife do not always remain cordial, yet Allah's law does not allow that the strained relations should continue indefinitely. Therefore it lays down the maximum period four months for a separation in which they legally remain husband and wife but practically live separate lives without any conjugal relations between them. Such a separation is called *Ila'* in the Shari'ah. During this period they must either make a reconciliation between themselves or part for good so that they may free to marry a suitable person of their liking.

From the words "Those who take oath . . . ", the jurists belonging to the Ḥanafī and Shāfi'ī schools of thought conclude that this period of four months applies only to those cases of separation which are made on oath; if they remain separate for any length of time without an oath, this law would not apply to them.

On the other hand, the Mālikī jurists are of the opinion that the maximum period of four months applies to all cases of separation. Imām Aḥmad bin Hanbal also supports this opinion.

Sayyidnā 'Ali, Ibn 'Abbās and Shaikh Ḥassan al-Baṣrī are of the opinion that this law applies only to that case of separation which is the result of strained relations, and does not apply to the case in which the husband and the wife agree to discontinue conjugal relations with mutual consent for some common good and at the same time keep cordial relations. There are other jurists who are of the opinion that the law of *ila'* would apply to every case of separation made on oath irrespective of the fact whether their relations remain good or bad; hence it should not go beyond the prescribed term of four months.

Some jurists interpret this to mean that if they break their oaths within four months and re-establish conjugal relations, in that case there would be no expiation *(Kaffārah)* for this; Allah will forgive the breach of their oath without expiation. But the majority of the jurists are of the opinion that expiation must be made in any case: *"Allahwill forgive and show mercy"* does not mean that the expiation will be remitted. It merely means that Allah will accept the expiation and forgive the wrong done against each other during their separation.

According to the verdict of Caliph 'Uthmān, 'Abdullāh bin Mas'ūd, Zaid bin Thābit and some other jurists, they can reunite only within four months. The expiry of this term itself is a proof that the husband has decided upon *Ṭalāq* (divorce). Hence after its expiry, divorce will automatically take place and the husband will forfeit the right of reunion. If, however, both of them agree, they may remarry. There is a verdict to the same effect from Sayyidna 'Umar, Sayyidnā 'Alī, 'Abdullāh bin 'Abbās and Abdallāh bin 'Umar and the jurists of Ḥanafī school have accepted the same.

The famous **Ṣaḥābī** Sa'īd bin Musayyib, and some others are of the opinion that after the expiry of four months, there shall be an automatic divorce but this will be a single revocable divorce and the husband will have the right to reunite within the period of *'iddah*, and if he does not reunite within this period, they may remarry if still they so desire.

On the other hand, 'Āishah, Abū-Dardā and many other jurists of Medina are of the opinion that after the expiry of four months, the case should be taken to a court so that the judge may order the husband either to reunite with his wife or divorce her.

Li'ān: Mutual Impercation

The natural outcome of the marriage is procreation. Children cement the relationship between the married partners. It is through the children that the progeny of a man continues. Marriage brings about legitimate children. This is the reason why Islam has forbidden *Ẓinā* and marriage is made essential. The children born out of marriage bear the name of the father as the Ḥadīth of the Prophet suggests:

الولـــد للفـــراش

"The child belongs to one on whose bed it is born."

In no circumstances should a husband intentionally deny the fatherhood of his child according to the above quoted Ḥadīth of the Prophet. If one merely depends on mere imagination of his enemies that the child is not his own, it is still unfair on his part to disown his child. Such a drastic step will prove to be very harmful for the future of the child as well as his mother. But, if at all, it is beyond any doubt that his wife has been dishonest and the child is born due to her intercourse with another man, the Sharī'ah, in such cases, does not want to thrust the responsibility of the child on to the husband of the woman, nor does it want to impose him on his property. This is where the provision of

Lia'ān or mutual impercation comes into force. The process of *Li'ān* has been clearly shown in *Sūrah al-Nūr* of the Holy Qur'ān:

«وَالَّذِينَ يَرْمُونَ أَزْوَاجَهُمْ وَلَمْ يَكُنْ لَهُمْ شُهَدَآءُ إِلَّا أَنْفُسُهُمْ فَشَهَادَةُ أَحَدِهِمْ أَرْبَعُ شَهَادَاتٍ بِاللَّهِ إِنَّهُ لَمِنَ الصَّادِقِينَ، وَالْخَامِسَةُ أَنَّ لَعْنَتَ اللَّهِ عَلَيْهِ إِنْ كَانَ مِنَ الْكَاذِبِينَ، وَيَدْرَءُوا عَنْهَا الْعَذَابَ أَنْ تَشْهَدَ أَرْبَعَ شَهَادَاتٍ بِاللَّهِ إِنَّهُ لَمِنَ الْكَاذِبِينَ، وَالْخَامِسَةَ أَنَّ غَضَبَ اللَّهِ عَلَيْهَا إِنْ كَانَ مِنَ الصَّادِقِينَ».

"And for those who launch a charge against their spouses, and have in support no evidence but their own, their solitary evidence can be received if they bear witness four times with an oath by Allah that they are solemnly telling the truth; and the fifth oath should be that they solemnly invoke the curse of Allah on themselves if they tell a lie. But it would avert the punishment from the wife, if she bears witness four times with an oath by Allah that her husband is telling a lie; and the fifth oath should be that she solemnly invokes the wrath of Allah on herself if her accuser is telling the truth."[48]

The difference between *Qadhf* and *Li'ān* is that the latter is restricted to the accusation put forward by the husband in respect of his wife. In the case of *Qādhf* four witnesses are required to give evidence to prove the accusation will be enough as laid down in the above verses of the Qur'ān. He has to swear in the name of Allah four times saying that he saw his wife committing adultery or that the pregnancy was not from him, and then swear the fifth time invoking Allah's curse *(La'nah)* on himself if he had accused her falsely. Likewise, the woman, if she were not guilty would also take oaths four times saying that she was not guilty of adultery and that her husband had lied. The fifth time, she would also invoke Allah's curse upon her if she were lying.

If she confessed her guilt, she would be given *hadd* punishment for *Ẓinā*. If the husband hesitated and refused taking the required oaths, she will be given the *ḥadd* punishment for *Qadhf*. According to Imam Abu Ḥanifah, if he refuses to take oaths, he should be imprisoned until he agrees to take oaths or the wife confesses her guilt,or that the husband withdraws the accusation or he divorces his wife. Imāms Mālik, Shāfi'ī and Aḥmad bin Ḥanbal take a different view. If the husband refuses to take the required oaths, he will be given *ḥadd* punishment for *Qadhf* which amounts to eighty lashes. If the wife refuses to take oaths of innocence, she will be deemed guilty of *Zinā* and will be given the *Ḥadd* punishment accordingly. Imām Abu Ḥanifah insists here too that she must be detained until she takes oaths.[49]

While the *Qāḍi* hears the suit, the husband will have two alternatives. He may retract or withdraw the charge before the end of the trials which will immediately bring the case to an end and there will be no need to take any other nor would there be any embarrassment for the wife. But if he persists in his attitude and takes the oath followed by the oaths of innocence of the wife, as we have described before, the suit for *Li'ān* will be deemed complete. There will be no need of pronouncement of divorce by the *Qāḍī* according to both Imām Aḥmad bin Ḥanbal and Imām Mālik.[50] But, according to Imām Abū Ḥanīfah, it will be essential then for the judge to pronounce divorce and dissolve the marriage. Imām Shāfi'i, however, takes a quite different view from the other Imams. He thinks that the moment the husband finishes taking his oaths of impercation, declaring that his wife had committed adultery and invoking the curse of Allah upon himself if he were a liar, he has given a heavy blow to the love and confidence that he had in his wife. Then *Li'ān* is complete the moment the husband finishes taking his five oaths.[51] Once marriage is dissolved by the *Qāḍi* after the due process of *Li'ān* stipulated in the Qur'ān, it will result into irrevocable divorce according to all the schools of Islamic Jurisprudence with the exception of Imam Abū Ḥanifah who opines that if later the husband declares that he had lied while taking oaths of impercation and that everything happened in the heat of the moment that husband will be given *Ḥadd* punishment. Thereafter they can remarry and the chīld will be given to him.[52]

---

1. Qur'ān, ch. 4:21.
2. Abū Dā'ūd, 13:3; also Sunan Ibn Mājah, vol. 1, 318.
3. *Kashf al-Khafā*, vol. 2, 302; also *Tafsīr al-Qurṭabī,* vol. 18, 149.
4. Qur'ān, ch. 4:35.
5. To understand the role of arbitrators in details, see Abū Zahrah, Muḥammad, *Al-Aḥwāl al-Shakhiṣiyyah*, Cairo, pp. 277-278.
6. Qur'ān, 4:130.
7. Qur'ān, 4:129.

8. Qur'ān, 2:226.
9. *Sharḥ al-Kabīr*, vol. 8, p. 234, also cf. Al-Sābūnī, 'Abd al-Raḥamān, *Ḥurriyyat al-Zawjayn fil Ṭalāq*, Cairo 1968, pp. 85-86.
10. *Mughnī al-muḥtāj*, vol. 3, p. 307.
11. Al-Nawawī, *Sharḥ 'alā Muslim*, vol. 10, p. 61.
12. Al-Dardūr, *Sharḥ mukhtaṣar Khalīl*, vol. 2, p. 423.
13. Abd al-Ḥākim Muḥammad, *Aḥkām al-Usrah*, p. 114.
14. *Al-Fawākih al-'Adīdah fī Fiqh al-Ḥanābalah*, vol. 2, p. 27.
15. *Bidāyat al-Mujtahid*, vol. 2, p. 43.
16. Al-Qayrawani *Risālah*, op. cit. ch. 32: *Bāb fil Nikāḥ wal Ṭalāq*, pp. 89-97.
17. Qur'ān, 4:129.
18. Qur'ān 4:130.
19. Ameer 'Ali, *The Spirit of Islam*, London 1965, pp. 243-44.
20. Qur'ān, ch. 65:2.
21. Sayyid Sābiq, *Fiqh al-Sunnah*, op. cit., vol. 8, p. 59.
22. Ibid, p. 62.
23. Ibid, p. 63.
24. Al-Ghazālī, *Iḥyā al-'Ulūm*.
25. These three months constitute the "iddah" period which is obligatory on such wives with whom the marriage has been consummated. "The women who are divorced shall wait concerning themselves until they have their courses thrice." Qur'ān, ch. 22:228.
26. Qur'ān, ch. 65:1.
27. Qur'ān, ch. 65:6.
28. Qur'ān, ch. 2:232.
29. Al-Qayrawānī, *Risalah*, op. cit. ch. 32: *Bāb fil Nikah wal Talaq*, pp. 89-97.
30. Ibid.
31. cf. Yussuf Ali, Holy Qur'ān, op. cit. page 90, Note 256.
32. Qur'ān, ch. 2:228.
33. Qur'ān, ch. 2:230.
34. Matthew, 19:6.
35. Ibrahim Abdel Hamid, *Dissolution of Marriage*, an article in *Islamic Quarterly*, vol. 3, 1956, pp. 166-75, 215-223; vol. 4, 1957, 3-10, 57-65, 97-118.
36. Al-Tirmidhi.
37. Qur'ān, ch. 2:229.
38. Tirmidhi, 9:25.
39. Qur'ān, 2:230.
40. Al-Qayrawānī, *Risālah*, ch. 33: *Bāb fil 'Iddah Nafaqah*, pp. 98-101.
41. Qur'ān, 33:4.
42. Qur'ān, ch.
43. Qur'ān, ch. 58:2.
44. Qur'ān, ch. 58:3.
45. Qur'ān, ch. 58:4.
46. Qur'ān, ch. 2:226-227.
47. Sayyid Sābiq, *Fiqh al-Sunnah* op. cit., Vol. 7, p. 137.
48. Qur'ān, ch. 24:6-9.
49. *Bidāyah al-Mujtahid*, vol. 2, p. 120.
50. Cf. *Ḥāshiyah al-Dasūqī*, vol. 2, p. 467.
51. *Bidāyah al-Mujtahid*, vol. 2, p. 121.
52. Cf. *Bidayāh al-Mujtahid*, vol. 2, pp. 120-121.

Chapter 12

Khul': Divorce at the Instance of Wife

Definition of Khul'

Khul' is derived from *Khul'-al-Thaub* releasing or removing the dress from the body, because a woman is a dress of a man, and vice-versa as is delcared in the Qur'ān: "The women are your dress and you are their dress".[1]

Just as Shari'ah provides for a husband to divorce his wife, the wife can also ask for divorce if sufficient grounds exist for it. If the husband is cruel, she can ask for divorce *(Khul')* and is not forced to tolerate what seems to be untolerable for her.

There do occur the cases of torture and maltreatment of the wife in the society where divorce is not allowed. Islam by allowing divorce initiated by the wife has helped the Muslim homes not to become miserable for children because of the limitless nagging and quarrelling between father and mother and the two partners are not condemned to life long unhappiness.

The Māliki Jurists define *Khul'* as *al-Ṭalāq bil'iwaḍ* or "a divorce by giving something in return",[2] and the Ḥanafi Jurists say that it is the end of a marital relationship with consent either with the utterance of the word *Khul'* or something that means the same.[3] The Shāfi'i Jurists say that "it is a separation sought with something given in return and with pronouncement of the word divorce or *Khul'*.[4] It can be achieved through mutual agreement of the two parties or through the order of the *Qāḍī* on payment by the wife to the husband a certain amount that does not exceed what was given to her as dower (*Mahr*).[5]

Guidance from Qur'ān and Sunnah on Khul'

The Qur'ānic injunction makes it clear that a wife is entitled to ask her husband for a divorce *(Khul')* if she fears cruelty or desertion from him. It lays down:

«وَإِنِ امْـرَأَةٌ خَافَتْ مِنْ بَعْلِهَـا نُشُـوزاً أَوْ إِعْـرَاضاً فَلا جُنَاحَ عَلَيْهِمَا أَنْ يُصْلِحَا بَيْنَهُمَـا والصُّلحُ خَيْرٌ وَأُحْضِـرَتِ الأَنْفُسُ الشُّحَّ وَإِنْ تُحْسِنُوا وَتَتَّقُوا فَإِنَّ اللّه كَانَ بِمَا تَعْمَلونَ خَبِيرا».

"If a wife fears cruelty or desertion on her husband's part, there is no blame on them if they arrange an amicable settlement between themselves; and such settlement is best; even though man's souls are swayed by greed. But if you do good practise self-restraint, Allah is well-acquainted with all that you do".[6]

It is narrated in the *Sunnan al-Baihaqī:*

اتت امـرأة النبي صلى الله عليـه وسلم وقـالت: اني ابغض زوجي واحب فراقـه، قال: «اتـردين عليـه حديقتـه التي اصدقك؟» قالت: نعم وزيادة، فقال النبي صلى الله عليه وسلم: «أما الزيادة فلا».

A woman came to the Prophet (S.A.W.) and said: "I hate my husband and like separation from him." The Prophet asked: "would you return the orchard that he gave you as a dower?" She replied: "Yes, even more than that." The Prophet (S.A.W.) said: "You should not return more than that."[7]

Thus when the wife becomes apprehensive that her husband fails to observe the bounds described by the Sharī'ah that is, cannot perform the duties imposed on him by the conjugal relationship, – she can release herself from the tie, by giving up whole or some property in return, in consideration of which the husband is to give her a *"Khul'"* and when they have done this, an irreversible divorce would take place with consent of each other. But if the wife fails to pay the compensation, there is yet another means to dissolve the marriage through, *"Mubārāt"*, according to which no compensation has to be paid, and a complete separation is effected, merely by mutual consent of the parties.

The compensation is a matter of arrangement between the husband and wife. The wife may return the whole, or a portion of the dower, but not anything more than the dower, if it has been paid, or she may make any other agreement for the benefit of the husband such as for instance, to nurse their child during its two years of suckling, or to keep and maintain the child for a fixed period, at her own expense after having weaned it. But this should be done in agreement with the husband.

Supposing the wife is an unfortunate woman who is subjected to abuse and threats by a brutal husband who really wishes that she may forfeit the whole of her *Mahr*, she need not forfeit the whole of her *Mahr*. She can go to the *Qāḍī* with a complaint against the husband and demand a formal separation. If her allegations are true, the *Qāḍi* will call upon the husband to repudiate her. In case he refuses to do so, the *Qādi* himself pronounced a divorce which will operate as a valid repudiation, and the husband will be liable for the whole of the deferred *Mahr*, if any. This is called "*tafrīq* or a legal separation."

The first *Khul'* case in Islam quoted by Imām Bukhari in the following words: the wife of Thābit bin Qais, came to the Holy Prophet and said 'O Messenger of Allah, I am not angry with Thabit for his temper or religion, but I am afraid that something may happen to me contrary to Islam, on which account I wish to be separated from him.' The prophet said: "Will you give back to Thabit the garden which he gave to you as your settlement?" She said: 'Yes'. Then the Prophet said to Thabit, "Take you garden and divorce her at once."[8]

This Ḥadīth clearly shows that Thābit was blameless, and that the proposal for divorce came from the wife who feared she would not be able to observe the bounds set by Allah, she will not be able to perform her functions as a wife. The Prophet here permitted the woman to release herself by returning to the husband the *Mahr* as compensation for the release granted to her.

All the jurists are agreed on the legality of *Khul'*. Imām Mālik[9] says that if a husband has forced his wife to enter into a *Khul'* the wife is entitled to get back the dowry, but the separation will be valid under Sharī'ah. The only Jurist who does not agree with the legality of *Khul'* is Bikr bin 'Abdallāh al-Muznī, a famous *Tābi'ī* scholar.[10] According to al-Shukāni, his view falls out of *Ijmā* (consensus).[11]

When can Khul' be Demanded

It should be noted that *Khul'* must only be asked in extreme circumstances. It must not be resorted to on flimsy grounds. The following Ḥadīth of the Prophet gives a warning to women who ask for *Khul'* without any reasonable ground:

قال رسول الله صلى الله عليه وسلم: «ايما امرأة سألت زوجها الطلاق من غير بأس فحرام عليها رائحة الجنة».

The Messenger of Allah has said: "If any woman asks for divorce from her husband without any specific reason, the fragrance of paradise will be unlawful to her."[12]

Ḥasan al-Baṣrī has also narrated a Ḥadīth from Abū Ḥurairah on the same issue:

«المنتزعات والمختلعات هن المنافقات»

"The women asking for separation and *Khul'* are hypocrites."[13]

Khul' is disliked *(Makrūh)* except that there is a fear that the limits imposed by Allah will not be observed if release is not sought.[14] According to al-Dasūqī, *Khul'* is lawful and not disliked.[15] The following are some of the causes, for which a wife can demand a divorce by authority of the *Qādī*. Where the wife has the right to prefer a claim of "*tafriq*" the husband is entitled to no compensation. Divorce may be granted by the *Qāḍī* for:

1. Habitual ill-treatment of the wife
2. Non-fulfilment of the terms of the marriage contract
3. Insanity
4. Incurable incompetency
5. Quitting the conjugal domicile without making provision for the wife
6. Any other similar causes which in the opinion of the *Qāḍī* justifies a divorce.

Compensation and 'Iddah for Khul'

Once the case goes to the court, it will first of all try to ascertain whether the wife really dislikes the husband so much that she cannot live with him any longer. Then if the court is satisfied that they cannot live together happily, it shall fix as compensation anything that it considers proper, and the husband shall have to accept that and divorce the wife. The jurists are generally of the opinion that the compensation should not exceed the dowry given by the husband.

As soon as *Khul'* is granted, the husband forfeits the right of reunion after the divorce because it has been bought by the wife. It is lawful for them to remarry with mutual consent.

According to the majority of the Mulsims, the term for *'Iddah* for the wife in the case of *Khul'* is the same as that of divorce. But Abū Dā'ūd, Tirmizi and Ibn Majah and other have related *Ahādīth* to the effect that the Holy Prophet prescribed only one monthly course as ther term for the wife after the divorce, and Caliph 'Uthmān decided a case in accordance with this.[16]

According to the Māliki school, *Khul'* is not confined to the utterance of any particular word. Some other words like *Fidyah, Sulh* and *Mubarat* can also be used. The word *Khul'* is specially used when a woman asks for a release by returning all that was given to her, *Sulh* refers to the part payment, *Fidyah* to over payment and *Mubārāt* means dropping the right that the wife had over her husband.[17] Ibn al-'Arabi has mentioned in his *Aḥkām al-Qur'ān* that Imam Malik has defined *Mubāra'ah to mean Khul'* (release) in cosideration of payment before the consummation of marriage, while *Khul'* is effected after consummation.[18]

Khul' of a Woman in Death Sickness

If a woman sought *Khul'* during her death sickness *(Marḍ al-Maut)*, and she died while still in ʿiddah, Khul' is still valid and the former husband, according to the Ḥanafi school,[19] will receive whatever is less out of the following three things:

1. An amount agreed to be given in consideration for *Khul'*
2. One third of the estate after paying her debts
3. His share of inheritance from her.

Ibn Rushd,[20] the Māliki Jurist has narrated from Ibn Nāfi from Imām Mālik that the *Khul'* in death-sickness will be valid with all of the one third (*Thulth*).[21] The Shāfi'i School also agrees with the validity of the *Khul'* in death-sickness, and the former husband will receive whatever is lesser than *Mahr al-Mathal* or one third of the estate of the deceased.[22] The Hanbali view on this issue is the same as the Māliki stand.[23]

The *Khul'* negotiated by anyone else other than the wife will be null and void according to the Ẓāhirī and the Hanbali schools, but it is valid according to the Ḥanafi, Māliki and the Shāfi'i schools. It is said in *al-Muḥalla*[24] that *Khul'* negotiated by father is void. Likewise, none is allowed to negotiate *Khul'* on behalf of an insane or mentally deranged woman or a minor girl whether he happens to be her father or a ruler or anyone else. According to the Shāfi'i school, there is no difference whether *Khul'* is negotiated by the father or guardian of the woman or a stranger.[25] The Ḥanafi school says that either the father or a stranger can negotiate *Khul'* only with the permission of the woman concerned.[26]

According to the Maliki School, *Khul'* negotiated by a minor or an insane woman is unlawful. If the father negotiates it on behalf of his minor or insane daughter, *Khul'* will be valid whether it is achieved through the father's property or that of his daughter, and whether it is obtained with or without her permission.[27] The Ḥanafi School considers the *Khul'* sought by an insane woman or a minor who is not a *Mumayyazah* as void.[28]

Can Khul' be given at any time?

At the outset, it will be fair to say that the conditions that apply to divorce *(Ṭalāq)* will also apply in *Khul'*. There are different opinions about the *Khul'* to be given in the period of menstruation. According to *Mukhtaṣar al-Nāfi'*[29], *Khul' can only be given in the period of purity (Tuhur)*. The Ibadis believe that it is an innovation *(Bidʿah)* to give divorce while the woman is menstruating.[30] The Ḥanafi's consider it *Makrūh* (disliked)[31] but the famous scholar Ibn ʿĀbdin said that it is not at all *Makrūh,*[32] since the Messenger of Allah did not ask the wife of

Thabin bin Qais about it when *Khul'* was granted to his wife through the intervention of the Prophet (S.A.W.).[33] Al-Kharashī, the Mālikī jurist says that when the woman has willingly obtained *Khul'* in consideration of payment, it is her right to do so even in the period of menstruation.[34] The Ḥanbalī jurists say that since *Khul'* comes about by mutual agreement of the two married partners, there is no harm even if it is given during menstruation.[35]

1. Qur'ān, ch. 2:182.
2. Ḥāshiyah al-Dasūqī, vol. 2, p. 406.
3. Ibn Najim, *Baḥr al-Rāiq*, vol. 4, p. 77.
4. *Nihāyah al-Muhtaq*, vol. 6, p. 47.
5. Al-Ṣābūnī, *Ḥurriyah al-Zawjain fil Ṭalāq*, op. cit., p. 495.
6. Qur'ān, 4:128. The commentators of the Qur'ān have also derived the rule in respect of *Khul'* from other Qur'ānic injunctions: Qur'ān, 4:20; 4:128; 4:130.
7. *Sunan al-Baihaqī*, vol. 7, p. 313
8. *Sahih al-Bukhārī*, 9:329.
9. *Al-Mudawwanah al-Kubrā*, 5, 22. Also *Tafsīr al-Qurṭabī*, 3, 138.
10. Fatḥ al-Bārī, 9, 346.
11. Al-Shaukānī, *Fāth al-Qadīr*, 1, 213.
12. Al-Shaukānī, *Fatḥ al-Qadīr*, 1, 2141 Also see Al-Mughnī, 8, 174.
13. Al-Baihāqi, *Al-Sunan al-Kubra*, 7, 376.
14. *Fatḥ al-Bārī*, 9, 346.
15. *Ḥāshiyah al-Dasūqī*, 2, 406.
16. *Ibn Kathīr*, vol. 1, p. 276.
17. *Bidāyah al-Mujtahid*, 2, 40; Al-Mudawwanah al-Kubrā, 5, 28. Here the words *Mukhtali'ah* and *Muftadiyah* are discussed by Imām Mālik.
18. Ibn al-'Arabi, *Aḥkām al-Qur'ān*, 1, 194; also see *Tafsīr al-Qurṭabī*, 3/145.
19. *Baḥr al-Rāiq*, 4/80.
20. *Bidāyah al-Muhtahid*, 2/41.
21. See also *Tāj al-Madhhab*, 2/291.
22. *Hurriyah al-Zawjayn fil Ṭalāq*, op. cit., Vol. 2, p. 555.
23. *Al-Mughni*, 8/215.
24. *Ḥurriyah al-Zawjayn*, 2/557; also see Al-Insāf, 8/389.
25. Ibid. p. 559.
26. *Bahr al-Ra'iq*, 4/97.
27. *Al-Muntazi' al-Mukhtār*, 2/435.
28. *Al-Mabsūt*, 6/180; also cf. *al-Bahr al-Rāiq*, 4/180.
29. *Muktasār al-Nafi'*, p. 227; see *Jāwahar āl-Kalam* 5/360.
30. *Sharḥ al-Nīl*, 3/556.
31. *Mukhtaṣar al-Qudūrī*, 2/23.
32. Ḥāshiyāh Ibn 'Ābdin, 2/428.
33. *Mukhtaṣar al-Muznī*, 4/51.
34. *Sharḥ al-Kharshī*, 3/169.
35. *Al-Mughnī*, 8/174.

Chapter 13

'Iddah: Period of Waiting Guidance from Qur'ān and Sunnah on 'Iddah

The word *'Iddah* is derived from the Arabic word *al-'Adad* meaning the number, in the terminology of the Shari'ah it means a period of waiting from re-marriage after the death of her husband or her separation or divorce from her. The Muslim Jurists have unanimously agreed on it essentially (*wujūb*),[1] since the injunction of the Qur'ān is quite explicit on the subject:

«وَالمُطَلَّقَاتُ يَتَرَبَّصْنَ بِأَنْفُسِهِنَّ ثَلاثَةَ قُرُوءٍ»

"The Divorced women shall wait concerning themselves for three monthly periods".[2]

The Holy Prophet (S.A.W.) had order Fāṭimah bint Qais as follows:

«اعتدّي في بيت أم مكتوم»

"Complete your *Iddah* period in the house of Umm Maktum".

The Sharī'ah emphasises on reconciliation as a better course than divorce for the married partners and gives them opportunity to mend their relations if they have gone sour. Therefore, the Holy Qur'ān prescribes a period of waiting after divorce has been pronounced so that a spell of temporary separation and suspension of conjugal relations may give the spouses time for rethinking and reconsideration in the interests of family and children, if any, of the question whether divorce should be revoked or made final and irrevocable. The *'iddah* has another important object to serve, that is it may make it known whether the woman is having a child of the former husband in her womb so that there may be no confusion about the paternity of such a child if the woman seeks to remarry. The Qur'ān says:

«وَالمُطَلَّقَاتُ يَتَرَبَّصْنَ بِانْفُسِهِنَّ ثَلاثَةَ قُرُوءٍ وَلاَ يَحِلُّ لَهُنَّ انْ يَكْتُمْنَ مَا خَلَقَ اللّهُ فِي ارْحَامِهِنَّ اِنْ كُنَّ يُؤْمِنَّ بِاللّهِ وَاليَوْمِ الآخِرِ - وَبُعُولَتُهُنَّ احَقُّ بِرَدِهِنَّ فِي ذٰلِكَ اِنْ ارَادُوا اِصْلاحاً - وَلَهُنَّ مِثْلُ الذي عَلَيْهِنَّ بِالْمَعْرُوفِ وَلِلرِّجَالِ عَلَيْهِنَّ دَرَجَةٌ - وَاللّهُ عَزِيزٌ حَكِيمٌ».

Divorced women shall wait concerning themselves for three monthly periods. Nor is it lawful for them to hide what God has created in their wombs, if they have faith in Allah and the last day. And their husbands have the better right to take them back in that period, if they wish to reconciliation. And women shall have rights similar to their rights against them, according to what is equitable but men have a degree (of advantage) over them. And God is Exalted in Power, Wise".[3]

The Different Kinds of 'Iddah

The duration of *'iddah* is prescribed by the Holy Qur'ān as follows:

«وَالـلاَّئي يَئِسْنَ مِنَ المَحِيضِ مِنْ نِسَـآئِكُمْ اِنِ ارتَبْتُمْ فَعِـدَّتُهُنَّ ثَلاثَـةُ اشْهُـرٍ والـلاَّئي لَمْ يَحِضْنَ وَاوُلاتِ الاحْمَـالِ اَجَلُهُنَّ اَنْ يَضَعْنَ حَمْلَهُنَّ وَمَنْ يَتَّقِ اللّهَ يَجْعَلْ لَهُ مِنْ اَمْرِهِ يُسْراً».

"Such of your women as have passed the age of monthly courses, for them the prescribed period, if you have any doubts is three months, and for those who have no courses (it is the same): For those who carry life (within their wombs), their period is until they deliver their burdens: and for those who fear God, He will make their path easy".[4]

The Qur'ān lays down that there shall be no *'iddah* for a woman who is divorced by her husband before he has consummated his marriage with her. It says:

«يَـآأيُّهَـا الـذينَ آمَنُوآ اِذَا نَكَحْتُم المُؤْمِنَاتِ ثُمَّ طَلَّقْتُمُوهُنَّ مِنْ قَبلِ اَنْ تَمَسُّوهُنَّ فَمَا لَكُمْ عَلَيْهِنَّ مِنْ عِدَّةٍ تَعْتَدُّونَهَا فَمَتِّعُوهُنَّ وَسَرِّحُوهُنَّ سَرَاحاً جَمِيلاً».

"O you who believe! when you marry believing women, and then divorce them before you have touched them, no period of *Iddah* have you to count in respect of them: so give them a present, and set them free in a handsome manner".[5]

But in the case of termination of marriage due to the death of the husband, the widows shall have an *'iddah* of four months and ten days. The extra period of forty days seems to have been added to provide for mourning by the widow. The Qur'ān says:

«وَالَّذِينَ يُتَوَفَّوْنَ مِنْكُمْ وَيَذَرُونَ أَزْوَاجاً يَتَرَبَّصْنَ بِأَنْفُسِهِنَّ أَرْبَعَةَ أَشْهُرٍ وَعَشْراً ـ فَإِذَا بَلَغْنَ أَجَلَهُنَّ فَلا جُنَاحَ عَلَيْكُمْ فِيمَا فَعَلْنَ فِي أَنْفُسِهِنَّ بِالْمَعْرُوفِ ـ وَاللَّهُ بِمَا تَعْمَلُونَ خَبِيرٌ».

"If any one of you die and leaves widows behind him they shall wait concerning themselves for four months and ten days: when they have fulfilled their term, there is no blame on you if they dispose of themselves in a just and reasonable manner. And God is well acquainted with what you do."[6]

The different kinds of '*Iddah* can be summed up as follows:

1. '*Iddah* of women who still menstruate: Three menstruations.
2. *Iddah* of women who have passed the age of menstruation: Three months.
3. '*Iddah* of a woman whose husband died: Four months and ten days.
4. '*Iddah* of a pregnant woman: Until she delivers a child.
5. No '*Iddah* for a woman whose marriage is not yet consummated.

Some of the scholars like Ibn 'Abbās have said that since Allah has made it obligatory for the woman whose husband dies to wait for four months and ten days, and has specified the period of waiting for the pregnant (woman) to last until she has been delivered, (it follows that) if the husband dies and the woman is pregnant she is bound by two periods concurrently just as she would be bound to fulfil any other two duties combined together.[7]

According to Imām al-Shāfi'ī,[8] the Messenger of Allah said to Subay'ah, daughter of al-Harith, who gave birth to a child a few days after her husband's death: "You are lawful (for marriage) and you may get married", this indicates that the '*iddah,* whether in the case of death or divorce, is to be fulfilled by (the expiration of) the required months – was intended to (bind) women who are not pregnant; but if they are pregnant the '*iddah* is dropped.[9]

Code of Conduct for a Woman in 'Iddah

The Jurists have difference of opinions about the giving out of the house of a woman in '*Iddah*. The Ḥanafī Jurists say that it is not lawful for a woman who is given the first and second divorce *(Raj'āh)* nor for a woman who is serving '*iddah* for *Bāin* form of *Ṭalāq* to go out of the house either during the day time or at night. But a widow can go out during the day time or at certain times at night, but must not spend the night anywhere except in the house. The difference is that in the case of a divorce, she has the right to be maintained from the property of the husband, and hence it is not allowed for her to leave the house of the husband as a wife. But, in the case of a widow, she is not entitled for the maintenance, hence she can go out to better her lot. According to the Ḥanbalī Jurists, she can go out during the day time whether she is in *'Iddah* of divorce or as a widow. Jābir has reported that his aunt was divorced three times, then she went out to cut the fruits of her date-palm. Someone met her and told her not to do so. She came to the Prophet and reported the matter to him. The Prophet replied:

«اخرجي فجذي نخلك لعلك ان تصدقي منه أو تفعلي خيرا».

"You may go out to cut the fruits of your date-palm so that you may give charity out of it or do something good with it."[10]

As a precaution, she should not go out at night without any necessity because many evils do happen in the dark hours of night, while during the day time she can go out to fulfil her necessities and buy whatever she needs.

She must not remarry during the period of *'Iddah. Aḥādīth* give clear instructions that widows should not wear ornaments, coloured and showy dresses, nor adorn themselves with any kind of make-up during this period.

According to Imām Abū Ḥanīfah, she will have the right to her maintenance and a dwelling place during the period of *'Iddah* of irrevocable divorce just as during the *iddah* of return, but in that case she will have to spend the period of *'Iddah* in the matrimonial home. The maintenance will be considered like a debt at the time of divorce. Imam Mālik and Imām Shāfi'i say that she will only be entitled to the dwelling place but not the maintenance except when she is pregnant. Imam Aḥmad bin Ḥanbal, on the contrary, says that she would have neither right to maintenance nor a dwelling place.

Treatment of Divorced Women During 'Iddah

The Holy Qur'ān prescribes the time when divorce shall be pronounced and the treatment that shall be given to the divorced woman during *'iddah*. It says:

«يَاآيُّهَا النَّبِيُّ اِذَا طَلَّقْتُمُ النِّسَاء فَطَلِّقُوهُنَّ لِعَدَّتِهِنَّ وَاحْصُوا العِدَّةَ وَاتَّقُوا اللّهَ رَبَكُمْ لا تُخْـرِجُـوهُنَّ مِنْ بُيُوتِـهِنَّ وَلا يَخْرُجْنَ إلاَ أَنْ يَأتِينَ بِفَاحِشَةٍ مُبَيِّنَةٍ وَتِلكَ حُدُودُ اللّهَ....».

> "O Prophet, when you do divorce women, divorce them at their prescribed periods, and count accurately their prescribed periods: and fear Allah your Lord: and turn them not out of their house, nor shall they themselves leave, except in case they are guilty of some open lewdness. Those are the limits set by Allah".[11]

It further lays down:

«فَاِذَا بَلَغْنَ اجَلَهُنَّ فَامْسِكُوهُنَّ بِمَعْرُوفٍ اوْ فَارِقُوهُنَّ بِمَعْرُوفٍ وَاَشْهِدُوا ذَوَىْ عَدْلٍ مِنْكُمْ وَاقِيمُوا الشَّهَادَةَ لِلَّهِ....».

> "Thus when they fulfill their term appointed *'iddah* either take them back on equitable terms or part with them on equitable terms; and take for witnesses two persons among you, endued with justice, and establish the evidence as before Allah".[12]

Thus, the divorced woman should live in the house of the husband until she finishes the *'Iddah*. It is not lawful for her to leave it, nor must the husband divorce her away from it. Even if she was not present in her matrimonial home at the time of the pronouncement of divorce or separation, it is essential for her to return to the house of the husband. The Qur'ān says: "And turn them not out of their houses, nor shall they themselves leave, except in the cases they are guilty of lewdness".[13] There is however, a difference of opinion as to whether a widow should pass the term in the house of the deceased or not. Sayyidnā 'Umar, Sayyidnā 'Uthmān, 'Abdallāh bin 'Umar, the four Imāms and many other great jurists are of the opinion that she should reside in the house of the deceased husband. Sayyidah 'Āishah, Ibn 'Abbās, Sayyidnā 'Alī and some other great jurists are of the opinion that she is free to pass the period wherever she likes.

Re-Marriage of Widows is Encouraged in Shari'ah

In religions like Hindusim and Jainisin, widow re-marriage is not permitted. Even if the husband dies immediately after her marriage, she has to remain a widow all her life bearing the taunts of her mother-in-law and sister-in-law. In the first place, she is held responsible for the death of the husband. It is believed that she brought an ill-omen as a result of which her husband died.

Islam, on the contrary, sympathises with the plight of a widow and encourages her to remarry and start life once again. The Holy Qur'ān says:

«وَالَّذِينَ يُتَوَفَّوْنَ مِنْكُمْ وَيَذَرُونَ اَزْوَاجاً يَتَرَبَّصْنَ بِأَنْفُسِهِنَّ اَرْبَعَةَ اَشْهُرٍ وَعَشْراً فَاِذَا بَلَغْنَ اَجَلَهُنَّ فَلا جُنَاحَ عَلَيْكُمْ فِيمَا فَعَلْنَ فِي اَنْفُسِهِنَّ بِالْمَعْرُوفِ وَاللّٰهُ بِمَا تَعْمَلُونَ خَبِيرٌ».

"If any of you die and leave widows behind, they shall wait concerning themselves four months and ten days: when they have fulfilled their term, there is no blame on you if they dispose of themselves in a just and reasonable manner. And God is Well acquainted with what ye do".[14]

Similarly, the Qur'ān says:

«وَلا جُنَاحَ عَلَيْكُمْ فِيمَا عَرَّضْتُمْ بِهِ مِنْ خِطْبَةِ النِّسَاءِ أَوْ أَكْنَنْتُمْ فِي أَنْفُسِكُمْ عَلِمَ اللَّهُ أَنَّكُمْ سَتَذْكُرُونَهُنَّ وَلَكِنْ لا تُوَاعِدُوهُنَّ سِرّاً إِلاّ أَنْ تَقُولُوا قَوْلاً مَعْرُوفاً وَلا تَعْزِمُوا عُقْدَةَ النِّكَاحِ حَتَّى يَبْلُغَ الْكِتَابُ أَجَلَهُ وَاعْلَمُوا أَنَّ اللَّهَ يَعْلَمُ مَا فِي أَنْفُسِكُمْ فَاحْذَرُوهُ وَاعْلَمُوا أَنَّ اللَّهَ غَفُورٌ حَلِيمٌ»

"There is no blame on you if ye make an offer of betrothal or hold in your hearts. God knows that ye cherish them in your hearts: but do not make a secret contract with them except in terms honourable, nor resolve on the tie of marriage till their term prescribed if fulfilled and know that God knoweth what is in your hearts, and take heed of Him and know that God is Oft-forgiving, Most. Forbearing".[15]

A definite contract of remarriage for the woman during her period of '*Iddah* of widowhood is forbidden as obviously unseemly, as also any secrecy in such matters. It would bind the woman at a time she is not fitted to exercise her fullest judgement. But circumstances may arise when an offer (open for future consideration but not immediately decided) may be to her interests, and this is permissible. In mystic interpretation the cherishing love in one's heart without outward show or reward is the true test of sincerity and devotion.

---

1. Sayyid Sābiq, Fiqh al-Sunnah, op. cit., vol. 8, p. 177.
2. Qur'ān, ch. 2:228.
3. Qur'ān, 2:228.
4. Qur'ān, 65:4.
5. Qur'ān, 33:49.
6. Qur'ān, 2:234.
7. This is the opinion of Ibn 'Abbās and 'Alī. See Shawkānī, *Nayl al-Awtār*, vol. VI, pp. 306-307.
8. Al-Shāfi'ī, *Risālah*, op. cit., p. 168.
9. See Mālik, Vol. II, pp. 589-90, Abū Dawūd, Vol. II, p. 293, Shāfi'ī, *Kitāb al-Umm*, Vol. II, pp. 205-206; Shawkani, *Nayl al-Awtar*, Vol. VI, p. 305.
10. Narrated by Abū Daūd and al-Nisāi.
11. Qur'ān, 65:1.
12. Qur'ān, 65:2.
13. Qur'ān, ch. 65:1.
14. Qur'ān, ch. 2:234.
15. Qur'ān, ch. 2:235.

Chapter 14

Al-Nafaqah: The Maintenance

What is Nafaqah?

Maintenance *(Al-Nafaqah)* is the right of one's wife and children to get food, clothing and a residence, some other essential services and medicine, even if the wife happens to be a rich lady.[1] Maintenance in this form is essential *(wājib)* according to the Qur'an, Sunnah and the consensus of opinion of the Jurists.[2] Where both spouses are above the age of puberty, it is the duty of the husband, and not that of a wife as happens in some Western countries nowadays, to supply his wife and children with food, clothes and lodging on a scale commensurate with the social position of the partners and in accordance with the customs and habits of the society in which they live.

Some jurists have given detailed instants of things to be provided as *Nafaqah*[3] during the time they were writing about it. These are to be adjusted in the light of modern necessities to suit the circumstances of the countries and their living standard. It will be the responsibility of a father to maintain his daughters until they are married, and sons until they reach the age of puberty. Likewise, it is a duty of every Muslim to maintain his parents and grand-parents, maternal as well as paternal if he can afford to do so. If it is possible and one has the means, one should look after the needs of even one's poor relatives. According to the Hanafi school every relative within the prohibited degrees is entitled to maintenance, if he is a child and poor, or if he happens to be infirm or blind and poor, if it is a female and that she is poor she should also be maintained whether she is a child or adult.

If the wife is a minor, she will be maintained by her father or guardian as we have seen before. The Messenger of Allah married A'isha two years before she reached the age of puberty and did not give her maintenance. But if the wife has not reached puberty but has submitted to her husband, according to the Māliki and Shāfi'i schools no maintenance is to be given to her.

According to Qadi Abu Yusuf, the Ḥanafi Jurist, if the wife is a minor and the husband accepts her in his house, it is essential for him to maintain her, but if she does not come to his house, he does not have to do so. But Imām Abū Hānīfah and his pupil, Imām Muḥammad, follow the same view as that of Māliki and Shāfi'i schools already mentioned before.

It is not essential to provide one's wife with maintenance in the following events:

1. If she packed and moved out of her matrimonial home to some other place without her husband's permission or without any religious cause.
2. If she travelled without his permission.
3. If she puts on Iḥrām for ḥajj without his permission. But if he went with her or she travelled with his permission the maintenance will be given.
4. If she refused sexual intercourse to her husband.
5. If she is imprisoned after committing a crime.
6. If the husband dies and she becomes a widow. In that case, her right of inheritence supervenes. This is the very reason why the widow is not entitled to maintenance during the *'Iddah* of death.

According to the Māliki and Shāfi'ī schools, if the husband failed or neglected to provide maintenance for the period of two years, the wife is entitled to dissolution of marriage, but in Ḥanafī school, inability, refusal or neglect to maintain are not sufficient grounds for dissolution. A wife is entitled to demand her husband, about to set out on a journey, either to give her; for the whole duration of his absence, an anticipatory allowance, or to give a power of attorney to another for her maintenance. The allowance will fall due at the same intervals at which the husband was in a habit of paying it.

Maintenance in the Modern Family

As we have already discussed, it is the husband who is supposed to provide for the family. If he cannot gain enough to support the family, or if his income is too low to provide for a relatively acceptable standard of living, and provided the wife is willing, both of them may work for gain. However:

1. The husband has the right to terminate the wife's working whenever he deems it necessary.
2. He has the right to object to any job if he feels that it would expose his wife to any harm, seduction or humiliation.

3. The wife has the right to discontinue working whenever she pleases.
4. Any gain from work realised by the wife belongs to the family and cannot be considered as her personal property.

When the wife is not employed, the household becomes her first occupation. By household it is meant the rearing of the children and all domestic services required for maintaining a clean and comfortable habitation. The Prophet (S.A.W.) says: "Cleanliness is a part of faith. Motherhood is highly commended in Islam and is the greatest value second to the worship of Allah *('Ibādah).*

Maintenance After Dissolution of Marriage:

The Holy Qur'ān points out the responsibility of maintenance in the cases of divorce in the following verse of *Sūrah al-Ṭalāq* (The Divorce):

«اَسْكِنُوهُنَّ مِنْ حَيْثُ سَكَنْتُمْ مِنْ وُجْدِكُمْ وَلَا تُضَارُّوهُنَّ لِتُضَيِّقُوا عَلَيْهِنَّ، وَإِنْ كُنَّ أُولَاتِ حَمْلٍ فَأَنْفِقُوا عَلَيْهِنَّ حَتَّىٰ يَضَعْنَ حَمْلَهُنَّ، فَإِنْ أَرْضَعْنَ لَكُمْ فَآتُوهُنَّ أُجُورَهُنَّ، وَأْتَمِرُوا بَيْنَكُمْ بِمَعْرُوفٍ».

"Let the women live in *'Iddah* in the same style as you live, according to your means: Trouble them not so that you make things difficult for them. And if they are pregnant, then spend you substenance on them (maintain them) until they deliver (the baby): and if they suckle your child, give them recompense: and take mutual counsel together, according to what is just and reasonable".[4]

The responsibility of maintenance of the husband is not only when she lives as a legal wife and towards his children by that wife, but it is important to maintain her even in the event of divorce.

There are some selfish people who may maltreat wives and make their lives miserable after pronouncing first divorce and when she is still in *'Iddah*. This is forbidden. She must be provided for on the same scale as he is, according to his status in life. There is still hope of reconciliation, and if not, yet the parting must be honourable. In the event of pregnancy, the Holy Qur'ān provides additional responsibility. No separation will be possible until after the child is born. Hence she must be properly maintained.

As for the child, its nursing, welfare and the home of the mother remains the duty of the father. If the mother's milk fails, or if such circumstances arise which bar the natural course of the mother's nursing her child, merits the father's responsibility to give the child to someone else to suckle at his own expense. This must not induce the father to cut down the reasonable maintenance to which the mother is entitled taking into consideration the circumstances.

The Holy Qur'ān further guides in the matter of maintenance in *Sūrah al-Baqarah:*

> "The mothers shall give suck to their off-spring for two whole years, if the father desires to complete the term, but he shall bear the cost of their food and clothing on equitable (just) terms".[5]

In the above injunction, the word *'rizq'* is mentioned which includes sufficient food, adequate dressing, and other necessary provisions.

The verse specifically mentioned the maintenance of the child so that selfish people may not use the child as an excuse for driving a hard bargain on either side, whether from the mother or the father.

> "No mother shall be treated unfairly on account of her child. Nor father on account of his child, an heir shall be chargeable in the same way."[6]

The father and the mother must conclude all the arrangements for maintenance of the child through mutual consent. They must agree to some course reasonable and equitable both as regards the period before wearing the maximum of which is two years. If a wet-nurse is to be engaged or if the child is to be fed on artificial milk and feed. Further guidance on the subject is offered in the following verse:

«لِيُنْفِقْ ذُو سَعَةٍ مِنْ سَعَتِهِ، وَمَنْ قُدِرَ عَلَيْهِ رِزْقُهُ فَلْيُنْفِقْ مِمَّا آتَاهُ اللّٰهُ، لَا يُكَلِّفُ اللّٰهُ نَفْسًا إِلَّا مَا آتَاهَا سَيَجْعَلُ اللّٰهُ بَعْدَ عُسْرٍ يُسْرًا».

> "Let the man of means spend according to his means: and the man whose resources are restricted, let him spend according to what Allah has given him. Allah puts no burden on any person beyond what he has given him. After difficulty, Allah will soon grant him a relief".[7]

As a practical religion, the Sharī'ah of Islam does not impose burden on either party. They must do their best in the interest of the child according to their means. If they act with honest integrity, Allah will provide a solution to the problem.

The necessity of providing maintenance is emphasised in the Farewell Pilgrimage address of the Prophet (S.A.W.) *(Ḥaj al-Widā'):*

> "Beware about your treatment of women. You have accepted them with the word of Allah, and have made lawful sexual relationship with them with the word of Allah . . . as you have a duty to provide them with reasonable maintenance and clothing."[8]

In a Ḥadīth narrated by 'Ā'ishah, once Hindah bint 'Utbah said to the Prophet: "O Messenger of Allah, Abū Sufyān is a miserly person. He does not provide for me and my son except whatever I take away myself secretly about which he does not know. The Prophet advised: "Take whatever is sufficient for you and your son in a reasonable way ."[9]

According to the Maliki Jurists, it will be the duty of the husband to provide an accommodation for his divorced wife, if he had consummated the marriage. No maintenance is due to a divorced woman, however, except where the number of divorce is less than three. But a pregnant woman, whether repudiated once or thrice is entitled to maintenance. A woman who separated from her husband under the system known as *Khul'*, shall not be entitled to maintenance except when she happened to be pregnant. But, any woman who is separated from her husband through *lian*, imprecation, cannot claim maintenance from that husband, even if she happens to be pregnant.[10]

A wife according to the Māliki school, observing the *Iddah* of mourning, is not entitled to maintenance. But she is entitled to accommodation if the house she happens to be staying in, belonged to her late husband or if the deceased had paid rents in advance.[11] Imām Abū Ḥanifah says that she will be entitled to her maintenance as well. A wife must not leave her house, on account of divorce or the death of her husband, until she has completed the *'Iddah* prescribed for the occasion.

In the Ḥanafi school of law, as laid down in *Durral-Mukhtar,* the wife will be treated as *asl* (root) and the child as *Far'* (branch) in establishing the priority in awarding maintenance although both are inseparable and their maintenance is *Wājib* according to the jurists of all schools.

The wife is not entitled to past maintenance except under the Shāfi'i school. The Shi'ites agree with the Shāfi'i in this regard.

In fixing the sum by way of maintenance, all the schools lay down the rule that the *Qāḍi* in exercising his direction should consider the rank and circumstances of both the spouses. But the following conditions must be fulfilled:[12]

1. It must be a valid marriage.
2. She submits herself to her husband and is obedient.
3. She gives him free access at all lawful times.
4. She does not refuse to accompany her husband when he travels unless she strongly feels that during the travel her person and her property are not safe.
5. When both parties can derive benefit from each other.

If the above conditions are not fulfilled she is not entitled to maintenance. The husband's duty to maintain commences when the wife attains puberty and not before.

Guardianship

In every human society and at all times in human history orphans, insane persons as well as minor children have been maltreated. Some unscrupulous people, including close relatives, have also misappropriated the funds of such unfortunate persons. In the *Jāhilliyah* society, before Islam, the cases of embezzlement and misappropriation were quite rampant. It was the society where might was right and the only law that prevailed was the law of the jungle. As a result, the guardians appointed from among the members of the family of the orphans, insane persons and minors, they always devoured out of their property. With the introduction of Islam special attention to the protection of the interest of these unfortunate persons was provided in order to minimize risks to which the person and property of these people were generally exposed. Under Sharī'ah there is no need of any formal appointment of a competent person to act as a guardian. One should be a sane and a matured person having fear of Allah (*Taqwah*) and sense of justice to act as a good guardian.

In sharī'ah guardianship is of three kinds:

(i) guardianship of person
(ii) guardianship of property, and
(iii) guardianship in marriage.

As far as the guardianship of person and property is concerned, the following guidance is available in respect of the person and property of the orphans. The Holy Qur'ān says:

Maintenance of Parents, Poor Relatives and Destitutes in general:

The Qur'ān and the hadith abound in the teachings in respect of the treatment of ones parents. In *Sūrah Banī Israīl* we have been commanded in the following words:

> "Thy Lord has decreed that you worship none but him and that you be kind to your parents. Where one or both of them attain old-age in your life say not to them a word of contempt nor repel them but address them in terms of honour and out of kindness, lower to them the wing of humility and say: 'my Lord bestow on them your mercy even as they cherished me in childhood.'"[13]

These words explain in clear terms that when the parents were strong and child was helpless the parental affection was showed on the child. Since the child has grown up and is strong and the parents have become weak and helpless, it is his duty to bestow similar tender care on the parents and maintain them. According to *Hidāyah* it is incumbent upon a man to provide maintenance for his father, mother, grand-fathers and grandmothers as they should happen to be in the necessitous circumstance.[14] If one happens to be in easy circumstances, he is duty bound to maintain his poor relations especially those who fall under the prohibited degree of relationship by consanguinity in proportion to the shares which he will inherit at the time of the death of such poor relations. A wealthy person is also required to help and maintain the poor and the needy living around him, without any distinction of caste, creed or colour, if he is in a position to do so.

Raḍā: Suckling

In order to ensure that children are properly fed, clothed and looked after, the Holy Qur'ān lays down rules in respect of *Rada* (Suckling). These rules are meant for safeguarding the interests of children both when the marriage between their parents continue and when such marriages end in divorces. It is in that if the marriage between parents continues, it is the responsibility of both of them to look after their child and not neglect it as it is incapable of taking care of itself.

If their marriage ends in divorce, they can agree to some reasonable and equitable arrangement for the care of their child. *Raḍā* or suckling is a duty of both parents and if they neglect it, they will be answerable to Allah on the Day of Judgement. The maximum period of suckling is two years. If the father of the child is afraid of neglect of the child on the part of the mother, he should have a wet-nurse. In the modern times this will include arrangements for artificial feeding. The injunction of the Qur'ān goes thus:

«وَالْوَالِدَاتُ يُرضِعْنَ اَوْلَادَهُنَّ حَوْلَيْنِ كَامِلَيْنِ لِمَنْ اَرَادَ اَنْ يُتِمَّ الرَّضَاعَةَ وَعَلَى
الْمَوْلُودِ لَهُ رِزْقُهُنَّ وَكِسْوَتُهُنَّ بِالْمَعْرُوفِ، لَا تُكَلَّفُ نَفْسٌ اِلَّا وُسْعَهَا لَا تُضَارَّ وَالِدَةٌ
بِوَلَدِهَا وَلَا مَوْلُودٌ لَهُ بِوَلَدِهِ وَعَلَى الْوَارِثِ مِثْلُ ذٰلِكَ فَاِنْ اَرَادَ فِصَالاً عَنْ تَرَاضٍ
مِنْهُمَا وَتَشَاوُرٍ فَلَا جُنَاحَ عَلَيْهِمَا وَاِنْ اَرَدْتُمْ اَنْ تَسْتَرْضِعُوا اَوْلَادَكُمْ فَلَا جُنَاحَ
عَلَيْكُمْ اِذَا سَلَّمْتُمْ مَا اٰتَيْتُمْ بِالْمَعْرُوفِ وَاتَّقُوا اللّٰهَ وَاعْلَمُوا اَنَّ اللّٰهَ بِمَا تَعْمَلُونَ
بَصِيرٌ».

"The mothers shall give suck to their off-spring for the two whole years, if the father desires to complete the term. But he shall bear the cost of their food and clothing on equitable terms. No soul shall have a burden laid on it greater than it can bear. No mother shall be treated unfairly on account of her child; nor father on account of his child. An heir shall be chargeable in the same way. if they both decide on weaning by mutual consent, and after due consultation there is no blame on them. If you decide on a foster-mother for your off-spring, there is no blame on you, provided you pay (the mother) what you offered, on equitable terms. But fear Allah and know that Allah sees well what you do."[15]

The points which become clear from the above verse of the Holy Qur'ān are as follows:

1. The period of giving suck is normally two years.
2. The responsibility for providing maintenance to the wife or former wife and for arranging suck for the child lies on the man. He shall bear the cost of food and clothing on equitable terms.
3. The woman who gives suck to her baby should not be maltreated by her husband.
4. The weaning of the child should be done by mutual agreement between the mother and the father.
5. If the man dies, his heirs will be responsible for maintenance of his widow and *raḍā* of his child.
7. If by any chance, the mother herself cannot give suck and she and her husband decide to employ a foster-mother, there is no harm. But the mother should still be given her maintenance.
7. Every Muslim should know that whatever he does Allah sees him all the time, therefore he should not treat his wife or former wife and his child unfairly.

Period of Suck

Suck is to be given for a period of two years at the end of which the child should be weaned. However, the period may be extended if there are special circumstances to warrant it. The Holy Qur'ān says:

> "And we have enjoined on man (to be good) to his parents: In travail upon travails did his mother bear him and his years twain was his weaning: (hear the command), show gratitude to me, to thy parents; to me is (thy final) goal."[16]

It says further

«وَحَمْلُهُ وَفِصَالُهُ ثَلٰثُونَ شَهْراً».

> "The carrying of (the child) to his weaning is a period of thirty months."[17]

Commenting on the last verse, 'Allāhmah Yusuf Ali says: "It leaves six months as the minimum period of human gestation after which the child is known to be viable. This is in accordance with latest ascertained scientific facts. The average period is 28 days, or ten times the intermenstrual period, and of course the average period of weaning is much less than 24 months."[18]

Orphans and their Guardianship

The person and property of orphans is generally exposed to many risks. Therefore, Islam gives special attention to the protection of the interests of orphans by their guardians. The Qur'ān says:

«وَيَسْأَلُونَكَ عَنِ ٱلْيَتَامَىٰ قُلْ اِصْلَاحٌ لَهُمْ خَيْرٌ وَاِنْ تُخَالِطُوهُمْ فَاِخْوَانُكُمْ
وَٱللَّهُ يَعْلَمُ ٱلْمُفْسِدَ مِنَ ٱلْمُصْلِحِ وَلَوْ شَاءَ ٱللَّهُ لَاَعْنَتَكُمْ اِنَّ ٱللَّهَ عَزِيزٌ حَكِيمٌ».

"They ask thee concerning orphans, Say: The best thing to do is what is for their good: If you mix their affairs with yours, they are your brethren; but Allah knows the man who means mischief from the man who means good. And if Allah wished, he could have put into difficulties: He is indeed Exalted in Power, Wise."[19]

«وَاٰتُوا ٱلْيَتَامَىٰ اَمْوَالَهُمْ وَلَا تَتَبَدَّلُوا الْخَبِيثَ بِالطَّيِّبِ وَلَا تَأْكُلُوا اَمْوَالَهُمْ اِلَىٰ
اَمْوَالِكُمْ اِنَّهُ كَانَ حُوباً كَبِيراً».

"To orphans restore their property (when they reach their age), nor substitute (your) worthless things for (their) good ones: and eat not their substance (by mixing it up) with your own for this is indeed a great sin."[20]

«وَلَا تُؤْتُوا ٱلسُّفَهَاءَ اَمْوَالَكُمُ ٱلَّتِي جَعَلَ ٱللَّهُ لَكُمْ قِيَاماً وَ ارْزُقُوهُمْ فِيهَا
وَاكْسُوهُمْ وَقُولُوا لَهُمْ قَوْلاً مَعْرُوفاً، وَٱبْتَلُوا ٱلْيَتَامَىٰ حَتَّىٰ اِذَا بَلَغُوا ٱلنِّكَاحَ فَاِنْ
آنَسْتُمْ مِنْهُمْ رُشْداً فَادْفَعُوا اِلَيْهِمْ اَمْوَالَهُمْ وَلَا تَأْكُلُوهَا اِسْرَافاً وَبِدَاراً اَنْ يَكْبَرُوا
وَمَنْ كَانَ غَنِيّاً فَلْيَسْتَعْفِفْ وَمَنْ كَانَ فَقِيراً فَلْيَأْكُلْ بِالْمَعْرُوفِ فَاِذَا دَفَعْتُمْ اِلَيْهِمْ
اَمْوَالَهُمْ فَاشْهِدُوا عَلَيْهِمْ وَكَفَىٰ بِاللَّهِ حَسِيباً».

"To those of weak understanding (orphans and others) make not over your property, which Allah has made a means of support for you, but feed and clothe them therewith, and speak to them words of kindness and justice."

"Make trial of orphans until they reach the age of marriage; if then you find sound judgement in them, release their property to them; but consume it not wastefully, nor in haste against their growing up."[21]

The words *'Your property'* are used in respect of an Orphan's property in *Sūrah al-Bāqrah*, verse 220. What is meant by it is that all property belongs to Allah and any one who possesses it or administers it, is merely a custodian. Ultimately all property belongs to the community and is for their good and it is for your support that is the support of the community it is only held in trust by an individual. The guardians are advised as to how he will administer the property of orphans: "If the guardian is well off let him claim no remuneration, but if he is poor, let him have for himself what is just and reasonable. When you release their property to them, take witnesses in their presence: but all sufficient is Allah in taking account".

These verses are very comprehensive in meaning. They teach the Muslim Community that in no case should a wealth, which is so important for the maintenance of life, be entrusted to such people as are feeble-minded and incapable of using or managing it properly, for they might, by its wrong use, spoil its cultural and economic system and in the long run its moral system as well. It is true that the rights of private ownership must be honoured, but at the same time they are not to be so unlimited as to allow one to use them in any way one likes and create social chaos.

As far as one's necessities of life are concerned, they must be fulfilled but none should be allowed to use these rights to the extent that is harmful to the collective moral, cultural and economic good of the community.

According to the verse, every owner of wealth should consider seriously before entrusting his wealth to anyone whether that person is capable of using it properly. On the larger scale, the Islamic State should take into its own custody the property of those who are found incapable of using it properly, or of those who may be using it in wrong ways but should arrange for provision of their necessities of life.

The Qur'ānic statements, "Make trial of orphans until they reach the age" gives guardians an additional responsibility to keep an eye upon them and go on testing their intelligence in order to see how far they have become capable of looking after their own affairs before giving them back their property.

In other words, two conditions of puberty and sound-judgement have been laid down for the return of their property to the orphans. As to the application of this first condition, all the Jurists are agreed, but in regard to the second condition there is some difference of opinion. Imam Abu Hanifah is of the opinion that if the orphan lacks capability when he reaches the age of puberty, his guardian may wait for a maximum period of seven years, and then he must return his property to him whether he shows signs of capability or not. But Imām Abū Yusuf, Imām Muhammad and Imām Shāfi'i are of the opinion that capability is a pre-requisite for the return of his property to the orphan. Probably these latter learned people were inclined to the opinion that the case of such a person should be referred to a Muslim *Qāḍi*, who would himself arrange for the management of the property of the one who has not acquired capability of management.

The guardians are further advised:

«وَاِذَا حَضَرَ الْقِسْمَةَ أُولُوا الْقُرْبىٰ وَالْيَتَامىٰ وَالْمَسَاكِينُ فَارْزُقُوهُمْ مِنْهُ وَقُولُوا لَهُمْ قَوْلاً مَعْرُوفاً».

"But if at the time of division, other relatives, or orphans, or poor, are present, feed them out of the property (although they have no legal share) and speak to them words of kindness and justice" 22.

"Those who unjustly eat up the property of orphans, eat up fire into their own bodies: they will soon be enduring a blazing fire".

The cause of revelation of this verse has been mentioned in the books of Aḥādīth. When Sa'ad bin Rubai'ah, a companion of the Prophet, was killed in the battle of Uḥud, his widow came to the Prophet with his two daughters and said: "O Messenger of Allah, these are the two daughters of Sa'ad, the one who got martyrdom in the battle of Uḥud. Their uncle has taken away all the property belong to Sa'ad and has left nothing for the children. Who will marry these girls? It was then that this verse was revealed to give warning to those who eat up the property of orphans.[23]

The Qur'ān urges upon people to be fair and just to orphans especially when they want to marry female orphans. It says:

«وَيَسْتَفْتُونَكَ فِي النِّسَاءِ قُلِ اللّٰهُ يُفْتِيكُمْ فِيهِنَّ وَمَا يُتْلٰى عَلَيْكُمْ فِي الْكِتَابِ فِي يَتَامَى النِّسَاءِ الَّتِي لَا تُؤْتُونَهُنَّ مَا كُتِبَ لَهُنَّ وَتَرْغَبُونَ أَنْ تَنْكِحُوهُنَّ وَالْمُسْتَضْعَفِينَ مِنَ الْوِلْدَانِ وَأَنْ تَقُومُوا لِلْيَتَامٰى بِالْقِسْطِ وَمَا تَفْعَلُوا مِنْ خَيْرٍ فَإِنَّ اللّٰهَ كَانَ بِهِ عَلِيماً».

"They ask thy instruction concerning the women, say: Allah does instruct you about them: and (remember) what has been rehearsed unto you (to be just in your dealings with women, orphans and children and those who are real requiring special consideration) in the Book, concerning the orphans of women to whom you give not the portions prescribed, and yet whom you desire to marry, as also concerning the children who are weak and oppressed: that you stand firm for justice to orphans. There is not a good deed which you do, but Allah is well acquainted therewith."[24]

It also says:

«وَإِنْ خِفْتُمْ أَلَّا تُقْسِطُوا فِي الْيَتَامٰى....»

"If you fear that you shall not be able to deal justly with the orphans . . . "[25]

The cause of revelation of this verse was that there was an orphan girl under the care of a man. She owned a date-palm. He married her just because she owned a date-palm and not because he loved her. It was on that occasion that this verse was revealed.

Hadānah: Custody and Guardianship of Minors

The custody of minor children and their guardianship belong to the following persons: According to the jurists a mother is entitled to the custody of a male child until seven years of age and a female child until she reaches the age of puberty. The Shī'ite law differs slightly from the Sunni law in this respect. A male child remains under the custody of the other until two years while the female child until seven years. After this specified age the father is the only guardian who looks after the welfare of his children. In the event of the death of the father his executor becomes their legal guardian. Even though the minor children are in the care of the mother, the father must not ignore his responsibility of supervising his children under the custody of their mother. In the absence of the mother, that is, if she is dead or if she is disqualified according to shari'ah, the custody of male and female children will be given to the following female relatives in the order of priority:

a) mother's mother,
b) father's mother,
c) mother's grand-mother,
d) father's grand-mother,
e) full sister,
f) utarine sister,
g) daughter of full sister,
h) daughter of utarine sister,
i) full maternal aunt,
j) utarine maternal aunt,
k) full paternal aunt.

Supposing there do not exist either the mother or she is disqualified and there are no female relations available the guardianship will devolve on the male relations on the following order:

a) father
b) nearest paternal grand-father
c) full brother
d) consanguine brother or any other paternal relative within the prohibited degree.

In the absence of legal guardians, the Qadi or the court will appoint the guardian for the protection of a minor's property.

Guardianship in Marriage:

For guardianship in marriage see the topic: *The Role of Guardian in Valid Muslim Marriage* in Chapter 7.

1. Sayyid Sābiq, *Fiqh al-Sunnah*, vol. 7, p. 85.
2. Ibid.
3. See for complete *Mukhtaṣar* of Sīdī Khalīl giving details of what a husband is obliged to provide for his wife.
4. Qur'ān, ch. 65:6.
5. Qur'ān, ch. 2:233.
6. Qur'ān, ch. 2:233.
7. Qur'ān, ch. 65:7.
8. Sayyid Sābiq, *Fiqh al-Sunnah*, vol. 7, p. 86.
9. Narrated by Al-Bukhārī and Muslim.
10. Al-Qayrawānī, *Risāl ah*, op. cit., ch. 33: *Bāb Fil'Iddah Wal Nafaqh*, pp. 98-101.
11. Al-Qayrawāni, *Risāl ah*, op. cit., ch. 33: *Bāb Fil'Iddah Wal Nafaqh*, pp. 98-101.
12. Sayyid Sābiq, *Fi qh al-Sunnah*, op. cit., vol. 7, pp. 88-89.
13. Qur'an ch. 17:23, 24.
14. Hidāyah, p. 147
15. Qur'ān, 2:223.
16. Qur'ān, 31:14.
17. Qur'ān, 46:15.
18. A Yūsuf 'Ali, *The Holy Qur'ān Text, Translation and Commentary*, 1370 (Beirut 1968).
19. Qur'ān 2:220.
20. Qur'ān 4:2
21. Qur'ān, ch. 4:5-6.
22. Qur'ān 4:8.
23. Al-Bukhārī, *Ṣaḥīḥ al-Bukhārī:* Kitāb al-Tafsīr.
24. Qur'ān, 4:127.
25. Qur'ān, 4:3

PART III

CRIME AND PUNISHMENT

Chapter 15

Criminal Law (Al-'Uqūbāt) and Punishment (Al-Ḥudūd)

The Criminal and the Society

It is rightly believed that at the height of glory of human civilization, satan comes to play his role. A man becomes *Zalum* and *Jahul* (Unjust and foolish)[1] in spite of the continuous guidance given by the Creator through His Messenger and Prophet throughout ages. No matter, how purified and reformed a given society becomes, crimes will still be committed though the difference would be that of degree. It is very essential for us therefore, to examine the problems of crime and the reasons for its prevalence, to study the personalities of these criminals as well as their psychology and nature in order to prevent the future crime rate. Wherever it is necessary to apportion the blame on the society, it is equally necessary to blame the structure of our social institutions and our leaders and the members of the society who helped in encouraging as driving the criminal to commit a particular crime. Ibn Hazam, while discussing the helpless condition of a man who is driven by hunger to eat the flesh of a dead and rotting animal or pork which is unlawful in Islam, says:

> "It is not lawful for a Muslim to eat these unlawful things even in helpless condition when his Muslim or *Dhimi* neighbours or members of society have lawful food and drink more than what they require, since it is obligatory *(Fard)* for such people to feed the hungry. In such a situation, he has a right to share food from the rich neighbours. If he has to fight in the course of getting his food and he is killed, the killer will have to face *Qaṣāṣ* (law of Equality). He will be considered among those who rebel *(Bāghī)*.

One who stops one's brother from getting his lawful right will be considered as involved in a rebellion. It was on this ground that Sayyidnā Abūbakar fought against those who refused to pay *Zakāt* (The Poor due).[2]

When the society denies the right of its individual members, it must be taken to task as the Qur'ān says:

«فأن بغت احداهما على الاخرى فقاتلوا التي تبغى حتى تفىء الى امر الله».

"If one group of them shows highhandness on the other, fight with them until they return to Allah's injunction".[3]

Society, in the religion of Islam takes preference over an individual, and hence it is the interest of society that over-rides the individual and not vice-versa. It is because of this reason that any crime committed against the peace and well-being of the society will be deemed as the crime against the Creator Himself. As we have seen before, society has not right to tyranize an individual member unless the individuals interests do not pose any threat to the rights of other individuals or the society.

It is against this background that Islamic Sharī'ah does not agree with the synthetic theory or test for determining the problem of abnormality and criminality. According to this synthetic theory, 'no act can be called a crime, if, at the time the act was committed the doer was suffering from mental derangement or morbid impulse of a really irressistible type that caused the loss of the mental or emotional equillibrium".[4]

Let us carefully examine the above view and then look at the narration in *Ṣaḥīḥ al-Bukhārī*.

When Sayyidna Ali says to Sayyidnā 'Umar: "Do you know from whom no good deed or evil are recorded and are not responsible for what they do: an insane person until he becomes sane; a child till he grows to the age of puberty; a sleeping person till he wakes".[5] The Shari'ah also agrees with the view that no act can be called a crime, if at the time the act was committed, the doer was suffering from some mental derangement, but does not generalise and consider every criminal to be mentally deranged or every criminal act merely an irresistible type of impulse. Crimes and sins often are the manifestations of human selfishness, avarise, revenge, caprice and egoism.

Benevolence, undoubtedly, is an ideal justice provided it does not open the way to temptation and encouragement to spread mischief in the world, *(Fasād fil arḍ)*. The crime rate will surely increase if no deterrent is provided by those who manage the affair of the society. The twentieth century of ours has seen the crimes plaguing the so called 'civilized' world of ours. Is it not a pity that one cannot move freely and fearlessly in the streets of western capitals in the evening where pickpockets, thieves, hooligans and evil elements of the society roam about to deprive people of their fundamental rights to move freely in the 'Land of Allah'! Last year, I attended a conference in New York, and then began a tour in the United States of America. I was advised by friends not to carry much money with me nor go empty-pocketted. On enquiry, I was told that if I carried plenty of money, a hooligan might meet me and take away everything that I carried; but, if he failed to find anything worth taking away from me, he might attack me in his desperate moments. The cure of this pathetic situation does not merely lie in dreaming about "rooting out the criminality of the offending human being, without destroying his humanity and the potential good within him."[6]

Dr. James Seth has said that the theories of punishment and interdependent are in no way mutually exclusive. According to him, in virtue of his manhood and personality, "the criminal must be convinced with the righteousness of the punishment."[7] But the question is, how are you going to convince the criminal who has committed a grave criminal ;act like homicide, armed robbery, adultery and *continuous* acts of theft of the righteousness of punishment. There was the law of Allah of which he was made aware right from his childhood in a Muslim family. The deterrent *Ḥadd* punishments that he saw and heard of should have made him aware of the gravity of the crime he was committing. But if satan, an open enemy to man (*'Aduwuj al-Mubīn*) convinced him more than "the righteousness of punishment", how can one stop others not falling into the same snare again. Can we do this through the campaigns? According to eminent thinkers like Hegel, punishment in itself tends to reform the offender.[8] The Islamic Shari'ah has provided two kinds of punishments, one leading to learn lesson and reform and re-educate one's self not to commit a similar crime and an opportunity to rehabiliate one's self as a good and harmless member of the society. This form of light punishment is called *Tazīr*, meaning putting to shame or disgracing the criminal for the criminal act he has committed against a member of the society, or, in other words, against the society itself. *Tazīr* is left to the discretion of a pious and learned judge *(Qāḍī)* whether it is in the form of flogging publicly, banishing or even a warning and admonitions to behave well next time.

The Shari'ah law does not sanction providing a criminal anice room instead of a cell in the prison house, good and tasty foods, furniture, television and radio sets and cosy gardens for sports.

Al-'Uqubat: Criminal Law

The penal or criminal law in Islam is called *al-'Uqūbāt* (singular, al-*'uqūbah*) which covers both torts as well as crimes. There is very little difference between the two. The Sharī'ah emphasises on fulfilling the rights of all individuals as well as the public at large. The law that gives the remedy to the public is a crime and if it is given to the individual it is a tort. The *'Uqūbāt* applies to Muslims, as well as non-Muslims alike in a

Muslim state. A Muslim will be punished for a crime committed even if it was done far away from the Islamic state. In an ultimate sense, it is a crime against Allah, and he will be punished once he came home or was brought back by the authorities of an Islamic state.

The *qāḍī* or a Sharī'ah judge has to abide by the law prescribed in the case of *'Uqūbāt*, and hence he is forbidden to impose a penalty other than that fixed by the Divine law in conformity with the injunctions of the Qur'ān and the Sunnah otherwise he will be an evil doer.[9]

Ḥudūd and Ta'zīrāt

Ḥadd Punishment only given when there is a violation of People's Rights

The word *Ḥudūd* is the plural of an Arabic word *Ḥadd*, which means prevention, restraint or prohibition, and for this reason, it is a restrictive and preventive ordinance, or statute, of Allah concerning things lawful *(Ḥalāl)* and things unlawful *(Ḥarām)*.

Ḥudūd of Allah are of two categories. Firstly, those statutes prescribed to mankind in respect of foods and drinks and marriages and divorce, etc., what are lawful thereof and what are unlawful; secondly, the punishments, prescribed, or appointed, to be inflicted upon him who does that which he has been forbidden to do. In Islamic jurisprudence, the word *ḥudūd* is limited to punishments for crimes mentioned by the Holy Qur'ān or the Sunnah of the Prophet while other punishments are left to the discretion of the Qāḍī or the rule which are called *Ta'azīr* (disgracing the criminal). The general word for punishment is *'uqūbah* derived from *'aqb* which means "one thing coming after another", because punishment follows transgression of the limits set by Divine Law. This is the reason why Islamic Penal Law is called *Al-Uqubat* as we have seen earlier. We should bear in mind that all the violations and breaches of Divine limits in a general sense are not punishable since the punishment is only inflicted in those cases in which there is violation of breach of other people's rights. As for example, if someone neglects his prayers *(ṣalāt)*, or does not observe fasts or perform pilgrimage when he has the means, they are not punishable. But if one does not pay Zākat or poor due, which is a charity as well as a tax from the rich to the poor, there will be punishment accorded to the defaulter. The Holy Prophet appointed officials to collect the Zakāt, which was received in the *bait al-māl* (public-treasury), thus showing that its collection was a duty of the Muslim state. Islamic history records that when certain Arab tribes refused to pay Zakāt, Sayyidnā Abū Bakr sent out troops against them, because the withholding of Zākat on the part of an entire tribe was tantamount to a rebellion against the Islamic state and the violition of the rights of the poor.

These crimes which are punishable in Sharī'ah are ones which affect the society. The Holy Qur'ān has enumerated them as murder *(Qatl)* dacoity or highway robbery *(Ḥirābah)* theft *(Sariqah)* adultery or fornication *(Zinā)* and accusation of adultery *(Qadhaf)*. We shall discuss in detail these crimes and their punishments, but it should be understood that the Holy Qur'ān lays down a general law for the punishment of offences in the following words:

«وَجَزَآؤُا سَيِّئَةٍ سَيِّئَةٌ مِثْلُهَا فَمَنْ عَفَا وَأَصْلَحَ فَأَجْرُهُ عَلَى اللّهِ إِنَّهُ لَا يُحِبُّ الظَّالِمِينَ».

"And the recompense of injury *(Sayyi'ah)* is punishment. *(Sayyi'ah)* equal thereto, but whoever forgives and amends, his reward is due from Allah for Allah loves not those who do wrong."[10]

This golden principle is of very great importance and applies both to individual wrong done by one person to another and also to the offences committed against society. There are a number of Qur'ānic injunctions concerning the punishment of offenders guiding the Ummah: "And if you punish then punish with the life of that with which you were affected; but if you are patient, it will certainly be best for those who are patient."[11] "And he who punishes evil with the like of that with which he has been afflicted and he has been oppressed, Allah will certainly help him."[12] "Whoever acts aggressively against you, inflict injury on him."[13]

While in the verses quoted above and similar other verses, there is a rule laid down for the individual wronged, that he should in the first instance try to forgive the offender provided he amends by forgiveness. According to these verses, if punishment of evil is to be given, it should be proportionate to the evil committed. Every civilised code of penal laws is based on this principle. It is an interesting point to remember that the Holy Qur'ān generally adopts the same word for punishment, as for the crime. Thus in chapter 42:40, both the evil and its punishment are called *sayyi'ah* (evil); in chapter 16:126 and chapter 22:60, the word used is a derivative of *'uqūbah* (punishment); and in chapter 2:194, the word used is *i'tida'* (aggression). The adoption of the same word evil for the crime and its punishment indicates that punishment itself, though justified by the circumstances, is truly speaking nothing but a necessary evil.

It is for this reason that the Muslims are asked to get their rights either on private or public grounds through the due process of law taking the matter up to the competent *Qāḍīs* (judge) court and not by taking law into their own hands. Otherwise they will be among the wrong-doers *(Ẓālimūn)*. In private defence too, they must be just in using the amount of force necessary. But in all cases, they must not seek a compensation greater than the injury suffered by them. The most they can do is to demand equal redress, i.e. the harm equivalent to the harm done to them and no more. But the ideal way is not to seek vengeance at all but reconciliation, forgiveness and making the offender aware of the gravity of his offence as long as it is not against the public and injurious to the entire society. In the latter case, the deterrent punishment will follow. The Qur'ānic injunctions gives this gospel of goodness in the following words:

«وَلَا تَسْتَوِي الْحَسَنَةُ وَلَا السَّيِّئَةُ ادْفَعْ بِالَّتِي هِيَ أَحْسَنُ فَإِذَا الَّذِي بَيْنَكَ وَبَيْنَهُ عَدَاوَةٌ كَأَنَّهُ وَلِيٌّ حَمِيمٌ».

"Nor can goodness and evil be equal. Repel evil with what is better: then will be between whom and you was hatred as it were your friend and intimate."[14]

But such goodness will only be granted to those who exercise patience, forbearance and self-restraint, who are really persons of the greatest good fortune.[15] They will be given their reward twice by Allah, their Creator, because they have persevered and have tried to avert evil with good.[16] In Sūrah 33, verse 96, Muslims are ordered specifically to repel evil with what is best.[17]

Muslims are thus taught to be forbearant *(ṣābirīn),* but they are equally asked to prevent repetition of crimes by taking steps and applying both physical and moral means. The best moral means is to turn hatred into friendship by forgiveness and love, as the Qur'ān says: "But if a person forgives and makes reconciliation, his reward is due from Allah, for Allah loves not those who do wrong."[18]

Allamah Yūsuf 'Ali, while commenting on this verse rightly says that "this active righting of wrongs, whether by physical or by moral or spiritual means, which are commanded as better, is an antithesis to the monkish doctrine, when you are smitten on the cheek, to turn the other also. This would not suppress, but encourage wrong-doing. It is practised by none but poltroons, and is preached only by hypocrites, or men who want to make slaves of others, by depriving them of the power of self-defence."[19] The doctrine of offering another cheek when one is smitten by anyone occurs in Matthew and Luke,[20] although it is not necessary for us to believe that this unnatural and unpracticable law was preached by Prophet Jesus.

Punishments for crimes can be divided into four broad categories:

a. Physical punishments which includes death sentence, amputation of hand, flogging and stoning to death.

b. Restrictions of freedom which includes imprisonment or sending one on an exile.
c. Imposition of fines.
d. Warning given by the Qāḍī.

Apart from these prescribed punishments for various crimes there are other ways of making the criminal feel that he has committed a great wrong. As for example, a man convicted of false accusation of fornication *(Qādhaf)* will be deprived of the right of giving a testimony *(Shahādah)*.

Prevention of Ḥadd Punishment in cases of doubt

Prophet Muḥammad has given the basic ruling in a Ḥādith:

> "Prevent the application of *Ḥadd* punishment as much as you can whenever any doubt persists."

Once this ruling was applied it reduced the number of *Ḥadd* punishments in the Muslim Countries like Saudi Arabia. When the benefit of doubt is resolved in favour of the accused supposing in case of theft *(Sariqah)*, a lesser punishment by *Ta'azīr* is given because the doubt relates to the criteria and not the conviction. In the case of adultery, if there is a little doubt, no *Ḥadd* punishment will be given at all.

In the case of theft, the accused should not be given the *Ḥadd* punishment all of a sudden. In a Muslim state, every individual is entitled to social security through the public treasury called *Bait al-Mal* where funds are collected from various sources including the obligatory collection of *Zakāt*. If a citizen is driven by force of circumstances since he could not earn his living for himself and his family due to lack of opportunities or was not taken care of through the funds of *Bait al-Mal*, the society will be considered at fault and no *Ḥadd* punishment will be given to the accused. This is in keeping with the decision of Caliph ʿUmar not to apply *Ḥadd* to those accused of theft during the period of famine in Medina.

Even the very process of law under the Sharī'ah curtails the number of *Ḥadd* punishments. According to the Mālikī school the accused in the case of theft, must be taken to the *Qāḍī*. In the Ḥanāfi school of law, it is required that it would be the complainant whose property is stolen to demand that the *Qāḍī* should consider applying the *Ḥadd* punishment of amputation of hand. But if the complainant forgives the accused and forgoes the recovery of his property, the *Ḥadd* punishment will not be applied, but, instead, *Ta'azīr* will be applicable.

At the most, the accused will be put to disgrace through the lesser punishment of lashes, fine, imprisonment or mere warning as the *Qāḍī* deems fit. In Ḥanafī school, if the person whose property is stolen asks the Qāḍi to deem the stolen property as donation to the accused, *Ḥadd* punishment of amputation will not be applied. The Mālikī and the Shāfi'i schools differ on this point and say that once the Qāḍi's Court is asked by the complainant to consider applying the *Ḥadd*, it is no longer left to the discretion of the Complainant to intervene at a later stage. They base their argument on a case decided by the Messenger of Allah himself.

Another factor in awarding *Ḥadd* punishment is the stipulation of *TWO* matured and just male witnesses of high moral probity. It is not always easy to find such witnesses present at the scene of the crime. If the accused confesses the crime, the punishment will be accorded. Even in this regard, Imām Abū Yusuf of the Ḥanafī school and Imām Aḥmad bin Ḥanbal say that two or even three sustained confessions are needed before conviction.

Apart from these measures, it must also be proved before giving *Ḥadd* punishment that in the event of theft, the accused did force open or break into the house and actually entered it. It is required that money, gold, silver, ornaments, diamonds and pearls and other valuables must be kept securely locked in a strong box and stores must be guarded and houses must be locked so as not to tempt the potential thief. If one failed to take enough precaution then he gets part of the blame for negligence which brought about the theft. In such cases where these requirements are not satisifed, but there exists sufficient ground for conviction *Ta'azir* will be applied instead of *Ḥadd* punishment. Besides, if the stolen property is food, fruit, grass or forest wood, *Ḥadd* punishment will not be applied at all.

Ḥadd punishments are awarded in the following seven cases:

1. Penalties exacted for committing murder, manslaughter or bodily harm;
2. Punishment for theft by the amputation of a hand;
3. Punishment for fornication or adulter: stoning for a married person, and one hundred lashes for an unmarried person;
4. Punishment for slander by eighty lashes;
5. Punishment for apostacy by death;
6. Punishment for inebriation by eighty lashes;
7. Punishment for highway robbery *(Qata al-Tariq)* by death, cutting off a leg and an arm from opposite direction or an exile according to the seriousness of the crime.

In the rest of the cases, *Ta'azīr* will be applied.

Ta'azir: Its meaning and application

Ta'azir literally means disgracing the criminal for his shameful criminal act.

In *Ta'azir*, punishment has not been fixed by law, and the Qāḍī is allowed discretion both as to the form in which such punishment is to be inflicted and its measure. This kind of punishment by discretion has been provided in special consideration of the various factors affecting social change in human civilisation and which vary on the basis of variations in the methods of commission or the kind of criminal conduct indicatable under the law. Offences punishable by this method are those against human life, property, and public peace and tranquility.

The general structure of the Criminal Law of the Muslims today *(al-Siyāsat al-Shara'ī)* is based on the principles of *Ta'azir*. In other words, *Ta'azirāt* form discretionary penalties inflicted by the judge himself, either for an offence whose punishment is not determined, or for prejudice done to one's neighbour. The punishment can take the form of lashes, imprisonment, fine, warning etc. To sum up, *Ta'azir* can be defined as follows:

«تأديب على ذنب لاحد فيه ولا كفارة».

"It is disciplinary punishment for a crime for which no specific *ḥadd* is prescribed nor any form of expiation."

Exceptions to Legal Responsibility

«وقال علي لعمر: اما علمت ان القلم رفع عن المجنون حتى يفيق وعن الصبي حتى يدرك وعن النائم حتى يستيقظ».

Sayyidnā 'Alī once said to Sayyidnā 'Umar: "Do you know that no deed good or evil are recorded (for the following) and are not responsible for what they do:

1. An insane person till he becomes sane:
2. A child till he grows to the age of puberty;
3. A sleeping person till he awakes. [21]

According to the above narration, we shall consider the legal liability or criminal responsibility in Sharī'ah.

The responsibility for the crime committed will be that of the criminal alone. His father, mothers, brother or any other relative will not be made to undergo punishment for crimes committed by him as happened during the Jāhiliyyah period before Islam. The Holy Qur'ān says that nobody will bear the burden of another. [22]

The only collective responsibility will be that of the family in respect of payments of blood money or damages resulting from a crime. In this case, the criminal, as well as his relatives on his father's side will be collectively responsible for *Diyah* (Blood money) or damages imposed for causing any physical injury.

The famous *waṣiyyah* or will left by Sayyidnā ʿAlī throws further light on this subject. When Sayyidna Ali sustained injury at the hands of ʿAbd al-Raḥmān bin Muljim, he called his sons to his deathbed and said to them: "Do not kill anyone except him who killed me. But wait; if I die from his blow, revenge me with a blow for a blow, and don't mutilate the criminal, for I heard the messenger of Allah say: 'Beware of mutilation even if it were an ailing dog'."

Criminal liability

A child will not be given *Ḥadd* punishment for a crime committed by him. Since there is no legal responsibility of a minor, i.e. children of all ages until they reach the age of puberty, the Qāḍī will still have the right either to admonish the jevenile delinquent or impose on him some restrictions which will help to reform him and stop him from committing any future crime. According to Abū Zaid al-Qayrāwanī a;-Mālikī, there shall be no *ḥadd* punishment for minors even in respect of levelling a false accusation of unchastity *(Qadhaf)* or in respect of committing fornication.[23]

If a person has committed a crime in the state of insanity, he will not be punished. Imām Abū Yusuf, says that "the *ḥadd* punishment can be imposed on the accused after his confession, unless it is made clear that he is not insane, or mentally troubled. If he is free from such deficiency, he should then be submitted to the legal punishment." It is therefore, most essential that the qāḍī (judge) assures himself of the sound mind of the criminal before he pronounces his verdict.

Sleep is considered to be a lesser death. If any crime is committed while still in sleep, one is not legally responsible for it provided it is ascertained that it was committed in a sleeping state. The case of Sayydinā ʿUmar's son ʿUbaid Allah, who committed adultery with a sleeping woman is mentioned in some details in the chapter on *Zinā*. While ʿUbaid Allāh was punished, the lady was acquitted.

The same principle will apply if one suffers from walking in sleep. Although he looks aware, he is still sleeping and walking. If one commits a crime in that state, he will not be legally responsible.

If any crime is committed under force or dur· ess, there will be no legal liability if it is proved that he did with a hadith which states "my community is excused for what it commits — The Holy Prophet has said: "My ummah will be forgiven for crimes it commits under duress, in error, or as a result of forgetfulness." No punishment will be given for crimes committed under such a state of mind as negating responsibility for a criminal act.

Notes

1. Qur'ān, ch. 33:72.
2. Ibn Ḥazam, *Al-Muḥallā*, vol. 6, p. 159, also see Yūsuf Qarḍāwī, *Al-Ḥalāl wal-Ḥarām fil Islām.*
3. Qur'ān, ch. *Al-Ḥujurat:* 9.
4. Shethna, Jehangir M. J., *Mental Abnormality and crime in Contribution to Synthetic Jurisprudence*, edited by M. J. Shethna, Bombay 1962, p. 255.
5. Bukhārī.
6. Sethna, M. J., *Society and the Criminal*, op. cit., motto quoted on the first page of the book.
7. Seth, J., *A Study of Ethical Principles*, Edinburgh 1911, pp. 322-323.
8. Cf. Ewing, A. C., *The Morality of Punishment*, London 1929, p. 75. Dr. Ewing has cited from studies in *Hegalian-cosmology*, p. 133.
9. Qur'ān, ch. 5:51.
10. Qur'ān, ch. 42:40.
11. Qur'ān, ch. 16:126.
12. Qur'ān, ch. 22:60.
13. Qur'ān, ch. 2:194.
14. Qur'ān, ch. 41:34.
15. Qur'ān, ch. 41:35.
16. Qur'ān, ch. 28:54.
17. Qur'ān, ch. 23:96.
18. Qur'ān, ch. 42:40.
19. Yūsuf 'Alī, *The Holy Qur'an*, op. cit., p. 1317.
20. Matthew V. 30; Luke VI: 29.
21. Al-Bukhārī.
22. Qur'ān, ch. 6:124.
23. Al-Qayrawānī, Risālah, op. cit., ch. 37: *Bāb fil aḥkām wal Ḥudūd*, pp. 121-130.

Chapter 16

Crimes and Punishments

A. Qatl (Homicide) and Qaṣāṣ (Law of Equality)

In no other religion in the world human life is considered to be so sacred that one man's murder is considered to be the murder of all the human race, and whoever saves a life it is as if he had saved the lives of all mankind.

«اَنَّهُ مَنْ قَتَلَ نَفْساً بِغَيْرِ نَفْسٍ اَوْ فَسَادٍ فِي الْاَرْضِ فَكَاَنَّمَا قَتَلَ النَّاسَ جَمِيعاً،
وَمَنْ اَحْيَاهَا فَكَاَنَّمَا اَحْيَا النَّاسَ جَمِيعاً ».

"that if any one slew a person – unless it be for murder or for spreading mischief in the land – it would be as if he (slew) the whole people: and if anyone saved a life, it would be as if he saved the life of the whole people."[1]

This is the way in which the legal injunctions of the Qur'ān have declared protection of human life. In *Sūrah Banī-Isrāil,* Allah has said:

«ولا تقتلوا النفس التي حرم الله الا بالحق».

"Do not kill a soul which Allah has made sacred except through the due process of law."[2]

In this verse, homicide has been distinguished from destruction of life carried out in pursuit of justice. Only a competent Qāḍī will decide whether or not an individual has forfeited his right to life by disregarding the right to life and peace of other human beings. Prophet Muḥammad (S.A.W.) has declared homicide as the greatest sin only next to polytheism *(Shirk)* . He said: "The greatest sins are to associate something or someone with Allah and to kill human beings."

One forfeits one's right to life in the following five situations:

1. Law of Equality (*Qaṣāṣ*) applied for a criminal who killed someone intentionally.

2. In the war of defence (*Jihād*) against the enemies of Islam, it is natural that some of the combatants will be killed.
3. Punishment of death to the traitors who try to plot to overthrow Islamic government *(Fasād fil arḍ)*.
4. A married man or a woman who is given *hadd* punishment for adultery *(Zinā)*.
5. Those who commit highway robbery *(Ḥirābah)*.

The crime of committing a murder of a Muslim is so very horrible that the criminal after getting his ḥadd punishment, still goes to hell and becomes an object of anger and curse of Allah:

«ومن قتل مؤمنا متعمدا فجزاءه جهنم خالدا فيها وغضب الله عليه ولعنه واعد له عذابا عظيما».

"If a man kills a believer intentionally, his recompense is Hell, to abide there is forever: and the wrath and curse of Allah are upon him, and a dreadful penalty is prepared for him."[3]

It is not merely the life of a grown up person, even the life of a child or even a child who is an embryo and not yet born must not be taken under any pretext whatsoever. No amount of poverty and hunger must drive a man or a woman to kill children. The Holy Qur'ān says:

«وَلَا تَقْتُلُوا اَوْلَادَكُم مِنْ اِمْلَاقٍ-نَحْنُ نَرْزُقُكُمْ وَايَّاهُمْ».

"Kill not your children on the pleas of want; – we provide sustenance for them and for you."[4]

It is not only that human life is sacred, but all life is sacred. Even in killing animals for food, a dedicatory formula *"Bismillāh, Allāh Akbar"* has to be employed. Killing embryos through abortion is becoming a fashion in the modern promiscuous society of today. Some medical practioners are also culprits of killing children in embryo in order to earn quick money. The parents of such a child yet to be born and the doctors who perform such operations are all guilty of this crime. These little children will be asked by Allah on the Day of Resurrection with great anger:

«وَاِذَا اَلْمَوْءُدَةُ سُئِلَتْ بِاَيِّ ذَنْبٍ قُتِلَتْ»

"When the female infant buried alive will be questioned for what crime she was killed?"[5]

The question in the above verses is directed to the pagan Quraish who used to commit female infanticide sometimes due to the imaginary fear of poverty and sometimes they felt ashamed to being addressed as 'father-in-law' when their daughters grew up. Hence, they used to kill their female children by burying them alive. In this world of sin, so much unjust suffering is caused through taking innocent lives without even a trace being left, by which offenders can be brought to justice. The present day killing through abortion is also done secretly and unnoticed by the society. In some countries, abortion is legalised. The crime was committed in the past and is still committed today in the guise of social plausibility in secret collusion. But in the spiritual world of justice, questions will be asked by Allah, and the victim who is dumb here will be able to give evidence on the Day of Judgement. The proofs will be drawn from the very means used for concealment of the crime.

Not only is the killing of others forbidden in Islamic Shari'ah, one even has no right to take his own life. Suicide is the work of a coward, and a great punishment awaits him in the Next World. The Qur'ān commands:

"Nor kill (or destroy) yourself".[6]

Apart from the Holy Qur'ān, the Holy Prophet dwelt upon it at length in his Farewell Pilgrimage *(Ḥajj al-Widā)* address on this subject:

«ولا تقتلوا انفسكم».

"O People! Your blood, property and honour is made completely forbidden upon one another. The respect for these things is such as it is the respect of this (Day of Pilgrimage), and the respect of the month of *Dhul Hajjah*, and the respect of this city (Mecca). Beware, let it not happen after me that you begin to take each others lives and be in the category of unbelievers".[7]

Acting on this exhortation himself, the Prophet further said:

"All the murders of the days of Jahiliyyah are under my feet (i.e. no revenge for them). First revenge which I forgive is of the killing of a member of my own family, the murder of the son of Rabiah bin al-Hadith, which was committed by Bani Hudhail. I forgive it."[8]

Sacredness of Life in Islam

In other words, life is so very sacred in Islam that it cannot be taken for sport or for any sacrificial or medical purposes.

As far as the question of taking life in retaliation for murder or the question of punishment for spreading corruption on this earth is concerned, it can be decided only by a proper and competent Qāḍī and his court. If there is any war with any nation or country, it can be decided only by a properly established government. In any case no human being has any right by itself to take human life in retaliation or for causing mischief on this earth. Therefore, it is incumbent on every human being that under no circumstances should he be guilty of taking a human life. If any one has murdered a human being, it is as if he has slain the entire human race.[9] These instructions have been repeated in the Holy Qur'ān in another place saying:

> "Do not kill a soul which Allah has made sacred except through the due process of law".[10]

Qaṣāṣ: The Law of Equality

The word Qaṣāṣ is derived from an Arabic word *Qaṣṣā* meaning he cut or he followed his track in pursuit, and it comes therefore to mean Law of Equality or equitable retaliation for the murder already committed. - The treatment of the murderer should be the same as his horrible act, that is, his own life should be taken just as he took the life of his fellow man. This does not mean that he should also be killed with the same instrument or weapon.

During the *Jahiliyyah* period before Islam; the Arabs were always prone to take revenge even if it was done from centuries. If a member of their clan or tribe was killed by a member of another clan, the revenge was taken by killing any innocent person belonging to the enemy clan. The chain reaction that would start would not end for generations. There is a famous incident recorded in the books of history that an old man, on his death-bed asked all his sons to come by his side and thus admonished them: "I am dying but I have not taken revenge from certain tribes. If you want me to achieve peace after death, take revenge on my behalf". The only love they had was for the life of their own clan. They used to demand the life of a man of the same rank from the clan of the murderer. At times, blood-feuds used to start and the lives of hundreds would be lost for the life of one person. If the murdered belonged to a higher rank, instead of taking his life, they would insist of taking the life of a totally innocent person of higher rank from his clan.

The injunctions on *Qaṣāṣ* in the Qur'ān are based on the principles of strict justice and equality of the value of human life:

«يَا أَيُّهَا ٱلَّذِينَ آمَنُوا كُتِبَ عَلَيْكُمُ ٱلْقِصَاصُ فِي ٱلْقَتْلَى-اَلْحُرّ بِٱلْحُرِّ، وَٱلْعَبْدُ بِٱلْعَبْدِ ، وَٱلْأُنْثَى بِٱلْأُنْثَى- فَمَنْ عُفِيَ لَهُ مِنْ اَخِيه شَيْءٌ فَاتِّبَاعٌ بِٱلْمَعْرُوفِ وَاَدَاءٌ اِلَيْهِ بِاِحْسَانٍ-ذٰلِكَ تَخْفِيفٌ مِنْ رَبِّكُمْ وَرَحْمَةٌ-فَمَنِ ٱعْتَدَى بَعْدَ ذٰلِكَ فَلَهُ عَذَابٌ اَلِيمٌ»

> "O you who believe! the law of equality is prescribed to you in cases of murder: the free for the free, the slave for the slave, the woman for the woman. But any remission is made by the brother of the slain, then grant any reasonable demand, and compensate him with handsome gratitude. This is a concession and a Mercy from your Lord. After this, whoever exceeds the limits shall be in grave penalty".[11]

In this verse, Islam has mitigated the horrors of revenge and retaliation which were practised in the *Jāhiliyyah* period or much of which is even prescribed in a slight modified form in the modern so-called civilised world of ours. Equality in retaliation is prescribed with a strict sense of justice, but it makes a clear provision for mercy and forgiveness. The brother of the slain can make remission on the basis of granting his reasonable demand and compensation with handsome gratitude.

Qaṣāṣ in the Books of Ahl Al-Kitāb

The law of *Qaṣāṣ* was not totally new to the *Ummah* of Prophet Muhammad. The followers of other religions who believe in the revealed books of Allah were also given the law of Qaṣāṣ:

« وَكَتَبْنَا عَلَيْهِمْ فِيهَا انّ ٱلنَّفْسَ بِٱلنَّفْسِ، وَٱلْعَيْنَ بِٱلْعَيْنِ، وَٱلاَنْفَ بِٱلاَنْفِ،
وَٱلاُذُنَ، بِٱلاُذُنِ وَٱلسِّنَّ بِٱلسِّنّ، وَٱلْجُرُوحَ قِصَاصٌ فَمَنْ تَصَدَّقَ بِهِ فَهُوَ كَفَّارَةٌ لَهُ
وَمَنْ لَمْ يَحْكُمْ بِمَا أَنْزَلَ ٱللّٰهُ فَأُولٰئِكَ هُمُ ٱلظَّالِمُونَ».

> "We ordained therein for them: 'Life for life; eye for eye; nose for nose; ear for ear; tooth for tooth, and wounds equal for equal.' But if any one remits the retaliation by way of charity it is an act of atonement for himself. And if any fail to judge by (the light of) what God hath revealed, they are (no better than) wrong-doers".[12]

The retaliation was prescribed in three places in the Pentateuch,* but there is no mention of mercy or forgiveness as it is in the verses of the Qur'ān. In Matthew v. 38, however, the Old law is quoted: eye for eye", etc. which mentions forgiveness, but the Qur'ānic injunction is more practical. This appeal for mercy is as between man and man in the spiritual world. Even where the injured one forgives,, the State or Ruler is competent to take such action as is necessary for the preservation of law and order in Society. For crime has a bearing that goes beyond the interests of the person injured since the entire Community is affected by it.[13] The Mosaic Law makes no mention of mercy, it is only found in the teachings of Prophet Jesus and Muḥammad. One can clearly see how the teaching of Prophet Jesus is gradually introduced as leading up to the Qur'ān.

The law of retaliation among the Israelites extended to slaying for slaying, wounding for wounding and mutilating for mutilating, but the Holy Qur'ān has expressly limited it to cases of murder only. It speaks of retaliation in wounds as being an ordinance of the Mosaic Law,[14], but it is nowhere prescribed as a law for the Muslims, who are required to observe it only in the case of the slain.[15] All the Islamic Laws were introduced gradually. In earlier days, retaliation was also ordered in some cases of wounds, but this was before an express commandment came and limited it to the cases of murder only. However, the relative or the person who suffers from the death of the murdered man can make a remission, and ask for diyah or blood-money instead. The blood-money can also take the place of a death sentence if it is proved that it was an unintentional killing. The Holy Qur'ān says:

> "And it does not behove a believer to kill a believer except by mistake, and whoever kills a believer by mistake, he should free a believing slave, and blood-money should be paid to his people unless they remit it as alms, but if he be from a tribe hostile to you and he is a believer, the freeing of a believing slave".[16]

In a case of murder in which the murderer's intention is doubtful, *Diyah* (blood-money) is to be paid.[17] And where the murderer could not be discovered, *Diyah* was to be paid from the state treasury.[18]

If a group of people kills one person jointly, all of them will be killed. If a person who is drunk kills another person, he is killed. But if a mad man kills a person, the *Diyah* should be paid by his relatives. Besides, an intentional killing or the intentional infliction of injuries committed as that exceeds one-third of a *Diyah*, or is equal to one-third. But if the amount to pay as compensation is less than one-third of *Diyah,* it must come from the minor's personal property.[19]

A woman shall be killed for killing a man, and a man shall be killed for killing a woman.[20] Likewise, whosoever is made to suffer the loss of both his hands is paid a whole *Diyah* as in a case of homicide. Similarly, in respect of a loss of both legs, and loss of both eyes, a complete *Diyah* is to be paid. And if a man is made to suffer the loss of one of these, he is paid half of complete blood-money. In respect of a nose whose cartilage separating the base of the nostrils, a complete blood-wit is to be paid. The same rule will apply when a loss of hearing is inflicted, or when loss of mental balance occurs, or when the backbone is broken or testicles are impaired or when the glands of the penis are destroyed, or when the tongue is made useless; or when the power of speech is deprived. For a destroying the two bosoms of a woman or the eye of the one-eyed person a full blood-wit will also be paid.[21]

The Procedure of Applying Ḥadd Punishment

It must be proved beyond any shadow of doubt that the murder was really committed by the criminal. No execution must take place in case of a homicide, except when men of integrity have given evidence, or where the murderer himself makes a confession or if the relatives of the deceased swore *'qasama'* oaths to confirm it. The relatives of the deceased will swear fifty times *(Qasama)*, after that, they will be entitled to have the accused executed. The oath is to be sworn by no less than two men in a murder case. And in respect of such an oath, never are more than one person executed. A *qasama* becomes necessary if the deceased declared that – on being wounded – so-and-so has my blood; or when one person testified against the accused, or when two people testified seeing the deceased being wounded if he survived all that and was able to eat and to drink.

When the plaintiffs failed to swear, the defendants are asked to swear and free themselves from liability. They do that fifty times. if the defendant was not able to get some of his kinsmen to swear with him, he swears alone fifty times. If the accusation of homicide is levelled against the group of people, each one of them will have to swear fifty times. But if kinsmen were suing in respect of a murdered kinsmen, fifty of them must swear once each. But if there were less than fifty, the surplus oaths were re-distributed to them. However, a woman does not swear in a murder case. The heirs will swear in the event of accidental homicide in direct proportion to the amount they inherit of the blood-wit, whether they are men or women. If the division should present a problem by producing fractions the person with the biggest share of the blood-wit shall be made to swear the extra oath.[22]

If the relatives of the deceased person came, while others did not show up, in respect of an accidental killing, those present shall swear the full number of oaths in a *qasama*. If afterwards others turned up, they swear in direct proportion to their share of the estate.

The litigants shall swear standing. *Qasama* oaths are not sworn in respect of wounds, nor among the scripturaries, nor a person killed between two rows of warring enemies. Nor when a dead body is found in the vicinity of some settlement. There cannot be any pardon in respect of a treacherous murder. A man can pardon in respect of his own murder, if it did not involve treachery. But in respect of accidental killing, he can only waive up to one third of the *Diyah*. If one of the sons of the victim in a homicide case decided to forgive the killer, the killer cannot be executed. The remaining heirs can than have their shares of the blood-money.

When in a homicide case the heirs comprise sons and daughters, the daughters are not empowered by law to waive this claim for *Qaṣāṣ* and grant pardon.

When a homicide is pardoned, he is to be given one hundred strokes of the cane and imprisoned for a year.

The blood-money in respect of people who have camels is to consist of one hundred camels. And in respect of people who have gold, is to be one thousand pieces.[23]

Al-Zinā (Adultery)

Zinā means sexual intercourse between a man and a woman not married to each other. It is immaterial whether one or both parties have their own spouses living or are unmarried. It is also immaterial whether it is with the consent of the parties. The word *Zinā* applies to both adultery (where one or both parties are married to a person or persons other than the persons involved in the sexual intercourse) and fornication where both parties are unmarried. Islam considers *Zinā* not only as a great sin but also as an act which opens the gate for many other shameful acts, which destroys the very basis of the family, which leads to quarrels and murders, which ruins reputation and property and which spreads numerous diseases, both physical and spiritual. Therefore, the Holy Qur'ān enjoins upon people:

«وَلَاتَقْرَبُوا الزِّنٰى اِنَّهُ كَانَ فَاحِشَةً وَسَاء سَبِيلًا».

"Do not come nearer to adultery for it is shameful (deed) and an evil, opening the road (to other evils).[24]

The Prophet (S.A.W.) has declared *Zinā* to be the greatest sin after *shirk* (associationisms). He says:

«قال عليه الصلاة والسلام: «ما من ذنب بعد الشرك اعظم من عند الله من نطفة وضعها رجل في رحم لا يحل له».

"There is no sin after associationism greater in the eyes of Allah than a drop of semen which a man places in the womb which is not lawful for him."[25]

There is another Ḥadīth which places *Zinā* next after associationism and the killing one's child for fear of poverty. It says:

«عن عبد الله بن مسعود رضى الله عنه قال: «يارسول الله اي ذنب اعظم؟» قال: «ان تجعل لله ندا وهو خالقك»، قلت: «ثم اي؟»، قال: «ان تقتل ولدك من اجل ان يطعم معك»، قلت: ثم اي؟ قال: «ان تزانى خليلة جارك».

'Abdullāh bin Mas'ūd reported: I asked the Prophet (S.A.W.), "O Allah's Apostle which is the biggest sin? He replied: To set up rivals with Allah by worshipping others though He alone has created you." I asked: "What is next?" He said: "To kill your child lest it should share your food." I asked: "What next?" He said: "To commit illegal sexual intercourse with the wife of your neighbour."[26]

There are some other *aḥādīth* in which murder is considered to be the greater sin as compared to adultery. Be that as it may, adultery is undoubtedly a very great sin. If allowed to go unchecked it may disrupt the social fabric of *Ummah*. For this reason severe punishment is reserved for this major crime in the penal law of Islam and great torments for adulterers in the hereafter. The Prophet (S.A.W.) is reported as saying that the dwellers of hell will have the punishment of smelling the most pungent smell emanating from the private parts of an adulterer. He is further reported to have said that if a person commits adultery, Allah will open for him in his grave eighty doors of hell from which will emerge scorpions and snakes to trouble him until the Day of Resurrection.

Islam abhors adultery and for that end enjoins upon Muslims to keep away from all those satanic things which lead a man to adultery. The first step towards adultery is provided by having a passionate look at an unknown woman. This is prohibited by the Prophet (S.A.W.) in the following ḥadīth:

«النظر الى النساء الاجنبيات من الكبائر».

"Even to look at an unknown woman (with a passionate look) is also a sin."

Other steps towards adultery are prohibited by the Prophet (S.A.W.) in another ḥadīth:

«قال عليه الصلاة والسلام: «زنا الرجلين المشى وزنا اليدين البطش وزنا العينين النظر».

"The adultery of legs is walking (towards an unlawful woman with bad intention) and the adultery of the hands is touching and patting (an unlawful woman) and the adultery of eyes if casting passionate glances (at a woman).

Punishment for Zinā

There are definite *Hadd* punishments mentioned in the Qur'ān and the Sunnah for adulterers. The Qur'ānic injunctions were revealed gradually and bit by bit so as to be easily acceptable to the new converts of Islam who were steeped in the vice of *Zinā* in the Arab Society of Jāhiliyya days. The first revelation merely spoke of the punishment of confining only the woman guilty of sexual offences in their houses until they died. It said:

«وَالَّتِي يَأْتِينَ الْفَاحِشَةَ مِنْ نِسَائِكُمْ فَاسْتَشْهِدُوا عَلَيْهِنَّ أَرْبَعَةً مِنْكُمْ فَإِنْ شَهِدُوا فَأَمْسِكُوهُنَّ فِي الْبُيُوتِ حَتَّى يَتَوَفَّاهُنَّ الْمَوْتُ أَوْ يَجْعَلَ اللَّهُ لَهُنَّ سَبِيلاً».

> "If any of your women are guilty of adultery, take the evidence of four (reliable) witnesses from amongst you against them; and if they testify, confine them to houses until death do claim them, or Allah ordains for them some (other) way."[27]

The second revelation covered both men and women and was a little specific regarding punishment for *Zinā*. It read:

«وَالَّذَانِ يَأْتِيَانِهَا مِنْكُمْ فَآذُوهُمَا فَإِنْ تَابَا وَأَصْلَحَا فَأَعْرِضُوا عَنْهُمَا - إِنَّ اللَّهَ كَانَ تَوَّاباً رَحِيماً».

> "If two persons among you are guilty of adultery, punish them both. If they repent and amend, leave them alone: for Allah is oft-returning, Most Merciful."[28]

The third revelation came with specific punishment for adultery. It reads:

«الزَّانِيَةُ وَالزَّانِي فَاجْلِدُوا كُلَّ وَاحِدٍ مِنْهُمَا مِائَةَ جَلْدَةٍ وَلاَ تَأْخُذْكُمْ بِهِمَا رَأْفَةٌ فِي دِينِ اللَّهِ إِنْ كُنْتُمْ تُؤْمِنُونَ بِاللَّهِ وَالْيَوْمِ الآخِرِ - وَلْيَشْهَدْ عَذَابَهُمَا طَائِفَةٌ مِنَ الْمُؤْمِنِينَ».

> "The woman and the man guilty of adultery or fornication, flog each one of them with a hundred stripes; Let not compassion move you in their case, in a matter prescribed by Allah, if you believe in Allah and the Last Day and let a party of believers witness their punishment."[29]

When this verse was revealed, it was understood that those guilty of adultery should be given one hundred lashes as a punishment. The Prophet (S.A.W.) clarified the injunction:

«خذوا عني خذوا عني فقد جعل الله لهن سبيلا - البكر بالبكر جلد مائة وتعذيبهن عاما - الثيب بالثيب جلد مائة والرجم».

> "Take from me accept from me, Undoubtedly Allah has now shown path for them (adulterers). For unmarried persons (guilty of fornication), the punishment is one hundred lashes and an exile for one year. For married adulterers, it is one hundred lashes and stoning to death."[30]

The above Ḥadīth shows that if the offender is not married, he should be given 100 lashes and should be exiled away from his home for a period of one year. If the offender is married, he should be given 100 lashes and should also be stoned to death. But some jurists are of the view that an offender is going to be stoned to death, there is no need to punish him with 100 lashes as the Prophet stoned to death two Jewish adulterers and did not punish them with lashes. This Ḥadīth is the fulfilment of Allah's promise to 'ordain some other way'.[31]

On the other hand, Sayyidnā ʿAli, the fourth Caliph, punished a woman with lashes on a Thursday and stoned her on Friday. He maintained that he gave lashes according to the command of Allah and stoned her according to the command of the Messenger of Allah.

The following conditions must be fulfilled before the *ḥadd* of stoning to death is applied:

1. The offender must be sane
2. He must be a Muslim
3. He must be married
4. He must have reached the age of puberty
5. He must be a free man and not a slave

The Method of Awarding Punishment

The idea behind awarding the seemingly harsh punishment is that it should ser ve as a deterrent to the society. A very grave responsibility lies on the *Qāḍī* (the Judge) before he gives verdict to stone the guilty person to death. This form of punishment is only accorded when it is proved beyond any doubt through the testimony of four reliable, and pious Muslim witnesses given at the same time, that they saw the guilty person actually committing the offence. The benefit of the slightest doubt in the statement of testimony of the witnesses should go in favour of the accused. The only other proof of the guilt of the accused may come in the form of four confessions which such accused makes completely voluntarily in one sitting. If he confesses three times but retracts his confession the fourth time, he should not be stoned. The man or woman confessing the crime must be sane, major, mature and married.

It is reported that the Prophet (S.A.W.) punished an adulterer when he bore witness against himself and confessed his sin.

It is narrated by Jābir ʿAbdallāh al-Anṣārī: A man from the tribe of Banī Aslam came to Allah's Apostle and informed him that he had committed illegal sexual intercourse and he bore witness four times against himself. Allah's Apostle ordered him to be stoned to death as he was a married person.*

Many scholars have said that because the Holy Qur'ān is silent on punishment by stoning to death, therefore this punishment is not justifiable. This is precisely what Caliph ʿUmar forestalled to do. Ibn ʿAbbās has reported:

عن ابن عبــاس رضى الله عنــه قال قال عمــر: لقــد خشيت ان يطول بالناس زمان حتى يقول قائل لانجد رجم في كتاب الله فيضلوا بترك فريضة انزل الله - الا وان الرجم حق على من زنى وقد احصن اذا قامت البنية، او كان الحمل او الاعتراف.

> "Umar said: I am afraid that after a long time has passed, people may say: "We do not find the verses of *Rajm* (stoning to death) in the Book of Allah." and consequently they may go astray by leaving an obligation that Allah has revealed. Lo! I confirm that the penalty of *Rajm* be inflicted on him who commits illegal sexual intercourse if he is already married and the crime is proved by witnesses or pregnancy or confession.[33]

Islam commands purity of sex life both for men and women, at all times of their lives. Therefore, punishment for *Zinā* is carried out openly so that it may be a deterrent for others int he society.

Punishment of Caliph 'Umar's Son: An Example

The Shari'ah does not favour any person whether a king or a slave, rich or poor, black or white. Once *Zinā* is proved against him beyond any doubt, punishment will be applied to him regardless of his station in life. The glowing example is that of the punishment given to 'Ubaid-Allāh, alias Abi Shamhah, the second son of Caliph Umar.

One day he passed by the house of a Jew, drank wine and got intoxicated. He saw a sleeping woman and committed *Zinā* with her. She became pregnant. When she got a son, she came to the Prophetic Mosque and placed the child in Caliph 'Umar's lap saying: O Commander of the Faithful, take this child as you have greater right over him than myself. Then she explained that it was the child of this son Abī Shamhah. Caliph 'Umar asked her whether it was legitimate. The lady replied: 'From my side, it is legitimate but from his it is illegitimate.' Then she told the whole story. The Caliph went home and confirmed from his son that he had committed the crime although he felt very much ashamed of it. The Caliph caught him by his collar to take him to the Mosque of the Prophet. Abī Shamhah asked him where he was taking him. The Caliph replied that he was taking him to the Companions of the Prophet in the Mosque so that I may take from you the right of Allah in this world before it is taken from you in the next world." Abī Shamham requested the Caliph to take right of Allah from him then and there so that he may not be put to disgrace in the presence of the Companions of the Prophet. Caliph Umar replied: "O son you have already disgraced yourself and your father. We must go in their presence." 'Umar ordered Maflah to give him stripes. When he was given seventy stripes, Abī Shamhah appealed to the companions of the Prophet to intervene. The companions requested 'Umar to stop. 'Umar replied: "O Companions of the Prophet, have you not read in the Qur'ān 'Do not show mercy over them." He was then given one hundred stripes as a result of which Abī Shamḥah died. Then Caliph ʿUmar took him to his house, gave him a bath and buried him. It should be noted here that most of the punishment carried out by the Prophet and the four Rashidun Caliphs were based on confession and not the proof.

Sodomy (Al-Liwāṭ)

Sodomy or homosexuality is an unnatural act of sex to satisfy one's passion. The people of Lūṭ from (Prophet Lot) were materially very advanced. In spite of the warning from Prophet Lot they committed sodomy.

The Qur'ān speaks of them in the following words:

وَلُوطاً اذْ قَالَ لِقَوْمِهِ أَ تَأْتُونَ ٱلْفَاحِشَةَ مَا سَبَقَكُمْ بِهَا مِنْ اَحَدٍ مِنَ ٱلْعَالَمِينَ - اِنَّكُمْ لَتَأْتُونَ الرِّجَالَ شَهْوَةً مِنْ دُونِ ٱلنِّسَاءِ - بَلْ اَنْتُمْ قَوْمٌ مُسْرِفُونَ».

> "We also sent Lūṭ: he said to his people: 'Do you commit adultery as no people in creation (ever) committed before you? For you practise your lusts on men in preference to women: you are indeed a people transgressing beyond limits'."[34]

When they did not heed the warning of their Prophet, they were ruined completely through a shower of brimstone[35] though a few remains of their towering buildings have survived until today.

According to the narration of al-Ṭibrānī and al-Baihaqī, Prophet Moḥammad (S.A.W.) is reported to have said:

قال رسول الله صلى الله عليه وسلم: «اربعة يصبحون في غضب الله تعالى ويمسون في سخط الله»، قيل له: ومن هم يا رسول الله؟ قال: «المتشبهون من الرجال بالنساء والمتشبهات من النساء بالرجال، والذي يأتى البهيمة والذي يأتى الرجال».

> "Four types of people get up in the morning while they are under the wrath of Allah and they sleep in the night while they are under the displeasure of Allah." He was asked: "Who are they, O Messenger of Allah?" The Prophet replied: "Those men who try to resemble women and those women who try to resemble men (through dress and behaviour) and those who commit sex with animals and those men who commit sex with men."[36]

Homosexuality is therefore a great sin in Islam. The Prophet (S.A.W.) is reported to have said:

قال النبي صلى الله عليه وسلم: «من قبل غلاما بشهوة عذب الله تعالى في النار الف سنة».

"One who kissed a boy with passion, Allah Most High will punish him for a thousand years in the fire of hell."

He is reported to have also said:

قال عليه الصلاة والسلام: «من مس غلاما بشهوة لعنه الله والملائكة والناس اجمعون».

"The Prophet said: 'One who touched a boy with passion, he will be cursed by Allah, the angels and all the people'."

The Prophet of Allah has also said:

عن ابن عباس رضى الله عنه ان رسول الله صلى الله عليه وسلم قال: «لا ينظر الله عز وجل الى رجل آتى رجلا او امرأة في دبرها».

"It is related by Ibn Abbas that the Prophet (S.A.W.) said: Allah Most High will not look at a man who committed sex with a man or a woman through her anus."

The Prophet (S.A.W.) further said this about unnatural relationships between two men or two women:

قال عليه الصلاة والسلام: «اذا آتى الرجل الرجل فهما زانيان واذا اتت المرأة المرأة فهما زانيتان».

"If a man commits an act of sex with a man, they both are adulterers and if a woman commits such acts with a woman, then both of them are adulteresses."

Homosexuality is on the increase in the *civilised* western world and homosexual clubs and unions are founded in the various countries of Europe and America which had only a few years ago considered homosexuality to be a major crime. If this is the sign of civilisation, freedom and liberation, the less said the better.

Punishment for Homosexuality (Liwāṭ)

All Muslim jurists agree that sodomy is a sexual offence but differ in their punishment. According to Imām Abū Ḥanīfa, the act of sodomy does not amount to adultery and therefore there is no punishment by *Ḥadd* to be given to the offender except *Ta'azīr*. According to Imām Mālik the *ḥadd* punishment will be applied whether the offender is married or not. he relies on the following Ḥadīth:

عن ابي هريرة قال رسول الله صلى الله عليه وسلم: «من وجد تموه يعمل عمل قوم لوط اقتلوا الاعلى والاسفل وفي قول الاخرى اقتلوا الفاعل والمفعول به».

It is reported by Abū Hurairah that the Messenger of Allah (S.A.W.) said: "If you find someone who is committing an act of the committment of lut (that is homosexuality), kill the one on top and one below" and in another statement it says: "kill the doer and the one with whom the act is committed."

'Abu Hurairah reports: That the Prophet (S.A.W.) said:"Imam Shafi'i, Abu Yusuf and Muhammad have said that if the offender is married the *hadd* of stoning to death will be applied, but if he or she is unmarried, only punishment by *Ta'azir* will suffice.

It is also a crime to have sex with one's wife in an unnatural way, that is through the back (anus). The majority of the jurists believe that *ta'azir* will apply since this is the case surrounded by doubt *(shubuhat)* and wherever there is a doubt, the *ḥadd* will not be applied.

Punishment for Bestiality

There are times when a human being falls to the level of beasts and commits sexual intercourse with an animal. According to Imāms Mālik, Abū Ḥānifa and Ẓāhir, only *Ta'azīr* shall be applied to the individual guilty of bestiality and not *hadd* punishment. The flesh of the animal which was the subject of bestiality is *(Ḥalāl)* when it is slaughtered. But Imāms Ḥanbal and Shāfi'ī hold that *ḥadd* punishment of stoning to death should be applied on the individual and the animal which was the subject of bestiality should also be killed; and its flesh is unlawful *(ḥarām)*. They rely on the following *ḥadīth* of the Prophet:

قال رسول الله صلى الله عليه وسلم: «اقتلوا البهيمة ومن آتاها».

"Said the Messenger of Allah (S.A.W.): 'Kill the animal and the person who committed sexual intercourse with it'."

Some other jurists also maintain that only an individual can be punished but not an animal since it has no guilty mind. When *Ḥadd* punishment is given *al-Ūlā*. Most of the *Ḥadd* punishment in the first century of Islam (*Qurun al-ula*) were given on confession made by the offenders. The person who committed adultery does not receive the *hadd* punishment except through such voluntary confession or through pregnancy which becomes evident or through the testimony of adult men of integrity and piety who witnessed the action like a *mirwad* in a *mukhula.* (A *mirwad* is the little stick for applying antimony to the eyelids. *Mukhula* is the container for kohl or antimony). These witnesses must see the action at the same time, and if one of them failed to complete the description, the three should receive *ḥadd* punishment for *qa dhf* or false accusation of fornication. There shall be no *ḥadd* punishment for anybody who is not mature.[37]

Punishment for Adultery in Sharī'ah, Its Conditions, Its Parity and Its Comparative Effects: and a Resume

At the Conference on *Muslim Doctrine and Human Rights in Islam*[38] between the Saudi Arabia scholars and European Jurists, the Muslim 'Ulamā gave the following arguments in favour of *hadd* punishment for adultery:

> "This penalty is prescribed only when the culprit, prior to his delict, had contracted a legal marriage, and if four witnesses known for their righteousness and their integrity, were present at the accomplishment of the sexual act, in a manner which could exclude the possibility of any doubt; it would not be sufficient namely, that they had seen the accused completely naked and stuck together."

The Delegation went on to say:

> "Here again, we agree with our guests on the severity of the punishment. Nevertheless, it is not imposed in Islam, unless the act, as we just said, was testified to by four objective and trustworthy witnesses. The testimony of one witness has no value before the law: in that case, the person is advised to refrain from making the denunciation, and condemned to be scourged, if he would continue in his accusations; the same thing happens, if there are only two, or even three witnesses. The primary condition, required by the Verse, is the presence at the moment of the act, of four witnesses who can be trusted, and have never been indicted. But if the act was accomplished in the presence of four witnesses, the judgement is that public order has been seriously offended. Whether legitimate or not, it is always improper for the sexual act to take place in public. This is why Islam reveals the most severe attitude against offenders of public order and morality.
>
> We suppose that, if such a thing had occurred in the street of the Capital of a civilised country, where complete sexual liberty is allowed, passers-by would have taken upon themselves to lynch the performers, even before the case could be laid before a court. Such people would be treated like beasts, and their lives would not deserve any more respect."

Then, the Delegation proceeded:

> "It must be noted, in the matter that the hard punishment of adultery was prescribed at the very beginning of the Islamic Message. There was, at that time, an urgent necessity to bring

society out of a system, where existed, in numerous walks, absolute sexual licence, and by the very fact, there was utter confusion with regard to paternity, into a new order, where procreative instinct would be regulated, and could be exercised only within the limits of legitimacy. And so, from the beginning of the Islamic predication, and during the whole life of the Prophet, not one single case of adultery was established by evidence of four eye-witnesses. Only one case was verified, through the spontaneous confession of the culprit eager to purify himself in this life, and so to escape punishment in the other. When, coming to the Prophet, he confessed his crime, and asked to be stoned to death, the Prophet turned his face and refused to listen. Since the act had been accomplished in secret, and thus public order and morality did not suffer, the matter concerned only the culprit, who, is his soul and conscience, had simply to beg the Lord's forgiveness. The man, however, earnestly renewed his confession and his request, so as to prove his sincerity towards God, and to deter others from committing the same crime; again, the Prophet turned his face. The same thing happened a third time, but when the culprit repeated his words a fourth time, the Prophet asked him if he had become insane, or had really admitted being guilty of the crime. First by refusing to listen, then by questioning the fact, the Prophet had long promoted him to retract, but the man so insisted, that in the end his demand had to be heard. At the moment of execution, however, he regretted his declaration and ran away; the punishment squad ran after him and killed him. The Prophet, then, pronounced his famous sentence: 'Would that you had left him alive: he would have repented, and God would have been merciful to him."

The Delegation continued:

"Thus Gentlemen, it was not possible to prove, by such evidence as is required, one single case of adultery at the time of the Prophet; and yet, it was an age of transition from general sexual licence to discipline and legality on this point. Fourteen centuries have elapsed since that most severe penalty was edicted, and we can strongly affirm that fourteen cases of stoning could hardly be numbered in all that time. In this way, punishment by stoning has remained what it always was, cruel in principle, but extremely rare in practice. But, through the very ruthlessness of this provision, Islam has prevented dislocation of family and confusion with respect to paternity. We surely admit that men are always men, but it remains that, under a secular legislation, where such a severe punishment, religiously motivated, is lacking, married people end to lose the fear of God, and are more tempted to fall in this crime. Generally speaking, the state of things prevailing in non-Muslim countries has caused the dissolution of family ties, and jeopardized the conjugal happiness, which Muslim husbands and wives, faithful to one another, to their religion, and to God, enjoy."

Commenting on the subject, His Excellency Doctor Dawalibi made the following observations. These were addressed in particular to the President of the European Commission, who had, before leaving for Saudi Arabia, heard from some people hostile to Islam the remark:

"So you are going to the country where they lynch women for adultery? If you please, Mr. President, report to these people what you have heard. You have neither heard that anyone had been stoned, nor seen any such thing in this Kingdom. It would be better for a society where the fear of God is enough to prevent both crime and punishment, thus securing integrity of the family and happiness of married couples, to prescribe a strict religious penalty in this matter, rather than rely on a secular legislation, which does not provide any similar penalty, but does not instill in man any fear of God either, and which, by the same token, causes many to lose the sense of the family. There inevitably follows offences to social dignity, and encouragement to crimes of the most dreadful and varied kinds, whereas, in Muslim countries, where God is openly reverred, and His Law sincerely enforced, nothing comparable happens."

Al-Qadhf: Defamation

Qadhf or defamation is an offence which comes into existence when a person falsely accuses a Muslim of fornication or doubts his paternity. It is a great crime in Islam and those who commit it are called wicked transgressors by the Holy Qur'ān which reads:

«وَالَّذِينَ يَرْمُونَ الْمُحْصَنَاتِ ثُمَّ لَمْ يَأْتُوا بِأَرْبَعَةِ شُهَدَاءَ فَاجْلِدُوهُمْ ثَمَانِينَ جَلْدَةً وَلَا تَقْبَلُوا لَهُمْ شَهَادَةً أَبَداً. وَأُولَئِكَ هُمُ الْفَاسِقُونَ».

"And those who launch charge against chaste women, and produce not four witnesses (to support their allegations), flog them with eight stripes. And reject their evidence even after. For such men are wicked transgressors."[39]

Every Muslim is supposed to guard the honour and respect of a fellowman and not bare the hidden failings of any other Muslim. if a person accuses a Muslim of adultery and cannot prove it by producing four witnesses who have seen the act being committed at the same time and at the same place, the accuser will be punished with eighty lashes. he will be considered a *Fāsiq* and as such his evidence will no longer be accepted whenever he comes forth to do so.

The Prophet also spoke of *Qadhf* as a great vice and warned Muslims to avoid it:

> "It is reported by Abu Hurairah that the Prophet (S.A.W.) said: 'Keep away from seven abominable acts.' He was asked 'O Messenger of Allah What are they?' The Prophet replied: 'Association of partners with Allah, the magic, killing someone which is forbidden by Allah except when it is with the injunction, eating of the usury, devouring the property of orphans, turning away from the day of Jihad in the path of Allah and the slander of chaste but indiscreet women'."[41]

'Ubāda bin al-Ṣāmit, who took an oath of fealty to the Prophet with a group of people reports that the Prophet included a prohibition against defamation:

عن عبادة بن الصامت رضى الله عنه قال: بايعت رسول الله صلى الله عليه وسلم في رهط فقال: «ابايعكم على ان لا تشركوا بالله شيئا ولا تسرقوا ولا تقتلوا اولادكم ولا تأتوا ببهتان تفترونه بين ايديكم واحلكم ولا تعصوني في معروف - فمن خطأ منكم فاجره على الله ومن اصاب من ذلك شيئا فاخذ به في الدنيا فهو كفارة له وطهور - ومن ستره الله فذلك الى الله ان شاء عذبه وان شاء غفر له».

> "I take your pledge that you will not worship anything besides Allah, will not steal, will not commit infanticide, *will not slander by forging false statement and spreading it,* and will not disobey me in anything good. And whoever among you fulfils all these, his reward is with Allah. And whosoever commits any of the above crimes and receives his legal punishments in this world, that will be his legal expiation and purification. But if Allah screens his sins, it is up to Allah who will either punish or forgive him according to His wish."

At times good and chaste women tend to be simple-hearted and indiscreet (*al-Ghafilat*). This may lead them in some problems through the evil manouvres of some selfish and jealous people. Such good natured women think of no evil and their innocent indiscretion may put them and those related to them in great difficulties. Such was the case of the mother of the faithful, 'Ā'isha Ṣiddīqa. A slanderous charge was spread about her in 5-6 A.H. This put not only her but also her husband, the Prophet himself, and her father Abū Bakr in the most painful predicament. It might have had most serious repercussions on the *Ummah* in its formative years and the great work in which the Prophet was engaged at that time. But, fortunately, Allah exposed the falsehood of the accusation through revelation.[41] In this connection the Qur'ān says:

«إِنَّ الَّذِينَ يَرْمُونَ الْمُحْصَنَاتِ الْغَافِلَاتِ الْمُؤْمِنَاتِ لُعِنُوا فِي الدُّنْيَا وَالْآخِرَةِ وَلَهُمْ عَذَابٌ عَظِيمٌ - يَوْمَ تَشْهَدُ عَلَيْهِمْ أَلْسِنَتُهُمْ وَأَيْدِيهِمْ وَأَرْجُلُهُمْ بِمَا كَانُوا يَعْمَلُونَ».

"Those who slander chaste women, indiscreet but believing are cursed in this life and in the Hereafter, for them is a grevious penalty on the day of judgement, their tongues, their hands, and their feet will bear witness against them as to their actions."[42]

According to Imāms Mālik and Ḥanbal, even if a person accuses someone merely by implication, it is sufficient to punish him with eighty lashes. But according to Imām Abū Ḥanīfa, Shāfi'ī, the accused should be asked about his intention and in making the accusation before punishment is awarded to him. It says that he did not mean to slander the woman then he shall be punished by *Ta'azīr only.*

Repentance of the Slanderer

The Holy Qur'ān says:

«إِلَّا الَّذِينَ تَابُوا مِنْ بَعْدِ ذَٰلِكَ وَأَصْلَحُوا فَإِنَّ اللَّٰهَ غَفُورٌ رَحِيمٌ».

"Unless they repent thereafter and mend their behaviour then Allah is oft-forgiving Most Merciful."

Therefore is the slanderer, after receiving the punishment of eighty lashes repents and assures that he would not engage in a similar activity in the future his civic right of giving evidence would be restored. But Imām Abū Ḥanīfa takes a different and more serious view and considers that neither the punishment of eighty stripes nor the incompetence for giving evidence is cancelled by repentance; but it removes only the spiritual stigma of being regarded as a "wicked transgressor".

Slander of one spouse by the other

If a husband puts forward slanderous accusations against his wife or a wife against her husband, the Holy Qur'ān lays down the following procedure:

«وَالَّذِينَ يَرْمُونَ اَزْوَاجَهُمْ وَلَمْ يَكُنْ لَهُمْ شُهَدَاءُ اِلَّا اَنْفُسُهُمْ فَشَهَادَةُ اَحَدِهِمْ
اَرْبَعُ شَهَادَاتٍ بِاللّٰهِ اِنَّهُ لَمِنَ الصَّادِقِينَ - وَالْخَامِسَةُ اَنَّ لَعْنَتَ اللّٰهِ عَلَيْهِ اِنْ كَانَ
مِنَ الْكَاذِبِينَ - وَيَدْرَؤُا عَنْهَا الْعَذَابَ اَنْ تَشْهَدَ اَرْبَعَ شَهَادَاتٍ بِاللّٰهِ اِنَّهُ لَمِنَ
الْكَاذِبِينَ - وَالْخَامِسَةَ اَنَّ غَضَبَ اللّٰهِ عَلَيْهَا اِنْ كَانَ مِنَ الصَّادِقِينَ».

"And for those who launch a charge against their spouses, and have (in support) no evidence but their own, their solitary evidence (can be received if they bear witness four times with an oath) by Allah that they are solemnly telling the truth. And the fifth (oath) should be that they solemnly invoke the curse of Allah on themselves if they tell a lie."

"But it would avert the punishment from the wife, if she bears witness four times with (an oath) by Allah, that he (her husband) is telling a lie. And the fifth (oath) should be that she solemnly invokes the wrath of Allah on herself if (her accuser) is telling the truth."[43]

In the context of permission granted by Islam to a husband for divorcing his wife, the case of slander of wife by the husband takes a colour entirely different from what it is in the Western Legal system. In the Western countries the spouses' decision of obtaining a divorce had to plead that the other spouse had been guilty of adultery and only on the basis of this plea could divorce be granted by court of law.

This was necessarily a potent reason for making false accusations. But in Islam there is no need to divorce. As such accusation by one spouse against the other is always a serious business in Islam to obtain divorce. Suppose a Muslim catches his wife in an actual act of adultery, which is not generally possible *it will still be essential for him to produce four pious witnesses who had seen the act.*

In most cases it will be difficult to find witnesses. Therefore, the husband will have to swear in the Shari'ah court four times to the fact of his wife's adultery and in addition invoke a curse on himself if he were not telling the truth. it will then be a *prima facie* proof of the wife's guilt. If the wife similarly swears her innocence four times and then she invokes a curse on herself if she were not telling the truth she will be acquitted of the charge. But if she refuses to take oaths, the charge will be deemed proved against her and she will have to face the punishment.

Whatever happens, once the oaths are taken, the marriage will be dissolved since it is quite impossible that the spouses would ever be able to live in peace and harmony after such an experience.

According to Abū Zaid al-Qayrawānī al-Mālik, there shall be no *ḥadd* punishment of minors either in respect of levelling a false accusation of unchastity *(Qadhf)* or in respect of committing fornication. Anybody who denied the paternity of another then the former shall receive the *ḥadd* punishment. Accusations of unchastity shall always be given the *ḥadd* punishment – even if they are veiled in innudendoes. If a man said to another 'O you homosexual' he shall receive *ḥadd* punishment. If a man levelled a false accusation against a group of people he shall receive one *ḥadd* punishment when all of them demanded it. Afterwards he is free and guiltless.[44]

If a man drank wine repeatedly or committed adultery repeatedly he is to receive only one *ḥadd* punishment – in respect of each of the repeated offences. This rule applies in respect of the person who levelled false accusations against a group of people. If a person is liable to receive *ḥadd* punishments and at the same time liable to be executed. The execution alone is sufficient for all that except where the *ḥadd* punishment is in respect of adultery, under such a circumstance the man must receive the *ḥadd* punishment and then be executed – later on.[45]

Al-Hirabah: Highway Robbery or Brigandage

Islamic teachings puts a great premium on the sanctity of human life and property. The Holy Qur'ān is a book of *Hidāya,* the perfect guidance for the entire mankind. The Islamic way of life is a constant whole and fosters both material and well-being and spiritual upliftment.

Therfore, a moral code of the Qur'ān is to be strictly adhered to in order to make human life on this planet worth living and peaceful. As the liberated members of the *Ummah* every member has to uphold the truth of God and should be free from any fear or slavery to human weaknesses of temptation, avarice, taking other's property or life by force of arms. As creative members of the *Ummah,* the Muslims should strive to bring about a society based on economic and social justice. The Holy Qur'ān speaks of the economic rights enjoined upon the Muslims: "And in their wealth there is acknowledged right for the needy and destitutes".[46] But this right is not to be misunderstood that the poor, needy, greedy or ambitious people should rob or steal their property.

Al-Ḥirābah or highway robbery is a serious crime according to the Holy Qur'ān. It is an exercise of a group of armed people or a single person who may attack travellers or wayfarers on the highway or any other place depriving them of their property through the use of force in the circumstances when the victims are away from receiving any immediate help. The Holy Qur'ān calls it "a war against Allah and His Messenger" and an attempt to spread mischief in the world.

The Holy Qur'ān describes robbery as a grave crime and its punishment are enumerated in the verse below:

«انَّمَا جَزَاءُ الَّذِينَ يُحَارِبُونَ اللّٰهَ وَرَسُولَهُ وَيَسْعَوْنَ فِى ٱلْاَرْضِ فَسَاداً اَنْ يُقَتَّلُوا أَوْ يُصَلَّبُوا اوْ تُقَطَّعَ اَيْدِيهِم وَاَرْجُلُهُمْ مِنْ خِلاَفٍ اَوْ يُنْفَوْا مِنَ ٱلْاَرضِ ذٰلِكَ لَهُمْ خِزْىٌ فِى ٱلدُّنْيَا وَلَهُمْ فِى ٱلاخِرَةِ عَذَابٌ عَظِيمٌ».

"The punishment of those who wage war against Allah and His Messenger, and strive with might and main for mischief through the land is: execution, or crucifixion, or the cutting off of the hands and feet from opposite sides, or exile from the land (imprisonment outside his hometown): That is their disgrace in this world and heavy punishment is theirs in the next world."[47]

While giving the causes for this revelation (*Asbāb al-Nuzūl*) for this verse, Imām Bukhāri reports that some people from the tribe of Ukul came to the prophet in Medina pretending that they wanted to accept Islam. They complained to the Prophet that the weather in Medina was not favourable to them and they suffered from ill-health. Thereupon the Prophet ordered that they should be taken outside Medina to stay where the weather was better for them and drink milk from the cattle belonging to the state.

They killed the keeper and ran away with the cattle. When the matter was reported to the Prophet, he ordered that they should be chased and brought back. This verse was revealed about this time.

Ḥirābah or robbery is not merely an offence against the human society but, according to the above verse of the Qur'ān, it is as if one is waging war against Allah and His Messenger through the use of sheer force. To wage war against a community may result in chaos and confusion and loss of peace of mind and heart. Waging war with the Creator and His Apostle is much more serious and amounts to a clear rebellion against the established principles of equity and justice and the respect for all. So anyone who disturbs or attempts to disturb that system of life is an outlaw and deserves capital punishment.

The Robbers or brigands are, therefore, those people who raise arms against innocent people with whom they have no previous enemity. The gravity of the act of brigandage remains the same whether it is committed in a city, village or desert and victims do not find help or they are prevented from crying for help.

In these circumstances the act of robbery or brigandage is complete according to Imām Mālik but Imām Abū Ḥanīfa differs from him on the point that if such an act is committed in a town, it will not amount to brigandage.[48] The brigands may be male or female as long as they are sane and adult. As soon as they confess of committing the act or if two adult Muslim witnesses give an evidence against them even if they were from those who were victims, the punishment is to be accorded.

The punishment for brigandage of highway robbery is spelt out in *sūrah al-Māida* in the verse we have quoted before. In this double crime committed against the state as well as the treason and the rebellion against Allah, four alternative punishments are mentioned, anyone of which is to be applied according the circumstances.

They include execution (i.e. cutting off the head or crucifixion or cutting off hands and feet from opposite sides or exile from the land [imprisonment outside his hometown]). According to Imām Mālik if the robber kills, he should be killed or crucified and the judge has no choice in that. If the offender robbed the property without killing, the judge then has a discretion either to kill, crucify or cut off his hand and leg from opposite sides. If the offender terrorises and frightens victims, the judge has his discretion either to execute or crucify or maim or banish him. If the offender is a woman, she must be executed. In any case, sincere repentance before it was too late was recognised as a ground for mercy but he will still be held responsible for all other offences other than robbery and has to account for the property of the innocent victims.

The Holy Qur'ān says:

«إِلَّا ٱلَّذِينَ تَابُوا مِنْ قَبْلِ أَنْ تَقْدِرُوا عَلَيْهِمْ - فَاعْلَمُوا أَنَّ ٱللَّهَ غَفُورٌ رَحِيمٌ».

> "Except for those who repent before they fall into your power; In that case, know that Allah is Oft-Forgiving, Most Merciful."[49]

What exactly constitutes the highway robbery or *Ḥirābah* differs from jurist to jurist. According to Imām Mālik, the robbery can be committed inside the town or outside the town. But Imām Abū Ḥanīfa says that there is no highway robbery if it is committed inside a town because the authorities are there to protect the citizens. The others say that it is the same whether it is committed inside the town or outside the town provided force is used. Imām Al-Shāfi'ī says that if the authorities are weak and cannot help or protect its citizens, armed robbery may be committed inside the town. The jurists have explained the act of *ḥirābah* in the following categories:

1. The robbers who could only kill but could not get away with their loot. Still it amounts to robbery.
2. If they killed and took away the property, it is robbery.
3. If they took away property with the use of force without killing.
4. Even if they only frightened without intention to rob, it still amounts to robbery.

All the jurists agreed that whenever a robber kills with the intention to rob and takes away the property he should be killed for his crime or crucified. But if he kills and cannot get away with the loot, he should be killed but not crucified. In the case when he takes away the property through the use of force but does not kill, his hand and leg on opposite sides must be cut off. But if he frightens only with the intention to rob and does not get away with the property, nor does he kill in the attempt, he should be exiled. All jurists agree that he should not be killed unless he kills the victim. The above punishments are also applicable to the women robbers with the exception that they should not be exiled since this can induce them to commit adultery which is another grievous offence. The judges are at liberty to award any of the punishments enumerated above in the case of a robber who takes away the property without killing and also in the case of frightening the victim.

Al-Dasūqī, a great Mālikī jurist, says that if a person forces a woman to have a sexual intercourse with the force of arms, the act will be deemed as committing *Ḥarābah*.

Treason and Conspiracy

The Qur'ānic verses (ch. 5:33-34) on robbery *(Qat al-Ṭarīq)* also includes the culprit who "spreads mischief" in the land of Allah, and are traitors and conspire against the interest of an Islamic state. The examples can be seen in the life history of the Prophet (S.A.W.) and the Rāshidūn caliphs.

There was the general clemency awarded to the general public of Mecca but the other side of the story tells us that in spite of the general clemency, eight persons were ordered by the Prophet himself to be executed on charges of conspiracy and *'fasād fil arḍ* (mischief in the land)'. The Prophet said:

> "Go and put to death all the named persons even if they are found behind the curtains of the Holy Ka'bah."

The persons ordered by Prophet Muḥammad to be put to death were: 'Abdallāh bin Sa'ad, 'Abdallāh bin Khatal, Huvairith bin Naqirs bin Wahab, Maqīs bin Sababah, Sarah (a woman), Akramah bin Abī Jabal and 'Abdallāh bin Khatal's two daughters. But only four out of the eight named persons could be put to death. Thus it stands as a fact of the history that even Prophet Muḥammad, famous for the general clemency awarded to the Meccans, and aptly known as *Raḥmat al-lil-'ālamīn*, did not hesitate in ordering the said persons to be put to death for 'being the conspirators and mischievous elements on the earth'.[50]

It is also interesting to note that when Prophet Muḥammad and his followers had just returned after the battle of the Ditch *(Khaybar),* the archangel Gabriel appeared and asked the Prophet to punish the violator of the pledge from the Jews of the Banū Quraisah tribe for their violation of the pledge and conspiring with the enemy while the battle of the Ditch was in progress. They only asked that their punishment should be left to the judgement of Sa'ad bin Mu'ādh of the tribe of Aus. The Prophet accepted their plea and made Sa'ad bin Mu'ādh the arbiter. Sa'ad gave his judgement saying that all the fighting men should be put to death, and that the women and children should become the slaves of the Muslims. The verdict was carried out.

Mr. Stanley Lane Poole, a famous scholar, in his selections from the Qur'ān writes about the execution as follows: "It was a harsh bloody sentence, worthy of the episcopal generals of the army against the Albigenesis, or the deads of the Augustinian age of Puritanism, but it must be remembered that the crime of these men was high treason against the state during the time of seige, and those who have read how Wellington's march could be traced by the bodies of the deserters and pillagers hanging from the trees, need not be surprised at the summary execution of a traitorous clan."

The Jews of Naḍīr Qayunqa' had been ordered to be expelled from the Islamic State of Medina on charge of conspiracy. The conspiracy and *'fasād fil arḍ'* can never be excused. When the news of attack on Medina came from the side of Khālid bin Sufyān Alhazli on 5th of Muḥarram in 4th Hijrah, Prophet Muḥammad sent 'Abdallah bin Anīs Jehnī al-Anṣārī to bring forth the head of the conspirator Khālid. 'Abdallāh did this job alone and was awarded the stick *('Aṣā)* of the Prophet.

Al-Sariqa: The Theft

In the year 632 A.D., the Holy Prophet Muḥammad delivered his Farewell Address in the *Ḥajj al-Widā*, i.e. Farewell Pilgrimage, on the plain of 'Arafāt'. He said: "Your lives and properties are forbidden to one another till you meet your Lord on the Day of Resurrecton". Islam has thus conferred the right of security of ownership of property. The Qur'ān declares: "Do not devour one another's wealth by false and illegal means".[51] *Sariqa* or theft also is an illegal means of acquiring another's property. A thief may be male or female and an act of theft is deemed complete by the *Fuqahā* when the following elements are present:

1. The property is taken away secretly.
2. It is taken away with criminal intention.
3. The thing stolen should be legally owned by the person from whom it is stolen.

4. The stolen property should have been taken out of the possession of its real owner.
5. The stolen thing should have already come under the possession of the thief.
6. The property should reach the value of *Nisāb* of theft.

The Holy Qur'ān has prescribed the following punishment for those who commit theft:

»وَالسَّارِقُ وَالسَّارِقَةُ فَاقْطَعُوا اَيْدِيَهُمَا جَزَاءً بِمَا كَسَبَا نَكَالاً مِنَ اللّٰهِ وَاللّٰهُ عَزِيزٌ حَكِيمٌ«.

"As to the theft male or female, cut off his hands or her hands: a punishment by way of example, From Allah, for their crime: and Allah is exalted in Power and Wise".[52]

The *Asbāb al-Nuzūl* or causes for the Revelation are mentioned in a narration of an incident of theft in the life time of the Prophet (S.A.W.). A man stole a bag of flour belonging to his neighbour and he took it and dumped it in someone's house. Since the bag was leaking, it could be traced. Meanwhile, the owner complained to the Prophet about his stolen property and suspected his neighbour which was really the truth. The Prophet did not like this idea that he suspected a Muslim neighbour for committing the theft. But when it was actually proved that the bag was stolen by the neighbour, he ran away into the bush and died. The above verse was revealed after this incident happened.

The punishment for committing theft in the time of earlier Prophets of Allah was very grave. During the period of Prophet ʿIsā (Jesus), anyone who was found guilty of committing theft and it was proved, was crucified.[53] The Biblical attitude towards punishment is summed up in the following statement: " If thy foot or thy hand offend thee, cut them off, and cast them from thee".[54]

The Shariʿah takes a more realistic view in punishing an offender. The idea behind the punishment is to provide a deterrent to stop the crime so that there may be established peace in the society. It is interesting to note that in this verse (Qur'ān, ch. 41:41) a male thief is mentioned before the female thief while in the verse concerning the sexual offences, the woman is first mentioned. Perhaps it may mean that in the offences of the thefts, it is usually men who take the lead in order to get rich quicker. Certainly, women are not lagging behind in this and all other crimes nowadays.

Islam wants to build a healthy *Ummah*. In order to establish peace in human society, theft is considered to be a grave crime and a sin. In a Ḥadīth of the Prophet, a thief is not a believer at the time when he is committing a theft:

Narrated Ibn 'Abbās: the Prophet (S.A.W.) said: "When an adulterer commits illegal sexual intercourse then he is not a believer at the time he is doing it; and when somebody steals, then he is not a believer at the time he is stealing."[55]

عن ابن عباس رضى الله عنه ان النبى صلى الله عليه وسلم قال: «لا يزنى الزانى حين يزنى وهو مؤمن ولا يسرق السارق حين يسرق وهو مؤمن».

Similarly, a thief is cursed by Allah as is mentioned in the following Ḥadīth:

Narrated Abū Huraira: The Prophet (S.A.W.) said: "Allah curses a man who steals a *Baiḍa* (an egg) and gets his hand cut off, or steals a rope and gets his hand cut off".

عن ابى هريرة عن النبى صلى الله عليه وسلم قال: «لعن الله السارق يسرق البيضة فتقطع يده ويسرق الحبل فتقطع يده».

The above Ḥadīth warns that right from the beginning when a man tries to lift small things, he should be disgraced and looked down upon. Ibn Hazm says that even for stealing an egg or a rope, the hands will be cut off. But the majority believe that it should reach one quarter Dīnār. The Ḥadith emphasises to discourage the crime of theft since from small thefts, one can become one day a great robber if he is not checked.

Although petty thefts are exempted from the punishment stipulated for theft in the Sharī'ah, the general opinion of the 'Ulama' based on the above injunction of the Qur'ān is that only one hand should be cut off for the first theft provided that the thief is a Muslim, an adult, sane and if it is proved beyond doubt that he has stolen the property from its proper place. The proof of stealing should be established beyond doubt. There must be two reliable male witnesses who should be good Muslims. They are required to testify against the accused or the accused himself confesses about the crime though he has every right to deny the charge levelled against him. The judge should be fully satisfied as to the crime and what has been stolen from where and when and the value of the stolen property.

As far as the stolen property is concerned, it must be movable and legally valuable and must have been kept in its usual custody and reaches the *Nisāb.*

If it does not reach *Nisāb*, there will be no hand punishment but it will be substituted by *Ta'azir*.

The jurists differ in their opinion about the *Nisab* which will confer the punishment of cutting the hands of a thiefup to the ankle. According to Imām Malik, a hand of a thief will be cut off when he steals something the value of which reaches ¼ of a dinar. He bases his opinion on the

Ḥadith of the Prophet which is reported by 'Āisha, the wife of the Prophet. Imām Abū Ḥanifah, on the contrary fixes the *Nisāb* for the punishment of cutting a hand on 10 dirhams and he bases his opinion as the tradition reported by Ibn 'Abbās:

Similarly the Muslim Jurists also differed in the case when the theft committed collectively by many thieves. According to Imām Mālik, if the property stolen reaches the *Nisāb*, one hand of each one of them should be cut off as their punishment. But Imām Abū Ḥanīfa says that if the stolen property is divided among them and the share received by each one of them reaches the *Nisāb*, the hadd will be applied and one hand of each one of the thieves will be cut off. If the share does not reach the *Nisāb*, only *Ta'azīr* will be applied. The following *Aḥādīth* of the Prophet throws further light on *Nisab:*

> Narrated 'Āisha: The Prophet (S.A.W.) said: "The hand of a thief should be cut off for stealing a quarter of a Dinar".

عن عائشة عن النبى صلى الله عليه وسلم قال: «تقطع يد السارق في ربع دينار».

> Narrated Ibn 'Umar: "The Prophet (S.A.W.) cut off the hand of a thief for stealing a shield that was worth three Dirhams".

عن ابن عمر قال: «قطع النبى صلى الله عليه وسلم في مجن ثمنه ثلاثة دراهم.

The *ḥadd* of cutting the hands is applied after the following conditions are fulfilled:

1. The person who has committed a theft must be sane.
2. He must be an adult.
3. He must not have been compelled to commit theft.
4. He must not be hungry while committing theft.

There are also conditions concerning stolen property which should be met with before cutting the hand off:

1. The stolen property must reach *nisāb.*
2. It must be valuable.
3. It must be in a custody.
4. It must be owned by someone.

In case the property stolen belongs to *Bait al-Māl* in which, it will be presumed that he has a share, or a father taking away a son's property or a wife from her husband's property. In these case the property will not be deemed as taken from custody *(ḥirz)* and it is doubtful that it really belonged to someone, only *ta'azīr* will apply.

Each case is to be decided taking into consideration the circumstantial evidences. The stolen property must be lawful and that it is removed completely from its normal custody. If one is permitted to enter a place, anything he steals in that place, the punishment is not then by *ḥadd*. According to Mālikī and *Ẓāhirī* schools, human beings cannot be subject to theft. Similarly, water, grass, sand and house cannot be stolen. Other Jurists say that human beings can be kidnapped or enticed by kidnappers. In this case, punishment is by *Ta'azir*. *Ḥadd* punishment will not be applicable in the case, of a child who stole his parent's property, or the parents who stole their son's property.

If a thief repents after he has committed the crime and amends his conduct, Allah turns to him in forgiveness. The Qur'ān says:

«فَمَنْ تَابَ مِنْ بَعْدِ ظُلْمِهِ وَأَصْلَحَ فَإِنَّ ٱللَّهَ يَتُوبُ عَلَيْهِ إِنَّ ٱللَّهَ غَفُورٌ رَحِيمٌ».

> "But if the thief repents after his crime and improves his ways, Allah turneth to him in forgiveness; for Allah is Oft-Forgiving, Most-Merciful".[57]

Once he repents after receiving his punishment, even his witness will be accepted as is mentioned in the following Hadith:

> Abut 'Abdallāh says: "If a thief repents after his hand has been cut off, his witness will be accepted. Similarly, any person upon whom any legal punishment has been inflicted repents, his witness will be accepted."[58]

قال ابـوعبـد الله: «اذا تاب السـارق بعـد ما قطـع يده قبلت شهادته وكل محدود كذلك اذا تاب قبلت شهادته».

It is important to note that any consideration of blood relationship or any other form of relationship were absolutely disallowed for interference in matters of justice. The mother of Muslims, or Lady Aisha, the wife of the Holy Prophet (S.A.W.) has reported that once a woman from the clan called Makhzūmī committed a theft. The influential members of the Quraishite were worried about the terrible punishment of the women from an important clan by cutting off her hand. In their consultations, they asked: "Who is going to speak on her behalf to the Prophet?" Someone replied: "Who could dare to do so except 'Uthman bin Zaid, who is so much loved by the Prophet?" They asked 'Uthman therefore to plead to the Prophet on behalf of the highly placed woman. When he spoke to the Prophet, he said: "Are you asking me to violate a decree of Allah?" Then the Prophet addresses the ṣaḥābah thus:

«انمـا هلك من قبلكم، انهم كانـوا يقيمـون الحـد على الـوضيـع ويتركون الشريف، والذى نفسى بيده لو فاطمة فعلت ذلك لقطعت يدها».

"The earlier communities before you were ruined and destroyed whenever a noble person was convicted of theft, they left him unharmed, but if the same thing happened to a lowly person, they exacted the punishment on him. By Allah, had Fatima stolen, I would have had her hand cut off."

It is worth mentioning here that Imām Abū Ḥanīfah was more liberal in his interpretations in respect of giving *ḥadd* punishment in case of theft as can be seen from the following comparative view of various schools of Islamic jurisprudence:

If a father steals a son's property, the *ḥadd* punishment of amputation of hand will not apply according to Imām Abū Hanīfah, but Imām Mālik says that the punishment will still be given to the father in such a case. If something is stolen collectively by many people and its value reached the *nisāb*, no-one's hand will be amputated, likewise, if any of the spouses steals property of the other, no *ḥadd* punishment will be applied according to Imam Abu Hanifah, but Imām Mālik says that the punishment will be given. If one's brother or uncle steals his property, Imām Shāfi'i, Imām Aḥmad bin Ḥanbal and Imām Mālik says that the *hadd* punishment will be applied to them, but Imām Abū Hānifah says that there will be no *ḥadd* punishment to such near relatives. if one borrows something from someone and then refutes that he ever borrowed it, he will face *ḥadd* punishment according to Shāfi'i, Hanbali and Mālikī schools, but the Ḥanafi school will not favour *ḥadd* punishment for such a defaulter. Likewise, if a man steals something and then becomes its owner by purchasing it or through gifts *(Hibah)*, there will still be *ḥadd* punishment according to the three schools except the Ḥanafī school.

Non-Mulsims who live as *Musta'min* under the protection of a Muslim state will not be given *ḥadd* punishment of amputation of hand in the event of theft according to Imām Abū Hanīfah, but the other three Imāms say that *ḥadd* punishment be applied to *Musta'minīn* as well. If someone steals shrouds of dead people, there will be no *ḥadd* punishment according to Abū Hanīfah, but Imām Shāfi'i, Imām Malik and Imām Aḥmad say that the *hadd* punishment will apply. The Ḥanafi school, similarly, will not give any *ḥadd* punishment in the event of stealing prompted by starvation, is punished by amputation of *ḥadd* punishment will still be given. The Ḥanafi school will not give any *ḥadd* punishment for the theft of wood or other perishable items, but all the other schools will award such *ḥadd* punishment for such theft.

The following resume presented by the Saudi Arabia *'Ulamā* in respect of *hadd* punishment for theft offers the practical side of the application of this deterrent in a Muslim country in the modern times.

Punishment for Theft: A Comparative View

> "Theft, with the exception of doubtful cases, as, for instance, stealing promopted by starvation, is punished by amputation of the hand. We are willing to admit, with the Jurists, that such a punishment is exceedingly harsh. It must be noted, however, that stealing in the West is most of the time perpetrated by force, and so frequently entails the murder of the victim. In such event, one wonders if it is better to have pity ont he hand of the thief rather than on the life of the assaulted person."

The debate went on:

> "Due to the harshness of this punishment in Islam, both the hand of the thief and the life of the victim have been protected, at one and the same time, and tranquility secured for all. The execution, which is done publicly serves to set an example.

At this point, Dr. Dawalibi made a comment:

> "I have been in this country for seven years", he said, "and I never saw, or heard of, any amputation of the hand for stealing. This is because the crime is extremely rare. So, all that remains of that punishment is its harshness, which has made it possible for all to live in perfect security and tranquility, and for those who are tempted to steal, to keep their hands whole. Formerly, when these regions were ruled by the French-inspired Penal Code, under the Ottoman Empire, pilgrims travelling between the two Holy Cities – Mecca and Medina, could not feel secure for their purse or their life, unless they had a strong escort.
>
> But when this country became the Saudi Kingdom, the Qur'ānic Law was enforced, crime immediately disappeared. A traveller, then, could journey, not only between the Holy Cities, but even from Al-Dahran on the Gulf to Jeddah on the Red Sea, and traverse a distance of more than one thousand and five hundred kilometres across the desert all alone in his private car, without harbouring any fear or worry about his life or property, be it worth millions of dollars, and he be a complete foreigner."

The Saudi Delegation resumed:

> "In this manner, in the Kingdom of Saudi Arabia, where Islamic Law is enforced, state money is transferred from one town to

> another, from one bank to another, in an ordinary car, without any escort or protection, but the car driver. Tell me, Gentlemen: in any of your Western States, would you be ready to transfer money from one bank to another, in any of your capitals without the protection of a strong police force and the necessary number of armoured cars?"

The speaker proceeded:

> "Only here, Gentlemen, in this country where Islamic Law is enforced, the American Minister of Foreign Affairs, Mr. William Rogers, during his visit last year, could, he and his suite, dispense with the armoured cars, which had been carried in by special planes, and which accompanied them in their tour of more than ten countries. Only here, Gentlemen , did the Government of the Kingdom not allow its visitors to go around in these cars. Eventually, Mr. Rogers spontaneously declined the guard of honour usually placed by the Government at the disposal of their foreign guests; he walked through the souks by himself, and confessed that, in this Kingdom, and in this Kingdom alone, one had such a feeling of security that one had no more need of a guard."

To conclude his report on the punishment of hand amputation for stealing, the speaker said:

> "If you consider the striking results with regard to security, public order, and general tranquility, which are the order of the day in this country, do you not agree, Gentlemen, that it is our duty to remain faithful to the commands of our Religion, to prevent similar infraction? Stealing is almost unknown in our Kingdom, when people, in the great Capitals of Western countries under secular regimes, have no more security for their lives or their possessions. I still remember, when I was in Paris in the summer, two years ago, a hold-up in one of the biggest restaurants, near the Cahmps Elysees: in front of hundreds of customers, stunned and motionless, gangsters managed to take off the whole cash. The next morning, all Parisian newspapers published the news."

Khmar: An Intoxicant

Wine-drinking, taking of alcohol or any intoxicating drug used is forbidden *(Ḥarām)* in Islam. The word for an intoxicant used in the Qur'ān is *Khamar* which is derived from *Khamara* meaning the covered or veiled thing. Thus it will mean any fermented juice of grape, barley, dates, honey or any other thing which may make one intoxicated after drinking. It may also include any liquor or thing which has the same property.

«الخمر ما خامر العقل».

"The intoxicant is something that puts a curtain on one's intellect."

Gradual prohibition introduced in Islam:

Drinking wine or the taking of an intoxicant is a great sin in Islam although there may possibly be some benefit in drinking it, but the harm, according to the Qur'ānic guidance, is greater than the benefit, especially when one looks at it from a social as well as an individual point of view. The Arabs, even after they had accepted Islam used to drink wine. They used to ask the Prophet many questions about it when the following verse was revealed:

«يَسْئَلُونَكَ عَنِ ٱلْخَمْرِ وَٱلْمَيْسِرِ قُلْ فِيهِمَا إِثْمٌ كَبِيرٌ وَمَنَافِعُ لِلنَّاسِ وَإِثْمُهُمَا أَكْبَرُ مِنْ نَفْعِهِمَا».

"They ask thee (O Prophet) concerning wine and gambling. Say: In them is a great sin, and some profit, for men; but the sin is greater than the profit." 59

The above verse only pointed out the evils of wine-drinking but did not prohibit it. Later, the Divine Revelation forbade its use partially as they were asked not to pray when they were drunk:

«يَاأَيُّهَا ٱلَّذِينَ آمَنُوا لَا تَقْرَبُوا ٱلصَّلٰوةَ وَأَنْتُمْ سُكَارىٰ حَتّىٰ تَعْلَمُوا مَا تَقُولُونَ».

"O you faithful, do not pray while you are drunk until you come to your senses and know what you say". 60

«يَاأَيُّهَا ٱلَّذِينَ آمَنُوا إِنَّمَا ٱلْخَمْرُ وَٱلْمَيْسِرُ وَٱلْأَنْصَابُ وَٱلْأَزْلَامُ رِجْسٌ مِنْ عَمَلِ ٱلشَّيْطَانِ فَاجْتَنِبُوهُ لَعَلَّكُمْ تُفْلِحُونَ إِنَّمَا يُرِيدُ ٱلشَّيْطَانُ أَنْ يُوقِعَ بَيْنَكُمُ ٱلْعَدَاوَةَ وَٱلْبَغْضَاءَ فِي ٱلْخَمْرِ وَٱلْمَيْسِرِ وَيَصُدَّكُمْ عَنْ ذِكْرِ ٱللّٰهِ وَعَنِ ٱلصَّلٰوةِ - فَهَلْ أَنْتُمْ مُنْتَهُونَ؟»

"O you who believe, wine and games of chance and idols and divining arrows are only an abomination, a handiwork of satan. Leave it aside in order that ye may succeed. Satan seeketh only to cast among you enimity and hatred by means of wine and gambling, and would keep you from remembrance of Allah and from prayer; will ye not then desist?" 61

The Jāhiliyyah Arabs before the advent of Islam were victims of these two vices. While intoxicated, they used to commit many a horrible crime which are recorded in the Books of history. They continued drinking after the advent of Islam until the Hijrah from Mecca to Medina in the year 632 A.D. Gradually, they were weaned away from this vice. The above verse contains the injunction on final prohibition of wine drinking.

According to Qatādah, the verse prohibiting wine-drinking was revealed after the battle of Aḥzāb which took place in the fourth or fifth year of the *Hijrah*. Ibn Isḥāq, the famous historian has also confirmed that it was revealed in the fourth year of Hijrah.[62]

Drinking: The Mother of all Evils:

The Prophet (S.A.W.) has referred to an intoxicant as the mother of all vices *(Umm al-Khabāith)*. In some parts of the world, many families are destroyed because of this evil. The habitual drunkards and drug-addicts cannot live without it, and in their desperate moments are ready to commit any crime.

قال رسول الله صلى الله عليه وسلم: «الخمر ام الخبائث فمن شربها لم تقبل صلاته اربعين يوما فان مات وهي في بطنه مات ميته جاهلية».

The Prophet (S.A.W.) said: "An intoxicant is a mother of all vices. Whosoever drinks it, his prayers *(ṣalāt)* will not be accepted (by Allah) for forty days. If he died and there is wine in his stomach, he has died the death of the Jahiliyya (the period before the advent of Islam)".

The prayers save a man from evil thought and action, as mentioned in the Qur'ān.[63] By doing this evil, a devotee stands to lose not only guidance from Allah but will lose the blessings and acceptance of his prayers for forty days and will move nearer to satan and fall in his net again and again.

This is the reason why, wine-drinking once started quickly becomes a habit and becomes difficult to get rid of. The Prophet (S.A.W.) has also called it an embodiment of all the sins:

قال رسول الله صلى الله عليه وسلم: «الخمر جماع الاثم».

The Prophet (S.A.W.) said: "The wine is an embodiment of all the sins." The Holy Prophet has described a drunkard as a cursed man:

The Prophet (S.A.W.) said: "A drunkard is a cursed person".

قال رسول الله صلى الله عليه وسلم: «شارب الخمر ملعون».

The wife and *Imām* (faith) cannot go together in one person and he is not a faithful *(Mu'min)* while he drinks wine as mentioned in the following *ḥadith:*

قال رسـول الله صلى الله عليـه وسلم: «من شرب الخمـر لا يجتمـع الخمـر والايمان في قلب امرىء ابدا».

The Prophet (S.A.W.) said: "The man who drinks wine, wine and *Imam* can never remain together int he heart of the same person."

قال رسول الله صلى الله عليه وسلم: «لا يشرب الخمر شاربها حين يشرب وهو مؤمن».

The Prophet (S.A.W.) said: "The man who drinks wine is not a believer at the time he drinks it."

The Qur'ānic legislations concerning the total abstinence from drinking wine or taking any other intoxicant gives Islam a degree of temperance unknown to any other creed. The Qur'ānic prohibition gives the Muslims a general stamp of soberiety unknown among the followers of any other religion. In Judaism, wine forms an integral part of their religious festivities and it is considered to be a sacred drink. In Christianity, only its abuse is condemned (Judg. 9:14) and it was never absent from the Church nor from its clergy , and that it attained enormous proportions among the latter in our own islands, and in the 8th and 9th centuries on the continent also'.[64] Thus it goes to the eternal glory of the Holy Qur'ān that wine drinking is condemned as 'a handiwork of Satan' *('aml al-Shaiṭān)* and a sin.

In one of the Traditions of the Prophet Muḥammad, he says: 'Every drink that intoxicates is prohibited *(Ḥarām)*. 65This means that every drink or drug that intoxicates is *ḥarām* (unlawful). In another Ḥadith, the Prophet says:

«كل مسكر حرام، وما اسكر الفرق منه فملء الكف منه حرام».

All intoxicants are unlawful of whatever thing a large quantity intoxicates, even a small quantity is prohibited. 66

From the above Ḥadīth, it is clear that hemp, hashish, opium, marijuana and other drugs are equally *ḥarām*. The Ḥanafī jurists, call the hemp smokers 'irreligious innovators' *(zindiq mubtadī)*.

The Prophet (S.A.W.) has said that Allah has cursed wine or an intoxicant, and the person who drinks it, the person who serves it, the person who sells it and buys it, the person who brews it, the person who gets it brewed and extracted, the person who carries it and the person to whom it is carried.[67] All the jurists of the four schools have a consensus that a drunkard must be punished through flogging. The Mālikī, the Ḥanafi and the Ḥanbali jurists say that the *ḥadd* punishment for wine-drinking will be eighty lashes, but the Imām Shāfi'ī says that the punishment will be forty stripes only. SayyidnāUmar also used to give punishment of eighty lashes and instructed Khālid bin al-walīd and Abū U baidah to do the same in Syria in his letters written to them. The punishment will be given if a person drunks accepts *(al-Iqrār)* that he has drunk or on the evidence of two just witnesses.

The jurists differ in heir opinions whether the *ḥadd* punishment will be given through smelling one's mouth. According to Imām Malik, if the mouth smells of wine, the *ḥadd* punishment of eighty strokes will be given. Imām Abū Ḥanifah and Imām al-Shāfi'i disagree on this point and maintain that the smell may be of something else which resembles wine. Therefore, *ḥadd* punishment will not be given to a child, or an insane or someone who was made to drink under duress.

Al-Riddah: Apostacy

Al-Riddah means rejection of the religion of Islam in favour of any other religion either through an action or through words of mouth. The act of apostacy thus puts an end to one's adherence to Islam. When one rejects the fundamental principles of faith *(īmān)* like faith int he Existence of Allah or the Messengership of His Prophet Muḥammad as contained in the credal statement of Islam, the *Kalimah al-shahādah.* Similarly the rejection of the belief in the Qur'ān as the Book of Allah or the belief of the message contained in it, or the belief in the Day of Resurrection, or Reward and the Punishment of Allah will all amount to apostacy. The rejection of the obligatory ritual practices, like *Salat* (prayers), *Zakāt* (giving of the poor-rate), *Ṣiyām* (Fasting in the month of Ramaḍan), and *Ḥajj* Pilgrimage will also amount to acts of *Irtidād.* Likewise, if one imitates the practices of non-Muslims in their prayers etc; it will be considered an act of apostacy.[67]

The following Qur'ānic verse explains the gravity of sin and the crime of apostacy:

كيف يهدى الله قوماكفروا بعد ايمانهم وشهدوا ان الرسول حق وجاءهم البينت والله لا يهدى القوم الظالمين - اولئك جزاؤهم ان عليهم لعنة الله والملئكة والناس اجمعين .

خلدين فيها لا يخفف عنهم العذاب ولا هم ينظرون - الا الذين تابوا من بعد ذلك واصلحوا فان الله غفور رحيم» .

> "How shall Allah guide those who reject faith after they accepted it and bore witness that the Apostle was true and the clear signs had come unto them. But Allah guides not the people unjust of such the reward is that on them rests the curse of Allah, of His Angels and of all mankind in that will they dwell; nor will their penalty be lightened, nor respite be their lot, except for those that repent (even) after that and make amends; for verily Allah is oft-forgiving, Most Merciful." 68

Ḥadd

The punishment for apostacy is prescribed in the following Ḥadīth of the Prophet:

عن ابن عباس رضي الله عنه، قال: قال رسول الله صلى الله عليه وسلم: «من بدل دينه فأقتلوه».

> It is reported by Abbas, may Allah be pleased with him, that the Messenger of Allah (S.A.W.) said: "Whosoever changes his religion (from Islam to anything else), bring end to his life.'"69

The punishment by death in the case of apostacy has been unanimously agreed upon by all the four schools of Islamic jurisprudence. But, if one is forced to pronounce something that amounts to apostacy, while his heart is satisfied with *Īmān* (faith), he will not be charged with apostacy in those circumstances. The Qur'ān says:

«مَنْ كَفَـرَ بِاللّٰهِ مِنْ بَعْـدِ ايمَـانه الَّا مَنْ اكْرِهَ وَقَلْبُهُ مُطْمَئِنٌّ بِالْايمانِ وَلٰكِن مَنْ شَرَحَ بِالْكُفْرِ صَدْراً فَعَلَيْهِمْ غَضَبٌ مِنَ اللّٰهِ وَلَهُمْ عَذَابٌ عَظِيمٌ».

> "Anyone who after accepting Faith in Allah, utters Unbelief, except under compulsion, his heart remaining firm in Faith; but such as open their breast to Unbelief, on them is wrath from Allah and theirs will be a dreadul penalty." 70

In the books of *Ahadīth*, the causes of revelation (*Asbab al-Nuzul*) of this verse are mentioned referring to the case of 'Ammar bin Yasir. 'Ammār's father Yasir and mother Sumayyah were subjected to unbearable tortures for their belief in Islam and love for the prophet, but in spite of the tortures they never recanted. 'Ammār was a young man of less mature age. In a weak moment, while suffering great tortures at the hands of the pagan Arabs and thinking of his parent's suffering uttered something that was construed as recantation, though his heart never wavered. Abū Jahl had made iron chains and had put them around his body in the hot summer days. The chains became hot like live charcoals due to the heat of the sun. In such desperate moments he said something which was reported to the Prophet. The Prophet thereupon said about 'Ammār:

عمار ملىء أيمانا من فرقه الى قدمه.

" 'Ammar is full of *Iman* from his head to his feet."

It was on this occasion that the above verse was revealed.

The other legal aspects concerning the effects of apostacy on marriage, divorce and inheritence are discussed in the respective chapters dealing with them.

Al-Firār Min Al-Zaḥf

Running Away from the Battlefield in Jihād

Whenever a Muslim joins the forces of *Jihād* for the cause of Islam, and one is already on the battlefield, fighting against the enemies, his running away from the ranks constitutes a great crime in *Shari'ah.* It is on the contrary, an occasion to stand firm according to the instructions of the leaders as thoughtfully planned in their strategy. It is a time to show bravery and lay down one's life for the defence of Islam, Muslims or to defend the rights on non-Muslims living in a Muslim state. Running away from the battlefield can endanger the fate of the *Ummah*. The following *Qur'ānic injunction shows how grave is the crime to flee the battlefield:*

«يَـا أَيُّهَـا ٱلَّـذِيْنَ آمَنُـوا اذَا لَقِيتُم ٱلَّذِينَ كَفَرُوا زَحْفاً فَلا تُولُّوهُمُ ٱلاَدْبَارَ وَمَنْ يُوَلِّهِمْ يَوْمَئِذٍ دُبُرَهُ الاَّ مُتَحَرِّفاً لِقِتَالٍ اَوْ مُتَحَيِّزاً الىٰ فِئَةٍ فَقَدْ بَآءَ بِغَضَبٍ مِنَ ٱللّٰهِ وَمَاوَاهُ جَهَنَّمُ وَبِئْسَ ٱلْمَصِيرُ».

"O you who believe, when you meet the Unbelievers in hostile way, never turn your backs to them. If any do turn his back to them on such a day – unless it be in a stratagem of war, or to retreat a troop (of his own) – he draws on himself the wrath of Allah, and his abode is hell, an evil refuge indeed." 71

The *ḥadd* punishment for this grave and dangerous crime of fleeing the battlefield is death according to the consensus of opinions of the Muslim jurists of all the schools. The law is in conformity with that enforced – virute and discipline in the modern armies. The soldiers are instructed to meet the enemy fairly and squarely, not rashly. The Arabic word *Zaḥf* used in the verse of the Qur'ān implies meeting in a hostile array of a well-planned proceeding towards a hostile army. The soldiers obey orders and work merely on reflection when they are in combat where there is no room for a second thought. The best motto then is death or victory. It may be death for himself, individually, but the *Ummah* will prosper through his sacrifice, and his reward will be that of a *Ghāzi*, if he survives the war, or will become a martyr in the cause of Allah, if he died in active service of Allah.

In the modern armies too, such defaulters are court-martialled and put to death or given very harsh punishments.

The Islamic concept of *Jihād*, and the circumstances in which it becomes permissible are fully discussed in a relevant chapter in this book.

---

1. Qur'ān, ch. 5:32.
2. Qur'ān, ch. 6:15.
3. Qur'ān, ch. 4:93
4. Qur'ān, ch. 6:151.
5. Qur'ān, ch. 81:8-9.
6. Qur'ān, ch. 4:29
7. Bukhārī, Abū Dāūd, Nisāī and Musnad Aḥmad have all reported this great address *(Khuṭbah)*.
8. Ibid.
9. Maudūdi, A. A., *Human Rights in Islam,* Leicester, 1976, p. 17.
10. Qur'ān, ch. 6:151
11. Qur'ān, ch. 2:178
12. Qur'ān ch. 5:48.
13. Exod. XXI: 23-25; Leviticus XXIV: 18-21 and Deut. XIX: 21.
14. Qur'ān, ch. 5:35
15. Qur'ān, ch. 5:45.
16. Qur'ān, ch. 2:178.
17. Qur'ān, ch. 4:92.
18. Abū Dāūd, 38:25.
5. Bukhari, 87:21.
19. Al Qayrawāni *Risālah,* op. cit., ch. 37: Bābfī aḥkāmal- *Da'wal Ḥudūd* ch. 37, pp. 121-130
20. Ibid.
21. Al-Qayrawānī, Risālah, op. cit., ch. 37: *Bāb fī ahkam al-Da'wal Ḥudūd*, pp. 121-130.
22. *Al Qayrāwanī, Risālah,* op. cit., see chapter: *Bab fi Aḥkam al-Dima Wal Ḥudud*, pp. 121-131
23. Al-Qayrawānī, Risālah, op. cit., pp. 121-131.
24. Qur'ān, 17:32.
25. Al-Bukhāri, Kitāb al Ḥudūd.
26. Al-Bukhāri, Sahih al-Bukhārī Kitāb al-Ḥudūd.
27. Qura'ān, 4:15.
28. Qur'ān, 4:16.
29. Qur'ān, 24.2.
30. Al-Bukhārī, Kitab al-Ḥūdud.
31. Al-Bukhāri, *Kitab al-Ḥūdud.*
32. Ibid.
33. Qur'ān, ch. 7:81.
34. Qur'ān, ch. 7:84
35. Al-Ṭibrānī and al-Baihaqī

37. Al-Qayrawānī, *Risālah* op. cit., ch. 37: *Bāb fī ahk ·am, al-Da'wal Ḥudūd*, pp. 121-130.
38. Conference on *Muslim Doctrine and Human Rights in Islam,* Ministry of Justice, Riyadh, March 23, 1972.
39. Qur'ān
40. Al-Bukhārī
41. For details of the incident see *Ṣaḥīḥ Al-Bukhārī.*
42. Qur'ān, 24:23-24.
43. Qur'ān, 24:6-9.
44. Al-Qayrawānī, *Risālah*, op. cit. ch. 37: *Bāb fī aḥkām al-Da'wal Ḥudud*, pp. 121-130.
45. Ibid.
46. Qur'ān, ch. 51:12.
47. Qur'ān, ch. 5:32.
48. For details, see *Nail al-Awtār*, Vol. 7, p. 336; also *Ḥāshiyah al-Dasūqī*, vol. 4, p. 348.
49. Qur'ān, ch. 5:34.
50. Ibn Hishām, *Seerah,* Vol. II, (Arabic Edition), pp. 271-272.
51. Qur'ān, ch. 2:188.
52. Qur'ān, ch. 5:41.
53. Cf. Matthew, 27:38.
54. Matthew, 18:8.
55. Al-Bukhārī; *Kitāb al-Ḥudūd.*
56. Qur'ān, ch. 5:42.
57. Al-Bukhārī: *Kitāb al-Ḥudūd.*

58. Conferences on *Muslim Doctrines and Human Rights in Islam* between Saudi Ulama and European Jurists, Ministry of Justice, Riyadh, March 23, 1972.

59. Qur'ān, ch. 2:219.
60. Qur'ān, ch. 4:43.
61. Qur'ān, ch. 5:91.
62. Sayyid Sābiq, *Fiqh al-Sunnah*, op. cit., vol. 9, p. 32.
63. Smith and Cheetham, Dictionary of Christian *Antiquities* vol. 1, p. 585.
64. Bukhārī, 74:3.
65. Abū Dāūd, 25:5.
66. Al-Nawawī, Muhammad bin 'Umar, *Tanqīh al-Qaul al Ḥathīth bi-sharḥ lubāb al-Hadith*, Cairo (undated).
67. Al-Ajūz, Aḥmad Muḥyi al-Dīn, *Manāhijal-Sharī'ah al-Islāmiyyah*, Beirut, 1969, vol. 1, p. 249.
68. Qur'ān, ch. 3:86-89. Also cf. Qur'ān, ch. 2:161-162.
69. Al-Bukhārī.
70. Qur'ān, ch. 16:106.
71. Qur'ān, ch. 8: 15-16.

PART IV

INHERITANCE AND DISPOSAL OF PROPERTY

Chapter 17

Mīrāth: Law of Succession

There are about thirty five verses of the Qur'ān which refer to *Mīrāth* (inheritance) or its derivatives in one form or the other. The word *Mīrāth* is specifically used in the following two verses:

«وَلِلَّهِ مِيرَاثُ ٱلسَّمٰوَاتِ وَٱلْأَرْضِ وَٱللَّهُ بِمَا تَعْمَلُونَ خَبِيرٌ».

"To Allah belongs the inheritance of the heavens and the earth; and Allah is well-acquainted with all that you do."[1]

In Sūrah al-Ḥadīd, the Qur'ān says:

«وَمَا لَكُمْ أَلَّا تُنْفِقُوا فِي سَبِيلِ ٱللَّهِ وَلِلَّهِ مِيرَاثُ ٱلسَّمٰوَاتِ وَٱلْأَرْضِ».

"And what cause have you why you should not spend in the cause of Allah? For to Allah belongs the inheritance of the heavens and the earth."[2]

Even the Prophets of Allah like Zakariyā have prayed to be given successors to inherit them:

«وَزَكَرِيَّآ إِذْ نَادَىٰ رَبَّهُ رَبِّ لَا تَذَرْنِي فَرْدًا وَأَنْتَ خَيْرُ ٱلْوَارِثِينَ».

"And remember Zakariya, when he cried to his Lord: O my Lord! Leave me not without off-spring, though you are the best of Inheritors".[3]

In legal terminology, *Mīrāth* means inheritance to be divided from the property of the deceased among his successors. The science of *Mīrāth* in Shari'ah gives rules which guide as to who inherits and who is to be inherited, and what shares go to the heirs. Thus, one of the most important branches of the Islamic family law is that relating to inheritance. The death of a person brings about transfer of most of his rights and obligations to persons who survive him and are called *wuratha*, that is heirs and representatives. Just as inheritance is called *Mīrāth* in Arabic.

The transmissible rights include all rights to property as well as rights, connected with property, and other dependent rights, such as debts, rights to compensation, etc. There are also the transmissible obligations those which are capable of being satisfied out of the deceased's estate. What is left after the last needs of the deceased have been satisfied, namely, after the payment of funeral expenses and the discharge of his obligations and debts, is to be distributed according to the law of *Mirath* as defined in the Qur'ānic injunctions.

The rules regulating inheritance in Sharī'ah are based on the principle that property which belonged to the deceased should devolve on those who by reason of consanguinity or marital relations have the strongest claim to be benefited by it and in proportion to the strength of such claim. The deceased may, however, leave more than one person so related to or connected with him that it would be difficult to say with regard to any one of them that his claim should altogether supersede that of the others. It is laid down in the Qur'ān "*of your parents and sons you do not known which of them are the nearest and of most benefit to you*".[4] Islamic Sharī'ah in those cases distributes the estate among the claimants in such order and proportions as are most in harmony with the natural strength of their claims.

In the Jahiliyyah period, the rules of inheritance excluded both women and children from inheriting from the estate left by their deceased relatives, because according to them only those who could go to the battle field in order to defend the clan were allowed to inherit. As far as a woman was concerned, she was considered to be the property of her husband's family, and she was to be included in the estate immediately after the death of her husband.

At the time when Muslims emigrated from Mecca to Medina, the law of succession was based on the Islamic relationship. A Muslim from Medina could inherit his Meccan brother in Islam until the time when this verse was revealed; verse 75, *Sūrah 8* which changed the rules from brotherhood in Islam to near relatives.

Essentials of Succession

The essentials of succession are as follows:

1. Deceased person
2. Heir
3. Estate

In most cases the estate is the most important part of the law of succession. But the Jurists differ in what amounts to property. The Ḥanafī school says that property excludes rights and that the rights are not inheritable as for example, if somebody enters into a contract of hire, should his heirs after his death inherit the contract also? According to the Ḥanafi school the contract lapses with the death of their father.

But the rest of the schools are of the opinion that rights are inheritable.

Conditions of Succession

There are three conditions of inheritance which must be satisfied:

1. The death of Prepositus
2. The survival of heirs at the time of death
3. The relationship which justify inheritance.

1. *The Death of Prepositus*

The death of Prespositus must be actual and clear either by real death or by the decree of the court in the case of a missing person.

2. *The Survival of Heirs*

It has to be proved that the heir or heirs are surviving at the time of the death of the Prepositus, before he or they are allowed to inherit.

In the case of an embryo, it will not inherit unless it is born alive. His share should be put aside pending his delivery but the share which is to be kept should be the share of a male child. But according to the Māliki school, the whole estate should be saved pending the delivery of the child before the distribution.

In the case where all the people died at the same time, and there is no way to determine who died first and who died later, then their estate should be inherited by their relatives who are surviving. The authority of this rule is that, after the battle of Yamāmah in which many Muslims died, Sayyidnā Abūbakar ordered Zaid bin Thābit to distribute their estate, to which Zaid distributed among their surviving relatives, as narrated by him.

قال زيد امرني عمر بتوريث اهل طاعون وكانت القبيلة تموت باسرها فورثت الاحياء من الاموات ولم اورث الاموات بعضهم من بعض.

Zaid (bin Thābit) said: "Umar ordered me to apportion the shares of victims who suffered from the epidemic of plague. There was a clan whose members had died. I apportioned the shares of inheritance from the dead for the ones alive since they do not inherit each other."

Man's sojourn on this earth is for a limited period, and then comes the appointed time not a minute earlier or a minute later. During the short span of his life, whatever he accumulates in this world will be left behind except the good actions which go with him. The property and belongings that he leaves behind go to his successors. Islam being the complete way of life the Holy Qur'ān contains rules for the disposal of intestate property.

A dying man or a woman, of his own free-will, must think of his parents and his next of kin, not in a spirit of injustice to others, but in a spirit of love and respect for those who have cherished him or whom he has cherished in this life. This should be done according to reasonable usage *(bil-ma 'rūf)*:

«كُتِبَ عَلَيْكُمْ اذا حَضَرَ اَحَدَكُمُ اْلمَوْتُ اِنْ تَرَكَ خَيْراً اْلوَصِيَّةُ لِلْوَالِدَيْنِ
وَاْلاَقْرَبِينَ بِاْلمَعْرُوفِ حَقّاً عَلَى اْلمُتَّقِينَ. فَمَنْ بَدَّلَهُ بَعْدَ مَا سَمِعَهُ فَاِنَّمَا آثْمُهُ عَلَى
اْلَّذينَ يُبَدِّلُونَهُ اِنَّ اْللّهَ سَميعٌ عَليمٌ».

"It is prescribed when death approaches any of you, if he leaves any goods, that he makes a bequest to parents and next of kin, according to a reasonable usage, this is due from Allah-fearing person. If any one changes the bequest after hearing it, the guilt shall be on those who make the change. For Allah hears and Knows all things."[5]

This was ordained long before the law of inheritance was revealed. Later the definite shares were laid down for heirs in *Sūrah al-Nisā.* These later verses limit the testamentary powers, as we shall soon see, but they do not abrogate it. Supposing there is an orphan grand-son among the kins in the presence of surviving sons, he will not inherit according to the intestate scheme and the testator might like to provide for him under the provision of above verses. Likewise, the injunctions cover grandfathers and great grandfathers and grandmothers or great grandmothers.

But according to a Ḥadith,[6] he cannot dispose of more than one third of his property and should not be partial to one heir at the expense of the others. It is in such cases that witnesses will come to play their just role.

The principle of inheritance of individual heirs is laid down int he following verse:

«لِلرِّجَالِ نَصيبٌ مِمَّا تَرَكَ اْلوَالِدانِ وَاْلاَقْرَبُونَ وَلِلنِّسَاءِ نَصيبٌ مِمَّا تَرَكَ
اْلوَالِدَانِ وَاْلاَقْرَبُونَ مِمَّا قَلَّ مِنْهُ اَوْ كَثُرَ نَصيباً مَفْرُوضاً».

"From what is left by parents and those nearest related there is a share for men and a share for women, whether the property be small or large, a determinate share."

A strict warning is given to those who are in charge of disposing and dividing of an estate to have the same fear in their minds as they would have if they had left a helpless family behind. They are asked to observe the principle of justice and be kind and helpful.[7]

The details of the shares of individual heirs is given in the following verse, but the above verse has five legal implications:

a) The inheritance is not meant for men only but women also have the right to inherit.
b) The property left behind by a deceased, however little it might be, must be distributed justly among the heirs. The ʿUlamā say that even if he has left a piece of cloth, it should be cut into equal number of pieces among the heirs unless one of the heirs buys their share.
c) The law of inheritance will apply to all kinds of property, movable or immovable or of any other kind.
d) The question of inheritance only comes up when the deceased has left any property.
e) The nearer relative precludes the distant relative from the inheritance.

The details of the shares of each heir is given in the following verse of the Holy Qur'ān:

«يُوصيكُمُ ٱللّٰهُ فِي أَوْلَادِكُمْ لِلذَّكَرِ مِثْلُ حَظِّ ٱلْأُنْثَيَيْنِ-فَإِن كُنَّ نِسَاءً فَوْقَ ٱثْنَتَيْنِ فَلَهُنَّ ثُلُثَا مَاتَرَكَ-وَإِنْ كَانَتْ وَاحِدَةً فَلَهَا ٱلنِّصْفُ وَلِأَبَوَيْهِ لِكُلِّ وَاحِدٍ مِنْهُمَا ٱلسُّدُسُ مِمَّا تَرَكَ إِنْ كَانَ لَهُ وَلَدٌ-فَإِنْ لَمْ يَكُنْ لَهُ وَلَدٌ وَوَرِثَهُ أَبَوَاهُ فَلِأُمِّهِ ٱلثُّلُثُ-فَإِنْ كَانَ لَهُ إِخْوَةٌ فَلِأُمِّهِ ٱلسُّدُسُ مِنْ بَعْدِ وَصِيَّةٍ يُوصِي بِهَا أَوْ دَيْنٍ-ءابَاؤُكُمْ وَأَبْنَاؤُكُمْ لَا تَدْرُونَ أَيُّهُمْ أَقْرَبُ لَكُمْ نَفْعًا، فَرِيضَةً مِنَ ٱللّٰهِ إِنَّ ٱللّٰهَ كَانَ عَلِيماً حَكِيماً».

"Allah directs you as regards your children's (Inheritance): to the male, a portion equal to that of two females: if there are only daughters, two or more, their share is two-thirds of the inheritance; if there is only one (daughter), her share is a half. For parents there is one-sixth share of the inheritance to each, if the deceased has left children, if there are no children, and the parents are the only heirs, the mother gets a third; if the deceased left brothers (or sisters), the mother gets a sixth. (The distribution in all cases is) after the payment of legacies and debts, you know not whether your parents or your children are nearest to you in benefit. These are settled portions ordained by Allah, and Allah is all-Knowing, All-wise."[8]

'Allāma Yūsuf ʿAlī', while explaining this verse rightly remarks that Muslim jurists have collected a vast amount of learning on this subject and this body of law is enough by itself to form the subject of life-long study.[9] This is quite true as the Shari'ah has dealt with the problems of succession in very minute details. "in these provisions, we find ample attention paid to the interest of all those whom nature places in the first rank of our affections; and indeed it is difficult to conceive any system containing rules more strictly just and equitable."[10]

Guidance from the Ḥadīth on Succession

The *Asbāb al-Nuzūl* or causes of revelation have been explained in the Ahadith of the Prophet. It is reported in the famous collection of Ḥadīth, viz. *Ṣaḥiḥ al-Bukhāri* in *Kitāb Al-Tafsir*[11] that this important verse on *Mirath* "Allah commands you as regards your children's inheritance" was revealed in the following circumstances.

عن جابر رضى الله تعالى عنه عادَ النبي صلى الله عليه وسلم وابو بكر في
بنى سلمة ماشيين فوجدني النبي صلى الله عليه وسلم لا اعقل فدعا بماء
وتوضأ منه ثم رش علي فأفقت وقلت «ما تأمرني ان اصنع في مالي يارسول
الله؟ فنزلت: «يُوصيكُمُ ٱللّٰهُ فِي اَوْلَادِكُمْ».

"Narrated Jābir: The Prophet (S.A.W.) and Abū Bakr came on foot to pay me a visit (during my illness) at Banū Salma's (dwellings). The Prophet (S.A.W.) found me unconscious, so he asked for water and performed the ablution from it and sprinkled some water over me. I came to my senses and said: "Allah's Apostle, what do you order me to do as regards my wealth?". So this was revealed: "Allah commands you as regards your children's inheritance."[12]

The causes of revelation of the verse 12 in *Sūrah al-Nisā* are mentioned in *Ṣaḥiḥ al-Bukhāri; Kitāb Al-Tafsir:* 102 are mentioned as follows:

«وَلَكُمْ نِصْفُ مَا تَرَكَ اَزْوَاجُكُمْ»

"in what your wives leave, your share is half."[13]

Narrated Ibn ʿAbbās: (In the pre-Islamic period) the children used to inherit all the property but the parents used to inherit only through a will. So Allah cancelled that what He liked to cancel and decreed that the share of a son was to be twice the share of a daughter, and for the parents sixth for each one of them (if the deceased had a child) and one-third third (if the deceased had no child).

So Allah cancelled what He liked to cancel and decreed that the share of a son was to be twice the share of a daughter and for the parents one sixth for each one of them (if the deceased had one child) and one-third (if the deceased had no child) and for the wife one-eighth (if the deceased had a child) or one-fourth (if the deceased had no child) and for the husband one-half (if the deceased had no children) or one-fourth (if the deceased had a child)."

Rights of Sharers

There are two classes of heirs, those who have specific shares *(farḍ)* mentioned in the Qur'ān, and the *aṣāba* that is those who are entitled to the remainders of the shares. They are as follows:

MALES who are entitled to succeed are son, son of son.

1. Son
2. Son of son how low so ever.
3. Father of the deceased.
4. Grandfather of the deceased how high so ever.
5. Brother of the deceased.
6. Son of the brother of the deceased.
7. Uncle, i.e. brother of the father of the deceased.
8. Son of Uncle, i.e. Son of the brother of the father of the deceased.
9. Husband.
10. Master who freed his slave.

These are only the male heirs

FEMALES

1. Daughter of the deceased.
2. Daughter of the son of the deceased.
3. Mother of the deceased.
4. Grandfather of the deceased for both sides.
5. Sister whether full, consanguine and uterine.
6. Wife of the deceased.
7. Freed slave (mistress) maulatunneamati.

These are the only females who are going to inherit.

ASḤĀB AL-FARĀ'IḌ

There are four males.

1. Husband of the deceased.
2. Father of the deceased.
3. Grandfather of the deceased.
4. Uterine brothers.

Their shares are ½, ⅙, ¼ and ⅓.

The females are:

1. Wife of the deceased.
2. Daughter of the deceased.
3. Daughter of the son of the deceased.
4. Mother of the deceased.
5. Grandmother of the deceased.
6. 3 sisters (full sister, uterine sister and consanguine sister).

Their shares are ¼, ⅛, ½ and ⅔.

The Shi'ities have the following classification of heirs, slightly different from the Sunnis:

A. *Nasab* (blood relationship), and
B. *Sabab* (special cause).

A. *Nasab* is divided into two groups:
 (i) *Dhū farḍ* (Qur'ānic heir) (a)
 (ii) *Dhū qarābāt* (blood relation, agnate or cognate) (b).

B. *Sabab* is also subdivided into two groups:
 (i) *Zawjiyyah* (the status of a spouse),
 (ii) *Wala* (special legal relationship).

Wala is of three kinds:

1. *walā* of 'itq (right of emancipation),
2. *walā* or *Ḍāmin al-jarīmah* (right of obligation for delicts committed by the deceased),
3. *wala* of *Imāmah* (right by virtue of religious leadership).

Table One

The male heirs among the *'Asābah* (Agnates) except husband and mother's brother.

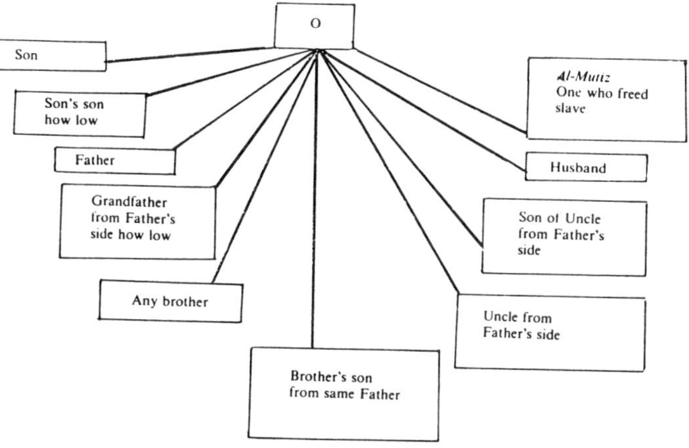

Table Two

The Female Heirs who are Dhawat al-Faraḍ except freed slave woman.

الوارثات وكلهن ذوات فرض الا المعتقة

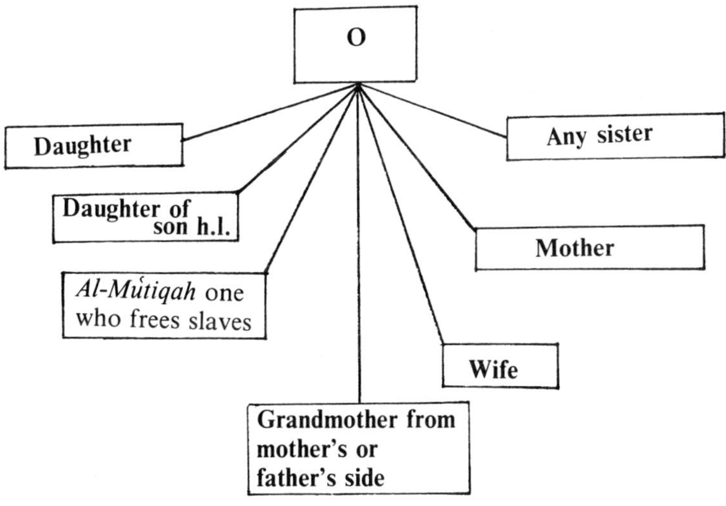

Table Three

The male and Female Heirs at the same time where they can be co-sharers.

الورثة عند اجتماع الصنفين

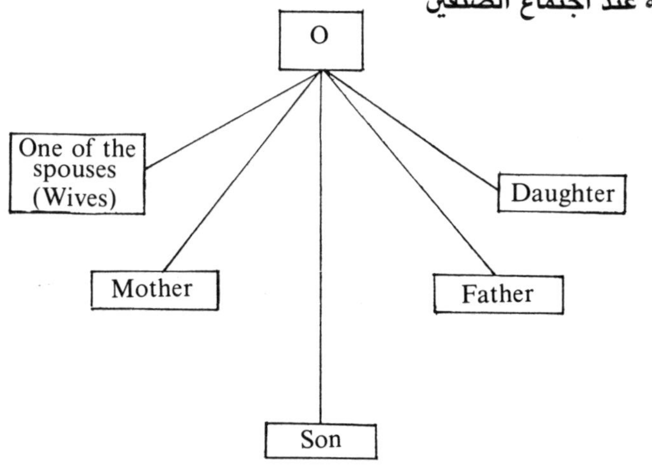

Table Four

The Heirs inheriting one half when there is no male residual heir among the female heirs.

ورثة النصف حيث لم يكن مع الأناث

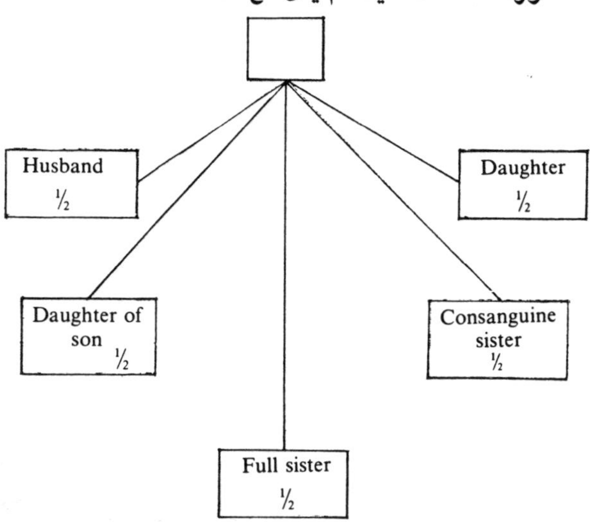

Table Five

The Heirs of 2/3 female heirs in the absence of male residual heirs inheriting with them - where they are brothers the rule will not apply

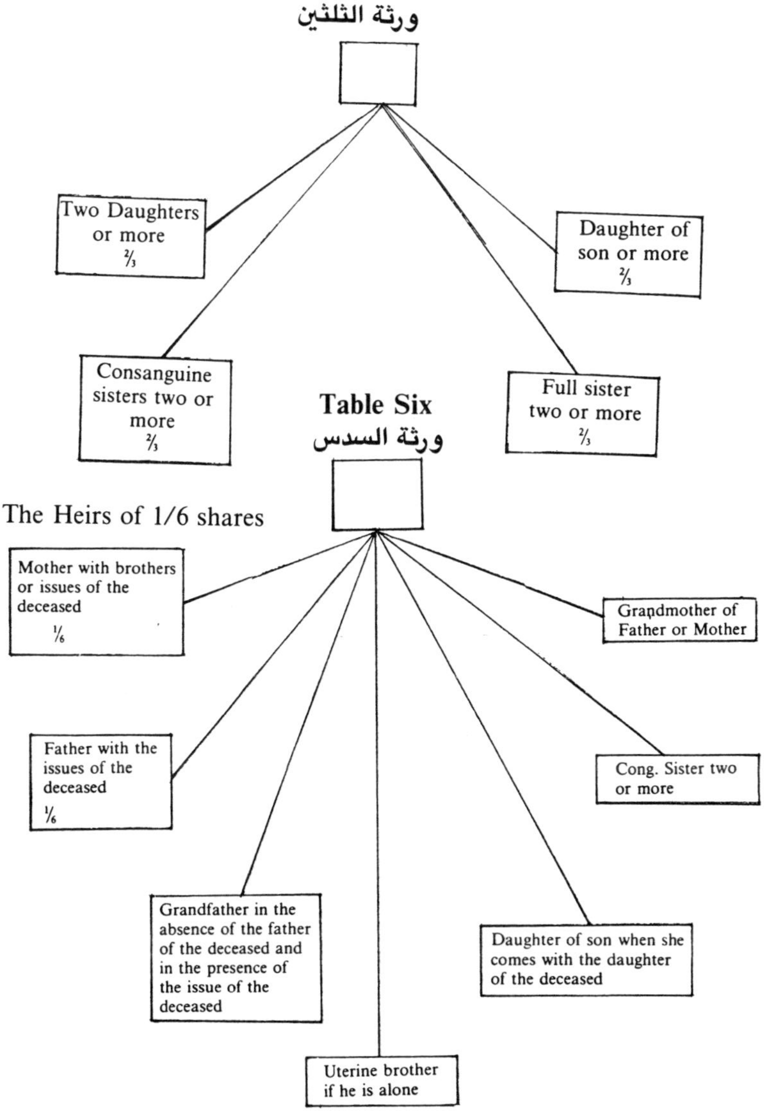

Note: The Prophetic Hadith says: "Give to the heirs their fixed shares and the remainder should be given to the nearest male agnate". Therefore, the father takes $\frac{1}{6}$ + R when he comes along with female issue.

Table Seven

Those who are no excluded totally from inheriting

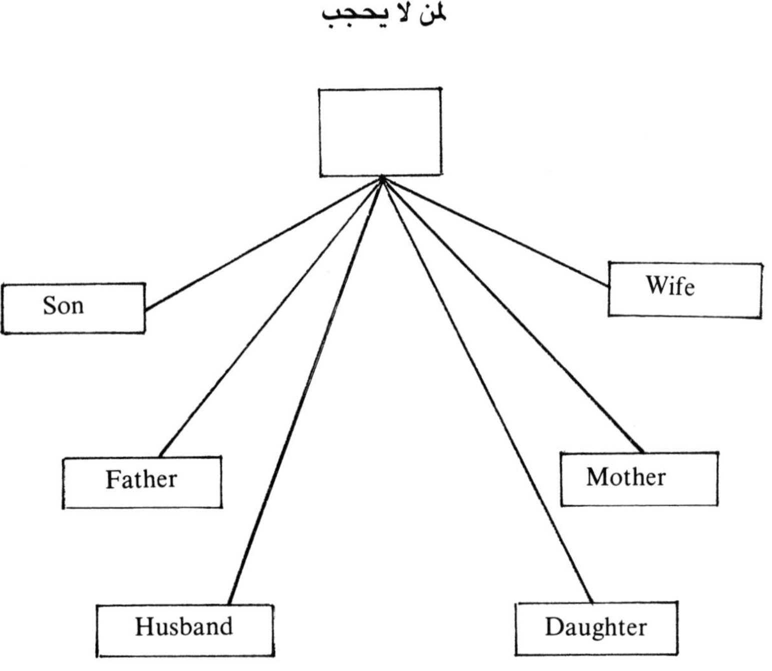

Table Eight

Those who are excluded by son or sons of the deceased

المحجوبين بالابن

المعتق

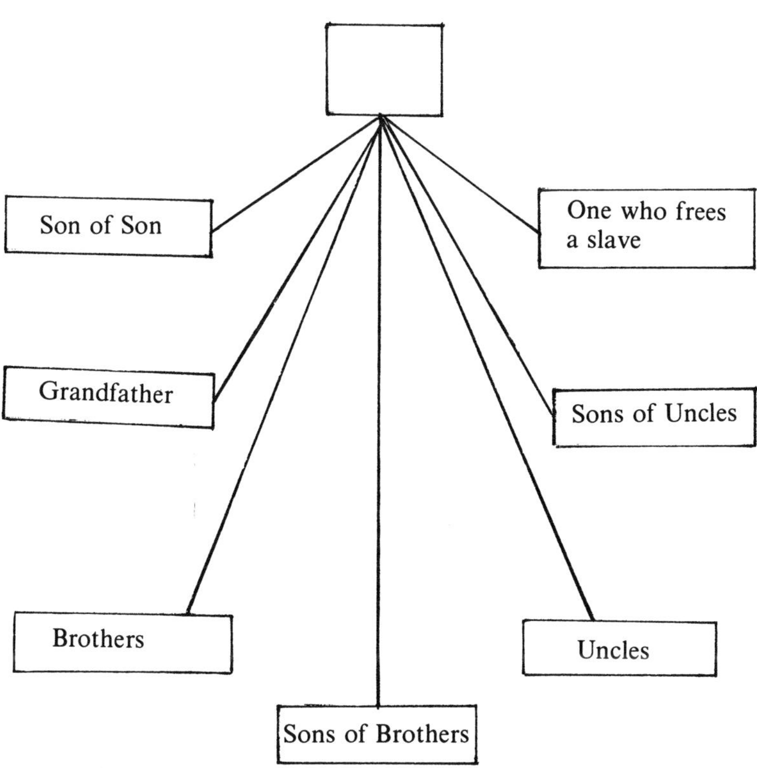

Table Nine

Those who are totally excluded by father of the deceased. They are seven.

المحجوبين بالاب

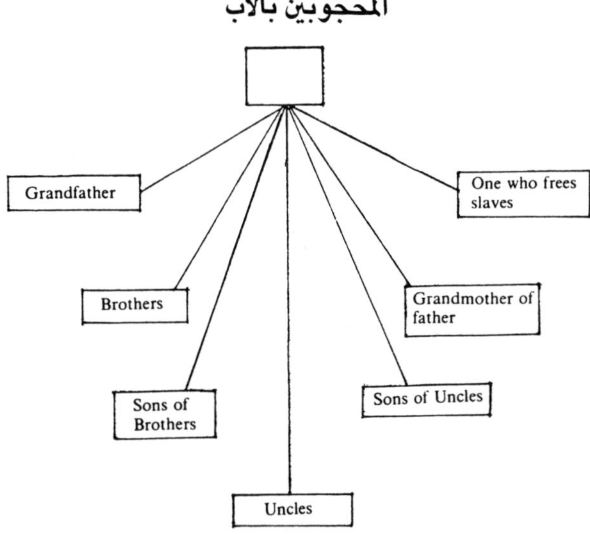

Table Ten

Those who are excluded totally by Grandfather of the deceased. They are six.

المحجوبين بالجد

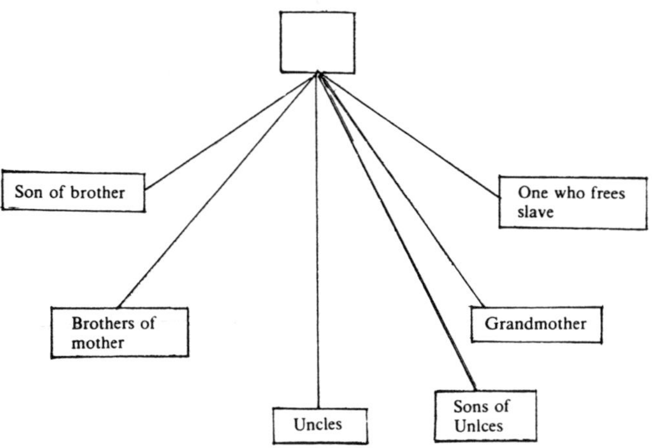

Table Eleven

Those who are totally excluded by full brother of the deceased. They are five.

المحجوبين بالاخ الشقيق

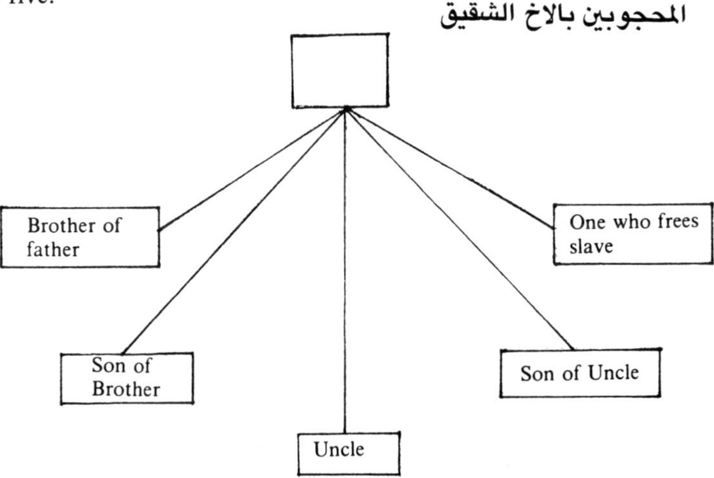

Table Twelve

Those who are totally excluded by consanguine brother of the deceased. They are four. المحجوبين بالاخ لأب

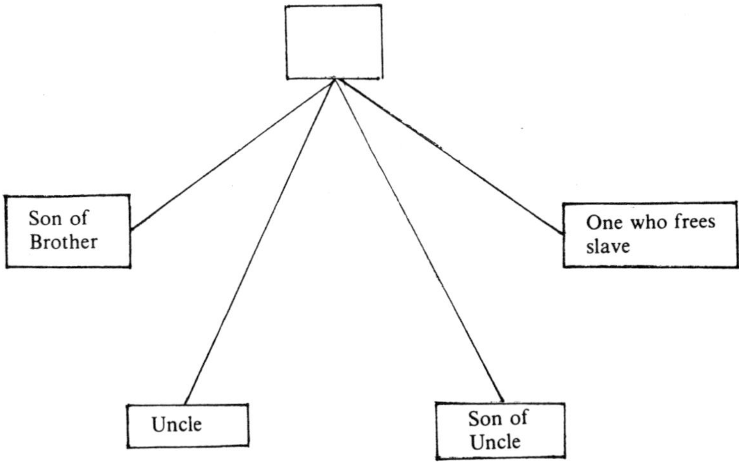

Table Thirteen

Those who are totally excluded by paternal uncle (full brother of the father of the deceased) المحجوبين بالعم الشقيق

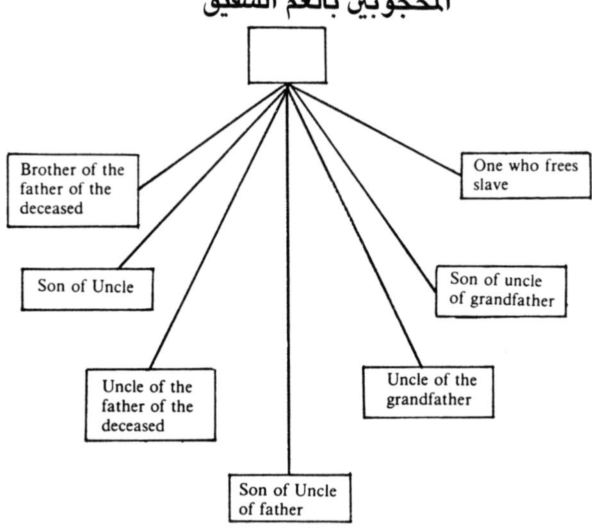

Table Fourteen

Those who are excluded by a consanguine brother of the father of the deceased. They are six.

المحجوبين بالعم لأب

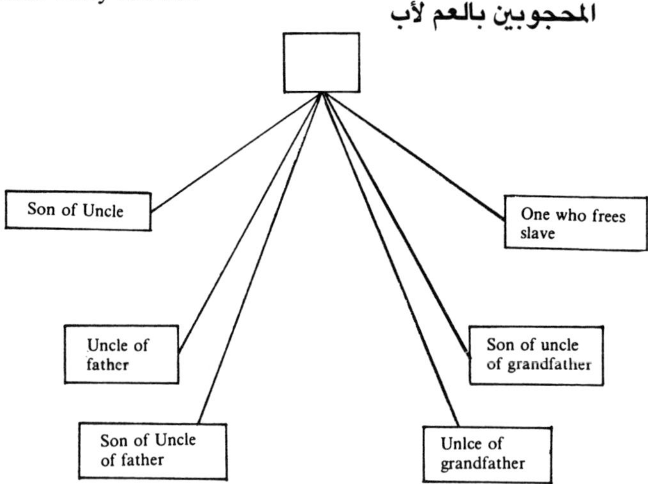

Table Fifteen

Those who are excluded by uncles and uncle's sons of the deceased. They are seven.

الحاجبون للاعمام وبنيهم

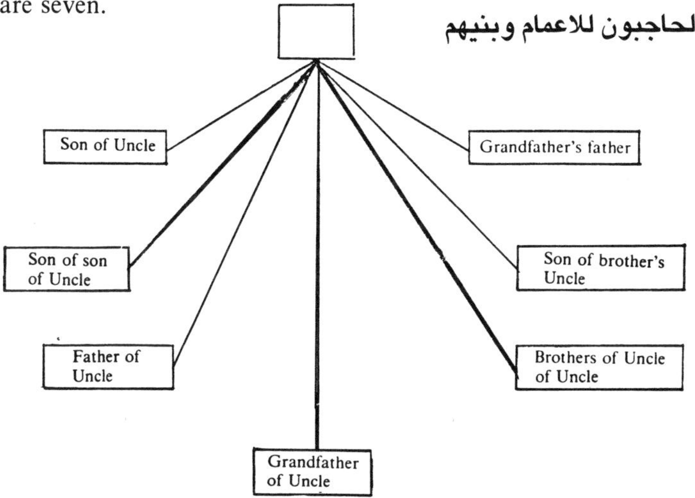

Table Sixteen

Those who are excluded by uterine brother of the deceased.

الحاجبون للاخ لأم الستة الاول الثلاثة الاول والسابع

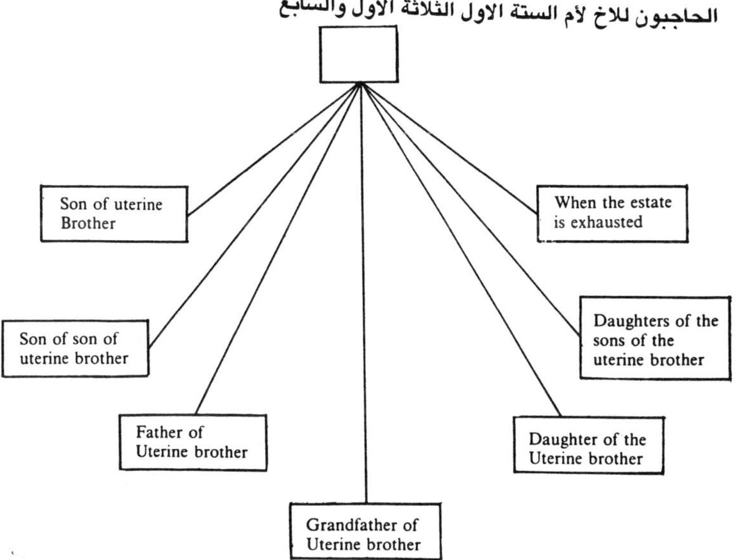

Impediments to Succession

According to some of the Jurists the ˙npediemtns to succession are six and other say they are ten, but the most essential and according to the majority, they are the following three:

1. Homicide
2. Difference of religion
3. Slavery

1. *Homicide (Al-Qatl)*

All Muslim Jurists agree that a murderer or killer shall not inherit. The exception was made by the extremist act known as *Khārijites* or *Khwārij* who argued that a killer has a right to inherit. Those who argued that a murderer or a killer shall not inherit relied solely on the following prophetic tradition:

«لا يرث القاتل»

"A murderer does not inherit"

Sayyidinā'Umar prevented a murderer of one's father from inheriting him. If such people are allowed to kill and then benefit from the estate of the victims, it will encourage incidents of homicide and also it would seem as if the accused person is allowed to benefit from the crime he has committed.

On the question whether the maxim, "the killer shall not inherit" is also application to *'waṣiyyah'*. The Māliki Jurists say that if the victim knows about the act and he did not withdraw the will, we should not prevent the killer from the will. But Imām Abū-Ḥanifah says he will apply the same restriction also on the wills.

The Māliki Jurists have provided the following two categories of murderers:

1. *Qatl al-'Amad':* Intentional murder;
2. *Qatl al-Khaṭā':* un-intentional murder.

The other three schools have added a third category of murder. It is called *Qatl al-Shubh 'Amad*, that is a murder neither intentional or unintentional.

Qatl al-'Amad is an intentional and premeditated murder, while an act of a mad and a minor will be considered as neither intentional nor un-intentional. According to Māliki Jurists it will not prevent them from inheriting while other Jurists say that it will prevent them from their right of inheritance.

The *Qatl al-Khaṭā'* is an un-intentional killing or killing through mistake or through the mistaken identity. The Māliki Jurists say that it will not prevent the killer from inheritance but that he will not inherit from the *diyyah* which he pays.

In the following cases of *Qatl* the right of inheritance will not be affected:

1. If it is lawful killing, as a result of exercising Judicial punishment resulting death, and on the battle Muslims and non-Muslims.
2. If killing is done during a *Jihad* of defence between Muslims and non-Muslims.
3. If killing result in self-defence.
4. In the case of any Justifiable killing according to Sharī'ah.
5. An act of a mad person and a minor.

As far as the Ḥanafī school is concerned, any killing whatsoever will prevent the right of *mirath* whether it is intentional or un-intentional with the exception of the following cases:

a. An act of a mad person or a minor.
b. The lawful killing in accordance to the verdict of the Qāḍi.
c. An indirect killing.
d. Any justifiable killing according to the Sharī'ah.
e. Killing as a result of self defence.

Imām Aḥmad bin Ḥanbal shares the same view with Imām Abū Ḥanīfah. But Imām Shāfī'i differs from all the other schools saying that any kind of homicide whatsoever will prevent *mīrāth,* whether it is lawful, justifiable, intentional, un-intentional, direct or indirect. Even a person connected with the death in any way will not be allowed to inherit.

2. *Change of Religion*

Change of religion will immediately prevent *mīrāth* subject to certain conditions. The following Ḥadīth emphasises on this point:

«لا يرث المسلم الكافرولا الكافر المسلم».

"A Muslim cannot inherit an unbeliever and an unbeliever will not inherit a believer".

The majority of Muslim Jurists opine that a Muslim will not inherit his deceased relative who happens to be a non-Muslim and vice-versa. Supposing a Muslim husband dies leaving behind his Jewish or Christian wife, she will not inherit him but she will be entitled through *Waṣsiyyah*, which will not be more than one-third of the net estate. Some Jurists say that the share must not be more than the share of her co-Muslim wives of the deceased husband.

Some of the *Ṣaḥabah* like Mu'adh bin Jabal, Muawiya bin Abu Sufyan and others are of the opinion that a Muslim will be allowed to inherit his non-Muslim relative, but a non-Muslim will not be allowed to inherit his Muslim relative. When Mu'āwiya became a Caliph, he introduced this rule in his courts, and it continued during the period of the Umayyad dynasty until the time of'Umar bin'abd'al-'Aziz who abolished the rule after proper consultations with the Muslim Jurists of that period.

Those who had adopted his opinion based on the following principle:

«الاسلام يزيد ولا ينقص»

"Islam increased and does not decrease".

The Shī'ite Jurists also supported the same view. As far as the inheritance between the followers of different non-Islamic religions are concerned, there are different opinions of the Jurists of different religions. Imām Malik and Imām Aḥmad bin Ḥanbal say that they will not inherit each other i.e., a Jew will inherit only a Jew, and a Christian will inherit only a Christian and so on.

They base their view on the following:

«لا توارث بين الملتبين».

"There will be no inheritance between two religions".

But Imām Abū Ḥanīfah, Imām Shāfī'i and Sufyān al-Thaurī say that they will not look into the difference of their religions and will consider them as one nations. Thus a Jew will be able to inherit a Pagan and so on.

The famous Jurist Qāḍī Shuraiḥ Ibn Abū Ya'lā and others have divided all the religions into the three following groups:

1. Religion of Islam: Muslims will inherit each other;
2. Christianity, Judaism and Sabiuns: they will not inherit each other;
3. The Zoroastrians and all other religions without any Divine Book will be treated as one group, and thus will inherit each other.

As far as the inheritance of an apostate is concerned, whether he happens to be killed according to *Ḥadd* punishment or dies a normal death, the majority of the Jurists of Hijāz, as well as Imām Mālik and Imām Shāfi'ī say that his estate will go to the public treasury basing their authority on the above quoted Ḥadith.

But the Ḥanafī Jurists of Kūfah and Basrah, the *Ṣaḥābah* like Sayyidna 'Alī and Ibn Mas'ūd supported Imam Abu Hanifah and Sufyān al-Thauri say that he can be inherited by his relatives. They arrive at this conclusion by applying *Qiyās* that since he is going to be inherited by *Bait al-Māl* (Muslim Treasury) because of his Islamic relationship, he is closer to his relatives than even to public treasury, because he has two relationships between him and his relatives while with the public treasury he has only one relationship which is Islam.

Imām Abū Ḥanīfah differentiates between a man and a woman in the case of apostacy. He says that if a man became *Murtad*, his estate which he gained during the time when he was a Muslim will be inherited by his Muslim Relatives, while the property which he gained while he changed his religion will go to public treasury.

But if a woman changes her religion, all her property will go to her relatives. Other Jurists do not make this kind of distinction between a man and a woman.

3. *Slavery*

All Muslim Jurists agree that slavery is a bar to inheritance. They will not inherit and they will not be inherited. If a slave died he will not be inherited by his relatives. because he, as a slave, owned nothing since all that a slave owned belonged to his master and he himself was treated as a property. Islam made it a great reward to free slaves as a meritations act and included it in expiation (*Kaffārah*). Thus there are no slaves today, hence the problem does not arise.

4. *Difference of Domicile*

This impediment was added by Imām Abū Ḥanīfah, and it is only applicable to the non-Muslims, i.e., if a non-Muslim who is living in one country dies, his relatives living in another part of the world will not be allowed to come and inherit the property and other rights of the deceased, unless they are citizens of the same country.

The Qur'ānic Guidance on the Administration of the Estate of a Deceased Muslim

Before distributing the estate of the deceased among heirs, it is required by Qur'ānic injunctions first to settle the claims of debts and other rights of Allah and His servants on the deceased as well as the will that he has left behind. The Qur'ān emphasises:

مِنْ بَعْدِ وَصِيَّةٍ يُوصِينَ بِهَا أَوْ دَيْنٍ.

مِنْ بَعْدِ وَصِيَّةٍ يُوصِي بِهَا أَوْ دَيْنٍ.

مِنْ بَعْدِ وَصِيَّةٍ يُوصِينَ بِهَا أَوْ دَيْنٍ.

"The distribution in all cases is after the payment of legacies and debts."[14]

Although the Qur'ān mentions *Wasiyyah* before claims, but all the Companions and Muslim Jurists agree on the view that the debts attached to the specific property or to a specific part of the estate like mortgage *(rahn)*, *zakāt* of crops and the *zakāt* on animals should be settled first. The Māliki school also shares the same view. While other Jurists do not concern with *Zakāt* until after the other claim on the dead person is settled.

a. The settlement of debts

Normal debts means the debts that are not secured or specifically attached to the estate i.e. loans or any other unsettled debts.

The Ḥanafi school divides debts into two groups: Firstly those debts which are proved by the admission of the dead person before the death-sickness *(maraḍ al-Maut)* either in writing or by any other way, and secondly the debt which was mentioned by the admission of the dead person while on death-sickness.

According to the Ḥanafi school, the first kind of debts must be settled first before the second one. It is likely that the dead person wanted to favour some of his relatives or the person who served him admitting the debt while on his death-bed. The other Jurists do not make this distinction.

The Ḥanafi school says that the funeral expenses must be settled first, before anything is taken from the estate of the deceased. Supposing a person dies leaving his estate on *Rahn* (mortgage), the majority of Jurists say that the *Rahn* must be settled first, but the Ḥanbali school opines that the funeral expenses will be considered first.

The Ẓāhiri on the contrary said that debts must be settled first because the funeral expenses is a responsibility of all the Muslims (Muslim Community) including the creditors.

The Shāfi'i say that the debts of Allah must be settled before the debts of individuals, while Imāms Mālik and Abū Ḥanifa say that the debts of the individuals must be settled before the debts of Allah. Imām Mālik further stipulates that the Zakāt will be paid only if it was requested by the deceased before his death.[15]

b. Funeral expenses

Islam preaches simplicity, particularly so when one dies. Every one is given a seamless shroud. Therefore, funeral expenses must be reasonable.

According to the Māliki school, where a wife dies leaving her husband, the husband is held responsible for her funeral expenses. If the man dies admittedly after her death, the responsibility will shift to the other surviving relatives who will inherit him.

According to the Ḥanafi school, the husband is responsible for a wife's funeral expenses even though he himself is dead and even if the wife is rich.

Imām al-Shaibānī says that if she is rich the funeral expenses will be paid out of her estate, but if she does not leave anything, the funeral expenses will be paid by her relatives because the marital relationship came to an end upon the death of her husband.

In the Shāfi'ī school of thought if the husband is rich, he is responsible for funeral expenses. The husband is likely to become rich by inheriting her too. But if she is rich, the funeral expenses will be paid out of her estate but excluding the share of the husband. If she is not rich, and the husband is not likely to become rich by inheriting her, the funeral expenses will be paid from the little she has left including the share of the husband. if she had left nothing her relatives will bear the expense. If she has no relatives it will be paid from the public treasury.

c. Waṣsiyyah: Wills

After taking our the funeral expenses and debts, i.e., the debts of the right of Allah and that of individuals, the *Waṣiyyah* or the will will be carried out. The *Waṣiyyah* will include all the gifts that are made during the death-sickness of the deceased, since the majority of the Jurists consider them all as wills. Both the wills and the gifts must not exceed the one-third of the estate of the deceased unless consented to by the heirs.

Notes

1. Qur'ān, ch. 3:180.
2. Qur'ān, ch. 57:10.
3. Qur'ān, ch. 21:89.
4. Qur'ān, ch. 4:11
5. Qur'ān, ch. 2:180-181.
6. A Ḥadīth narrated by Sa'īd bin Abī Waqqās.
7. Qur'ān, ch. 4:7.
8. Qur'ān, ch. 4:11.
9. Yūsuf 'Alī, A., *The Holy Qur'ān, Text, Translation and Commentary*, Beirut, 1968, p. 181.
10. Macnaughten, *Principles and procedures of Mohammeden law, quoted by A. Majid Daryabadi in Holy Qur'ān, Vol. 1, Lahore 1957. p. 149.*
11. *Ṣaḥīh al-Bukhārī: Kitab al-Tafsir: 101*
12. Qur'ān, ch. 4:11.
13. Qur'ān, ch. 4:12.
14. Qur'ān, ch. 4: 11-12.
15. Cf. Abū Zaharah, *Aḥkām al-Tarakat wal Mawārith,* Cairo p.

Chapter 18

Shares of Each Heir

The following details of the share of each sharer is given under the Law of *Mīrāth* in Sharī'ah. No other religious Law has given these minute details as given in the Sharī'ah. So much work has been done on this subject by the Jurists over centuries that we are even surprised to see the huge volumes left by them for posterity. The encouragement of learning these books came from the Prophet who once said that the mastery of Law of inheritance equals to one half of the religious knowledge. We shall discuss and summarise *these* shares in the following pages.

A. Shares Allotted to Parents

1. The rights of parents are emphasised in various chapters of the Qur'ān. As far as the shares of the parents from the property left behind by their son is concerned, each one of them will have one-sixth of that which he has left if the deceased has left behind a child. If both parents are alive and there also are children, both father and mother take a sixth each. If one of them is alive, he or she takes a sixth and the rest goes to children.
2. If the deceased has left no child, and the parents are the only heirs, then his mother will get one-third and the father will get the remaining two-thirds.
3. If the deceased has left no children but only sisters and brothers, his mother in that case will have one-sixth and the father gets the residue as the father excluded collaterals.
4. The same overall principle, as we have seen before, that all distribution will take place only after the legacies and debts, including funeral expenses, are first paid out of the property left behind by the deceased.
5. The Qur'ānic injunction also makes it very clear that both children and parents of the deceased always get some share if they survive, but this will be determined by the number of the heirs in these

categories. Both parents and children are so equally near related to you, and in point of benefit either of this world or the next, one does not know which are nearest to us, as emphasised in this verse of the Holy Qur'ān. Therefore these are settled portions ordained by Allah for them.

The following Qur'ānic injunction is in respect of the shares of the husband or wife of the deceased:

«وَلَكُمْ نِصْفُ مَا تَرَكَ اَزْوَاجُكُمْ اِنْ لَمْ يَكُنْ لَهُنَّ وَلَـدٌ-فَـاِنْ كَانَ لَهُنَّ وَلَـدٌ فَلَكُم اَلرُّبُع مِّما تَرَكْنَ مِنْ بَعْدِ وَصِيَّةٍ يُوصِينَ بِهَا اَوْ دَيْنٍ، وَلَهُنَّ اَلرُّبُعُ مِمَّا تَرَكْتُمْ اِنْ لَمْ يَكُنْ لَكُمْ وَلَدَ-فَاِنْ كَانَ لَكُمْ وَلَدٌ فَلَهُنَّ اَلثُّمُنُ مِمَّا تَرَكْتُمْ مِنْ بَعْدِ وَصِيَّةٍ تُوصُونَ بِهَا اَوْ دَيْنٍ، وَاِنْ كَانَ رَجُلٌ يُورَثُ كَلاَلَةً او امْرَأَةٌ وَلَهُ أَخٌ اَوْ أُخْتٌ فَلِكُل وَاحِدٍ مِنْهُمَا اَلسُّدُسُ-فَاِنْ كَانُوا اكْثَرَ مِنْ ذلك فَهُمْ شُرَكَاءُ فِي اَلثُّلُثُ مِنْ بَعْدِ وَصِيَّةٍ يُوصَى بِهَا اَوْ دَيْنٍ غَيْرَ مُضَارٍ-وَصِيَّةً مِنْ اَللّهِ وَاللّهُ عَلِيمٌ حَلِيمٌ».

"In what your wives leave, your share is a half, if they leave no child. But if they leave a child, you get a fourth after payment of legacies and debts. In what you leave, their (your wives) share is a fourth, if you leave no child. But if you leave a child, they get an eighth after payment of legacies and debts. If the man or woman whose inheritance is in question, has neither ascendants nor descendants, but has left a (uterine) brother or a sister each one of the two gets the sixth; but if more than two they share in a third, after payment of legacies and debts; so that no loss is caused (to any one). Thus it is ordained by Allah and Allah is All-Knowing, Most-Forebearing".[1]

Of the heirs there are some whose shares or portions have been fixed in the Qur'ān. These are called *Aṣḥāb al-farā'id* or "shares" as commonly translated. They are altogether *twelve* in number, four males and eight females: father, father's father how high soever, half-brother by the mother, the husband, the wife, daughter, son's daughter how low soever, full sister, consanguine sister, uterine sister, mother, and true grandmother, that is, grandmother in whose line of relationship to the decease no false grandfather intervenes.

The shares of the "sharers" in the inheritance are either one-half, one-fourth, one-eighth, two-thirds, one-third or one-sixth. The husband has one-fourth when there is a child or son's child how low soever and one-half when there is no child or son's child; the wife has one-eighth when there is a child or son's child and one-fourth when not; the daughter's share is one-half when only one or more daughters and no son, they take two thirds when only one or more daughters and no son, they take two thirds between them; the son's daughter takes one-half if only one and there is no child or son's son; if there are two or more son's daughters they take two-thirds when there is no child or son's sons; and the son's daughter takes one-sixth when there is one daughter or a higher son's daughter and no son; the sister takes one-half when she is only one and there is no son or son's son. If there are two or more sisters, they take two-thirds under the same circumstances; the consanguine sister takes one half when only one and there is no son, consanguine brother or sister; if there are two or more consanguine sisters under the same circumstance they take two-thirds and the consanguine sister takes one-sixth when there is one full sister but no son, etc., or consanguine brother; the mothers share is one-sixth when there is a child or son's child or two or more brothers or sisters and one-third when not, but she takes one-third only of the remainder after deducting the wife's or the husband's share when there is a wife or husband and the father; the true grandmother has one-sixth when she is not excluded the father takes one-sixth; the grandfather's share is one-sixth when he is not excluded and the uterine brother or sister gets one-sixth when only one and no child or sons child; father or true grandfather; and if there are two or more of them they will get two-thirds in the same circumstances. Under certain circumstances some of the sharers become residuaries or take both as sharers and residuaries.

Father's Share

In the case where father is coming with only mother and wife or husband, he will take the residuary after the share of wife and mother are given in accordance with the doctrine of *Umariyyataini* which will be explained later.

If there is nobody to inherit with him he will get the whole of the estate. The father also inherits $\frac{1}{6}$ + R when there is a female issue.

Mother's Share

As it is the case of father with children, mother will also get one-sixth as her share. But, she will be entitled to one-sixth in the presence of two or more brothers and sisters even if they are Uterine, full, or consanguine or mixed, but one alone will not restrict her to one-sixth.

She will get one-third of the residuary share in the case where she is coming together with father and wife or husband. After taking away the share of husband or wife from the rest of the estate, she will get one-third while father will take the rest on the basis of the doctrine of *Umariyyatāni*. With this discussion, it is essential for us to understand the case of *Umariyyatāni*.

The Umariyyatani Case

The case of *Umariyyatāni* occurred during the Caliphate of Sayyidnā 'Umar, the second Caliph, when he decided a case regarding the inheritance between father, mother and husband, and again between father mother and wife. it is also referred to as *Al-Gharrawani II*.

The most important thing to note in this case is the share of a mother when there are:

1. Mother, father and husband.
2. Mother, father and wife.

In normal circumstances, we have seen the shares of the mother is either 1/6 or 1/3 of the total estate. But taking into consideration the case of *Umariyyatani*, it will be different with the mother. In this case, the mother will take 1/3 of residue after taking away the shares of the wife, or the husband.

F	H	M	F	M	W
R	½	⅓ of R	R	⅓ of R	¼

In the normal circumstancs, where there are father, mother and husband or wife, the shares will be like this:

F	H	M	F	M	W
R	½	⅓	R	⅓	¼
1	3	2	5	4	3

When one looks carefully at the first example, one sees that the share of the mother is more than the share of the father. In the normal rule where a female is coming together with a male, the share of a male is to be double the share of a female as in the case of sons and daughters or brothers and sisters; or the share to be equal as in the case of father and mother in the presence of children.

In the second example also the normal rule did not apply, because the mother's share is so near to the share of the father.

The majority of the Muslim Jurists say that the rule is not eminently by suitable to Muslims. Therefore the rule to be applied is that of *Umariyyatāni*. If the husband or wife takes his or her share, whatever remaining should be divided between the father and the mother.

The mother will get 1/3 while the father will take the rest. They referred to the Qur'ānic verse which says that if the father inherits, the mother will get 1/3 while the father will take 2/3. This is applied only where two of them are going to inherit together. But in the case where they are coming with either husband or wife, the mother will get 1/3 of residue. Some *Sahabah* and the Jurists like Ibn'Abbās, Dāūd al-Ẓāhiri, Sayyidnā 'Ali, Mu'ādh bin Jabal and Qāḍi Shuraiḥ are of the opinion that the Qur'ānic rule must be left untouched. Qur'ān says that the absence of children and brothers or sisters, the mother will get ⅓ of the total estate, therefore, it must be applied as is commanded.

Ibn Sīrīn agrees with Sayyidnā 'Umar on the first example where father is coming with mother and husband, but he does not accept the second formula where the father comes with mother and wife because in that case, as he maintains, the father gets more than the mother. Therefore the rule must be amended.

F	M	H
R	⅓	½ according to Ibn 'Abbās
2	4	6
F	M	H
R	⅓ of R	½ according to Umariyyatāni

B. Shares Allotted to Children

1. Whatever the parents leave after their death, their children and nearest kins have the rights over their property which should be shared according to the guidance from the Qu'rān.
2. The power of testamentary disposition extends over only one-third of the property; the remaining two-thirds are distributed among heirs.
3. The Qur'ānic injunctions have made it clear that there is a share for men and a share for women. This is because the women and minor males were denied inheritance not only in pagan Arabia but also in the law of the Bible. According to Cheyne and Black's *Encyclopaedia Biblica*, "Women appear to have been universally and in every respect regarded as minors so far as rights of property went – only sons, not daughters, still less wives, can inherit".[2] Looking at the Qur'ānic injunctions it becomes clear that "the male will have as much as the portion of two females". As Sir Muḥammad Iqbāl has rightly remarked, this is not determined because of many inferiority inherent in her 'but in view of her economic opportunities, and the place she occupies in the social structure of which she is a part and parcel'.[3]

He further says that while daughters according to Muslim law "is held to be full owner of the property given to her both by the father and the husband at the time of her marriage; while further she absolutely owns her dower money which may be prompt or deferred according to her own choice, and in the term of which she can hold possession of the whole of her husband's property till payment, the responsibility of maintaining her throughout her life is wholly thrown on the husband.

Besides, the Islamic Sharī'ah has put greater economic responsibility on man while a woman's role is comparatively much lighter.

4. But if among the off-springs of the deceased, the daughters are the only heirs, and they are more than two, they will have two-thirds of the share. If she is only one, she will have one-half.

5. All distribution takes place only after the legacies and debts, including funeral expenses, have been paid.

C. *Shares Allotted to Husband and Wives*

The following shares are allotted according to the Qur'ānic injunctions in the above verse:

1. When the wife dies, the husband takes half (½) of his deceased wife's property if she leaves no child. The residuaries get the rest of the property.
2. If the deceased wife leaves a child, the husband gets only one-fourth (¼)
3. As we have seen before, the female share is generally half of the male share. The widow, therefore, gets one-fourth of her deceased husband's property, if he leaves no children.
4. If he leaves children, the widow gets only one-eighth.
5. If the widows are more than one, their collective share is one-fourth if there are no children. But if there are children, their collective share is one-eighth from which they divide equally. The Bible was less kind to the widow as it does not place her among her husband's heirs. In Judaism, the Jewish widow was a charge on her children or if she has no children, she would depend on her own family.[4]
6. The golden rule of inheritance still remains the same. That all distribution will only take place after the legacies and debts including funeral expenses are already paid.

Husband will receive ½ of the estate of the deceased in the absence of male or female children or son of daughters. He will get ¼ in the presence of sons and daughters or son of son or daughter of son.

The spouses will inherit each other subject to the following two conditions: *Firstly* the contract of their marriage should be a valid one. What is essential for the purpose of mirath is not the consummation of the marriage but the very contract of marriage. Any woman claiming the *mīrāth* has to prove the validity of her marriage in accordance to either Mālikī school or any other Sunni school: The other schools say that the marriage must have been solemnized in accordance to their own schools only.

According to the Māliki school, if a marriage is contracted during the death-sickness, neither of the spouses will be allowed to inherit after the death of one or the other. But some other Jurists say that if the contract is with the agreement of the other inheritors, the widow will be allowed to inherit.

The other condition to be satisfied is that the spouses will have to prove that death, either in fact or by law, that means that they are together or in the case of a woman she has to prove that she is divorced but is still serving her ʿiddah period and that the divorce is *revocable* (raj ʿī). If the divorce is given during *Maraḍ al-Maut* (the death sickness) of the husband, she will be allowed to inherit, on presumption that the husband perhaps divorced her in order to prevent her from that right of inheritance.

The Māliki school has taken quite a different view altogether; they say that the woman will inherit whether the divorce is revocable (Raj ʿī) or not, or whether the husband intended to prevent her from her right of inheritance or not, or whether she is serving the *ʿiddah period*, or she has finished her *ʿiddah*. If she has remarried to another husband, she will still be allowed to inherit the husband provided that he died due to sickness.

The husband will not inherit her if the wife died in such condition. According to the Ẓahari school, if the divorce is final she will not be allowed to inherit, even if it is proved that the husband divorced her intentionally to prevent her from her right of inheritance.

The Shāfiʿi school partly agrees with Ẓāhiri school and partly with the Ḥanafi's on this issue. The Ḥanafi view is that she will be entitled to inherit the husband if she is still serving her *ʿiddah period.*

The Ḥanafi school holds that she will inherit even if she has finished her *iddah* provided that she did not get remarried.

If the divorce has resulted due to the woman's request or due to compulsion, then one cannot be accused of preventing her from the mirath. It is interesting to note that Sayyidnā Uthmān gave *mīrāth* to the wife of ʿAbdulraḥmān Ibn Auf, and Sayyidnā ʿAlī gave *mīrāth* to the wife of ʿUthmān.

The following examples will help to further elucidate the shares:

1. When a wife dies leaving her husband and other heirs the inheritance will be divided as follows:

p

H	F	S of D	D of D	
½	R	=	=	= 6
3	3	0	0	= Equal Unity

2.

	P		
H		S	
1/4		R	= 4
1		3	= Equal Unity

3. When a husband dies leaving his wife and without issue, then the inheritance will be divided as follows:

	P			
2		No.	Child	4
1/4				
1	+	0	4	3 less than unity

4. Suppose the husband leaves children the inheritance will be divided as follows:

	P		
W		S	out of 24
1/8		R	
1		7	= 24 equal unity

5. Suppose there are no issues or issue and that the widows are more than one, the inheritance will be divided as follows:

P		
4 wives	No.	Child out of 24
1/4		
3		= 9 less than unity

The problem is that how can we divide 3 to 4 widows? To avoid fractions we use 'Taṣḥīḥ', that is, 3 × 4 (No. of widows) 12. Then 12 divide by 4 will get 4.

Suppose there are issues? It will look like this:

P			
4 Wives	S		
		out of 4	
1/8	R		
1	3		4 equal unity

Let's apply 'Taṣḥīḥ' 4 × 3 = 12 and 4 × 2 = 63 + 12 = 75. Each of the W she gets 3 = 12 and the son will get 63 out of 75 nothing remaining.

D. Shares Allotted to Daughter of Daughters

Daughter will receive if she is only one daughter in the absence of a son inheriting the father. But if there are two more daughters, they will receive 2/3 in the absence of a son. When a daughter is coming with son or sons they will inherit the sons will have double the share of daughters.

E. Shares Allotted to Daughter of Son

Daughter of the son will inherit in the absence of the proper son and daughter, or, son of son who is in the same class with her or any son from upper class. But if the son is from lower class, he will not effect her, she will inherit 2/3 if there are two or more daughters in the absence of the son, son of son, etc. . .

She will receive 1/6 share if there are one or more daughters in the presence of one proper daughter, or any daughter in the upper class. Here the daughter of the son will take 1/6 after the proper daughter has taken her 1/2 share to complete the share of females. Which is 2/3.

Example one:

S.	D ½
Here there is SS.	5D of son ⅙
S, SS, and SSS excluded	
(2) S.	D
Here also no SS.	½ D of son
son	
daughter, SS, & SSS,	⅙ of D of son of son
(3) S.	D
Here also there is SS	DS ½
There is no	
S, D, SS, DSS, SSS.	DSSS ⅙

If there is only SD she will get 1/2 and DSSS from lower class will receive 1/6 to complete 2/3 of the female share.

As an *AṢĀBA,* she will inherit as together with a male, either from her class or from lower class to support her they will inherit on the principle of:

«لِلذَّكَرِ مِثْلُ حَظِّ ٱلأُنْثَيَيْنِ».

"To the male, a portion equal to that of two females".[5]

1. If there is SS of the same class they will inherit on the principle of *Lil-Dhakar".*[6]

SS	SD	SS	2DS
⅔	⅓	½	¼ each

2. When she is supported by a male from lower class e.g.,

S	SD	⅔
SS	DS	
SSS		

In the above example, there is no son, but there are two daughters. In that case 2/3 is allocated to females. Since there are daughter of son and son of son of son, the SD will get nothing and the SSS will receive the share of *AṢĀBA.* The Jurists are of the opinion that DS is closer than the SSS, hence it will be an injustice to exclude her and give share to the other who happens to be from lower class. Therefore, according to them, he will go and support her and they will inherit on the principle of "*Lil-Dhakar*".[7] The daughter of the son will be excluded totally in the presence of the son or any male child from the upper class, i.e., any male coming from the upper class will exclude all the other lower classes, whether they are male or female.

Let us see the following examples to eludicate our point:

Zaid died and left behind

1.

S	SD		SSS
½	⅙	*AṢĀBA*	

2.

D	SD		SS
½		*AṢĀBA*	*"Lil-Dhakar"*

4. A died leaving:

H	M	F	D	SD	SS
1/4	1/6	1/6	1/2		*Asaba*
3	2	2	6		= 13
					12

5. A died leaving:

W	2D	2 SD	SSD	SSS
1/8	2/3		R	

A male child will support females who happen to be in the same class with him and also to those who are in the upper class.

F. Shares Allotted to Uterine Brothers and Sisters

The uterine brother or sister if he or she is only one, will receive 1/6 in the absence of any child, whether son or son and daughter or SS or SD. If there are any of the children either male or female, they will exclude him or her.

Similarly, they will inherit with the ascendants of the deceased person. If they are two or more mixed, they will share equally from 1/3. Sometimes they share the 1/3 with full brothers or full sisters or with full brothers and sisters as in the following cases:

a) X died leaving behind:

M	2FB	3US
1/6	R	1/3

b)

H	M	2US	UB	3FB
1/2	1/6		1/3	R
6	2		4	0

c)

W	H	US	UB	BFB
1/4	1/6		1/3	R
3	2	4		3

d)

H	2	(2UB 2US. 2FB 2FS) mixed
1/2	1/6	1/3

H	M	2UB	FB		
$\frac{1}{2}$	$\frac{1}{6}$		$\frac{1}{3}$		

f)

H	M	2UB	2US	mixed &	2FS
$\frac{1}{2}$	$\frac{1}{6}$		$\frac{1}{3}$		$\frac{2}{3}$

This provides us with a proper case of '*awl*. Whenever H., M., 2UB or US or 1UB or 2UB may come with full brother and full sister, they will share the 1/3. It is essential that there is a full brother so that he will agnatise them. In this case, if we follow the normal rule the division will occur as follows:

H	M	2UB or US 1US or 1 UB	FB & FS
$\frac{1}{2}$	$\frac{1}{6}$	$\frac{1}{3}$	R O

The Jurists are of the view that here it is unfair to give those who are having relationship with the deceased only from mother's side and still prevent those who are having the relationship on both sides. This is known as *AL-ḤIMĀRIYYAH* or *HAJARIYYAH* or *YAMMIYYA*.

But where there is father or daughter of the son they will exclude both the full and uterine brothers. The grandfather will also exclude the uterine brothers and sisters.

If there is only one uterine brother coming together with the full brother and sister, then it will be a straight forward case since UB will receive 1/6 and the rest will go with the full brother and sister as residue. The Jurists of Medina and Kūfah differ in their opinions on this issue. Sayyidna Umar and Zaid bin Thābit, the two Companions, followed by the views of Imām Mālik and Imām Shāfi'i adopted the rule that when the UB or US is coming with the full brother and sisters, they will share the 1/3. They argue that how they can the less nearer brothers inherit preventing those who are nearer in relationship with the deceased.

The other Companions of the Prophet like Sayyidna 'Alī, 'Abdallāh Ibn Mas'ūd and others followed by Imām Abū Ḥanifah, Imām Ahmad, Dā'ūd al-Ẓāhirī, Sufyān al-Thaurī and others opposed the above view and said that the rule must be left as it is in the Qur'ān.

Allah has said in the Qur'ān that the UB & S are to get 1/3. Whatever remains will go to the full brothers as residue. No one should try to change this injunction.

For example, in this case of:

H	M	UB	10FB	&	10S
$\frac{1}{2}$	$\frac{1}{6}$	$\frac{1}{6}$	R	=	$\frac{1}{6}$

All the Muslim Jurists adopted the above case. The Ḥanafī school asked as to why the first group also adopted the same without applying *Qiyās*, while in this case too one UB is getting the same share as that of 30 brothers and sisters?

H	M	UB	FB	W	10UB	FB
½	⅙	⅙	R = ⅙	¼	⅓	R
				3	4	5

The other Jurists replied that they did not wish to interfere in such cases because sometimes the full brother gets more and sometimes he gets less.

According to Ibn ʿAbbās, however, they will share according to the principle "To the male a portion equal to that of two females".[8] While other Jurists are of the opinion that they will share equally because the verse of the Qur'ān in this regard begins with the message of equality and we should not end up with inequality.

«وَإِنْ كَانَ رَجُلٌ يُورَثُ كَلَالَةً او امْرَأَةٌ وَلَهُ أَخٌ اَوْ أُخْتٌ فَلِكُلِّ وَاحِدٍ مِنْهُمَا اَلسُّدُسُ فَإِنْ كَانُوا اَكْثَرَ مِنْ ذٰلِكَ فَهُمْ شُرَكَاءُ فِي اَلثُّلُثِ».

G. Shares Allotted to Full Brothers and Full Sisters

1. If full sister is only one, she will inherit 1/2 in the absence of inheriting children, father or grandfather and full brother.
2. If there are two or more full sisters, they will share 2/3 in the absence of inheriting children, full brother, father, and grandfather.
3. They will inherit as *AṢĀBA* in the presence of full brothers and will divide according to the principle of "For male equal to that of two females".
4. In the case where a full sister is coming with daughter or daughters or daughter of the son, she will inherit as an *AṢĀBA* after taking their shares. This will be treated as an exceptional case:

D	FS	D	2FS			
½	R = ½	¼	r = ½			
2D	2FS	2D	2FS	D	D	SFS
⅔	R = ⅓	⅔	R = ⅓	½	⅙	R = ⅓

If one daughter or more are coming with full brother and also co-existing with uterine sisters, they will share the 1/3 equally in a joint group *Al-Mas'alah al-Mushtarikah*):

H	M	UB	FS	FB they share the 1/3 equally.
½	⅙		⅓	

In the case where she comes with Grandfather, he will agnatise here as the full brother will do.

The authority of giving sister residue if she comes with daughters is that of the Ḥadīth which was narrated by ʻAbdallāh bin Masʻūd. He said that the Prophet (S.A.W.) decided a case where there were D and DS. He gave complete the share of the female which is 2/3. And the residue was given to full sister.

Another authority is that, someone came to Abū Mūsā al Ashʻarī the Governor of Kūfah in the presence of Sulaimān Ibn Rabiʻah. He asked Abū Mūsā about the inheritance of D, DS and FS as to what each of them will get? The Governor replied that the daughter will get 1/2 and the sister will get the residue, and he excluded the DS. He asked the questioner to go and ask ʻAbdullāh bin Masʻūd to confirm this decision. When he informed ʻAbdallāh bin Masʻūd what the Governor had said, ʻAbdallāh replied:

> "I would have gone astray if I were not one of those guided (by the Prophet). I would adjudicate just as it was judged by the messenger of Allah. For the daughter, it is one half and for the daughter of the son is one sixth thus completing two-thirds. Whatever is remaining will go to the sister".

When they went and informed Abū Mūsā what ʻAbdallāh bin Masʻūd had said, Abū Mūsā told them not to ask him anything as far as that learned person (i.e. ʻAbdallāh bin Masʻūd) was alive among them.

Muʻāz bin Jabal also decided a similar case during the days of the Prophet (S.A.W.) where there was a daughter and full sister. he gave 1/3 to the daughter and the residue which was 1/4 to the full sister.

ʻAbdallāh bin ʻAbbās differed with the rest of the Jurists in the case of *Mīrāth* of full sister. He said in a case where the full sister came with the daughter that she will not get anything, either as one of the *Aṣḥāb al-Farḍ* or as *AṢĀBA*. He quoted the Qur'ānic authority that *AṢĀBA* will inherit only in the absence of the children, and in this case there was already a child. As far as the *AṢĀBA* are concerned, they must be male or both the male and female. He will not allow only a female alone to act as *AṢĀBA,* because it will then be contrary to the Qur'ānic injunction. He once decided a case of a D and FS and gave the D 1/2 and excluded the FS. At this point, when he was told that Sayyidnā ʻUmar had decided such a case and gave D 1/2 and FS 1/2, Ibn ʻAbbās said that the decision of Sayyidnā ʻUmar will not bind him, since there is the authority of the Qur'ān to be followed.

H. *Shares Allotted to Consanguine Sister*

1. In the absence of children, father, full brother or sister, and consanguine brother, the consanguine sister will receive 1/2.

2. If they are two or more, they will receive 2/3 provided they are not excluded and not agnatised.
3. If the presence of one full sister, they will receive 1/6.
4. If she is agnatised by consanguine brother, she will share as *AṢĀBA*.

She will be excluded by S, SS, F, FB, 2FS, one full sister if she is acting as AṢĀBA and daughter or daughter of the son, and also if they are not agnatised by either consanguine brother or grandfather.

She can inherit as *AṢĀBA* when she comes with con-brother, or grandfather, or with D or DS int he absence of full sister:

2D	FS	2D	C.S	2D	FS	C.S
⅔	R = ⅓	⅔	R = ⅓	⅔	R = ⅓	EX.

Supposing a man died leaving:

FS	10CS	(⅙) to complete the ⅔ of ⅙ of the woman
½		

5. She will inherit as *AṢĀBA* when she comes with grandfather. The grandfather will agnatise her, but he will do it only if she is going to get something.

H	C.S	G.F
½		

2FS	CS	2FS	COS	CB	2FS	CS	GF
⅔	0	⅔		R		O R	

I. The Share Allotted to Grandmother

Grandmother will inherit 1/6 of the total estate and their number must not exceed four. They may be grandmothers either paternal or maternal, i.e., mother of the mother and her mother, and mother of the father and her mother. This definition of grandmother is according to the Māliki school. Although the Ḥanafī school limits the category of grandmothers who will inherit to the mother of the father, the mother of the mother and the mother of the father of the father.

According to Imām Mālik the grandmothers cannot be more than two, and where there are two of them, they will share the 1/6. The Ḥanafī school, on the other hand, says that there is a possibility of having three grandmothers coming together and still they will share the 1/6. As for example:

M/MM (They will all share the 1/6 according to the Ḥanafī school.)
M/MF
M/FF.

The Māliki school excludes MFF but agrees with the Ḥanafi school on MMM they say that this is in accordance with the *Sunnah* of the Prophet (S.A.W.). About the MMF Imām Mālik agrees with the Ijtihad of Sayyidnā'Umar who allowed the MMM and the MMF to share the 1/6. But for the MMF, he said that she was not going to inherit because there was no authority available on this. The Maliki view of preventing MFF from inheritance seems to be contrary to the opinions of the great *Ṣaḥābah* like Zaid bin Thābit, Sayyidnā 'Ali and Ibn'Abbās and also the Ḥanafi Jurists.

Those who can exclude the grandmother are:

1. Mother will exclude MM and MF and their mothers;
2. Father will exclude only MF and her mothers, but will not exclude MM or her mothers;
3. The nearer from the mother side, i.e., MM and her mother will exclude those who are remote from the mother's side and also from the father's side.

According to the Ḥanafi school, the nearer the relation will exclude all those who are remote from any other side although the Māliki school takes quite a different view. This argument is based on the degree of relationship.

The Māliki school, on the contrary, says that the person inheriting through the process of *Ijtihād* cannot exclude one who is inheriting in accordance with the *Sunnah*, i.e., MMF will inherit according to *Ijtihād* while MMM will inherit according to the *Sunnah* of the Prophet (S.A.W.). The different of opinion in mind, is merely marginal.

J. Share Allotted to Grandfather

1. If the grandfather is the sole survivor, he will get the whole of the estate.
2. If the grandfather comes with other male issues, e.g., son, son of son, he will inherit 1/6 of the net estate.
3. If he comes with female issues, e.g., daughter, daughter of son, he will be entitled to 1/6 + residue.
4. If he comes with brothers whether full or consanguine and/or sisters, he will be left to his choice, either to take 1/3 of the estate or to be treated as brother. For example if he chooses to be counted as brother:

GF	FB	SONB	GF	GF	2FS
½	½	½	½	½	½

In the above example he is treated as a brother since it is more advantageous for him to be treated in that way.

But if he is coming with 2FB or Cons, or 4FS or Cons, it will be the same whether he choses to be a brother or to take 1/3 as his share. But in the case where he is coming with more than 2FB or more than 4FS or Cons, he is going to be given the share that suits him the most.
5. Supposing he is coming together with the group of both FB and Cons B, he will either take 1/3 or be counted as a brother, but here although the Cons B will not inherit because he is excluded by the full brother, still the full brother will count him on his side in order to prevent the grandfather from getting more than 1/3. As for example:

GF	FB	CONSB
1/3	1/3	1/3
	2/3	

If he is counted as brother, when they share equally but the full brother will go round and receive the share of the consanguine because he will not inherit in the presence of FB.
As for example:

GF	FS	CONB
2/5	1/5	2/5

In this case, after every one of them has got his share, the full sister will go back and insist that she must get her specific share as specified in the Qur'ān. Thus she will reduce the share of CMB to make her own 1/2 share 1/2, and the CNB will be left with 1/10 as residue. The case will then be like this:

GF	FS	CNB
2/5	1/2	R = 1/10

6. If the grandfather is coming with other Qur'ānic sharers he will be entitled to the best of the three things:

a) 1/6 of the total estate; or
b) 1/3 of the residue after the other Qur'ānic sharers have received their shares; or
c) he will be counted as brother.

GF	FB	W
1/6	R	1/4
2	7	3
	12	

GF	FB	W
1/3 R	of R	1/4
1	2	1
	4	

1.

GF	FB	W
	3/4	1/4
3	6 6 3	2
	8	

GF	FB	M	W	GF
	5/12	1/3	1/4	
5	5	8	6	
		24		

As a brother, it is better for him.

2.

GF	FB	M	H
1/6	R	1/3	1/2
1	0	2	3
		6	

In this case having this 1/6 is better for him.

2D	FB	GF	2D	FB	GF
2/3	R	1/6	2/3		1/3
4	1	1	4	1	1
	6			6	

All these examples are according to the decisions of Zaid bin Thābit and Mālik bin Anas.

M	FS		GF
1/3	.	2/3	
3	2	4	
	9		

In the case where Grandfather is coming with full sisters or consanguine sisters. the shares will be as follows:

1.

M	GF		FS	or	CONS
1/3		R			

This is according to Imām Mālik and Zaid bin Thābit.

2.

M	GF	FS	or CONS
1/3	R	EX	

This is according to Sayyidnā Abūbakar and 'Abdallah bin 'Abbās.

3.

M	GF	FS	or CONS
1/3	R	1/2	

This is according to Sayyidnā 'Alī.

Imām Mālik is of the view that when a sister comes with grandfather, she will not inherit as Ṣāḥib-al-Farḍ, but she will be agnatised by the grandfather in the following order:

H	M	GF	FS	(Lil-Dhakar)[9]
1/2	1/3	R = 1/6		

As far as the Mālikī is concerned, it does not give grandfather anything less than 1/6 and in the above case the residue will be 1/6. In this case the grandfather will get in reality something less than 1/6.

Imām Mālik says that she will be given her specific share and the grandfather will be given his own share which is 1/6. All of them will then bring their shares together and add them and then divide according to the principle of "For male equal to two females".[10] In this following order:

AKDARIYYA:

H	M	GF	FS
1/2	1/3	1/6	1/2

They will add 1/2 and 1/6 together and then divide it.

Lil-Dhakar: i.e. Male will have equal to two females

H	M	GF		FS
1/2	1/3	1/6		1/2
			1/6	
9	6	2	1	
		18		

H	M	GF		2FS
1/2	1/6		1/3	
6	2	2	2	
		12		

If the grandfather is coming with FB, the case will be treated differently when he comes with FS.

H	M	GF	FB
1/2	1/3	1/6	R = 0

In this case the GF must be given his 1/6 which will not be shared with FB. Since the R = 0, the FB will get nothing.

According to Sayyidnā 'Umar:

H	FS	GF	M
½	½	⅙	⅓

This is in fact a case of *'Awl.*

In the case where there is:

H	M	GF	CONB	UB
½	⅙	R = ⅓	Ex.	Ex.

This is the view of Imām Mālik which is known as "*shubh al-Mālik*". In this case Imām Mālik differed from Zaid bin Thābit as follows:

H	M	HG	CONB	UB
½	⅙	⅙	R = ⅙	Ex.

In such a case the grandfather will not allow the Cons B to take the residue, due to the presence of the grandfather, the Cons Brother is getting something since grandfather excluded the Uterine brother. Since he will get nothing due to his absence, he will get nothing even in his presence.

K. Shares Allotted to the Kalālah

Kalālah are those who inherit the deceased who dies leaving neither ascendants nor descendants. The word Kalālah, according to Sayyidnā ʿUmar, the second Caliph, was difficult to define since it was not defined in the life-time of the Prophet. The Caliph ʿUmar wished that the Holy Prophet had defined these three terms. One is concerning *Khilāfah*, the second is concerning *Ribā* (usury) and the third is *Kalālah.* It is concerned with the inheritance of a person who has left no descendants or ascendants however distant, but only collaterals with or without a widow or a dower. If there is a widow or widower surviving, she or he takes the share as already defined, before the collaterals come in.

If the deceased has left no ascendants or descendants but has only left a brother or a sister, each one of them gets one-sixth of the property.

But, if there are more than two, they divide equally out of one-third.

The Concept of 'Awl

'Awl was neither known nor practiced during the time of the Prophet (S.A.W.) or during the Caliphate of Sayyidnā Abūbakar, the first Caliph. Such a case arose during the time of Sayyidnā ʿUmar the second Caliph, who decided it after the consultation and agreement of the *Ṣaḥābah* (the Companions of the Prophet).

The first case that came to Sayyidnā ʿUmar concerned the inheritance when there were two full sisters, and a husband. Sayyidnā ʿUmar said:

"By Allah, I do not know which of you Allah has put first and which comes next"

Sayyidnā' Umar then invited the Companions of the Prophet (S.A.W.) and asked their advise on this case, saying that if he gave the two sisters their specified share, the husband will not get his specified share, but if he gives the husband his share, the sisters will not get their share.

What should he do? There are differences of opinions as to who suggested *'Awl*. Some say that it was Companion 'Abbās, while others said it was Sayyidnā 'Ali some others say that it was Zaid bin Thābit who suggested *'Awl*.

The case of *'Awl* is suggested in a hypothetical proposition that if a man died leaving six dirhams, and there were two people claiming their debt from the estate, one of them is claiming three dirhams and the other is claiming four dirhams, we have to adopt the rule of bankruptcy and divide it proportionally. Sayyidnā 'Umar then agreed to this proposition. Then Al-'Abbas said: "This is then the rule to be applied here". Husband will get 1/2 and the two full sisters will get 2/3:

H	2FS
$\frac{1}{2}$	$\frac{2}{3}$
3	4
	7

Therefore, the husband gets 3/7 and the two full sisters 4/7.

Some said the first case of *'awl* was that of H FS US and others said H FS M.

All the Ṣaḥabāh (Companions) agreed with the case except Ibn Abbās, after the death of Sayyidnā'Umar. When asked why he did not discuss it with'Umar during his life time, his reply was that it was because of'Umar's personality and the respect he had for him. He was then asked what was his solution in such a case, Ibn'Abbās replied saying that some time, some of the heirs inherit as *Aṣḥāb al farāiḍ* like mother, husband and wife. They will be given priority in the matter of inheritance. Sometimes, sisters too inherit as *Aṣḥab al faraid* and sometimes as *asaba* and sometimes they are excluded totally. Others, like uterine brothers and sisters if they are not inheriting as *aṣḥāb al farāiḍ* they will also be excluded totally. He then said, I swear by Allah, if 'Umar had given priority to those whom Allah had given priority, and delayed those whom Allah has delayed, there would not arise any problem of *'Awl* at all. Ibn'Abbās said, those whom Allah has given priority are those who inherit as *aṣḥāb al farāiḍ*. If they shift from a specific share, they will go to a specific share, and those who will be transferred from a specific share to something less than that i.e. to *asaba*, they are those who are delayed.

Ibn Shihāb al-Ẓuhrī said that if the decision of Ibn ʻAbbās was not preceded by judicial authority of Sayyidnā ʻUmar, nobody will differ with Ibn ʻAbbās.

In the case where the shares of heirs are less than the estate, the priniple of *al-radd* will be adopted.

In the case where the shares are more than the *Aṣl* (original estate), *ʻAwl* will be applied. The total of the shares then will be used as a new *Aṣl*, e.g.:

1.

2FS	H original *aṣl* is 6 and the new *asl* is 7
⅔	½
4	3

2.

H	2FS	M	US	(original *aṣl* is 6, and the new *aṣl* is 9).
½	⅔	⅙	⅙	
3	4	1	1 = 9	

3.

H	2F	M	2US	(original *asl* is 6, and the new *asl* is 10).
½	⅔	⅙	⅔	
3	4	1	2 = 10	

4. Jurists observed that out of seven *asl* is only in 6, 12, and 24; that is where *ʻawl* will occur.

H	2FS	2US	M

This is known as *"al-Shuraiḥiyyah"* decided by Qāḍī Shuraiḥ.

5.

W	2D	M	F

This case is known as *"al-Minbarrīyyah"* decided by Sayyidnā ʻAlī.

The following provides a good example of *Radd:*

D	DS	W	M		
½	⅙	⅛	⅙	*asl*	24
12	4	5	4		23

This is the case of *radd*, because, in this case, the total of the inheritors are less than the *aṣl*.

The following are examples of *Tasib:*

W	D	2FS
⅛	½	R

(*Aṣl* 8 in order to give every sister her share multiply every number plus the *asl* by 2 in order to give every one of his own share.)

As for example *aṣl* 8 is mulitplied by 2 *asl* is 16. Therefore, every sister will get 3 as her share.

W	D	2FS
1/8	1/2	R
1	4	3
2	8	6

8DS	M	F
2/3	1/6	1/6 × R
4	11	1
8	2	2

Aṣl is 6 is multiplied by 2 *aṣl* is 12. Each D will get one out of 12.

H	5FS
1/2	2/3

Aṣl is 6, new *aṣl* is multiplied by 5. Therefore, *aṣl* is 35. Each full sister will get 4/35.

FDS	3GM	3FS
2/3	1/6	R
4	1	1
12	3	3

Aṣl is 6 is multiplied by 3 *aṣl* is 18. Therefore everyone will get his share.

6DS	2GM	3FS
2/3	1/6	R
4	11	1
12	3	3

Aṣl is 6 multiplied by 3 *asl* is 18. Therefore everyone of them will get his own share.

AW	3GM	4FS		4FB
1/4	1/6		R	
3	2		7	
36	24		84	

Aṣl is 12 mulitplied by 12 *aṣl* is 144.

Each of the 4FB will get 14/84
Each of the 4FB will get 7/84
Each of the 3GM will get 8/84
Each of the 4W will get 8/84

3GM	4W	2UB	5CB
1/6	1/4	1/3	R
2	3	4	3
10	15	20	15

Aṣl is 12 multiplied by 5 aṣl is 60.

Representation to the Estate of Deceased Man

Professor Anderson, in his book *Islamic Law in the Modern World*[11] has unjustly criticised the rule against representation as causing much hardship. He thinks that this rule is pre-Qur'ānic origin, which is not true at all. The reason why this rule was not over-ruled by the Prophet says Anderson, was that he himself was debarred from succeeding to his grandfather. Thus, in order he might not be suspected of personal, bias or motives, he did not change the rule. I wonder from where did Professor Anderson bring this argument which is not at all convincing. There are many things which the Prophet did, even at the cost of being assumed biased, provided he once became guided or convinced that the thing was for the good. For example, he said that nobody will succeed him as whatever a Prophet of Allah leaves is for the poor.

In fact, the more plausible reason behind the survival of the rule against representation seems to be the fact that the law of inheritance in Islam is very much connected with the provisions of wills and gifts, and a defect in one may be corrected by another. Thus, a person who has been adversely affected by this rule may be compensated by a gift or bequest.

But there may arise, situations in which the execution of a gift or will may not be possible. In such cases, the rule against representation may really cause hardship. Take the example of a grandfather who dies suddenly as a result of heart collapse. So common these days, and could not find time to make a gift or bequest in favour of a son of his pre-deceased son. According to Muslim Law, the son of a pre-deceased son gets nothing of his grandfather's estate. Now the grandson is wholly dependent upon the mercy of other relatives who have inherited. If they chose to ignore him, the grandson could do nothing. In such cases there is a need to do something to protect the said grandson. But this must not contrary to the provision of the *Sharī'ah*.

In recent years, several Islamic countries have made provisions to mitigate hardships of the son of a pre-deceased son. Such provisions were enacted by Egypt, then by Syria, followed by Morocco and Pakistan. The first three mentioned countries envolved a system of "obligatory Bequests'. Under this heading, the "Egyptian Law of Testamentary Dispostion", for example, provides that a *grandfather must make a bequest to grand-children of their pre-deceased children.*

This bequest should be of what the pre-deceased child would have inherited, on intestacy, had he survived.

It has been provided that such "obligatory Bequests" *(Wa-siyah al-Wājib)* should not exceed the bequeathable third. In case the grandparent fails to make such a bequest, its existence would be *presumed* by the court. The "obligatory Bequests" have a priority over the regular bequests.

In Morocco, such "obligatory Bequests" operate only in favour of the child of a pre-deceased son, and not of daughter. This is rather strange. In the matter of inheritance, the daughters have the right. If something is done to remedy the son, the same must apply to the daughter.

In Pakistan, section 4 of the *Muslim Family Laws Ordinance,* 1961 provides:

> "in the event of the death of any son or daughter of the propositus before the opening of succession, the children of such son or daughter, if any, living at the time the succession opens, shall per stripes receive a share equivalent to the share which such son or daughter, as the case may be would have received if alive."

This is a pure innovation *('Bid'ah)* and goes contrary to the spirit of the *Shari'ah.*

Rules of Exclusion from Inheritance

According to the principles of the *Sharī'ah* exclusion is based on three main principles:

1. "Nearer in degree excluded one who is remoter". (e.g., excludes son's son; father excluded grandfather).
2. "A person who is related to the deceased through another is excluded by the presence of latter". (e.g., father excludes brother.) There is however one exception to this rule. That is a mother does not exclude brother or sister.
3. "Full blood excludes half blood". (e.g., full sister excludes consanguine sister.) The exception to this rule is that the uterine relations are not excluded on this ground.

The total exclusions under the *Sharī'ah* will be enforced on the following grounds:

a) *Change of Religion:* According to the *Sharī'ah* a non-Muslim cannot inherit from a Muslim. If a Muslim changes his or her religion, he or she is excluded from inheritance.
b) If one causes the death of another either intentionally or unintentionally, he cannot inherit from the deceased. There is a

difference between the Ḥanafi and Māliki Legal systems. The Ḥanafis say that if an act is committed by an infant or insane person which causes the death of another person, this does not exclude such an infant or an insane person from inheritance.

Moreover, the act causing the death should be of direct nature; for example, when a person has dug a well into which another falls, or placed a stone on the road against which another stumbles and is killed in consequence are not sufficient causes for exclusion.

The Māliki Jurists say that one who intentionally kills or causes the death of another, directly or indirectly, will be precluded from any right to inherit from him, while one who kills another by accident, even by a direct act, such as shooting a pistol or flinging a bomb, will not suffer any such deprivation.

Shīʿās say that the homicide must be intentional, but the absence of intention should be clearly proved.

c) *Slavery:* Both under the Shīʿā and Sunnī Laws, the status of slavery is a bar to succession, although this does not apply nowadays, since the institution of slavery is abolished world over.

d) *Illegitimacy:* A bastard, in Ḥanafi Law, cannot inherit from the father; he could, however, do so from the side of the mother.

In the Shīʿites, on the other hand, illegitimacy acts as a factor for total exclusion, and a bastard is not allowed to inherit either from mother or father. A distinction is, however, drawn between a child of fornication and a child whose parentage has been disallowed by the father, that is, a child of impercation. In the case of fornication, the child is excluded from inheritance; while a child of impercation, is allowed to inherit from the side of the mother. The Sunni Law does not recognise this distinction. The child of fornication and impercation are both regarded as illegitimate, and inherit from the mother's side.

Likewise, the son of a uterine brother does not inherit. And a germane brother excludes a consanguine brother who is preferred to the son of a germane brother takes precedence over the son of a consanguine brother. And, the son of a consanguine brother excludes a consanguine paternal uncle. Further, the consanguine paternal uncle excludes the son of a germane paternal uncle. Further, the son of a germane paternal uncle excludes the son of a consanguine paternal uncle. This is so, that the nearer excludes the more remote.[12]

The children of sisters, however the strength of the bloodtitle, do not inherit, nor can the offspring of daughters, the same rule applies to the daughters of the brother, however the strength of the blood-tie, nor can the daughters of the paternal uncle. Furthermore the maternal grandmother does not inherit, nor can the paternal uterine uncle. Similarly, a slave or anyone not completely emancipated cannot inherit.[13]

Nor can there be mutual right of inheritance between a Muslim and a non-Muslim. The following persons also do not inherit. These are: the son of the uterine brother, the maternal grandfather, the mother of the mother's father, the father; that is the deceased's father. Also uterine brothers do not inherit if they co-exist with the paternal grandfather; nor can they inherit in the presence of the agnatic descendent, male or female. The sibling also do not inherit in the presence of the paternal grandfather. Also the heir who caused the death of the deceased intentionally does not inherit in the estate nor in the blood-wit, nor can he inherit in the blood-wit in the case of an accidental killing, but can inherit from the estate. Whoever is disqualified to inherit from an estate, cannot himself exclude others.[14]

A woman repudiated three times by her husband who is in his death sickness, shall inherit the husband if he dies in that sickness, but the husband himself cannot inherit her. Similarly she can still inhrit him, even if it was a single repudiation if he happens to die from that illness; and even if she has completed her *'Idda* period. In the event of a person in good health repudiating his wife once, there shall be mutual inheritence between them should either of them die before she completed the period of *'Idda*. But there can be no mutual inheritance, should either of them die, after she completed the *'iddah* period.[15]

Where a man in his death sickness married a woman; and if either should die, there can be no mutual inheritence.

The mother's mother is entitled to one-sixth in the net estate so is the father's mother, but if they co-exist, then they share the one-sixth. But when the mother's mother is nearer in degree then she is given priority, because the share is given to her by the text. But where the paternal grandmother is nearer in degree both shall share the one-sixth equally.[16]

According to Mālik more than two grandmother's cannot inherit. He allows only the father's mother and the mother's mother, how high soever.[17]

However, it is reported that Zaid Ibn Thābit had allowed three grandmothers to inherit. That is one from the side of the mother and two from the father's side. They are the mother's mother, the father's father's mother. But it has not been noticed as part of the practice of the rightly guided Caliphs to allow more than two grandmothers to inherit.[18]

Al-Ḥajb wal Ḥaram: Prevention from Inheritance

Ḥajb means prevention. In Sharī'ah, the term is used where a person is prevented from *mirath* because of some impediments. One who comes under this category will either be totally or partially excluded. The total exclusion is called *"Ḥajb Ḥarmānī"* and the partial exclusion is termed *"Ḥajb Nafsānī"*. According to Muslim Jurists, the total exclusion does not apply to sons and daughter's father, and mother, and husband and wife. But the others will be subject to total exclusion, e.g., the daughter of the son in presence of son or two daughters; brothers from father's side or grandfather's side and so on. It is also the view of the Jurists that if an heir is excluded on the ground of impediment, he will be considered as if he does not exist at all. His physical presence will not effect others. As for example, if there is a mother and two Christian brothers, they will not prevent mother from getting 1/3, but if the brothers are Muslims they are only prevented partially by the presence of the father. They will thus pull her from the range of 1/3 to the range of 1/6.

'Abdullāh bin Mas'ūd says that the presence of either one who is prevented totally or partially will effect the other, e.g., son who had murdered someone, will effect the others. In a case where there are son, mother and father, the presence of the son who has killed will effect them and will bring them down to the area of one sixth.

The Scheme of Al-Radd (Return)

After giving away the shares of the sharers, if there is any residue left and there is no residuary heir, the residue reverts to the sharers in proportion to their shares. This is called *Radd* in Sharī'ah.

The Jurists have differences of opinion on the question of *al-Radd.* Some of them are of the view that the residue will go to public treasury *(Bait al-Māl)* in the case of *Radd* while others say that it will be divided among the Qur'ānic sharers.

Zaid bin Thabit was of the opinion that where the *Radd* is applied the residue will go to the public treasury. Imam Malik has adopted this opinion. Imām Shāfi'ī and Ibn Ḥazm also agree with the same view. They have said that Allah has specified for every heir his specific share in the Qur'ān. If we add anything to it, we are exceeding the laws of Allah.

Imām Shāfi'ī says that in the verses of the Qur'ān, Allah has mentioned sister and has given her a maximum of 1/2 if she is alone. If she is given the total share by applying *Radd*, we are in fact acting completely against the clear rule of the Qur'ān.

The majority of the Companions of the Prophet and the *Tābi'ūn* and

Imāms Abū Ḥānifa and Aḥmad bin Ḥanbal as well as the Shī'ites have adopted the principle of *Radd*. They quote the following verse as their authority:

Jurists who adopted *Radd* said that the remainder will go to Qur'ānic heirs excluding spouses. The Ḥanafī Jurists take a different view and say that if we don't find anybody other than the spouses, it is better to give them the remainder, rather than giving it away to the *Bait al-Mal.*

Sayyidnā 'Uthmān bin 'Affān and Jābir ibn Zaid are of the opinion that we should apply *Radd* to all the Qur'ānic heirs including the spouses.

'Abdāllāh bin Mas'ūd says that we should apply *Radd* but should exclude spouses, daughter of the son in the presence of proper daughter, Uterine sisters and brothers in the presence of mother. Consanguine sister in the presence of full sister and the grandmother. 'Abdallāh bin 'Abbās, on the contrary, excluded spouses and the grandmother. The following examples will explain the scheme better:

Example 1:

If X died leaving only one Qur'ānic heir, i.e., daughter, she will take 1/2 as a Qur'ānic share and 1/2 by way of *Radd.*

Example 2:

Where there are more than one Qur'ānic sharers who are in the same category, i.e., two daughters, they will take the entire estate 1/2 each.

Example 3:

Where there is more than one person but of different categories, e.g.:

D	DS	M	
$\frac{1}{2}$	$\frac{1}{6}$	$\frac{1}{6}$	*asl* = 6
3	1	1	= 5 divided: by 5
= $\frac{3}{5}$	$\frac{1}{5}$	$\frac{1}{5}$	

Example 4:

In the case where there is a spouse involved is the most difficult of all problems, i.e.:

H	D	or	W	D
$\frac{1}{2}$	$\frac{1}{4} \times R$		$\frac{1}{8}$	$\frac{1}{2} \times R$

H	D	M	
$\frac{1}{4}$	$\frac{1}{2}$	$\frac{1}{6}$	12
3	6	2	11
1	3		

= 1	$\frac{1}{4} \times 3$	$\frac{1}{4} \times 3$	
=	$\frac{9}{4}$	$\frac{3}{4}$	multiplied all by 4 to remove
= 4	9	3	the fraction *aṣl* = 16

Example 5:

W	*M*	*3D*	
$\frac{1}{8}$	$\frac{1}{6}$	$\frac{2}{3}$	24
3	4	16	23
1		7 8	
= 1	$\frac{1}{5} \times 7$	$\frac{4}{5} \times 7$	
= 1	$\frac{7}{5}$	$\frac{28}{5}$	multiply by 5
= 15	21	84	*asl* = 40 mulitply by 3
= 15	21	84	120

Example 6:

W	*2GM*	*6US*	
$\frac{1}{4}$	$\frac{1}{6}$	$\frac{1}{3}$	12
3	2	4	9
1		3	4
= 1	$1 \times \frac{1}{3}$	$2 \times \frac{1}{3}$	
= 1	1	2	4

Dhaw Al-Arḥām: Uterine Relations

The *Dhaw al-Arham* or Uterine heirs are those who are neither Qur'ānic sharers nor the residuary or agnetic heris. *Dhaw al-Arḥām* literally means kindred who are female agnates and cognates, whether male or female. The *Dhaw al-Arḥām* form a vast and complicated class of heirs.

The *Dhaw al-Arḥām*, therefore, constitute the following:

Descendants:

1. Daughter, children and her descendants.
2. Children of son's daughter, however h.l.s. and their descendants.

Ascendants:

3. False grandfathers, h.h.s.
4. False grandmothers h.h.s.
5. Full brother's daughters and their descendants.
6. Consanguine brother's daughters and their descendants

Descendants Grandparents, True or False:

8. Full paternal aunt and her descendants.

9. Consanguine paternal aunt and her descendants.
10. Uterine paternal uncles and aunts and their descendants.
11. Full paternal uncle's daughters and their descendants.
12. Consanguine paternal uncle's daughters and their descendants.
13. Uterine paternal uncle's children and their descendants.

The famous learned Companions of the Prophet like Zaid bin Thābit as well as jurists like Imām Mālik, Shāfi'i and Ẓāhirī are of the opinion that these *Dhaw al-Arḥām* have no place in Islamic scheme of *Mirath*. Hence, they will not inherit in any circumstances. The majority of the *Ṣaḥābah*, the Jurists of Kūfah and Baṣrah including Imām Abū Ḥanīfah, on the contrary saye *Dhaw al-Arḥām* will inherit. Imam Mālik, Imām Shāfi'ī and other Jurist's opinions are rigid since they say that the question of shares of *mīrāth* canot be settled by the use of *Qiyās* or analogical deduction. It must be based on the Qur'ān, the *Sunnah* and *Ijmā'* or the consensus of opinion of the *'Ulamā*. Ḥanafi Jurists also base their argument on the Qur'ān the *Sunnah* and *Ijmā.'* They maintain that in the Qur'ān, the following verse speaks of the rights of *Dhawa al-Arhām*.

«واولوا الارحام ببعضهم اولى ببعض في كتاب الله للرجال نصيب مما ترك الوالدان والاقربون–والنساء نصيب مما ترك الوالدان والاقربون».

A Missing Person's (Mafqūd) Right of Inheritance

When someone is missing and his whereabouts cannot be traced what will happen to his property?

The Muslim Jurists say that according to the concept *Istis'ḥāb* we shall presume that the person is still alive until the contrary is proved. According to rules governing *mīrath*, no one is going to be inherited until he is definitely proved dead, and no one will be allowed to inherit until it is proved that he is still alive when the prepositus died. Therefore according to *Istis'ḥāb* the person is not to be inherited until his death is declared either by evidence or by a decree of a Court.

About the missing heir, Imām Mālik and Abū Ḥanīfah say that if his relative dies after he is declared missing until he is declared dead, he has no entitlement to inherit, but he will surely inherit those of his relatives who died before he was declared missing. As far as his own estate is concerned, it is to be kept until he is declared dead. It is after declaration that his relatives will inherit.

According to Imām Shāfi'ī and Aḥmad bin Ḥanbal, the missing person will be entitled to inherit all his relatives who have passed away after him, his share is to be added to his original property until the time when court declares him dead. Imāms Mālik and Abū Ḥanifah say that the evidence of *Istis'hab* is considered only as a shield to protect his estate, but will not entitle him to inherit others; but Imam Shafi'i and Imām Aḥmad bin Ḥanbal say it helps to protect his estate as well as gives him right to inherit others.

It will be both a shield as well as a sword. If such a case arises, it can be solved in two ways. If we assume that the missing person is either alive or dead, and his daughter dies leaving husband, mother, father's sister and father who missing, the following sharing will take place:

H	M	FS	F	(who is missing)
½	¼ of R	ex	R of R	6
3	1	0	2	
½	⅓	½	0	6
3	2	3	0	8

(assuming that he is dead)

In the above case we adopt the *asl* to be 24 and multiply the first one with 4 and the second one with 3 and give every one his minimum share.

If a missing person is alive, the shares will be divided as follows:

H	M	FS	F	(who is missing)
½	⅓ of R	ex	R of R	
3	1	0	2	6 × 4
12	4	0	8	24
3	2	3	0	8 × 3
9	6	9	0	24

In the above case we presume that the missing person is alive and his share is to be reserved until he is declared dead. The husband will get 9 as his minimum share, the mother will get 4 as her minimum share and the full sister will be excluded by the father.

1. Qur'ān, ch. 4:12

2. Cheyne and Black, *Encyclopaedia Biblica*, 4 Vols., Black, London cc. 2724, 2728.
3. Iqbāl, Dr. Sir Muḥammad, *Reconstruction of Religious Thoughts in Islam*, Lahore, pp. 236-237.
4. Letournean, *Evolution of Marriage*, pp. 259-269.
5. Qur'ān, ch. 4:11.
6. Ibid.
7. Qur'ān, ch. 4:11.
8. Qur'ān, ch. 4:11.

9. Qur'ān, ch. 4:11.
10. Qur'ān, ch. 4:11.

11. Syed Khālid Rashīd, *Muslim Law*, Lucknow 1979, p.
12. Al-Qayrawānī, *Risālah*, op. cit., ch. 39: *Bāb al-Farāid*, pp. 137-145.
13. Al-Qayrawānī, *Risālah*, op. cit., ch. 39: *Bāb al-Farāid*, pp. 137-145.
14. Ibid.

15. Al-Qayrawānī, *Risālah*, op. cit., ch. 39: *Bāb al-Farāid, pp. 137-145.*
16. *Ibid.*
17. *Ibid.*
18. *Al Qayrawānī, Risālah*, op. cit., ch. 39: *Bāb al-Farāid*, pp. 137-145.

Chapter 19

Disposal of Property

A. *Waṣiyyah: Bequest*

In the *Jāhiliyyah* period, before Islam, Arabs disposed of their property as they liked as no law concerning bequest or inheritance existed to guide them. They could make bequest in favour of any one, depriving their own parents, children and wives. At times the bequest was made in favour of rich and influential members of the clan.

Waṣiyyah comes from its Arabic root *wasa* which means he conveyed. In other words *waṣiyyah* means a gift of property by its owner to another contingent on the giver's death.[1] The legal Qur'ānic injunctions in respect of bequest or will was revealed in *Sūrah al-Baqarah* (ch. 2: 180-182) where it says that it is the responsibility of the pious and Allah-fearing persons to leave *wasiyyah* behind. But these verses were revealed when no law was yet fixed in the matter of inheritance. Later in *Surah al-Nisa'* a complete guidance was given to Muslims concerning inheritance and fixed portions for each heir. The Islamic law in respect of inheritance and will is further clarified by the Holy Prophet in his ahadith in the following manners:

The prophetic hadith, reported on the authority of Sa'd bin Abi Waqqas says:

> "I was taken very ill during the year of the conquest of Mecca and felt that I was about to die. The Propet visited me and I asked: "O Messenger of Allah I own a good deal of property and I have no heir except my daughter. May I make a will, leaving all my property for religious and charitable property?" He (the Prophet) replied: "No." I again asked may I do so in respect of ⅔ of my property? He replied "No." I asked: "may I do so with one half of it?" He replied: "No." I again asked: "May I do so with ⅓ of it?" The Prophet replied: "Make a will disposing of one third in that manner because one third is quite enough of the wealth that you possess. Verily if you die and leave your heirs rich is better than leaving them poor and begging. Verily the money that you spend for the pleasure of Allah will be rewarded, even a morsel that you lifted up to your wife's mouth."[2]

The Islamic Law in respect of inheritance and bequest is further clarified

1. The bequest *(waṣiyyah)* can be made only for 1/3 of the entire property and no more.
2. No one can make a bequest in respect of any legal Qur'ānic heir. In other words, those relatives whose portions are fixed in the Qur'ān, one cannot increase or decrease them through bequests nor can one deprive a legal heir through any bequest.

In spite of the clear guidance in respect of shares of inheritance in the Qur'ān and the Sunnah, *Waṣiyyah* still remains an operative injunction up to the maximum of one-third of one's property but should be done with strict sense of justice and equity. This provision can be used for those who are helpless but are not Qur'ānic recipients of shares like the children of those sons or daughters who have already died during the life-time of their grandfathers. Similarly there may be some really needy persons outside the family circle whom one wishes to help through bequests or wants to spend some money on public welfare which he is afraid his wealthy heirs, will not willingly give away after his death if he did not make adequate provision through his bequests.

In the verses of injunctions concerning inheritance, it is made clear that the shares will be distributed only after the debt left behind by the deceased is paid and the bequest is carried out.[3] There is a consensus of opinion of the *'ulamā* that although bequest is mentioned before the debt, the debt should first be paid and then the bequest, then will follow the distribution of the shares to the heirs. The point that has been emphasised in verse 12 of *Surah al-Nisa* is that the man undergoing debt or making bequest should remember that Allah is watching him and knows all his intentions. He is not borrowing money or making bequests in order to deprive the Qur'ānic sharers of their legitimate shares after his death. The temptation to do so becomes greater in respect the collaterals *(Kalālah)* when the deceased has no children or parents and the property is to be given to the distant relatives. He might think that rather than property going to collaterals, it is better that he gives it away through bequests or through the pretext of debt. This will be against the spirit of the law of *Mīrāth.*

A Muslim who owns property is given permission to bequeath his property for a charitable object or to anyone excepting a legal heir. This is called *waṣiyyah*. The making of a will is specially recommended. The Holy Qur'ān speaks of the making of a will as a duty incumbent upon a Muslim when he leaves sufficient property for his heirs.[4] The Holy Prophet is reported to have said: "It is not right for a Muslim who has property to bequeath, that he should pass two nights without having a written will with him."[5] But this duty, or right, is subject to certain limitations. In the first place, not more than one-third of the property can be disposed of by will,[6] and secondly, no will can be made in favour of an heir.[7] But, as expressly stated in the Holy Qur'ān, the making of a will is incumbent only on well-to-do people. The reason for limiting the bequest to one-third is clearly stated in a Hadith of the Prophet: "That one should leave his heirs free from want is better than that they should be begging of other people."[8] And the reason for excluding the heirs is that no injustice may be done to certain heirs at the expense of others. A *wasiyyah* which is against these princiles would be ineffective to that extent. It may be added that if a property in respect of which a bequest is made is encumbered with a debt, the debt is payable before the will is executed. If the amount of the *waṣiyyah* exceeds one-third, it will not be executed except where the heirs give their consent.[9]

On who makes *waṣiyyah* is called *al-Mūṣī* in Arabic. It should be noted that the *wasiyyah* takes effect only after the death of *al-Mūṣī*. For a valid *waṣiyah,* he must be a *Mumayyiz*, i.e. the person who will differentiate between what is good or bad. He should realise that he is really doing good and not depriving anyone of his due rights and that he is not disobeying Allah. This condition is specified by the Mālikī school. The Hanafi school on the contrary, rejected the *wasiyyah* made by *mumayyiz* equating it with a gratuitous contract. Imām Mālik says that we prevent the *Mumayyiz* from making the gratuitous contracts only to prevent his property upon which he will depend on. Since the *wasiyyah* will only take place after his death, there is no need of preventing him. The same rule will apply in the cases of a person who is mentally deranged or insane *(al-safīh)*.

The person in favour of whom the *wasiyyah* is made, must be capable of ownership whether he exists or is capable of existing, whether insane or sane, adult or minor. If he is not capable or receiving it like minors or insane persons, it can be accepted by his guardian on his behalf. The only essential condition is that he must not be among the heirs, unless with the agreement of the other heirs. The Mālikī Jurists have based their authority on the Ḥadīth of the Prophet:

«ان الله قد أعطى كل ذي حق حقه-فلا وصية للوارث».

The Māliki school also allows the *waṣiyyah* in favour of a dead person knowing that the person is actually dead. The *waṣiyyah* in fact is intended to go to his heirs. *Waṣiyyah* can also be made in favour of a mosque for its maintenance. In such a case it will be the *waqf* for the mosque for all time to come. The *waṣiyyah* can be made in favour of an animal although the animal is not capable of having anything. It will really mean that the *wasiyyah* is made to the person taking care of the animal to feed and look after it. *Waṣiyyah* can also be made to the heir to give out Zakāt if it is due out of the estate. But if the *waṣiyyah* for the payment of Zakāt is for the past years, it will be to the proportion of the one-third of the *waṣiyyah*.

Imām Muḥammad Idris al-Shāfi'i has discussed the following two verses of the Holy Qur'ān showing an example of abrogating *(Nāsikh)* and abrogated *(Mansūkh)* verses and the role of Sunnah and *Ijmā'* in deciding the rule of law on *Waṣiyyah*.[10]

The verse 180 of *Sūrah al-Baqarah* says:

كُتِبَ عَلَيْكُمْ اِذَا حَضَرَ اَحَدَكُمُ الْمَوْتُ اِن تَرَكَ خَيْراً الْوَصِيَّةُ لِلْوَالِدَيْنِ وَالْأَقْرَبِينَ بِالمَعْرُوفِ حَقّاً عَلَى الْمُتَّقِينَ».

"It is prescribed for you, when death draws near to one of you, and he leaves behind some property, that he makes a bequest in favour of his parents and relatives according to resonable usage; an obligation on the God-fearing."[11]

The verse 240 of *Sūrah al-Baqarah* says:

«وَالَّذِينَ يُتَوَفَّوْنَ مِنْكُمْ وَيَذَرُونَ اَزْوَاجاً وَصِيَّةً لِأَزْوَاجِهِمْ مَتَاعاً اِلَى الْحَوْلِ غَيْرَ اِخْرَاجٍ فَاِنْ خَرَجْنَ فَلَا جُنَاحَ عَلَيْكُمْ فِي مَا فَعَلْنَ فِي اَنْفُسِهِنَ مِنْ مَعْرُوفٍ - وَاللّٰهُ عَزِيزٌحَكِيمٌ».

"And those of you who die, leaving widows, let them make bequest for their widows, provision for a year without expulsion (i.e. residence); but if they leave, there is no fault in you what they may do with themselves honourably. Allah is All mighty; All-wise."[12]

Thus Allah provided (legislation) for the inheritance of parents as well as for near relatives whether together with them or as successors, and for the inheritance of the husband from his wife and the wife from her husband.

The two foregoing verses may be interpreted either to confirm bequests for the parents and the near relatives, bequest for the wife, and inheritance together with bequests, so that inheritance and bequests are lawful; or that the legislation concerning inheritance abrogates that concerning bequests.[13]

Since both interpretations are possible, it is obligatory upon the learned *'Ulamā* to find an evidence in the Book of Allah as to which of the two is valid; if nothing is found in the text of the Book of Allah they should try the Sunnah of the Prophet. If such an evidence is found, it should be accepted, as if accepted from Allah by virtue of His command to obey His Messenger.

We have found that those learned in legal interpretation and the authorities in the campaigns of the Prophet – whether from the tribe of Quraysh or other tribes – are agreed that in the year of the conquest of Mecca (8 A.H./630 A.D.) the Prophet said:

> "No bequest to a successor (is valid), nor shall a believer be slain for (the blood of) an unbeliever."[14]

This tradition has been transmitted from those who have heard it from the authorities on the (Prophet's) campaigns. So this is a transmission by the public from the public and is therefore of greater authority than the transmission of one (individual) from another. Further, we have found that the scholars are agreed on the acceptance of this tradition.

We have concluded that the Holy Prophet's ruling: "No bequest for an heir" is valid. As Imām Shāfi'ī has said, it means that legislation on inheritance has abrogated that on bequests for the parents and the wife, on the strength of the information related by those learned in matters concerning the (Prophet's) campaigns, interrupted traditions from the Prophet, and the agreement of the Jurists.

A great number of Jurists also have held that the legislation concerning bequests for relatives was abrogated and is no longer obligatory; for whenever they are entitled to inherit, they are so by virtue of the law of inheritance; but when they are not entitled to inherit, it is not obligatory that they should inherit by a bequest.

Ṭāwūs bin Kaysān and a few other authorities, however, held that the legislation concerning bequests for parents has been abrogated, though it was confirmed for relatives not entitled to inherit. So it is not permissible for him who bequeaths to do so to persons other than relatives.

It also indicates that the bequest of the deceased cannot exceed one third of his estate.

Bequests to parents are no longer valid, since their right to inheritance as successors is confirmed. A bequest made by a deceased to anyone – if he is not a successor – is valid. It is commendable if the deceased leaves a bequest to his relatives.

Opinions differ whether the provision of a year's maintenance with residence, for a widow is abrogated by the share which the widow gets (one-eighth or one-fourth) as an heir[15] Yūsuf ʿAlī does not think it is abrogated.[16] The bequest (where made) takes effect as a charge on the property, but the widow can leave the house before the year is out, and presumably the maintenance then ceases. Thus, as we have seen, *waṣiyyah* offers to the testator a complementary means of enabling some of the poor relatives who are excluded from inheritance to obtain a share in his property according to the law of succession. The will or bequest also offers an opportunity to the testator to recognize the services rendered to him by a total stranger whom he wants to reward although such power given to the testator is not exercised to the injury of the lawful heirs. Hence, the testator can not exceed while making his will to the limit of ⅓ of his property. It is unfortunate that some western scholars, as well as Muslim scholars influenced by these western scholars, try to explain the Qur'ānic restriction about the limit of one-third. They conjecture that probably the restriction was influenced by Roman law as mentioned by Fyzee[17] and Ameer ʿAlī.[18]

Any Muslim who is sane and a major and has some property can make a will. Any will or bequest made during *mard al-mant*, death sickness, is not valid. Likewise, a person who has taken poison or has tried to commit suicide by some other means makes a will it will not be considered valid. The will can be made either orally or in writing. It is desireable, however, that it should be rendered in writing. If the will is in writing it may not be signed and if it is signed it may not be attested. What is really important is that the intention of the testator must be very clear. even a dumb person who can not speak can make valid wills through gestures. Will can be made in favour of a male or female, Muslim or non-Muslims as long as they are capable of holding property. Even an unborn child, who can not be a legatee as he is in the womb, if he is born within six months from the date of making the will he can validly avail the benefit of the bequest made in his favour. The jurists of alls schools of Islamic jurisprudence are of the opinion that the bequest made by Muslims to non-Muslim is valid. The Shāfiʿi jurists, however, differ in their view on this subject. An apostate can not be a legatee. It is permissible to make a valid will in favour of educational, charitable and religious institutions. Once the will or *waṣiyyah* is made, it can be revoked by the testator either by a subsequent will or through express or implied statement made orally or in writing. The implied revocation of a bequest is made when the testator subsequently acts in such way that the revocation can be inferred. As for example, he makes a will in respect of a parcel of land. Subsequently he buildings a dwelling place on it. In this case, by implication he has revoked the will. If the testator has made a will and then makes another will subsequently on the same property in favour of another person, the previous will becomes null and void.

In conclusion it can be added that *waṣiyyah* is optional both on the part of the testator as well as the beneficiary. The testator may or may not make the bequest as he pleases, while the beneficiary is free either to accept it or reject it. Every will or bequest made by a person during his life time is valid and becomes executable after his death only.

B. Hibah: Gift

Hibah means gift from one living person to another without usurping or neglecting the rights of his descendants and near relatives and must be an immediate and unqualified transfer of the corpus of the property without any return *(iwaḍ)*. In other words, it is a transfer of a determinate property without an exchange with a definite proposal on the part of the person who gives the gift and acceptance on the part of the person to whom the gift is given. Valid *Hibah* under Islamic Law must take care of the three main ingredients:

1. There must be declarations of the gift by the person who wants to give it away.
2. The person to whom the gift is given must accept it either by himself or through an agent.
3. The possession of the gift should be delivered by the donor to the person receiving it.

The law governing *hibah* does not specify that it must only be given to a destitute or poor person, a gift can also be made in favour of a rich man. The poor people, in reality, are more deserving, and it is encouraged that they should also be made recipients of gifts.

The Ḥadīth of the Prophet emphasises on making a habit of exchanging gifts since it is beneficial in generating mutual relationship and strengthens love and affirmity and takes away rancour. The Prophet has said:

« تهادوا تحابوا ».

"Exchange gifts among yourselfs and thus strengthen mutual love, with each other."[19]

There are some other *ahadith* of the prophet on which the law of *hibah* is based. The Prophet has said: "Give present to one another, because a present removes grudges." He further says:

> "If any one seeks to take back a gift he is like a dog who returns to its vomit. An evil example does not apply to us."[20]

The Qur'anic injunction of spending in the path of Allah (*infaq*) which is mentioned in *Sūrah al-Baqarah* especially encourages Muslims to offer gifts.[21] Any gratuitous transfer of property which is made with the intention of obtaining its reward in the next world is called *Sadaqah*, but if something is brought to a donee in order to show one's respect for him, it is *hibah*, a present or a gift. *Hibah*, therefore, is an immediate and unqualified transfer of ownership of a determinate object which is done in the life time of the transfer without obtaining an equivalent for it. In other words, it is the transfer of the right of property in that substitute (*tamlīk al-'Ain*) by one person to another without any consideration or equivalent (*'iwaḍ*). Gift is therefore an act of liberality by which the proprietor bestows a thing without the intention of receiving anything in exchange.

The giving and accepting of gifts is thus recommended by the Prophet very strongly. One must not despise even the smallest gift.[22] *Hibah* is also allowed in favour of a son, but it is recommended that similar gifts should be made in favour of other sons and that there should be an equal treatment with all children.[23] The husband can make a gift to his wife, and the wife can give a gift to her husband, or other than husband.[24] Gifts from, and in favour of, non-Muslims can also be made.[25] A gift can be compensated.[26] *Hib bi-sharṭ al-'iwaḍ* i.e. a gift can be made on the condition that the receiver shall give to the donor some determinate thing in return for the gift are also allowed. The *hibah* is complete when the receiver has accepted it and taken possession of the gift. It is not allowed for a person to revoke the *hibah* when it has been accepted by the receiver.[27] While a will is allowed only to the extent of one-third of the property, no such limitation exists on *hibah*, because in this case the owner divests himself of all rights in the property immediately, while in the case of a will (*waṣiyyah*) not the owner but the heirs are deprived.

It should be noted that a gift, an alm, or any pious endowment is incomplete unless they are taken over by those to whom they are given. If the benefactor should die before such formal taking over is effected, they shall be treated as part of the legacy except where these are taken over while the deceased is sick. Under such a circumstance they can be executed so long as they do not exceed one-third of the legacy and the beneficiaries and not heirs of the legacy.

Is Gift a Charity?

A gift to a relative or a poor person is like an alm and cannot be withdrawn. If any person gave an alm to his son, he cannot take it back. But he is permitted to take back a gift that he gave to his minor son, as long as he did not use the property in getting married or gave the money on loan, nor indeed, converted the object of the gift into something else. A mother can withdraw her gift as long as the father remained alive. But if the father dies, she cannot then take back the gift she previously made to her son. Likewise, a gift made to an orphan cannot be withdrawn.[28] In a gift made to a son who has attained maturity, the father cannot effect *hiyaza* i.e. take possession of the article already gifted. Once something is given as a charity, it cannot be withdrawn nor can it revert back to him, except through inheritance *(Mīrāth).* There is no harm on the part of a person who gave an alm of a cow, sheep or goat to drink its milk, but he cannot buy back things he gave as alms. While one gives a gift, and the giver accepts something in return, the receipient shall have the option of either giving to the donor some article of equal value or return the gift immediately.

Besides, it is reprehensible for a father to give some of his children all his property. However, he is permitted to give away some of it. Also a man is permitted to give away to poor people the whole of his property.

If one made a gift which was not taken over by the person to whom it was given and the donor became sick or was declared bankrupt, it will now be unlawful for him to accept the gift. But in case the man to whom the gift was made dies, his heirs can claim it from the donor if he was not declared bankrupt.[29]

When the donor and the recipient reside in the same house the process of the gift is complete even without the physical transfer of the object of the gift, like a gift from husband to his wife, a father to his child, mother to her son and a guardian to his ward.

Who Can Make a Gift?

Every Muslim who has reached the age of maturity and is mentally sane is capable of making a gift. The gift should be made without exercising any force or under duress. This is essential for the donor to know the consequence of his act. A person on his death-bed in the last minutes of his life cannot make a valid gift because, in reality, it is neither *Hibah* nor *Waṣiyyah*. Supposing a gift is made during the *Marḍ al-Maut*, it will be considered at the time of sharing the inheritance and in any circumstances will not exceed one third of the estate, after paying the funeral expenses and debt as required by the injunction of the Qur'ān, and if the shares of the inheritance have no objection to giving out such a gift. This is so because the property of a man on deathbed actually becomes the property of the heirs. While making a gift, one must be just and must not deprive some of his heirs of their legitimate rights.

Gifts can be made in favour of any living person who is capable of holding property. Gifts can also be made in favour of a child in the womb of his mother, a mosque building, a school or any charitable institution. Gifts can also be made to only non-Muslim. Imām Abū Ḥanifah says that a fit of *mushā'* property which means joint and undivided property subject to the right of more than one individual is invalid if it is done of the co-sharers. But his disciples Imām Abū Yūsuf and Imām Shaibānī hold that it is valid. Imām Abū Ḥanīfah's point of view was that when several persons own a property jointly no one is in a position to predicate that his interest is attached to any specific property out of it. Therefore, *hibah* or gift by one of the co-sharers in such a property is likely to create some confusion (*shuyū'*, the word from which *mushā'* is derived) in its enjoyment by all the co-sharers.[30] In the case when gifts are made to two or more persons jointly or if the gift is made by two persons jointly to one person the Ḥanafī jurists hold that it is still valid. As we have seen before, Imām Abū Ḥanīfa does not hold that such gift is valid in the former case. The *musha'* gifts are not encouraged simply because without proper division of the divisible things, disputes and complications would arise in the enjoyment of the objects of such gifts. Therefore, it is essential in the case of *hibah* that its quantity should be known property. If the specification is not given, it is bound to give rise to confusion.

According to the Mālikī school of Islamic jurisprudence, a gift made in favour of a near relative or a poor person will be considered a charitable donation. Hence such gifts will remain irrevocable. The person giving an ordinary gift to a child or a minor may take it back if he so likes, but if the gift is made the basis of his or her marriage it becomes irrevocable. Similarly, a mother can revoke a gift given to her child as long as the father of the child is alive. But if the father dies, the gift becomes irrevocable since any gift given to an orphan cannot be revoked.[31] According to the Shāfi'ī school of jurisprudence, once the gift is validly made nobody can retract it except the father. According to the Ḥanafī jurists, any revocation of a gift is considered abominable in any circumstance whatsoever. But if the delivery of the possession of gift has not been given, it can still be revoked. Once the delivery of the possession of the gift is done, its revocation will not be possible unless a decree has been issued by the Qāḍī or that the donee has consented to it.[32]

In Islamic legal terminology, *waqf* means "tying up of the property in perpetuity" so as to prevent it from becoming the property of a third person. The *waqf* property thus belongs to Allah, and no human being can alienate it for his own purpose.[33]

In Islam it is incumbent upon every muslim to give *ṣadaqah* that is charity, out of one's property. While the payment of *zakāt* of 2½% is obligatory and becomes the right of the poor and the needy and which is to be paid from one's savings on which a year has passed, *ṣadaqah* is to be given at any time from one's property. The establishment of *waqf* property came into existence in order to organize and institutionalise the voluntary charities. Although there are no Qur'ānic verses specifically mentioning *waqf* or the establishment of *waqf* property, the provision is covered in a large number of verses scattered throughout the Holy Qur'ān on the theme of *Infāq fī Sabīl Allah* meaning 'spending in the path of Allah'.

The history of the establishment of *auqāf* started right in the time of Prophet Muḥammad when the very first mosque and Islamic centre was built by the Prophet in Medina, the city par excellence, in the first year of Hijrah. The Prophetic Mosque or *Masjid al-Nabawī* as it is called was built on a parcel of land belonging to two orphans.

Inspite of the Prophet's insistence to pay for the land, the orphans insisted that they would not accept the price from the Prophet but would take it from Allah in the next world. The establishment of *Awqāf* continued in the prophet's time when 'Uthmān, who later became the third Caliph, bought a well and made it a trust property for the charitable use of all and sundry in order to relieve Muslims of the difficulties imposed by Jews who banned Muslims to draw water from another well. Prophetic tradition mentions the three things that a man can leave behind which will benefit him after his death: the establishment of welfare institutions like digging up of a well, canal or building of a hospital, erecting an educational institution; a scholar writing a book from which people will benefit even after his death and pious children who will pray for the parents after their death. This hadith encouraged the companions of the Prophet to 'tie up' part of their property for people's welfare. Hence 'Umar bin al-Khaṭṭāb bought a land in Khayber area. He went to the Prophet and asked his guidance in order to make the most pious use of it. The Prophet replied:

> "Tie up the original property and devote the usurfrcut to human beings which is not to be sold or made the subject of gift or an inheritance. Bring the produce to your children, or relatives and the needy in the path of Allah."[34]

Imām Bukhārī, the famous compiler of *Ṣaḥīḥ al-Bukhārī*, has also narrated a *ḥadith* which supports the institutions of *waqf*. Abū Ṭalḥa gave his choicest piece of land to the Prophet known as Bairuha orchard in Medina. The Prophet gave it back to him advising that he should make it an endowment for his relatives. Abū Ṭalḥa there upon gave the orchard as a charity to Ubayy and Ḥassan.[35]

The specific Prophetic direction in respect of waqf is contained in the following words which sum up the definition of wāqf:

> "Retain the original (property) itself and endow its fruits in the path of Allah."

Every wealthy Muslim who is not a minor nor an insane has right to create a *waqf* provided he is the owner of the property he is dedicating. He should not work under dur ess to do so nor should he be defrauded in creating a *wāqf*. Any waqf created in *marḍ al-maut*, that is death illness is not valid because by then the property is almost passing in the hands of his heirs. The *wāqif*, that is the person who creates the *wāqf*, must not dedicate more than one-third of his estate as *waqf* property unless his heirs give the consent to do so. The objective for which the *wāqf* is set up must not be against the principles of Islam. In other words, a Muslim must not create a *wāqf* in favour of idol worshippers or a temple or a deity since this will conflict with the fundamental principle of *Tauḥīd* (monotheism) of Islam.

There exist slight differences of opinions among the jurists about the type of property that can be dedicated as a *wāqf*. Imām Abū Ḥanīfa, the founder of the Ḥanafī school says that only the immovable property can be made *wāqf*. His eminent disciple Imām Abū Yūsuf also agrees with his master but makes an exception when he says that the beasts of burden and weapons of war can also be dedicated as *wāqf*. The view of another eminent disciple of Imām Abū Ḥanīfa namely Imām Muḥammad is quite different from the view of his master and his colleague. He agrees with other Imams and famous jurists and holds that all articles or movables that can be subject to the dealings and transactions of man can be made *wāqf*. The jurists, particularly Imām Abū Ḥanīfah, say that to establish *wāqf* is supererogatory (*mustaḥab*), but is not essential (*wājib*).

C. *Waqf*

Waqf literally means detention *(Ḥabas),* but its legal meaning is the dedication of a property or giving it away in charity for the benefit of certain property[36] for a good purpose other religious, pious or charitable. Actually, it is a detention of a specific thing from the ownership of the appropriator, and devoting or appropriating its profits or charity on the poor or for other good objects. According to Imām Muḥammad Idrīs al-Shāfi'ī, Imām Mālik and two disciples of Imām Abū Ḥanīfah, Abū Yūsuf and Imām Muḥammad *(Ṣāḥibayn)*, *Waqf* signifies the extinction of the appropriator's ownership int he thing dedicated and the detention of the thing in the ownership of Allah *('alā ḥukum milk-Allāh)* in such a manner that its profit should be made use of for the good of mankind from beginning to the end.[37]

The Jurists say that to establish *Wāqf* is supererogatory *(mustaḥab)*, but is not essential.[38]

The establishment of *wāqf* in other words, extinguishes the right of the *wāqif* (dedicator) and transfers its ownership to Allah.[39]

When such *waqf* is created, a pious person or a group of people are appointed as the managers of the *wāqf*. In some places, they are called *Mutawwalī*, but the property of the *wāqf* does not vest in the managers. Once a *wāqf* is created, it will always remain *wāqf* property and cannot change its character. Since it is created for a pious object, the *wāqf* property is not to be sold or given to someone as *an* inheritance or a gift. Since *wāqf* is created for general welfare, it is of two kinds.[40]

a) *Wāqf al Ahli:* Family wāqf
b) *Wāqf al-Khayri:* Welfare wāqf

Waqf al Ahlī is created for the security of the welfare of near relatives of the dedicator *(wāqif)* and his family to ensure that they get their needs from it for all their life, and then reverts to the welfare of the poor people after their death. It can be made of both moveable and immovable property.

Wāqf al-Khayrī is created to cater for the needs of the orphans, destitutes, blind people and the handicapped, likewise, such *wāqfs* can be created for maintaining mosques, schools, hospitals, grave yards and other places of public welfare.

In conclusion, it should be noted that the establishment of the philantrophic *wāqf* is only voluntary and not an obligation like the payment of Zakāt.

The following conditions must be satisifed in the creation of *wāqf*:

1. The subject of *waqf* must belong to the *wāqif* (dedicator) at the time of dedicating the property.
2. The person dedicating a *wāqf* must not be a minor or a person of an unsound mind.
3. *wāqf* of *Mushā'a* or undivided share in the property may form the subject of *waqf* but for the purpose of a mosque or a burial ground, it is not valid.
4. The purpose for which the *wāqf* is created must be one recognised by the Sharī'ah.
5. The object of *wāqf* must be shown with reasonable certainty.
6. Any *wāqf* made by a will or during *marḍ al maut* (Death illness) cannot operate on more than one-third of the net assets without the

consent of the heirs.

7. A *wāqf* created by a will shall not be invalid simply because there is a clause that the *waqf* shall not operate if a child is born to the *wāqif*. Since a will can be revoked or modified at any time before death. The same will apply to a *wāqif* which is created by a will.

The institution of *Waqf* assumed rigid legal form in the second century hijrah.[41] The large *auqaf* which were established during the Ummayad periods were supervised by the Qāḍis. It was during this period that *Diwān al-Naẓr fil Maẓālim* that is *Bureau to inspect the grievances* was established which apart from looking at the miscarriage of justice was entrusted with the responsibility of supervising the *waqf* property and its administration.[42] During the Abbasid caliphate the Qadis continued the supervision of *auqāf*.[43] In most muslim countries today, in *Mutawallis* are appointed to the *Auqaf*.

Hundreds of *Awqāf* dating from the Umayyad and ʿAbbāsid period of Islamic history have come down to us. In most of parts of the muslim world, a number of schools, colleges, hospitals, orphanages, mosque-buildings and scholarship funds are run through the help of the *Waqf* properties. It is really surprising that in some West African countries like Nigeria, Ghana, Chad, Niger and other neighbouring countries such *Awqāf* foundations are not yet established. Looking at the successful public welfare activities carried out through *Awqāf*, it is strongly recommended that Muslims in these countries should work towards the establishment of *Awqāf*. At present, a large number of *Auqaf* exist throughout the Muslim world. In India alone there are more than 100,000 Muslim *Auqāf* valued at more than a billion Indian rupees.[44]

D. *Shufa': The Right of Pre-Emption*

The word *Shufa'* in Arabic means 'conjunction' since it refers to the land sold which is conjuncting to the land of the *Shāfi'* or the pre-emptor i.e. the person claiming the right of pre-emption. In Islamic legal terminology it means becoming an owner of land sold for the price at which the purchaser has bought although he may not be consenting to it.[45] In the *Ṣaḥīḥ* of Imām Muslim, a prophetic tradition is narrated as follows: "Any one who has a co-sharer in a house or date palm-grove he should not sell it till he has the permission of his co-sharer but if he is willing to take it (buy it) he may pre-empt it, but if he does not wish to take it he should leave it." Imām Bukhāri has also reported *ahādīth* of the prophet on the same theme in his *Ṣaḥīḥ* in the following words: Ṭalḥa bin 'Abdullāh asked the Prophet: O Prophet of Allah I have two neighbours. Which one of the two shall I sell the share first. The Prophet replied: to the neighbour whose door is nearer to your door.[46]

The underlined principle behind *Shufa'* is the expediency and desire to prevent the introduction of a stranger among co-sharers and neighbours of a certain locality who are likely to cause inconvenience or vexation. If the law of *Shufa'* is not applied it is likely to damage the beauty and comfort of the inhabitants and their privacy in their enjoyment of their property rights. The right of *Shufa'*, therefore, does not exist in respect of any movable property but it only exists in respect of the land and what is naturally included in it e.g. buildings, trees, fruits etc. It does not amount to the right to repurchase from the seller but in reality it amounts to the right of substitution which entitles the pre-emptor to stand in the shoes of the person who sells it.

The right of pre-emption, according to the Hanafi jurists, can only be exercised by the owner who has undivided share in the property sold. This right can not be exercised by a tenant no matter for how long he must be staying in the premises. The Shāfi'ī jurists are of the opinion that the right of *Shufa'* can only be exercised in respect of a sale which means an immediate transfer for a definite price including, however, a mortgage by conditional sale whenever it becomes absolute. The shi'ite jurists say that the right of pre-emption does not arise if there happen to be more than two co-owners.

The Mālikī jurists have set up a time limit about exercising the right of pre-emption. They say that the pre-emptor must sue within one year of the sale but the Shafi'i and the Shi'ite jurists are of the opinion that the pre-emptor must sue with all reasonable speed. The Ḥanafī jurists say that the pre-emptor must make three specific demands for his right of pre-emption.

The right of *Shufa'* it should be noted, has not been mentioned in the text of the Holy Qur'ān but certainly the prophetic guidance contained in the hadith make reference to this right. In reality this is the right of good neighbourliness in which case a neighbour tries to save his neighbour an embarrassment and problems which may otherwise be caused because of the nearness of the house or property or land situated to each other. As we have seen, it simply amounts to the right which the owner of an immovable property possesses to acquire by purchase another immovable property which has been sold to another person. The neighbour must be consulted before such sale is executed since he has the first right either to purchase that property or to have reasonably good people as owners of property in this neighbourhood.

Categories of Pre-emptors:

Shāfi' al-Sharīk: Whenever the right of pre-emption is in respect of a partner in the property of the land which is sold commonly it is called *Shāfi' al-Sharīk*. This right is derived from the prophetic ḥadīth which says: "The right of *Shufa'* holds in a partner who has not divided off and taken separately his share."

Shāfi al-Khalīt: Whenever this right is in respect of a partner in the immunities and appendages of the land it is called *Shāfi' al-Khalīṭ*. This right is derived from the prophetic hadith which says: "A neighbour of a house has superior right to that house; and the neighbour of lands has superior right to those lands; and if he be absent, the seller must wait his return: provided, however, that they both participate in the same road."

Shāfi' al-Jar: Whenever such right is in respect of a neighbour it is called *Shāfi' al-Jar*. This right is derived from the prophetic hadith which says: "A neighbour has a right superior than that of a stranger in the lands adjacent to his own."

The following conditions are strictly to be adhered to while claiming or awarding the right of *shufa'*:

1. If there are a number of pre-emptors claiming the right of *shufa'*, a partner in property would be preferred to a partner in immunities and a partner in immunity is preferred to a neighbour. If the first relinquishes his right the second becomes entitled to it. When the second one gives up his right then the third, that is a neighbour, is entitled to pre-empt the property. This can be illustrated in a case when a large building is situated in a blind street and is jointly owned by two persons. When one of them sells the share the right of *shufa'* will logically be claimed by the partner in the building. Supposing he reliquishes his right, the people living in that street will claim the right without any distinction since they share the passage leading to that building. If they all give up their rights then the right will automatically devolve on to the neighbour who lives right behind the building.
2. If a non-Muslim buys a house from another non-Muslim not paying in cash but in commodities like wine and pigs, and if the right of *Shufa'* was claimed by another non-Muslim there is no harm in his substituting himself for the previous buyer by paying with the same commodity that is wine and pigs. But if the right of *Shufa'* is claimed by a Muslim he cannot, from the point of view of Shari'ah, pay in terms of wine and pigs. he can only pay in cash.[47]
3. There does not exist any right of pre-emption in auqaf, the pious endowments and establishments. In this case neither the person or persons managing the *wāqf* property (*mutawawli*) nor any beneficiary can claim this right.
4. There is no right of *shufa'* in the agricultural lands belonging to

Bait al-Māl, that is the public treasury.

The right of *shufa'*, it should be emphasised, exists only at the time of executing the sale and only in *'aqqār* that is immovable property only. This right is awarded on demand (*ṭalab*). A decree is to be obtained from the Qāḍī or judge as regards the ownership of the property only after a valid sale and after a cessation of the seller's ownership in the property sold is established. if the sale is invalid the right of pre-emption does not exist. Similarly, there is no right of pre-emption when the property is acquired by inheritance or gift or the property is given as dower or on hire. The right of *shufa'* can be claimed by Muslims and non-muslims alike, male or female, major or minor. For minor the father or guardian would claim the right.

The demand or *ṭalab* made by the person who is claiming the right of pre-emption is divided in the following three categories:

1. *Ṭalab al-Muwāthibah:* This means that the demand is made immediately. As for example, the moment that the person who is claiming the right of *shufa'* comes to know about the sale of the property, he must claim his right immediately without losing any time. Supposing he remains silent without making a *ṭalab* or claim of his right, the right would be extinguished. Imām Muḥammad al-Shaibānī, the Ḥanafī jurist is of the view that there is no harm if the demand is made at any time during the meeting in which the information of the sale is received. There is no special formulae in which the demand is expressed. It will be quite appropriate if the words or sentences show clear intention to exercise the right of pre-emption.
2. *Ṭalab al-Ishhād:* This means that the demand is made with invocation of witnesses. In this case the person claiming the right of *shufa'* calls witnesses to attest his demand which will provide him with proof in case the seller denies that demand was ever made. The pre-emptor then can call his witnesses to testify that he did make the demand in the presence of witnesses as soon as he heard of the sale. Thus, he did not abandon his right when he heard of the news of the sale before he rose from the meeting in which the news of the sale of the property reached him.
3. *Ṭalab al-Khaṣūmah:* This is a claim of the right of *shufa' by litigation. In this case, a person claiming the right of pre-emption petitions the judge to order the purchaser of the property to surrender it to him. This mode of claim is also known as Ṭalab al-Ṭamalluk* which in actual sense means obtaining the decree of the Qāḍī or the judge. The right of pre-emption will not be annulled if the pre-emptor is not in a position to litigate the matter due to illness or imprisonment. As far

as possible he should appoint an agent but if he is unable to do so the right of pre-emption will still exist and he can claim it later.

The right of *shufa'* becomes null and void when it is abandoned voluntarily (*Ikhtiyārī*). Once the sale has taken place, the pre-emptor says in no uncertain terms that he has made his right of pre-emption void or that he has waived the right of pre-emption. The right is rendered null and void necessarily (*ḍarūrī*) when the pre-emptor dies after making the demands and before taking possession of the property. In this case, the Hanafi jurists are of the view that the claimant's right is extinguished by his death. But if the seller of property dies the pre-emptor can still demand his right from the heirs of the owner of the property. If the seller of the property gives the property as a gift to the buyer, and brings witnesses while doing so, the right of pre-emption is invalidated. Likewise, when the owner of the property gives the property in *sadaqah* to someone the right of pre-emption is invalidated.

The right of *shufa'* is not exercised or claimed by many people in some Muslim countries (like West Africa) simply because they are unaware of such right. It is, therefore, the duty of the *'Ulamā* and the jurists to educate masses so that the right of *shufa'* may be properly claimed.

Notes

1. See *Durr al-Mukhtār*, vol. 4, p. 397; also see *Hidayah*, vol. 4 p. 466
2. Bukhārī ch. 55, Ḥadīth 2.
3. cf. Qur'ān, ch. 4:11-12.
4. cf. Qur'ān, ch. 2:180.
5. Bukhārī, ch. 55, Ḥadith 1.
6. cf. Bukhārī, ch. 55, Ḥadīth 2 and 3.
7. Abu Daud, ch. 17, Hadith 6.
8. Bukhārī, ch. 55, Ḥadīth 2.
9. Qayrawānī, *Risālah*, op. cit., ch. 35 *Bāb al-waṣāyā*, pp. 113-115.
10. Al-Shāfi'i, *Risālah*, op. cit., pp.
11. Qur'ān, ch. 2:180.
12. Qur'ān, ch. 2:240.
13. cf. Ṭabarī, Tafsīr, Vol. III, pp. 384-96; V. pp. 250-62.
14. Abū Dāūd, Vol. III, p. 113; Shawkānī, *Nayl al-Awtār*, Vol. VI, p. 43; Shāfi'ī, *Kitāb al-Umm*, Vol. IV, pp. 27, 36, 40.
15. Qur'ān, ch. 4:12.
16. Yūsūf 'Alī, *The Holy Qur'ān*, op. cit., note 273.
17. Fyzee A.A.A., *Mohammedan Law*, p. 348.
18. Ameer Ali, *Muslim Law*, 1938, p. 366.
19. See Musnad Abū Ya'lā and *Jāmī' Ṣaghīr*, Vol. 1, p. 454.
20. *Mishkāt* vol. 2, 645 and 647.
21. Qur'ān. ch. 2:215, for further definition of *Hibah* cf. Ibn Asim, *Tuhfat al-Ḥukkām*, rule 1191; *Ḥidāyah* vol. 3, p. 291.

22. Bukhārī, 51:1.
23. Bukhārī, 51:12.
24. Bukhārī, 51:14-15.
25. Bukhārī, 51:28-29.
26. Bukhārī, 51:11.
27. Bukhārī, 51:30.
28. Al-Qayrawānī, *Risālah*, op. cit., ch. 36: *Bāb fil Shuf'ah wal Hibah* pp. 116-120.
29. Al-Qayrawani, *Risalah*, op. cit., ch. 36: *Bab fil Shuf'ah wal Hibah*, pp. 116-120.
30. *Fatāwā 'Ālamgiri* vol. 4, p. 526.
31. Ibn 'Āsim, *Tuḥfat al-Ḥukkām*, No. 1212 and 1213.
32. *Fatāwah 'Ālamgīrī*, vol 4, p. 537; *Durr al-Mukhtar* vol 3, p. 499.
33. For detailed study of *waqf*, see shalabi (Dr.) Muḥammad Muṣṭafā, *Muḥāḍarat fil wāqf wal waṣiyyah*, cairo 1956, p. 9.
34. *Tirmidhī* and *Bukhārī.*
35. *Ṣaḥīḥ al-Bukhārī* — see *Waṣāyā*, ch. 17.
36. This is the view of Imam Abū Ḥanīfa. See Ibn'Ābdīn. *Ḥāshiyah Radd al-Muḥtār*, vol. 3, p. 493.

37. See Al-Shāfi'i, *Kitāb al-Umm*, vol. 3, p. 281; *Al-Baḥr*, vol. 5, p. 209; *Sharḥ al Bājī lil Muwaṭṭā*, vol. 6, p. 122.
38. This is the opinion of Imām Abū Ḥanīfah.
39. For detailed study of the concept of *wāqf*, see Shalabi, Dr. Muḥammad Muṣṭafā, *Muḥāḍarāt fil waqf wal Wasiyyah*, Cairo 1956, p. 9.
40. Al-Ili, 'Abdal-Ḥakīm Ḥasan, Al-Ḥurriyat al-'Āmmah, Cairo 1974, pp. 505-506.

41. Khālid Rashīd, *Wakf Administration in India*, New Delhi 1978, P. xviii.
42. Von Kremer, *The Orient under the Caliphs*, translated by Khudā Buksh, University of Calcutta, 1920, P. 285: also c.f. Khalid Rashid op. cit, P. xix.
43. Ameer Ali, *The short history of Saracenes*, London, 1951, P. 422.
44. Khalid Rashid, *Muslim Law*, Lucknow, 1979, P. 140. This statement is quoted an the authority of Professor Humayun Kabir at one time Minister of Scientific Research and Cultural Affairs and *Auqaf* in India.
45. For Definition of Shufa see *Durr al-Mukhtar* vol. 4 p. 126; *Hidaya* vol. 3, p. 561 and *Fatāwah 'Ālamgīrī* chapter 7.
46. For further details of aḥādīth on the same subject see *Muwaṭṭā* of Imām Mālik p. 371 and *Musnad* of Imām Abū Ḥanifah, p. 308.
47. cf. *Fatāwa 'Ālamgiri*, vol. 5, p. 383.

PART V

THE ECONOMIC SYSTEM

Chapter 20

Tijarah: Trade and Commerce

Guidance from the Qur'ān and Sunnah on Islamic Economic System

There are a number of Qur'ānic injunctions which have encouraged Muslims to engage themselves in lawful and wide range of trade and commerce. Some of the injunctions specially mention trade as *"Fadl Allāh"*, the bounties and excellence of Allah. There are a number of *Aḥādith* of the Prophet which also support the Qur'ānic injunctions. In order to do successful trade, Muslims have been asked to undertake travelling and long journeys.

«وَاٰخَـرُونَ يَضْـرِبُـونَ فِي ٱلْاَرضِ يَبْتَغُـونَ مِنْ فَضْلِ ٱللَّهِ وَاخَرُونَ يُقَاتِلُونَ فِي سَبِيلِ ٱللَّهُ»

"Some people will travel in seeking bounties of Allah (through trade) and some people will travel to fight war of defence (jihad) in the path of Allah."[1]

There are so many bounties of Allah mentioned in the Qur'ān, and one of them is the use of seas, oceans and rivers which help in internal and external trade and movements of goods and commodities.[2]

«وَتَرَى ٱلفُلْكَ فيهِ مَوَاخِرَ لِتَبْتَغُوا مِنْ فَضْلِهِ وَلَعَلَّكُمْ تَشْكُـرُونَ»

"And you see the ships there in that plough the waves (sail in the sea) in order that you may seek thus the bounties of Allah so that you may be thankful."[3]

Allah has also helped in blowing the air to sail the sea for way-farers seeking the bounties of Allah through trade:

«وَمِنْ آيَاتِهِ اَنْ يُرْسِلَ الرِيَاحَ مُبَشِّرَاتٍ وَلِيُذِيقَكُمْ مِنْ رَحْمَتِهِ وَلِتَجْرِىَ الْفُلْكُ
بِاَمْرِهِ وَلِتَبْتَغُوا مِنْ فَضْلِهِ وَلَعَلَكُمْ تَشْكُرُونَ»

"Among signs is this, that He sends the winds, as heralds of glad-tidings, giving you a taste of His Grace and Mercy, that the ships may sail majestically by His command and that you may seek of His Bounty: in order that you may be grateful."[4]

In *Sūrah al-Jum'ah* Muslims have been warned that their engagement in trade and business must not make them negligent of their duties to Allah, their Creator. As soon as the call for Friday's prayer is given, and likewise call for other prayers as well, we are asked to close our business and answer the call earnestly and loyally and submit to Allah:

يَا أَيُّهَا الَّذِينَ آمَنُوا اِذَا نُودِىَ لِلصَّلوٰةِ مِنْ يَوْمِ الْجُمُعَةِ فَاسْعَوْا اِلَىٰ ذِكْرِ اللّه
وَذَرُوا الْبَيْعَ - ذَلِكُمْ خَيْرٌ لَكُمْ اِنْ كُنْتُمْ تَعْلَمُونَ»

"O you who believe! when the call is proclaimed on Friday for prayer has been earnestly to the remembrance of Allah, and leave off business and traffic: that is best for you if you but knew."[5]

Apart from prayers, the Mosque provides for believers a meeting place, a place of consultation where social contacts are also established. A brother comes closer to a brother and thus it helps in cementing the relationship even outside the Mosque. After the prayers, we are asked to disperse in the land of Allah and continue our trade and transactions and earn our livelihood in the *ḥalāl* way:

«فَإِذَا قُضِيَتِ الصَّلوٰةُ فَٱنْتَشِرُوا فِى ٱلْأَرْضِ وَابْتَغُوا مِن فَضْلِ اللّهِ وَٱذْكُرُوا
اللّهَ كَثِيراً لَعَلَّكُمْ تُفْلِحُونَ»

"And when the prayer is finished, then may you disperse through the land, and seek the Bounty of Allah (through trade, business and undertaking lawful professions): and celebrate the praises of Allah so that you may prosper."[6]

But we are reminded that the business and trade must not make us forget our responsibility towards Allah and His servant while counting capital and profit at all times. During the time of the Prophet, once he was delivering a sermon and people heard the voices of a trade-caravan arriving. Some people rushed away without listening to the *Khutbah* (sermon) of the Prophet in order to carry out their trade with the incoming caravan. Therefore, the following verse was revealed as a reproach:

«وَاِذَا رَاَوْ تِجَارَةً اَوْ لَهْواً انفَضّوُا اِلَيْهَا وَتَرَكُوكَ قَائِماً قُلْ مَا عِنْدَ اَللّه خَيْرٌ مِّنْ اللَّهْوِ وَمِنَ اَلتِّجَارَةِ وَاللّهُ خَيْرُ الرَّازِقِينَ»

"But even when they have some bargain or some amusement they disperse headlong to it, and leave you standing. Say (O Prophet): 'The blessings from the presence of Allah is better than any amusement or bargain. And Allah is the best to provide for all needs."[7]

The Messenger of Allah himself had engaged in trade on behalf of Lady Khadījah, and has encouraged business through his own practice. He once said:

«التاجر الامين الصدوق مع الشهداء يوم القيامة»

"A trustworthy and an honest and truthful businessman will rise up with martyrs on the day of Resurrection."[8]

In yet another Ḥadīth, he has said:

«التاجر الصدوق الامين مع النبيين والصديقين والشهداء»

"A truthful, and trustworthy trader will rise up with the Prophets, the righteous and the martyrs."[9]

The wise words of the Prophet has given honest trading such a high status that those engaged in it are likened with the martyrs who gought and gave their lives in *Jihād fī sabīl Allāh* (war in the path of Allah). An honest trade will rise up with martyrs also means that if he continued his trade without deceiving people and without practicing usury and adhered to other principles of lawful trade, then it would be construed as if he passed his life waging *"Economic Jihād"*.

How should trade and business be carried out

The following code of conduct for Muslim traders is given in the Holy Qur'ān:

«يَـاأَيُّهَـا الَّـذِينَ امَنُـوا لَا تَأْكُلُوا اَمْوالَكُم بَيْنَكُم بِالْبَاطِلِ اِلَّا اَنْ تَكُونَ تِجَارَةً عَن تَرَاضٍ مِنْكُمْ»

"O you who believe, eat not each other's property by wrong means, but let there be amongst you trade and business through mutual good-will."[10]

The above verse of the Holy Qur'ān has set down an important principle concerning trade *(al-Tijārah)*. Every Muslim should live his life as if he is always in the presence of Allah. We have to think that we hold all the property as a trust from Allah, whether the property is in our own name or in someone else's name or belongs to the entire community. The Qur'ānic words *"the wrong methods (bil-bāṭil)"* refer to those practices which are against *Sharī'ah* and thus unlawful morally. The trade should be such that in the process there should be an exchange of benefits as profits without exercising any unlawful pressure or fraud on another party. There should be no bribery or usury in the trade.

The Qur'ānic verse emphasises on good-will in the trade which means that there should be no displeasure or disagreement between the parties in business relationship. In bribery or usury, one often thinks that there is no harm practising bribery or usury, with full agreement between the parties. In reality, even this agreement has come about by force of circumstances. In fact, there is still a great deal of concealed 'pressure' to enter into such an agreement just as it happens in gambling where there is seemingly an agreement between the gambling parties but in reality, that sort of tacit agreement has come about as a result of false hopes in their minds that they are going to win. One will not participate in gambling with the hope of losing.[11] Likewise, in fraudulent practices in trade there also seems to be an agreement between parties but it is not so as the loser in the fraud was unaware of the actual fraud. Had he known about it, he would have certainly refrained from it.

In *Sūrah al-Baqarah*, similar injunction occurs and believers are asked not to use their property to corrupt judges or others who are in authority with the intention of eating up wrongfully and knowingly other people's property.

«وَلَا تَأْكُلُوٓا أَمْوَالَكُم بَيْنَكُم بِالْبَاطِلِ وَتُدْلُوا بِهَآ إِلَى الْحُكَّامِ لِتَأْكُلُوا فَرِيقًا مِّنْ
أَمْوَالِ النَّاسِ بِالْإِثْمِ وَأَنتُمْ تَعْلَمُونَ»

"And do not eat up each other's property by wrong means, not use it as bait for judges, with intent that you may eat up wrongfully and knowingly a little of other people's property."[12]

Although the above verse speaks of corrupting the judges and other authorities in acquiring someone's property, many such cases arise out of contractual trade agreements between two parties and the cases to the the court of law where the influential party through the help of bribes win the case wrongfully and thus acquire someone else's property.

The Qur'ānic injunction puts a stop to such practices. Even though the court may order in favour of the wrong party, it will not become lawful *(Ḥalāl)* for him as the Ḥadith of the Prophet testifies:

«انمــا انــا بشــر وانتم تختصمــون الى ولعــل بعضكم يكون الحق بحجته من بعض، فأقضى له على نحو ما اسمع منه - فمن قضيت له بشيء من حق اخيه فانما اقضى له قطعة من النار».

"There is no doubt that I am a human being. It is likely that you may bring a case to me and one of the parties among you may be stronger in putting forward argument as compared to the other, and I may decide the case in his favour from whatever I have heard. But one who acquired something from his brother's right due to such verdict, in reality he acquires nothing but a piece of hell."

As it is a human weakness, greed and temptations everpower man, particularly the greed of wealth and property. According to a Ḥadīth, a man gets older and two things become younger in him – the desire to collect more wealth and live longer. Ordinarily, honest men and true believers in Allah are content with whatever they get. In their trade and business they are straight forward and they establish right with justice as commanded by Allah:

«وَاَقيمُوا ٱلْوَزْنَ بِالقِسْطِ وَلاَ تُخْسِرُوا ٱلْمِيزَانَ»

"So establish weight with justice and fall not short in balance."[13]

Every Muslim must be honest in every matter, such as weighing out things which he is selling and in all other dealings with other people. He must not cheat by showing specimen of a good quality and then selling inferior stuff, or giving less weight than agreed upon.

Every Muslim is asked to earn his livelihood in a lawful manner. If one collects property through unlawful means and then gives out charity *(Ṣadaqah)* and Ẓakāt to the poor and needy, it will not be acceptable to Allah. On the contrary, he will be deemed to have committed a sin.

«من جمع مالا من حرام ثم تصدق به لم يكن له فيه اجر وكان اجره عليه».

"Whosoever gathered unlawful riches and then gave out in charity, he will have no reward; on the contrary he will have to bear the burden of his evil deed."[14]

Any property earned in an unlawful manner and through *haram* means, will have no blessings from Allah, and whatever property he leaves behind for his proginy, also becomes a source of greater problems in this world and the next world. Allah, our Creator, does not wipe out evil with evil or dirt with dirt. Any property earned with evil means continues its evil effect for generations to come. The lawful property acquired with lawful means will have its blessings which will become perceptible even among one's children.

The Messenger of Allah has said:

«لا يكسب عبدا مالا حراما فيتصدق به فيقبل منه. ينفق منه فيبارك له فيه، ولا يتركه خلف ظهره الا كان زاده الى النار ان الله تعالى لا يمحوا السيء بالسيء ولكن يمحو السيء بالحسن، ان الخبيث لا يمحو الخبيث».

"When a servant of Allah earns property in an unlawful manner and then gives it in charity, it will not be accepted of him. There will be no blessing in that he spends and that he leaves behind (for his dependants) but it becomes a provision for the fire of hell. In reality, Allah does not wipe out evil with evil, but erases evil with good action. Undoubtedly, dirt does not clean dirt."

When we try to understand the Divine injunctions and their further explanations given by the Prophet in his *Aḥādīth,* it becomes clear that the Divine laws strike at the very root of the evils resulting from the modern form of capitalism. They enjoin rules or morality upon man in his earning and spending and hold him responsible for the well-being of his fellowmen. Hoarding is thus condemned,[15] and usury forbidden;[16] extravagance is denounced[17] and moderation enjoined.[18] Wealth is not to be devoured in vanity[19] but is to be developed by fair means and through traffic and trade so that it is used for the welfare of the community, hence no cause for socialism.

The Qur'ān thus enjoins the cardinal values of equity, justice, mutual co-operation and self-sacrifice for re-organising the socio-economic milieu of the Islamic society. The Holy Prophet has said: "If allah makes anyone in charge of some job of the Muslims and he neglects their requirements, He will also neglect him in time of his need." He has further said: "An office is a trust; it is a humiliation except for those who rise equal to the task and pay everyone his due." Again, "if somebody in a community sleeps hungry until the next morning, Allah will withdraw His security from that community." It was on this basis that Caliph 'Umar declared: " 'Umar, the son of Khaṭṭab would be answerable to Allah if a camel starves to death along the Euphrates."

A study of the teachings of the Qur'ān and the Holy Prophets sayings suggests the objective of setting up an economic order which enforces justice, stops exploitation and sets up a contented, satisifed society. Islamic state, in a nutshell, is a real welfare state. What the early Islamic governments did to achieve this objective can be a subject of a voluminous book.

Directions for Sale Transactions

Men and women are allowed to engage in lawful trade in the Sharī'ah.

In the Ḥadith, men and women are mentioned as selling to and buying from one another. In other words there is no sex disqualification.[20] All are equally entitled to do trade, hence while a transaction is being carried on with one man, another should not intervene.[21] The Sharī'ah allows an auction.[22]

Hoarding any food item is unlawful.[23] It is through this inhuman practice that the society suffers a lot. The cattle seller is prohibited from leaving them unmilked for some days before selling, so that they may fetch a higher price.[24] This is a mere deception. Fruits or crops must not be reaped before they are in a fit condition because it may give rise to disputes.[25] The fruits on trees can only be sold if they are property valued.[26] The imaginary sale of things, when there are no goods to deliver, are totally prohibited.[27] Likewise, one should not sell what one does not possess. The sale of land is generally discouraged, and it is recommended that one should not sell his land or another house with the same money. The taking of oaths in sale transactions is also expressly forbidden. This practice is very rampant in many Muslim countries where traders keep on taking oaths to describe their merchandise and their prices.

The Holy Qur'ān as we have seen before, lays stress on honest and straight forward dealing in the very earliest revelations: "Woe to the defaulters, who, when they take the measure out to others or weigh out for them, they are deficient."[28] "And give full measure when you measure out and weigh with a fair balance; this is fair and better in the end[29] and weigh things and do not act corruptly in the earth making mischief.[30] The Ḥadith of the Prophet also lays stress on honest dealing, so much so that if there is any defect in a thing it must be pointed out to the intending buyer.[31] The Holy Prophet is himself reported to have written to 'Adda' ibn Khālid as follows: "This is the writing by which Muḥammad, the Messenger of Allah, has made a purchase from 'Adda' ibn Khālid, the barter of a Muslim with a Muslim, there is no defect in it nor any deception nor an evil."[32]

According to another Ḥadīth he is reported to have said: "If the two parties speak the truth and make manifest, their transaction shall be blessed, and if they conceal and tell a lie, the blessing of their transaction shall be obliterated.[33]

Trade in all forms must be clean and honest. If one carries it out according to the guidance of the Qur'ān and the Sunnah, he will see Allah's blessings even though he may not be able to amass fabulous wealth. After all, as the Holy Prophet has said, nine parts out of ten of one's recommended livelihood lies in trade and commerce.

Trade was so much encouraged by the Messenger of Allah that when the *Muhājirūm* (immigrants) went to Medina due to the unbearable persecution of the Meccan pagans, the *Anṣār* (Helpers) became their brothers in faith, and not only gave them a shelter but also distributed their belongings into half and gave them to *Muhājirūn*. Sa'd bin Rabi' al-Anṣārī divided all his property into two parts and gave one part to Abd al-Raḥmān bin 'Auf. 'Abd al-Rahmān said to Sa'd: "Brother I do not need all this. Show me if there exists any market place (where) I can do my business" Sa'd informed him that there was a big market of Bani Qayunqa'. Next day, Abd al-Raḥmān bin 'Auf went to this market with cheese and butter, and later became a very successful business man and used his property for the cause of Islam. Abd al-Rahman was merely following the examples of the Prophet, Abūbakar, 'Umar, and other companions of the Prophet who were engaged in lawful trade at one time or the other in their lives.

As long as there is not tyranny, deceit, hoarding, cut-throat competition, transaction involving usury, every Muslim is encouraged to do trade and business. The only trade that is declared unlawful is that of dealing in wine and other intoxicants, pigs and things made out of it, idols and images.

It is unlawful, as al-Qayrawānī says, in trading to swindle, cheat or lie in respect of price, or to deceive. Nor is it lawful to hide defects; nor is it lawful to mix a commodity of poor quality with one of good quality. Further, it is not lawful to a seller to hide some nature of his commodity, mentioning of which can stop the buyer from buying it or hiding a defect the mention of which can lower the price.[34]

Here it is pointed out that Allah is the real owner of all things and man only a legal owner, more appropriately, a trustee with unsufructary rights. Private property is, indeed, a trust in possession and one has to deal with it as is expected of a trustee. By the transfer of such property the owner cannot give better rights than he has for himself.

Law of Contract

The Arabic word for contract is *al-'aqd* which literally means an obligation or a tie. It is an act of 'putting a tie to a bargain'. When two parties enter into contract, it is called *al-in'iqād*, that is joining or tying up the offer and the acceptance together. The obligations thus arising out of contract are called *'Uqūd*. We are asked through Qur'ānic injunction to fulfil all our obligations:

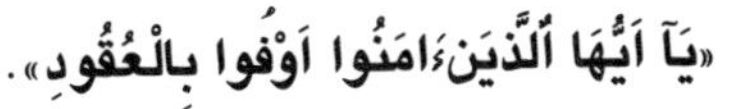

"O you who believe, fulfil all obligations."[35]

The word *'Uqūd* used in the Qur'ān is very meaningful and comprehensive. All human beings are required to fulfil *'Ḥuqūq Allāh,* the rights of Allah, by observing *salat* (Prayers), *Ṣaum* (Fasting), *Ẓakāt* (Poor-due) and *Hajj* (Pilgrimage) and the *Ḥuqūq al-'Ibād*, the rights of the servants of Allah like good neighbourliness, kindness and mercy to all human beings (and even animals). Thus the term *'Uqud* has a much wider connotation as compared to the term "contract" in common law.

Milk or Ownership in Islamic law refers to a relationship between a man and his property which is under his control to the exclusion of other claimants. One may have physical possession of the property *(Milk al-Yad)* or right of disposal of the property *(Milk al-Taṣarruf)* or may have the proprietary rights *(Milk al-Ragabah).*

The Law of Contract centres round the property (al-Māl)

Māl is something that exists and can be held in use and be beneficial at the time of need. Air and water cannot be secured and hence, cannot constitute *māl.* Likewise grass and wild trees would not be considered as *māl.* The usufruct of the property will also be included in *māl*, as for example, the rent to be collected by the landlord from his tenant in respect of the house let to him.

Consideration

In the Sharī'ah, a contract is made only when one party offers something to another party for some consideration and such other party accepts the offer. The offer and aceptance must be made in a free manner. The consideration must be lawful. The parties must also agreed upon their rights and duties.[36]

Offer

An offer is the first stage of making a contract. The offer can be made in a number of ways:

1. It can be made verbally *(Bil Kalām).* This kind of offer is to be made in the same meeting.
2. It can be made in writing *(Bil Kitābah).* This form of offer becomes effective as soon as the letter leaves the person offering and will remain valid until received by the recipient. The offer must be replied to immediately.
3. It can be made through a message sent with some person *(Rasul).* Whose honesty is not doubted and the offer is accepted, it will be a good acceptance. The Mālikī, Shāfi'ī and Ḥanbalī Jurists are of the opinion that the offer must be made by the owner of the property in return of due consideration. But the Hanafī Jurists say that it can

come from either party.

4. It can be made through signs and gestures particularly in those cases where the person offering is deaf or dumb or when the recipient does not understand the language of the person offering. The Māliki school regards as valid the known signs made by even a perfect peson since the main idea is that the person offering should communicate the offer. Most jurists believe that the known signs of dumb persons made to constitute an offer are valid, but there are some Jurists who consider signs and gestures invalid as modes of making an offer.

5. It can be made by conduct *(Fil)*. An offer made through the delivery of goods is valid according to the Māliki school. But an offer cannot be made through silence. If the contracting person keeps silent while he is expected to express himself, it will be deemed as a valid contract.

Withdrawal of an offer

The time between the making of an offer and its acceptance is called *Majalis al-'Aqd.* The Ḥanafi and Ḥanbali jurists say that the person offering has the option to withdraw his offer before it has been accepted. Since the person who is to receive, has been given the chance to make up his mind whether to accept or reject the offer, it seems equitable that the person offering should also have the right to withdraw his offer before acceptance is made. It is likely that the person offering might have made some mistake or forgotten to include something in his offer, therefore he can quickly withdraw his offer while the other party is still busy in making up his mind whether or not to accept it. But the Māliki School takes a different view and says that once the offer is communicated to the recipient the person offering has no right to withdraw the offer because he ought to have made up his mind before making an offer, but will not be permitted to change it later on.

Consideration

Consideration is an essential ingredient of a valid contract. Anything which is impossible to attain cannot form a valid consideration.[37]

Consideration must be lawful. Therefore, wine, pork etc., which are not lawful in Islam cannot be offered as consideration. A contract by a Muslim to sell grapes or dates for preparing wine, will be invalid according to the Māliki and the Ḥanbali schools. Likewise, the sale of weapons to robbers or rebels will be void.

Competency of parties

The parties who want to enter into a contract must be legally competent to do so. A minor (one who has reached the age of puberty), or a slave, or an insolvent,or a person of unsound mind, or an intoxicated person cannot enter into a contract. Likewise, a person suffering from death illness (*maraḍ al-Maut*) cannot make a valid contract.[38]

Termination of contract

The contract can be terminated by the mutual consent of the parties according to the terms stipulated in their contract, or on the basis of the nature of the contract. Some contracts are terminated unilaterally, while there are others which would need the agreement of the parties. If the consent of one of the parties has been obtained to the contract in a manner which makes it unfree due to coercion, undue influence, fraud, misrepresentation or mistake then such party may avoid the contract at his option; but the other party cannot do so.

The contract of sale –ʿaqd al-Bayʿ

The contact of sale *(al-Bay)* means the delivery of a definite object which possesses legal value in exchange for something equivalent in value (called the price). The concept of sale also includes barter (i.e. exchange of one thing for the other of equivalent value) although there are a number of limitations on this. Price may be paid immediately on delivery of goods sold, or it may be paid after delivery of goods bought has been made, or goods may be delivered immediately and the price may be paid later. It is possible to postpone the payment of price as well as delivery of goods.

The seller *(Mushtarī)* and the buyer *(bāʿi)* are referred to by one generic name *al-ʿAqid.* The *ʿAqid* must possess the following qualifications:

1. He must be a *mumayyiz,* i.e. he must be able to understand the implications of the contract of sale. Thus an insane person or a minor who does not understand the implications of the contract of sale will not be a *mumayyiz*. However, according to all the schools (except Shāfiʿi) of Islamic Jurisprudence if a minor is *mumayyiz* the contract is valid.
2. He must be capable of disposing of his property.
3. He must be free to use his own discretion *(Mukhtār)* i.e. he must not be working under coercion, undue influence, misrepresentation, fraud or mistake.

The subject matter of sale

1. It must be owned by the seller of his agent.
2. It must be in a position to be delivered. The sale of a bird in the air or fish in the water is void.
3. It must be lawful *(Ḥalāl)* and wholesome *(Ṭahīr)*. The sale of

unwholesome things like wine, pig and dead animal (except fish) is void.

Ḥawālah: Assignment of Debts

Some contracts are assignable. As for example, if A lends some money to B, A may, by contracting with assign the claim to C. This is called *hawalah*[39] (i.e. assignment or transfer). Imām Mālik approves of such assignment but other Jurists of Shāfi'i and Ḥanbali schools oppose it, while the Ḥanafis allow it in exceptional cases. But all the Jurists permit A to sell his claim against B to anyone A likes or to make a gift of it to any person other than the debtor, B. The following are the conditions requisite for a valid *ḥawālah*:

1. The debt which is the subject matter of the contract must be a lawfully subsisting obligation.
2. The original creditor (A) and debtor (B) must mutually agreed that the debt should be paid by B to C, the assignee debt which constitutes the object of the transfer.
3. The debt must have fallen due, even though it consists in the price to be paid by a slave for his freedom; but it is not necessary that the debt owed to the transferor should have fallen due.
4. Both debts must consist in objects of the same kind, equal in quantity and quality; there are several opinions however, as to the varying fineness of coins.
5. The two debts must not consist of foodstuffs which have been purchased.

The Gharar Sale (Bay'al-Gharar)

The *Gharar* sale is a kind of sale in which uncertainty is involved, such as the sale of fish or birds before they are caught or produced by the vendor. The Messenger of Allah has forbidden the *gharar* sale, the sale of dry dates for ripe dates except the sale of *'Arayā.* Where two or more distinct articles are the objects of a single sale, the price of each should be individually known and determined, otherwise the transaction is void for uncertainty *(Gharar).* The *gharar* sale in other words, involves speculative risks in contract.

نهى رسول الله صلى الله عليه وسلم عن بيع الحصادة وبيع الغرر.

"The Messenger of Allah forbade the sale through fraudulent means or the gharar sale."

The *gharar* sale resembles the present sale of future goods recognised by Sale of Goods Acts in the Common Law Countries.

The Muzābanah and 'Ariyyah Sales: A Misunderstanding Removed

The Aḥādīth in *Muwaṭṭā* of Imām Mālik on the subject of *Muzābanā* sale are as follows:

حدثنى يحى عن مالك عن نافع عن عبد الله بن عمران ان رسول الله صلى الله عليه وسلم نهى عن المزابنة بيع الثمر بالتمر كيلا

"It is reported by Yaḥyā from Mālik from Nāfi'from 'Abdullāh bin'Umar that the Messenger of Allah (may peace be upon him) forbade the *Muzāban* sale; and *Muzābana* is the sale of unripe fruits on the tree against the dried fruits." [40]

In another *Ḥadīth*, Muzābana sale is mentioned as:

«المزابنة اشتراء الثمر بالتمر فى رؤوس النخل»

Muzābana is a general rule while *'Ariyya* is an exception in the principles of contract of sale. *Muzābana* form of contract can be applied in any commodity, but *'Ariyya* is only applicable in the case of sale of fruits for dried dates. *Muzābana* is possible in any form of crop in the field to be sold. For example in case of wheat crops, grapes, dates with approximate weight *(Kail)*. Dry fruits and fresh fruits cannot be bartered, othrwise it becomes *Muzābana*.[41] It is classified by the following Ḥadith:

عن سعد ابن ابى وقاص سمعت رسول الله صلى الله عليه وسلم يسئل عن اشتراء التمر بالرطب فقال لمن حوله «ان ينقص رطب اذا كيس»، قالوا: نعم. فنهى عن ذلك

The Hadith on *'Ariyyah* sale mentioned in the *Muwaṭṭā* is as follows:

حدثنى يحى عن مالك عن نافع عن عبدالله بن عمر عن زيد بن ثابت ان رسول الله صلى الله عليه وسلم ارخص لصاحب العربة ان يبيعها بخرصها

Imām Shāfi'ī says in his book *Kitāb al-Umm* that a man may purchase unripe fruits in return for ripe dates on a condition that when it is ripe, he will get it from him by giving *tamar* immediately[42] because he needs it.

Imām Mālik says that *Tamar* may be given afterwards *(Muwajjalan)*. The difference lies in time. *'Ariyya* was a special permission given in the case of dealing between a rich man and a poor man, particularly when a rich person wanted to give the unripe dates to his poor neighbour as a *ṣadaqah* (charity), but it becomes cumbersome that the man keeps on coming in his compound to see whether fruits are ready. Besides, he may need dry fruits urgently hence the rich person can give ripe fruits and buy unripe ones by approximation so as to save him from trouble. Imam Ahmad bin Hanbal reports from Sufyān Ibn Ḥasain that *'ariyya* used to be given to the needy who could not wait until they became ripe.

Hence a permission *(Rukh..ṣah)* given in Ḥadith that a poor man can sell by whatever he may get.[43] Yaḥyā bin Sa'īd Anṣāri further defines it that *'Ariyyah* is that a man buys unripe fruit to feed his children ripe but undried fruits. So he may calculate roughly with dried dates and may buy it. This is a special dispensation.[44] Imām Mālik says that during the time of famine, the Arabs used to give *ṣadaqah* to the poor people of some trees full of unripe dates just as owners of herds of camels and goats used to give one or two of them to drink their milk.[45] Imām Mālik confines *'Ariyyah between Muwhūb lahu* and *wahib* only, but Imām Aḥmad bin Ḥanbal says it can be given to any one.[46]

Imam Malik further says that *'Ariyya* is that fruits which are in someone else's orchard. The owner of land does not like frequent visits by the owner of one or two trees, then the owner of land and more trees can give dried dates for the approximate fruits on the tree. This is also permissible.[47] Imām Mālik's view is based on the principle of *Taḍarrur*, so that one may not interfere in someone else's property. According to Imām Mālik:

العريه ان يعرى الرجل نخله، ثم يتأذى بدخوله عليه فرفض له ان يشتريها منه»

It will be clear from these examples, therefore, that to regard the *Muzābana* sale and the *'ariyya* sale as the same is to misunderstand completely their provisions and significance as stipulated in the *Ahadith* in the two types of sale.

After discussing *Muzābana* and *'Ariyya* contracts, professor Coulson says in his book *A History of Islamic Law:*

> "The *Muwaṭṭā* here simply reflects the stage of a *rough and uneasy compromise* between the comparatively liberal and practical outlook of the earliest scholars and the rigid approach of the doctrinaire group."[48]

One is at a loss to find 'an uneasy and rough compromise' in such a simple and straight forward Prophetic solution and special dispensation in the matter of *'Ariyyah.* For a Muslim scholar, it is difficult to see such watertight compartments between the imaginary 'doctrinaire group' and 'earliest scholars' which did not exist during that period. To us they were all *Salaf al-Ṣāliḥīn* our pious predecessors who, we believe, were pure and who strictly followed the foot-steps of the Messenger of Allah and depended solely on the Book of Allah and Sunnah of His Messenger.

The Doctrine of Khiyār al-Majlis

"Each of the parties to a contract of sale has the option against the other party as long as they have not separated". *This Ḥadīth of the Prophet* expresses the doctrine known as *Khiyār al-Majlis*, which gives the parties to a contract, duly completed by offer and acceptance, the right to repudiate the agreement during the session *(majlis)* of the bargain. Imām Mālik comments on this Ḥadīth in the following words: "Here in Medina we have no such known limit and no established practice for this" and the points he then proceeds to discuss show that for Imām Mālik a contract was binding as well as complete immediately mutual agreement had been reached. Professor Coulson remarks on the point of view of Imām Mālik in the following words: "This is one of the many occasions on which the law expressed in the reported precedents of the Prophet or later authorities was rejected by the early Medinan scholars when it ran counter to their currently accepted doctrine."[49] He erroneously brands the above quoted Hadith of the Prophet as merely "the alleged statement of the Prophet".[50]

Professor Coulson falls into a grave error of assuming that Imām Mālik was in a habit of rejecting the Prophetic traditions and the authority of the Prophet's precepts expressing Islamic Law. *The Muwaṭṭā*, on the contrary shows that Imām Mālik always quotes a Ḥadīth or a precedent of *Khulafā'al-Rāshidūn* or very prominent *sahabah*. Many Muslim scholars of the past have considered the *Muwaṭṭā* as a book that has rendered a great service to the cause of collection of *Aḥādīth* even long before.

Imām Bukhārī and Imām Muslim and other scholars of Hadith began to compile their authentic manuals of Ḥadīth much later. As we have seen before, great scholars like Imam Shāfi'i have rated the *Muwaṭṭā* as a book 'the most authentic book after the Book of Allah'.

The misunderstanding in the above example of our learned friends arises out of the statement of Imam Mālik in the *Muwattā* in the matter of *Khiyār al-Majlis*, which is as under:

وليس لهذا عندنا حد معروف ولا امر معمول به

"There is no such known limited an established practice for those here (in Medina)."[51]

The above statement does not in the least disregard or reject the most authentic Ḥādith the Prophet (S.A.W.) quoted in the beginning of the chapter 38 *(bāb Bay' al-Khiyār)*. Imām Mālik has only stated the fact as to what operated in his time in Medina. It should be pointed out that it is typical of the Mālikī school that *'amal ahl al-Medina'* (the practice of the people of Medina)[52] is very much relied upon. Even so, the practice of the people of Medina, which Imām Mālik mentioned here, was based on the Sunnah of the Prophet (S.A.W.). It was the learned and pious and Imam's view that Medina was the birth-place of the Prophet, the nerve centre of the *Ummah*, the centre where important legal verdicts were given by the Prophet and the Righteous Caliphs, the place where the companions and their followers lived and taught strictly according to the *Kitāb Allāh* and the Sunnah of the Prophet. Hence, the practice of the people of Medina could not really be contrary to the Sunnah of the prophet especially during the early period in which Imām Mālik lived and taught.

As far as the doctrine of *Khiyār al-Majlis* is concerned, other schools of law have contested the validity of the doctrine itself.[53] Even there were some scholars like Ibn Ha j ar who were of the opinion that the doctrine does not contradict *'amal ahl-Medina'* because it had been the view of Ibn'Umar, Sa'īd bin al.Musayyib, Al-Ẓuhrī and Ibn Abī Zib who were eminent leaders in their ages in Medina.[54]

The Forbidden Contracts of Sale

The following contracts of sale are forbidden in the Sunnah of the Prophet. They are self explanatory:

1. *Two transactions in one sale:*

نهى النبى صلى الله عليه وسلم عن بيعتين في بيعه.

"The Messenger of Allah has forbidden making one contract of sale into two transactions of sale."[55]

2. *Extra condition attached to a sale:*

نهى رسول الله صلى الله عليه وسلم عن بيع وشرط.

"The Messenger of Allah has forbidden to attach an extra condition with a sale transaction."[56] The contract must not be combined with a conditional agreement.

3. *Sale of what one does not own:*

نهى رسول الله صلى الله عليه وسلم ان ابيع ما ليس عندى.

"The Messenger of Allah forbade me to sell a thing which is not my property."[57]

4. *Al-Mulāmisah and Al-Munābidhah Sales:*

نهى رسول الله صلى الله عليه وسلم عن الملامسة والمنابذة

"The Messenger of Allah forbade me to sell a thing which is not my property." or selling something that is not apparent and seen clearly."[58]

5. *Al-Najash forbidden:*

نهى رسول الله صلى الله عليه وسلم عن النجش

"The Messenger of Allah has forbidden dishonesty and bad behaviour in transaction."[59]

6. *Talaqa Rukbān:*

نهى رسول الله صلى الله عليه وسلم عن تلق الركبان

"The Messenger of Allah has forbidden to go out of the town and meet the caravan and do trade with them through tricking the people of the town."[60]

This sort of trade can lead to fraudulent practices such as buying things at a very cheap rate in order to sell at an exhorbitant price since the people of the town would not be able to discover the actual price. It might also be to deceive the caravan traders by offering them a low price until they come to the town and discover that they were cheated. Similarly, during the famine period, the traders might go out to nearby villages to buy food-stuff from simple villagers at a nominal price without telling them the current market price in the town.

7. *Bai' Ḥadīr Lilbādi:*

نهى رسول الله صلى الله عليه وسلم ان يبيع حاضر لباد.

"The Messenger of Allah has forbidden that a city dweller fraudulently acts as a self imposed agent for sale and purchase of the simple villagers."

This Ḥadīth refers to two types of transactions: a cunning city-dweller has a lot of merchandise in the city which he could easily sell. But, in order to gain big profits takes the commodity to sell in the villages although the city-dwellers are badly in need of those things. Secondly, he tries to stop the direct sale between the villagers and the city-dwellers, and becomes a self-imposed agent on behalf of the villagers and buys commodities on their behalf at an exhorbitant price.

Shirākah: Partnership

The word sharing and partnership in activities has occured several times in the Qur'ān – Moses prays to Allah to make Hārun, his brother, his partner in his great mission to Pharaoh:

هارون اخى اشدد به ازرى وَاَشرِكْهُ فِى اَمْرى

"Harun (is) my brother; add to my strength through him, and make him share my task."[61]

Sharing the estate in *Mirāth* as partners is mentioned in *Sūrah al-Nisā:*

«فَاِنْ كَانُوا اَكْثَر مِنْ ذٰلك فَهُمْ شُرَكَاءُ فِى الثُّلُث»

"But if (they are) more than two, they are sharers (*Shuraka*) in a third."[62]

Shirakāh or partnership contract signifies the conjunction of two or more persons to carry on a business to share the profits by joint investment. In the widest sense of the term *Shirākah*, the partnership exists where property is held in common between two or more co-proprietors. A person thus alienates an undivided share of his property, in return for an undivided share of the property of another each having a right to administer the whole.[63]

The *Shirākah* may be effected in a specified amount of capital or in labour on contribution of labour and skill or in credit where no capital is contributed and the partners buy and sell on credit on understanding that they shall share the profits. There may be a *Shirākah* of mixed characters in cases of capital and labour, Agricultural farms and labour and so on and so forth.[64]

Shirkāh al-'Inān: Limited Partnership

Shirkāh al-'Inān is a limited partnership in which on partner is not allowed to do anything without his co-partner.

Shirkah al-Abdān: Association of Bodies or Labour Association

Islamic Law allows two or more persons to associate themselves for the exercise of a profession or a handicraft. The profits will be practically equal for the partners with a view to lending mutual assistance even through the associates work separately. Imām Mālik says in *Mudawwanah al-Kubrā* that the stock of tools may be provided by each partner in such labour associations, but the other Jurists say that the tools will be owned by the association or hired by the association at common expense. In this kind of *Sharikah,* any payment received or engagement entered upon by one of the associates for some work done or to be done binds the other, and the payment remains at their risk even after the dissolution of the *Sharikah*. It will be illegal for one of the associates to hold a greatly predominant share in the stock of tools by one of the associates of the *Sharikah.*

Qirad: Dormant Partnership

Qirad agreement is a contract by which a person entrusts funds to a trader *(amil)* in order that he shall trade with it, subject to the lender having a share in the profit.[65] Thus, in *Qirad*, the capital is handed over to an agent to trade with, and the contract comes into force when the agent starts his trading journey. *Qirad* was encouraged by the Prophet himself, and it was a common form of trading in the early days of Islam. The commercial enterprises in the time of the Prophet used to be organised under the charge of a caravan leader commissioned by one or more rich persons of the society.

In the contract of dormant partnership, a certain fixed capital is handed over to agent on condition that the person entrusting it shall participate in the profits in certain proportion. The dormant partner remains the owner of the capital. The agent is only in possession by virtue of the trust reposed in him. He is only held responsible for negligence or the breaking of the rules of the contract.

Capital in Qirad Partnership

In the dormant partnership, the capital should not consist of a debt owed by a debtor to his creditor nor should it consist of a pledge or of a security. That is, the debtor or the holder of the pledge should not be the agent and the creditor should not be the dormant partner. Capital should not consist of debased coins nor of goods which the agent has taken upon himself to realise because in these cases the value of the capital cannot be strictly determined. It is prohibited in a *Qirad* contract that all there is of the enterprise are turned upon the agent. The dormant partner will continue to remain the owner of the capital. The agent is only in possession by virtue of the trust reposed in him. In *Qirad* partnership, the risk for the enterprise should not be thrown upon the agent, otherwise the contract will become invalid. It is prohibited that the shares should not remain ambiguous or fake, otherwise, it will create confusion later on. The agent will be required to perform his duties in good faith taking into consideration the good of the entrepreneur. He should take the same amount of care as he would do if the concern were solely his own.

Difference between Ordinary Partnership and the Qirad Partnership

The ordinary partnership has its existence where the partners live. The shares involved in ordinary form of partnership are small. All the partners place an active part in the concern and each contributes its share of the capital. In the *Qirad* or dormant partnership, on the other hand, a capitalist furnishes the funds but the active agent operates the concern almost without control. The agent can be far from the place where the contract was entered into. In the *Qirad* partnership the capital must consist as a general rule in cash but in the ordinary form of partnership it is not so.

Muḍārabah: Co-Partnership

Ḍarb fil arḍ or moving about in the land of Allah seeking for trade or work is mentioned in *Sūrah al-Baqarah.*[66] Perhaps, the word *Muḍārabah* is derived from this Qur'ānic phrase.

Mudarabah, in legal terminology, is a contract in which certain property or stock *(Rās al-Māl)* is offered by the owner or proprietor *(Rabb al-Māl)* to the other party to form a joint partnership in which both parties will participate in profit.[67] The other party is entitled to a profit in lieu of his labour since he is giving to manage the property *(Muḍārib).* It is a contract of co-partnership. It is proposed by Muslim economics that the Islamic interest – free banking system can best be established on the principles of *Muḍārabah.*

Wakālah: Agency

The word *Wakil* appears about twenty four times in the Holy Qur'ān. In the following verse in *Sūrah al-An'ām,* it is used to convey the meaning "a person responsible for arranging one's affair":

«وَكَذَّبَ بِهِ قَوْمُكَ وَهُوَ الْحَقُّ قُلْ لَسْتُ عَلَيْكُمْ بِوَكِيلٍ»

"But your people (O Prophet) reject you though it is the Truth. Say: "not mine is the responsibility for arranging your affairs".[68]

The same word is further repeated in verse 107 of the same *Sūrah* to convey the same meaning:

«وَمَا أَنْتَ عَلَيْهِمْ بِوَكِيلٍ»

"Nor are you set over them to dispose of their affairs."[69]

In Islamic Law, *Wakālah* or agency arises where one person authorises another to replace him in the exercise of his civil rights. The person thus authorised is called *wakil. Wakil* can be entrusted with all acts which can be done by a representative, such as concluding or rescinding a contract, collecting a sum due, assigning a debt or discharging a debtor, even though the amount of the debt be unknown to all three. Once one appoints his *wakil*, the latter should not make any formal admission unless he has full powers. The principle cannot delegate his *wakil* to take an oath on his behalf, nor can he appoint an agent to commit an illegal act. A general agent can be appointed to deal with all matters, on behalf of the principal except the principal's divorce, or for giving consent to the marriage of the principal's virgin daughter or to sell the principal's house. If he is a special agent, his powers will be limited according to the instructions given by the principal.

Obligations of a Wakīl

A *wakil* will be responsible to sell or buy for the price, and should declare clearly to the third party: "I am sent by my principal Mr. M in order to that, you may sell to him this and this". He will be responsible for any breach of warranty in the thing already sold, unless the buyer has been informed that the vendor was acting simply as an agent for Mr. M. He must accept only legal tender as the payment, or if the principal has *authorised, he may accept as barter in a halal* manner. He must, however, conform to the current market price, otherwise the principal is not bound to ratify his transactions.

It is essential for the wakil to comply with the instructions given by his principal, otherwise the latter may refuse to accept the purchase or part with merchandise. Likewise, if the thing is bought at a reduced price or has some defect. He should also comply with his principal's instructions as to the time and place of the purchase or sale, nor should he raise or reduce the price of the commodity for which limits are agreed and fixed although fluctuations up to five percent (5%) will be tolerated. If the *Wakil* exchanges food-stuff from food-stuff or has exchanged gold for gold, the principal may rescind the sale. The principal is bound to ratify a sale or puchase made by his *Wakil* under more favourable but lawful terms.

The *Wakīl* cannot sell to himself the wares which are given to him for sale, nor can he sell them to one of his wards under his guardianship although he is allowed to sell to his wife since, in Islamic Law, it is only the person of the spouses that are in common, not their personalities. A Muslim must not appoint a Jew, a Christian or an enemy of his debtor as his agent in the transactions of sale and purchase although there are differences of opinion on this subject looking at the complex nature of modern society.

If the principal and his *wakīl* have independently of each other sold the same goods, the first sale in point of time shall be considered valid provided the subsequent sale was not followed by immediate delivery. The *wakīl* must obtain a receipt for the payment of the principal's debt, otherwise, in case of complaints, the *wakīl* will be held liable. The principal will remain the vendor's debtor so long as the vendor has not received his purchase money.

Ḍamān: Guarantee

Ḍamān or guarantee is a form of contract by which the third person constitutes himself liable for the debt of another. He is called *Ḍāmin.* According to Islamic Law, a person who becomes *ḍāmin* or surety must be enjoying full civil rights. A married woman or even a sick person can become *ḍāmin* to the extent of the responsibility of the value of the disposal of the third of the property. Such a surety *(ḍāmin)* may be given for a debt which is not yet due and may be paid at once provided it is one which can be legally extinguished before it has fallen due. The extension of period may be sought by the *ḍāmin* provided the debtor is solvent. If he has the means to discharge the debt, it will be considered illegal to ask for such an extension through surety. A *Ḍāmin* or a surety can withdraw so long as the loan has not been made, but he cannot withdraw prior to the creditor taking an oath as to the existence of the debt. The debt in question must be such that it can be discharged by the surety. The *ḍāmin* has his remedies if his principal proves to be a defaulter. He can sue him in the court of the *Qāḍī* for what he has paid either in money or in kind but he will have to prove that such payment was made. Everything that discharges the obligation of the principal debtor also discharges the obligation of the *ḍāmin* (surety). If the surety dies, the payment of the debt that he has guaranteed is to be made chargeable upon his estate. A surety can be sued as long as the debtor is present and solvent. In the case where several persons constitute themselves as sureties for one debtor and for one and the same debt, the creditor can only claim from each co-surety the amount each has given guaranty for unless they have constituted themselves jointly and severally liable.

Ijārah: Hire

The contract of hire in Islamic Law is called *al-Ijārah* which is derived from an Arabic word *ajar* meaning remuneration or reward.

When one party sells to the other the temporary enjoyment of moveable property other than ships and animals in return for a price it is called *al-Ijārah.*[70] The price should be in proportion to the temporary enjoyment sold. The famous Mālikī scholar and jurist al-Dardır says that the words *Ijārah* and *ajar* are synonymous.

Ijārah is referred to in the Qur'ān in *Sūrah al-Qaṣaṣ* in respect of hiring the services of Moses by Jethro on the recommendation of his daughter after Moses had helped them in watering their flocks:

قَالَتْ اِحْدٰهُمَا يَاَبُتِ اسْتَاْجِرْهُ اِنَّ خَيْرَمَن اُسْتَاْجَرْتَ اْلقَوِىُّ اْلَامِينُ - قَالَ اِنّي
اُريـد اَنْ اُنكِحَـكَ اِحْـدَى اْبنَتَّى هَاتَـيْنِ عَلٰىَ اَنْ تَاْجُرَنى ثَمَـانِىَ حِجَـجٍ - فَاِنْ
اَتْمَمْتَ عَشْراً فَمِنْ عِنْدِكَ.

> "Said one of the girls: O my father, hire him on wages: Truly the best of men for you to employ is the man who is strong and trustworthy. He said: 'I intent to wed one of these my daughters to you, on condition that you serve me for eight years; but if you complete ten years, it will be grace from you'."[71]

The ships are excluded from the above definition of *Ijārah* because transport sea can only form the object of a conditional contract which is termed as *Miyārah,* the chartering of a ship.

For *Ijārah* to be valid, the ingredients essential are the lesser and the lessee, the thing which is to be hired, the price or remuneration for the hire, the consent of the hire. The contracting parties must be legally capable to enter into the *Ijārah* contract and there must be proper stipulation of price or remuneration.

The remuneration for hire is to be paid day by day but in the following cases, it is to be paid in advance:

1. If it consists of a definite object.
2. If there has been a stipulation to that effect.
3. If it is a local custom to do so.
4. If it is for hire of any animal for some definite journey which is not yet commenced.

The same value will apply in cases of modern means of transport.

The Ijarah contract will be void if it is combined with a conditional agreement, e.g. a person agrees to grind corn subject to his receiving the barn, or that he agrees to weave cloth in return for a proportional share of the cloth. The contract will be null and void if in a letting agreements of land, the rent is given in the form of food-stuff. The remuneration or salary in *Ijārah* contract may be fixed in proportion to the work to be done. A lesser may hire from his lessee the things he has let. A master who takes an apprentice may stipulate that the apprentice shall engage himself for one year.

The hired servants, workmen or persons hiring moveables will be considered as simple bailees, and hence, the risk will not be at their charge as long as there has been no negligence on their part. The caretaker of houses or workmen working for their employer or brokers or agents shown to be honest persons or sailors whose ship has been lost due to an act of Allah will not be deemed responsible for the loss or damage.

An agreement in respect of *Ijārah* can be rescinded if the hirer or lessee is evicted or if a workshop is closed by order of the government authorities or if a hired wet-nurse becomes pregnant or falls ill and is unable to nurse the child. The *Ijārah* agreement ceases on the death of the workmen engaged, but can not cease on the death of an employer.

Likewise, the *Ijārah* agreement ceases if the thing hired out is lost but not on the death of a person who has hired it. Where disputes arise is respect of a verbal letting agreement of land or houses, and neither side can prove their allegations, each party shall be called upon to make oath and the *Ijārah* contract shall be annulled.

Taḥkīm: Arbitration Contract

Taḥkim or Arbitration contract is that form of contract in which it is agreed that in case of any dispute or disagreement in the terms of contractual agreement, it will be settled through the appointment of a *ḥakam* or arbitrator.[72]

---

1. Qur'ān, ch. 73:20; 35:12; 62:10.
2. Qur'ān, ch. 73:20.
3. Qur'ān, ch. 35:12.
4. Qur'ān, ch. 30:46.
5. Qur'ān, ch. 62:9.
6. Qur'ān, ch. 62:10.
7. Qur'ān, ch. 62:11.
8. Ibn Mājah and al-Ḥākim.
9. Al-Hamimand al-Thirmidhī.
10. Qur'ān, ch. 4:29.
11. Maudūdī-Tafhim al-Qur'ān, (Urdū), vol. , p.
12. Qur'ān, ch. 2:188.
13. Qur'ān, ch. 55:9.
14. Ibn Khuzaimah, Ibn Ḥabbān and Al-Ḥākim.
15. Qur'ān, ch. 104:2.
16. Qur'ān, ch. 2:275.
17. Qur'ān, ch. 17:26.
18. Qur'ān, ch. 17:29.
19. Qur'ān, ch. 4:2.
20. Bukhārī, ch. 34, Ḥadīth 67.
21. Bukhārī, ch. 34, Ḥadīth 58.
22. Bukhārī, ch. 34, Ḥadīth 59.
23. Bukhārī, ch. 34, Ḥadīth, 54.
24. Bukhārī, ch. 34, Ḥadīth, 64.
25. Bukhārī, ch. 34, Ḥadīth, 85.
26. Bukhārī, ch. 34, Ḥadīth, 75, 82 and 83.
27. Bukhārī, ch. 34, Ḥadīth, 61.
28. Qur'ān, ch. 83:1-3.
29. Qur'ān, ch. 17:35.
30. Qur'ān, ch. 26:181-183.
31. Bukhārī, ch. 34, Ḥadīth 19.
32. Ibid.
33. Ibid.

34. Qayrawānī, *Risālah*, op. cit., See chapter: *Bāb fil buyū'wa mā Shakala al-Buyū'*, pp. 102-112.
35. Qur'ān, ch. 5:1.
36. Cf. Sahnūn, *Mudawwanāt al-Kubrā*, 15:197; Shāṭibī, *Muwaffiqāt fī Uṣūl al-Sharī'ah*, vol. 2, pp. 248-264; Kāsānī, *Al-Ṣanāi'wal Badā'i*, 7, 171.
37. Al-Jawzī, Ibn Qayyim, *I'lām*, vol. 3, p. 96; also see Al-Shātibī, *Muwaffiqāt*, op. cit., vol. 2, p. 327.
38. Al Shāfi'i, *Kitāb al-Umm*, vol. 3, p. 194; *Al-Mughnī:* vol. 4, p. 525; Kāsānī, *Al-Bādai*, cit., vol. 1, p. 170.
39. Al-Minhāj, p. 174; *Durr al-Mukhtār*, vol. 3, p. 201.
40. Mālik bin Anas, *Al-Muwatta*, ed. Muḥammad Fuad 'Abdul Bāqī, *Kitāb al-Buya* Ḥadith 23, Cairo (undated), p. 386. For further discussion on *Muzabana* and relevant *Aḥādīth*, see Bukhārī, *Bāb Bay al-Rutul bit tamar illa fil 'arāyā*. Also cf. Imām Shāfi'ī, *Risalah* (ed. Aḥmad Muḥammad Shākir), para 906.
41. Cf. Shaukānī, *Nail al-Awtār*, op. cit., p. 224.
42. Shaukānī, *Nail al-Awtar*, Cairo (undated), vol. 5, p. 227.
43. Shaukānī, *Nail al-Awtar*, vol. 5, p. 227.
44. Ibid, 227.
45. Ibid, 226.
46. Ibid, 226.
47. Tahawī reports from Imām Mālik. cf. Shaukānī *Nail al-Awṭār*, op. cit., p. 226.
48. Coulson, *A History of Islamic Law*, Edinburgh 1971, p. 44.
49. Coulson, *A History of Islamic Law*, Edinburgh 1971, p. 46.
50. Ibid.
51. *Muwatta*, op. cit., p. 416.
52. Ibid.
53. For an exposition of this see A. A. 'Abdallāh, *Khiyār al-Majlis or Option of the Meeting Place* (an unpublished article).
54. Ibid, also see Ibn Ḥajar, *Fatḥ al-Bārī Sharḥ Ṣaḥīḥ al-Bukhārī*, vol. 4, pp. 276-277.
55. Al-Nisāi and al-Tirmidhi.
56. Al-Ṭibrān.
57. Al-Tirmidhi.
58. Al-Bukhārī.
59. Al-Bukhārī.
60. Al-Bukhārī.
61. Qur'ān, ch. 20:31-33.
62. Qur'ān, ch. 4:12.
63. This is the definition given by Ibn Arfa', see *Mukhtaṣar* of Sīdī Khalīl, op. cit., p. 193.
64. For details, see *Al-Mughnī*, vol. 5, p. 111; *Minhāj*, p. 179; Durr al-Mukhtār, vol. 2, p. 546.
65. Definition given by Ibn 'Arfa in *Mukhtaṣar* of Khalil. Also cf. Ruxton, F. H., *Maliki Law*, London 1916, p. 227.
66. Qur'ān, ch. 2:273.
67. Al-Mahjūbi, *Sharh Wiqāyah*, Lahore, vol. 3, p. 816.
68. Qur'ān, ch. 6:66.
69. Qur'ān, ch. 6:107; The word *Wakīl* is further used in the same sense in ch. 10:108 and ch. 39:41.
70. Qur'ān, ch. 28:26-27.
71. This is the definition of Ibn 'Arfa as quoted by Sīdī Khalīl in his *Mukhtasar*.
72. *Minhāj, p. 181; Sharḥ Wiqāyah*, vol. 3, p. 740.

Chapter 21

Distribution of Wealth

Ill-gotten Wealth

Money or property which is acquired through unfair means, is positively unclean and unlawful, and anyone who makes use of it or spends it on his needs does himself a great harm. As the Holy Prophet has warned, his prayers will not find acceptance with Allah, his supplications will not be answered, his petitions will not be granted, and in case he does good deeds they will avail him nothing. In the Next world, there will be no share for him in the special favours of Almighty Allah.

The Prophet has narrated about a man who after undertaking a long and tedious journey arrives at his destination in such a state that his hair is dishevelled and his body is covered from head to foot with dust. He raises up his hands towards the heavens and cries out, 'O Lord! O my Preserver!' but his sustenance is of the impure and he has been brought up on what is polluted ; – how can his prayer be granted when such is the case?"

The above Ḥadīth amply demonstrates that when a person draws his livelihood from impure means his prayers no longer remain worthy of being answered. Another Ḥadīth of the Holy Prophet reads: "If a person buys cloth for ten dirhams and one of them is stained (i.e. it has been earned dishonestly), none of his prayers will be accepted by Allah as long as he wears it." In another Ḥadīth, he says, "The flesh gathered on one's body by means of unclean earning deserves to be thrown into the fire of hell". On the basis of these strict principles of Islam economy, it will not be lawful, for one to liquidate one debt with another. When one sells a commodity at a price to be paid later, one must not buy it back at a lower price either with cash or to be paid at a date earlier than that date fixed first; nor buy it back at a higher price to be paid at a date later than the date fixed for the first agreement. But it is permissible to buy back the property for a price to be paid on the date fixed first.[1]

There will be no harm in buying commodities in a sack when the contents were described and made known. But it is not lawful to buy cloths that can not be unfolded or described or at night in the darkness, where people cannot look at it or recognise its contents. Similarly, it is unlawful to sell an animal at night in the darkness. One must not outbid the bid of his brother Muslim, and that is when the contracting parties are about to reach an agreement, nor at the beginning of making an offer.[2]

It will also be unlawful to sell fish while still at large, in rivers or pools. Nor is it permissible to sell a foetus while still in its mother's womb; nor is it lawful to sell what is in the wombs of other animals. It will not be lawful to buy in advance the off-spring of what the foetus of a she-camel shall bear; not to sell, the semen of male camels which shall produce young, when they cross female ones.[3]

It will be equally unlawful to exchange ripe dates with dried ones or rasins with grapes. In this respect neither greater nor equal amounts can be received in the exchange. No ripe juicy ones for dried fruits of the same type. This is prohibited because it involves selling or exchanging a thing in return for something which is unknown.[4]

It is ensured by Shari'ah as already mentioned in the above lines, that the trader must not exploit the buyer. The government in the later centuries took interest in the market condition and thus there developed in an institution of *ḥisāb,* the department of inspection which was responsible for stopping adulteration, underweighing, over-work by employers, employment in risky jobs, encroachment on the thoroughfares, unhealthy trades, unlawful professions and cruelty to animals.

Such departments were headed by *muḥtasibs*. There are numerous instances to suggest that the government intervened if the rules of justice and fairplay were violated. The Holy Prophet's treaties with the *Thaqīf, Ḥawazin* and the people of Najrān required a ban on the transactions involving uncertainty. The Holy Prophet not only appointed an inspector to ensure that the unlawful transactions were avoided but also himself visited during his life time the market places advising the traders to observe moral principles in trade. His successors, the *Khulafā al-Rāshidūn*, were also active in controlling malpractices in trade and commerce. Serious actions were taken against adulteration of any kind. Minting of coins was regulated as to prevent debasement and dishonesty and save the general public from being degraded. Most of the rulers later and the Caliphs in Islamic history were vigilant about prices of different markets, and divided various institutions to control the harm ensuing from the hands of selfish and greedy traders and trade companies.

Warning to selfish and dishonest traders

The following traditions of the Prophet (S.A.W.) speak of the eternal punishment for selfish and dishonest community of traders:

Wathilah bin Asāqa says that once the Messenger of Allah came to us and said:

«يا معشر التجار، اياكم والكذب»

"O you traders, beware of telling lies (in your business) transactions."[5]

Some traders are habituated to swear in the name of Allah while selling their commodities.

The Prophet has said about them:

"There are three persons towards who Allah will not look on the Day of Ressurrection, nor would they be cleansed of their sins, and they will be the recipients of painful punishment. One of them would be the person who sold his goods by swearing falsely."[6]

The following narration is in respect of a bedouin who sold his goods but used to swear in the name of Allah:

«مـر اعـرابي بشـاة فقلت تبيعها بثلاثة دراهم؟ فقال لا والله، ثم باعها فذكرت ذلك لرسول الله صلى الله عليه وسلم فقال: فباع آخرته بدنياه».

"A bedouin was passing by with a goat. I said to him: 'Would you sell this goat for three dirhams?' He replied: 'By Allah, No.' Then he sold it when I narrated this to the Messenger of Allah, he said: 'He (the bedouin) sold his Next world for this world'."[7]

Al-Ribā: The Usury

One such evil means of acquiring wealth which is described in the Holy Qur'ān in no uncertain terms is *'Al-Ribā'* the Usury, a practice prevalent in the *Jāhaliyya* period, the pre-Islamic era, and equally prevalent in the modern time, the *neo-Jāhaliyya* age. In order to satisfy their lust and gain more wealth, some people say: "Trade is like Usury" and see no difference between the two, but the former is permitted in Islam and the latter forbidden completely. With this introduction, we shall examine the Qur'ānic injunctions forbidding usury and the guidance from the Sunnah of the Prophet Muḥammad (S.A.W.) on the same subject.

The Qur'ānic injunction contained in Sūrah *al-Baqarah* says as follows:

«الَّذِينَ يَأْكُلُونَ الرِّبَا لاَ يَقُومُونَ إِلاَّ كَمَا يَقُومُ الَّذِي يَتَخَبَّطُهُ الشَّيْطَانُ مِنَ
الْمَسِّ ذَلِكَ بِأَنَّهُمْ قَالُوا إِنَّمَا الْبَيْعُ مِثْلُ الرِّبَا وَأَحَلَّ اللَّهُ الْبَيْعَ وَحَرَّمَ الرِّبَا
فَمَنْ جَاءَهُ مَوْعِظَةٌ مِنْ رَبِّهِ فَانْتَهَى فَلَهُ مَا سَلَفَ وَأَمْرُهُ إِلَى اللَّهِ – وَمَنْ عَادَ
فَأُولَئِكَ أَصْحَابُ النَّارِ هُمْ فِيهَا خَالِدُونَ».

"Those who devour usury will not stand except as stand one whom the devil by his touch has driven to madness. That is because they say: *Trade is like usury*, but Allah has permitted trade and forbidden usury. Those who after receiving direction from the Lord, desists, shall be pardoned for the past; their case is for Allah (to judge); but those who repeat (the offence) are companions of the fire; they will abide therein (forever)."[8]

Those who practice usury are ungrateful and wicked:

«يَمْحَقُ اللَّهُ الرِّبَا وَيُرْبِي الصَّدَقَاتِ، وَاللَّهُ لاَ يُحِبُّ كُلَّ كَفَّارٍ أَثِيمٍ».

"Allah will deprive usury of all blessings, but will give increase for deeds of charity for he loves not creatures ungrateful and wicked."[9]

True believers must give up the practice of usury immediately:

«يَا أَيُّهَا الَّذِينَ آمَنُوا اتَّقُوا اللَّهَ وَذَرُوا مَا بَقِيَ مِنَ الرِّبَا إِنْ كُنْتُمْ مُؤْمِنِينَ»

"O you who believe, fear Allah and give up what remains of your demand for usury, if you are indeed believers."[10]

If one does not stop the evil practice of usury, he is given a notice of war from Allah and His Messenger:

«فَإِنْ لَمْ تَفْعَلُوا فَأْذَنُوا بِحَرْبٍ مِنَ اللَّهِ وَرَسُولِهِ، وَإِنْ تُبْتُمْ فَلَكُمْ رُءُوسُ أَمْوَالِكُمْ
لاَ تَظْلِمُونَ وَلاَ تُظْلَمُونَ».

"But if you do not do (what is prescribed in the verse 278) take notice of war from Allah and His Apostle: but if you turn back you shall have capital sums: deal not unjustly, and you shall not be dealt with unjustly."[11]

The promise of prosperity in this and the Next World is given to those who stop this evil practice:

« يَا أَيُّهَا الَّذِينَ آمَنُوا لاَ تَأْكُلُوا الرِّبَا أَضْعَافاً مُضَاعَفَةً وَاتَّقُوا اللَّهَ لَعَلَّكُمْ
تُفْلِحُونَ».

"O you who believe devour not usury, doubled and multiplied but fear Allah; that you may really prosper."[12]

Those who devour usury are the rejectors of faith:

«وَاَخْـذِهِمُ الـرِّبَـوا وَقَـدْ نُهـوُا عَنْهُ وَاكِلْهِمْ اَمْوَالَ النَّاسِ بِالْبَاطِلِ وَاَعْتَدْنَا لِلْكَافِرِينَ مِنْهُمْ عَذَاباً اَلِيماً».

"That they took usury although they were forbidden and that they devoured men's property wrongfully. We have prepared for those among them who reject Faith a grievous punishment."[13]

Wealth does not increase but decreases in a long run by practising usury:

«وَمَا اَتَيْتُمْ مِنْ رِباً لِيَرْبُوَ فِي اَمْوَالِ النَّاسِ فَلاَ يَرْبُوا عِنْدَ اللّٰهِ وَمَا اتَيْتُمْ مِنْ زَكوةً تُرِيدُونَ وَجْهَ اللّٰهِ فَاُولئِكَ هُمُ الْمُضْعِفُونَ»

"That which you lay out for increase through the property of (other) people, you will have no increase with Allah: but that which you lay out for charity, seeking the countenance of Allah (will increase): it is those who will get a recompense multiplied."[14]

There are a number of *Aḥādīth* of the Prophet (S.A.W.) which condemn usury.

The Prophet (S.A.W.) has pronounced Allah's curse on those involved in the practice of usury:

«عن جابر قال لعن رسول الله (ص) اكل الربا وموكله وكاتبه وشاهديه وقال هم سواء».

Jabir reported: "The Apostle of Allah cursed the one who accepted usury, the one who paid it, the one who recorded it, and two witnesses to it, saying that they were all alike."

The following Ḥadīth explains unsurious transactions:

عن ابى سعيد الخدرى قال قال رسول الله (ص) الذهب بالذهب والفضة بالفضة، والبر بالبر والشعير بالشعير، والتمر بالتمر، والملح بالملح، مثلا بمثل يدا بيد فمن زاد او استزاد فقد اربى-الاخذ والمعطى فيه سواء».

Narrated Abū Saʿīd al-Khuḍrī said the Apostle of Allah: "Gold is to be paid by gold, silver by silver, wheat by wheat, barley by barley, dates by dates, and salt by salt, like by like, payment being made on the spot.

If anyone gives more or asks for more, he had dealt in usury. The receiver and giver are equally guilty". (Muslim). Even receiving a gift after giving a loan amounts to usury:

عن انس عن النبى (ص) قال: «اذا اقرض الرجل الرجل فلا يأخذ هدية».

Narrated Anas, said the Apostle of Allah: "When a man makes a loan to another he must not accept a present."[15]

One dirham of usury is a greater crime than adultery:

عن عبدالله بن حنظلة قال قال رسول الله (ص): «درهم ربا يأكله الرجل وهو يعلم اشد من ستة وثلاثين زنية».

Narrated ʿAbdallāh bin Hanzala, the Messenger of Allah said: "A dirham which a man knowingly receives in usury is more serious (a sin) than thirty-six acts of adultery."[16]

Usury ultimately leads to poverty:

عن ابن مسعود قال قال رسول الله (ص): «ان الربا وان كثر تصير الى غل».

Narrated Ibn Masʿūd the Messenger of Allah said: "Even though usury be much it leads in the end to penury." (Bahaqi and Ibn Mājah)

The Prophet has forecast as to what will happen as is the case today:

عن ابى هريرة عن رسول الله (ص) قال: «ليأتين على الناس زمان لا يبقى احد الا اكل الربا فأن لم يأكله اصابه ممن خسارة»

Narrated Abu Huraira the Messenger of Allah said: "At time is certainly coming to mankind when only the reciver of usury will remain and if he does not receive it some of its smoke will reach him."[17]

Usury was not new in Arabia

Even before the advent of Islam, the system of usury prevailed in the Arabian Peninsula, and the entire economy was based on it. Let no one imagine that it was simply a question of isolated transactions between individuals. The Quraysh undertook a considerable trade with Syria in the summer and the Yemen in the winter. The capital of the Quraysh was invested in this trade. Let us not forget that the caravan of Abū Sufyān which the Muslims ambushed at the battle of Badr and then evaded them, to be replaced by Allah with something better for them, contained a thousand camels loaded with good. If usury had simply been practised in restricted individual dealings, and had not been a comprehensive system of economic life, it would not have deserved the repeated and scorching attack made on it by Almighty Allah in the Qur'ān, and the pursuance of that attack by the Prophet in the *Ḥadīth.*

This capital, this commercial activity, this economy all were based on the system of usury. Shortly before the mission of the Prophet, the economies of various countries came to be gathered into this system, as for example in Medina, where the economy was dominated by the Jews. Usury was in fact the basis of the economic system of the Jews.

This was the economic "reality" on which the life of the land was based. Then Islam came, denying and rejecting this unjust and criminal system, and setting forth in its stead a new basis: that of *Zakāt*, of the goodwill loan, of cooperation and mutual solidarity.[18]

The thoroughness of the Prophetic condemnation of usury which was made after the dawn of Islam, leaves no room for any part, however indirect, in the Islamic transaction. The Apostle of Allah cursed the receiver (literally, the eater) of interest, and the clerk who writes the bond, and the two witnesses thereof, and declared them all as equally culpable. Other traditions record that the Prophet (S.A.W.) forbade the barter of a heap of date of an unknown weight for a specified quantity. Similarly, Muslims are forbidden to sell the fruit upon their trees, before it is ripe, even when the two parties are willing to take the risk.

Thus all that the Book of Allah and the Sunnah have prohibited of the transactions aims at the realisation of equity and at the prohibition of injustice, whether light or grave. These aspects according to Ibn Taimiyyah, include: "appropriation of the property of others unjustly, or by usury and gambling." Certain aspects of usury and gambling, in particular, which the Prophet (S.A.W.), has forbidden are for example:

a) Selling of commodities or lands not possessed by the seller.
b) Selling of animals still unborn.
c) Selling of birds not yet hunted and of fish not yet caught.
d) Selling the *Musarrat*, the ewe of which has not been milked for a long time, to impose on the buyer falsely that its milk is always abundant.
e) Selling of commodities of which the defects have been disguised.
f) Selling of commodities while allowing the buyer to touch them only, without seeing (or examining) them.
g) Selling a piece of cloth (or dress) without exposing it adequately to the buyer.
h) Selling of commodities haphazardly without weighing or measuring.

i) selling agricultural produce not yet ripened.

j) Prearranging with a man to bid a high price for a commodity, so as to induce others to buy it at a lower (but still a high) price.

k) Selling the fruits before they show any sign of ripening.

Added to all these are also prohibited all kinds of invalid partnerships, such as partnerships in cultivating a tract of land in return for the products of a certain piece of it.[19]

Besides, as al-Qayrawānī has mentioned in his *Risālah*, the selling of silver with silver in direct exchange in which one of the parties gives more than he receives, is also considered as usurious. It was also considered usury, to sell gold with gold, yet again one of the parties giving more than he received. It is not lawful to exchange silver with silver or exchange gold with gold except in equal quantities in direct and immediate exchange. The exchange of silver with gold shall be considered usury, except when done with immediate effect. In respect of foodstuffs such as cereals, legumes and similar things, which can be stored, all kinds of foodstuffs and condiments, it is unlawful to exchange those of the same type, except by giving equal quantities and with immediate effect. It is not lawful for one party to delay compliance with these rules. It is not lawful to exchange foodstuff with foodstuff, whether of the same type or not and whether of the type that can be stored or not, when one or both parties are permitted to delay compliance with meeting their obligation.

There is no harm in exchanging fruits and vegetables and other things than cannot be stored, while one party gives more to the other even if they are of the same type, through direct exchange. It is not lawful for one party to give more to the other in respect of commodities of the same type and which can be stored, such as dried fruits and other condiments, foodstuffs and drinks, except water alone.

As for commodities of different types of grain, fruits and foodstuffs, there is no harm in one party giving more to the other, in direct immediate exchange.

In exchanging commodities of one type it is not lawful for one party to give more than it receives except in respect of vegetables and fruits.[20]

Wheat, barley and huskless barley are considered as one category, in respect of lawfulness and unlawfulness. Raisins of all types are considered as one type. Similarly dried dates are all considered one type also. Legumes are considered to consist of many types in respect of trading. But Imām Mālik held a different view on this. Imam Malik considered legumes to consist of one type for the purpose of alms-giving. The flesh of quadruples whether tame or wild is considered to be of the same type. Further, the flesh of all birds is considered to consist of one type. Again, the flesh of all acquatic animals is considered to be of the same type. Any fat extracted from the flesh of animals regarded as one type is considered like the flesh to be of one type. The milk of that type mentioned as well as the cheese and ghee are all considered as one type.

Whoever buys foodstuffs it will not be lawful for him to sell it off before he takes it over, if the purchase is done through weighing, measuring or counting. However, he is permitted to do that if he bought the foodstuff en bloc. The same rule applies to all foodstuffs, condiments and drinks, with the exception of water alone.

Now, if the commodity to be sold happens to be drugs or legumes from which oil cannot be extracted, then it will not be unlawful to be sold before it was received after purchase. In trading such legumes one party can give more than it receives of that same commodity.

There is no harm for foodstuffs bought on credit to be sold before they are taken over. There is no harm in joint purchase of resale at cost price or revocation of a sale of measured foodstuffs before it is taken over.

Every sale or hire or rentage contract which involves some hazard or uncertainty in respect of price or the object of sale, or uncertainty int he time payment shall be due, is not lawful

It is not lawful for a sale to involve uncertainty nor is it lawful to sell an unknown commodity. Besides, it is not lawful to sell a commodity payment of which shall be due at an unknown time.

Here it may be mentioned that the Shari'ah does not tolerate any profit which is stipulated at the time of contract (i.e. pre-determined profit) because apart from being *riba* it is risky in that it may not at all be realised, or even realised, it may be less than the stipulated amount.

Distribution of Income and Wealth

The Islamic policy of distribution of wealth through *Mīrāth, Zakāt, Ṣadaqāt,* etc., helps a lot in discouraging accumulations and concentrations in few hands. It assures that in the process of distribution none of the factors of production exploit the other. The land owners, the labourers and the owners of capital jointly share in their production. As a practical religion and way of life, it compulsorily retains a portion of this produced wealth for those who are detained from contributing their share in production due to any social, physical or economic handicap.

The Holy Prophet and the Rāshidūn Caliphs achieved this goal through prohibiting a very large number of exploitative and unjust techniques in trade and commerce. A study of Ḥadīth literature is suggestive of those measurers which include disciplinary restrictions on landlord and the farmer, the employer and the employee and the producer and the trader. Our study on prohibition of *Ribā* has explained some of these measures.

We shall examine some other aspects in the following pages.

Al-Amānah: The Trust

The law of Allah categorically declared: "Do not devour one another's wealth by false and illegal means."[21] If someone deposits his property as a trust with some trustworthy person, he is duty bound to look after this property just as he would look after and protect his own. A man who keeps someone's property in trust is *Amin*, a trustworthy person. Because of his integrity, honesty, sincerity and faith in Allah, he does not devour another's wealth by false or illegal means nor does he change someone's superior thing for something inferior. The Holy Prophet's life offers us the best model as he was given an honorific title *Al-Amin* even by those people who had not accepted Islam because of his great qualities as a trustworthy man. Even on the day of Hijra from Mecca to Medina, he made sure and handed over all the trust property to his cousin, to return to their rightful owners.

The Holy Qur'ān speaks about *Amānah* (Trust) in the following words:

«اِنَّ اللّٰهَ يَأْمُرُكُمْ اَنْ تُؤَدُّوا الْاَمَانَاتِ اِلَىٰٓ اَهْلِهَا وَاِذَا حَكَمْتُمْ بَيْنَ النَّاسِ اَنْ تَحْكُمُوا بِالْعَدْلِ اِنَّ اللّٰهَ نِعِمَّا يَعِظُكُمْ بِهِ اِنَّ اللّٰهَ كَانَ سَمِيعاً بَصِيراً»

> "Allah does command you to render back your trusts to those to whom they are due; and when you judge between man and man, that you judge with justice. Verily, how excellent is the teaching which He gives you. For Allah is He who hears and sees all things."[22]

The trustee is charged with a great responsibility in Islam. His duty is to guard the interest of the person on whose behalf he holds the trust and to render back the property and accounts when required according to the terms of the trust. This duty of keeping trust is linked with the sanction of the Religion of Islam which requires a higher standard than even stipulated by common law. The Qur'ān says:

«فَاِنْ اَمِنَ بَعْضُكُمْ بَعْضاً فَلْيُؤَدِّ الَّذِى اؤْتُمِنَ اَمَانَتَهُ وَلْيَتَّقِ اللّٰهَ رَبَّهُ»

> "And if one of you deposits in trust a thing with another, let the trustee (faithfully) discharge his trust, and let him fear his Lord."[23]

The Islamic concept of life is such that all our human life in this world must be lived as in the presence of Allah who sees all our actions, knows fully our thoughts and intentions. Any breach of trust or bad intentions will be accounted for, if not in this world, on the day of Judgement. The

Ḥadith of the Prophet enumerates the signs of the hypocrite, one of which is a man who becomes dishonest in the matter of trust deposited with him:

> Abu Hurairah reported on the authority of the Prophet. He said: "The signs of the hypocrites are three: when he speaks, he lies; and when he makes a promise, he breaks it; and when he is charged with a trust, he becomes dishonest."[24]

The Qur'ān injunction further emphasises upon keeping the trust in the following words:

«يَا أَيُّهَا الَّذِيْنَ آمَنُوا لَا تَخُونُوا اللّٰهَ وَالرَّسُولَ وَتَخُونُوا اَمَانَاتِكُمْ وَاَنْتُمْ تَعْلَمُونَ»

> "O ye that believe! betray not the trust of Allah and the Apostle, nor misappropriate knowingly things entrusted to you."[25]

The trust referred to in this verse may be of various kinds: (1) property, goods, credit, etc. (2) plans, confidences, secrets, etc.; (3) knowledge, talents, opportunities, etc.; which we are expected to use for our fellow men. Men may betray the trust of Allah and His Apostle by misusing property, or abusing the confidence reposed in them or the knowledge or talents given to them.

Al-Dayn: The Debt

In human life, there comes ups and downs. There are periods of trials from Allah as He says in the Qur'ān: "We surely test you with aught of fear and hunger and diminuation in riches and lived and fruits, and bear though the glad-tidings unto the patient."[26] In such circumstances, believers are asked to remain patient. When one has a family to look after or some sudden need arises of borrowing money for keeping the business going, one is required to go to friends, neighbours, relatives or philanthropic people to ask for a loan. The Holy Qur'ān has laid down principles concerning the repayment of loans and debts.

The guidance from the prophetic traditions also support the Qur'ānic teachings on this subject. We shall first consider the Qur'ānic injunctions in this regard.

«اِنَّ اللّٰهَ يَاْمُرُكُمْ اَنْ تُؤَدُّوا الْاَمَانَاتِ اِلٰى اَهْلِهَا».

> "Allah does command you to render back the trust of the prople."[27]

In Islam debt is also the trust which should be returned to its owner, Imām al-Bukhārī has used this verse as the caption of a chapter (Bukhārī vol. III) concerning repayment of debt.

The Holy Qur'ān has guided Muslim in respect of lending and borrowing in *Sūrah al-Baqarah* in the following manner:

«يا أيها الذين آمنوا اذا تداينتم بدين الى اجل مسمى فاكتبوه وليكتب
بينكم كاتب بالعدل ولا يأب كاتب ان يكتب كما علمه الله فليكتب وليملل
الذى عليه الحق وليتق الله ربه ولا يبخس منه شيئا فان كان الذى عليه
الحق سفيها او ضعيفا او لا يستطيع ان يمل هو فليملل وليه بالعدل
واستشهدوا شهيدين من رجالكم فان لم يكونا رجلين فرجل وامرأتان ممن
ترضون من الشهداء ان تضل احدهما فتذكر احداهما الاخرى ولا يأب
الشهداء اذا ما دعوا ولا تسئموا ان تكتبوه صغيرا او كبيرا الى اجله ذلكم
اقسط عند الله واقوم للشهادة وادنى الا ترتابوا الا ان تكون تجارة حاضرة تديرونها
بينكم فليس عليكم جناح الا تكتبوها واشهدوا اذا تبايعتم ولا يضار كاتب ولا
شهيد وان تفعلوا فانه فسوق بكم واتقوا الله ويعلمكم الله والله بكل شىء
عليم»

"O you who believe! when you deal with one another, in lending for a term named, write it down (in a document), and let a scribe write it down justly between you, and let not the scribe refuse to write according to what Allah has taught him. Let him fear Allah, his Lord, and diminish nothing from it (i.e. from what he owes). But if the person who owes be insane or infirm or unable himself to dictate, then let his guardian dictate justly. And call to witness two witnesses of your men, but if both be not men, then a man and two women of those you agree upon as witnesses, so if one of the two makes an error, the one thereof shall remind the other, and let not witnesses refuse when they are called on. And be not weary of writing it down, be it small or bid, with the term thereof. This is the most equitable in the sight of Allah and the most confirmatory of testimony and nearest that you may doubt, except when it be a ready merchandise that you circulate between you (i.e. hand to hand and not on credit), for then there shall be no blame on you if you do not write it down. And call witnesses when you bargain with one another; and let not the scribe come to harm nor the witness; and if you do, verily it will be wickedness in you. Fear Allah and Allah teaches you; and Allah is Allah-Knower."[28]

The verse on the injunction of debt and its repayment is among the detailed verse of commandments *(āyāt al-aḥkām al Mufaṣṣal).*

The above verse says:

1. When money or something is lent for a specific term, it should be written down in a document.
2. The scribe who is called upon to write should not refuse since Allah has gifted him with the art of writing. He should write exactly what is dictated.
3. The person taking oath should dictate.
4. Supposing such a person is ignorant of the ordinances or statutes and if he does not know what dictation is or cannot dicate well or he is

of an immature age or senile or a foreigner who is ignorant of the language of the land, then his guardian or agent should dictate justly.

5. Two witnesses from amongst the Muslims should be called to witness the deed. They must be adult and of unimpaired reason, freemen and should be of good character. The disputes, if any, are to be decided on the testimony of these witnesses, and not on the strength of the written document, the role of which is only secondary or subsidiary.

6. If two male witnesses are not available, then one Muslim man and two Muslim women should be invited as witnesses. When we compare this with the Jewish code where the testimony of a woman is inadmissable, we realise the practical view Islam has taken about the witnesses.[29]

7. In the entire affair, the parties concerned should fear Allah and do justice.

The Guidance from the Sunnah

1. Intention in taking debt:

عن ابى هريرة رضى الله عنه عن النبى صلى الله عليه وسلم قال: «من اخذ اموال الناس يريد ادائها ادى الله عنه، ومن اخذ يريد اتلافها اتلفه الله».

Narrated Abu Huraira, the Prophet (S.A.W.) said: "Whoever takes the money of the people with the intention of repaying it, Allah will repay it on his behalf, and whosoever takes it in order to spoil it, then Allah will spoil him."[30]

2. *Payment of Debt is Most Essential*

قال ابو هريرة رضى الله عنه قال رسول الله صلى الله عليه وسلم: «لو كان لى مثل احد ذهباً ما يسرنى ان لا يمر على ثلاث وعندى منه شىء الا شىء ارصده لدين».

Narrated Abū Hurairah, Allah's Messenger (S.A.W.) said: "If I had gold equal to the mountain of Uḥud, it would not please me that it should remain with me for more than three days except an amount which I would keep for repaying debts."[31]

3. *Debt may lead to sin*

عن عائشة رضى الله عنها اخبرت ان رسول الله صلى الله عليه وسلم كان يدعوا فى الصلاة ويقول: «اللهم انى اعوذ بك من المأثم والمغرم» فقال قائل ما اكثر ما تستعيذ يارسول الله من المغرم؟ قال: «ان الرجل اذا اغرم حدث فكذب ووعد فأخلف»

Narrated 'Āisha, Allah's Apostle used to invoke Allah in prayer, saying: "O Allah, I seek your refuge from all sins, and from getting into debts." Someone said: "How often you seek Allah's refuge from being in debt, O Allah's Apostle?" He replied: "If a person is in debt he tells lies when he speaks, and breaks his promise when he makes a promise."[32]

4. *Repayment of Debts by a Wealthy Person*

عن ابى هريـــرة رضى الله عنـــه يقـول: قال رســول الله صلى الله عليـــه وسلم: «مطل الغنى ظلم».

Narrated Abū Hurairah, Allah's Messenger (S.A.W.) said: "Procrastination in repaying debts by wealthy persons is unjustice."[33]

Al-Rahn: The Mortgage

Al-Rahn literally means a proof or something that has been held in pledge. The word *rahinah* occurs in the Holy Qur'ān in the following verse:

«كُلُّ نَفْسٍ بِمَا كَسَبَتْ رَهِينَةٌ»

"Every soul will be held in pledge for its deeds."[34]

In Sharī'ah Law, it means holding something that has a value while giving something on debt. The Qur'ān has laid down this condition in the following verse:

"If you are on a journey, and cannot find a scribe, a pledge with possession *(rihānun Maqabūḍah)* may serve the purpose. And if one of you deposits a thing on trust with another let the trustee faithfully discharge his trust and let him fear His Lord. Conceal not evidence; for whoever conceals it, his heart is tained with sin. And Allah knows all that you do."[35]

Where parties cannot trust each other, something should be deposited as security, a convenient form of closing the bargain as mentioned in the above verse.

Mortgage is allowed in Sharī'ah as is shown by the action of the Prophet:

عن عائشة رضي الله عنها ان النبي صلى الله عليه وسلم اشترى من يهودي الى اجل ورهنه ذرعا من حديد

Narrated 'Āisha: "The Prophet (S.A.W.) purchased food grains from a Jew on credit and mortgaged his iron armour to him."[36]

The thing mortgaged must possess value. If the time stipulated while giving a debt on security expires, the debt can be recovered from the mortgaged property. There are three essential requisites for a valid mortgage:

1. The presence of the mortgagor and the mortgagee.
2. The thing to be mortgaged and the debt to be given in lieu of it.
3. Consideration and acceptance. e.g. The Mortgager says: "I give so much amount as a debt on mortgage of such and such a thing for such and such a period." The mortgagee must accept the condition.

A valid mortgage must satisfy the following three conditions:

1. Both the mortgagor and the mortgagee must have the legal capacity to possess and dispose of the property. Therefore, the mortgage of an insane person or a minor will not be valid.
2. While making the agreement terms of the mortgage must be expressed, eg. "I loan you a certain amount for a certain period in lieu of this mortgage."
3. The debt as well as the mortgaged property should not be unlawful commodities whose transactions are forbidden under Sharī'ah, like wine, pigs, etc.

If the mortgaged things happened to be birds then the eggs will belong to the mortgagor. Likewise honey as well as the rent of the house all belongs to the mortgagor. But the animals still in embryo, wools and hairs of the animal will all remain with the mortgagee. When a horse is given as a security, the mortgagee will be allowed to use it for riding as a compensation for feeding it. Similarly a milch-animal's milk will be allowed to the mortgagee when he feeds the animal.[37] Hence it is evident that when agricultural land or a house is mortgaged, the mortgagee can also derive benefit from it when he pays land-revenue or house-tax, or spends money on the upkeep of the property.

The agreement of mortgage will be considered incomplete until the article pledged is taken over. A witness in this regard is of no consequence so long as the witness failed to see the transfer of the article mortgaged. Responsibility for damage or loss of the article mortgaged shall be borne by the mortgagor. But the mortgagee only makes good what is lost while in his possession. He does not make good what is lost while in possession of others.[38]

Bayt al-Māl: The Centre of the Financial Organisation of the Ummah

Bait in Arabic means a House and *Māl*, the property. *Bait al-Māl,* therefore, means the treasury of the public. The very concept of the *Bayt al-Māl* is the concept of trust: the wealth of *Bayt al-Māl* is to be treated as Allah's wealth or Muslims' wealth, as against the imperial treasury as used to be known during the medieval period. This concept implied that monies paid into the treasury were Allah's trust and the common property of all the Muslims and that the Caliph or a ruler was in the position of a trustee, whose duty it was to spend them on the common concerns of all Muslims while allowing for himself nothing more than a fixed stipend.

The concept of the Islamic state and the establishment of *Bait al-Māl* are inseparable. The word *Bait al-mal* does not occur in the Qur'ān as such, but the sources from which the funds flow into the *Bait al-mal* are all mentioned in one way or the other in the Holy Qur'an. The institution however is mentioned frequently in the *Ahadith* of the Prophet. The *Bait al-māl* came into being in the life term of the Prophet immediately after the coming into existence of the Islamic state of Medina. It developed fully in the time of the *Rashidun* Caliphs, particularly the second Caliph 'Umar bin al-Khattab.

The sources from which funds are collected in the *Bait al-māl* are as follows:

A. *Zakāt:* One of the pillars of Islam which demands that 2½ or 1/40 the part of our savings should be given the poor and needy as a poor-rate. These funds were collected and managed in the *Bait al-mal* of Muslims for the welfare of the *Ummah*. The *zakāt* is only payable by Muslim subjects from their cash property, trade merchandise and herds of cattles. The non-Muslims are exempted from the payment of *Zakāt.*

Being one of the five pillars of Islam there occur a number of verses of injunctions on *Zakāt* in the Qur'ān:

1\.

"And they pray regularly and give Zakat."[39]

2\.

"Tie be to the polytheists who do not give Zakat and disbelieve in the life after death."[40]

3\.

"My mercy is spread on all things. So I shall write it for those who are righteous and give Zakat and believe in our signs."[41]

4\.

"Whatever Zakāt you give to seek pleasure of Allah, such people will increase their property two-fold in the Next world."[42]

B. *Ṣadaqah or Infāq Fī Sabīlillāh*

Ṣadaqah is a voluntary charity given by individuals over and above the payment of the compulsory *Zakāt* to relieve the problems and sufferings of fellow-human beings. According to the *Aḥādīth, ṣadaqqh* must be given in such a way that 'even the left hand of the donor does not know what the right hand gives'.

The word *sadaqah* and *Infāq fī-sabīlillāh* occur several times in the Holy Qur'ān:

1.

> "And in their property is the right of the beggar and those devoid of riches (i.e. poor)"[43]

2.

> "And spend in the path of Allah and do not throw yourselves with your own hands into destruction."[44]

3.

> "O you who are believers, spend from the pure things that you have earned."[45]

4.

> "You give to your relative his right and to the poor and a way-farer."[46]

5.

> "O you who believe, spend from what we have given you."[47]

C. *Jizzyah*

The *Jizyyah* is an annual tax levied on non-Muslim citizens living in the Islamic state. Just as the Muslims pay the compulsory *Zakāt,* the non-Muslims pay the *Jizyyah*. In return, it will be the duty of the Muslim state to protect their lives and property like any Muslim citizen. The payment of *Jizyyah* will exhonerate them from fighting for the cause of the state and render any military service to the nation. The Muslims in spite of their payment of *Zakāt,'Ushr* and *sadaqat* will still be required to take up arms if needed for the protection of the *Ummah* as well as the non-Muslim citizens. The *Jizyyah* collected will go to the *Bait al-Māl.*

The Qur'ānic injunction in respect of *Jizyah* is as follows:

> "Fight those who believe not in Allah nor the Last Day, nor hold that forbidden which has been forbidden by Allah and His Apostle nor acknowledge the religion of truth, even if they are the people of the Book, until they pay the *Jizyah* with willing submission, and feel themselves subdued."[48]

D. *Kharāj: Kharāj* is a tax levied on the producer of the landed property owned by the non-Muslims in the Islamic state. Just as the Muslims pay *'Ushr,* the non-Muslims are supposed to pay *kharaj* to the *Bait al-Māl.* According to Imām Abū Yūsuf, *Karaj* is a kind of *Fay.*[49] The Qur'ānic injunction on *Fay'* is as follows:

"What Allah has bestowed on His Apostles (and taken away) from the people of the townships, belongs to Allah — to His Apostle and to kindred and orphans, the needy and the way farer; in order that it may not merely make a circuit between the wealthy among you."[50]

B. *'Ushr:* The taxation to be paid on the produce of the landed property of the Muslims at the rate of ten per cent if it is through natural rainfall in an Islamic state is called *'Ushr.* But if the water has been supplied through irrigation, it will be at the rate of 20%.[51] This amount is to be paid in the *Bait al-Māl* which will cater for the welfare and needs of the individuals as well as the *Ummah* as a whole. The Qur'ānic injunction in respect of *'Ushr* is as follows:

"And render the dues that are proper on the day that the harvest is gathered."[52]

F. *Khums:* A certain percentage of whatever a Muslim army gets as a booty *(ghanīmah)* after fighting war with enemies and gaining victory over them is called *Khumus. Likewise, a certain percentage of the income from the natural resources, mines, petroleum and other natural hidden treasures owned by individuals is also called khumus.* Such proceeds go to the *Bait al-Māl* and is used for the welfare of the nation. The injunction of the Holy Qur'ān in respect of *Khums* is as follows:

"And know that out of all the booty that you may acquire in war, a fifth share is assigned to Allah and to the Apostle, and to near relatives, orphans, the needy, and a traveller."[53]

G. *Fay':* *Fay'* is the property captured from the enemy forces without fighting any battles with them. Such property, if acquired, will go to the central funds of the *Bait al-Māl.*

The Qur'ānic injunction in respect of *Fay'* is contained in *Sūrah al-Hashr,* verse 7, as mentioned before.

H. *Ḍarā'ib:* *Ḍarā'ib* are the general taxes which the Islamic state deems fit to impose on its citizens to carry out some public welfare works or when the state needs funds in the event of any emergency. The proceeds go to the *Bait al-Māl.* The following verse also includes a sanction of such taxes:

"You give to your relative his right and to the poor and the way farer."[54]

'Abdallāh bin 'Umar has said:

"In your property, there are other rights other than Zakāt."[55]

I. *Wāqf:* These are the religious trust and the proceeds from these religious trust properties go to the *Bait al-Māl.* The further details about *wāqf* are given elsewhere in this book.

J. *'Ushūr:* *'Ushūr* constitutes the revenue collected from the proceeds out of the trade and business carried our by all the citizens of the Islamic state irrespective of their religious beliefs. This revenue also goes to the *Bait al-Māl.*

K. *Kira āl-Arḍ:* The income generated from the government is called *kira' al-ard,* and it goes to the central funds of the *Bait al-Māl.*

L. *Amwāl al-Fāḍilah:* Any income from the government owned natural resources is called *Amwal al-Fāḍilah* and goes to the *Bait al-Māl.*

The estate left behind one who has no heirs

If a Muslim dies and leaves behind an estate but no heir to inherit the property, or does not leave any will behind or any other claimant, the property will go to the *Bait al-Māl.*

Ibn Ḥazm al-Ẓāhirī, the celebrated author of *al-Muḥallā* has said: "If the income of *Bayt al-Māl* or State Treasury falls short of the needs of the poor, the *Amir* or Head of the State can compel the rich to provide the poor with the indispensable food and the necessary clothing to protect them against the heat of the summer and the cold of winter and a shelter to save them from rain, heat and storm."[56] According to the Caliph 'Umar each and every individual Muslim has a right in the property of the *Bait al-Māl* whether he exercises it or not.[57] This is how Islam provides social security.

Again, on the authority of Abū Sa'īd al-Khuḍrī, the Prophet is reported to have said: "He who has extra means of transport, let him pass it on to him who has none; he who has surplus food, let him give it to him who has no food." The Prophet continued enumerating different kinds of property to such an extent that Abū Sa'īd thought he had no right to own whatever is surplus.[58] It is reported by Muḥammad, the son of Caliph 'Alī, that his father (Ali) said: "Allah had charged the rich with a duty to satisfy the needs of the poor and if they are left hungry and naked due to the negligence of the rich, then the rich shall be severely punished by Allah."[59] The Caliph 'Umar is reported to have said: "Had I known what I came to to know later, I would have taken all the surplus (wealth) from the rich to distribute it among the poor and the immigrants."[60]

The Right of the Poor and the Handicapped

As promised in the Qur'ān, "Allah will deprive usury of all blessings, but will give increase for deeds of charity."[61] Thus, Islam lays great stress on the relief of poverty by the rich:

> "The poor and the unfortunate have a right in their (the rich peoples') property."[62]

It is not considered to be a favour by the rich if they help the poor; on the other hand, it is a duty of the rich and prosperous men to take part in the economic uplift of the poor. The Qur'ān condemns all those who go on collecting wealth but do not spend it for charitable purposes:

> "And those who go on hoarding gold and silver and do not spend it in the way of Allah, give them warning of a great punishment."[63]

The Holy Qur'ān reminds us that in the past many nations were destroyed because the rich and well-to-do among them did nothing to better the condition of the poor, tried to keep them in a state of poverty and treated them with great disrespect and indignity. The Prophet Nuh (Noah), when he began to remind the rich people of his nation of their duties towards the poor, he was told by the well-to-do sections:

> "Does your religion demand of us that we should give up worshipping what our fathers worshipped and what we should not be free to do whatever we like with our wealth and property?"[64]

This shows that in all ages the Prophets of Allah preached that men are not free to use and spend their wealth as they liked, but that the poorer sections of the people have a right in their wealth and possessions. The Holy Prophet was a great friend of the poor and treated them with great respect and kindness. He not only instituted the system of *Zakāt* as ordained by Allah to relieve poverty, but also stressed the fact that if a man has paid his *Zakāt,* his duty towards the unfortuate members of the community has not ended. He is still required to help the poor and the needy. A Ḥadīth of the Holy Prophet says:

> "If a man brings up and educates an orphan, he will be as near to paradise as the fingers of a hand are near to each other."

In another Ḥadīth, the Prophet has said:

> "A man who helps and spends his time and money in looking after widows and the poor, holds the same position in the eyes of Allah as one who fights in the holy war, or fasts every day and prays the whole night over a number of years."

The Prophet has made no distinction in these traditions between a Muslim and a non-Muslim. In fact, he used to help many Jews in Medina out of the *Zakāt* funds which were collected by the State from only the Muslims. Similarly, Caliph Umar, was of the opinion that the word *Miskīn,* used in the Qur'ān for the poor, means the non-Muslim poor, while *Fuqarā* means the poor Muslims. So both should be helped. In the treaty of Hira, Khālid bin Walīd made an express promise to the Christians that if there was an old man or woman among them, or a disabled person or a blind man, the Muslim Government would grant him or her a pension for life from the *Bait al-Māl.* This is because Islam stands for the good and happiness of all mankind, Muslims and non-Muslims alike. The Muslims have been ordered to work for the uplift of all mankind and to show by their conduct that their minds and hearts are free from national or religious hatred.

While Muslims must not live an extravagant life, those who are blessed with the bounties of Allah are not expected to live in rags, for the Prophet has said that Allah likes to see traces of His bounty of His Servant.

Miserliness condemned in Sharī'ah

Miserliness is considered to be a sin in Islam. Islam does not believe in merely collecting property and living a miserly life. A generous man is considered to be a friend of Allah according to the teachings of the Prophet. He is closer to Allah, a beloved of men and is closer to the paradise. The message of the Qur'ān is quite clear in respect of wealth and wealthy men:

> "And render to the kindred their due rights, as (also) to those in want, and to the wayfarer, but squander not (your wealth) in the manner of a spendthrift."[65]

In the Jewish scriptures, this refinement of kindness to those in want and alos to travellers and wayfarers (i.e. total strangers whom you come across) finds no place. Even the command "to honour thy father and mother" comes after the ceremonial observance of Sabbath. With Muslims, the worship of Allah is linked up with kindness – to parents, kindred, those in want, those who are far from their homes though they may be total strangers to us. The mention of kindness is not merely verbal. They have certain rights which must be fulfilled.

The miserly persons are the brothers of *Shaiṭān,* the Devil, and hence are always ungrateful to Allah like *Shaiṭān.*

The Qur'ān further says about misers:

> "Verily spendthrifts are brothers of the Evil ones; and the Evil one is to His Lord Ungrateful."[66]

Begging: An unlawful act

Muslims are asked to struggle to earn their lawful livelihood, and not merely depend on charity. The upper hand that gives is better than the lower. Hence a Muslim is required not to sit idle or live in a secluded corner of a jungle or a monastery shunning his responsibility towards his wife and children. As the Holy Qur'ān says:

> "That Man can have nothing except what he strives for. That the fruit of his striving will soon come in sight."[67]

It is good to put ones trust in Allah but that does not mean that he should shun the struggle to get a lawful livelihood. The Qur'ān says:

> "It is He who has made the earth subservient to you so that you can work on its shoulders and eat out of its provisions."[68]

In the above words of the Qur'ān it is made clear that the earth is made by Allah and we are asked to get the benefit out of it from our efforts so that we can till and plough and get bumper harvest. Likewise, we may exploit the mineral resources out of it for our benefit but all these will need efforts on our part. Merely sitting down cross-legged with reliance on Allah without doing any effort will not bring forth neither harvest nor the rich mineral wealth. Similarly, one should not depend merely on charity. He can turn to it as the last resort when in spite of his efforts he is unable to get the necessities of life. The Prophet has said:

> "Charity is not lawful for a rich man neither is it lawful for a healthy and able man."[69]

The Prophet has also discouraged begging in many other traditions in very strong terms:

> "If a man begs without any dire necessity as if he puts live charcoals on his hands."[70]

The Prophet has also said:

> "If a man extended his hands before people in order to beg so that he can become rich, his face would be terribly wounded on the day of resurrection and he will be given hot stones of hell for his food."[71]

In yet another Ḥadīth, the Prophet has said:

> "Whosoever makes himself habituated of begging, he will meet Allah in such a horrible condition that there will be no flesh on his face (on the day of resurrection)."[72]

The Prophet has asked to under hardship and collect wood from the jungle and sell it to earn a living rather than go around begging.

The only time begging can be permitted is when a man is hard pressed and there is no other way to survive than asking for help. Truly speaking, it will be the responsibility of the Muslim society to look after the have-nots and the destitutes living in their localities. One of the purposes of the five-time daily prayers in Islam is that the Muslims should meet each other and understand the need of the fellow man living int he neighbourhood. One may realise that they are handicapped in some way and are not in a position to look after their family, they should provide for their needs without begging.

A good Muslim should be his brother's keeper. The exceptional circumstances in which a man is permitted to beg are recorded in

Ḥadiths quoted by Imām Muslim. Abi Bishar Qabīsah bin Al-Mukhāriqah who reported: "I accepted the responsibility as a guarantor in a certain case. I went to the Messenger of Allah and begged from him (in order to fulfil his promise as a guarantor). The Prophet replied wait until the property of ṣadaqah arrives, then I shall give you something. The Prophet said: Oh Qabisah it is not lawful to beg except for three categories of people (1) that a man who accepts to be guarantor on someone's behalf (and has no money to pay). It is lawful for such a man to beg until such time that he gets the required amount. Immediately after than he should stop begging. (2) That a man whose property is destroyed because of calamities. It is permissible for such a man to beg until such time that he receives enough means in order to get his livelihood. (3) The third category of person is one who is starving and three people of his locality confirm that he is really starving. In such circumstances it is permissible for him to beg until he gets enough as his livelihood. Except for these circumstances, if any one begs and gets something he eats unlawful *(Ḥarām)*.[73]

Al-Rishwah: The Bribery

Al-Rishwah or bribery is offered or promised to be offered to someone in order to influence him or persuade him to do something wrong in favour of the giver. Thus, bribery is given to deprive someone of his right or to bring undue pressure on him or to tyrannise someone or to free a criminal or to get his punishment reduced or to pervert justice in any other form.

Al-rishwah is Dishonesty

The bribery is a form of dishonest practice in order to usurp the rights of people. The Prophet therefore has said:[74]

قال رسول الله صلى الله عليه وسلم: «لعن الله الراشي والمرتشي والرائشي بينهما».

"Allah has cursed one giving bribe and one receiving bribe as well as the go-between."

It is essential for the administrators and civil servants who are employed in the collection of *ṣadaqah, zakāt, jizyah* and other forms of annual taxes imposed by the government not to accept any gift from people because it also amounts to accepting a bribe in order to give relief either for full payment of the tax or to get under-assessed or to gain time for the payment. The Prophet sent ʿAbdallāh bin al-Luthbiyyah Azdi to collect the *Zakāt* from Bani Sulaim tribe. When the account was to be rendered ʿAbdallāh reported: "This much amount was collected as the *zakāt* while the remaining was given as a gift." On hearing this, the Messenger of Allah said:

«فهلا جلست في بيت ابيك وامك حتى تأتيك هديتك ان كنت صادقا؟»

"If you were sitting in the house of your father or your mother would any one give you that gifts if you are really truthful?"

Such gifts are not to be accepted and if at all given, they should be paid into public treasury *(Bait al-Māl).*

A true believer will neither give bribes nor accept any gift during the tenure of his office as an administrator. In the Caliphate of Abū Bakr, Khālid bin al-Walīd has imposed annual *Jizyah* tax on the people of Hirah in Syria. The inhabitants of Hirah were so much impressed by the justice of the Muslims and their cordial relationship and good behaviour that they insisted on sending gifts to Abū Bakr. When it was very difficult for Kalid to persuade them not to do so, he at least accepted the gifts and later counted it as a part of the compulsory tax and reduced the actual amount of payment and thus, sent it to the *Bait al-Māl.* Caliph Umar also sent to all his governors the following message:

«اياكم والهدايا فأنها من الرّشي»

"Beware of the gifts because they form part of bribe."

The Caliph 'Umar's statement is very correct when we think of the point of view of our modern society where bribery is so very rampant – given and taken in the name of gifts. The pious caliph 'Umar bin 'Abdulaziz flatly rejected to accept any gifts. Someone said to him that the Messenger of Allah used to receive gifts, he replied:

«كانت له هدية ولنا رشوة لانه كان يتقرب اليه لنبوته لا لوليته ونحن يتقرب الينا للولاية».

"It was a gift for him alright but for us it is actually a bribe since people wanted to come closer to him because of his priesthood and not because of his rule while they wish to come closer to us because of our sovereignty."

In other words, the Prophet used to accept a gift and give it away to the poor people. Those who brought gifts to him did not have any ulterior motive. While in the case of the rulers in the later days the intention of giving gifts was no other than to secure undue and unjust favours.

This does not prohibit the mutual exchange of gifts among friends and relatives. According to the prophetic traditions, gifts help to remove rancour and increase love and affection. The Messenger of Allah has also said: "Exchange gifts, this will increase your love." The taking of gifts by the government officers and administrators in the process of discharging their duties is thus forbidden under Shari'ah. The Prophet has warned: "There will come the period when bribe will be made lawful by people through gifts, and murder through admonitions."

The Devastating Effects of Modern Economic System

While solving the economic problem of man, one has to be realistic in one's approach to human life on this planet. It is true that a man has various economic needs in life, it is not necessary to exaggerate its importance to the extent that it is reckoned as the whole problem of life. A man is not to live by bread alone. Therefore, it will be a blunder to share our lives, our ethical and moral values, our culture and society on economic foundations. A Muslim saga has rightly remarked that a man does not live to eat but eats to live and survive.

If we attempt to build our society on economic foundation alone, it would really mean that a man's position is being reduced to a grazing animal. A purely materialistic society, as we can see in the Western world of today, the spiritual and moral values of life are lost sight of, and in such a society only the selfish thrive. The business motives and commercial ideas are applied in social conduct and thus a man's role has been reduced to that of an economic animal.

As a result, people forget that they were merely custodians over their property and not real masters and that the wealth was to be acquired by lawful means and not through dishonesty and treachery. The wealthy people, forgetting their role of *Khalifa* of Allah on earth, began to describe their motto of life as "money, more money and yet more money". They have multiplied their necessities of life over and above their real needs. This has created artificial requirements of self-indulgence and they struggle hard all their lives for their fulfilment. Their necessities have grown so much that they have devised evil methods of increasing their wealth through hoarding, giving less weight and supplying inferior commodity, cut-throat competition, usury, selling human blood, pornography, cinema halls, prostitution markets, highway robbery, etc. They have drowned themselves in intoxication and self-forgetfulness and thus have created an artificial necessity for a large number of men to prepare liquor, cocain, opium, help and grow marijuana. Because of their ill-gotten wealth, adultery has been made a necessity for which an army of prostitutes, and dishonourable agents have been recruited. Wild music has become an urgent need for which an army of musicians, dancing girls, drum-beaters and manufacturers of such instruments have to be patronised. This, in turn has required an army of actors, and actresses, showy and tight dress-designers to stitch tight jeans, mini-dresses and unisex dresses. In order to satisfy their artifically created needs, they have needed more wealth which in turn have bred professional criminals and their active agents. It is in order to satisfy their lust that all illegal dishonest ways of earning have been legalised by them and everything has been named a 'business' *(al-tijārah).*

The Modern Banking System and Interest-free Muslim Banks

The idea of usury is quite evident in the concept of modern bank interest. The rate of interest as defined by modern economists is the price of money, the price at which money can be borrowed and determined like other prices, by the interaction of the forces of supply and demand.[75]

Originally, usury meant any premium paid for the use of money. Nowadays, it means the practice of demanding an exorbitant premium of interest. Attempts were made, particularly by the Romans, to provide maximum rates of interest, but they were unsuccessful. Later, usury being condemned by the Christian Church, it was allowed to fall into the hands of the Jews. Borrowing with interest is now unfortunaely a world-wide phenomenon.[76]

Thomas Erskine writing in 1809 A.D. says: "The crime of usury before the Reformation (i.e the 16th Century) consisted in the taking of any interest for the use of money and now in taking a higher rate of interest than is authorised by law."

Since then, all the modern Banks function on the basis of interest. Every business man in need of loans is driven by force of circumstances to borrow from the Banks which charge high rates of interest.

It is argued by most of the*'Ulamā* that the interest given by the banks on the deposit account is *riba,* and likewise one who receives loans from the banks on interest also give *riba* to the banks.

Coulson in *"A History of Islamic Law"*[77] and some brain-washed Muslims confuse the trade and *Riba* which have been differentiated in the Holy Qur'ān. He gives the following definition: *"Ribā:* Basically, interest on a capital loan. In classical doctrine, however, the term covers many forms of gain or profit which accrue as the result of a transaction and which were not precisely calculable at the time of the transaction being concluded." The correct and clear definition would be: "Any amount of interest on capital, or an unfair gain in a transaction." Even the double contract arrangement was not acceptable to all schools of theology, but it was taken over by Medieval Europe under the name of *Mohatra (from Arabic Mukhāṭarah,* risk*)*, together with the *Suftajah,* bill of exchange.[78]

Muslims were the first to lay down the true foundation of proper trade and even banking in modern civilization. Hence, the present day banking terminology is permeated with Arabic words and expressions. The very word Cheque is originally Arabic. Its etymology goes back to *sakk* (pl. *Sukūk*). To quote a few others we might mention traffick and trafficking whose origin was *tafrīq*; buy was *bai;* the French word acheter, is *ishtara;* and the word tarriff, *ta'rīfah,* and many others. Although we gave them all these words, we are not responsible to give the ugly words like "interest" and "usury". They are purely of Western invention because the Islamic economic system rightly avoided them. Usury was not in practice in Muslim banks, otherwise the Europeans would have borrowed these terms and incorporated them in their own terminology like the other terms mentioned above. Indeed, cheques go back to the time of Caliph 'Umar bin al-Khaṭṭāb. He was the first to draw a cheque (634-644 A.D.). Al-Ya'qūbī, an eminent Muslim historian who died in 897 A.D., mentions in his history,[79] *Inna Umar Ibn al-Khaṭṭab kana awwala man sakka wa Khatama asfala al-sikak"* (Umar ibn Al-Khaṭṭab was the first to draw cheques and put his stamp underneath and sign them). Al-Jahashiyari, who died in 942 A.D., makes similar statement with regard to Harun al-Rashid: *"sa'alahu'l Fadhlu 'an yasukka bi-hadha'l-mablaghi bi Khaṭṭih'* (Al-Fadhl asked him (i.e., Al-Rashīd) to draw a cheque in his own hand with regard to this sum of money (which was a million dirhams).

Ibn Miskawaih (d. 1030) in his *Tajārīb al-Umam* mentions that salaries of the army were paid by cheques. One of the charges made against Muḥammad bin Dawud is that he paid the army in cash and not in cheques. From that time onwards the custom of using cheques by the people, as a whole, became quite familiar. Centres of money exchange were established by the Muslim merchants in different parts of the Muslim world. Muslim dynasties ruled all over the world and inherited this well established banking system, but they never engaged in the practice of *ribā* or interest without which the modern banks, as the general impression is given to all of us, cannot work. [80]

The interest-free commercial transactions of Medieval Muslim society seems to have baffled and surprised many Western scholars, who believe that it is simply unworkable in the modern times. The following passage from savory explains our point:

"In the important area of commercial law, the Shari'ah was hampered by what at first sight appears to be an unsurmountable handicap. I refer, of course, to the Qur'ānic prohibition, which is quite specific, on the taking of interest *(ribā).* Such a prohibition would appear to be totally divorced from the realities of trade and commerce in a free society. Yet the classical theory of Islamic law, as developed by the Jurists, far from affording any relaxation, of this ban, made it even more rigid.

The jurists evolved the doctrine that any speculative transaction, any transaction which resulted in the 'unjustified enrichment' of one party, was forbidden. If a profit were made, it should be given to the poor. This doctrine was derived from Qur'ānic phrase 'God will abolish interest and cause Charity to increase.' In the case of barter deals there are two principles involved, according to the Jurists: first, the two amounts to be traded must be equal in weight or quantity; second, there must be no time lag in the completion of the transaction, because during the interval the value of one commodity might fluctuate, and this would permit one party or the other to make a speculative gain."[81]

"Since the whole principle of usury was so expressly prohibited in the Qur'ān, people were naturally reluctant openly to act in defiance of the Qur'ānic injunction. On the other hand, trade was vitally important to the Medieval Islamic world, and so the Jurists developed a whole series of complicated 'stratagems' or 'devices' known as *ḥiyal* (for example, partnerships etc.) to enable people to get around the law."

It is really not true to say partnerships, etc., were devices to get around the law. In that case, we might classify even free trading as a "stratagem" to get around *riba.* There is a point at which *ribā* and "profiteering" and "speculation" stop and lawful profit starts. Even in trade, Muslim jurists have limited the amount of profit made by a reasonable percentage.

A thorough study of the Islamic Development Bank, in which twenty-three Muslim countries have participated will one day convince the European scholars that the Islamic interest free Banks can also function profitably.

In Muslim countries or where Muslims form a sizeable community, they can easily avoid *Riba* by constructing such banks. We thank Allah, that some Islamic Banks have been set up in recent times. From available reports, it seems that these banks are becoming successful. Professor Nejātullāh Ṣiddīqī's book *Banking Without Interest*"[82] provides guidelines in this direction. Professor Siddiqui has rightly said in the preface of his book that "by prohibiting interest Islam had endeavoured to do away with a hideous form of tyranny and injustice prevalent in the human society. The institution of interest is a great challenge to all those who are trying to revive and reconstruct the Islamic way of life in the modern times. In the modern Economic system interest, and enterprises based on interest, occupy a key position. The whole Banking system rests on interest. It is, therefore, imperative that for the reconstruction of the Economic system on the Islamic pattern, an Interest-less Banking system should be established and run successfully.

Obviously, the Banking system renders a few fundamental, beneficial and essential services without which no modern developed economy can be conceived. There is also a concensus of opinion among the Muslim economists on the point that even without interest a Banking system can be organised to discharge all the usual functions performed by modern Banking systems based upon interest. These experts also agree that the re-organisation of Banking on the Islamic pattern can be brought about on the Islamic principles of *Muḍāarbah* (a joint enterprise) and *Sharakat* (partnership) but so far it had not been described in details how a Banking system would be established on these principles and how "Interestless Banking" would discharge all the functions of modern banks."[83]

While describving the Islamic Economic system, Muhammad Muslehuddin has said that the economic policy of Islam occupies an intermediate position between the doctrines of 'Bourgeouis Capitalism and Bolshevik Communism.'[84]

Sir Hamilton Gibb also remarks that 'Within the Western World, Islam still remains the balance between the exaggerated opposites. Opposed equally to the anarchy of European Nationalism and the regimentation of Russian Communism, it has not yet succumbed to that obsession with the economic side of life which is characteristic of present-day Europe and present day Russia alike . . ."[85]

Islamic Bank: A New Economic Order for the Modern World

The efforts to establish the **Islamic Bank** at Makkah, the heart of the Muslim World has shown new horizons of hope to Muslims. It will help to set up the New Islamic Economic Order, based on the divine principles which the world has more or less forgotten due to the lethargy of Muslims themselves.

The Islamic Bank can function as the central bank for the Muslim world. Operating with entirely new functions and principles, it would be more simple and just, as well as free from interest and the complex loopholes of the current financial transactions.

A few guidelines for an ordered and centralised economic pattern of the world, that could be ordained through the Islamic Bank are suggested below:

1. The world Muslim currency should be immediately established. It may be given the name of Dīnār and its value should be fixed equivalent to about 15 US dollars.
2. The value of one barrel of crude oil should be fixed at one **Dīnar.** In this way the oil reserves would turn into the monetary reserves.
3. In foreign currencies, the oil price should be gradually

increased with an index based on the rate of inflation (price-hike) on a selected number of **Technical Essentials.**

These may include Heavy Machinery Manufacturing Plants, Electronic Nuclear Equipment and Installations, Petro-chemicals and Synthetic Polyniers, cost of studies in world's selected institutions of Technical learning, Fertilizers, Food grains, life saving medicines and Equipment. This measure will keep on revaluing the **Dinar,** in parity with the level of raising inflation and the price increasing tendencies of the industrialised world, and will save the Muslim world from its harmful effects.

4. All other Muslim countries whose economy depends on the export of their Natural Resources in the raw state, must establish standard export prices for their items in terms of the **Islamic Dīnārs.**

5. All the Islamic countries must see and contain in all their requirements for development, including Education, to Technology and Ideology. They should be able to process their natural resources, mostly to meet their own requirement. They should export only a portion of these resources at reasonable standard prices to non-Muslim countries. They should, however, trade preferentially among themselves.

6. All the surplus wealth of Muslim countries must be deposited with the **Islamic Bank**, operating on the following basic principles of Islamic Economy:

   a. No interest in any form.
   b. Maximum utilization of wealth and measure to check its concentration in few hands.
   c. Annual deduction of Zakāt on the deposit.

7. The major functions of the **Islamic Bank** should be to invest its contributions, both at home and abroad. The investments should be organised by a Body of Experts, selected from the Muslim World strictly on the basis of merit and Taqwa.

8. Another Body of Experts should be formed to prepare an **International Price List of the Technical Essentials Dīnār.** No member of the Muslim world community, should pay a price higher than that. The body should also set up an **International Standard** of good quality for these goods.

9. The **Islamic Bank** should give interest free **Dīnār Loans** to the Muslim countries for their development projects. It should however, receive an **Inflationary Compensation**, if a price-Hike occurs in the Technical Essentials, at the time of repayment.

10. The **Islamic Bank** should also deduct **Annual Zakāt** on the stagnant wealth that could be used as **Aid** to the poor Muslim countries.[86]

An economic order based on the Muslim monetary system and principles of the **Islamic Bank** shall:

a. Set oil reserves and other Natural Resources of the Muslim World as monetary reserves.

b. Make **Islamic Dinar** as the stablest and foremost currency of the world.

c. Relieve the Islamic world from its dependence on foreign currencies, as it will assess all the importable commodities in terms of hard **Islamic Dinars.**

d. Serves as a bridge between the **Barter Trade System of the Communist World** and the **System of Payments in Disbalancing exchange rates** of the **Capitalist World.**

---

1. Al-Qayrawānī, *Risalah*, op. cit., ch. 34: *Bāb fil Buyū'wa mā Shakala al-Buyū,*'pp. 102-112.
2. Ibid.
3. Ibid.
4. Ibid.
5. Al-Ṭibrānī.
6. Al-Muslim.
7. Ibn Ḥabbān.
8. Qur'ān, ch. 2:275.
9. Qur'ān, ch. 2:276.
10. Qur'ān, ch. 2:278.
11. Qur'ān, ch. 2:279.
12. Qur'ān, ch. 3:130.
13. Qur'ān, ch. 4:161.
14. Qur'ān, ch. 30:39.
15. Bukhārī.
16. Dārqutnī and Aḥmad.
17. Abū D'āūd, Aḥmad and Nisāi.
18. Sayyid Quṭb, *Ḥādhā al-Dīn (This Religion of Islam)* Gray, Indianapolis (undated), page 61-62.
19. Cf. Ibn Taimiyyah on *Public and Private Law in Islam or Public Policy in Islamic Jurisprudence.* Translated from Arabic by Omar Farrukh, Beirut, 1966, pp. 179-180.
20. A-Qayrawānī, *Risālah*, op.cit., See *Bāb Fil Buyū'wa mā shakala al-suya,* pp. 102.112.
21. Qur'ān, ch. 2:188.
22. Qur'ān, ch. 4:58.
23. Qur'ān, ch. 2:283.
24. Bukhārī, 2:23.
25. Qur'ān, ch. 8:27.
26. Qur'ān, ch. 2:155.

27. Qur'ān, ch. 4:58.
28. Qur'ān, ch. 2:282.
29. cf. Cohen's *Everyman's Talmud* (Dent. London), p.326. It says "The witnesses must be men, not women or minors." See also *Jewish Encyclopaedia* (Frank and Wagnallel, New York,) vol. v, p. 177.
30. Bukhārī, 3:572.
31. Bukhārī, 3:574.
32. Bukhārī, 3:582.
33. Bukhārī, 3:585.
34. Qur'ān, ch. 74:38; also see ch. 2:283.
35. Qur'ān, ch. 2:283.
36. Bukhārī, 3:570.
37. Bukhārī, 48:4.
38. Al-Qayrawānī, *Risālah*, op.cit., ch. 36.
39. Qur'ān, ch. 2:44.
40. Qur'ān, ch. 41:87.
41. Qur'ān, ch. 7:156.
42. Qur'ān, ch. 30:39.
43. Qur'ān, 51:19.
44. Qur'ān, 2:191.
45. Qur'ān, 2:268.
46. Qur'ān, 30:38.
47. Qur'ān, 2:255.
48. Qur'ān, ch. 9:29.
49. Abū Yūsuf, *Kitāb al-Kharāj*, p. 23.
50. Qur'ān, ch. 59:7.
51. Abū Yūsuf, *Kitāb al-Kharāj*, p. 69.
52. Qur'ān, ch. 6:141.
53. Qur'ān, ch. 8:41.
54. Qur'ān, ch. 30:38.
55. Al-Muḥallā, vol. 6, p.158.
56. Ibn Ḥazam, *al-Muḥallā*, vol. 6, p.156.
57. Abu'Ubaid, *al-Amwāl*, p.304.
58. Ibn Ḥazm, *Al-Muḥallā*, op. cit., pp. 157-158.
59. Ibid, p.158.
60. Ibid.
61. Qur'ān, ch. 2:276.
62. Qur'ān, ch. 51:19.
63. Qur'ān, ch. 5:24.
64. Qur'ān, ch. 8:88.
65. Qur'ān, ch. 17:26.
66. Qur'ān, ch. 17:27.
67. Qur'ān, ch. 53:39-40.
68. Qur'ān, ch. 67:15.
69. Tirmidhī.
70. Al-Baihaqī and Ibn Khuzaimah.
71. Tirmidhī.
72. Unanimously agreed Hadith.
73. Muslim, Abū Dāūd and Al-Nisāī.
74. Narrated by Aḥmad, al-Ṭibrānī.
75. Hanson, J. L. *Monetary Theory and Practice*, London, 1974, p. 180.

76. Alington, C. A., *The New Standard Encyclopaedia*, 1932, p. 1254. (see article on Usury).
77. Coulson, *A History of Islamic Law*, op. cit. p.239.
78. Schacht, *Encyclopaedia of Islam*. Article on *Riba* p. 1150.
79. Ya'qūbi, *Tārīkh*, vol. II, pp.132-133.
80. Ibn Maskawaih, *Tajārib-al-Umam*, vol. 3, p. 45.
81. Sabory, R.M. *Introduction to Islamic Civilizations*, p. 59.
82. Siddiqui, Nejatullah, *Banking Without Interest*, Lahore 1973; also see Qureshi, Anwar Iqbal, Islam and the Theory of Interest, Lahore 1946.
83. Ibid.
84. Muslehuddin, Muhammad *Economics and Islam*, Lahore, 1974, p. 55.
85. Gibb, Sir Hamilton, *Whither Islam*, London 1932, p. 379.
86. Some of these suggestions were given by *The Voice of Islam*, vol. 25, No. 6-7, March-April, 1977.

Chapter 22

The Concept of Lawful (Ḥalāl) and Unlawful (Ḥarām) in Sharī'ah

The Shari'ah has given clear guidance in respect of lawful and unlawful based on the teachings of the Qur'ān and the Sunnah. It is not any human being who decides what is lawful and unlawful, not even the Prophet through his own personal judgement. What is *Ḥalāl* is declared through the Qur'ānic Injunctions, and believers are asked to accept it as lawful. Likewise nobody has an authority to declare any food, drink, dress or trade and business as *ḥarām* or unlawful.

The Institution of Islam says:

«قل من حرم زينة الله التي اخرج لعباده والطيبات من الرزق قل هي للذين آمنوا في الحياة الدنيا خالصة يوم القيامة كذلك نفصل الايات لقوم يعلمون. قل انما حرم ربى الفواحش ما ظهر منها وما بطن والاثم والبغى بغير الحق وان تشركوا بالله ما لم ينزل به سلطانا وان تقولوا على الله ما لا تعلمون».

> "Say: Who hath forbidden the beautiful (gifts) of Allah, which He hath produced for His servants, and the things, clean and pure, (which He has provided) for sustenance? Say they are, in the life of this world, for those who believe, (and) purely for them on the Day of Judgement. Thus do We explain the Signs in detail for those who understand. Say: The things that my Lord has indeed forbidden are: Shameful deeds, whether open or secret; sins and trespasses against truth or reason; assigning of partners to Allah for which He has given no authority; and saying things about Allah of which you have no knowledge."[1]

The basic principles in the matter of all restrictive ordinances is that a thing which is not disallowed is deemed to be lawful, as the well-known juridical dictum has it. *Al-ibāha aslan fil-ashyā,*' i.e. "Lawfulness is a recognised principle in all things." In other words, everything is presumed to be lawful, unless it is definitely prohibited by law. There are some jurists who have held the contrary view that everything is unlawful unless the law declares it to be lawful, but this view is, on the face of it, absurd and impossible; moreover it is against the clear principle laid down in the Holy Qur'ān, that everything has been created for the benefit of man, which leads to the only possible presumption that everything can be made use of by him, unless a limitation is placed by law, on the use.

The dictum that everything is presumed to be lawful, unless it is definitely prohibited by Sharī'ah, is based on the following verse of the Holy Qur'ān:

«هُوَ الَّذِي خَلَقَ لَكُمْ مَا فِي الْأَرْضِ جَمِيعاً ثُمَّ اسْتَوَىٰ إِلَى السَّمَاءِ فَسَوَّاهُنَّ سَبْعَ سَمٰوَاتٍ وَهُوَ بِكُلِّ شَيْءٍ عَلِيمٌ».

"It is He (Allah) who has created for you all things that are on earth; moreover His design comprehend the heavens, for He gave order and perfection to the seven firmaments; and of all things He has perfect knowledge."[2]

It further says:

«أَلَمْ تَرَوْا أَنَّ اللّٰهَ سَخَّرَ لَكُمْ مَا فِي السَّمَوَاتِ وَمَا فِي الْأَرْضِ وَأَسْبَغَ عَلَيْكُمْ نِعَمَهُ ظَاهِرَةً وَبَاطِنَةً».

"Do ye not see that Allah has subjected to your (use) all things in the Heavens and on the earth, and Has made His bounties flow to among you in exceeding measure, (both) seen and unseen?. Yet there are among men those who dispute about Allah, without knowledge and without guidance and without a Book to enlighten them."[3]

Of all these bounties of Allah, the lawful and the unlawful are clearly shown, as the Ḥadīth says:

«ما احل الله في كتابه فهو حلال، وما حرم فهو حرام، وما سكت عنه فهو عفو - فأقبلوا من الله عافية فان الله لم يكن ينسىء شيئا - وتلا وما كان ربك نَسِيّاً».

"Wherever Allah has declared lawful in His Book is lawful, and wherever He has declared unlawful is unlawful, and wherever He has remained silent are forgiven. Then accept those bounties of Allah because Allah does not forget anything. Then the Prophet recited the verse (of Sūrah Marryam): Your Lord never forgets anything."[4]

Those things which are made unlawful are enumerated in details in the Holy Qur'ān:

«وَقَدْ فَصَّلَ لَكُمْ مَا حَرَّمَ عَلَيْكُمْ».

"He (Allah) has enumerated in details whatever is made unlawful for you."[5]

Allah has fixed limits in respect of everything, and through the guidance of His Messenger given in the Sunnah, every aspect is fully explained to us. We are asked, according to a Ḥadīth in *Dārqutnī* not to enter into unnecesary discussion about those things which are not mentioned at all. The Prophet said:

«ان الله فرض فرائض فلا تضيعوها وحد حدودا فلا تعتدوها وحرم اشياء فلا تنتهكوها، وسكت عن اشياء رحمة بكم غير نسيان فلا تَبحَثوا عنها».

"Allah has made obligatory deeds essential, don't waste them, and He has fixed limits, do not cross them. Whatever He has declared as unlawful, do not violate them, and He has kept quiet about certain things, it is a sort of mercy for you, don't enter into unnecessary discussion about them."[6]

We should not fabricate any excuses to make lawful what is already declared as unlawful. It will be an act of mere hypocrisy to do so since what is declared as unlawful by Allah and His Messenger will remain unlawful till the last Day. The Jews, according to the Holy Qur'ān, tried to find excuses in order to render whatever was unlawful as lawful. The Holy Prophet (S.A.W.) advised the Muslims thus:

«ترتكبوا ما ارتكب اليهود وتستحلوا محارم الله بأدنى الحِيَل».

"Whatever the Jews did, you do not do it just as they tried to render lawful wherever Allah has declared unalwful merely by giving flimsy excuses."

What is unlawful for a Caliph, a King, an Emperor, a Ruler, is equally unlawful for a pauper. What is unlawful for an *Imām* is also unlawful for his follower. There is no double-standard in the Sharī'ah of Islam. Arabs and non-Arabs are equal before the law, and that is *Ḥarām* for one will always remain *Ḥarām* for the other.

Not only that the Sharī'ah declares theft unlawful for Muslims, it is equally unlawful for non-Muslims as well. The thing that is stolen, whether is belongs to a Muslim or non-Muslim is still unlawful.

We have no responsibility in respect of a non-Jew. They attribute a lie against Allah and they already know about it."[7]

The Jews are asked not to catch fish on Saturday, but they tried to change what was *Ḥarām* by tricking themselves. They used to dig ditches on Friday so that fishes might accumulate in them and then they might (collect them on Sunday). To fabricate such excuses is utterly unlawful in the Sharī'ah of Islam.

It is unfortunate that some Muslims have begun to follow the footsteps of the Jews and hypocrites by finding flimsy excuses to make lawful what is already declared as unlawful in the Qur'ān and the Sunnah. The two most attractive things for the Muslims in the modern times are wine-drinking and eating of Usury. In respect of wine, they have found some beautiful name for some drinks and have started drinking. The Prophecy of the Messenger of Allah is confirmed int he modern times:

«ليستحلّن طائفة من امتى الخمر يسمّونها بغير اسمها».

"A group of my *Ummah* will name wine something else in order to name it lawful."[8]

Likewise, he has said about the Usury which has come true today:

«يأتي على الناس زمان يستحلّون الربا باسم البيع»

"A time will come on people when they will declare usury lawful under the name of trade."[9]

No matter how good intentioned one might be, it does not change an unlawful act into lawful and vice-versa. Similarly the means to obtaining *haram* is also *ḥarām* in Islam. Anything that helps an act of adultery, theft, brigandage, murder is also *ḥarām.* One who brews, sells and distributes wine is also committing as act of *ḥarām.* A witness in the case of Usury deed, an agent, the lender and borrower of usury are also committing unlawful acts.

Between the categories of clearly lawful and unlawful, there are things which are of doubtful nature. As a matter of *Taqwah* (piety), one should try to keep away from them. The Prophet has advised:

"The lawful is made clear and the unlawful is also made clear, and in between lie the acts which are doubtful about which most people do not know whether it is lawful or unlawful. One who kept away from it in order to safeguard his religion and honour, he will remain in peace. But if one is involved in doubtful things, it is too remote to fall a victim to unlawful things. Like a shepherd who grazes his herds in forbidden ground, it is possible to enter into it. Remember that every king has a forbidden grazing ground, and beware that Allah's forbidden grazing ground means the unlawful things."[10]

There are limited in a man's life when he finds himself in a very difficult situation. He may be so very destitute that he may not be able to get his lawful bread. In spite of all his efforts, he might not find a job. Surely, in such circumstances, it is his Muslim neighbours and the entire Muslim society which has really failed him in spite of the systems of *Zakāt* and *Ṣadaqah* in Islam. How is it possible for one to remain hungry in an Islam society? In case, one finds himself in an utterly helpless situation and his wife and children are facing starvation, he may, out of necessity, partake of what is even clearly declared unlawful *(Haram).* This rule will apply to other human necessities as well:

«فَمَنِ اضْطُرَّ غَيْرَ بَاغٍ وَلاَ عَادٍ فَلا أِثْمَ عَلَيه، إنَّ اللّٰهَ غَفُورٌ رَحِيمٌ».

"But if one is forced by necessity, without willful disobedience, nor transgressing the limits, then is he guiltless. For Allah is oft-Forgiving, Most-Merciful."[11]

Injunctions in Respect of Ḥalāl and Ḥarām Food

A *Mu'min* that is a believer is one who willing accepts Allah as his Creator and the obedience of Allah as the mode of his life and strives to seek His pleasure in all his actions in this world. A *Mu'min* also believes that there is going to come another life after the present mundane existence. He also believes in the Day of Judgement and that whosoever obeys the commands of Allah and His Prophet is sure to have a good life in the hereafter and that whosoever violates these commands shall have to bear eternal punishment.

In Islam, a believer is not left without any guidance. The Qur'ān lays down values and norms for all moral actions, including eating and drinking. The Holy Qur'ān says that one should eat 'the lawful and clean things out of what is in the earth.'[12]

«يَـا أَيُّهَـا ٱلنَّـاسُ كُلوُا مِمَّا فِي ٱلاَرْضِ حَلاَلاً طَيِباً وَلاَ تَتَبِعُوا خُطُوَاتِ ٱلشَّيْطَانِ انَّهُ لَكُمْ عَدُوٌ مُبِينٌ».

"O you people, Eat of what is on earth, lawful and good; and do not follow the footsteps of the devil (the Evil one), for he is to you an avowed enemy."

In this verse, there is a general instruction given to all and sundry, Muslims, people of the Book (Jews and Christians) as well as the pagans concerning food and drinks. The Creator asks all the Creatures to follow His command and eat what is pure, clean, wholesome, nourishing and pleasing to the taste. All these qualities are beautifully summed up in the word *'Ṭaiyib'* in the above verse of the Qur'ān. The injunction contained in this verse is that the Jahliyya practices dating before the dawn of Islam should be rejected. All the restrictions they had wrongly imposed should be broken since they are based on superstitions. Whatever they have made lawful or unlawful is because of their own imaginations, the handiwork of satan.

The pagan Arab custom of eating congealed blood is nothing but an example of a shameful custom. It was the blood on the animal sacrificed that they used to smear on the walls of Ka'aba and it was the blood that they used to eat fried as their delicacy.

The same emphasis on eating of the good things *(Tayyib)* is given in verse 172 of the *surah al-Baqarah* of the Qur'ān:

«يَا أَيُّهَا الَّذِينَ آمَنُوا كُلُوا مِنْ طَيِّبَاتِ مَا رَزَقْنَاكُمْ وَاشْكُرُوا لِلَّهِ إِنْ كُنْتُمْ إِيَّاهُ تَعْبُدُونَ».

"O you who believe, Eat of the good things that we have provided for you, and be grateful to Allah, if it is Him you worship."[13]

The above verse is particularly addressed to the believers who have faith in Allah and His Messenger. They are asked to do so and be grateful to Him, since gratitude for Allah's gifts is one of the forms of worship *('Ibādah).* Those who have faith have been told that if by accepting Islam, they have accepted the Divine law just as they claimed, then they should shun all those superstitious beliefs and restrictions on certain foods in the days of the *Jāhilliyah* period. These were not ordained by Allah but by the Quraishite priests, the Jewish rabbii and the monks. The Holy Prophet's Ḥadīth says on the same subject:

«من صلى صلواتنا واستقبل قبلتنا واكل ذبيحتنا فذلك مسلم».

"Whosoever prayed our prayers, faced our Qiblah and ate food slaughtered by us, he is a Muslim."

According to the above Ḥadīth, a man who prays and faces the Qiblah does not absorb himself completely in the Ummah of Islam until he leaves all the *Jahiliyyah* practices concerning food and drinks and be free from all the shatters of the superstitions which were established by his forefathers. If he continues with the past practices in spite of the fact that he prays facing the Ka'abah, he is not a true Muslim.

The following Qur'ānic injunctions explain clearly the foods which are unwholesome physically, morally and spiritually:

«إِنَّمَا حَرَّمَ عَلَيْكُمُ الْمَيْتَةَ وَالدَّمَ وَلَحْمَ الْخِنْزِيرِ وَمَا أُهِلَّ بِهِ لِغَيْرِ اللَّهِ فَمَنِ اضْطُرَّ غَيْرَ بَاغٍ وَلَا عَادٍ فَلَا إِثْمَ عَلَيْهِ إِنَّ اللَّهَ غَفُورٌ رَحِيمٌ».

> "He has forbidden you only carrion, blood and the flesh of swine and that over which is invoked the name of other than Allah. But he who is driven by necessity, neither craving nor transgressing, it is no sin for him. Lo! Allah is forgiving, Merciful."[14]

When one is forced by necessity and eats unlawful food without willful disobedience to the injunctions of Allah concerning foods and drinks, then he is guiltless. But in this verse, the permission for the use of unlawful things is given *conditionally.* The following three conditions should be kept in mind:

1. The man who ventures to eat the unlawful must be put really in a helpless state and was driven by utter necessity to save his life and that of his dependants. As for example, on account of hunger or thirst his life was in danger and there was nothing available except unlawful food, or due to illness, there was no way of saving his life except eating that food as a remedial prescription.
2. There was absolutely no intention to break the law of Allah in eating the unlawful food but he was driven by necessity.
3. Even if one had to eat the unlawful food out of utter necessity, it should not be taken more than necessary. Supposing a few morsels of food or a little drink of water can save one's life, it should not be used more than that quantity.

«حُرِّمَتْ عَلَيْكُمُ الْمَيْتَةُ وَالدَّمُ وَلَحْمُ الْخِنْزِيرِ وَمَا اُهِلَّ لِغَيْرِ اللّٰهِ بِهِ وَالْمُنْخَنِقَةُ
وَالْمَوْقُوذَةُ وَالْمُتَرَدِّيَةُ وَالنَّطِيحَةُ وَمَا اَكَلَ السَّبُعُ اِلَّا مَا ذَكَّيْتُمْ وَمَا ذُبِحَ عَلَى
النُّصُبِ وَاَنْ تَسْتَقْسِمُوا بِالْاَزْلَامِ - ذٰلِكُمْ فِسْقٌ».

> "Forbidden unto you (for food) are the dead-meat, and blood and flesh of the swine, and that over which is invoked the name of other than Allah, and the strangled, and the dead through beating, and the dead through falling from a height, and that which has been killed by (the goring of) horns, and the devoured of wild beasts, unless you have cleansed (by slaughtering) it in the proper, lawful way, while yet there is life in it, and that which has been immolated unto idols. And (forbidden is it) that ye swear by the divine arrows. This is an abomination."[15]

In the *Sūrah al-An'ām,* the food which are declared unlawful are further mentioned in the following verses:

«وَلَا تَاْكُلُوا مِمَّا لَمْ يُذْكَرِ اسْمُ اللّٰهِ عَلَيْهِ وَاِنَّهُ لَفِسْقٌ - وَاِنَّ الشَّيَاطِينَ
لَيُوحُونَ اِلٰى اَوْلِيَائِهِمْ لِيُجَادِلُوكُمْ - وَاِنْ اَطَعْتُمُوهُمْ اِنَّكُمْ لَمُشْرِكُونَ».

> "And eat not of what wheron Allah's name hath not been mentioned, for Lo, it is abomination. Verily, the satans are ever inspiring their friends that they may wrangle with you. But if you obey them, ye will be in truth idolaters."[16]

«قُلْ لَا أَجِدُ فِي مَا أُوحِيَ إِلَيَّ مُحَرَّماً عَلَىٰ طَاعِمٍ يَطْعَمُهُ إِلَّا أَنْ يَكُونَ مَيْتَةً أَوْ دَماً
مَسْفُوحاً أَوْ لَحْمَ خِنْزِيرٍ فَإِنَّهُ رِجْسٌ أَوْ فِسْقاً أُهِلَّ لِغَيْرِ اللَّهِ بِهِ فَمَنِ اضْطُرَّ غَيْرَ
بَاغٍ وَلَا عَادٍ فَإِنَّ رَبَّكُم غَفُورٌ رَحِيمٌ».

"Say thou (O Prophet): I find out not in that which hath been revealed unto me ought forbidden unto an eater that eat thereof, except it will be carrion, or blood poured forth, or flesh of swine, for that verily is foul, or an abomination over which is invoked the name of other than that of Allah, then whosoever is driven (by extreme and uncontrollable hunger) thereto, neither lusting nor transgressing, verily thy Lord is Forgiving, Merciful."

«وَعَلَى الَّذِينَ هَادُوا حَرَّمْنَا كُلَّ ذِي ظُفُرٍ وَمِنَ الْبَقَرِ وَالْغَنَمِ حَرَّمْنَا عَلَيْهِمْ
شُحُومَهُمَا إِلَّا مَا حَمَلَتْ ظُهُورُهُمَا أَوِ الْحَوَايَا أَوْ مَا اخْتَلَطَ بِعَظْمٍ - ذَٰلِكَ
جَزَيْنَاهُمْ بِبَغْيِهِمْ وَإِنَّا لَصَادِقُونَ».

"And unto those who are Judaised we forbade every animal with cloven hoof; and of the bullock and the goats we forbade unto them the fat thereof, save that which is borne of their backs or entrails or that which sticketh to the bone. Thus we awarded them for their rebellion, and verily we are Truthful."[17]

From the above Qur'ānic injunctions it is clear that a true Muslim should abstain from eating the following kinds of foods:

1. The flesh of swine or a pig (i.e. Pork)

Swine is a dirty animal whose foul habits and coarse-feeding are well known. When one sees them in those conditions, it makes their flesh repulsive. Moreoever, eating the flesh of swine may become a cause of glandular fever and leprosy. The ancient Egyptians and Pheonicians as well as the Jews regarded swine as it is mentioned by Hastings in his Dictionary of the Bible (Vol. iv. p. 633).

The Bible's abhorrence of swine is clear no matter may be the practice of the modern 'Christian' world. The flesh and blood of swine are described as characteristically heathed and repulsive. 'And the swine . . . he is unclean to you.'[18] 'And the swine . . . It is unclean to you; ye shall not eat of their flesh, nor touch their dead carcase.'[19] There also occurs similar references in Mark: 11-12 and Matthew: 7-6.

The Holy Qur'ān refers to swine as *'Khinzir'* which is a contemptuous term. The same is true in English also as the word 'swine' is applied to 'a low, greedy or vicious person' (New Standard Dictionary of English Language, New York). The shorter Oxford Dictionary describes 'swine' as 'applied as robriously to a sexual, degraded or coarse person; also as a mere term of contempt or abuse, and 'swinish' is described as 'gross specially', the word 'pig' is applied to a person 'selfish, mean, unclean and vile'.

For a true believer *(Mu'min)* all these above explanations are unnecessary since he firmly believes in the commandments of the Qur'ān which categorically forbid the eating of the flesh of swine (pork, bacon, or ham).

2. The dead or rotting flesh

For a Muslim, eating of the carcase of dead and decaying flesh is forbidden. The Holy Qur'ān describes this in a word *'Maitata'* which signifies even 'that which has not been slaughtered in the manner prescribed by law'.

3. Blood poured from an animal by force

Eating and drinking of blood is also forbidden. Some people like to collect blood and boil it and turn it into a cake looking like liver and then eat it. This is forbidden in Islam.

4. The flesh of a strangled animal

The flesh of any animal which is strangled to death is forbidden for a Muslim.

5. The flesh of an animal beaten to death

The flesh of an animal which is beaten to death is also forbidden.

6. The flesh of an animal which dies through a fall.

If an animal dies through a fall from a height, its flesh is forbidden for a Muslim.

7. The flesh of an animal which is smitten to death with the horn

If an animal is smitten to death during a fight with another animal which knocks it with its horn, its flesh is forbidden for a Muslim.

8. The flesh of an animal a part of which is eaten by a wild beast

If a part of the flesh of an animal is eaten by a wild animal it is forbidden for a Muslim. This is highly unhygienic.

9. The flesh of an animal which dies a natural death

If an animal dies through sickness or otherwise, its flesh is also forbidden for a Muslim.

10. The flesh of an animal slaughtered for the worship of an idol.

Islam is purely a montheistic religion and any form of polytheism *(shirk)* is considered as the greatest of sins. The Holy Qur'ān says that an animal which is slaughtered in the name of any idol or demi-god is forbidden for a Muslim. This means that the animal is slaughtered for the worship of that idol whose name is recited while slaughtering it. According to the Hadith of the Holy Prophet, a Muslim should say *Bismillāh Allāhu Akbar* (In the name of Allah, Allah is the Greatest) while slaughtering an animal (Bukhārī, ch. 73, Ḥadīth 9).

No animal except fish and locust are lawful unless they are slaughtered according to the Islamic law namely by drawing the knife across the throat and cutting the jugular vein and wind-pipe repating at the same time the formula given before. The *Dhabḥ* is of two kinds:

Dhabḥ al-Ikhtiyārī: This is the voluntary slaughter of an animal reciting the name of Allah while driving the knife across the throat.

Dhabḥ al-Iḍṭirārī: This is the slaughter through necessity affected by wounds as in the shooting of birds and animals. In this case the prayer formula *(Bismillāh Allāh Akbar)* must be said at the time of the discharge of the arrow from its bow or the shot from the gun.

11. The Beats of prey with canine teeth

Abū Tha'labah said: "The Messenger of Allah, may benedicition and salutation of Allah be upon him, forbade all beasts of prey with canine teeth" (Bukhārī, ch. 72, Ḥadīth 29). According to the *Mishkāt,* the birds of prey with claw are also included in the above. (Mishkāt, ch. 19, Ḥadīth 2). The animals like donkey, lion, dog, tiger, hyenas, crocodiles, leopard and lizards are also forbidden according to the following Ḥadīth:

« عليكم بهذا القرآن - ما وعدتم فيه من حلال احلوه وماوجدتم فيه من حرام محرمة الا لا احل لكم حمار الاهلى وكل ذي ناب من السبع».

According to *Hidāya,* all quadrupeds which seize their prey with their teeth and all birds that seize it with their talons are unlawful for Muslims in normal circumstances.

It is lawful to make use of the wool and hair of a dead animal. Similarly, it is lawful to make use of that which is removed from animals while they are alive. But what is considered better in the Mālikī view, is for such things to be washed first, before they are used.

It is not lawwful to make use of the feathers of a dead bird, its horn, its nails and teeth. It is reprehensible to use the tusks of elephant. However, there are conflicting views with regards to that.

If a mouse should fall into a quantity of butter, or oil or honey, all of which are in liquid form, and dies in them; they must be thrown away, and must not be eaten. However, there is no harm in using the oil, or something of that sort in which a mouse died such as fuel for a lamp but only to be used in places other than mosques. **Mosque** must be free from any such things which are mixed up with filth.

If however, the butter, the oil and the honey, were in a solid state, the dead mouse, and the oil or honey, which is around it, should be thrown away, and the remainder may be used for food.

But Sahnun, one of the most most famous Maliki jurists, is of the opinion that, if the dead mouse, had been in the foodstuff for a long time, such liquid foodstuffs must be thrown away.[20]

Hunting for the purpose of sport only is detestable in the eyes of Sharī'ah. But hunting for a purpose other than sport is lawful. Every game killed by a trained dog or trained falcon which are set upon an animal or bird whose flesh is lawful will still be lawful food for consumption.

Similarly, it is lawful to eat the flesh of the game your falcon or dog has brought and the prey is dead and you are not able to slaughter it in the normal Islamic way.

Every game you are able to catch, through using your arrow or spear, you are free to eat its flesh. If you are able to take hold of it before it is dead, you can then slaughter it in the normal way. But if it died of its own before you are able to slaughter it, you can nevertheless eat its flesh if it is indeed killed by your arrow. However, if the hunter finds the game already dead, and his arrow having hit a vital spot in the body of the game, there shall be no harm in eating the flesh of such game.[21]

If one slaughters an animal for the purpose of sacrifice or another other purpose and he forgets to pronounce the formula: "In the name of Allah", it is permissible for such an animal to be eaten. But if one amoits to pronounce the formula deliberately, the animal thus slaughtered must not be eaten.

Similarly, the hunter who forgets to pronounce the formula: "In the name of Allah" at the time he lets loose a falcon or a dog at a game, the flesh of such a game killed can be eaten by Muslims. If, however, hit omits to pronounce the formula deliberately, the flesh of the game thus killed shall not be wholesome.

An animal killed for the purpose of sacrifice, on the occasion of *'Īd-al-Kabīr* or for the purpose of doing expatiation for an error in pilgrimage rites or on slaughtered on the occasion of naming a child must not have any part of it sold.

A man is permitted to eat the flesh of the beast he slaughtered for the purpose of sacrificing on the occasion of *'Īd-al-Kabīr*. But it is better for him to give away part of it, as alms. However, it is not obligatory upon a person to give away part of the flesh as alms.

A pilgrim must not eat the flesh of an animal he slaughters, for the purpose of making a sacrifice to atone – for an error he committed, in the pilgrimage rites, nor does he eat of the flesh of the animal he slaughters to compensate for a game he kills while in a state of *iḥrām*. He should not eat the flesh of the animal he vowed to slaughter, for the sake of the poor. He should not eat of the flesh of an animal he intended to sacrifice voluntarily, as a mark of piety; before such an animal reaches the place it is supposed to be killed.[22]

Notes

1. Qur'ān, ch. 7:32-33.
2. Qur'ān, ch. 2:29.
3. Qur'ān, ch. 31:20.
4. Al-Ḥākim
5. Dārqutnī.
6. Qur'ān, ch. 6:119.
7. Qur'ān, ch. 3:75.
8. Aḥmad bin Ḥanbal.
9. Ighathan al-Lahfan, vol. 1, p. 352.
10. Bukhārī, Muslim and Tirmidhi.
11. Qur'ān, ch. 2:173.
12. Qur'ān, ch. 2:168.
13. Qur'ān, ch. 2:172.
14. Qur'ān, ch. 2:173.
15. Qur'ān, ch. 5:4.
16. Qur'ān, ch. 6:121.
17. Qur'ān, ch. 6:145-146.
18. Le. 11:7.
19. Dt. 14:8.
20. See Al-Qayrawānī, *Risālsh,* op. cit., ch. 29.
21. Al-Qayrawānī, ʿAbdallāh Ibn Abi Zaid, Risāllah, Zaria, 1976, see Chapter 29 *Bāb fil Daḥāya wal Dhabāiḥ*. pp. 78-83.
22. Ibid.

PART VI

EXTERNAL AND OTHER RELATIONS

Chapter 23

Al-Siyar: International Law

In the ancient times, there was nothing like international law as such. Whatever elements of international law existed in their legal system, there was nothing international nor law in it. It was considered as a part of politics and solely depended on the manoeuvres and machinations of the statesmen. Even the Iroquois had some notion of international law as they sent and received envoys, and they knew very well the rights of war and peace but still they continued eating their prisoners.[1] In other words, we cannot consider the ancient system as international law since it was not based on right principles. The rules of international law worked out by the ancient people applied only to a limited number of states or city-states inhabited by people of the same race or following the same religion, or speaking the same language. As for example, the Greeks who were merely influenced by the Phoenician culture were so very narrow-minded that their international law could only be applied between the city-states of the Greek Peninsula. According to their law, non-Greeks were considered barbarians. As Aristotle once said: "the nature intended barbarians to be slaves of the Greeks."[2]

Plato had advised his countrymen to be more lenient in their mutual treatment, but he could not tolerate non-Greeks who could be treated mildly. The Greek City States had formed a kind of league of nations and were instructed not to destroy any town or cut running water int he time of war or peace, but this principle was to be applied strictly within the city-states. Later, the Romans also evolved their own legal system. The new system us as advanced as the Greek system but did not go far enough. As far as the life and property of a citizen of a state which had not a treaty relation of friendship with Rome was concerned, the inhabitants of that city could be made slaves and their properties could be seized. The Roman law of war remained very much the same, recognising no right for the belligerent, and using nothing but discretion regarding the non-Roman enemy. The only people who were treated honourably were the ambassadors.[3] Even the *Jāhiliyyah* Arabs, before the advent of Islam, had some form of international law. The Arab chiefs used to visit foreign rulers and sent and received ambassadors.[4] The Yemenites sent envoys to Madyan to ask for Persian help against the Abbysinians. These Yemenites used to receive the ambassadors of several foreign rulers including the Byzantine empire.[5]

The *Jāhiliyyah* Arabs too sent envoys to solicit the return of the Muslim refugees to the court of Emperor Negus of Abbyssinia in the year 612 A.D.[6] In spite of these rules of international relations, applied only whenever it served their purpose, they proved to be very cruel in their treatment meted out to other people with whom they had no such relations.

After the advent of Islam, the Muslims were the first to accord a dignified place to the international law in the Sharī'ah. *Al-Siyar* – thus created both rights and obligations and the international law became a branch of study as an independent science under the name *al-siyar.* It made no discrimination among foreigners and dealt equitably with the non-Muslim states of the entire world.[7]

The Sharī'ah has enshrined in itself the principles of Islamic International Law right from its inception and as early as 150 years after the Hijrah, it regulated the conduct and behaviour of the Muslim state in war, peace and neutrality. The general concept on international law restricts its jurisdictional application to nations only but the concepts of Islamic international law in the Shari'ah regulated not only the conduct of the Muslim state with other states, but also the relationship of non-Muslim states and non-Muslim individuals living in the Muslim state.

The object was to enlarge the concepts of Islamic international law to encompass all public functions conducted by the state or its citizens in any intercourse not necessarily subject to private regulations in the performance of the public needs or functions. As Dr. Ḥāmidullah puts it, "When Islam came and founded a state of its own, the earliest name given by Muslim writers to the special branch of law dealing with war, peace and neutrality seems to have been Siyar the plural form of Sirat meaning conduct and behaviour."[8]

The Muslim Jurists are of the opinion that the term *al-Siyar* to connote international law was first used by Imām Abū Ḥanīfah (d. 150 A.H.), the founder of the Ḥanafi school, while delivering his series of lectures on the theme of international law. Imām Moḥammad al-Shaybani (d. 188 A.H.), the famous pupil of Imām Abū Ḥanīfah and a famous scholar attached to the 'Abbāsid Caliphate has rendered the services of editing and recording these lectures in his famous books '*Kitāb al-siyar al-ṣaghir*' and '*Kitāb al-saiyar al-kabīr*'. These books of *al-siyar,* among other things, discuss the behaviour of Muslims in dealing with non-Muslims, the covenanted people *(ahl al-Dhimmah)*, the resident aliens, the apostates, the rebels and so on and so forth.[9]

The word Sirat, when it was used without adjectives meant the conduct of the Prophet more specially in his wars.[10] Later it came to be used for the conduct of Muslim rulers in international affairs.[11] In the works of European jurists of the Middle ages like Grotious, Puffendorf and others, one notices that they intentionally excluded the Muslims and the Science of al-Siyar from all community of interest from the Christian nations of Europe. Their law originated in the necessity of regulating the relations of the new sovereign states which arose because of the urgent need of temporal unity of Christendom. The later European jurists, out of necessity, thought that their international law was limited to Christendom only, and then enunciated broad principles to include others as well. Some Muslim scholars think that "these European principles were just echoes of the time. Moreoever, their human modifications for civilization came only after they intensively borrowed Islamic principles by the impact of Muslim Spain, the Crusades and earlier Ottomans."[12]

The impact of *al-siyar,* the Muslim international law can be properly assessed from the fact that the earliest European writers on international law like Pierre Bellow, Ayala, Victoria, Gentiles and others, all hailed from Spain or its neighbour Italy, and were influenced by Islam and Muslims during the period of renaissance which came about as the impact of Islam on Christendom. The famous author Grotins was born in Holland but he had also read and was influenced by Muslim International Law as can be seen from his discovery that postilimium was known to Muslim Law.[13]

The Fundamental Human Rights under Siyar

The fundamental human rights of man in Shari'ah rest on the premise than man is the Khalifa of Allah on earth and hence the center of the universe.

The fundamental difference between human rights in Islam and those of the famous Declaration of Human Rights adopted by the United Nations General Assembly is that the former are binding on every Muslim state while the latter are mere declarations binding on nor state or country. One of the purposes of the United Nations, according to Article 1 of its Charter, is to provide and encourage respect for human rights. Later the General Assembly adopted two agreements,[14] which are known as the "Covenant on Civil and Political Rights" and the "Covenant on Economic, Social and Cultural Rights". The former covenant includes the following rights:

a. The right of life and liberty and security of person
b. The right of privacy
c. The right to marry and found a family
d. The right to education
e. Freedom of thought, conscience and belief
f. Freedom of expression of opinion
g. Freedom of movement
h. Right to a peaceful assembly and association
i. The right to fair trial and equality before law
j. The right to be free from arbitary arrest and detention.

Unfortunately, the above rights and freedom granted by the covenant are not binding on any state. The states which voluntarily sign the covenent would be legally obliged to abide by its provisions. In recent times, we have seen some states which have signed the covenant but have not implemented all of its provisions. As far as these rights are concerned, they are taught to every Muslim through the divine scriptures which provide necessary guidance to the believers to develop all his faculties in a manner that will benefit him for his great task as the viceregent of Allah on earth. We shall discuss all the fundamental human rights in Islam granted to Muslims and non-Muslims alike in the following chapters.

Since we have discussed the characteristics of Sharī'ah, we should bear in mind that individual freedom is sacred within the ethical limits imposed by the Sharī'ah, and it will be considered sacred only as long as it does not conflict with the larger social interest or as long as the individual does not transgress the rights of others.[15]

Treaty Relations in Sharī'ah

The Prophet was the greatest politician and did not forget to respect the treaties and pledges, but he held on the contrary a great importance to the strict observance of the terms of treaties entered into by Muslims. Sometimes in observing the terms of treaties, he had to forego the advantage of his little Commonwealth of Islam which functioned on the principles of Sharī'ah.

One Ḥuzaifa-bin-Yaman could not migrate to Medina with the Prophet. He entered into a contract with the Quraish he would not fight against them, and in consideration thereof he remained free from molestations at Mecca. Subsequently, at the Battle of Badr, he joined the Prophet to fight against the Quraish. The Prophet was informed of the solemn contract between Huzaigah and the Quraish. The Prophet consequently ordered him to refrain from attacking the Quraish in fulfilment of his contract.

Once the Quraish sent Abū Rafi' as their ambassador to the Prophet. When he came to Medina he was greatly influenced by the intrinsic force of Islam and expressed his willingness to accept it. The Prophet could not accept his declaration at that time, as the detaining of an ambassador on any ground whatsoever is breach of international law.

The importance of observing the terms of treaties, pledges and pacts with non-Muslims under the Sharī'ah is sanctified in Islam and stands above all other considerations. As for example, non-Muslims are entitled to Diyah (blood-money) if they happen to be in treaty relations with Muslims, while there is no provision of Diyah to the relatives of a Muslim who belongs to a people with no treaty relations with the Muslims.

The best example of this can be seen in Ḥudaibiyah when the Prophet (S.A.W.) entered into a treaty relation with non-Muslims even though the terms of the treaty were unfavourable to Muslims. Suhail was negotiating the terms of the treaty with the Prophet on behalf of the Quraishites while his son, Abū Jandal, who had accepted Islam and was persecuted by the Quraishites for having done so managed to escape the hands of the enemies. It was verbally agreed between Suhail and the Prophet (and not yet written down or sealed) that a Muslim should not aid another Muslim against a non-Muslim who enjoyed the protection of a pledge even for a religious cause. The Qurān says:

«وَإِنِ ٱسْتَنْصَرُوكُمْ فِي ٱلدِّينِ فَعَلَيْكُمُ ٱلنَّصْرُ إِلَّا عَلَىٰ قَوْمٍ بَيْنَكُمْ وَبَيْنَهُمْ مِيثَاقٌ».

"But if they seek your aid in religion, it is your duty to help them, except against a people with whom you have a treaty."[16]

While still the treaty was in the process of negotiation, and the Prophet had agreed on the above, Abū Jandal fled the non-Muslim Meccans and came for refuge to the Muslims. The moment Suhail saw his son, he declared: "O Muḥammad, the matter between you and myself has already been settled." To this the Prophet replied: "You speak the truth." When Abū Jandal heard this, he should: "O Muslims, am I to be returned to the idolaters to be deprived of my religion?" But Abū Jandal was returned to the non-Muslims according to the terms of the treaty although many Companions of the Prophet raised their objection.

The practice of dealing with the non-Muslims continued during the period of Muslim rule in most countries and any case of injustice should be considered as a deviation and a sign of weakness on the part of the individual ruler. Imām Abū Yūsuf, an eminent jurist and the famous disciple of Imām Abū Ḥanīfah says about the treaty rights of the non-Muslims: "We shall take from them only what was mutually fixed at the time of peace-making. All terms of the treaty shall be strictly adhered to and no additions would be permitted."[17]

---

1. *Esprit des Lois;* Paris 1860, liver ch. 3, p. 7.
2. See *Politics*, book I, ch. 7.
3. cf. Oppen Heim International Law, 4th Edn. vol. 1, pp. 59-61.
4. Ṭabari, *Tarīkh* vol. 1, p. 1537, also see Masʿūdi, *Murūj al-Dhahab*, vol. 4, p. 250.
5. Nadvi, Sulaiman *Ard al-Qur'an*, vol. 1, p.319.
6. Ibn Hishām, pp. 217-221.
7. Ḥamidullah, Moḥammad, *Introduction to Islam*, I.I.F.S.O. Publication to the Kuwait 1970, p. 188-189.
8. Ḥamidullah, Muiḥammad, *Muslim conduct of State*, Lahore, 1973, p. 10.
9. Al-Sarakhsī, *Al-Mabsūt*, vol. 10, p. 2.
10. Al-Sarakhsī, *Al-Muhīt*, vol. 1, fol. 567 a, b. (MS. Waliud Dīn, Istanbul, No. 1356).
11. Ḥamīdullāh, op. cit. p. 21.
12. Qādrī, Anwār Aḥmad, *Islamic Jurisprudence in the Modern World*, Lahore, 1973, pp. 277-278.
13. De Jire•Belli, X, 3, v. quoted by Dr. Ḥamīdullāh in *Muslim Conduct of State*, Lahore 1937, p. 72.
14. See critical analysis given on this topic by, Anwer, Beg, *Civil and Political Rights in Islam*, No. 1-2, vol. 14 *Al-Ittiḥād*, January-April 1977, p. 41.
15. For further details on this subject, see Doi, A. Rahman I., *Non-Muslims under Sharīʿah*, Maryland, 1980.
16. Qur'ān, ch. 8:72.
17. Abū Yūsuf, *Kitāb al-Kharāj*, Cairo, p. 35.

Chapter 24

Non-Muslims and the Sharī'ah

Non-Muslims and Islamic Nationality

The non-Muslims who live in an Islamic state and enjoy all their human rights which are enshrined in the Shari'ah care called Ahl al-Dhimmah or Dhimmis, the covenanted people. The Dhimmis living in an Islamic state are guaranteed the protection of their life, property and honour exactly like that of a Muslim. The rights given to a Dhimmī are of an irrevocable nature. It becomes every Muslim's religious duty to protect life, property and honour of a non-Muslim since it forms a part and parcel of faith (Īmān).

The word Dhimmah literally means pledged *(al-'Ahd)*, guarantee *(al Ḍamān)*, safety *(al-Amān)*.[1] The non-Muslims are called Dhimmis because they are under the pledge of Allah, the pledge of the Messenger of Allah, and the pledge of the Muslim community so that they can live under the protection of Islam. In other words, they are under the protection of Muslims and their guarantee. The pledge of security and guarantee given to the non-Muslims is like the political nationality[2] given in the modern times on the basis of which people acquire all their rights as the nationals of a certain country and become liable to responsibilities. The Dhimmis from this point of view are "the people of the abode of Islam" *(ahl Dār al-Islam)*[3] and hence the possessors of Islamic Nationality (*al-Jinsiyyah al Islāmiyyah*).[4]

Non-Muslims under the Jurisdiction of a Muslim State

The Muslim Jurists have classified the Non-Muslim citizens under different categories.[5] The most prevalent view is that there are the first three kinds of non-Muslims who may be found in any Islamic State:

1. *The Dhimmis:* These are the *Ahl al-Dhimma* or those who accept the hagemony of a Muslim State whose matters are to be decided with the terms of the appropriate treaty. Muslim State is duty bound to abide by all the terms of such a treaty.
2. *The 'Conquered People':* These non-Muslims are those who fought against Muslims until they were defeated and they were

overpowered. They automatically become the *Dhimmah* or responsibility of a Muslim State. They will pay a fixed amount of *Jizyah* tax and their lives, property, honour and places of worship will be protected in lieu thereof.

3. Those non-Muslims who cleared happen to be residing in the Muslim State as its citizens.
4. Non-Muslims residing temporarily in a Muslim country, e.g., tourists or temporary sojourners.
5. Resident aliens who have opted voluntarily to live in a Muslim State.

It is essential to remove some misconceptions about these distinctions in the Shari'ah between Muslims, Dhimmis and non-Muslims. Some Scholars tend to give the misleading analogy of this distinction and compare it with the Roman concept of Jurisdiction in the Jus Civile or the Roman Pax Romana. It should be remembered that non-Muslims are not outside the jurisdiction as is the case with Jus Civile. Likewise, Muslims are not supposed to consider themselves as the "Lords of the population of the globe" as they are not arbis Romanus but merely "Servants of Allah" *('Ibād Allāh)* and even as rulers, they merely the custodians of Allah's property and not the absolute owner because everything existing in the heavens and the earth belong to Allah. The non-Muslims therefore, are equal before the law in every aspect. The distinction in the terms of 'Muslims' and 'non-Muslims' merely remains one of political administration and not of human rights.

Since the Dhimmis are under Dhimmat-Allah, they enjoy complete religious, administrative and political freedom – a right guaranteed to them in return for their loyalty and the payment of a reasonable tax called *Jizyah* which will be utilized in the defence and administration of the state.6

Muslims and non-Muslims: Guidelines from the Qur'ān

It is a wrong presumption that since an Islamic state is based on a definite ideology, the state will annihilate the non-Islamic elements within its fold. There are guidelines in the Qur'ān and the Sunnah which speaks of strengthening and cementing the relationship between Muslim and non-Muslim citizens. The basic foundation of this relationship is referred to in the Qur'ān in the following words:

«لَا ينْهٰكُم اللّٰهُ عَنِ ٱلذَّيَن لَمْ يُقَاتِلوُكُمْ فِي الدّينِ وَلَمْ يُخْرِجُوكُمْ مِنْ دِيَارِكُمْ اَنْ تَبَـرّوهُمْ وَتُقْسِطـُوا اِلَيْهِمْ اِنَّ اللّٰهَ يُحِبُّ ٱلْمُقْسِطِينَ – اِنَّمَا يَنْهٰكُمُ اللّٰهُ عَنِ الذَّيَن قَاتَلوُكُمْ فِي الـدّينِ وَاَخْـرَجُـوكُمْ مِنْ دِيَارِكُمْ وَظَاَهَرُوا عَلٰى اِخْرَاجِكُمْ اَنْ تَوَلوَّهْمُ – وَمَنْ يَتَوَلَّهُمْ فَاُولَئِكَ هُمُ الظَّالِمُونَ».

"Allah forbids you not with regard to those who fight you not for your Faith nor drive you out of your homes, from dealing kindly and justly with them: For Allah loves those who are just. Allah only forbids you with regard to those who fight you for your Faith and drive you out of your homes and support others in driving you out, from turning to them (for friendship and protection). It is such as turn to them (in these circumstances), that do wrong."[7]

According to the above verses of Sūrah al-Mumtaḥanah, Muslims are asked to deal with unbelievers kindly and justly unless they are rampant and out to destroy Muslims and their Faith as was shown by the example of Prophet Muhammad in the treaties of Hudaibiyah and Medina.

The best example of such treatment can be seen in the life time of the Prophet. In the early days of Islam, Muslims had to migrate fromt heir place of birth because of the persecution at the hands of non-Muslim pagan Meccan. Qutailah bint ʿabd al-ʿUzza, the mother of Asmā bin Abūbakr and the wife of Abubakr, who later became the second Caliph, did not migrate from Mecca to Medina in 622 A.D. nor did she accept the religion of Islam. After the treaty of Ḥudaibiyah, when Meccans visited medina, Qutailah came to Medina to see her daughter. ʿAbdallāh bin Zubair, the illustrious son of Asmā narrates that Asmā first refused to see her non-Muslim mother. When she asked the Prophet whether or not she could see her non-Muslim mother, the Prophet asked her to see her and treat her well.[8]

From the above incident, the jurists have deduced that it is essential for every Muslim to treat with respect one's parents, brothers and sisters and other relatives no matter what their faith is. They should also try to help them in the hour of need, provided they do not profess to be the open enemies of Islam.[9]

As far as the people of the Book, that is Jews and Christians, are concerned, they have been given a special position in the Qur'ān since their religions were originally based on the Heavenly Books like Torait and Injil. The Qur'ān says in respect of Ahl al-Kitāb:

«ولا تجادلوا اهل الكتاب الا بالتي هي احسن الا الذين ظلموا منهم وقولوا امنا بالذي انزل الينا وانزل اليكم والهنا والهكم واحد ونحن له مسلمون».

"And dispute you not with the People of the Book, except with means better (than mere disputation), unless it be with those of them who inflict wrong (and injury), but say: 'We believe in the Revelation which has come down to us and in that which came down to you; our God and your God is One and it is to Him we bow (in Islam)'."[10]

In order to achieve their purpose as standard bearer of Allah, Muslims are required to find true common ground of belief, as stated in the latter part of the above verse, and also to show their kindness, sincerity, truth and genuine anxiety for the good of others, that they are not cranks ore merely selfish seeking or questionable aims. But those who are deliberately trying to wrong or injure others will have to be treated firmly, as we are guardians of each other. With them there is little question of finding common ground or expecting patience, until the injury is prevented or stopped.

Fundamental Rights of Non-Muslims

The fundamental rights of non-Muslims in an Islamic State are of two kinds:

1. Their protection from all external threats.
2. Their protection from all internal tyranny and persecution.

The first kind of protection is the same as in the case of Muslims. The head of state and those in authority are bound to look after the interest of all citizens using all the force at their command. The famous Malikite Scholar Imām al-Qurafi[11] quotes the statement of Ibn Hazm from his book Marātib al-Ijmā:

> "If enemies at war come to our country aiming at certain Dhimmi, it is essential for us that we come out to fight them with all our might and weapons since he is under the protection of Allah and His Messenger. If we did anything less than this, it means we have failed in our agreement for protection.

This principle of the Shari'ah was amply demonstrated by the famous Shaikh Ibn Taimiyyah when the Tartars had invaded Syria. The Shaikh went to see Qatlushah to spare the sufferings of people. he agreed to do so with the Muslims but refused to treat non-Muslims in the same way as Muslims. The Shaikh said that it would not please them since the Jewish and Christian families were under their protection.[12]

The more important protection is to accord to non-Muslim citizens is from internal high-handedness, persecution, tyranny and injustice. The Muslim citizens are duty bound to spare their hands and tongues from hurting the non-Muslim citizens.[13] They must not keep enmity or hatred against them, since Allah does not like tyrants but gives them a quick punishment in this world or gives them a greater punishment in the next world.[14] There are a number of verses of the Holy Qur'ān warning wrong-doers and the following saying (Aḥādīth) of the Prophet (S.A.W.) warn Muslims against any high handedness towards the non-Muslim citizens.

«من ظلم معاهدا او انتقصه حقا او كلفه فوق طاقته او اخذ منه شيئا بغير طيب نفس منه، فأنا حجيجه يوم القيامة».

> "Whoever persecuted a Dhimmi or usurps or took work from him beyond his capacity, or took something from him with evil intentions, I shall be a complainant against him on the Day of Resurrection."[15]

The Prophet also said:

«من آذى ذميًا فأنا خصمه، ومن كنت خصمه خاصمته يوم القيامة».

> "Whoever hurts a Dhimmī, I shall be his complainant, and for whosoever I am a complainant, I shall ask for his right on the Day of Resurrection."

The Prophet also said:

«من آذى ذميا فقد آذاني، ومن آذاني فقد آذى الله».

> "One who hurts a Dhimmi, he hurts me; and one who hurts me, hurts Allah."[16]

Some Muslim jurists like 'Ibn-'Ābdīn (d. 1836 A.D.) have argued that since Muslims are given a responsibility to protect the blood and property of non-Muslims and since the persecution of weak persons at the hands of the strong is considered as one of the greatest crimes, the persecution of non-Muslims in an Islamic state will be considered to be a greater crime than the persecution of Muslims by non-Muslims.[17]

Muslim–non-Muslim Relationship in the time of the Prophet

When Muḥammad (S.A.W.) started to preach openly about Tauhid, i.e. monotheism – that is the belief that there is only One Lord for the whole universe, and that is Allah, and that none has the right to be worshipped, but Allah – the pagan aristocracy of Mecca turned against him and his followers. Members of the pagan aristocracy were so deeply sunk in the depth of ignorance that they could not accept any supremacy over their imaginary idols of wood and stone of which *Lat, Manāt, Uzzah and Hubal* were their source of happiness and sorrow, reward and punishment.

But a good number of eminent Quraishites rallied round the Holy Prophet (S.A.W.) and the inveterate enemies of Tauhid started inflicting torture and injuries upon the Holy Prophet and his followers so that others would not dare to join them in their religious mission. But the number of the Holy Prophet's followers grew which was an indication of a serious revolutionary movement against their mode of worship, unjust ways of life and their very existence as the custodians of the Ka'aba.

To save their own institution from destruction, the Quraish started persecuting Muslims; it was then that the Holy Prophet advised his followers to seek in the nearby Christian Kingdom of Ḥabasha (Ethiopia).

He told his followers: "If you go to Abyssinia (Ethiopia) you will find a king under whom none is persecuted. It is a land of righteousness where Allah Almighty will give you relief from what you are suffering."[18]

Consequently, in A.D. 615, a small group of eleven men and four ladies including Uthman bin Affan and his wife Ruqayia (daughter of the Holy Prophet), ʿAbdal Raḥmān bin ʿAuf, and Zubair bin ʿAwwām, crossed the Red Sea and reached the hospitable shores of Ethiopia. It was followed by another batch of eighty-three men and eighteen ladies under the leadership of Jafar bin Abu Talib (cousin of the Holy Prophet and brother of Syedina Ali). This emigration is referred to as the first hijrah in the history of Islam.

The news that these Muslims were kindly received and lived under the protection of Najashi, the King of Habasha filled the Quraish with dismay and subsequently they deputed Abdallah bin Rabīʿand Imr bin ʿAas with precious gifts to the king to request that the fugitives might be returned. The Quraish were well-acquainted with Abbyssinia through trading relations. The king of Abyssinia granted an audience to the deputed Quraish and told them he would himself examine the refugees. The Quraish expected their prospects for the morrow to be excellent. The king summoned the refugees in the presence of the Christian bishops and asked: "What is the religion for which you have abandoned your people and yet have neither adopted mine nor any other known religion?"

Jaʿfar bin Abu Talib answered in words that reflect the Arab life before the birth of the Holy Prophet Muḥammad (S.A.W.) and the early message of Islam:

> "O King, we were a barbarous nation, worshipping idols, eating carrion, disregarding every feeling of humanity, committing shameful deeds, killing our blood relations, forgetting our duty towards our neighbours, the strong men among us devouring the weak, we knew no law save that of the jungle. Such was our state until Allah sent us an Apostle, from amongst ourselves, with whose lineage, integrity, trustworthiness, excellence of character and purity of life we were fully aware.
>
> "He summoned us to Allah, to believe in His unity, to worship Him and abandon the stones and idols which we and our fathers worshipped in His stead. He commanded us to speak the truth, to be faithful in our trusts, to observe our duties to our kinsfolk and neighbours, to refrain from forbidden things and bloodshed, from committing immoralities and deceits, from consuming the property of orphans and from slandering virtuous women. He order us to worship God and associate no other with Him, to offer prayer, give alms, and observe fast. So we trusted in His word and followed the teaching he brought us from Allah. (This is our fault), and for this reason our countrymen turned against us and persecuted us to try and seduce us from our faith, that we might abandon the worship of our God and return to the worship of idols."[19]

The king asked Jaʿfar bin Abū Ṭālib what did Prophet Muḥammad say about Jesus Christ. Jaʿfar quoted the texts from the Qur'ān, Sūrah

"Maryam". (This Sūrah was revealed before the first Muslim hijrah to Ethiopia).[20]

Being satisfied to his enquiries, the king saw no reason to listen to the demands of the Quraish, and returned their gifts saying "If you were to offer me a mountain of gold, I would not give up these people who have taken refuge with me."

The Quraish ambassadors returned empty-handed, and the Holy Prophet held the Habessins (Abyssinians) in considerable affection. he blessed the king and his progeny. He is reported to have said, "Leave the Habessins in peace so long as they do not take the offensive."[21]

Afterwards, Muḥammad (S.A.W.) wrote a letter to the king about his mission, which was the Holy Prophet's first letter about Islam to any non-Muslim king. That letter was brought to Ethiopia by Umru Ibn Ummayia. The king received the letter with reverence and "the Najashi declared his belief in the Prophet's mission."[22]

The Muslims who had taken refuge in Ethiopia lived in peace under the protection of the king. Some of the emigrants returned to Mecca when conditions improved at home for a great number of the Quraish had joined the Holy Prophet in his righteous mission.

Friends and foes, Muslims and non-Muslims, were all alike to the Holy Prophet and to His laws. He followed the Qur'ānic injunction – "Let not hatred of a people incite you to act unjustly, that is neater to piety." "Verily Allah enjoins to do justice and kindness – O you who believe, be upholders of justice, bearers of witness for Allah's sake, though it be against yourselves or parents or near relations."[23] The Qur'ān again says: "When you speak, then be just though it be against a relation."[24]

Once a Muslim thief was brought to the Apostle of Allah, He ordered his hand to be cut off on trial. His companions considered it a very severe sentence. Then the Prophet said: "Had she been (my own daughter) Fatima, I would have certainly cut off her hand."

Once in a trial between a Muslim and a Jew, he gave a decision in favour of the Jew who at once exclaimed: "By Allah, you have decided with truth." He did not fear that by this act he would alienate the sympathy of the clan to which the Muslim belonged.

Once a respectable lady of the Makhzūm tribe committed a theft. She was brought before the Prophet under arrest. When the companions saw her and considered her respectability, they requested the Prophet to let her off. The Prophet abhorred the idea of distinction and passed order for cutting off her hand.

Once a ruffian of Banū Tha'alaba tribe killed an Anṣāri all of a sudden. The heirs of the murdered Anṣari demanded surrender of his son and revenge of murder. The Prophet prohibited it and said: "A son is not guilty for the crime of his father."

When the whole of Arabia except Khaiber came under the sway of the Prophet, the Khaiber Jews one day murdered a companion unjustly at Khaiber. The Prophet could not find out who the culprit was. Consequently, he paid compensation of one hundred camels to the heirs of the murdered person from the State Wealth.

The Holy Prophet used to do justice according to the law to which the complainant belonged. Once a Christian of the Banū Quraiẓa tribe was killed by a Christian of the Banū Nazīr tribe. In a complaint before the Prophet, he enforced the law of the Torah – Life for life.

In disputes between the Jews, Muslims and other tribes, the Prophet was the final Court of Appeal. Before his death, the Prophet announced publicly: "If I owe anything to anybody, he may claim it. If I offended anybody, he may take revenge." In response, a man named Sarf claimed some dirhams. They were at once paid to him.

Sakhar was a Muslim who accepted Islam after Ṭāyif was conquered. He was the chief of his tribe. Once the infidel Mugīrah complained to the Prophet that Sakhar had kept his aunt detained with him. The Prophet at once ordered Sakhar to hand over Mugirah's aunt to him.

Prophet's Advice to His Caliphs about Non-Muslims

The non-Muslims must be treated with leniency and must not be oppressed by any ruler and must not be taxed beyond their capacity and nothing should be taken from them except for a duty encumbering them."[25] The prophetic tradition emphasises on this point: "Whoever oppresses a non-Muslim subject or taxes him beyond his capacity, then I shall be the opposite part to him in the litigation."[26] The second Caliph of Islam, Sayyidnā 'Umar bin al-Khaṭṭāb is reported to have said the following in the last moments of his life:

> "I exhort my successor regarding the treatment to be meted out to the covenanted people by the Messenger of Allah. They should receive the fullest execution of their covenant, and their life and property should be defended even if it requires to go to war (with oppressors), and they should not be taxed beyond their capacity."[27]

The Khulafā'al-Rashidun (the right-guided Caliph) used to enquire about non-Muslims whenever people came to see them from the neighbouring countries or provinces. Whenever any complaint came fron non-Muslims, they used to give their urgent attention to it in order to ensure that justice was done to them. It is narrated by Al-Ṭabarī in his famous historical work that Caliph 'Umar used to question the delegates concerning the condition of non-Muslims and used to ask if any Muslim had hurt the feelings of non-Muslims in their countries. Once he asked some delegates to narrate the treatment of non-Muslims at the hand of Muslims in their home towns. They replied:

»ما نعلم الا وفاء«.

"We do not know except fair treatment by fulfilling their pledge."[28]

The religion of Islam and the Shari'ah has emphasised a great deal on the rights of the non-Muslims so much so that any Muslim who violates any of their right is deemed to have committed a grave sin. Many atrocities have been committed in the name of religion in many parts of the world. In Hinduism, for example, if a non-Hindu, whether a Muslim or a Christian, eats in a plate, the plate becomes 'unholy' and needs to be washed. Similarly, the blood of a Brahmin is consider superior to the blood of a low-caste Hindu (Shudra) who is born to serve the Brahmin.

The world has also seen the differentiation between man and man on the basis of geographical area. In Roman law, if a man belonging to one city-state entered into another city-state, he was captured and treated as a slave. The same is also true if the basis was the colour of skin, as is the case in apartheid South Africa today, that only a white man can enjoy certain rights and privileges and a black man cannot even sit and eat with a white man. In all these cases, the basis is merely "an accident of nature and belongs more to the animal instinct than to the nationality of man."[29]

Islam rejects all these man-made distinctions even if they are given religious colouring. The only unifying factor in Islam is the identity of ideas which solely depends on the choice of man and not upon the accidents and hazards of birth, race, colour and geographical location. All men are equal in Islam, and even if one does not choose to follow the religion of Islam, he has every right to live in peace and tranquility in a Muslim state or Muslim majority areas as an honoured citizen with all rights and privileges. Neither the religion of Islam nor the Shari'ah can be forced on any one against his will according to the teachings of the Qur'an and the Sunnah of the Prophet.

The main emphasis of the Shari'ah is on the sanctity of a legal due process concept to guarantee life, liberty, property and honour of every human being. Therefore, Muslim law is the fair regulation of the conduct of the faithful in this world and in the world hereafter. Mutatis mutandis, Muslim international law aims at the fair regulation of the Muslim state in its foreign relations. As Dr. Bassouni puts it: "It is directed also to the individual Muslim state and any non-Muslim state."[30] The Shari'ah is the unifed source of moral precept and it prevents a duality of moral standards in national versus international affairs because in Islam what sanctions the individual's private conduct also sanctions the individual's public conduct."[31]

According to the Shari'ah, the entire mankind is one nation and Muslim should think of the rights of all human beings. All the human rights granted by the Sharī'ah are meant for the welfare of the world. The human rights under Sharī'ah were promulgated 1,400 years ago. When one looks at Articles 1-30 of the universal Declaration of Human Rights, it seems as if they are the reflections of the aims and objectives of the Shari'ah. All the rights like the right to an honourable life, the right to practice any religion of one's choice, the right to any employment and choice of work, the right to a decent wage and the giving of the wage even before the perspiration of the worker dries up, the right to own property, the right to social security, the right to obtain basic necessities like food, clothing and shelter are all guaranteed by Sharīah.

The individual is viewed by Islam both as a single and unique unit and also as a part and parcel of a composite unit, i.e., mankind. It is this sublime concept which is reflected in the way Sharī'ah deals with non-Muslims in general and the non-Muslim minority in particular. Freedom of religious practice, personal status matters, citizenship and protection of life, liberty and property and only some examples of specific guarantees that have to be afforded to the non Muslims and the 'minorities' who live under the protective covenant of an Islamic state. We shall endeavour to discuss these aspects in the next chapter.

---

1. Cf. Al-Qardāwī Yūsuf, Ghayr al-Muslimīn fī Mujtamá al-Islāmī, Cairo, 1977, p.7.
2. Ibid.
3. Al-Sarakhsī,Sharh al-Siyar al-Kabir, vol. 1, p. 140, Ibn Qudāmah,Al-Mughnī, vol. 5, p. 516; Al-Kasani, Al-Badai'wal Sanai', vol. 5, p. 281.
4. 'Audah,'Abd al-Qādir, Al-Tashrī ál-Janāi al-Islamī vol. 1, p. 307; Also Zaidān, Ábd al-Karīm, Ahkam al-Dhimmiyyin wal Musta'minin fi Dar al-Islam, pp. 63-66.
5. Maulanā Abul Álā Maudūdī has given the first three in the above list as categories of non-Muslims (see Rights of Non-Muslims in Islamic State, Lahore, 1976, p.6). The categories 4 and 5 also come under the jurisdiction of a Muslim State. Cf. Hamidullah, M. Muslim Conduct of State, Lahore, 1973, p. 112.
6. Abū Zahrah, Muḥammad, Al-Jarīmah Wal 'Uqūbah fil-Fiqh al-Islām, Dār al-Fikr al-Arabi, undated, p. 189 (footnote).
7. Qur'ān, ch. 60:8-9.
8. This incident is recorded in Musnad Aḥmad, Bukhārī and Muslim. Also see the details in Maudūdī's Tafhīm al-Qur'ān (Urdu), Delhi 1975, pp. 433-434.

Page

436

[9]Al Jaṣṣās, *Aḥkām al-Qur'ān*; also *Rūḥ al-Mu'ānī*.

[10]*Qur'ān, ch. 29:46.*

[11]*Imām al-Qarāfī Shahāb al-Dīn/Abul 'Abbās Aḥmad bin Ibrīs al-Mālikī, Al-Furūq,* Cairo 1346, vol. 3, pp. 14-15.

[13]Al-Qarḍāwī, Yūsuf, *Ghayr al-Muslimīn fil Mujtama' al-Islāmī,* Cairo, 1977, p. 10.

[14]Ibid.
[15]Ibid.

[16]Abū Daūd and Baihaqi. See *Al-Sunan al-Kubrā,* vol. 5, p. 205. Narrated by *al-Khaṭīb* with authentic *Isnād.*

[17]Al-Ṭibrānī.

[18]Ibn 'Ābdīn, Muḥammad Amīn, *Radd al-Mukhtār 'alā Durral-Mukhtār,* Cairo 1327 A.H., quoted by Al-Qarḍāwī, op. cit., p. 12.

[19]Qur'ān, ch. 8, verse 72.
[20]Abū Yūsuf, *Kitāb al-Kharāj,* Cairo, p. 35.
[21]Ibn Hishām, *Sīra,* Cairo, 1937, p. 343.

Chapter 25

Jihād

Jiḥād is derived from the Arabic word *al-Jaḥd* meaning a struggle or striving, and the word *Jaḥāda* means 'he has struggled or exerted himself'. *Jiḥād* does not necessarily mean resorting to the use of sword and the shedding of blood as is misunderstood by some people. The word *Jihad*, therefore, is so comprehensive that is also includes a striving and undergoing hardship and forebearing in great difficulties, while standing firm against one's enemies. The actual words for war in Arabic are *al-Ḥarb* and *al-Qitāl.* In the Qur'ān, therefore, the word *Jihād* as a Holy War, is used in respect of waging it for defence against any aggression or taking an offence in unavoidable circumstances when the onslaught of enemies is imminent. These circumstances alone can make a war morally justifiable.[1] The Prophet was asked in the Qur'ān to spread the religion of Islam and invite people to Allah with "wise counsel and good admonitions."[2] His main mission in Mecca was to invite people to Allah acting on Allah's command and undergoing persecution at the hands of the pagans. His companions, the early Muslims, also tolerated untold hardships because of their profession and dedication to the new religion of Islam.

«وَاصْبِرْ لِحُكْمِ رَبِّكَ فَإِنَّكَ بِأَعْيُنِنَا».

"Now await in patience the command of Your Lord: for verily you are in our eyes."[3]

The man of Allah must strive his utmost to proclaim the message of Allah. As far as the result is concerned, it is not in his hands or in his command. He has to wait patiently in the knowledge and with conviction that he is not forgotten by Allah, but he is constantly under the eyes of Allah, under His loving care and protection. He must continue in his good word undaunted.

The Qur'ān further says:

«فَاصْفَحْ عَنْهُمْ وَقُلْ سَلَامٌ فَسَوْفَ يَعْلَمُونَ».

"But turn away from them and say 'peace'! But soon shall they know."[4]

The persecution of the Quraishites was so much that he is consoled in the above verse to turn away from them, and was assured by Allah that the truth will prevail soon. In *Sūrah al-Jāthiyah,* the Prophet was asked to console his followers in those days of trouble:

«قل للذين آمنوا يغفرون للذين لا يرجون ايام الله».

"Tell those who believe, to forgive those who do not look forward to the Days of Allah."

The Days of Allah here will mean those days when truth will reign supreme and evil will be destroyed. The Prophet was not commanded to do away with evil with another evil or torture with another torture or fight those who were opposing his call and invitation to the wa y of Allah or fight those who were persecuting believing men and women. The Qur'ān instructed them in the following words in such unbearable circumstances:

«ادْفَعْ بِالَّتِي هِيَ أَحْسَنُ السَّيِّئَةَ نَحنُ أَعلَمُ بِمَا يَصِفُونَ».

"Repel evil with that which is best: We are well acquainted with things they say."*

When the situation went out of control the Prophet was asked to migrate with his companions and followers to a peaceful place, Medina, away from Mecca. It was in Medina where the verses of *Jihād* were revealed to the Prophet because the enemies of Islam did not want to leave them at peace in Medina in spite of the fact that the Prophet and his followers were away from them. It was imperative in such circumstances to defend the cause of religion, new Islamic culture, and the newly found capital of the Islamic state. The first word that was revealed on *Jihād* was the following:

«أُذِنَ لِلَّذِينَ يُقَاتَلُونَ بِأَنَّهُمْ ظُلِمُوا وإنَّ اللَّهَ عَلَىٰ نَصْرِهِمْ لَقَدِيرٌ. الَّذِينَ أُخْرِجُوا مِنْ دِيَارِهِمْ بِغَيْرِ حَقٍ إلَّا أَنْ يَقُولُوا رَبُّنَا اللَّهُ».

"To these against whom war is made, permission is given to fight, because they are wronged; and verily Allah is Most Powerful for their aid; they are those who have been expelled from their homes in defiance of right – for no cause except that they say, 'Our Lord is Allah'."[6]

Permission for Jihād only given after the Hijrah

The permission for *Jihād* was given on account of the following three reasons:-

1. The innocent Muslims were persecuted in the early days of the Prophet's mission for no other fault of theirs except for saying that Allah is one, and for establishing a system quite different from the pagan system of Arabia.
2. If the permission of *Jihād* were not given after the Hijrah, the enemies would have destroyed the mosque of the Prophet, the place of worship in which the name of Allah alone was pronounced. The non-believers would have persisted in their tyranny in order to force people to give up their belief in Allah and the Last Day.
3. The permission for *Jihād* was especially granted at that time so that the order of Allah can be established firmly on earth –*! besides, the institutions of prayers (ṣalāt),* poor-rate *(zakāt)* were just established. The enemies wanted to destroy these newly found institutions.

If the permission for *Jihād* were not given, the Meccans would have forcibly stopped the work of *daʿwah* by inviting people on the right path and stopping them from following the wrong path *(Amr bil Maʿrūf* and *Nahy 'anil Munkar).* Therefore, it was precisely in the second year of *Hijrah* that *Jihād* was obligatory in the following words:

«كُتِبَ عَلَيْكُمْ ٱلْقِتَالُ وَهُوَ كُرْهٌ لَكُمْ وَعَسَىٰ أَنْ تَكْرَهُوا شَيْئاً وَهُوَ خَيْرٌ لَكُمْ وَعَسَىٰ أَنْ تُحِبُّوا شَيْئاً وَهُوَ شَرٌّ لَكُمْ وَاللَّهُ يَعْلَمُ وَأَنْتُمْ لَا تَعْلَمُونَ».

"Fighting is prescribed for you, and you dislike it. But it is possible you dislike something which is good for you, and that you love a thing which is bad for you. But Allah knows and you know not."7

Jihād is *farḍ kifāyah* which means that it is not obligatory on every Muslim at all times, but if some of them answered the call to do away with their enemies, it will be deemed an obligation has been fulfilled by the rest of them. The other obligatory acts like *Īmān* (faith), *Ṭahārah* (Purification), *Ṣalāt* (Prayers), *Zakāt* (poor-rate), *Ṣiyām* (fasting) are *farāʾiḍ 'ainiyyah,* meaning that every individual is duty-bound to fulfil these obligations at all times. The following injunctions of the Qur'ān makes the above point more clear:

«وَمَا كَانَ ٱلْمُؤْمِنُونَ لِيَنْفِرُوا كَافَّةً فَلَوْلَا نَفَرَ مِنْ كُلِّ فِرْقَةٍ مِنْهُمْ طَائِفَةٌ لِيَتَفَقَّهُوا فِي الدِّينِ وَلِيُنْذِرُوا قَوْمَهُمْ إِذَا رَجَعُوا إِلَيْهِمْ لَعَلَّهُمْ يَحْذَرُونَ».

"Nor should the believer all go forth together: If a contingent from every expedition remained behind, they could devote themselves to studies in religion, and admonish people when they return to them, that thus they may learn to guard themselves against evil." 8

The Qur'ān further says:

«يَا أَيُّهَا الذَّينَ آمَنُوا خُذُوا حِذْرَكُمْ فَانْفِرُوا ثُبَاتٍ اَوِ انْفِرُوا جَمِيعاً.

"O You who believe, take your precautions, and either go forth in parties or go forth all together." 9.

In a Ḥadīth, narrated by Muslim, the Messenger of Allah has said:

«عن ابي سعيد الخدري ان رسول الله صلى الله عليه وسلم بعث بعثا الى بني لحيان من هذيل، فقال: لينبعث من كل رجلين احدهما، والاجر بينهما».

"It is reported by Abū Sa'īd al-Khuḍrī that the Messenger of Allah (Ṣ.A.W.) sent a delegate to Banū Lahyān from Ḥudhail, and said that one person out of two should be sent (for Jihād) and that all will receive the reward."

According to the above *Ḥādith* , if it was made compulsory that each one of them should go for *Jihād* the other necessary social and worldly welfare would have suffered. That is why only some of them were asked to fulfil the obligation.

In the following circumstances, *Jihād* will become *farḍ 'ain:*

1. If a man goes for *Jihād,* and is stationed in the battle-field, it will then be obligatory for him to continue fighting. He should not run away then. Otherwise he will create confusion and the whole strategy will fall apart. The Qur'ān says:

«يَا أَيُّهَا الذَّينَ آمَنُوا اذِا لَقيتُمْ فِئَةً فَاثْبُتُواَ».

"O you who believe, when you meet a force, be firm." 10.

It further says:

«يَا أَيُّهَا الذَّينَ آمَنُوا اذِا لَقَيتُمْ الذِّينَ كَفَرُوا زَحْفاً فَلا تُوَلُّوهُمُ اْلاَدْبَارَ».

"O you who believe, when you meet the unbelievers in hostile array, never turn your backs to them." 11

2. If enemies attack an enclave of Muslims, it will be obligatory for every resident of that place to come out and repel their enemies. Otherwise, the enemies will wipe them out and ruin their villages and their cities. The Qur'ān says:

«يَـا أَيُّهَـا الـذَّينَ آمَنُـوا قَاتِلوُا الذَّينَ يَلُونَكُمْ مِنْ الْكُفَّارِ وَلْيَجِدُوا فيكُمْ غِلْظَةً وَاْعَلمُوا اَنَّ اللّهَ مَعَ اْلمُتقِّينَ».

"O you who believe, fight the unbelievers who gird you about, and let them find firmness in you: and know that Allah is with those who fear Him." 12.

3. When the just and pious ruler orders someone to join the forces of *Jihād,* it will be obligatory for him to join without hesitation. The following hadith narrated by Ibn ʿAbbās says:

«لا هجرة بعد الفتح، ولكن جهاد ونية، واذا استنفرتم فأنفروا».

"There is no Hijrah after the conquest of Mecca, but there is still *Jihad* and intention for it. If you are asked to join forces, you must fulfil your obligation."

In other words, the obligation for *Hijrah* has been cancelled by this Hadith, but still migration from the 'abode of war' *(Dār al-Ḥarb)* to the 'abode of peace' *(Dār al-Aman)* is not cancelled. It will become obligatory for one to migrate when one fears that his religion is not safe by continuing living in a hostile place. Similarly, when a just leader demands that one should go out for *Jihād,* he must not refuse. The Qur'ān says:

«يَا أَيُّهَا الَّذِينَ آمَنُوا مَا لَكُمْ إِذَا قِيلَ لَكُمُ انْفِرُوا فِي سَبِيلِ اللّٰهِ اثَّاقَلْتُمْ إِلَى الْأَرْضِ أَرَضِيتُمْ بِالْحَيَاةِ الدُّنْيَا مِنَ الْآخِرَةِ فَمَا مَتَاعُ الْحَيٰوةِ الدُّنْيَا فِي الْآخِرَةِ إِلَّا قَلِيلٌ».

"O you who believe, what is the matter with you, that when you are asked to go forth in the cause of Allah, you cling heavily to the earth? Do you prefer the life of this world to the Hereafter? But, little is the comfort of this life as compared with the Hereafter." 13

On Whom is Jihād Obligatory?

Jihād is obligatory on the following categories of people:

1. a Muslim
2. a male
3. sane
4. one who has reached the age of puberty
5. a man who has sufficient means to maintain his family until he returns from the *Jihād.*

In other words, it is not obligatory for a non-Muslim, a woman, a child, a blind man, an old man and a sick person. The Qur'ān says:

«لَيْسَ عَلَى الضُّعَفَاءِ وَلَا عَلَى الْمَرْضَىٰ وَلَا عَلَى الَّذِينَ لَا يَجِدُونَ مَا يُنْفِقُونَ حَرَجٌ إِذَا نَصَحُوا لِلّٰهِ وَرَسُولِهِ مَا عَلَى الْمُحْسِنِينَ مِنْ سَبِيلٍ وَاللّٰهُ غَفُورٌ رَحِيمٌ».

"There is no blame on those who are infirm, or ill, or who find no resources to spend (on the cause) if they are sincere in their duty to Allah and His Apostle; no ground of complaint can there be against such as do right; and Allah is oft-Forgiving, Most Merciful." 14.

It further says in *Sūrah al-Fatḥ:*

«لَيْسَ عَلَى ٱلاَعْمٰى حَرَجٌ وَلاَ عَلَى ٱلاَعْـرَجِ حَرَجٌ وَلاَ عَلَى ٱلْمَـرِيضِ حَرَجٌ وَمَنْ يُطِـعِ ٱللّٰهَ وَرَسُـولَـهُ يُدْخِلْهُ جَنَّـاتٍ تَجْرِي مِنْ تَحْتِهَا ٱلاَنْهَارُ وَمَنْ يَتَوَلَّ يُعَذِّبْهُ عَذَاباً اَلِيماً».

"No blame is there on the blind, nor is there blame on the lame; nor on one who is ill (if he joins not the *Jihād*): but that he obeys Allah and His Apostle, Allah will admit him to Gardens beneath which rivers flow; and he who turns back, Allah will punish him with a grevious penalty." 15.

ʿAbdallāh bin ʿUmar has said:

«عـرضت على رسـول الله صلى الله عليـه وسلم يوم احـد وانا اربع عشرة سنة فلم يجزني.»

"I appealed to the Messenger of Allah to allow me to join force on the day of Uḥud and I was 14 years old (the Prophet) did not allow me." 16.

Likewise Aishah asked the Prophet: 17.

«قلت يا رسول الله على النساء جهاد؟ قال لا قتال فيه: الحج والعمرة».

I asked: "O Messenger of Allah is there any *Jihād* for women?" The Prophet replied: "There is *Jihād* for them in which there is no fighting that is (the performance of) the pilgrimage and the ʿUm rah."

The women can render their services in *Jihād* by giving water to the warriors and bandaging and nursing the wounded ones. One of the traditions of the Prophet discusses the priority of the actions *(aʿmāl)*. When the prophet was asked about the action dearer to Allah, he replied: "The performance of prayers at its time." Then he was asked which one came next, he replied: "goodness to parents". He was again asked which came next, he said: "*Jihād* in the path of Allah". In other words, if the parents are old, and need the services of their son, it is better that he attends to them rather than going to participate in *Jihād*. 18.

There are differences of opinion of the jurists whether the hypocrites, drunkards and non-Muslims will be allowed to participate in *Jihād*. We have an evidence that 'Abdallāh bin Ubayy and his hypocrite companions went out in *Jihād* with the Prophet. Likewise Abī Maham al-Thaqafī was a drunkard but still he fought in the well-known *Jihād* against Persia. The Jurists have particularly differed about the participation of non-Muslims. Imām Mālik and Imām Aḥmad bin Ḥanbal say that they should not join the *Jihād* absolutely. Imām Malik says that if non-Muslims happen to be the servants in the houses of Muslims, they will be allowed. Imām Abū Ḥanifah says that non-Muslims can also help, but the orders of the Muslim Commandant will be necessary for them to follow. Imām Shafi'i says that their participation will be allowed although he has stipulated some condtions.

Jihād Against One's Carnal Desire

Jihād is not merely limited to the use of force. There can also be a *Jihād* through speech and writing particularly when the wrong doer is the established authority. In the following Ḥadith it is mentioned that to speak up for truth is the best *Jihād.*

«قال رسول الله صلى الله عليه وسلم: افضل الجهاد من قال كلمة الحق عند سلطان جائر».

"The Messenger of Allah has said: 'The highest kind of *Jihād* is to speak up for truth in the face of a Sultan (government or other authority or any leader) who deviates from the right path'."

It is reported that once the Prophet was returning from the *Jihād* to Medina and he said to his companions on the way: 'We are returning from the smaller *Jihād* to the greater *Jihād."* The companions were surprised to hear this because they were in fact returning from active fighting and now they were going to Medina, a peaceful place. The Prophet here meant that actual fighting was a smaller *Jihād* but fighting against one's carnal desires is the greater *Jihād.*

We should bear in mind that once a revolutionary movement is launched to change a corrupt system it will definitely create an opposition from those who have some vested interest. They will resent the new order and use all the foul means at their disposal to crush the new movement. This was the reason why religion of Islam in those early days had to face great opposition right in Mecca, the place of its birth. Similar situations can arise at all times since the battle between right and wrong is note merely confined to any time or geographical region or any nation. Islam allows great latitude to its opponents to understand and respond to its teachings. With this object in mind it takes Mulsim through a stage of tolerance and endurance but it does not encourage them to suffer tyranny indefinitely or fall on easy prey to opponents. The period of suffering thus becomes a period of training to enable them to confront tyranny. Whenever the truth arises the falsehood disappears eventually. Muslims are asked to follow strictly the covenants and treaties entered into by their leaders even though sometimes their terms may go against them just as it happened in the case of the Treaty of Ḥudaibiyah between the Prophet and the Meccans. But if the enemies do not adhere to the terms stipulated in the treaty, the *Jihād* will be fought. Thus the military actions taken by Muslims will amount to establish peace through the *Jihād* like a tailor who cuts a nice piece of cloth into smaller pieces only to design it and shape it into a beautiful dress.

When one looks at the conquests of Napoleon or Hitler or the British, Dutch, French and German colonial masters, they were all meant for depriving free nations of their inborn freedom. The *Jihād* in Islam has never been fought for mere territorial gain and colonialism. If there was any desire on the part of the *Mujāhidūn* it was to spread what they considered to be the truth wherever they were invited by the rulers or oppressed people of distant lands.

Many non-Muslim biographers of the Prophet have tried to paint a sombre picture of the Prophet of a man with a sword in one hand and the Qur'ān in the other. When one really studies the events which led to the battles of the Prophet in the 10 years of military actitivies in the Medinan period the total loss of life incurred was 255 Muslims only as against 759 enemies of Islam. With this small number of casualties Islam had spread over a million square miles and still all opposition was suppressed. If at all these *Jihād* movements were merely inspired to convert people to other faith into Islam by force, they would have left behind a lot of records of atrocities just as we find in the case of religious wars of other religions. It will be interesting to note that the total number of prisoners taken in all the *Jihāds* of the Prophet were only 6,564 prisoners of war out of whom only two were executed for definite crimes committed by them, while 6,347 were released. The remaining 215 prisoners probably accepted Islam and became one with the Muslim *Ummāh*.

Code of Conduct for Mujāhidīn in Jihād

Jihād can be fought with one's property and with one's life as is specified in the Qur'ān:

«إِنَّ الَّذِينَ آمَنُوا وَهَاجَرُوا وَجَاهَدُوا بِأَمْوَالِهِمْ وَأَنْفُسِهِمْ فِي سَبِيلِ اللَّهِ»

"Those who believed, and adopted exile, and fought for the Faith, with their property and their persons."[19]

The following Ḥadīth further stresses the point:

«عن ابى سعيد الخدري قال: يارسول الله اي الناس افضل؟ ، «قال: من يجاهد في سبيل الله بنفسه وماله».

"It is reported by Abū Sa'īd al-Khudrī that the Prophet was asked: 'O Messenger of Allah, which of the persons is more excellent?' The Prophet replied: 'One who engages in *Jihād* in the path of Allah with his soul and his property'."

The *Jihād* property, truly speaking, means the spending of one's property to ensure the needs of those who join the forces of *Jihād (Mujāhidīn)* and their dependents like providing of the clothing, food, weapon, means of transport and medical provisions.

The Prophet has said:

«قال رسول الله صلى الله عليه وسلم: من جهز غازيا حتى يستقل كان له مثل اجره حتى يموت او يرجع».

"The Messenger of Allah said: 'One who provides the needs of a warrior for as long as he engages in *Jihād*, he will have a reward equal to his (the warrior) until he dies or returns (from the *Jihād*)'."

It is essential that the commander of the forces of *Jihād* is chosen by the Islamic authorities carefully. He should be a pious Muslim, a wise and matured man, well disciplined, and a brave man who commands respect of his soldiers and who takes foresighted decisions in planning a strategy against the enemy forces. The Muslim forces are instructed notr to enter into the fighting until the enemies proclaim the war and once the enemies incline towards peace, Muslims should at once agree to it as the Qur'ān says:

«وَاِنْ جَنَحُوا لِلسَّلْمِ فَاجْنَحْ لَهَا وَتَوَكَّلْ عَلَى اللّٰهِ اِنَّهُ هُوَ السَّمِيعُ الْعَلِيمُ».

"But, if the enemies incline towards peace, do you also incline towards peace, and trust in Allah! For He is the one that hears and knows (all things)."[20]

Muslims engaged in *Jihād* must make sure that the civilians of the area where they are waging war have certain rights which must be observed in all circumstances. Their lives, property and freedom must be protected. There should be no cases of high handedness on the part of any *Mujāhid.* There should be no devastation of houses and crops through killing and burning. The old people, invalids, women and children must not be killed in any circumstances. No places of worship should be demolished, nor the Priests of any religion be killed. The following advice of Sayyidna Abubākar, the first Caliph, given to Yazīd bin Abū Sufyān while the latter was engaged in *Jihād* on the coasts of Syria provides us with a strict code of conduct of Muslim armies followed in the past:

«اذا سرت فلا تعنف اصحابك في السير، ولا تغضب قومك، وشاورهم في الامر، واستعمل العدل وباعد عنك الظلم، والجور، فانه ما افلح قوم ظلموا، ولا نصروا على عدوهم، واذا أنتصرتم على عدوكم فلا تقتلوا وليدا، ولا شيخا، ولا امرأة، ولا طفلا،ولا تقربوا نخلا، ولا تحرقوا زرعا، ولا تقطعوا شجرا مثمرا ولا تغدروا اذا عاهدتم، ولا تنقضوا اذا صالحتم، وستمرون باقوام في الصوامع، رهبان ترهبوا لله، فدعوهم وما انفردوا اليه، وارتضوه لانفسهم، فلا تهدموا صوامعهم، ولا تقتلوهم، والسلام».

"When you travel, do not drive your comrades so much that they get tired ont he journey. Do not be angry upon your people and consult them in your affairs. Do justice and keep them away from tryanny and oppression, because a community that engages in tyranny, does not prosper, nor do they win victory over their enemies. When you become victorious on your enemies, do not kill their children, old people and women. Do not go even closer to their date palms, nor burn their harvest, nor cut the fruit bearing trees. Do not break the promise once you have made it, and do not break the terms of treaty, once you have entered into it. You will meet on your way people in the monasteries, the monks engaged in the worship of Allah, leave them alone and do not disperse them. Let them please themselves and do not destroy their monasteries, and do not kill them. May Peace of Allah be upon you."21.

Prisoners of War and Their Treatment

The Sharī'ah stipulates that the prisoners of war must be treated well. They must not be tortured or punished. They deserve kindness, and good care while in captivity of Muslims. Provisions must be made for their nourishing food and necessary clothing. The Qur'ān says:

«فَإِمَّا مَنًّا بَعْدُ وَإِمَّا فِدَاءً».

"Thereafter is the time for either generosity or ransom."22.

In other words, once the prisoners of war are captured, either treat them well without troubling them, or release after getting ransom on them. This is the reason why Islam has made the giving of food to the prisoners as a virtuous deed for the believers, just as the Qur'ān declares:

« وَيُطْعِمُونَ الطَّعَامَ عَلَىٰ حُبِّهِ مِسْكِينًا وَيَتِيمًا وَأَسِيرًا».

"And they (the believers) feed, for the love of Allah, the indegent, the orphan and the captive."23.

The Prophet and through him the Muslims are further instructed:

«مَا كَانَ لِنَبِيٍّ أَن يَكُونَ لَهُ أَسْرَىٰ حَتَّىٰ يُثْخِنَ فِي الْأَرْضِ تُرِيدُونَ عَرَضَ الدُّنْيَا
وَاللَّهُ يُرِيدُ الْآخِرَةَ وَاللَّهُ عَزِيزٌ حَكِيمٌ».

"It is not fitting for an Apostle that he should have prisoners of war until he has thoroughly subdued the land. You look for the temporal goods of this world; but Allah looks to the hereafter: and Allah is exalted in might, Wise." 24.

An ordinary war may be for territory or trade, or to capture prisoners of war, revenge or military glory or for an "temporal goods of this world". Such a war is condemned in Sharī'ah. But a *Jihād* is fought under strict conditions, under a righteous Imām, purely for the defence of faith and Allah's Law. All baser motives, therefore are strictly excluded. The greed of gain in the shape of ransom from captives has no place in the *Jihād* movements.

It should also be noted that seventy prisoners of war were taken in the Battle of Badr, the first *Jihād* in Islam. They were soon freed, and some cases those who were literate were asked to teach in lieu for their release. Among the prisoners taken were the Prophet's uncle 'Abbās and Sayyidnā 'Ali's brother 'Aqil, who afterwards became Muslims. 'Abbās was an ancestor of the founder of the celebrated 'Abbāsid Dynasty which played such a notable part in Islamic history. In the case of all prisoners, if there was any good in their hearts, their very fight against Islam and their capture led to their being blessed with Islam. Thus Allah's Plan works in a marvellous way, and evolves good out of seeming evil. The Qur'ān says:

«يَا أَيُّهَا النَّبِيُّ قُل لِّمَن فِي أَيْدِيكُم مِّنَ الْأَسْرَىٰ إِن يَعْلَمِ اللَّهُ فِي قُلُوبِكُمْ خَيْرًا
يُؤْتِكُمْ خَيْرًا مِّمَّا أُخِذَ مِنكُمْ وَيَغْفِرْ لَكُمْ وَاللَّهُ غَفُورٌ رَّحِيمٌ».

"O Apostle! say to those who are captives in your hand: 'If God findeth any good in your hearts, He will give you something better than what has been taken from you, and He will forgive you: for God is Oft-Forgiving, Most Merciful'." 25.

This verse gives a consolation to the prisoners of war that in spite of their previous hostility, Allah will forgive them in His Mercy if there was any good in their hearts, and confer upon them a far higher gift than anything they have ever lost. This gift in its highest sense would be the blessing of Islam.

The kindness must be shown to the prisoners of war, one must not start thinking that if we show kindness to them, and release them, they will again create problems for the *Ummāh*. The matter should be left to Allah:

«وَإِنْ يُرِيدُوا خِيَانَتَكَ فَقَدْ خَانُوا اللَّهَ مِنْ قَبْلُ فَأَمْكَنَ مِنْهُمْ وَاللَّهُ عَلِيمٌ حَكِيمٌ».

"But if they have treacherous designs against you, (O Apostle) they have already been in treason against Allah, and so hath He given (You) power over them. And Allah is He who hath (full) knowledge and wisdom."[26]

If the kindness shown to them is abused by the prisoners of war when they are released, it is not a matter for discouragement to those who showed the kindness. Such persons have in their treachery shown already their treason to Allah, in that they look up arms against Allah's Apostle, and sought to blot out the pure worship of Allah. The punishment of defeat, which opens the eyes of some of their comrades evidently did not open their eyes. But Allah knows all, and in His wisdom will order all things for the best. The believers have done their duties in showing such clemency as they could in the circumstances of war. For them "Allah suffice".[27]

---

1. Cf. Qur'ān, ch. 22:39-40 and ch. 2:190, 193.
2. Qur'ān, ch. 16:125
3. Qur'ān, ch. 52:48.
4. Qur'ān, ch. 43:89.
5. Qur'ān, ch. 23:96.
6. Qur'ān, ch. 22:39-40.
7. Qur'ān, ch. 2:216.
8. Qur'ān, ch. 9:122.
9. Qur'ān, ch. 4:71.
10. Qur'ān, ch. 8:45.
11. Qur'ān, ch. 8:15.
12. Qur'ān, ch. 9:123.
13. Qur'ān, ch. 9:38.
14. Qur'ān, ch. 9:91.
15. Qur'ān ch. 48:17.
16. Al-Bukhārī and Muslim.
17. Aḥmed bin Ḥānbal and al-Bukhārī
18. Cf. Al-Bukhārī and Muslim.
19. Qur'ān, ch. 8:72.
20. Qur'ān, ch. 8:61.
21. Al-'Ajūz, *Manāhij al-Sharī'ah al-Islāmiyyah,* op.cit., Vol. 1, p. 345.
22. Qur'ān, ch. 47:4.
23. Qur'ān, ch. 76:8.
24. Qur'ān, ch. 8:67.
25. Qur'ān, ch. 8:70.
26. Qur'ān, ch. 8:71.
27. Qur'ān, ch. 8:62, Yūsuf 'Alī's note 1238 on verse 8:71.

Chapter 26

Sharī'ah in the Fifteenth Century of Hijrah: Problems and Prospects

The aim of Sharī'ah is to make people happier in this world and the Hereafter. Therefore, it follows that Islamic Jurisprudence must be considered indivisible, or an integral whole, because adopting a part thereof and dropping the other part would not be conducive to the achievement of its objectives and purpose. Any study of Qur'ānic texts containing these laws and rules reveals that any violation of them invokes two sanctions: one secular and the other celestial. For instance, a brigand is punished by death or by chopping off some of his limbs, or by crucifixion or exile – all these are mundane penalties to be added to heavy punishment in the Hereafter.[1]

Likewise, scandalous talebearing and accusation of chaste women are punishable in this world and the Hereafter.[2]

Similarly, intentional murder has two penalties: retaliation in this world and torture in the Hereafter.[3]

Thus all laws issuing from Islamic Jurisprudence invoke two sanctions and are indivisible and inseparable. But, in recent times, there are some Muslim rulers and scholars who contend that some of the Islamic provisions should not be utilised. They contradict their own belief that all the provisions of Islamic jurisprudence are permanent in nature and application. The champions of this view, in fact, are inclined not to apply the Sharī'ah laws from fear of foreign indignation or some other similar reasons.

At times, in medical practice, a minor symptom leads to a general check up which in turn uncovers a major ailment only indirectly related to the original symptom. A similar sequence can occur in social sciences as well. Thus the present declaration by Pakistan to introduce Sharī'ah, and the Islamic Revolution in Iran again emphasising on establishment of Sharī'ah system have caused worldwide commotion. It has also precipitated a closer look by Western countries and the powerful news media of the Western world towards Islam as a Religion and Sharī'ah as a system of law of the *Ummah*.

For the last two hundred years or so the Shari'ah has been represented by the Western World as a barbarous system of law, totally impracticable in the modern age. This false propoganda had caught the imagination of the elites in the Muslim countries owing to the brain washing that they received in Europe where most of them were educated. Things had reached such a low in the Muslim countries that many of their so-called 'Muslim' rulers were openly indulging in debauchery, drinking and other diabolical activities. And, in fact, it was this elitist class which was repeating *ad nauseauit* the European bogey of Shari'ah being 'impracticable'.

Many voices were raised in favour of Sharī'ah in the past but they were mostly curbed by either the colonial Masters of the Muslim countries or the brain-washed Muslim rulers. However, in the wake of the era of decolonisation and a changed power structure in recent years, a new wave has come in the Muslim world. The young generation in its thirties and forties have again embarked upon its quest for Islamic identity whose glaring example is afforded by Pakistan and Iran. This has set them upon doing a little soul-researching in order to so reshape their legal systems as would numerate the Islamic values.

The realistic choice seems to have narrowed down to Islamic Sharī'ah because of the fact that the so-called 'modern', 'progressive' and 'enlightened' man-made laws of the Western World have only led to increases in crime-rate, in broken-homes, in mental diseases, in chaos and confusion.

Western Influence in the Muslim Countries

The influence of the Western World was first felt in the Muslim countries with the coming of imperialism in the early 19th century. So far the Muslim lands had a definite legal system guiding them in all aspects of public, private and international dealings. This system was none other than the *Sharī'ah*. The laws of European origin were thrust upon the countries occupied by the British, French or Dutch imperialists against the will of the people and the laments of the *'Ulamā*. But gradually the Muslims who were trained under the influence of these new rulers were given the opportunity to proceed for higher studies in European countries. Thus, the imperialists found their supporters from the distant lands occupied by them, and those indigenes, in turn, influenced the masses and to some extent even the *'Ulama*. It was a long and arduous process of change but ultimately the colonialists succeeded. The *'Ulamā* were quietened and a compromise was struck which resulted into the Anglo-Mohammedan or Franco-Mohammedan law.

The first influence of the common law or European legal system on the Muslim Society was found in the fields of public law including constitutional and criminal law as well as the civil and commercial transactions. The European rulers were clever enough not to bring about the changes in the personal law of the Muslims at once.

The Ottoman empire, the then seat of the Islamic Caliphate was the first to be influenced by the European legal system in the 19th century through the capitulations which the Western powers introduced in respect of their citizens who were residing in the Middle East as the civil servants and traders. In countries in South and South-East Asia and East and West Africa, the colonionalists had made their in-roads as traders. Here the European system of commercial law was applied under the capitulatory system. The Ottoman empire introduced its first so-called 'reforms' which are well known as the *Tanzimat* between 1839 and 1876. By 1850 they fully introduced commercial law based on French commercial code. As if this was not enough, in 1858 they adopted French penal code which replaced the Hadd punishments of the Shari'ah. The Ottoman empire, the strongest Muslim power, was followed by Egypt where, in 1875, they adopted the French penal law replacing the Sharī'ah and French commercial law. While doing so, they tried to strike a compromise between the colonial legal system and the Islamic legal system. Later, the Italian and German influences also crept in the Muslim countries. Towards the end of the 19th century, that is by 1875 and 1883, three-quarters of the legal system in Muslim lands was derived from the European legal system. In India, the Shari'ah system which was practised during the centuries of Moghul rule was replaced by Indian penal code in 1862. By 1899, Sudan also became a victim. The last to be affected by the European legal systems were the countries of Maghreb, Morocco and Tunisia and Nigeria in West Africa. The colonial rule was established in Tunisia by France in 1891 and in Morroco in 1912. The Northern Nigeria was taken over by 1912. Lord Macaulay declared in India that the Islamic legal system was out-moded and did not provide any justice whosoever while Lord Lugard in Nigeria declared that the Sharī'ah system was "repugnant to natural justice and humanity."[4]

The Egyptian martyr 'Abd al-Qadir 'Audah has vividly portrayed the picture of Egypt and other Muslim countries in the following words: "Consequent to the introduction of European law of Muslim countries special courts were established. The judges of these courts were appointed from among Europeans or indigenous scholars who had never studied Islamic jurisprudence. The new courts considered themselves entitled to assume jurisdiction over all kinds of litigation; a jurisdiction which, practically speaking, left inoperative and neglected the analogous decisions of Islamic jurisprudence, especially since the newly-formed courts did not apply any but their own laws. Besides, educational authorities had established special schools to teach the new philosophies of law. Naturally, such schools gave full attention to the study of the European codes, neglecting Islamic jurisprudence, except in the instance of a few matters such as *Wāqf*. This attitude led to a lamentable end, inasmuch as nearly all the jurists, who were among the elite of the educated, were kept ignorant of the principles of Islamic law. It is lamentable because this ignorance is equivalent to their ignorance of the Jurisdiction and rules of their religion, which is the religion of all countries claiming to be Islamic. This same ignorance led to the introduction and integration of the meagre provisions cited from European law, though these were diverse from the implications of Islamic jurisprudence, in some cases. For instance, the Egyptian penal law stipulated that all its provisions should be applied without prejudice to any way to the rights of individuals as established by Islamic Jurisprudence. But despite this express provision, Egyptian jurists felt no need to acquaint themselves with the details of the rights declared by Islam.

They confined their competence in the study of individual rights to what was inscribed in the French legal system and to what the French jurists have expounded, validating them on the same legal bases as did the French. Egyptian jurists went far in this direction, being influenced by two factors:

First: They did not study Islamic jurisprudence and knew nothing of its principles and provision:
Second: They bound themselves by the views and precedents of the European jurists generally, and the French specifically, allowing what they allowed and prohibiting what they prohibited. It goes without saying that the European jurists knew absolutley nothing about Islamic jurisprudence."

Among the European-educated Muslim elites are those who believe that Islamic jurisprudence is primarily the result of juristic innovations. If one submits to them an Islamic theory of jurisprudence that was unknown to man-made jurisprudence till date, they would express their astonishment at the Muslim jurists who could reach levels of judicial competence in the seventh and eighth centuries that other jurists could not reach or conceive of until the nineteenth or twentieth centuries! Imāms Abū Ḥanifāh, Mālik, Shāfi'ī and Aḥmad bin Ḥanbal and their disciples could think of matters thirteen centuries ahead of the European jurists of the present century. But those who believe that Islamic jurisprudence is the invention of jurists are undoubtedly as mistaken as those who believe that those jurists themselves were capable of preceding human thought. The correct viewpoint is that Muslim jurists, despite their vast erudition and profound reflections, did not really introduce novelties from their own imagination, nor were they above human standards with respect to their meditative faculties.

The fact is that they found within their grasp a system of jurisprudence Divinely-enriched with theories and comprehensive principles and they explained and analysed them to the fullest. They did nothing more than what any jurist and genuine thinker would try to do by collecting all the available data and assigning to each theory what is relevant to it and tabulating under each principle what belongs to it. If there had been any innovation or precedence of thinking, it would have been the innovation of Islamic jurisprudence which was itself ahead of human rational development, and which revealed the most perfect theories for the purpose of guiding human beings towards exaltation and perfection by raising them to its elevated standards.

In spite of the multifarious advancement of Muslims in all branches of human knowledge, some Western scholars, while commenting on the flourishing Civilisation of the Muslim states in the Middle Ages, have said what an average Muslim, with a little knowledge of Islamic history, will feel reluctant to accept as a true picture."[5] If it is said of Europe that the European Christian states and society had remained basically static, it will be absolutely true. The contribution of Islam and its civilisation to Europe was so great that it really helped to achieve whatever they could achieve during the period of renaissance due to the influence of their encounter with Muslims and due to fresh ideas pouring from the presence of Muslims in Europe. Arguing from this false premise, the Western scholars have maintained that because Muslim states and society had remained basically static, the Shari'ah law had proved able to accommodate itself successfully to such internal requirements as the passage of time had produced. But the pressure which now (i.e in the nineteenth century) arose from without confronted Islam with an entirely different situation.

Because of the rigidity of the Sharī'ah and the dominance of the theory of *taqlīd* (or strict adherence to established doctrine), an apparently irreconcilable conflict was not produced between the traditional law and the needs of Muslim society, in so far as it aspired to organise itself by western standards and values. Accordingly there seemed, initially at any rate, no alternative but to abandon the Sharī'ah and replace it with laws of western inspiration in those spheres where Islam felt a particular urgency to adapt itself to modern conditions."[6]

This is wholly untrue as the pressures of adopting western legal system, which was based on concepts and institutions fundamentally alien to the religion of Islam and to the Sharī'ah, came not from the Muslims but from the western colonialists. The Muslims did not aspire in the beginning of the colonial rule to change their Islamic legal system nor did they wish to adopt western standards and values. The pages of history are filled with many examples of the opposition of Muslims to the forced change in their religious law. But the centuries of foreign dominance changed the situation drastically. The western imperialist found Muslim natives to help their cause apart from their government pressures to adopt the new system of law. As a result, whatever little of the Sharī'ah that continued in force in the Muslim countries was found only in the area of family law but there too certain so-called 'reforms' were introduced. In all the Muslim countries, with the exception of Saudi Arabia, the hybrid system of law which was neither Sharī'ah nor purely European law is in practice till today. It is only in the late seventies that efforts are being made by certain Muslim nations to re-introduce Sharī'ah but there too exist many hurdles in the way which we will examine later.

The Myth of Neo-Ijtihad and the Changes in Sharī'ah Law

Many a Muslim country after independence has adopted legal concepts from abroad without regard to their suitability for the Islamic social milieu and the basic spirit of the religion of Islam. Since Anglo-Muhammedan and Franco-Mohammedan legal systems have operated side by side with whatever was left of the Sharī'ah during the pre-Independence period in the Muslim world, conflicts have often arisen. The Sharī'ah and the Western common law cannot be fused together completely nor will it be allowed by the *Ulāma* of Islam and well-meaning Muslims. This is the reason why the mixed law has not been able to command the respect of Muslims. It is my candid belief that if the process of *Ijmā', Qiyās, Maṣāliḥ al-Mursalah, Istiṣlaḥ* and *Istidlāl* are properly made to work, the Sharī'ah will meet the challenges and the necessities of the modern life.

After the second World War, Muslim countries began to gain independence from colonial masters of Europe. Some new Muslim states declared Islamic law as their source of legislation. Muslim and non-Muslim scholars like Dr. 'Abd al-Razzāq al-Sanhurī and Professor Anderson were invited to advise them in the process. Dr. Sanhurī drafted civil codes particularly as regards the law of contract and property for Egypt, Syria, Iraq and Libya. Professor Anderson was invited by Ḥabīb Bourgiba of Tunisia and Sir Aḥmadu Bello of Nigeria to advise on Islamic Legal system. In their march towards modernisation and secularization Egypt and Tunisia, in 1955 and 1956 respectively, abolished the Sharī'ah courts entirely.

The law of personal Status which was still based on Sharī'ah is now administered by a unified system of national courts along with the civil and criminal law.

In Algeria the French legal system influenced the country so much that the courts of the *Qāḍis* act as courts of the first instance and the appeals are to be made to judges who are sitting in the ordinary civil courts. In India the remnant of the Sharī'ah law has been put in the hands of ordinary civil courts for the last two hundred years and the final appeal was only to be made to the judicial Committee of the Privy Council. In the craze for modernization, the entire Sharī'ah was entrusted to be administered in the hands of incompetent lawyers who were solely versed in Common law but certainly were not competent to administer the Sharī'ah. The fusion of the two systems resulted into confusion which will take a long time to be removed from the minds of the Muslim elites. Many of the laws based on the Qur'ānic injunctions and the Sunnah of the Prophet were deliberately "reformed". Since the judges did not possess sound knowledge of the Sharī'ah, they tried to formulate novel principles by way of supplement to the traditional Islamic law in the name of so-called justice and equity. They considered Sharī'ah as rigid, harsh and inequitable under modern conditions and hence they thought it was necessary for them to temper with the divine law. The following examples would show how the so-called "reformers" without any sanction from the Book of Allah and the Sunnah tried to "modernize" and "reform" categories in which these countries can be divided as follows:

1. The countries which have retained the practice of Sharī'ah unchanged and uncodified as far as the Sharī'ah family law is concerned since Islamic penal law is not practiced anywhere except in Saudi Arabia.

Table 1

Country	*Muslims in Majority or minority*	*Present state of Islamic family law*
Afghanistan	overwhelming majority	unchanged and uncodified
Bahrein	overwhelming majority	unchanged and uncodified
Burma	minority	unchanged and uncodified
Ethiopia	strong minority	unchanged and uncodified
Gambia	majority	unchanged and uncodified
Ghana	majority	unchanged and uncodified
Gold Coast	minority	unchanged and uncodified
Kuwait	overwhelming majority	unchanged and uncodified
Libya	overwhelming majority	somewhat changed and codified
Maldive	overwhelming majority	unchanged and uncodified
Mali	majority	unchanged and uncodified
Mauritinia	overwhelming majority	unchanged and uncodified
Nigeria	majority	unchanged and uncodified
Qatar	all-Muslim	unchanged and uncodified
Saudi Arabia	all-Muslim	unchanged and uncodified
Sierra Leone	strong minority	unchanged and uncodified
Somalia	overwhelming majority	unchanged and uncodified
Yemen	overwhelming majority	unchanged and uncodified
Yugoslavia	strong minority	somewhat changed but uncodified (applicable subject to certain legal enactments governing) all Yugoslav citizens

Pakistan has started its efforts to re-adopt Sharī'ah recently.[7]

See the Islamic Law *(Enforcement of Niẓām-Muṣṭafā)* Law Times Publications, Lahore 1979.

2. The countries where the Sharī'ah has been changed through modern legislative process, thus subjecting the Islamic Institution to regulatory measures. Many Muslim and non-Muslim scholars call these changes "Law Reforms".[8]

Table 2

Country	*Years of reform*	*The aspect of Muslim Law already changed and codified*
Algeria	1959	Consent of parties to marriage, solemnization of marriage, divorce, rights of children
Brunei	1955	Betrothal, marriage, divorce, maintenance, matrimonial offences.
Ceylon	1951	Registration of marriage, marriage-age for women, guardianship, bigamy, divorce by husband, dissolution of marriage by court.
Cyprus	1951	All aspects of the law of marriage and divorce.
Egypt	1920, 1923, 1929	Marriage-age, women's rights, divorce, 'iddah', period of gestation, custody of children matrimonial disputes and some aspects of the law of inheritance and bequests.
India	1929, 1937, 1939 (the whole of India) 1876, 1920, 1935, 1942, (particular states)	Dissolution of women's marriage by court, registration of marriage, amount of dower, marriage-age, gestation, effect of apostacy on marriage and inheritance.
Indonesia	1946, 1947, 1955	Registration of marriage, marriage-age, divorce by husband, delegated divorce.
Iran	1931, 1937, 1948, 1967	Some aspects of the law of marriage and divorce.
Iraq	1959, 1963	Bigamy, marriage-contract, maintenance, divorce by husband, dissolution of marriage by court.
Jordan	1951	Some aspects of the law of marriage and divorce.
Lebanon		Some aspects of the law of marriage and divorce.

Malaysia	1949 to 1964	Betrothal, guardianship in marriage registration of marriage, divorce by husband delegated divorce, bigamy, dissolution of marriage by court, family disputes, matrimonial offences.
Morocco	1957 to 1958	Some aspects of the law of marriage and divorce, including bigamy, dissolution of women's marriage by court; some aspects of the law of intestate and testimony succession, including orphaned grandchildren's right to inheritance.
Pakistan	1961 to 1962	Registration of marriage, effect of apostacy on marriage and inheritance, divorce by husband, bigamy, dissolution of women's marriage by court, orphaned grandchildren's right to inheritance, life estates.
Singapore	1957 to 1960	As in Malaysia and Brunei.
Sudan	1916 to 1960	Guardianship-in-marriage, divorce by husband, dissolution of women's marriage by court, period of gestation, spouse-relict's rights to inheritance, some special cases of inheritance, bequest to heirs.
Syria	1953	Some aspects of the laws relating to marriage, divorce, inheritance and bequest.
Tunisia	1956	Some aspects of the laws relating to marriage, divorce, inheritance and bequest.

1. See Tahir Mahmood, *Family Law Reform in the Muslim World,* New Delhi 1972, pp. 270-272.

3. In countries where Sharī'ah has been abandoned and replaced by the modern law applicable to all people irrespective of their religious allegiance.

In countries like Saudi Arabia there has been no departure from Sharī'ah in any law or enactment whether civil or criminal. All other legislations there must conform to the Qur'ān and the Sunnah of the Prophet and the conduct of the *Ṣaḥābah* (Companions of the Prophet).[9] In spite of the efforts made in codification of Islamic Law in 1957, the Saudis did not put it into practice due to the opposition of the *'Ulamā*. The other countries where to a lesser degree Shari'ah continues to operate include Qaṭar, the two Yemens, Bahrain and Kuwait. The application of Sharī'ah is confined to civil aspects only since the penal law of Sharī'ah has been either diluted or completely changed. In all the countries of Africa, mentioned in the above tables, the Sharī'ah criminal law is not applicable but the Mālikī Family Law operates unchanged. These countries are Nigeria, Niger, Senegal, Mauritania, Mali, Guinea, Chad, and Gambia. In most countries of Asia, except Afghanistan and Maldive, Sharī'ah Family Law still operates according to the Ḥanafī School in the former and the Shāfi'ī School in the latter. But here too changes have been made which are termed as 'Law Reforms'.

The greatest victims of secularization have been the countries like Turkey and Albania where most of the laws both civil and criminal are secularised following the influences from the European countries. Once the Ottoman empire came to an end these countries abandoned Shari'ah totally. In his over-enthusiasm, Kemal Attaturk persecuted the *'Ulamā* and created the hatred towards Sharī'ah in the masses. As a result, some western scholars believe that 'both in theory and practice the Turkish version of Islam today is different from other Muslim peoples'.[10]

It is an irony of fate that the more Attaturk tried to make Turkey equal in its status with any European country by thrusting the European style of life on his people, the more European leaders despised Turkey as "a sick man of Europe". Likewise, the Muslim populations in the Soviet Union, who are of Turkish origin, are governed by secular family law. There is not even an inch of Shari'ah left intact in any form. The Muslim minority in the Philippines is also subjected to secular family laws. The two countries in Africa, where the drastic secularization has been enforced are Kenya and Tanzania. In spite of the fact that Zanzibar has a predictably a Muslim population, as unifed marriage law has been forced upon them recently. In all the remaining Muslim countries, the Islamic penal system has been abandoned completely while the Islamic Family Law has been tampered with or, as the modernists put it, it has been 'reformed'.

Out of the three divisions that we have made of the Muslim countries or the countries where Muslims are in sizeable minorities, we have nothing much to say about the countries which have totally abandoned Sharī'ah aping the western countries and their legal system in their leaders' search for indentity with the so-called 'civilised' western world. The few countries which have retained Shari'ah either in all spheres of their legal system or in Personal Status alone had to face great challenges to defend the cause of Sharī'ah. But the third category of countries where the so-called reforms are introduced in the Shari'ah Family Law, great damage is done since the modernists have attempted to change the Shari'ah to suit their imaginations. In the process, they have rejected or twisted the legal injunctions of the Qur'ān and the guidance from the Prophet's Sunnah. We shall discuss here these so-called 'reforms' in various aspects of the Islamic law of Personal Status in various countries.

ʿAllāmah Muḥammad Iqbāl, the Poet of the East, has rightly depicted the picture in the following couplets:
"They do no change themselves but wish to change the Qur'ān; How misguided are these theologians of the Holy sanctuary; These slaves (of Western Imperialism) think that the Book of Allah is faulty; Since it does not teach the Believers the path of Slavery."

Marriage with non-Muslims

Islamic law allows marriage with the women of *Ahl āl-Kitāb* 'People of the Book' but not vice-versa.[11] In Turkey, there is no such bar. A Muslim man can marry any one belonging to any religion. In Cyprus where Turkish Family Law of 1951 is applicable, there is a slight difference as regards this aspect of law. It provides that marriage of Muslim women with non-Muslim men is prohibited.[12] In both Lebanon and Israel, the Ottoman law of family rights of 1917 continues to be applicable to the Muslims. It declares the marriages of a Muslim woman with a non-Muslim man as void but it is silent about the marriage of a Muslim man with a non-Muslim wife belonging to any religion whatsoever. There is no distinction between *Ahl al-Kitāb* and polytheists and unbelievers.[13]

Taʿaddud al-Zawjāt: Polygamy

Islam allows polygamy in special circumstances provided justice is done to all the wives but does not permit it at will. At the same time the Holy Qur'ān, the Sunnah and the conduct of the *Ṣaḥābāh* show quite clearly that polygamy was practised in the time of the Prophet, the *Rāshidūn* Caliphs and in subsequent periods. Thus, Sharī'ah is not against limited polygamy which must not exceed more than four wives. Polygamy can prove to be a remedy for many evils in the modern promiscuous society of ours.

It is true that at times the rationale of the Qur'ānic injunctions[14] of polygamy and the conditions attached to it were misconstrued and misued by some Muslims all over the Muslim World. But, the same is equally true of the misuse of some other lawful provisions made by Shari'ah. This is not peculiar with Muslims alone as it is a general human weakness that there are always some people who flagrantly violate the principles of ethics and morality and other aspects of natural law and justice. The modernists, however, clamped down on the provision of polygamy and imposed various un-Islamic restrictions on bigamous marriages which they proudly call 'reforms' in Islamic Law. According to the Syrian law of personal status of 1953, article 17, prior permission of the court will be required for a bigamous marriage desired by the husband is capable of doing equal justice between the co-wives.[15] It is Iraqi Law of Personal Status of 1959, article 3 (iv) and the Malaysian Law sections 37 have imposed similar restrictions on a Muslim wishing to marry a second wife. All these countries require that the husband must be financially capable to maintain more than one wife before the court could grant him permission to take a second wife. Iran and Iraq even went to the extent that the person desiring to marry a second wife must obtain permission of the court which must declare that the husband is capable of doing equal justice between the co-wives.[15] It is simply impossible for any court to find out that the husband is capable of doing equal justice between the co-wives or not, when the Qur'ān specifically mentions that no matter how you desire to do equal justice between your wives you will not be able to do so. In Iraq, there is yet another condition imposed that there must be some "lawful benefit" involved in the proposed bigamous marriage.[16]

In Pakistan, prior permission of an Arbitration Council is required before taking a second wife according to the Muslim Family Law Ordinance, 1961. It is only the Arbitration Council which will decide whether the marriage is necessary and just.[17] If the husband violates the provision he will have to pay forthwith the entire amount of dower to the first wife and it would furnish a ground for dissolution of her marriage by the Court.[18] In Turkey, the civil code of 1926 has forbidden completely a bigamous marriage.[19] If at all such marriage is contracted, the court is given the power to declare the marriage invalid.[20] Except when the first marriage was lawfully dissolved before the person concerned took the second wife. The Turkish Family Law (Marriage and Divorce), 1951 of Cyprus, the court is empowered to declare a bigamous marriage as invalid in all cases without any exception what-so-ever.[21] Tunisia too declared a bigamous marriage totally forbidden in the code of Personal Status of 1956. If at all someone contracted the second marriage in Tunisia, he will have to face legal penalties. One would also incur the legal penalties if one married a second wife in Iran, Iraq, and also Pakistan without seeking prior permission.

Talāq: Divorce

The other law which the so-called 'reformers' thought needed change was the law of divorce. Divorce is mentioned as "most hated of the things permitted by Allah" in one of the Ahadith of Prophet Muḥammad. The marriage in Islam is a contract which should be made to work as far as it is humanly possible and following the guidance of the Book of Allah and the Sunnah of the Prophet.

There are a number of devices to repair strained relations. If these do not work, it is better to bring the marriage to a peaceful end rather than dragging on indefinitely, making the matrimonial home a hell and making children suffer untold hardships. The modernists here too interferred with the Qur'ānic injunctions and precepts of the Prophet. Changes were introduced in Turkey, Cyprus, Tunisia, Algeria, Iraq and Iran in the Islamic Law of Divorce. If a husband wants to divorce his wife, he must apply to the court of law first. A unilateral divorce is not possible. In Turkey and Cyprus, it is only the court which can dissolve a marriage as is required by Civil Code of 1926 and Turkish Family Law of 1951. In Tunisia and Algeria, the court may dissolve a marriage in pursuance of a mutual agreement between the spouses.[22] The Tunisian Law has empowered the court to grant a divorce if it is insisted upon by either party.[23] Under the Iraqi Law of Personal Status of 1950, a unilateral divorce pronounced by a husband, which is neither effected by nor registered with the court, will be considered inoperative. By usurping the right of a Muslim, who happens to be adult and sane, the Indonesian and Pakistani 'reformers' have introduced the intervention of Civil Officials in the matter of unilateral divorce. It is required in Indonesia that when a divorce is desired by the husband, he shall first apply to the Consultation Bureau in the Ministry of Religious Affairs or to the Marriage Council. In Pakistan a husband who has divorced his wife shall, immediately thereafter, give notice thereof to a local civil official who shall then constitute an Arbitration Council. The divorce shall not be effective until the expiry of 90 days from the date of the said notice.[24]

In order to impose a further check on the husband's power of unilateral divorce the so-called 'reform' law in Syria, Tunisia and Morocco imposed on the husband the liability to pay to the divorced wife an additional indemnity by way of compensation.[25]

In my view, these restrictions are imported from the European legal system which has not helped the Europeans to reduce the rate of divorce or maltreatment between spouses. The changes have not helped the Islamic society in any way.

Tabannī: Adoption

There is no adoption in Islamic Law. If a person adopts a son or a daughter, the Sharī'ah will not confer on the adopted person the Status or rights of a natural son or daughter. According to the Qur'ān,[26] if a person is not someone's real son he does not become his natural son merely by virtue of a declaration. The Turkish Code lists the categories of relationship which constitutes impediment to the marital union which includes the blood relations in the direct line as well as the relations by marriage. Adoption also features in this code as one of the impediments of marriage.[27] It was a *jāhiliyyah* practice before of Islam that a person would adopt someone's child as his own child. But adopting someone's child as one's own, the real heirs to the property of a man are deprived of their shares. It is an unjust and unfair practice and a great departure from the Shari'ah.

In Cyprus neither the fosterage nor adoption is mentioned by the Cypriot law as a bar to marriage.[28] In India, so long as a Muslim who establishes the custom of adoption does not make a declaration, he will be governed by the customary law of adoption.[29]

Apostacy

According to Shari'ah apostacy by one of the spouses brings an end to a valid Islamic marriage, but in India the Anglo-Mohammedan law provides that renunciation by a Muslim wife by conversion to a different faith or otherwise, shall not by itself operate to dissolve her existing marriage.[30] The Act of 1939 does not make any change in the law relating to the effect of a Muslim husband's apostacy on his marriage with a wife who continues to be a Muslim. The Muslim Family Law Ordinance of 1961 says that if a Muslim wife renounces Islam that in itself shall not operate to dissolve her marriage with the Muslim husband. The provision remains unchanged in Pakistan but a husband desiring to divorce his wife on the grounds of denunciating of Islam would follow the requirements of the Muslim Family Law of Ordinance.[31]

Waṣiyyah: Bequest

The introduction of obligatory bequest in favour of an heir has become a controversial issue for quite some time. According to the Ḥanbalī and Ḥanafī Schools of Islamic Jurisprudence, a bequest in favour of an heir will be considered valid provided other heirs consented to it. The Mālikī School considered such a bequest as invalid while the two shades of opinion of the Shāfi'i jurists support both Māliki and Hanafi views. The famous Egyptian scholars like Moḥammad Abduh, Rahid Rida and Qāsim Amin, while suggesting changes in certain aspects of the Shari'ah Law in respect of Family relations included the obligatory bequest as their solution to the problem.

Shaikh al-Marāghī, then the rector of Azhar University, also made his proposals for reform in the Family Law. As a result, the Egyptian Law of 1946 stipulated that a bequest in favour of an heir is valid and effective without regard to the consent of any other person.[32] If we examine this carefully, the new law is neither in conformity with the Ḥanafi and Ḥanbalī Schools nor the Mālikī and Shāfi'i Schools. It is a departure from the traditional Sharī'ah Law.

Obligatory Bequest

The doctrine of representation demands that nearer relations exclude remote relations. Hence, if a son of propositus is living at the time of his or her death, a grandson cannot claim any share in the estate left by the propositus. The orphan grandchildren thus had a misfortune which could easily be remedied through *waṣṣīyyah* or bequest up to one-third of the estate of the deceased as stipulated in the Holy Qur'ān. But the Egyptian Law of Bequest, 1946, introduced obligatory bequest in favour of the orphan grandchildren.[33] This is undoubtedly a departure from the Shari'ah. The Western scholars have made a hue and cry and branded the Sharī'ah as unjust on this issue. When the Egyptian law was passed, professor Anderson said: "This ingenious device does not in any way affect the structure of the Islamic Law intestate succession which it leaves completely untouched while it yet makes provision for orphan grandchildren."[34] It is not true to say that it leaves the Qur'ānic law of succession untouched. The Syrian Law of Personal Status 1953 goes a step further when it stipulates in respect of obligatory bequest as follows: "The grandchildren shall not be entitled to any obligatory bequest if they otherwise inherited from their father's ascendants nor if any of them left a legacy or a gift which is equal to an amount of that of the obligatory bequest." But then it confuses the issue and goes contrary to the Sharī'ah when it says that "where a man has less than the due obligatory bequest, the balance shall be made up."[35]

The Tunisian code has also enforced the principle of obligatory bequest but the benefit is available only to the first generation of grandchildren, male or female. The Moroccan code of personal status of 1958 stipulates that when a person dies, first son having died before him, bequest of an amount laid down in the following articles shall be binding on him from a third of his estate in favour of the grandchildren, if any.

The amount of such a bequest shall be equal to the share which their father would have received if presumed to have died after the deceased, provided that it shall not exceed one third of the estates.[36] Pakistan has also introduced the so-called reform on the obligatory bequest by introducing the presumptive share of a child who is dead at the time when succession is to be shared per *stirpes* by its own issues living at that time. One wonders what would happen if the surviving issues happen to be girls! This is an example of twisting the Shari'ah in order to accommodate one's imaginations.

"Widow's Lien"

A widow after her husband's death was given a privileged position in regard to her claim for unpaid *Mahr* against her deceased husband's estate. Under the Shari'ah, a widow in such circumstances ranks as one of the creditors and receives the unpaid *Mahr* before the shares of the inheritance are given to the appropriate heirs. But the Anglo-Mohammadan law in India gave the widow special privilege to her claim since it was comparable to what obtained in the English law as "a widow's lien". She was allowed against the Qur'ānic law to retain possession of her husband's estate.[37]

These are some examples of changes effected in the Divine law. Surprisingly enough, the modernist 'reformers' call these changes based on the myth of *Neo-Ijtihād.* In my view, there only exists the process of *Ijtihād* which was employed by the *Ṣaḥābah, Tābiūn* and *Tab 'Tābiūn* who solely depended on the exercise based on the Qur'ān, Sunnah and the conduct of the Companions of the Prophet. If one begins to term one's mere imagination in re-interpreting the principles of Shari'ah as *Neo-Ijtihād*, he is really guilty of changing the Divine Law.

Are the 'Law Reforms' Really Reforms or Deviation from Sharī'ah?

While examining all the 'reforms' in all aspects of Family Law of Shari'ah, it becomes quite evident that the reforms are truly speaking a departure from the Divine Injunctions contained in the Qur'ān and the Sunnah of the Prophet.

The Holy Qur'ān has warned those who fail to apply the Sharī'ah in the following strong words:

«ومن لم يحكم بما انزل الله فاولئك هم الفاسقون».

"And if any fail to judge by the light of what Allah has revealed, they are not better than those who rebel."[38]

«ومن لم يحكم بما انزل الله فاولئك هم الظالمون».

> "And if any fail to judge by the light of what Allah has revealed, they are no better than the wrong-doers."[39]

«وان لم يحكم بما انزل الله فاولئك الكافـــرون».

> "And if any fail to judge by the light of what Allah has revealed, they are no better than unbelievers."[40]

Besides, man-made laws, as we have seen are restricted by the current needs of individuals and societies, and they change in accordance with the evolution of the society. The more sophisticated the society becomes, the more need for new laws is felt. The new legislation is usually enacted by the rulers or government who rectify and change laws when they feel it is necessary. Thus, one society creates the laws and enacts them in view of meeting its own requirements which may not be applicable to other society. Such laws become subordinate to men and their further evolution depends on him. But, the objective of Shari'ah is to organise and direct the society, to cultivate the right kind of individual and to establish the ideal state and the ideal world. It is for this reason that its provisions are much more in advance of the standard of societies at the time they were inspired. It is my candid belief that they are still ahead of our contemporary conditions. Allah in His kindness and mercy has saved searching humanity much unproductive strain by revealing the Divine Law orienting people to do good deeds and lead virtuous lives and towards achieving exaltation and human perfection.

As we have noted before, the Sharī'ah was not revealed for limited application for a specific age. It will suit every age and time. It will remain valid and shall continue to be, till the end of this life on earth. Its injunctions were coined in such a manner that they are not affected by the lapse of time. They do not become obsolete, nor do their general principles and basic theories need to be changed or renovated. The generalised construction and elasticity of Sharī'ah allows even for bringing under their jurisdiction any unprecedented new case, even though it is not possible to expect its occurrence at the beginning of revelation. Hence, the provisions of Islamic jurisprudence are not susceptible to change or substitution as are other laws and legislation.

This is the reason why any deviation from such comprehensive code would be subject to Divine indictment:

> ". . . Then is it only a part of the Book that you believe in, and do you reject the rest? But what is the reward for those who among you behave like this but disgrace in this life? And on the Day of Judgement they shall be consigned to the most grevious penalty."[41]

Siyāsah al-Shar'īyyah and the Qur'ān Concept of "Those in Authority"

At the very outset, it should be borne in mind that Islamic Laws and rules are of two categories: The first consits of *Aḥkām* or legal injunctions set down for religious and spiritual purposes. These include the rules of faith and worship. The second category comprises the rules and laws administering and organizing the state, the government and the community, as well as the relations between individuals and their communities. These include the rules of human behaviour, criminal laws, laws of civil status, constitutional laws, international laws, etc. Thus, Islam combines the secular and the spiritual. It is a religion that embraces spiritual and secular life simultaneously. As faith and belief are one part of Islam, the government is the second integral part. Caliph 'Uthmān Ibn 'Affān had truly expressed this fact by saying: "Allah urges by the Ruler what may not be urged by the Qur'ān". But, such a ruler must be pious *(Muttaqī)* and Allah-fearing who tries to base his pronouncements on the teachings of Islam.

The Islamic laws are often changed using the technique of *Siyāsah al-Shari'yyah.*

Siyāsah literally means politics and *Shari'yyah* means something that concerns the Shari'ah. It is a technique through which certain so.called reforms were introduced in Shari'ah as an escape from the application of strict Shari'ah pinciples. Under the guise of *Siyāsah al-Shari'yyah,* certain Muslim states have tried to abandon the principles of Shari'ah law not by express supercession but by directing its courts that they shall not entertain any case based on such principles. In the course of time, these Shari'ah principles became obsolete.

When some Muslim states tried to apply reforms under the pretext of *Siyāsah al-Shari'yyah* they maintained that they were acting in conformity with the following Qur'ānic verse:

«يا ايها الذين آمنوا اطيعوا الله واطيعوا الرسول واولى الامر منكم»

"O you who believe, Obey Allah and obey the Apostle of Allah and those who are placed in authority among you."[42]

The question, however, arises as to who are the people in authority referred to in the Qur'ānic verse: Are they political leaders and statesmen? Certainly not. It is likely that there may come up some so-called Muslim rulers and leaders who may be victims of various vices and may impose regulations which may go contrary to the Qur'ān and Sunnah. Should we obey them simply because they are placed in authority over us? The Sunnah of the Prophet guides us in such situation in the following words:

«لا طاعة لمخلوق في معصية الله».

"There is no obedience due to any creature (no matter who they are) if they order to sin against Allah."

The Prophet has also said:

"He who commands you to sin, has no authority over you."

In reality, in the sphere of law, "those who are placed in authority" will mean those *'Ulamā* and *Fuqahā* who have authority in knowledge of the Book of Allah, the Sunnah of the Prophet and the conduct of the *Sahabah*, the companions of the Prophet.

It is a bitter fact that the majority of those who popularised this concept of *Siyāsāh al-Shar'iyyah* in the Muslim world happen to be the Egyptian *Ulama* who are respected throughout the world because of their association with *Al-Azhar*, an ancient seat of learning in Cairo.

But, during the colonial period these *'Ulamā* were the first who supported to so-called 'modernisation' of Egypt and even Islam by their rulers.

It will not be out of place to discuss here the fact that though Sharī'ah confers upon the ruler the right to legislate, this right is not absolute. In fact, it is a right restricted to this condition: that whatever the ruler may legislate must be compatible with the texts, spirit and general principles of the Shari'ah. Consequently, such a restriction confines the right of legislation to two categories:

1. Executive legislation, intended to guarantee the implementation of the provisions of Sharī'ah. In this case, legislation takes the shape of rules and regulations similar to those presently issued by government officials in the course of their daily responsibilities, for the purpose of ascertaining the execution of the relevant laws.
2. Organisational legislation, intended to organise the society, protect it and meet its needs in accordance with Shari'ah. Generally, such legislation is not called for except in such cases where there are no relative provisions in Sharī'ah administering them. In any circumstance, legislation by rulers must be in harmony and in agreement with general principles and the spirit of the Shari'ah. It is the Ijmā' of the 'Ulamā that all acts of the rulers are legitimate so long are they are within the framework of Shari'ah and compatible with its judicial decisions and spirit. Then, and only then, would the ruler be acting within his rights and accordingly, should be obeyed. Moreover, if he acts otherwise, issuing laws which contradict the Sharī'ah, his acts or laws become illegitimate and objectionable. This statement is based on the Qur'ānic verses:

> "O you who believe, obey Allah, and obey the Apostle and those placed in authority among you. If you differ in anything among yourselves, refer it to Allah and His Apostle."[43]

> "Whatever it be wherin you differ, the decision thereof is with Allah."[44]

In most of the Islamic countries, since the last century, rulers have been formulating codes of laws in the various legislative matters on the same pattern as that followed by European countries. As a matter of fact, they copied European constitutional, criminal, civil, commercial and other codes without reference to Islamic jurisprudence except in a few minor matters such as *Waqf* and the like. It is only fair to admit that many of these codes do agree with the basics of Islamic jurisprudence and do not contravene its general principles. But it is only fair as well to state that some of these codes run contrary to our jurisprudence established on principles opposed to it. For instance, certain of the said codes allow adultery in most cases and consumption of alcoholic beverages while Islam categorically prohibits both.

Enforcement of Niẓām-e-Muṣṭafā: A Ṣtep in the Right Direction

The present development in the Muslim world augur well for the new century of Hijrah. There are some Muslim countries in which efforts are being made to enforce the Sharī'ah. The enforcement of *Niẓam e-Muṣṭafā* in Pakistan is a fine example. While one is happy about this development, there is still need for cautious optimism. As President Ziā-ul Haq has said on the eve of introduction of *Niẓam-e-Muṣṭafā* or Shari'ah law, efforts have been made to reform the society which is exposed to complacency for a very long time. The preamble of the prohibition (enforcement of Hadd) order 1979 reads: "that it is necessary to modify the existing law relating to prohibition of intoxicant so as to bring it in conformity with the injunctions of Islam set out in the Holy Qur'ān and the Sunnah."

Ḥadd and *Tazir* punishments are to be accorded to the Shari'ah. The offence against property (enforcement of *Ḥudūd*) ordinance, 1979 says in respect of punishment of theft liable to *Ḥadd:*

1. Whoever commits theft is liable to *Ḥadd* for the first time shall be punished with amputation of his right hand from the joint of the wrist.
2. Whoever commits theft liable to *ḥadd* for the second time shall be punished with the amputation of his left foot up to the ankle.
3. Whoever commits theft liable to *ḥadd* for the third time, or any time subsequent thereto, shall be punished with imprisonment for life.

These are laudable attempts and we hope that these laws, once fully implemented, will reform the society. In respect of the offence of *Zinā* (enforcement of *Ḥudūd*) by *Niẓam-e-Muṣṭafā* ordinance No. VII of 1979 gives the following punishment if it is proved that the crime was really committed: A person guilty of *'zinā* or *'zinā-biljabr'* shall if he is not an adult, be punished with imprisonment of either description for a term which may extend to five years, or with fine, or with both, and may also be awarded the punishment of whipping not exceeding thirty stripes. Provided that, in the case of *'zinā-bil-jabr'* if the offender is not under the age of fifteen, the punishment of whipping shall be awarded with or without any other punishment. However, the punishment for *Zinā* does not seem to be according to the requirements of Sharī'ah. Perhaps, the government of President *Ziā-ul Haq* is cautious knowing the weakness of the society where the *hadd* punishment of Sharī'ah has not been applied for a very long time. It was perhaps, intended to arouse public sentiment against the Sharī'ah. Whatever may be the cause the punishment cannot be properly termed as the Sharī'ah punishment.

Takhayyur: Need for the Modern Islamic Society

Takhayyur literally means choice. In the language of *fiqh*, it means liberty of an individual Muslim to be governed by the law of any of the four schools of Islamic jurisprudence. As opposed to *Takhayyur* is the concept of *Taqlīd* that is following strictly the law of the school on which one is born. In other words, one who is born in a Ḥanafī home follows strictly the Ḥanafī laws and in a Mālikī home follows the Mālikī Laws. The moment that one begins to exercise his liberty to be governed by the law of another school other than his own, there is usually hue and cry. Some people begin to call him *Ghair-Muqallid* (unorthodox).

The Muslim countries have now come closer to each other due to the modern means of quick transport. The newly found oil wealth in some Muslim countries have attracted Muslims following different schools from other parts of the world to travel and work and live in these countries. Thus, it has increased a great deal on interchange of ideas among Muslims living in different parts of the world. *Takhayyur*, hence, offers a solution in a case of conflict of law. The doctrine of *Takhayyur* is not a new one. In the first place there was nothing like any particular school of law in the time of Prophet Muḥammad, the four *Rāshidūn* Caliphs as well as the early *Tābi'ūn*. Opinions on minor issues differed even during that time but according to the Prophetic traditions they were considered as "Differences of opinions among my *Ummah* is a sign of mercy of Allah". Even the great Imams themselves, loved each other and accommodated each others points of view. Why then should the doctrine of *Takhayyur* not work in the modern world of ours? Just as we did not call the early Muslim as *Ghair-Muqallid*, we have no right to brand the present day Muslims who exercise their right of *Takhayyur* either *Muqallid* (the person obliged to follow authorities of the school in which he is born) or *Ghair-Muqallid.*

If this is achieved, *Sharī'ah* will be more easily acceptable and practicable all over the Muslim world. To some extent the gap has been bridged as the principle of *Takhayyur* has assumed greater importance in modern times, but still many *Qāḍīs* all over the Muslim world are not well disposed to apply the laws of other schools. The result of *Takhayyur* will provide a harmonious and easy process of justice since the founders of all the schools of Islamic Jurisprudence, in reality, had no other goal in front of their eyes except the welfare of the *Ummah*. Thus, *Takhayyur* can bring about *Talfiq* which literally means piecing together or patching up through combination and fusion of juristic opinions of diverse nature. But, in all these processes there should not be allowed any departure from the spirit of the teachings of the Qur'ān and the Sunnah. *Takhayyur* and *Talfīq,* therefore, will bring about the reforms necessary to suit the modern conditions. In this case, one will be be driven to English, French or German legal systems and borrow from them in order to find a solution to our legal problems. Any attempt of *Ijtihād* to re-interpret the Islamic legal principles with the use of *Takhayyur* and *Talfiq* to suit the changed social conditions of our time will not be objected to, but mere change and departure from the Qur'ān and Sunnah in order to import French, English or Italian law and call it *Neo-Ijtihād* will amount to disbelief.

The Qāḍi, once *Takkayyur* is accepted, will be at liberty to apply an opinion other than that of the school to which they were traditionally bound. *Takhayyur* is applied in the Suddan by the Sudanese Mohammedan law courts organisation and Procedure Regulations.[46] Truly speaking, a lot of problems will be automatically solved if the *Ummah* in the present times understands the importance of the concept of *Takhayyur* and if its voluntary application is left to the *Qāḍis* of proven ability, knowledge, maturity and above all *Taqwah*, fear of Allah.

The modern courts, in many Muslim countries, where the Judges are either non-Muslims or Muslims trained in common law with marginal knowledge of Islamic law cannot be entrusted with this grave responsibility. A truly learned *Qāḍi* in Islamic Jurisprudence, as propounded by the four schools of *Fiqh,* will endeavour to make an electic choice between the corresponding legal principles of the various schools and will enforce one of the solutions given by various great

Muslim Jurists. He may even choose a lesser known juristic view over a well-known principle provided it will help the cause of equity and justice on which the Shari'ah lays a great emphasis.

The Shari'ah, particularly its application in public law, has been so much out of use for such a long time that people feel scared at the thought of bringing it back as a living system of law which can be practised today. Their attitude is like that of a misguided and emotional father who gives his ailing son suffering from typhoid the solid food thinking that he will be cured quickly and get quick energy. He only laments when his child eventually dies. During the colonial period, even some learned *'Ulamā,* like Shaikh Muḥammad 'Abduh of Egypt, became victims of an inferiority complex and called their obnoxious imaginations as intellectual re-interpretation of various Sharī'ah issues and called it fresh *Itjihād* or *neo-Itjihād.* It is really very unfortunate that some Muslim scholars during their stay abroad while working on their doctoral dissertations accepted this new and unIslamic term as a newly found treasure.

It is really a pity that most discussions on common law systems *vis-a-vis* the Sharī'ah are conducted in a haze of misinformation: There are few areas of so-called controversy between the application of the *Ḥadd* punishment in the Sharī'ah so much of what everyone "knows" is not really so.

It is, therefore, a duty of every Muslim to disseminate the knowledge of Sharī'ah both among Muslims as well as non-Mulsim all over the world.

The risks of re-introduction fo Shari'ah in Muslim Countries are very much less than its critics allege, and indeed would be sufficient ground for its rejection if the amalgamated Anglo-Mohammedan system had fewer risks than the Sharī'ah. But, their anti-Shari'ah lobby, for example in Pakistan, where Islamic Law was recently introduced created a hue and cry. The bureaucratic elites had acquired bad habits like drinking alcohol and the western style of life. If Sharī'ah were to be fully implemented, they would face great hardships. Even they enjoyed the blessings of the past regime and even before that period the past rulers had similar vices. Anyone who genuinely wanted to carry out the Islamic system had a marathon task ahead of him since the first opposition that he would face would come from those 'brain-washed' elites. This case-study of Pakistan holds particular relevance for other Muslim countries who wish to tread on this arduous path.

At present, there is wide spread though not complete support for the Sharī'ah by Muslim masses everywhere. But, because of the wrong propoganda against Sharī'ah that once it is fully brought into practice, streets of the Muslim world will be flooded with people whose hands are cut-off, or scenes of stoning to death and flogging in public will be witnessed frequently. Because of these imaginary dangers many Muslim 'elites' advocate to continue the 'more human' system of common law.

Clearly there is only one well-defined path for Muslims in the fifteenth century of Hijrah. While countries can make technological advancement and learn modern techniques from the western world or wherever they are available, it is clear that each Muslim country will have to make real efforts to re-educate the Muslim masses concerning the Islamic value system, and make them aware of the fact that the Shari'ah can operate even in the modern so-called 'advanced' society of ours.

The colonial era has pumped a wrong notion in the minds of Muslim intelligentia that Sharī'ah is outdated and cannot fit in the modern society of ours. What is rellay needed on the part of all Muslims is a sense of dedication, fear of Allah, sincerity of purpose and the easily forgotten fact, which Islam so much emphasises, the life after death and the Day of Resurrection and the Day of Judgement. In order to better our lives in this world as well as the next world, there is no other course open to us but to re-adopt Shari'ah.

In conclusion, I would like to quote the message of Shaikh 'Abdul Qādir 'Aduah to the Muslim scholars to awaken them from their deep slumber.

"Muslims scholars for long have disregarded their Islam. They have never censured any attitude violating Islam, nor tried to repel and revoke any injunction than came contrary to the principles of Islam. They have never even convened a meeting to encourage the re-institution of Islamic jurisprudence. Rulers have committed felonies, allowed the forbidden, shed blood, raped women, spread mischief and transgredded the limits enjoined by Allah, while the scholars have never so much expressed indignation and opposition to such actions. They uttered only the sounds of silence, as if Islam did not require them to invite others to do the good and forbid what is wrong *(Amr bil Ma'rūf wa Nahya'anil Mukar)* and did not make it incumbent upon them to give counsel to the rulers so that they might apply the laws of Islam. Man-made laws have been enforced in Muslim countries, though they contradited Islamic provisions, nullified Islamic commands, allowed what Allah has prohibited and prohibited what Allah has allowed. Yet, Muslim scholars were not disturbed by this violation of their religion nor were they perturbed about their own future though they earned their living at the expense of Islam. They did not even hold meetings to discuss the tragic turn of events relative to their own destiny and the future of their religion."[47]

We sincerely hope that the fifteenth century Hijrah which has brought new challenges, and opportunities to the Muslim *Ummah* will establish Islam as a social, political, economic and moral reality which it really is.

---

1. Qur'ān ch. 5:36.
2. Qur'ān, ch. 2:19.
3. Qur'ān, ch. 2:178; ch. 4:93.
4. Coulson, *A History of Islamic Law*, Edinburgh 1971, p. 157.
5. Coulson, N.J. *A History of Islamic Law*, op. cit., p. 149.
6. Coulson, N.J. *A History of Islamic Law*, op. cit., pp. 149-150.
7. See the Islamic Law *(Enforcement of Niẓam-Muṣṭafā)* Law Times Publications, Lahore 1979.
8. See Tahir Mahmood, *Family Law Reform in the Muslim World*, New Delhi 1972, pp. 270-272.
9. Fundamental law of Hejaz, see articles 5-6.
166.
10. Smith W.C., *Islam in Modern History*, New York, 1963, p. 166.
11. Qur'ān, ch. 2:221.
12. Turkish Family Marriage and Divorce Act 1951, section 7, 1c.
13. Ottoman Law Family Rights 1917, Article 52-58.
14. Qur'ān, ch. 4:3.
15. Iranian Family Protection Law 1957, article 14; Iraqi Law of Personal Status of 1959, art. 3 (iv).
16. Iraq Law of Personal Status of 1959, art. 3 (iv).
17. Pakistan Muslim Family Law Ordinance 1961, section 6.
18. Dissolution of Muslim Marriage Act 1939, section 2 (ii).
19. Turkish Civil Code, 1926, article 93.
20. Ibid. article 112.
21. See section 8, section 19.
22. Tunisian Code of Personal Status 1926, art. 30; Algerian Marriage Ordinance 1959, art. 6.

23. Tunisian Code of Personal Status 1956, article 31.
24. Muslim Family Laws Ordinance 1961 of Pakistan, section 7.
25. Tunisian Code of Personal Status 1956, article 31; Syrian Law of Personal Status 1953, article 117, Moroccan Code of Personal Status 1958, article 60.
26. Qur'ān, ch. 33:4-5.
27. See Turkish Code, Article. 92.
28. Turkish Family Law 1951, section 7.
29. Muslim Personal Law (Sharī'ah) Application Act, 1937, section 3.
30. Act of 1939, section 4.
31. Dissolution of Muslim Marriages Act, 1939, section 4.
32. The Egyptian Law of 1946, article 37.
33. Law of Bequest 1946, articles 76-77.
34. Anderson, Recent Reform in the Islamic Law of Inheritance 141 CLO 1956 p. 358.
35. The Syrian Law of Personal Status, 1953, section 2575.
36. The Moroccon Code of Personal Status, 1958, Articles 266-267.
37. See Fyzee, A. A. A., *Outlines of the Mohammedan Law,* Oxford, 1955.
38. Qur'ān, ch. 5:50.
39. Qur'ān, ch. 5:48.
40. Qur'ān, ch. 5:47.
41. Qur'ān, ch. 2:85.
42. Qur'ān, ch. 4:59.
43. Qur'ān, ch. 4:59.
44. Qur'an, ch. 22:10.
45. 'Audah, 'Adbul Qādir, *Islam Between Ignorant Followers and Incapable Scholars,* I.I.F.S.O. Publication, Kuwait, 1971.
46. The Sudanese Mohammedan Law Courts Organisation and Procedure, Section 53.
47. 'Audah, 'Abdul Qādir, *Islam Between Important Followers and Incapable Scholars,* I.I.F.S.O. Publication, Kuwait, 1971, pp. 105-108.

Index

A

B

M

Letter Sent by the Prophet (S.A.W.) to Non—Muslim Rulers

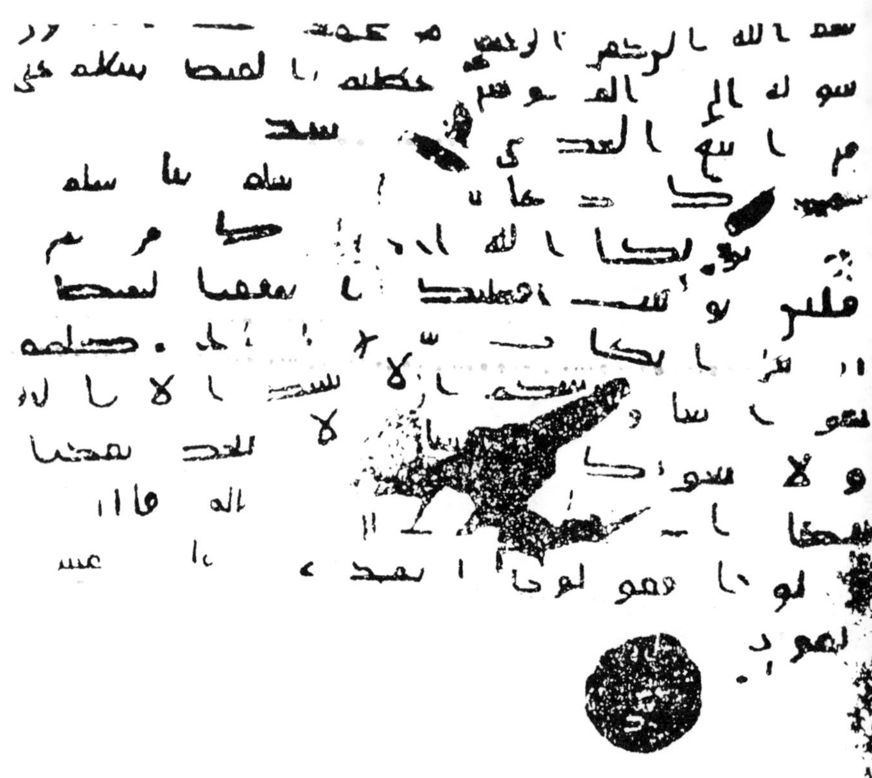

A Letter Sent to Maqoqas Misr Bin Yamin

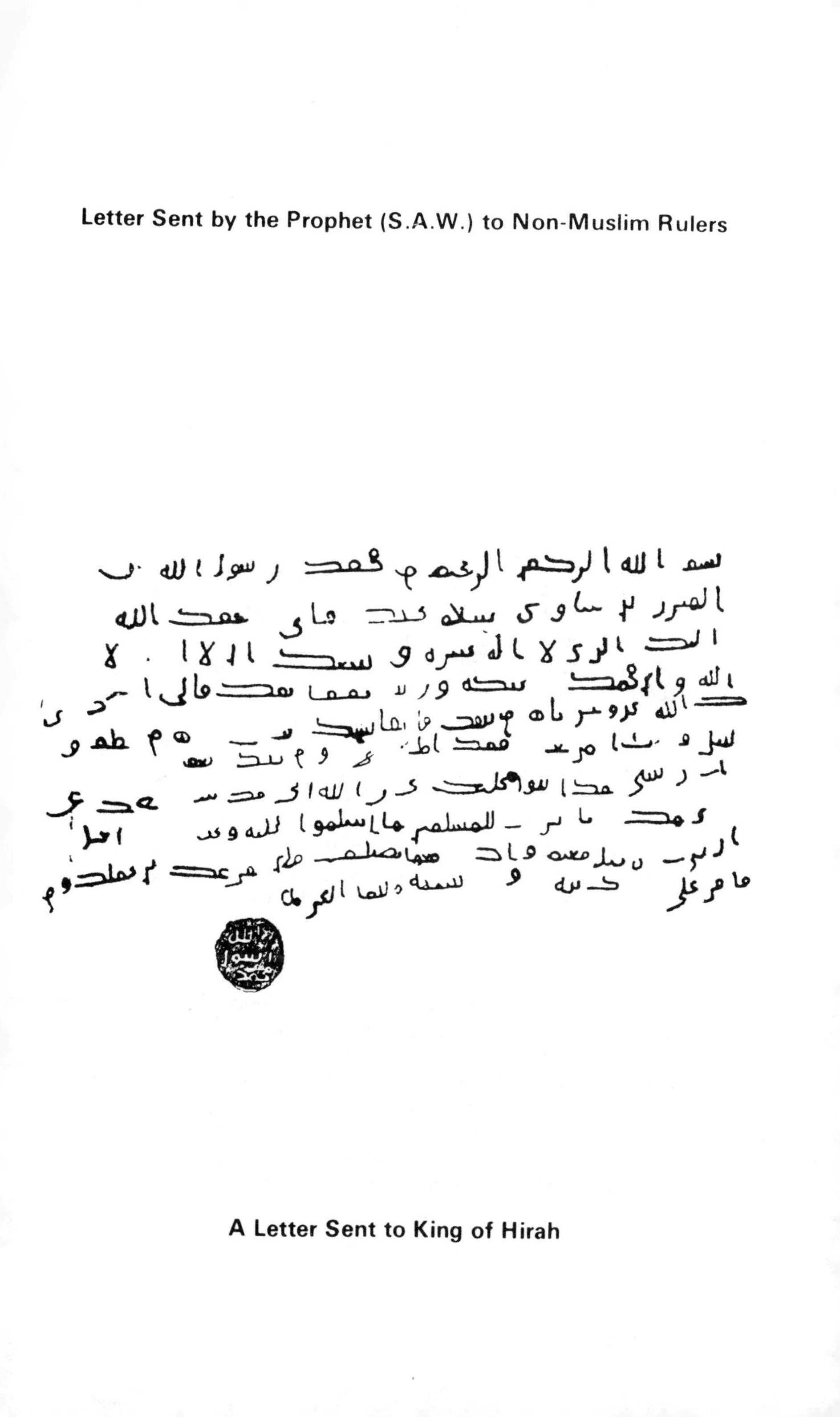

Letter Sent by the Prophet (S.A.W.) to Non-Muslim Rulers

A Letter Sent to King of Hirah

About the author:

Professor Abdur Rahman I. Doi, born in an Islamic environment in Himmatnagar (India) started his early education in *Madrassah.* He secured his B.A. (Hon.) in the first class from the University of Bombay and was awarded a gold-medal. He passed his M.A., examination in the first-class from the same University and was awarded a gold-medal. The University of Bombay then awarded him a merit scholarship to join the University of Cambridge as a research scholar. In England he had enormous opportunity to work on Arabic and Islamic manuscripts deposited in various libraries. He obtained his Ph.D. degree in 1964. He revived the Muslim Students' Association at the University of Cambridge which was lying dormant for many years after Sir Muhammad Iqbal's departure.

In 1965, he took up his appointment at the University of Nigeria, Nsukka, where he designed, introduced and taught the courses in Islamic studies. In 1967 he moved to the University of Ife as a research scholar in the Institute of African Studies. Later on he became Head, Department of Religious Studies and Philosophy at Ife. When the department was split into two he became the Head, Department of Religious Studies. In 1977 he was appointed as Professor and Director, Centre for Islamic Legal Studies, Ahmadu Bello University, Zaria, the position which he still holds.

Professor Doi has served on many Committees and Boards concerned with Islamic studies and Shari'ah. He was once the Editor-in-Chief of Nigerian Journal of Islam. At the moment he is Chairman, Editorial Board of *Shari'ah Law Reports* and Editorial Board *Journal of Islamic and Comparative Law.* He is a member of Editorial Boards of various journals abroad including *The Search: Journal on Arabic Islamic Studies,* Miami, (U.S.A.). He is Vice-President of *Nigerian Association for study of Religion.* He is a foundation member with the Colleges of Islamic Legal Studies in the various states of Nigeria. He has contributed at least 100 articles to well known periodicals in Islamic studies. His books include: *Women in Shari'ah; Non-Muslim in Shari'ah; Shari'ah in the 15the Century Hijrah; Islam in Nigeria; Introduction to the Qur'an; Introduction to the Hadith; The Cardinal Principles of Islam;* and *Prayers from Qur'an and Sunnah.*

He has attended a number of international conferences on Islam including *The First World Conference on Muslim Education, Conference on Islamic Social Science,* Riyadh.